30,00

D0205405

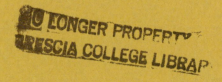

THE ECONOMICS OF
POPULATION GROWTH

The Economics of
Population Growth

JULIAN L. SIMON

PRINCETON UNIVERSITY PRESS

PRINCETON, NEW JERSEY

For My Grandmother

Fanny Goodstein

Who never went to school
But whose life made her family and community richer
Economically and spiritually.
    And for the many many women and men
In the poor populations of the world
Who are like my grandmother

CONTENTS

vii

CONTENTS

CONTENTS

CONTENTS

CONTENTS

CONTENTS

LIST OF FIGURES

Unless otherwise noted, figures that have been taken from books and articles indicated as sources are reproduced with the permission of the author and the publisher.

LIST OF TABLES

Unless otherwise noted, tables that have been taken from books and articles indicated as sources are reproduced with the permission of the author and publisher.

xvii

PREFACE

WHEN THIS book was begun in 1968, I believed that rapid population growth was the major threat to the world's economic development. And this book was intended as a contribution to understanding and combatting that problem.

By 1970, however, my reading on the effects of population growth had led me into confusion. The formal economic theory of population (which, except for Coale and Hoover, adds little to Malthusian diminishing returns) states that higher population growth implies a lower standard of living. But the available empirical data—the cross-sections and time-series of nations presented by Kuznets and Easterlin, together with the historical allusions of Sauvy and Clark—did not confirm that theory.

Shaken by this contradiction between the bare theory and the bare facts, I sought a reconciliation. Several ideas offered possibilities for a resolution: the theory of von Thunen, recently developed by Boserup, that population growth in poor countries induces people to change their agricultural practices; Kuznets' suggestion that a larger population in developed countries produces faster technological development; and the Resources for the Future demonstration that increased demand for resources induces a larger supply of resources. And, of course, it is possible that poor raw data on nations' growth might be responsible for the contradiction between Malthusian theory and the empirical results.

The results of my struggle to effect a reconciliation are presented in Part I. First come empirical analyses of population growth's effects in less-developed and more-developed countries, both at the aggregate level of national growth rates and at the more detailed level of microeconomic phenomena. Then building on these empirical results, Part I binds up the theory—the classical elements together with the ideas that go beyond Malthus—in such manner that the expanded theory is reasonably consistent with itself, with our understanding of reality, and with the data.

Part II, which analyzes the effects of economic conditions upon fertility, reaches conclusions that are reasonably conventional and value-free. But as with Part I, much of Part III—which discusses policies and methods for reducing fertility—is out of the mainstream of thought about population economics. As I worked on the managerial and marketing economics of fertility-reduction programs I decided—as had so many before me—that per-capita income by itself is not a sufficient criterion for population policies. Therefore, Part III of the book develops fertility-reduction strategies in the context of a wider view of welfare economics than the popular criterion of the average income of the current population. It offers methods of making national decisions about how much to spend for fertility-reduction programs, and how to use the funds most effectively, without losing sight of a country's own welfare objectives rather than simply implementing the welfare objective urged by outsiders.

The data, arguments, and conclusions found in Parts I and III may be (though I hope they are not) over-weighted toward the benefits of population growth. But the disadvantages of population growth have received much attention recently, whereas the benefits have been almost ignored. One of my aims, therefore, is to help achieve a better balance. My personal values may also be at work here, having evolved from concern only about the standard of living and what I thought was an unmitigated bad effect of population growth upon per-person income, to a belief that the number of people who can enjoy a good life is important as well as the economic level at which they live. More fundamentally, I came to recognize that I believe—except in rare cases—that life is worthwhile to those living it, for India's poor just as for the affluents of the West. This belief is quite the opposite of that held by many influential contemporary writers, authors of popular works (e.g., Ehrlich, 1968) as well as authors of technical economic studies (e.g., Meade, 1955). Given the prevailing climate of opinion, however, whatever critical attention this book receives will surely take care to counteract any bias in the direction of population growth's benefits.

As you assess the possible bias in this book, I hope that you will keep in mind that I reached the conclusions and beliefs that I now hold because of the facts and analyses contained in this book, rather than because I started with an ideological predisposition toward them. As I have said, I began this work with the presently prevailing popular view: that population growth is a menace to the world. It was this concern over that supposed menace that led me to the study of population economics in the first place. Furthermore, my early articles in this field were straightforward efforts to help reduce population growth.

The initial change in my views was caused by the empirical facts about the observed simple relationship of population growth to economic growth. These facts did not and do not persuade me that population growth is good; the data are too weak for that. But they were strong enough to cause me to distrust the Malthusian theorizing which is the basis of almost all academic strictures about population growth's ill effects. It was only after my attempts to make sense of the facts together with the existing theories that I was led to question the prevailing view, and to inspect my own values. One does not change one's mind easily about a subject like this, especially when one has made a professional investment in a viewpoint. In short, it was not my beliefs that led me to view the facts as I now see them; rather, it was the facts that led me to my present viewpoint.

Furthermore, I began to work in the field of population economics for the same reason that many others do: I thought population growth, along with all-out war, to be one of the two fearsome threats to mankind and civilization. So I respect the motivation and intentions of many of those people with whose conclusions and recommendations I no longer agree.[1]

Population has always been an emotional topic, and those emotions affect intellectual views and their acceptance. The tone and main conclusions of this book are not popular at the moment, either with the public or with economists and other professional students of population. The usual fate of technical books outside the consensus is that they are simply ignored, whether they are good or bad. This is in contrast to the reception of several recent examples of patently unscientific works about population that express a popular emotion and therefore are accepted widely—even though they are almost unanimously damned by specialists in the field. I hope that these fears about this book's reception are unfounded.

The topics and methods in this book are quite varied. Studies include micro-economics and macro-economics, empirical and theoretical analyses, on subjects ranging from agricultural techniques to contraceptive techniques to advertising techniques, with sources in half a dozen different literatures. An integrated examination of the economics of population growth demands great breadth of knowledge, but demand does not always create supply. Therefore, I hope that you will forgive my inadequacies where I touch on your particular specialty.

The book also suffers from unevenness in treatment. A few of the chapters are mostly critical summaries of the work of others (especially Chapters 10 and 14–17), whereas most of the chapters are new work. And the new work is narrower and deeper than the critical work. As a result the book is not a seamless evenly flowing statement of the economics of population growth. After I began the book I met vast lacunae where there seemed to be no satisfactory existing work. Therefore, I set out to fill some of these gaps with original studies. When they were included into the book, they were over-developed relative to the survey material, and in time they came to dominate the book. Arthur Lewis once wrote that the proper place for new ideas is in journals and not books. I hope, however, that on balance this treatment is nevertheless useful to the reader and does some justice to the material.

---

[1] But I find it harder to respect the motivation of those people who are against population growth for reasons typified by the car bumper sticker "Having Trouble Parking? Support Planned Parenthood."

On the other hand, the book is not just a collection of unrelated studies. It systematically attempts to cover all the major topics in the economics of population growth: Descriptive and normative, the more-developed countries and the less-developed countries, and the effects of population growth on income level as well as the effect of income level on population growth.

Now I shall end this preface on a hopeful note: Since Malthus and his frightening analysis, economics has been known as "the dismal science." The analysis in this book leads away from dismal conclusions, and points out that population growth can contribute to a better future. So the economics in this work is cheerful rather than dismal. My traverse from simple Malthusianism to the conclusions contained here shifted my worldview from pessimism to optimism. Now I believe that we need only forestall war to achieve a bright future for mankind.

Jerusalem, July, 1975

ACKNOWLEDGMENTS

THIS BOOK has been a long time in the making. I first wrote the title "The Economics of Population Growth" on a notepad in a hotel bathroom in Jerusalem in January, 1968. Then my wife was pregnant, our two tiny children were sick, snow had cut the city's communications, we knew not a soul and were all miserable. Now more than seven years later we —now five—are again in Jerusalem, well and happy and among friends. For that change in our circumstance I am most grateful.

During the long course of the book's development many people gave me that most valuable of gifts, their attention and thought. Bonnie Birnbaum, Ronald Lee, Adam Pilarski, George Simmons, J. J. Spengler and James Sweet read most of the manuscript and rendered valuable advice. Roberta Cohen, Anne Credicott, Israel Luski and Dan Weidenfeld programmed and ran the simulation models described in Chapters 5 and 13 and provided indispensable assistance; all contributed ideas as colleagues beyond what one may expect of research assistants. And at a crucial moment Carlos Puig helped us solve a thorny programming problem.

I received useful comments about various chapters in conversation and correspondence with, among others: Yoram Ben-Porath, Ester Boserup, Brian Boulier, Glen Cain, John Caldwell, James Carey, Ansley Coale, Dennis DeTray, Folke Dovring, Richard Easterlin, Stanley Engerman, Stephen Enke, Tomas Frejka, Robert Gillespie, Geoffrey Hawthorn, Robert Herdt, Edgar Hoover, Bert Hoselitz, Sheila Johannson, Allen Kelley, James Kocher, Simon Kuznets, Nathaniel Leff, Cynthia Lloyd, Frank Lorimer, Judah Matras, James Millar, Larry Neal, Goran Ohlin, Warren Robinson, Warren Sanderson, T. Paul Schultz, Rita Simon, Vladimir Stoikov, Louis Werner, Harold Williamson, Jr., and Robert Willis.

I appreciate permission from the following publications to reprint revised portions of my articles that appeared therein and are used here in the chapters indicated: *Demography,* Chapters 18 and 19; Carolina Population Center Monograph Series, Chapters 14–17; *Economic Development and Cultural Change,* Chapters 12 and 13; *Population Studies,* Chapter 20; *Economic Journal,* Chapter 21; *Studies in Family Planning,* Chapter 22; *Review of Economics and Statistics,* Chapter 10.

Many helpful people typed parts of this manuscript. Sylvia Farhi, Olga Nelson and Kay Rinewalt deserve special mention, however, for their thoughtful and skillful work which often went beyond typing. And Judith Blumberg did various bibliographic tasks sensibly and well.

The State of Illinois has been generous toward education and research at the University of Illinois and other state institutions. The work described in this book has benefited from that generosity, especially the computer time that was used and the research assistance for which the Graduate College Research Board of the University of Illinois provided funds. I am also grateful to the Departments of Business Administration and Economics at the University of Illinois, Urbana, and the Jerusalem School of Business Administration of the Hebrew University for their support with the secretarial services that were essential in getting this work done. The Center for Population Research of the National Institute of Health supported work discussed in Chapters 14–17 under grant NIH-NICHD-71-2034. Aside from those chapters, however, the research described in this book is not fashionable now and did not find outside support. Therefore I am especially grateful to the State and the University of Illinois for their support.

LIST OF SYMBOLS

$A_{F,t}$ the level of the technological know-how in use in agriculture at time t in the country being analyzed; productive efficiency in agriculture

$A_{G,t}$ industrial know-how

ART complex of natural resources, economies of scale, and technological knowledge

B_t fertility schedule; numbers of births in year t to the age-cohorts, composed of the various $b_{j,t}$ (defined below)

C_t the number of consumer equivalents

$D_{F,t}$ the set of indifference curves

EFF_t the effective labor force; the number of workers weighted by their education

$E_{j,t}$ mortality rate for cohort j in year t

F designates agricultural sector

G designates industrial sector

$H_{j,t}$ health adjustment to work expended by cohort j in year t

J_t social overhead capital (infra-structure) such as roads

$K_{F,t}$ privately-owned farm capital at time t, most of which is land

$K_{G,t}$ industrial capital

L_t the number of adult-male-equivalent workers *available* at time t

$MEN_{j,t}$ number of males of age j as of year t

$M_{F,t}$ the total number of man-hours worked in agriculture in year t

$M_{G,t}$ total hours worked in industry

N_t cultivated land in acres

$P_{G,t}$ and $P_{F,t}$ prices of industrial and farm goods, respectively

POP_t total population in year t

$Q_{F,t}$ agricultural output in year t, *not* including any saving and investment in agriculture

$Q_{G,t}$ industrial output *including* investment goods

R_t natural resources available for use in year t

S_t total resources spent on physical investment and education

W_t the wage level

$WOM_{j,t}$ number of females of age j as of year t

XED_t expenditure on education

Y_t total income; aggregate output

$\dfrac{\hat{Y}}{C}$ the aspired-to income per consumer equivalent

Z_t proportion of potential work hours that are actually worked in a given year t

$\alpha, \beta, \gamma \ldots$ parameters

$a_1, a_2 \ldots$ parameters

$b_{j,t}$ births to cohort age j in year t, ½ male and ½ female

e_L elasticity of labor force, L, with respect to children born

e_s elasticity of the saving ratio, s, with respect to number of children

xxvii

g_t female labor participation rate
$h_{j,t}$ effective health-adjusted work force
j index for age of cohort or persons
s_t ratio of saving to output
w ratio of children age 20 and under to adults age 21–60

FOREWORD

by Joseph J. Spengler

PROFESSOR Simon's *The Economics of Population Growth* is a path-breaking work, not merely in terms of challenging particular studies incorporated in it but above all in its espousal of a number of theses that run counter to currently prevailing opinion. It may be counted upon, therefore, to prompt critical response, to sharpen the population debate, and to stimulate progress both in economic demography as a whole and more specifically in the analysis and formulation of demographic policy. Professor Simon advances what may be treated as a new paradigm in the Kuhnian sense—a paradigm consisting in great stress on dynamic social processes underlying population growth, associated with such growth, or consequent upon it.

Professor Simon's thesis not only demands but surely will give rise to intense examination, widespread as well as critical. Not only do his findings run counter, in their net impact, to dominant opinion in the field of economic demography; they also, in their emphasis upon the longer-run rather than the shorter-run impact of events and policies, are at variance with current tendencies on the part of social scientists to stress the immediate future, allegedly at the expense of the longer-run future.

The book is divided into three parts, the first dealing with the economic effects of population growth, the second with the effects of economic conditions on fertility, and the third with the implications of diverse policies for population growth and its control. Critical reactions to Professor Simon's findings are likely to be concentrated, though not exclusively, upon the thesis presented in Part I where he is especially concerned with the feedback effect of population growth upon economic growth in advanced as well as less-developed countries.

The reader of Professor Simon's book is advised to familiarize himself with what Schumpeter might have called Simon's vision of the "total population problem" before plunging into the study. Fortunately a semblance of this vision may be inferred from the introductory chapter, together with Chapters 23–24 and the Appendix, in which objections to some of the book's conclusions are anticipated and rebutted. Given this summary view, Simon's conclusions, together with their development, are easy to grasp as a whole. Moreover, it illuminates the author's interpretation of the significance of variation in an economy's degree of modernization for the feedback of population growth upon economic growth. Simulation models are employed to describe the underlying response mechanisms.

The author attempts to serve the interests of both the general reader with a limited background in population study and readers with professional interests. Accordingly, what amount to reader guides are supplied in the introductory chapter. Every reader, of course, stands to benefit from the intensive array of figures, tables, and bibliography with which this work is equipped. The historically minded reader will be pleased not only because Professor Simon's fundamental concerns harken back to the Malthusian controversy and the origins of population theory, but also because attention is focused upon longer-run rather than shorter-run demographic changes. Indeed, a fundamental aim of the book "is to enlarge the time span within which the economics of population growth is commonly discussed, both by lengthening the horizon within which conditional analyses of the future are made and by pushing the historical record back to earlier times than are usually adduced in the discussion."

Although we have already suggested the author's main contributions, attention may be called to the numerous ways in which, as he points out in Part I, population growth may or does influence agricultural and non-agricultural growth and conditions, the supply of effort, and various economies of scale. In Part II he discusses *inter alia* the effect of income redistribution upon fertility, along with the effect of passage of time upon the response of fertility to increase in income. In Part III he examines the relevance of economic welfare theory and cost-benefit analysis to decisions respecting population growth, together with diverse methods of increasing contraceptive usage.

Duke University, *Durham, North Carolina*

THE ECONOMICS OF
POPULATION GROWTH

CHAPTER 1

Introduction to the Issues
and to the Book

OVERVIEW

MODERATE POPULATION growth has positive effects on the standard of living in the long run (after, say, 30 to 100 years) in both more-developed and less-developed countries—as compared to a stationary population and to very fast population growth. But of course *any* additional person adds a burden to parents and society in the short run. Therefore, whether one judges that population growth is good or bad—whether parents and society opt for more or less children—rationally depends upon how the importance of the long run is weighted relative to the short run. This is the central point of the first part of this book. Empirical data are presented concerning the various relevant strands in this argument. Then the strands are woven into simulation models from which the general conclusions are drawn.

The second part of the book reviews and summarizes data on the effect of economic level upon population growth. Taken together with the first part, the second part implies that Malthus and neo-Malthusian works such as *The Limits to Growth* are wrong with respect to human society in the assertion that there is a "constant tendency in all animated life to increase beyond the nourishment prepared for it" (Malthus, 5th ed., 1817/1963, p. 1). To put my argument in Malthus-like terms: If population has a tendency to increase geometrically, output has a tendency to increase geometrically and at least as fast—without apparent limit. Others have reached the same conclusions, but this book adduces empirical evidence and makes use of quantitative analysis to argue the point.

The third and last part examines the framework of welfare economics and values within which population policy decisions are made. It finds that many recommendations for policies are now being made whose implications are not known to the recommenders, and that may be inconsistent with their policy values. This third part of the book also offers some economic and marketing analysis to aid birth-control campaigns in countries which decide that the short-run disadvantages of additional population growth outweigh the long-term advantages.

THE INTELLECTUAL BACKGROUND

As a branch of science, population is very much an economic subject. The causes and consequences of population changes are of interest to sociologists, anthropologists, and psychologists, too. But the most important phenomenon in the study of population is *change in population size*. And change in population size is important mostly because it affects the *resources* available to people. Whether a given group of people (and their descendants) are richer or poorer in food, manufactured goods, space, and other resources depends heavily on population size. Resources are the central reason population study is important, and resources are the subject matter of economics.

Malthus[1] was the fount of the systematic economic study of population.[2] Though his central point was simple, Malthus has been much misinterpreted and wrongly extrapolated, perhaps because of some unfortunate illustrations and secondary passages. This has led to sterile disputes between wrongly named "Malthusians" and "Anti-Malthusians."

The essence of Malthus' point of view, to paraphrase Carr-Saunders (1925, pp. 23–24), is that though every new mouth that comes into the world is accompanied by a pair of hands, the new hands will not produce as much on the average as the hands already in existence. The output per person is thereby lowered. The reason why the additional hands produce less than the previous pairs of hands is that the amount of land is fixed at any given moment, and more hands working on the same amount of land will produce less per pair of hands.

Malthus also offered a theory of population history which Baumol called "the magnificent dynamics" because of its enormous historical scope. The analysis starts with a "progressive state" that has somehow raised production per capita above bare subsistence:

> The progressive state is characterized by a high level of investment (accumulation) which generally serves to increase total production but which also tends to keep up wages. This in turn leads to an increasing population. Because land is fixed in quantity there are diminishing average returns to additional labor in production. As population increases wages therefore tend to eat up the total product after rent payment and thereby reduce the profitability of investment until the

---

[1] Some modern economists condenscend intellectually to Malthus as a muddle-headed theorist on matters other than population. It is therefore interesting to note Keynes' claim that Malthus had a more correct vision of the economy than any other economist for the next hundred years. ". . . The almost total obliteration of Malthus's line of approach and the complete domination of Ricardo's for a period of a hundred years has been a disaster to the progress of economics. If only Malthus, instead of Ricardo, had been the parent stem from which nineteenth-century economics proceeded, what a much wiser and richer place the world would be to-day!" (Keynes, 1951, pp. 117, 118, 120). Perhaps future writers will judge that Malthus' original notion about population economics—the notion to which his name is so firmly attached—is really the least sound of his major ideas.

[2] This book gives only snatches of the history of economic population theory. The history is summarized well by Spengler (United Nations, 1953, Chapter 3).

inducement to invest disappears and the stationary state is attained (Baumol, 1951, p. 13).

Hence economics was called "the dismal science."

Malthus' work provoked reply and controversy throughout the nineteenth century. One line of criticism began with the observation that during the eighteenth and nineteenth centuries in England, its overseas extensions, and some parts of Europe, population rose rapidly but the standard of living *also* rose. One explanation offered was that a greater division of labor was possible with a larger population. Another suggestion was that the independent pace of technological progress in advanced countries had been and would be greater than the pace of population growth. Malthus' first edition, and all of Ricardo's editions, however, asserted that technological progress would *not* be rapid enough to permit population growth unconstrained by death: The "law of . . . nature . . . implies a strong and constantly operating check on population from the difficulty of subsistence. This difficulty . . . must necessarily be severely felt by a large portion of mankind . . . And the race of man cannot, *by any efforts of reason,* escape from it . . . misery is an absolutely necessary consequence of it" (Malthus, 1798/1959, p. 5, italics added).[3] Those who believed that technological progress could and would win a "race" with population growth were naturally more sanguine about the future than was the Malthus of the first edition.[4]

Some critics of Malthus found hope in the belief that people would increasingly limit births voluntarily—as Malthus, in the first edition,

---

[3] It should be noted that such an assumption about the rate of technological progress is not a necessary element of Malthus' theoretical system, as Malthus himself seemed to think it was.

[4] Does or does not history confirm Malthus' conclusions that in the long run economic welfare is a stationary series of fluctuations at and above subsistence? The answer must depend upon the length of the time period one looks at, as well as one's extrapolations into the future. For 2,000 years in India and China prior to the nineteenth or twentieth centuries, Malthus' description fits the facts. And population growth almost surely brought Malthus' positive check into operation regarding "the world's greatest civil war, the Taiping Rebellion" in China in the middle of the nineteenth century. P. Ho says that "Although the factors contributing to the rebellion were many, there can be little doubt that the pressure of population was one of the most basic" (1959, p. 274). But Malthus' reasoning does not fit the rise and fall of the empires of Rome, Persia, and others west of India. Most commentators even suggest that population growth *slowed down* at the height of Rome's glory. For example, Baron speaks of "Roman society . . . with its wide practice of birth control and even abstention from matrimony. . . . Perhaps in no other period of history was there such a high percentage of unmarried men and women" (Baron, 1952, vol. II, p. 209).

And if one takes as one's observation period for India and China the last 2,000 years *including* the twentieth century, plus the last few centuries in Western countries, then Malthus' prediction is apparently wrong. But again, as history advances progress may either continue or man may return to near-subsistence living. The point is that Malthus' analysis and prediction cannot be confirmed or falsified without specifying a place and a time span, which Malthus did not do.

only *hoped* they might. But by the time of the second and subsequent editions of his essay Malthus came to agree that people really *might* limit families voluntarily—which, it should be noted, is equivalent to the assumption that technological progress could win a "race" with population growth. "Thoughout the whole of the present work I have so far differed in principle from the former, as to suppose the action of another check to population which does not come under the head either of vice or misery; and, in the latter part I have endeavored to soften some of the harshest conclusions of the first Essay" (Malthus, 1803, p. xii of Irwin edition). Malthus even offered historical examples of voluntary fertility control, e.g., the delay of marriage in Scandinavia in response to population pressures (1803, p. 81).

The shift in Malthus' theoretical position after his first *Essay* did not mean that his predictions had completely reversed: "I believe that few of my readers can be less sanguine than I am in their expectations of any sudden and great change in the general conduct of men on this subject" (5th ed., 1817/1963, p. 271). But there is much less of this pessimism in the fifth edition than the first, and Malthus allowed himself to end the fifth edition with the following:

> From a review of the state of society in former periods, compared with the present, I should certainly say that the evils resulting from the principle of population have rather diminished than increased . . . it does not seem unreasonable to expect that they will be still further diminished. . . .
>
> On the whole, therefore, though our future prospects respecting the mitigation of the evils arising from the principle of population may not be so bright as we could wish, yet they are far from being entirely disheartening, and by no means preclude that gradual and progressive improvement in human society, which, before the late wild speculations on this subject, was the object of rational expectation. To the laws of property and marriage, and to the apparently narrow principle of self-interest which prompts each individual to exert himself in bettering his condition, we are indebted for all the noblest exertions of human genius . . . (5th ed., 1817/1963, p. 289).

This view allows for the contributions of both the check of "moral restraint" and the technological progress due to "the noblest exertions of human genius." And it projects an improving trend into the future. So Malthus himself was a powerful critic of "Malthusianism."[5]

---

[5] In general, Malthus' well-considered later position is much at variance with the position held by most of those people today who use his ideas for their theoretical base, and in my judgment he is much better-grounded and wiser by far than the modern "Malthusians."

6

Then there were those who, like Godwin (1820) believed that mankind's fate is fixed by his social institutions and not by the immutable laws of Malthus' theory. Godwin believed that if mankind would reorganize itself properly (and quite differently from the then-prevailing state of society in England and Europe) there would be no natural constraints upon population growth for a long time.[6] In the same line of thought were (and are) the Marxists. They believe that population could be too great only under capitalism, and they argue that a socialist economy could make productive use of as many people as would be born. (Just as the simplest elements of Malthus' original theory are the mainstay of most contemporary population-control discussions, the argument about the relationship of population growth to changes in social organization is heard today in form almost unchanged from Godwin. At the 1974 U.N. World Population Conference in Bucharest the Chinese opposed Western calls for a fertility-reduction policy, insisting that there is no population problem as such but rather only a failure of some societies and governments to come to grips with the problem of economic development.[7])

For a few decades beginning at the end of the nineteenth century and continuing through the 1920's, there was a Golden Age in the economics of population, marked by exceptional contributions from Cannan (1928), Dalton (1928), Robbins (1927), Wicksell (1928), and others. Some of the work displayed a very wide general grasp of the subject (e.g., Dalton, 1928). But the focus mainly was on the concept of the "optimum population." Whereas Malthus' theory was a two-variable dynamic model of

[6] The Godwin-Malthus argument is a fundamental issue in social thought. Malthus' reply to Godwin is as follows: "The great error under which Mr. Godwin labours, throughout his whole work, is, the attributing of almost all the vices and misery that prevail in civil society to human institutions. Political regulations, and the established administration of property, are, with him, the fruitful sources of all evil, the hotbeds of all the crimes that degrade mankind. Were this really a true state of the case, it would not seem an absolutely hopeless task, to remove evil completely from the world; and reason seems to be the proper and adequate instrument, for effecting so great a purpose. But the truth is, that, though human institutions appear to be the obvious and obtrusive causes of much mischief to mankind, they are, in reality, light and superficial, in comparison with those deeper-seated causes of evil which result from the laws of nature" (1803, p. 367).

[7] "We hold that the fundamental reason for the present poverty and backwardness in many developing countries in the Asian and Far East region as well as in other regions lies in the policies of aggression, plunder and war pushed by imperialism, colonialism and neo-colonialism, and in particular, by the super-powers, which seriously destroy these countries' productive forces. The decisive condition for changing this situation of poverty and backwardness is to get rid of aggression and oppression by imperialism, colonialism and neo-colonialism, to combat big-power hegemonism and power politics, to strive for and safeguard national independence and to develop the national economy independently.

"In our view, it is erroneous to say that the poverty and backwardness of the developing countries stem mainly from over-population and that a population policy is of fundamental significance and plays the main role in solving the problem of poverty and backwardness" (*Ta Kung Pao*, April 19, 1973, p. 10).

the interrelated effects of income and population growth, the "optimum population" notion is a static examination of the trade-off between the gains from division of labor and economies of scale, on the one hand, and the loss from diminishing returns to additional labor with a given stock of capital, on the other hand. This notion was in accord with the economics of its time; and the optimum-population theorizing was very neat even if not useful.[8]

Then economists lost interest in the subject of population. The old bugaboo of over-population no longer seemed frightening. In Western Europe population growth seemed to have ceased, and economists were then little aware of the underdeveloped world. In the absence of perceived threat from population increase, the interest of economists naturally dried up. Then Keynes (1937) and others suggested that increase in population is beneficial and perhaps even necessary as a stimulant to investment and overall demand (viz. Hansen, 1939). But this did not lead to much increase in the subject's attraction for economists.

As economists ceased studying population, sociologists and social psychologists gained interest. The desire to *stimulate* Western population growth in the 1930's was an important cause of interest for these social scientists. And after the subject fell into the hands of the sociologists, it remained there.

As economists more and more focused their attention on the economic growth of less-developed countries (LDC's) in the 1950's and 1960's, however, population growth forced itself on their awareness because it was thought to impede economic growth. In the low-income countries there has been rapid reduction in infant mortality and in mortality from endemic diseases. The fertility rates that kept population stable or growing only slowly when mortality rates were high remained as they were or increased, and the combined result has been a rapid increase in population. This extraordinary phenomenon has led to a spate of work whose starting point was Coale and Hoover's (1958) simulation of population growth's effect on India. Somewhat later came a renewed macro-economic interest in the role of population growth in the economies of more-developed countries (MDC's), an interest stimulated by concern about pollution, the environment, and natural resources.[9] And in the past few

[8] Myrdal called the concept of the population optimum "one of the most sterile ideas that ever grew out of our science" (1940, p. 26). But though the concept has ceased to be used much in economics, where it was developed, ecologists continue to discuss it.

[9] In the last few years biologists, and especially ecologists, have come to be very interested in population growth, and have dominated the discussion of population in the mass media. This will be discussed at greater length in Chapter 23 and the Appendix. At all times, however, the biologists have emphasized the role of resources in their thinking about population; their point of view is therefore very much economic. The best known example is Ehrlich's *The Population Bomb* (1968).

8

years there has burgeoned a microeconomic literature on the analysis of fertility, migration, mortality and marriage, much of it in the spirit of the "new consumer economics" which Becker brought to bear on demographic problems (1960; 1965). This book, then, appears at a time when economic interest in population is high, but before the literature is consolidated into a consistent integrated whole.

The Book's Organization and Findings

Now about this book. Population and economic welfare comprise a mutually interacting system, as Malthus taught us. But for purposes of analysis the system is separated into its component parts. Part I of the book discusses the effects of population change upon economic level and economic growth. That is, Part I inquires whether per-worker output and per-capita income will be influenced positively or negatively by increments of population, under various conditions. The issue is discussed first for countries that are already industrialized (MDC's) and then for those that are now industrializing or have hardly begun the industrialization process (LDC's). In both cases, the crucial question is the extent to which population growth has a positive feedback effect on economic growth and whether that positive feedback is great enough to eventually offset the negative effect. The main negative effect is much the same in both cases: An increase in the number of people working with a given amount of capital (including land) initially produces less output per worker.

The positive feedback effects from population growth are *not* the same in MDC's and LDC's. This is the main reason that the cases are discussed separately (MDC's in Chapters 3–6, and LDC's in Chapters 7–13). In MDC's increased numbers of people can have positive effects through increased knowledge and economies of size. But economies of size probably are less important in LDC's because of the lesser sophistication of their economies. The positive economic effects of population growth in LDC's are transformations of the individual and the society—for example, increases in work time and changes in production practices. Because there is much better intellectual foundation for understanding the positive effects in the MDC's than in the LDC's, the MDC's can be covered in four chapters, whereas the LDC's require seven.

The main aim of Part I is to assess these positive feedback effects in relationship to the negative ones. Technological progress constitutes a major part of the positive feedback. A key element in Part I is that the relationship between population growth and technological progress is

9

not a race between two independent forces, as so many writers[10] have suggested it is, but rather it is a system in which technological progress is to an important degree *a function of* population growth—the strength and nature of the connection being a central matter to assess.

Part I begins with a general discussion in Chapter 2 of the most important economic-demographic variables. In Chapters 3 and 4 estimates are made of the specific parameters necessary for the analysis of more developed countries, and the special topics of natural resources and pollution are discussed in Chapter 5. A simulation model for MDC's embodying these parameters is then constructed in Chapter 6. The crucial feedback effect of population growth upon the level of productivity is embodied in two alternative ways. The first approach utilizes the notion of the "residual" found in empirical studies of productivity change; the residual is made a function of the labor force, because it seems reasonable to assume that the size of the labor force influences the amount of invention and innovation. The second approach takes advantage of "Verdoorn's Law" which asserts that the change in productivity is a function of total output (and total output obviously is a function of population size). It is reasonable to suppose that output in Verdoorn's Law is an empirical representation for the influence of the size of labor force upon productivity, and hence the two approaches describe the same phenomenon. And in fact they give similar results.

The main finding for MDC's is that an increment of population in the MDC world would have at first a negative effect, but would come to have a net *positive* effect on per-worker income in less than a century, and perhaps in less than half a century—say, after 30–80 years.

Less-developed countries are then taken up. First, a general model is sketched in Chapter 7, and each of the variables is considered theoretically and empirically in Chapters 8–12. In addition to the likely negative effect of population growth upon the rate of monetized saving (Chapter 10), positive effects are found for the effect of population size and growth upon the rate of nonmonetized saving in agriculture (Chapter 11), and upon such social infrastructure as roads (Chapter 12). The latter effect is particularly important because of the crucial role that roads play in increasing the production and distribution of food, and the avoidance of famines such as that in the Sahel and Bangladesh. An increase in family size is also found to have a strong positive effect upon the amount of work done and output produced by the parents (Chapter 9). Then in Chapter 13 the equations and parameters are combined into a numerical

---

[10] "The fundamental conception of the *race* between technological progress and diminishing returns has stayed in the center of our growth theories . . ." (Fellner, 1963, p. xii, italics added).

10

simulation which considers the effects of various rates of population growth on per-worker output under various sets of conditions.

The main conclusion drawn from the LDC model is that moderate population growth has much better long-run economic effects than either a stationary population or very fast population growth. (In the short run, stationary population size is associated with a higher standard of living than is positive population growth, but the difference is surprisingly small.) The main factors accounting for the better long-run performance of moderate population growth as compared to stationary population growth are the additional work input by parents in response to increased needs of more children, higher industrial investment in response to higher demand, and economies of scale. (Of course nothing said here is intended to de-emphasize the short-run burden of additional children upon their families, and upon educational and other public facilities, until the system has time to adjust.)

Another finding (Chapter 8) is that the growth of Western economic civilization was both pushed by population growth and pulled by independent invention, rather than mostly being accomplished by one or the other force alone, as two schools of thought (described in Chapter 6) believe it was.

Part II considers the causal relationship running in the other direction, from economic condition to fertility. (It is only after both of these simultaneous mutually interacting influences are understood that one can try to understand the over-all effect of a change in either economic condition or in a population variable such as fertility.) More-developed and less-developed countries are discussed separately. And for each class of countries, the short-run effect of income—holding constant the effect of income-influenced forces such as education and urbanization—is taken up separately from the long-run total effect of changes in economic conditions (the latter including the effects through such forces as income and urbanization). Part II mostly surveys the extensive literature on the subject, and provides some general conclusions.

A central policy question considered in Part II is the extent to which fertility increases in response to a rise in income so as to counteract the rise in income. This "trap" was the heart of the Malthusian theory: An improvement in food production was thought to produce enough additional people to exhaust the improvement and to eventuate in the original level of subsistence living and high death rates. But the truth of this hypothesis depends upon—in addition to the possible positive effects of population—the *extent* to which fertility responds positively to increases in income level. It is concluded that it would be extremely unlikely that an increase in fertility could be of sufficient short-run magnitude to reverse economic gains of contemporary sizes.

11

The most important fact presented in Part II is the long-run decline in LDC fertility that follows upon economic development and an increase in LDC income. This effect is exactly the opposite of that assumed by the Malthusian model.

A special policy topic taken up in Part II for both MDC's and LDC's is the likely effect on fertility of economic incentives to have more or fewer children.

Part III considers some welfare and policy issues involved in the economics of population growth. Chapter 18 inquires into the welfare economics of population growth. It concludes that the welfare judgment one makes about additional people depends on such values as the importance of the short run versus the long run, whose welfare one wishes to take into account in which proportions, and what one believes is the importance to be attachèd to human life at poorer and richer standards of living. The judgment also depends, of course, on the economic outcomes one expects from population growth in various situations (the subject discussed in Part I). This implies the conclusion that the welfare effect of an increment of population is indeterminate in the presence of various widespread differences in value judgments and scientific analyses.

Part III then discusses some technical issues in the economics of population planning, including an analysis of the per-capita-income criterion (Chapter 19); the technique of cost-benefit analysis for population-control campaigns (Chapter 20); the appropriate concept of the value of an averted birth (Chapter 21), where perhaps unexpectedly this more general macro-economic method, free of the flaws of partial-analysis methods, leads to much *higher* estimates of the value of an expected birth of the order of $300 at 1956 prices at 5% and 15% rates of discount; and a study of birth-control marketing strategies (Chapter 22).

The reader may at first think it peculiar that the latter chapters in Part III discuss the economics of population reduction even though Chapter 18 argues that the welfare impact of additional children is scientifically indeterminate without controversial value judgments. But many countries are indeed prepared to make the value judgments that imply fertility reduction (though it is less clear that countries understand the long-run consequences of a stationary population versus moderate population growth well enough to make the decision in a thoroughly enlightened way). Chapters 20–22 are intended as technical assistance to nations which wish to reduce their population rate in furtherance of their own aims and values. I find no inconsistency in trying to help others achieve their aims even though I might not have the same goals were I in their places. Furthermore, birth-control campaigns to date use voluntary rather than coercive methods. They help couples have the number of children they want, and they thereby enhance people's power of choice and their ability to achieve the sort of family life they seek. Of that I am wholeheartedly in favor.

The general reader who wishes to skip background studies and general discussion and wants to find out what is new in this book should go directly to the conclusions in Chapter 23. If one is coming completely fresh to economic demography, Chapter 2 should then be a useful introduction. Otherwise, the general reader might proceed directly to Chapters 6 and 13 but omitting the formal aspects of the models, and then go to the welfare-economics discussion in Chapter 18. Readers who are primarily interested in the models of the effects of population growth on MDC and LDC economies but who demand documentation for the assumptions made in Chapters 6 and 13 will find that documentation in Chapters 3–5 and 8–12 respectively.

This book mostly discusses national units (though not particular countries) rather than the world as a whole, for several reasons. First, most policy decisions concerning population are made for nations rather than for the world. For example, Iranian leaders decide whether or not Iran will set up a birth-reduction program, and they do so in consideration of the needs of Iran rather than in consideration of the world's needs. Second, countries (and even small areas within countries) are quite independent in many ways. Third, the barriers to migration from one country to another imply that the country rather than the world as a whole is the appropriate unit of analysis. Fourth, autarky and striving for independent self-sufficiency may not be good things in themselves but sometimes they are necessary, at least for the time being. For these reasons it makes sense to study population at the level of the nation rather than at the level of the world.

Nations are classified for discussion into the two conventional classes of more-developed (MDC) and less-developed (LDC). In the former class are included: (1) most nations in Western Europe, Japan, and Oceania; and (2) nations with per-capita incomes over $1,000 (in 1976). Any nation whose economy might sensibly be analyzed with a Keynsian framework obviously falls into the MDC category, though the converse need not be so. While this classification is not perfect, the reader is not likely to be in much doubt about how to classify any particular nation for purposes of analysis in this book.

The most important population variable discussed in this book is the difference in total population size resulting from different birth rates, including such consequences of differences in birth rates as differences in labor-force proportions. Change in total population size as a function of migration will be discussed relatively little because in the second half of the twentieth century international migration runs a distant second in importance to birth rate differences.[11] Differences in mortality rates are discussed mostly as parameters rather than as variables, because it is doubtful that mortality will consciously be manipulated by civilized states for purposes of economic welfare alone.

TIME, PARADOXES, AND POPULATION: GROWTH'S REAL EFFECTS

A fundamental aim of this book is to enlarge the time span within which the economics of population growth is commonly discussed, both by lengthening the horizon within which conditional analyses of the future are made and by pushing the historical record back to earlier times than are usually adduced in the discussion. There is a single reason for both extensions: To understand and to take into account the slower-moving but crucial forces, together with the immediate-action factors, that connect population and economic welfare.

We are, at the time of this writing, in the midst of general concern over population growth. At the bottom of the concern are two commonly accepted ideas: (1) Population is on a geometrically increasing curve and is now "exploding" in size; (2) More people pressing on limited natural resources will keep us poor or make us poor. But things are not so simple. One crucial fact is that the history of population growth is not a history of steady geometric increase. Rather, population history has been a series of rises and falls, as Figure 1–1 shows for the lower Diyala basin in Iraq (one of the places for which our historical knowledge is fullest) and as Figure 1–2 shows for Egypt. The Roman Empire and

---

[11] Migration would also demand a large and special treatment, on a level of aggregation somewhat lower than the treatment of fertility. These are some of the ways in which the phenomena of migration and fertility differ for analytical purposes:

1. By the time of maturity, additional native children differ less on the average from the rest of the adult population than do immigrants, in such economic aspects as labor skills, education, and wealth endowment. The impact of immigrants therefore is disproportionately on a few industries. Analysis of the effects therefore requires close and complete analysis. For a rare successful example of such analysis see Jones and Smith (1970).

2. Immigrants usually have less claim than average on the nation's existing wealth. This means that if an immigrant produces more than his wage, everyone else benefits on the average because the owner of the capital with which he works increases his take. But an additional native is more likely to have a claim on both his salary and on capital's share of his additional output.

3. Immigrants tend to arrive after childhood, and hence the public part of their education costs are saved to the public.

4. Immigrants are culturally different, which has complex social effects. (These social effects can be good or bad, but usually only the bad side is discussed.)

5. The effect of immigration *can* be analyzed for one country, as can fertility. But it is more meaningful to broaden the analysis to include both the sending and the receiving countries, as well as the combined system of both sets of countries and their populations taken together. The welfare answers and the policy prescriptions differ depending on the context of analysis one chooses.

14

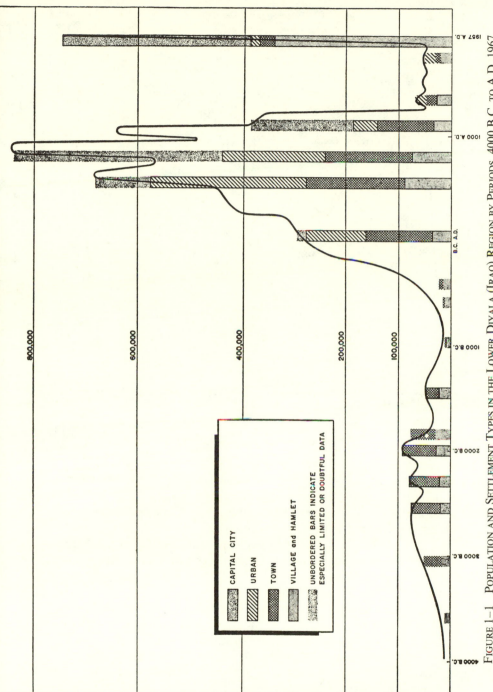

FIGURE 1–1 POPULATION AND SETTLEMENT TYPES IN THE LOWER DIYALA (IRAQ) REGION BY PERIODS. 4000 B.C. TO A.D. 1967

SOURCE: Adams, 1965, p. 115.

CAPITAL CITY

URBAN

TOWN

VILLAGE and HAMLET

UNBORDERED BARS INDICATE
ESPECIALLY LIMITED OR DOUBTFUL DATA

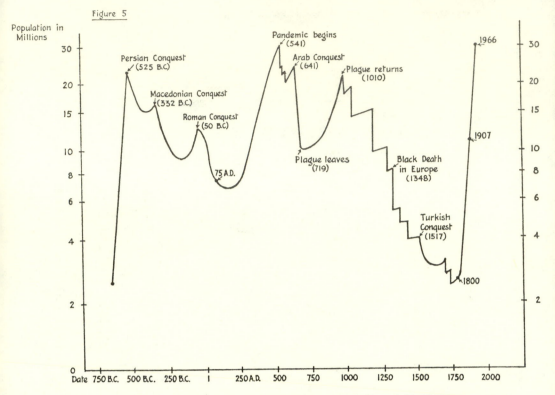

Figure 5

FIGURE 1–2   THE POPULATION OF EGYPT, 664 B.C. TO A.D. 1966
SOURCE: Reproduced from Hollingsworth, 1969, p. 311.

Europe are among the other places where sharp declines and rises in
population are known to have occurred. An especially sharp depopulation occurred in Mexico and the Caribbean after the Spanish arrived;
this may be seen in Figure 1–3. Another piece of complicating evidence
is that those times in history when population has been at or near peaks
have generally been the most prosperous times, and the recent centuries
in Europe and the West have seen the greatest economic *and* population
growth rates in history until then.

   These historical observations make one doubt the simplistic conventional system based on connections of population, natural resources plus
capital, and economic welfare; history forces us to look deeper for the
other forces that explain it. And it makes sense that these less obvious—
and slower acting—forces must be included in models for analysing
future possibilities if the models are not to lead us into error. If the models
are to embody these slower-acting factors and show their effects, their
horizons must be longer than the thirty-year or fifty-year horizons with
which economic-demographic models usually work.

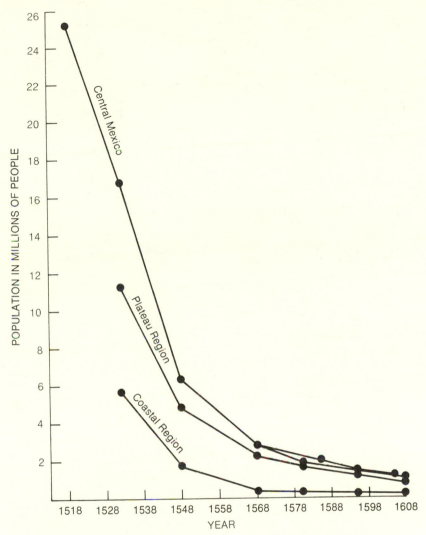

FIGURE 1–3   THE POPULATION OF MEXICO, CENTRAL MEXICO ALONE, AND
THE PLATEAU AND COASTAL REGIONS OF CENTRAL MEXICO, 1518–1608
SOURCE: Cook and Borah, 1971, pp. viii, 82.

The history of demographic predictions is another reason that we should
aim at humility and take care to avoid fear-motivated over-reactive
policies. For example, in the 1930's most Western countries worried very
much about an expected decline in population. The most extensive investigation, undertaken by some of the world's best social scientists, was
done in Sweden. The dotted lines in Figure 1–4 show how the future
looked to them then. *All* of their dotted-line hypotheses about the future—
intended to bracket all of the conceivable possibilities—turned out to be

17

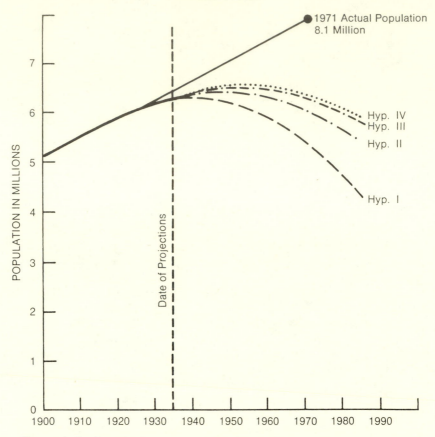

FIGURE 1–4   SWEDISH POPULATION, 1900–85, ACCORDING TO FOUR HYPOTHESES
MADE IN 1935 AND ACTUAL POPULATION IN 1971

SOURCE: A. Myrdal, 1941, p. 80; originally, Population Commission, Report on Demographic Investigations.

far below the actual course of population growth, as shown by the solid line; that is, the future turned out far better from the point of view of those scientists than any of them guessed it might. And if they had successfully brought about effective fertility-increasing programs, as they recommended, the results would have been contrary to what they *now* want. It may well be that we are now at an analogous point in history, with the difference that population growth is popularly thought to be too fast rather than too slow as in the 1930's.

The economics of population suffers as a study from the fact that it seems simple whereas in fact it is very complex. First, there is the paradox mentioned above that population growth which may appear detrimental

18

in the short run may be beneficial in the long run, even by the same measures of welfare. Second, there is the paradox that the increased use of such natural resources as oil and iron because of increased population and increased demand generally does not increase their scarcity from an economic point of view, because of the induced creation of new supplies for the same needs (see Chapter 5). Finally, there is the paradox that though vastly improved health will increase population growth in the short run, it will almost surely reduce population growth in the long run. Better health and lower child mortality make it possible for parents to achieve the family sizes they wish with fewer babies. This lessens the chance of over-shooting the mark and having more children than families wish. Therefore better nutrition—the main agent in improving health— may turn out to be the most effective investment in adjusting population size in poor countries to the desires of individuals and their nations.

Paradoxes like these make it important not to accept the answers of the simplest models of population, natural resources plus capital, and economic welfare. The simple and sensational answers obtained may well be wrong and could cause serious damage to civilization and mankind.

We must have the courage to accept that populaton economics is a complex subject, where one man's problem is another man's solution and where most people's long-run interests are likely to be best served by intellectual humility and undogmatic policies.

PART I

The Effects of Population Growth
on Economic Conditions

INTRODUCTION

PART I of this book aims to assess the effects of an increment of population—that is, faster or slower population growth—upon economic level and economic growth. The moder-developed and the less-developed countries are considered separately.

Chapter 2 reviews the basic concepts, first giving a comparative-statics analysis of each of the important variables separately, and then offering a sketch of the general model for such an inuqiry. Chapter 2 may be omitted by readers who are already familiar with economic-demographic studies.

Chapters 3 and 4 discuss in detail each of the variables that go into a numerical simulation of the effect of population growth in a more-developed economy. Both theory and available analytical evidence are brought to bear on each variable so as to build as solid an estimate of each parameter as is presently possible.

Chapter 6 constructs a specialized simulation model appropriate for the MDC world, and solves it numerically for a variety of assumed values. The main finding is that in almost all the simulated cases an increment of population leads, within 30–80 years, to a higher per-worker income than would otherwise prevail. That is, a higher population growth rate is apparently economically beneficial in the MDC world in the long run.

The subject of MDC's is dealt with in only four chapters, as compared to seven for LDC's. One reason for this relative brevity is that much of the necessary material is available elsewhere, and therefore need not be developed here. Another reason is that the positive effects of population growth are simple and easier to understand in MDC's than in LDC's. In MDC's, the feedback effect does not involve fundamental psychological or sociological transformations of the society, but rather stems mostly from economies of scale and the external effects of increased knowledge. But in LDC's, much of whatever positive economic effects flow from increased population growth are part of "modernization"—changes in attitudes and behavior and production practices. It is very difficult to understand such transformational changes and to estimate their likely magnitudes. Whereas the supply of labor may be considered exogenously determined in MDC's, in LDC's the amount and kind of productive work done by the population is a function of population size and growth. The demand side of the system therefore must be included. This is a major complication, and it is the most important reason why the discussion of LDC's is protracted relative to the discussion of MDC's.

Chapter 7 develops a specialized model for LDC countries that is appropriate both to the pre-industrial stage and to the industrializing stage. Arguments are given in that chapter for the choice of variables and the underlying scheme whereby the model is solved by society, but the equations are not specified in form or in parametric values. Chapter 8 studies the role of feedback caused by population growth, relative to the role of autonomous invention, in the economic growth of Western Europe and elsewhere. It is hoped that this inquiry carries independent interest for the understanding of history. But its main aim is to give historical perspective to the feedback process for use in contemporary models. Chapter 9 examines the evidence for quantitative estimates of the behavior change in LDC agriculture that population growth may be expected to produce; because the effects of population growth must differ over places and times, the appendix to Chapter 9 makes a case study of a single locale, villages in India, attempting to make parameter estimates that would fit this one particular place. Chapter 10 discusses the effect of LDC population growth on the accumulation of industrial capital. It reviews the economic-demographic models that have been based on capital effects, and extracts from them and from the available empirical studies parameter estimates that may be used for a more general model. Then Chapter 11 investigates and estimates the effect of population growth on agricultural investment. The effect of population increase on private agricultural investment is then compared to the effect on industrial investment; the comparison suggests that the two effects may be of the same general magnitude but in opposite directions. Chapter 12 studies the effect of population growth on investment in social capital, with emphasis on transportation.

Finally, Chapter 13 pulls together all the material on LDC's into a numerical simulation. It concludes that moderate population growth leads to a higher material standard of living in the long run than does either a stationary population or very fast population growth, while in the short run the advantage of the stationary population is very slight. The main mechanisms by which the moderate population growth produces better results in LDC's are increased work input, demand-induced industrial investment, and increased social infrastructure together with economies of scale.

The Effect of Population Growth
on the Economic Level:
Background, Comparative Statics, and
General Dynamic Model

THE BACKGROUND[1]

[Mr. Longways]:	"True; your mother was a very good woman—I can mind her. She were rewarded by the Agricultural Society for having begot the greatest number of healthy children without parish assistance, and other virtuous marvels."
[Mrs. Cuxsom]:	"Twas that that kept us so low upon ground—that great hungry family."
[Mr. Longways]:	"Ay. Where the pigs be many the wash runs thin."
	(Thomas Hardy, *The Mayor of Casterbridge*, p. 89)

THE BROAD outline of the history of population and economy is reasonably simple. The story begins with a country that has a high birth rate and a high death rate. Togo, for example, has a birth rate of 55 per thousand and Finland in the mid-eighteenth century had a birth rate of up to 45 per thousand, in comparison to a birth rate of 14 per thousand in Sweden in the early 1970's. Viewed differently, the average woman in Sweden now has a little over two children, while the average woman in Togo has over 6 children.

In earlier years the death rate in countries such as Togo at present and such as Finland in the eighteenth century was high enough to keep the population from growing rapidly, if at all.[2] But in most LDC's declines in death rates have already occurred and may be expected to continue, and declines will soon occur in the rest of the LDC's. The death rate in Togo in 1960–64 was 29 per thousand, so a substantial gap between death rates and birth rates already exists. And in Mauritius the death rate fell from 29.6 to 8.0 since 1931–35, and life expectancy at birth rose from 33 years to 64 years; mortality in Togo may well continue to fall in the future in the pattern of Mauritius.[3]

---

[1] This chapter contains little new material and may be skipped by readers who are well-acquainted with economic-demographic studies. The chapter is intended mainly for the reader who comes fresh to the subject.

[2] The birth rate is now probably higher in Togo than in earlier years, if the experience of other countries is a guide. See Chapters 14 and 16.

[3] Data are from Gille (1949–50), Stolnitz (1965), and *Population Index*, various issues up to 1974. The accuracy of such estimates is, of course, not great, but this will not affect the argument here.

Demographers believe that the birth rate in LDC's will also decline correspondingly with the death rate. They believe so because this was the experience in the past in Europe, its overseas extensions, and Japan, and because more recently the birth rate has declined sharply in such places as Singapore, Hong Kong, Taiwan, Mauritius, Barbados, Korea, Costa Rica, Reunion, and Martinique (many of which, it should be noted, are islands.) But unfortunately for the theory of the demographic transition, birth rates have not yet fallen much if at all in some countries where death rates (and especially infant mortality rates) have fallen greatly. That is, a fair number of non-European countries have not behaved in accordance with the pattern of Europe—as yet, anyway (but see Oechsli and Kirk, 1975). Nevertheless, let us proceed for the moment as if the demographic transition is a fair description of reality.

As compared to a high birth rate and a high death rate, a combination of a lower death rate and a lower birth rate is surely a good thing in itself—for the human reason of less travail and grief required to raise a family of any given size, as well as for economic reasons. Raising children who then die early is an appalling waste, both in economic[4] and emotional terms.

With respect to LDC's, the important demographic-economic question for scholars and for national planners is this: How will a larger or smaller fertility rate affect the course of the demographic transition and of industrialization? Will more births delay or prevent economic growth, or are more births a help? And how great is the expected effect of an increment of population on economic growth and on the standard of living during and after demographic transition? This is the question which the book addresses with respect to LDC's. The answer provided by the empirical explorations together with the simulation is that in the short run a very low population growth rate is rather advantageous. But in the long run—say, after 75–150 years—moderate population growth does better than either a stationary population or very fast population growth.

With respect to MDC's, the focus of the inquiry is different. Where the death rate is low and the birth rate is also low, further decline in the death

---

[4] Hansen (1957) multiplied the number of deaths in each age-bracket of children by the estimated total expenditures on children of that age prior to their death. For India the result was about 3% of national income as of 1951, and in the United Kingdom and United States it was about 0.1% of national income in 1951 (down from perhaps 0.3 or 0.4 in 1931). The figure for India is much less than the much-quoted figure of "22% of our national income" of Ghosh (1946), but it is still large enough to be very important, being of the same magnitude as total annual growth in GNP in India.

Another approach is to calculate the increase in the average cost of raising one person who will be alive at age 18. The higher is mortality during childhood, the greater the expenditure on children who will not live to age 18. Sauvy figured that while child mortality raises the cost less than 1% in MDC's, it was raised by 15–20% in India as of 1921–30. (Mortara, quoted by Sauvy, calculated 10% for India using a different cost structure. Sauvy, 1969, pp. 238–39).

rate is no longer a central economic issue.[5] But population may still grow at a faster or slower rate, and in fact it may not grow at all and may even decline. The various population-change possibilities have different implications for the MDC economy, as we shall see, for some of the same reasons and also for some quite different reasons than in LDC's. To ascertain the likely effects of different population-change regimes on economic growth in MDC's is our task with respect to MDC's. Two quite different simulation approaches, using the most plausible empirically based estimates for knowledge feedback and other parameters, suggest that after 30–80 years faster population growth comes to have a higher standard of living than slow or no population growth.

Because many of the principles of population analysis are the same for LDC's and for MDC's, this chapter now takes up the relevant variables in the abstract. The chapter also sketches a general model for understanding the dynamic effects of all the variables together. The chapters that follow separately investigate the over-all effect of population change in LDC's and MDC's. The rest of this chapter should be considered as a theoretical introduction to the substantive analyses that follow.

The Comparative Statics of Population Growth and the Economy

The most important idea in the analytical economics of population comes from Malthus and can be stated in a single sentence: *Ceteris paribus*, the more people the lower the per-capita income (PCI). This proposition derives from the "law" of diminishing returns: Two men cannot use the same tool at the same time or farm the same piece of land without reducing the output per worker. A related idea is that two people cannot nourish themselves as well as can one person from a given stock of food. And when one considers different population sizes resulting from different birth rates, the proposition is reinforced by the fact of a lower proportion of workers in the larger population.

The reader should not, however, leap too quickly or too violently to a belief in this conclusion which depends entirely upon the *ceteris paribus* assumption. Here are two observations intended to keep you in a state of suspended judgment for a while: (1) If population had *never* grown to the millions and billions, but rather had remained in the hundreds or thousands on this earth, it is pretty clear that we would still be primitive hunters and gatherers of food. (2) Some of the most densely populated places on earth are among the richest.

---

[5] In the future, lengthening of the span of time people spend at various physiological ages may become an important matter, however. I hope someone will investigate this question soon.

Much later discussion is devoted to considering the various factors compounded in the *ceteris paribus* clause which, if the factors are *not* held equal, might reverse the Malthusian conclusion above—or might reinforce it. This resembles asserting that, *certis paribus*, two objects will fall to the earth with the same speed (in a vacuum this will be the speed of gravity), and then considering the factors that might make one object fall slower than the other, or even rise (e.g., a balloon).

First, we will examine in more detail the operation of the law of diminishing returns (or to put it another way, the effect of sheer numbers). Then, we will consider the age-distributional and labor-force-proportion issue. After that we turn to some other factors, still in a comparative-statics framework, that might mitigate or reinforce these two primary forces. The discussion in this chapter is in very general terms. Empirical evidence bearing on most of these relationships is given in later chapters.

The Effect of Sheer Numbers

Simply adding more people to a population affects consumption directly. It also affects consumption indirectly through the effect on production per worker. The former effect is quite simple: If there is only one pie, the pieces will be smaller if it is divided among more eaters. The experience of the hippies in San Fancisco in 1967 illustrates this problem:

> Most hippies take the question of survival for granted, but it's becoming increasingly obviously as the neighborhood fills with penniless heads, that there is simply not enough food and lodging to go around. A partial solution may come from a group called the "Diggers," who have been called the "worker-priests" of the hippy movement and the "invisible government" of the Hashbury. The Diggers are young and aggressively pragmatic; they have set up free lodging centers, free soup kitchens and free clothing distribution centers. They comb the neighborhood soliciting donations of everything from money to stale bread to camping equipment.
>
> For a while, the Diggers were able to serve three meals, however meager, each afternoon in Golden Gate Park. But as the word got around, more and more hippies showed up to eat, and the Diggers were forced to roam far afield to get food. Occasionally there were problems, as when Digger Chieftain Emmett Grogan, 23, called a local butcher a "Fascist pig and a coward" when he refused to donate meat scraps. The butcher whacked Grogan with the flat side of his meat cleaver (*New York Times Magazine*, May 14, 1967, p. 121.)

This consumption effect occurs most sharply within a family. When there are more children, each one gets a smaller portion from the family's

28

earnings, if earnings remain the same rather than being increased by additional work to make up for the additional children's needs.

On the production side, consider a low-income country that possesses a given amount of land and a given quantity of factories and other fixed industrial capital at a given point in time. If the country has a large rather than a small labor force, the production per worker will be lower with the larger labor force than if the labor force were smaller. The reason is the classical argument: diminishing returns. If the number of workers is larger and the amount of capital (tools or land) is the same, output is less than proportional to the number of workers. That is, each worker has, on the average, less land or tools to work with, and hence average production per worker will be lower, even though the *total* production will be higher.

In the industrial sector the effect of diminishing marginal returns to a fixed stock of capital is obscured by the apparently fixed technological ratio: one man (or N men) to one machine. But even in the simplest case where one and only one man works at a machine (assuming all machines to be in use) an increasing number of workers leads to diminishing marginal returns—in fact, to zero marginal returns—because an added man has no machine with which to work and hence he produces nothing. Therefore, there is a lower average output per worker, because the same output is now divided by the sum of the original workers plus the added but unproductive workers. In the less extreme case where larger numbers of workers result in more daily hours of use per machine, the marginal return to additional workers also is likely to diminish because there is less time for the machine to be serviced and repaired; that is, more of the working-shift time will be used for repairs and servicing.

There has been much discussion about the possibility that marginal productivity in agriculture is *zero* in crowded LDC's. But by now there is general agreement that crops will always benefit *somewhat* from additional labor spent on them during almost any part of the growing season, so that the marginal productivity of additional *man hours* in agriculture is not zero (T. W. Schultz, 1972, p. 352). Even in the most densely settled countries there is always a shortage of workers at harvest time. (During the off seasons, of course, agriculturalists work relatively few hours per week. It is this phenomenon that has led many observers to think that marginal productivity is zero. This pool of potential work could aid economic development in LDC's if actual work output could be obtained from it, especially on infrastructure investment projects.) The fundamental Malthusian fact remains, however: In agriculture as in industry there are diminishing returns to additional workers.

So we have seen that the *ceteris paribus* effect of sheer numbers depresses per-capita income in two ways: more consumers dividing any given amount of output, and less output per worker because there is less capital for each worker to produce with.

The Age-Distribution Effect

The discussion until now has implicitly compared populations of different sizes but alike in all other respects—alike especially in the proportions of each population at each age. But policy-makers are never faced with a choice between populations with similar age distributions; one does not obtain populations of any size instantly as one calls up and buys either ten pounds or twenty pounds of sugar. Rather, to the extent that a nation can choose, it mostly chooses between higher and lower birth rates that will lead to populations of different sizes only after some time. And the process of reaching one population size or another inevitably results in different distributions of age groups in the population.

Consider two countries that have similar populations at the outset. The country that is headed for a larger population must have more babies this year than the other country, while all other age groups remain the same in the two populations; therefore, there is a higher proportion of children aged 0–1 in the population that is now, and will be in the future, larger. Furthermore, if two populations grow at constant but different rates over time, the faster-growing population will always have a higher proportion of children at each age, and therefore a higher proportion of all children below the working age, than the slower-growing population. To put this another way, faster population growth means a larger proportion of the population too young to work. This smaller proportion of workers must mean a smaller output per capita, *ceteris paribus*. Therefore the effect of sheer numbers, and the age distribution that occurs in the process of getting to higher numbers, both work in the same direction, causing a smaller per-capita product.

Readers not trained in demography may be surprised, as I was wn first came to study this material, at the *extent* of age-distributional du ferences. For example, in 1955–56, 44% of the population of Costa Rica was younger than fifteen years old, compared to 24% in Sweden (Dorn, 1963, p. 24). Age-distributional differences between Mexico and Sweden in 1970 are shown in Figure 2–1. Figure 2–2 summarizes the age-distribution data for the world as of 1960–65 (as well as the birth rates, the death rates, and rate of natural increase). And the proportions of the *male* populations who are within the prime labor-force years of 15 and 64 was 70% in Sweden in 1940, and 53% in Brazil in 1900 (United Nations, 1956, p. 15). That is, there were over 30% more male workers in Sweden than in Brazil relative to the total population. The economic effect of such differences is clearly not trivial. And this is the result of the age-distribution on only the *male* labor force.

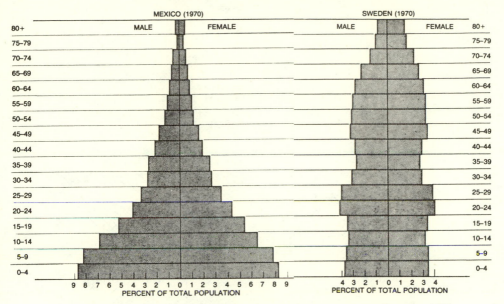

FIGURE 2–1 COMPARISON OF AGE DISTRIBUTIONS IN MEXICO AND SWEDEN, 1970
SOURCE: Reproduced from Freedman and Berelson, 1974, pp. 38–39.

When one also takes the women into account, the effect of age-distribution on the proportion of people in the labor force is even greater. The more children that are born per woman, the less chance she has to participate in the labor force outside the home. For example, in the 1920's and 1930's when most Israeli *kibbutzim* were near bare subsistence, strong pressure was often brought upon parents not to have more than two children so that women could continue to work on jobs other than child-rearing (Kanovsky, 1966, p. 38).

So an increased number of children has two negative age-distributional effects upon output (income) per capita: a smaller proportion of persons of labor-force age, and a decrease in the number of women free to leave home for work.

The Need for Public Facilities

If a given population were instantly enlarged by, say, 10% in all age groups, there would be 10% more people wanting to use the village well or the city hospital or the resort beach. An increase in the demand for such freely provided public services inevitably results in (1) an increase in the number of people who are denied service; (2) a decrease in the amount of service per person; or (3) an additional expenditure by the government to increase the amount of facilities available. If the 10% population increase also resulted in a 10% increase in the number of

31

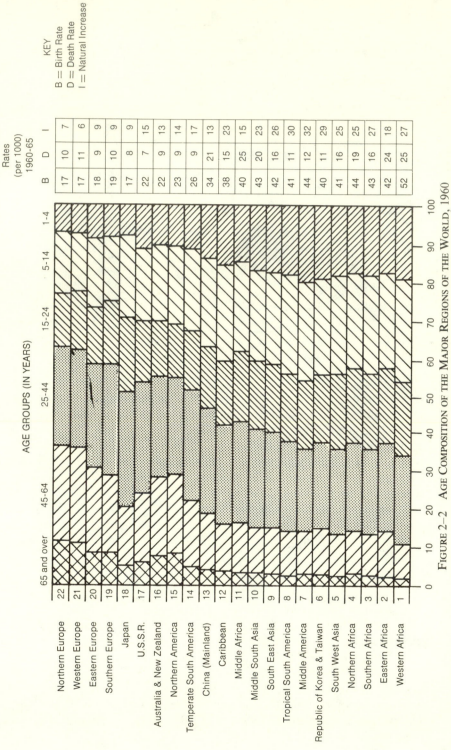

FIGURE 2–2 AGE COMPOSITION OF THE MAJOR REGIONS OF THE WORLD, 1960

SOURCE: Prepared by Bourgeois-Pichat, 1966, p. 44 from data in UN, 1963, Appendix B, Table I, and Appendix C, Tables I, II, and III.

people working, and if the productivity of the added people was as great, on the average, as that of the original population, then the added population would have no effect on per-capita income. But such a compensating increase in production is not likely to be the case. The demand for public facilities—especially schools—is likely to occur *before* people find work and become productive; even with respect to the immigration of adults, the immigrant uses the facilities of the custom house before he even enters the country. Even after the additional children join the labor force, the addition of more potential workers is likely to lower the average worker's productivity because of the diminishing-returns effect discussed earlier—at least in the short run and in LDC's—and hence the added workers will not be able to contribute as much in taxes to support public facilities as the average person formerly did.

As a result of the increased demand for public facilities, the average level of services received is likely to be lower, the average person receiving less education and less health care than otherwise. But also important is that funds are likely to be diverted from other sorts of projects on this account. Some tax moneys that might have gone into harbors or communications systems may instead go to the education and health care of the incremental people.

The Rate of Saving

Output per worker—and hence the income per capita—depends upon the amount of capital available for each man to work with (though output per worker does not *only* depend on the amount of capital, of course.) To obtain a stock of capital people must save some part of their incomes. Therefore, the amount that is saved from present income influences future PCI and consumption.

Saving can take place directly by individuals and businesses. Additionally, some of the money extracted as taxes from individuals can be saved by government. Let us first focus on individual saving.[6]

A father's marginal utility for money is often assumed to be greater with five hungry children than with three. That is, his "need" for money seems greater. Hence he is assumed to spend more and save less. This line of argument implicitly assumes that the individual's earning opportunity is fixed, so that the number of children does not affect his work decisions. It also assumes that additional children have an effect upon him such that he gives higher priority to *immediate* consumption than to *later*

---

[6] It is important to understand that from the standpoint of saving and investment, the *rest* of society is not directly affected by whether a man spends $50 per year on each of 6 children, or $150 per year on each of 2 children. Only if he spends *less* than $300 *in total* on the 2 children, whereas he would spend $300 if he had 6, does the society at large gain any benefit from his smaller family through individual saving.

consumption.[7] The warrant for the crucial latter assumption is simply the psychological guess that more children mean more pleas, requests, and demands of the parents who make the decisions to save or spend, a pressure which shifts the parents' preferences in such a way that they spend a larger proportion of their income in the present period than they otherwise would. But, then, one may also speculate about an opposing effect. With more children, people may forego some luxuries in the present in order to save for the children's future needs, as, for example, a college education. Such conflicts in the theory imply that the existing theory is not very helpful.

There is still another reason why theorizing about saving cannot by itself get us very far: The assumption that income is fixed, rather than variable in response to the number of children, may well be unrealistic. Men—and women, too, after their children are no longer young—work more if they have more children. The assumption of a fixed income is particularly inappropriate in the context of subsistence agriculture. Much of agricultural saving—especially new land clearance and construction of irrigation systems—is done with the farmer's own labor, and is usually *additional* to the labor he would otherwise expend in raising his crops. Population growth is likely to have a positive effect on this sort of saving, and hence upon the community's stock of capital.

In sum, even if the assumption about the effect of demands of more children upon preferences and decision-making is correct, theory cannot even tell us whether the saving effect out of given income is on balance negative or positive, or if it is negative, whether it is bigger in total than the opposite effect of people working harder when they have more children. Hence one must refer to empirical data to know how much effect, if any, more children have upon total saving, or upon saving as a proportion of income. A variety of such data for MDC's and LDC's is presented in Chapters 3 and 10–11, respectively.

The effects of more children on *governmental* savings may also be important. It is often assumed, *ceteris paribus*, that in poor societies governments have less power to tax when people have more children, because the competition in the family between feeding children and paying taxes is then more acute. One might also reason the opposite, however: If there are more children than otherwise, governments might be able to extract *more* in taxes because people recognize more need for taxes to buy additional schools and other facilities. The number of children may also affect the *kinds* of investments governments will make. For example, an

---

[7] This latter assumption may also imply that he prefers to spend more now rather than save so that he can later rise to a *higher* level of consumption. In terms of the life-cycle consumption theory, more children cause consumption to be shifted forward in time, which also implies less total consumption over the decision-maker's lifetime.

increase in children may induce a government to invest more than other-wise, but investment in the sort of capital that will quickly increase the production of goods might decline.

THE EFFECTS OF SCALE

The absolute size of a country, as well as the density of population per unit of area, can influence the efficiency of economic activity in many dif-ferent ways. First and foremost in the thinking of economists since Adam Smith, larger population implies a bigger market, *ceteris paribus*. A bigger market is likely to bring bigger manufacturing plants that may be more efficient than smaller ones, as well as longer production runs and hence lower set-up costs per unit of output. A larger market also makes possible greater division of labor and hence an increase in the skill with which goods and services are made. Specialization can also occur with respect to machinery. If the market for its goods is small, a firm will buy a machine that can be used in the production of several kinds of products. If its market is larger, the firm can afford to buy a separate more specialized machine for each operation. Larger markets also support a wider variety of services. If population is too small, there may be too few people to constitute a profitable market for a given product or service. In such a case there will be no seller, and people who do need the product or service will suffer from not being able to obtain it. Economies of scale also stem from learning. The more radios or bridges that a group of people produces, the more chance they have to improve their skills with "learning by doing."

The effect of a country's population size on its productive efficiency depends on its physical and political circumstances. One such factor is the extent to which a country is economically integrated with its neighboring countries. If the borders do not much restrict the flow of trade, and if transportation is good and cheap, then the size of the country itself is less important. Monaco does not suffer from lack of division of labor because it is so well integrated with France: it need not produce a wide range of goods and services itself, but rather can import most of them from France while specializing in its export commodity, the use of its casino. Israel, on the other hand, has little trade with any of its bordering Arab states and hence must conduct more activities within its own borders than if it could trade with its neighbors. Its absolute size is therefore more relevant than if it were economically integrated with the rest of the Middle East. Another factor affecting the absolute size of population required for efficiency is the stage of economic development. The less advanced is a society, the fewer specialties at which different people can work. That is, smallness has less of a depressing effect on a very backward country, *ceteris paribis*, than on a country further along in industralization.

Increased population must be accompanied by an increase in total income for there to be a bigger market, and more babies do not automatically mean a bigger total income, especially in the short run. But when the increment of population reaches the age at which it begins to work, under almost any reasonable set of assumptions total income and total demand will be larger than otherwise.

A bigger population also causes to be profitable many major social investments that would not otherwise be profitable (e.g., railroads, irrigation systems, ports). Such construction may be a function of population *density* per given land area. For example, if an Australian farmer cleared a piece of land very far from the nearest neighboring farm, he might have no way to ship his produce to market, as well as having difficulty in obtaining labor and supplies. But when more farms are established nearby, roads will be built which will link him with markets in which to buy and sell. Such reasoning lay behind the desire of Australia for immigrants and a larger population, as it was for the American West in the last century. Public administration and safety forces (e.g., fire departments) are other social activities that can often be carried on at lower cost per person when the population is larger.

There may also be *diseconomies* of increased scale. Congestion is such a diseconomy. As there is an increase in the number of sellers and activity in, say, a city's wholesale fruit-and-vegetable market, transacting one's business *may* become more difficult because of confusion and reduced space per unit of transaction. This sort of diseconomy is very much like the concept of diminishing returns to land that is at the heart of Malthusian reasoning. This phenomenon *ultimately* must occur as long as there is some factor of production—be it land for the farmer, or the market area for the wholesalers—that remains fixed in size. But if that factor can be increased, then the diseconomies of scale (especially congestion) can be avoided or reduced.

Another possible source of diseconomies is a smaller propensity to work cooperatively for the good of the group as the group gets larger (Olson, 1965).

In view of the fact that there are a variety of forces associated with scale that effect economic activity in opposite directions, the net effect of the size of the economy and the density of settlement can only be known empirically. A variety of relevant empirical data for MDC's and LDC's are presented in Chapters 4 and 12 respectively.

THE EFFECT OF POPULATION GROWTH ON HEALTH

The health of the citizens of a country is obviously one of their central welfare concerns. Feeling healthy is at least as valued as anything else an economy can provide. Health also is a central issue in the functioning of the economy. Healthy people can and do work much harder and better than sick people. Prevalent illness is a crucial barrier to the economic development of poor countries.

Additional population in very poor countries is likely to affect the level of health. At the family level, there is a direct reduction of each person's share of foods of all kinds, which can lead directly to developmental damage and indirectly to death through predisposition to disease. There will also be a reduction in maternal and paternal care, but in what circumstances this has ill effects is not clear. If a relatively smaller population leads to a relatively higher per-capita income, one would deduce that a better level of health in LDC's would also follow, because families could then afford better nutrition and health care.

But increased population density can also have beneficial effects upon health. Malaria, for example, flourishes where population is sparse and much moist land is not cultivated; increased density removes breeding grounds (see Chapter 12). Higher population density also increases the availability of health facilities. So we do not know a priori whether the net effect on health of increased populations will be positive or negative.

THE FEEDBACK EFFECT OF INCOME ON POPULATION GROWTH

The foregoing discussion of important elements in the population-income nexus is not complete without the effect of income on population size and growth. All else being equal—especially tastes—the effects of income on fertility and mortality are positive and negative respectively. But except in the very short run, other factors do not remain the same as income changes. Hence, the long-run effect of an increment of income on fertility is complex. This topic is taken up in considerable detail in Chapters 15 and 16. It is also worth mentioning here, however, that in some sorts of analyses population change may be considered exogenous, especially if fertility is to be a policy control variable. The feedback effect is then ignored. In the long run, however, population change clearly is a function of economic change, in which case the entire system must be studied as a whole.

A GENERAL DYNAMIC MODEL FOR THE STUDY OF THE ECONOMICS OF POPULATION GROWTH

If the economist is to be worth his keep he must attend to the *size* and *importance* of effects. Furthermore, if several influences operate concurrently, he must concern himself with the *over-all* effect, rather than with the size of the effect of any one variable assuming that all the rest of the variables are constant—which they are not. Such an over-all assessment requires study of the interaction of the variables with each other and with other variables. In such a case one can only obtain a satisfactory over-all assessment by constructing an integrated model of the economy under discussion, and then comparing the incomes produced by the economy under various conditions of population growth.[8]

An integrated assessment requires a dynamic model of the economy. One must compromise between the greater complexity of a more realistic model, and the greater distortion of a more abstract and less realistic model.

The starting point of such an integrated dynamic model is a production function that shows how output is related to the factors of production. The production function includes all the forces that affect output, such as labor of various kinds, capital of various kinds, other resources, the knowledge used in the productive process, and so on. In a study of population in LDC's it is often useful to work with two subparts of the overall production function, an agricultural production function and an industrial production function. Overall production (or income), Y, in year t may then be written[9] as

$$Y_t = f_F(M_{F,t}, K_{F,t}, A_{F,t}, \text{education, health, } \ldots \text{ other factors})$$
$$+ f_G(M_{G,t}, K_{G,t}, A_{G,t}, \text{education, health, } \ldots \text{ other factors}),$$

where M = number of man-hours of labor expended in sector F or G at time t

K = physical capital in sector F or G at time t

A = know-how and level of productive efficiency in sector F or G at time t

F = subscript indicating the agricultural sector

G = subscript indicating the industrial sector.

The inputs to the production function—especially the amounts of capital and labor and the level of productive efficiency in the system at each point in time—must then be allowed for. The amount of labor expended, M, depends on the size of the potential labor force L. In turn, the total amount of potential labor obviously depends on the number of births and deaths in previous years, the current level of health, and such other factors as the extent to which women go out to work—which may in turn be affected by the birth rate. That is,

$$L_t = f(\text{MEN}_{j=0, t=-65}; \text{MEN}_{j=0, t=-64}; \ldots \text{MEN}_{j=0, t=-15};$$

$$\text{WOM}_{j=0, t=-65}; \text{WOM}_{j=0, t=-64}; \ldots \text{WOM}_{j=0, t=-15}; \ldots E_{t=-65};$$

$$E_{t=-64}, \ldots E_{t=0}; \text{health; other factors}),$$

where $\text{MEN}_{j,t}$ and $\text{WOM}_{j,t}$ = number of men and women of age j in

[8] The implications of saying that one population size is *better* than another is an issue whose roots are philosophic and not economic; this issue will be discussed in detail in Chapter 17.

[9] A complete list of the notations used in the book may be found on pages xxvii and xxviii.

year t, respectively, and E_t = the mortality schedule in year t. The proportion of the potential labor that becomes actual man-hours of work depends upon people's tastes for goods and leisure, among other things, or

$$M_t = f(L_t, \text{tastes}).$$

The *distribution* of labor into agriculture and industry is obviously complicated but must be reckoned; it surely depends heavily on the stage of industrial development of the country.

The amount of physical capital in existence at any one time, t, is a function of the amount of capital at time $t-1$ plus the *net* saving in period $t-1$, assuming savings are invested. This identity may be written

$$K_{t+1} = K_t + S_t.$$

Next the model must indicate how changes in physical capital (i.e., savings) come about. Saving is surely affected by the overall economic level of the society. It also may be affected by increments of population, though a priori it is not clear whether the effects of population increases would be positive or negative,

$$K_{t+1} = K_t + f(Y_t; \text{POP}_t - \text{POP}_{t-1}; \text{other forces}).$$

where POP = total population size. Just *how* saving depends upon the total product, and also upon other factors in the economy such as family size and level of living, is very important in determining what happens in our model and in reality; it is also very difficult to estimate empirically.

Changes in technology (A) must also be accounted for. The influence of per-capita income, total demand (D) and population size upon technology are relevant in this model, as are some other factors, too.

$$A_t = f\left(\frac{Y}{\text{POP}}; D; \text{POP}; \text{other forces}\right).$$

Education is an important influence, of course. Economists think of education as contributing to the "stock of human capital" embodied in people and societies. Though this factor is crucial in economic growth, we know very little about the relationship of human capital to the productivity of physical capital.

This completes the list of major influences that must enter into a dynamic model of the effect of population on the income level over time. In any specific model a good many other factors also must be taken into account, of course, as will be seen in the specific models used in this book. A general model of LDC's (where the agricultural sector is relatively large) also requires a mechanism to allocate labor and capital to the industrial or agricultural sector. The likely mechanism in LDC's is people's tastes for leisure versus agricultural goods versus industrial goods. A schematic diagram of this general model is seen in Figure 2–3.

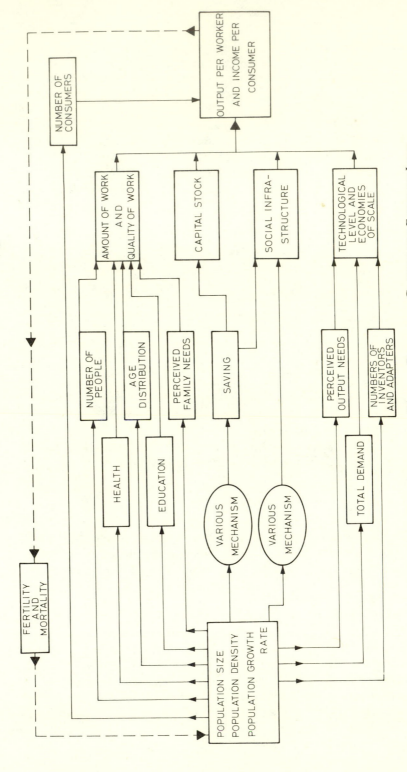

FIGURE 2–3 THE MAIN CONNECTIONS BETWEEN POPULATION GROWTH AND ECONOMIC LEVEL

Empirical data relevant to the estimation of the effects of all these influences will be presented in the rest of the chapters of Part I.

The Family Analogy

The analogy of the family is sometimes a satisfactory intuitive shortcut to understanding the effects of population growth. For example, if a family decides to have an additional child, there is less income available for expenditure on each of the original family members, just as with a country as a whole. The family may respond to the additional "need" by the parents working more hours for additional pay, just as with a nation. The family may find itself saving less, to pay for the additional expenses, *or* saving more to pay for expenses such as education that are expected later, and so it is for the nation as a whole. The additional child has no immediate economic advantages to the family, but later it may contribute to the parents and other relatives. Like a nation, the family must balance off the later economic benefits and the immediate noneconomic psychic benefits against the immediate cost of the child. The main way the family model diverges from that of the nation is that the additional person contributes to the stock of knowledge and the scale of the market of the society as a whole, whereas the family is not likely to benefit from such an effect.

The family model goes wrong, however, when it directs attention away from the possibility of new resource creation. For example, if a family starts with a given plot of land and an additional child is then born, it seems as if there will be less land per child when the children grow up and inherit the land. But the family can increase its *effective* land by irrigation, multiple-cropping, and other means, and *some* families respond by opening up whole new tracts of land. Hence the result of an additional child is not simply the decrease in land or other natural resources that appears to be inevitable when one looks at the family as a static closed system, but rather there may be an increase in resources caused by the coming of the additional child.

The Relationship between Growth, Size, Density, and Rate of Growth

The title of this book refers to population *growth*. But throughout the first and third parts of the book, the empirical data are most often data on population *size* and population *density*. This requires some explanation. Another necessary distinction is that between population increase and the rate of growth.

In social science, a cross-section of observations at a particular time is frequently used as a proxy to estimate the effects of a change over time of

41

a given entity. Here a sample of countries of *different sizes at a particular moment* is often taken as a proxy for a sample of periods during which a given country is at different total population sizes. Of course there are many sorts of hazards in reasoning from the cross-section to the individual history, all of them well documented in books on research methods (e.g. Simon, 1969, Chapter 19). But cross-sectional data are too often all we can get, and therefore we employ them up to the limit (but hopefully not beyond the limit) of their usefulness.

A sample of countries of different population sizes may be a good proxy when we are considering such matters as the relationship of population size to the cost of the central government. But there are many factors that we would not expect to be the same in countries of equal population but unequal land areas, for example, the state of agriculture. In such a case, comparison of countries of different population sizes *and* different areas would be misleading. For those cases where land area is important we are likely to turn to population *density* in various countries as a proxy for population growth in a given country, because population per unit of area (i.e., density) allows for differences in total area. But in cases where land area is not important, density is a defective proxy because it does not distinguish between different total populations.

Lastly, let us consider the concepts of the *amount* of population growth and the *rate* of population growth. First, let us notice that though we often talk loosely about amounts of population growth without specifying the period of time in which the increase is to take place, precise discussion always must include such a specification of the time period, (e.g., 20 years or 200 years). And if both the amount of growth and the time period are specified, we can immediately calculate the *average rate of growth* for the situation in question. Generally there is no difference between the concepts of *amount* of growth and *rate* of growth.

Sometimes, however, one is interested in *different* rates of growth *within* a given period. For example, it makes a difference to an economy and society whether during a given century, say, all the population growth takes place within the first half of the century and none during the second half, or instead the population growth is steady throughout the century. If there are several possibilities of this sort, then it may be useful to introduce the notion of rates of growth within the period along with the notion of the overall (or average rate of) growth in the period. But this is usually not necessary in the discussion in this book.

A last note: The subject of this book is the over-all economic *level*. No attention is given to the effects of population growth upon income *distribution*, either as a variable of interest in itself or as a force that might affect the level of economic activity. Lindert's work (forthcoming,

Chapters 6 and 7) suggests that increased fertility may have a considerable effect in widening the income distribution in the United States.

Summary

Chapter 2 restates the question of Part I: What are the main effects of population growth upon the economies of LDC's and MDC's? In the context of LDC's the issue is whether population growth slows or speeds the demographic transition and industrialization. In the context of MDC's the issue is the effect of population growth on the rate of increase of per-worker income.

The traditional Malthusian conclusion about the effect of population growth upon the economy is not supported by the empirical facts about the relationship of population growth to economic growth in LDC's and MDC's, as will be seen in later chapters. This suggests that the Malthusian model is lacking some crucial element or elements, which leads us to a search for more satisfactory models. The key elements in more complete models of the effect of population growth are reviewed briefly in this chapter. Then a very general dynamic model is sketched out. Subsequent chapters in Part I present data on these variables with respect to LDC's and MDC's, and develop specialized models based on these facts.

CHAPTER 3

The Influence of Population Growth on Income in Developed Economies: Data, Theories, and Micro-Economic Variables

INTRODUCTION: DATA AND THEORIES

There are two contradictory lines of thought about the effect of population growth upon per-worker income in rich countries. On the one hand, classical analysis using the standard economic concepts of saving, demand, and the production function suggests that an increment of population *reduces* per-worker income—once the nation or combination of nations is large enough so there are no important economies of scale, and given full employment and high-plateau life expectancies (see, for example, Malthus, 1803; United Nations, 1953, pp. 27–32, 36–39, and references cited therein; Meade, 1955, Phelps, 1968). The central operative mechanism is the Malthusian concept of diminishing returns to labor, as discussed in the previous chapter and as set forth in the model to be described shortly.

On the other hand, the empirical evidence suggests that at least in MDC's, population growth does not hinder and perhaps *helps* economic growth. One piece of historical evidence is the concurrent explosion in Europe of both population and economic development from 1650 onward. The failure of France to excel economically despite its low birth rate in the past 100 years is an important vignette in this history. A fuller picture is given by the samples of countries in Tables 3–1 and 3–2, which display decadal rates of growth of population and output per capita for contemporary MDC's for which data is available for periods of roughly 90–115 and 43–70 years, respectively. No strong relationship appears, as the four-way analyses of Tables 3–3 and 3–4 show.

Regressions of the rate of economic growth on the rate of population growth (summarized in Table 3–5) do yield negative coefficients for both the century and the half-century data. And the t ratio for the former even reaches -1.2. But these results should be interpreted as showing neither a negative nor a positive relationship between the variables, for these reasons: (1) The shorter period's regression coefficient is clearly insignificant statistically ($t = .36$), though the data should be better and the effect more pronounced over the shorter period; (2) The slopes—or the differences between the actual mean rates of decadal growth of per capita income, and the calculated rates of per-capita income growth at

44

TABLE 3–1

POPULATION GROWTH AND OUTPUT GROWTH OVER A
CENTURY IN CONTEMPORARY MDC'S

Country	Period	Population growth rate per decade	Output per-capita growth rate per decade
France	1861–70 to 1963–66	3.0	17.0
Sweden	1861–69 to 1963–67	6.6	28.9
Great Britain	1855–64 to 1963–67	8.2	13.4
Norway	1865–69 to 1963–67	8.3	21.3
Denmark	1865–69 to 1963–67	10.2	20.2
Germany	1850–59 to 1963–67	10.8	18.3
Japan	1874–79 to 1963–67	12.1	32.3
Netherlands	1860–70 to 1963–67	13.4	12.6
United States	1859 to 1963–67	18.7	17.3
Canada	1870–74 to 1963–67	19.0	18.7
Australia	1861–69 to 1963–67	23.7	10.2

SOURCE: Kuznets, 1971, pp. 11–14.

TABLE 3–2

POPULATION GROWTH AND OUTPUT GROWTH OVER HALF A
CENTURY IN CONTEMPORARY MDC'S

Country	Period	Population growth rate per decade	Output per-capita growth rate per decade
France	1896 to 1963–66	3.5	18.6
Great Britain	1920–24 to 1963–67	4.8	16.9
Belgium	1900–04 to 1963–67	5.3	14.3
Italy	1895–99 to 1963–67	6.9	22.9
Switzerland	1910 to 1963–67	8.8	16.1
Germany	1910–13 to 1963–67	10.4	20.5
Netherlands	1900–09 to 1963–67	14.2	15.1
United States	1910–14 to 1963–67	14.2	18.4
Australia	1900–04 to 1963–67	18.8	13.1
Canada	1920–24 to 1963–67	19.4	20.9

SOURCE: Kuznets, 1971, pp. 11–14.

zero population growth (the regression intercept)—are small in absolute terms. This implies that a change in the population growth rate has little economic impact; (3) Removing the "overseas offshoot" countries, as Kuznets thinks appropriate, greatly reduces even the weak association shown in these regressions (Kuznets, 1971, p. 23n); (4) The R^2's are small, suggesting that population growth rates do not explain much of the differences in economic growth rates.

45

TABLE 3–3

RELATIONSHIP OF POPULATION AND ECONOMIC GROWTH RATES IN
CONTEMPORARY MDC'S: 90 TO 115 YEAR PERIOD

Top half population growth rate, Top half economic growth rate: 2 countries	Bottom half population growth rate, Top half economic growth rate: 3 countries
Top half population growth rate, Bottom half economic growth rate: 3 countries	Bottom half population growth rate, Bottom half economic growth rate: 2 countries

TABLE 3–4

RELATIONSHIP OF POPULATION AND ECONOMIC GROWTH RATES IN
CONTEMPORARY MDC'S: 43 TO 70 YEAR PERIOD

Top half population growth rate, Top half economic growth rate: 2 countries	Bottom half population growth rate, Top half economic growth rate: 3 countries
Top half population growth rate, Bottom half economic growth rate: 3 countries	Bottom half population growth rate, Bottom half economic growth rate: 2 countries

TABLE 3–5

REGRESSIONS OF INCOME GROWTH ON POPULATION
GROWTH IN THE LONG RUN

Period (1)	Number of observations (2)	Mean rate of growth of population per decade (and standard deviation) (3)	Mean rate of growth of per-capita income per decade (and standard deviation) (4)	Regression coefficient of column 4 on column 3 (and t ratio) (5)	Inter-cept (6)	R^2 (7)
90–115 years	11	.191 (s.d. = .07)	.122 (s.d. = .06)	−.40 (t = −1.2)	.239	.129
43–70 years	10	.110 (s.d. = .05)	.200 (s.d. = .06)	−.15 (t = −.36)	.217	.015

SOURCE: Tables 3–1 and 3–2.

Another source of evidence is the contemporary cross-sectional relationship of population growth and economic growth. Kuznets arranged the post-World War II data (mostly for the early 1950's to 1964) for 21 MDC's as shown in Table 3–6. For these countries as a group he found a significant inverse rank-order correlation of −.434. But when Kuznets

TABLE 3–6

ANNUAL RATES OF GROWTH OF POPULATION AND TOTAL
AND PER-CAPITA PRODUCT, NON-COMMUNIST DEVELOPED
COUNTRIES (INCLUDING JAPAN), POST-WORLD WAR II PERIOD
(MOSTLY FROM THE EARLY 1950's TO 1964)

Average rates for groups of countries arrayed in increasing
order of rates of growth of population (%)

Groups	Population (1)	Per-capita product (2)	Total product (3)
1. 1–4	0.29	3.66	3.96
2. 5–8	0.65	3.60	4.28
3. 9–13	0.94	5.07	6.05
4. 14–17	1.46	3.49	5.00
5. 18–21	2.19	2.02	4.25
Average, 21 countries	1.10	3.64	4.77

SOURCE: Kuznets, 1967, p. 191.

excluded the "overseas European extension" countries—Canada, the
United States, Australia, and New Zealand—he found an insignificant
positive correlation, and he regards the latter as the more meaningful
result. Again, the overall impression is that neither a positive nor a
negative relationship is shown by the data (see also Easterlin, 1967).
Chesnais and Sauvy (1973) found no correlation between demographic
and economic growth among 16 "capitalist" countries of Europe in
the 1960's.

These sets of empirical data suggesting that the simple Malthusian
theory does not fit the facts in MDC's have naturally provoked explanations.[1] One set of explanations has suggested that population growth
has been a "challenge" which has evoked the "response" of increased
effort by individuals and societies. There certainly is a variety of evidence
that people can and do make special efforts when they perceive a special
need. Examples[2] include: (1) Firms and other institutions cut costs
when business goes bad. Many academic readers have, during the contemporary budget difficulties of universities, seen their universities find
pockets of money that could be transferred to more pressing needs
without being missed in their previous budget allocations. In industry
this usually takes the form of firing under-utilized people and closing

[1] Excellent discussions of this topic may be found in Myrdal (1940, Ch. 6), Kuznets
(1960), and Sauvy (1969).

[2] This point of view was clearly stated by J. Davis (1953).

inefficient departments and branches.[3] Studies of organizational slack have documented this phenomenon (Cyert and March, 1963; H. Simon, 1957). (2) During wartime, people and industries usually increase production far beyond what was thought possible before the war, by new exertions. And after World War II, Germany and Japan accomplished economic "miracles"—in large part by making the extra effort of working hard and saving a large proportion of income. The post-revolutionary history of the U.S.S.R is another example. (3) There is evidence that farmers in poor countries work harder if they have bigger families, as will be discussed at length in the LDC section, Chapters 7–12. But such a challenge-and-response mechanism is hard to work with scientifically; it provides too convenient a *deus ex machina* for any hard-to-explain situations.

Another set of explanations adduces the positive advantages of proportionately more *youth* in the labor force. Youth has several advantages: (1) In contrast to an older worker, a younger worker produces relatively more than he consumes, largely because of increases in pay with seniority whether or not there is increased productivity with seniority. (2) Each subsequent cohort of people in MDC's enters the labor force with more education than the previous generation. Hence a larger proportion of youth implies an increase in average education of the labor force, *ceteris paribus*. (3) Younger workers are thought to save a larger proportion of their income than older workers.

Still another set of explanations argue that growth in population creates additional *opportunities* which facilitate changes in the MDC economy and the society. This has several aspects: (1) Necessary reduction in size of organizations and work forces is always painful and difficult. But when the whole economy is growing, a facility or work force

---

[3] As an example of how industry can respond to need is "the story of how the giant Boeing aircraft manufacturing concern survived a sudden crisis when it lost two thirds of its world market six years ago. . . . Within a couple of months Boeing's manpower was cut to less than a quarter. Thousands of salary reductions were negotiated, right up to top management level. . . .

"In order to save tax, work was moved out of handsome new premises into dismal old buildings. Computer costs were cut to one third, after the machines had been programmed to assess their own efficiency. In 1969, Boeing employed about 60 'indirect' people—in finance, planning, engineering, industrial relations, supervising and such like jobs—for every 100 production workers. During the massive labour reduction drive, it began to lay off all indirect people who could be in any way dispensed with.

"'During this period'—Jack Steiner, Boeing's head, [said] . . . we quit mowing the lawn, quit weeding the flower beds and supplied barely enough water even to keep the shrubs alive. We studied the washrooms to make unnecessary plumbing facilities unavailable, and therefore not subject to cleaning. We were quite ruthless, and in this case quit scrubbing the lavatory floors until a good case of fungus appeared'" (*Jerusalem Post*, Oct. 24, 1974, p. 7).

that needs reduction can be reduced in relative size by leaving it the same absolute size. Sauvy makes this point with an example:

> Take universities for example. The state of knowledge at a given moment may require eighteen chairs in one faculty and twelve chairs in another. A little later knowledge may develop so that the numbers should become even. If the number of students and the financial resources are constant, the answer should be to create three new chairs in the second faculty and suppress three in the first. But the second action may be very unpleasant and may not be carried out, so that the university will no longer be equal to the needs. However, if the numbers of students and the financial resources are to increase by 20 per cent, they can be directed towards the creation of six chairs in the second faculty, thus establishing the correct balance without having to amputate the first faculty (Sauvy, 1969, p. 195).

In U.S. universities in the 1970's the cessation of growth of the student bodies has meant that there are many fewer new appointments to be made. This phenomenon strikes particularly hard at the number of young professors who can be appointed. It is demoralizing to aspirants for the Ph.D., and it is causing screams of anguish from senior professors who can no longer easily obtain offers elsewhere which they can use as levers to get their salaries raised. (2) Where new occupational needs arise, they can be more easily filled if there are more as-yet-untrained youths that will learn these occupations.[4] For this reason, as well as the previous one, population growth facilitates changes in sizes of industries and occupational structure. (3) When the total economy is growing relatively faster—as it will in an MDC with a relatively large labor force—physical capital can more easily be found for new investments without having to shift capital out of old investments. This is the physical counterpart to the human-capital phenomena discussed in points (1) and (2) above. (4) Investment is less risky when population is growing more rapidly. If housing is overbuilt or excess capacity is created in an industry, a growing population will take up the slack and remedy the error,[5] whereas without population growth there is no source of remedy for the miscalculation. Hence a growing population makes expansion investment and new entrepreneurial ventures more attractive by reducing risk—as well as by increasing total demand, of course.

---

[4] Kuznets observes "greater mobility of a growing than of a stagnant labor force" (1960, p. 326) ". . . new entrants and younger members of the labor force . . . are most responsive to economic opportunities and are readily available for many of the growing sectors in the economy" (1965, p. 15).

[5] "Possible errors of overoptimism . . . carry few penalties" (Kuznets, 1965, p. 15).

49

Still another explanation is that a faster-growing population increases the internal mobility of the labor force. The greater mobility is caused by a larger number of job opportunities, and by more people in the young age groups which tend to be more mobile. Internal mobility is of great importance in improving the allocation of resources, that is, the matching of people to jobs. About such internal mobility Kuznets wrote: "We cannot exaggerate the importance of internal mobility and of the underlying conditions for the efficient mechanism used in the modern economy to allocate and channel human resources" (1965, p. 16).

None of the above arguments about the benefits of population growth in MDC's will find place in the numerical model to be described in the next chapter, because it would be exceedingly difficult to quantify any of these effects at present. The rest of this chapter and chapter 4 will be devoted to discussion of those forces that will be embodied in the model constructed and run in chapter 6. These include the effect of population growth in MDC's upon saving, and the effect of children on the supply of labor (this chapter), and the importance of economies of scale in production, the effect of population growth upon the advance of knowledge and technological practice, and the effect upon the amount of education children obtain (chapter 4).

The Effect of Incremental Children on Saving as a Proportion of Income

Capital is the crucial element in the classical analysis. The amount of capital depends largely on the amount of saving and investment,[6] depreciation being important but secondary. Therefore, it is necessary to estimate the relationship of population growth to the rate of saving. This section summarizes the available evidence.

Family Budget Surveys

Budget surveys over a cross-section of families are one source of evidence. Typically, families are classified by income; within each income bracket, family size is the independent variable and savings the dependent variable. Brady (1956, reviewed in Coale, 1960) examined six surveys over sixty years in the United States. She concluded that the elasticity of consumption with respect to family size is about $\frac{1}{6}$. If one assumes that the marginal propensity to consume is .88, her finding translates into an elasticity of -1.2 for saving.[7]

---

[6] In MDC's I shall assume that savings equal investment, and net concepts will be used rather than gross concepts.

[7] That is, if a 6% increase in family size produces a 1% increase in consumption from .88 to .89, the reduction in saving is one-twelfth or about 8%, and the elasticity is 8%/6% = 1.2.

Eizenga allowed for the effect of age and income with a technique of "multiple standardization" before estimating the effects of family size on savings from family cross-section data. He estimated that in 1950 savings in the United States would have been about $31 less if the family had 5 children rather than 4, and about $50 less for the average family with 6, 7, 8, or more children than for the family with 4 children (1961, p. 90). Relative to per-family income in that year, these amounts do not seem large from any point of view. These estimates may be biased downwards, however, because of the nature of the sample.[8]

Kelley (1971) studied the relationship of the savings rate to family size in a survey of United States workers in 1889. The context is more akin to a contemporary LDC than to a contemporary MDC, however, and hence the results are discussed in Chapter 10.

There are several reasons why the relationship between family size and saving observed in budget surveys may not be causal or meaningful for purposes here:

1. If more children cause higher *absolute* income—as they well may after the first few years following a birth, as the father's labor effect comes to be bigger than the mother's labor-force effect—the *proportion* saved in the budget cross-section is biased downward.

2. Within cultural groups there may be something analogous to the "common set of factors residing in the political and social institutions of a country and in the views governing the behavior of its inhabitants [that] determines both the economic performance and its demographic patterns" (Kuznets, 1965, p. 29). To the extent that this is so, one should not interpret the observed relationship between family size and the savings ratio as a causal relationship.

3. An overwhelming proportion of the investment (saving) in an MDC like the United States is not directly discretionary within households and hence is not likely to be closely linked to family size. Kelley summed up the situation:

> First, private capital formation—agriculture, nonfarm unincorporated businesses, corporations, and households—tends to be financed with resources *internal* to the sector of investment. During the period 1900–1956, internal sources financed over 80 percent of the private sector's new capital. Second, Duesenberry has shown that for the period 1939–1949, over 70 percent of the household savings was in the form of residential construction, retirement funds, and insurance. Third, the quantitatively most important sector, corporations, overwhelmingly financed its own investment. In the period 1900–1920, internal

---

[8] Consumer surveys must also contain an upward bias because they customarily omit social security which—like pension-fund saving—is fixed outside the family independently of the family size.

financing in the corporate sector provided some 85 percent of the invested capital resources; this ratio increased to over 95 percent by 1930–1955. Finally, the overall proportion of private capital formation taking place in the corporate sector has increased over time. At the turn of the century corporations accounted for around 40 percent of total private investment; currently this proportion exceeds 60 percent. In summary, the joint trends toward increasing internal financing and the rising quantitative importance of the corporate sector suggests that even if demographic factors had strongly influenced household savings rates—an hypothesis questioned above on theoretical and empirical grounds—the impact of population on over-all savings could well have been low (Kelley, 1971, pp. 44–45).

The influence of family size on the desire for less savings could make itself felt indirectly, however, by way of household pressures or institutional policies through stock markets. This indirect effect cannot be learned well by an intra-country study; only cross-national studies can offer a clue to this.

4. Budget surveys are also unlikely to capture the effect of the birth rate on business investment through increases in demand for goods and services, either by family entrepreneurs or by incorporated businesses. The increase in total sales due to the incremental future workers and their increased spending raises the expected return on investment, and hence brings some investment projections above where the cut-off would otherwise be with lower population growth. This implies that, *ceteris paribus*, higher population growth would cause higher rates of business saving. And given that business investment is the dominant element in private investment, the over-all effect of population growth on private saving-and-investment might well be positive.

Cross-National Comparisons

In a cross-sectional comparison of countries, Leff (1969) estimated the elasticity of saving with respect to dependent children to be −.43 in MDC's, when controlling for per-capita income and other variables. Leff's method is sound though, of course, the regression analysis may be mis-specified.[9] In comparison, Denton and Spencer (1974) found no dependency effect in the 21 OECD countries.

---

[9] It is well to keep in mind the contradictory results obtained by the international multivariate cross-section studies of related matters, such as the connection of income and family size. On the latter, some studies have found a negative coefficient (Russett et al., 1964; Adelman and Morris, 1966; Rao and Dey, 1968), others a positive coefficient (Weintraub, 1962; Adelman, 1963; Heer, 1966; Friedlander and Silver, 1967). Hence any single study of this sort should be treated with caution.

Long-Run Time-Series Evidence

The notion of an inverse savings-family size relationship receives no support from U.S. history. The sharp decrease in family size in the last 100 or 50 years was not accompanied by an increase in the proportion of saving to income. (But because so many other things also changed during that period of time, it would be most unwise to interpret these data as showing that fewer children produce *less* saving.) And in a study of Canadian time series from 1928 to 1971 (excluding 1940–46) Denton and Spencer found no effects of age distribution upon consumption.

Business-Cycle Time-Series Evidence

The evidence from business cycles and long economic swings would seem to be relevant here. A positive relationship between population growth and business activity would seem to suggest that an increase in the number of children tends to produce an *increase* in saving. But though time series for population movements and cyclical business activity have often been displayed together (e.g., Losch, 1937; Kuznets, 1958; Easterlin, 1968, pp. 37–40), no causal effect from population to business activity—even to construction activity—has been shown. One reason is purely statistical, especially in the United States: Immigration has been a large part of the U.S. population increase, and it is quite unclear how much of the strong correlation between immigration and construction[10] is due to the pull exerted on immigration by the job market, and how much is caused by the new demand caused by the population growth.

A similar question exists about the direction of the relationship between fertility and business activity. These relationships might be better understood with population movement lagging *behind* changes in economic activity, but this has not been explored.

Upon consideration of the magnitudes involved, however, it is extremely unlikely that even a big change in the birth rate could cause a change in business activity large enough to show up immediately in business activity. Assume an impossibly large sudden jump in an MDC from a birth rate of 15 per 1,000 to a birth rate of 30 per 1,000. Assume also that a baby has the very high consumption "needs" of .5 of an adult consumer and that his parents respond by increasing their total consumption in such a way that their expenditure per-consumer-equivalent stays the same, rather than falling—by decreasing savings by that full amount. Even under these extreme conditions, total consumption would rise by only $(.030 - .015).5 = .0075$, or less than 1%. A change of this size

---

[10] A problem with examining the behavior of just one sector of the economy is that an increase in population might simply shift demand from one sector to another.

is far too small to show up amid the much greater changes taking place over the business cycle. (This also implies that the effect running from business activity to birth rate is likely to be the more important cause in the relationship of the two variables over the business cycle.) Over longer cycles, the effects of higher birth rates have time to add up substantially but even over longer cycles it would be difficult to find the effect statistically. Hence, one should not hope to learn much about the effect of fertility increase on savings and investment from time-series data.

Other Considerations About Savings

1. The aspect of saving behavior in connection with population which has caught the interest of most theorists (e.g., Cassell, 1932, discussed in Kuznets, 1960; Meade, 1955; Modigliani, 1966; and Phelps, 1968) has been the life-cycle effect. If a population's earners are relatively young, on the average they will save more than an older population because saving takes place earlier in life than does dissaving. But one should not interpret this phenomenon as suggesting that an increase in fertility will increase saving, because this comparison omits the possible effect of the pre-labor-force years on saving behavior. At the level of aggregation used in growth theory, it would be extremely difficult to relate saving to the effect of an incremental birth. Furthermore, that sort of analysis deals in proportions rather than in total saving, and it is the latter which is of interest here. Hence, this life-cycle aggregate analysis is not fruitful here.[11]

2. An increase in family size clearly increases total saving in at least some cases. An example: The Hutterites of North America who live communally in colonies "do not believe in practicing birth control, and so they continue to increase and thus to create the need for additional colony sites. The colonies need more and more cash in order to buy more and more land. This reduces the amount of cash available for other things. . . Young colonies starting out, or any colony unable to realize the levels of productivity needed for saving, will be helped by others" (Bennett, J., 1967, pp. 164–165).

3. The relationship of savings to family size is likely to change as a country becomes more modern. New needs for saving arise and old substitutes for personal saving disappear. For example, contemporary middle-class families feel a strong need to save for the college educations of their children, and an increase in offspring might increase saving on this account. Furthermore, the additional children are not thought of

---

[11] For the same reason, Clark's finding (1967, p. 268) across a sample of countries of no relationship between population growth and the savings ratio, holding per-capita income constant, is not helpful for our purposes here.

as reducing the parents' need for retirement saving, as in pre-modern times. These are two strong reasons to expect the savings-family size relationship to be more positive in richer, more modern economies than in poorer situations.

4. The general theory of consumption and savings is most complex and unsettled at present. One cannot say with much certainty what will be the effect of an increase in income of any sort (e.g., short-run, long-run, windfall) on saving and consumption. And in particular the relationship of family size to saving must be even more complex and unsettled than consumption theory in general.

Summary of the Effect of Population Growth upon Saving

To sum up the effect of population growth on savings in MDC's: The time-series evidence suggests no relationship. The household-budget surveys suggest a negative effect, but do not capture the effects of business investment, government investment, or complex interrelationships. The cross-national data agree with the household data in suggesting a negative sign, though such cross-sections also have deficiencies. Given that two very different and complimentary techniques give estimates with the same negative sign and the third method shows no relationship, the effect probably is negative.

Based on the above discussion, a wide variety of parametric estimates will be used in the simulation model, centering around Leff's estimate — an elasticity about $-.50$ — and including elasticities of -1.0 and 0.

The Effect of Incremental Children on Labor Supplied by Mother and Father

This section takes up the effect of additional children on the total work supplied outside the home by the children's parents. First let us consider the effect of incremental children on the work supplied outside the home by the *mother*. The basis is the body of work on the U.S. Census of 1960 by Bowen and Finegan (1969), Cain (1966), and Sweet (1970) as well as Landsberger's (1971) work with survey data collected by the National Bureau of Economic Research and the University of Michigan's Institute of Social Research. The effect is greatest in the years right after the children are born. By the time children are age 12, there is no observed difference between the labor-force participation of the incremental mothers and of matching women who did not have the incremental births—due surely to a trade-off between the labor-increasing effect of a greater "need" for money, and a labor-reducing effect of the continued need for care by the child. There may also be a negative effect from decay of the woman's skills while she is out of the labor force for one more baby.

55

To obtain an order-of-magnitude estimate for use here, assume that each woman will have *at least one child* in any case, and that each incremental baby means that the mother will for two years more than otherwise have a child under twelve. Hence for two years less than otherwise she will have no child under 12, the child's age at which labor-force participation ceases to be much affected by the presence of the child. This means that for each incremental child there will be two years of mother's labor force participation at, say, 15% rather than the same two years at, say, 42% labor-force participation (Sweet, 1968, p. 99). About two-thirds of all women who work are full-time workers, and we shall assume part-time workers work half-time. Rough calculations then suggest that an incremental baby results in an over-all loss of $2(.42 - .15)$ $(5/6) = .45$ years of work, or .225 of a worker "lost" to the work force in each of the two years after an incremental baby is born.

Another approach is to figure that women with children under 6 work an average of 5.6 hours, whereas women with no children under 18 work an average of 15.5 hours (Sweet, 1968, p. 130). This suggests a loss of a total of 10 hours' work a week for two years, or again $2(10/44) = .45$ years of work. And Landsberger's (1971) estimates from NBER and University of Michigan survey data even suggest *much* smaller negative effects for mothers of small children than those computed from the U.S. Census data.

The over-all effect computed here may seem to be small. If this is so, it is largely due to the assumption—reasonable, in my judgment, given the present incidence and trend of childlessness in the United States— that women will have at least one child. (There is a very big difference in the propensity to work between women with no and with some children, but much less difference among propensities to work of women with different positive parities.) Even this small estimate probably is biased upward, because some women choose to have more children on account of an already-made decision not to work rather than vice versa. If so, it is wrong to interpret the observed difference in labor-force participation as completely caused by the number of children. Still another reason why the true net negative effect of children on women's work is probably less than the estimate of .45 work years per child is that women who work often employ substitutes to do their domestic chores.

Now we move from the mother to the father. The positive labor-force effect of additional children on men, and also perhaps on some groups of women whose children are 12 or over, receives less emphasis than the negative effect on women, perhaps because the linkage seems less mechanical and more psychological, being a shift in preferences concerning work. Yet Bowen and Finegan's work on labor force participation is shot through with examples of "need"-increasing labor supply (for example, the strong effect of husband's income on wife's propensity to work). Another example of the effect of changed need is Clark's finding that the greater the war damage a country suffered in World War II, the higher its rate of saving after the war (1967, p. 268). The fuzziness of the phenomena that cause a positive effect here should not lead us to downgrade their importance.[12]

From the 1/1000 1960 U.S. Census tape I regressed men's hours worked per week on the number of children men have, holding constant with subclassification and multiple regression the men's education, race, age, occupation, and residence area. For white men an additional child is associated with approximately .2 additional hours of work per week. If one assumes a 44 hour week and 25 years of work after the incremental baby is born, then $.2/44 \times 25 \approx .10$ additional work years result per child.

Here are some other relevant estimates: a) Hill (1971) found that among the poor white head-of-household respondents to the 1967 U.S. Survey of Economic Opportunity, more children are associated with considerably more hours worked. For example, having a third child is associated with 219 extra hours of work yearly, a fourth child with 170 extra hours, and a fifth child with 122 extra hours; or about $5\frac{1}{2}$, $4\frac{1}{4}$ and 3 extra weeks of work a year, large effects indeed (p. 384). b) From the aforementioned NBER and Michigan survey data, where there is less error in the dependent variable because people are asked directly about number of weeks worked per year (page 55). Landsberger estimated, respectively, .49 and 2.0 extra weeks of work per extra child under 6. These estimates should be more reliable than the Census data. c) In Israel's 1971 Survey of Manpower data on hours worked the previous week, Gayer (1974) found that for each additional child, the head of the family

---

[12] (1) In the United States, Glaser and Rice (1959) find that there is an inverse relationship between employment (a reasonable proxy for income) and rates of property crime in the period 1930–56. (2) The data on moonlighting suggest that, other things being equal, relative economic status is important in explaining people's choices between leisure and money (Guthrie, 1965; 1966): (a) Men with working wives moonlight less. A working wife is an important economic asset; the man whose wife works is richer than the man whose wife does not, and hence he works less. (b) Men with "disorderly work histories" moonlight more. A man with little job security has poorer prospects in present-value terms than the man whose job is secure, and hence he works more. (c) Even subjective poverty leads a man to work more. Wilensky (1963) found that men who feel less well off than their parents are more likely to moonlight. Taken together, the moonlighting data support the view that the poorer a man is, the more sensitive he is to economic opportunity. (d) The higher the economic status of college students in sororities at Berkeley, the lower their "achievement orientation," as measured by such variables as high grades and intention of working after graduation. Working for high grades in school can be interpreted as giving up leisure to increase later income (Selvin and Hagstrom, 1963).

worked an extra 149 hours per year, i.e., more than three extra hours per week, an increase of about 7% in work for each child. It is note-worthy that the increase in the father's work time is more than three times the decrease in the mother's work time (42 hours per year) per child, so the additional baby apparently increases the total work done. d) And in a study of Israeli daily time-budget data, Gronau (1974) found that fathers spend an additional 4% more time working per addi-tional child age 0–5 or 6–12.

Other relevant evidence comes from moonlighting. According to Guthrie's summary of the literature (1966), during the years when men have young children—between the ages of 24 and 44—the rate of moonlighting is relatively higher. And the incidence of moonlighting among a sample of army men is strongly affected by the number of children they have. The most impressive data, however, come from the U.S. monthly labor force survey (Perella, 1970). There is a strong and regular association between number of children under 18, and the multiple job-holding rate among heads of households:

Number of Children	Percent Holding Two or More Jobs
No children under 18 years	6.0
1 child under 18 years	7.8
2 children under 18 years	8.9
3 or 4 children under 18 years	10.5
5 children under 18 years	11.3

Crude calculations on that data indicate that an extra child is associated with an increase of about 1% in the amount of moonlighting work done each year by the child's father, or about four-tenths of an hour per week on the average. (It is also relevant that almost three times as many moonlight jobs than regular jobs are self-employment. Such enterprise must be good for any economy and society.) The phenomenon of over-time work is particularly important in Great Britain, constituting 14% of factory workers' total labor in 1969 (*The Economist*, January 2, 1971, p. 46). Figure 3–1 makes clear that British men in the ages with fatherly responsibilities work the most overtime. This is consistent with the idea that an increase in children increases the amount of labor parents supply in the labor force.

Another way to estimate the effect of an additional child upon the amount of work done by fathers is by way of aggregate data on the relationship between average hours worked and per-capita income. An additional child immediately lowers per-capita income even if father's

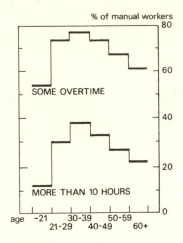

FIGURE 3–1 OVERTIME AND WHO WORKED IT IN ENGLAND
SOURCE: Reproduced from *The Economist*, January 2, 1971, p. 46.

output and income remain the same, in two ways: (1) the numerical effect of increasing the denominator in per-capita income by one head, and (2) by reducing the mother's income. Lower per-capita income then induces more work.

The strong relationship between people's economic circumstances and their willingness to work is shown by Figure 3–2, which plots the average work week in U.S. industry since 1850 against per-capita income. Much the same relationship is seen in an all-country sample in Figure 3–3.

From a sample like that in Figure 3–3, Winston estimated an elasticity of −.1 for hours worked with respect to per-capita income. That is, an increase (or decrease) of 10% in income causes a decrease (or increase) of 1% in hours worked. From this one may deduce the elasticity of hours worked with respect to the number of children. The third child in a family implies a reduction of 25% in per-capita income; whereas the family's income was formerly divided among four persons, it is now divided among five persons when the third child is born. This implies a (−.25)(−.1) = +.025 elasticity of father's hours worked with respect to additional children. This estimate may be biased upwards because an additional child is not a full consumer-equivalent during much of his childhood.

The model uses the low "conservative" estimate derived from the 1960 Census data tape—.2 hours per week more male labor per additional child for 22 years after the child's birth, or a total of .10 additional work

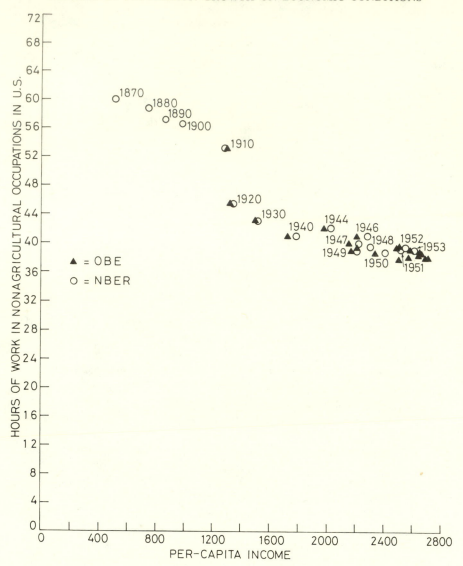

FIGURE 3–2   THE RELATIONSHIP OF PER-CAPITA INCOME TO THE LENGTH OF WORK WEEK
IN NON-AGRICULTURAL OCCUPATIONS IN THE UNITED STATES, 1870–1960
SOURCES: Work week, De Grazia, 1962, Table 1; per-capita income, *Historical Statistics of the U.S.*

years per child—because the work was completed before the higher estimates became known to me. But in the context of this model, the size
of the labor-force effects is not of major importance.

To summarize: for an additional child, the loss in women's labor is a
total of .45 years, and the gain in men's labor is .10 years, a difference of

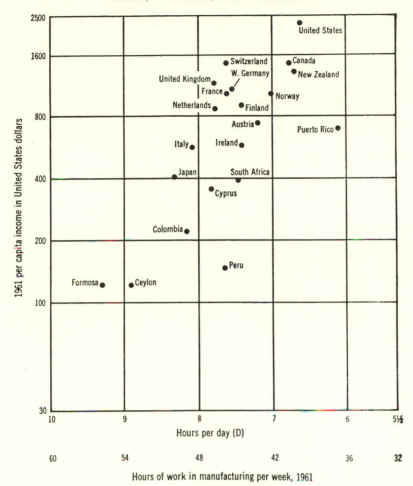

FIGURE 3–3   HOURS OF WORK IN MANUFACTURING PER WEEK IN A
CROSS-SECTION OF COUNTRIES, 1961
SOURCE: Kindleberger, 1965, p. 6.

.35 man years. However, the losses through the mothers occur at an earlier time than do the gains through the fathers. Hence the net loss (if the estimates are right) is greater than the difference of .35 man-years suggests. On the other hand, the market value of men's work is much greater.

The parents'-labor-force effect is introduced into the simulation model in Chapter 6 as follows: By the reasoning given earlier, for each baby born, .225 of a worker is removed from the model's labor force in the first and second years of each incremental child's life. Each father is estimated to offer .25% more work per incremental child, or an increase of .0025 of a worker, and hence that much work is added in each of 25 years following the incremental child's birth. The total effect is small, though even this small magnitude is biased by the omission of an allowance for the difference between the mean salaries of men and women—at least to the extent that those differences represent differences in skill levels.[13] On the average, women earn about 61% of what men earn per hour of work (Fuchs, 1967, p. 39).

SUMMARY

This chapter has discussed the effects of MDC population growth upon saving and upon labor-force participation. The next chapter considers economies of scale due to population growth, and the knowledge and technological-change effects of population growth. Both chapters are summarized at the end of Chapter 4.

[13] I am grateful to Allen Kelley for pointing this out.

Macro-Economic Influences of Population Growth on Income in Developed Economies

ECONOMIES OF SCALE IN PRODUCTION[1]

THE PREVIOUS chapter discussed the main micro-economic effects of population growth in MDC's. This chapter considers the main macro-economic effects—economies of scale, and changes in knowledge and technology.

General

Despite the fact that economies of scale are indissolubly linked with advances in knowledge, it may be useful to examine some of the evidence from studies that have attempted to isolate the effect of scale on efficiency.

Most economic inquiries regarding economies of scale have sought to learn the most efficient size of *firm* within industries, to determine whether larger firms are more efficient than smaller ones. The methods used have been various, and the results are hard to interpret. But in any case, the studies of firm efficiency are not germane to our purposes. To see why, consider an industry in which even a small country's market would be large enough to support at least one firm of the largest size found in big countries. This apparently implies that there are no economies to be gained in that industry by being a country with a larger population. But the existence of several firms of that size may lead to greater efficiency on the average than if there is only one firm, due to the interaction of the firms. These efficiencies may come from "external" effects such as improvements in techniques that all firms share, or they may come from the quickening effect of competition. In any case, the implication is that the appropriate unit of analysis is the efficiency of *countries as wholes*—or next best, the efficiency of the various industries within countries. We shall first review the evidence in industries, and then move on to countries as wholes.

Changes in Productivity in Industries over Time

One method is to relate the rates of change of productivity *over time* in

---

[1] General discussion of this topic may be found in Chapter 2. Discussion that pertains more to LDC's is found in Chapter 12.

various countries to their rates of change of labor input. The typical regression model is

$$\begin{pmatrix} \text{change of productivity in country } i \\ \text{during period } t, \text{ in logarithms} \end{pmatrix} = a + b \begin{pmatrix} \text{change of total labor input in country } i \\ \text{during period } t, \text{ in logarithms} \end{pmatrix}$$

This method was pioneered by Verdoorn, whose b coefficient was a remarkable .50 (Clark, 1967, p. 1960) which gave rise to Verdoorn's "law" that productivity goes up as the square root of total output. Clark used the same method on a larger sample and obtained a coefficient of 0.18, much lower than Verdoorn's estimate. Fabricant (1963, pp. 50–51) summarized the results of several cross-sections of time-series studies conducted by others. In a sample of somewhat less than 20 countries, over several decades the correlation between growth of physical output and output per man in individual industries is perhaps .7 or .8. When capital and other inputs are also included in the analysis, the correlation is somewhat lower, perhaps .6 or .5, according to Fabricant.

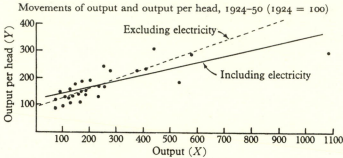

Movements of output and output per head, 1924–50 (1924 = 100)

Including electricity $Y_c = 113 \cdot 3 + 0 \cdot 23(X)$; standard error $= 35 \cdot 6$, $r = +0 \cdot 81$
Excluding electricity $Y_c = 94 \cdot 4 + 0 \cdot 34(X)$; standard error $= 31 \cdot 4$, $r = +0 \cdot 82$

FIGURE 4–1   OUTPUT AND OUTPUT PER HEAD IN VARIOUS
INDUSTRIES IN ENGLAND, 1924–50
SOURCE: Reproduced from Salter, 1966, p. 123.

The most recent study in this tradition is that of Salter (1969), who worked with changes in output and productivity per worker over 1924–50 in 28 industries in Great Britain. The correlation between the change in output and the change in productivity (output per head) is 0.81 (1966, p. 110) as shown in Figure 4–1. The corresponding correlation for the 1954–63 period is 0.69 (1966, p. 202). And a similar analysis for the 1923–50 period for 27 industries in the United States yielded a correlation of 0.62 (1966, p. 166). The elasticity (calculated at the medians) for the 1924–50 sample is .26 if the electrical industry is included, .39 if it is not. For the 1954–63 period, the elasticity is .43.[2]

[2] The medians and regressions come from Salter, 1966, pp. 107 and 123, 197 and 210, for the earlier and later periods respectively.

An important flaw of the time-series studies for the purpose here, however, is that there may well be causal effects in both directions between growth in market size (output) and growth in productivity. The time-series data show both effects together though we are presently interested only in the effect of growth in market size upon growth in productivity (the economies of scale). The resulting bias is upward. That is, the elasticity relevant to purposes here is likely to be lower than the estimates derived from, say, Salter's work.

Cross-National Productivity Comparisons

The tradition of work begun by Rostas (1948) has tried to remove the effect of technical change upon total output from the analysis by comparing two countries—usually the United States and Great Britain—at the same date. The model is:

$$\left(\frac{\text{Efficiency of U.S. industry } i \text{ in year } t}{\text{Efficiency of U.K. industry } i \text{ in year } t} \right) = f \left(\frac{\text{Scale of production of U.S. industry } i \text{ in year } t}{\text{Scale of production of U.K. industry } i \text{ in year } t} \right)$$

After omitting localized industries such as ice cream, Frankel (1957) obtained a correlation of .7 between relative efficiency and relative scale. Paige and Bombach (1959) used more industries than Frankel, and a different method, but obtained a similar rank correlation of .789 (p. 69).

Clark carried this work up to 1963, as shown in Figure 4–2. He finds that the slope of these data is "in the neighborhood of 0.5," which is quite consistent with Verdoorn's "Law."

Frankel (1957, pp. 64–68) developed other statistics that confirm the strong positive effect of market size upon productivity. When capital per worker and size of plant are held constant, the correlation between output per worker and market size goes up to .79. In a particularly telling analysis, he showed that the output per unit of *fuel input* is strongly positively affected by the market size—a correlation of .72 in the adjusted sample of U.S. and British industries. And when fuel input per worker and size of plant are held constant, the correlation rises to .90 (though Frankel warns of sampling instability). These fuel-input data are particularly interesting because they avoid problems of differences in skills of workers that might be present in the cross-country comparison. Fuel is the same in both countries, and if less fuel is needed per unit of output where markets are relatively larger, this would seem to show conclusively that relatively large markets result in relatively high productivity.

The rank correlation for output and productivity for 22 American and Canadian industries was .76 in 1955, implying that the size of the market "appears to be the most important single factor" accounting for differences between U.S. and Canadian productivity (Young, 1955, cited by Balassa, 1961).

65

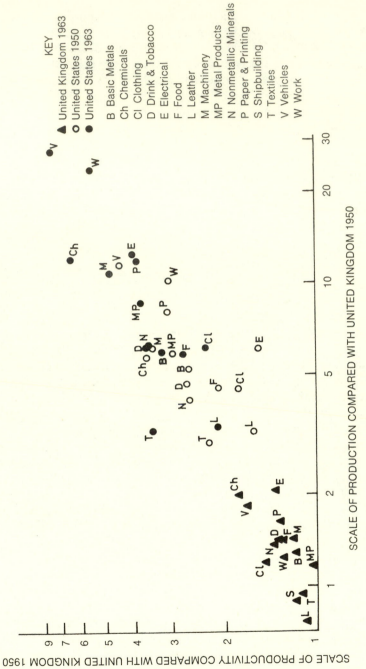

KEY

▲ United Kingdom 1963
○ United States 1950
● United States 1963

B Basic Metals
Ch Chemicals
Cl Clothing
D Drink & Tobacco
E Electrical
F Food
L Leather
M Machinery
MP Metal Products
N Nonmetallic Minerals
P Paper & Printing
S Shipbuilding
T Textiles
V Vehicles
W Work

SCALE OF PRODUCTION COMPARED WITH UNITED KINGDOM 1950

SCALE OF PRODUCTIVITY COMPARED WITH UNITED KINGDOM 1950

FIGURE 4–2   THE EFFECT OF SCALE UPON PRODUCTIVITY
SOURCE: Reproduced from Clark, 1967, p. 265.

Stigler (1961) used Frankel's data and a Cobb-Douglas function to estimate the elasticity of productivity with respect to output. The sum of the coefficients for capital and labor was 1.27, which implies an elasticity of .27, and substantial economies of scale. A regression using relative *prices* and relative outputs yielded a similar elasticity of .34. Fabricant (1963) warns us, however, that, in his judgment, any relationships drawn from these data are overstated for various technical reasons.

Chenery and Taylor (1968) conducted a time-series-plus-cross-section regression analysis of the development patterns of about fifty countries with 10–15 observations each. (Most of the countries are LDC's, but the pattern seems similar in both MDC's and LDC's.) For the manufacturing sectors that were expected to show economies of scale, the effects of reduced scale amount to between 25% and 50% in terms of "reduction in value"—very substantial indeed.

In summary, the evidence from cross-country studies suggests that economies of scale, at least in industry, are of the same order that Verdoorn found for within-country studies, that is, that productivity goes up as the square root of total output.

Economies of Scale in Governments

Now let us consider a single industry, the government. It is in the government sector that one would at first think there are substantial economies of scale, because of the one-to-a-country nature of parliaments, premiers, and so on. But upon examination of the matter across countries, E. Robinson concluded: "If one considers the problem as a whole, the economies of scale in relation to the administration, provision of public services, and the defence of a nation are probably on balance advantageous to a large nation, but, with the single exception of defence, are probably not of great significance." (1963, p. 239) And the largest nations seem to spend proportionally the most for defense, implying that even in the public sector economies of scale seem to be unimportant for our purposes.

Data on government units within countries would also seem to be relevant. Prest (1963) reports that in Australia, the Commonwealth Grants Commission studied the relationship of sizes of state to costs of education, health and hospitals, and law and order. The estimated cost per person was 12% lower in the three larger states (average 2.5 million people) than in the two smaller states (average 439,000 people), and it was 6% lower in the larger states than in South Australia (834,465 people). But these cost differences were said to stem not from differences in sparsity of population, but rather from total population size and differences in proportion of dependents; the latter factor muddies the point for purposes here.

With respect to hospitals alone:

> . . . the smaller the population the greater the need for excess capacity in hospital beds and other medical facilities in order to provide for random fluctuations in illness and injury. Despite the large population of the United States, the problem of efficient hospital size is still an important one. Nearly all observers are agreed that there are economies of scale in the production of short-term general hospital services up to a size of at least 200 beds (and possibly 500). However, at present, almost 40 per cent of the short-term patient days in the United States are provided in hospitals with fewer than 200 beds.
>
> In general, the cost of producing medical care (adjusted for quality) goes down as population size increases. (Fuchs, 1971, p. 226).

A good many studies of the determinants of public expenditures in the United States have included variables for population density and for the population size of municipal units. Miner's excellent survey of the literature[3] (1963, pp. 43–48) reports that a wide variety of results have been found, depending on whether state or local expenditures are considered, which other variables are included, and so on. Miner concludes that "density is negative in its impact on state spending and positive in its effect on city spending. The higher costs of police and fire protection in the cities is offset in the state analysis by the negative influence of density on highway and school expenditures" (p. 47). All in all, there seems no on-balance evidence of economies (or diseconomies) of scale with respect to population density in the state-and-local-government sector.

Aggregate Economies of Scale in Production

The ultimate interest here is in scale economies for the economy as a whole. After carefully reviewing the sorts of materials discussed above, plus others, in the context of his study of inputs to production and growth in a sample of European countries and the United States, Denison (1967, pp. 298–301) estimated a yearly gain from economies of scale of .36% for the United States over the period 1950–62, and a yearly gain of .93% for Northwest Europe. In both places, growth of the national market accounted for most of the economies, and independent growth of local markets for only a small part. The greater economies of scale in Northwest Europe stem from the fact that the increase in consumption was (during 1950–62) composed relatively heavily of income-elastic consumer-

---

[3] I am grateful to Walter McMahon for bringing this reference to my attention.

durable goods.[4] It must be noted that Denison included in his economies-of-scale calculations only those economies from changes in *production* scale, and he excludes gains in knowledge; the latter are estimated separately.

For the purposes of the present model, the economies of scale must be related to population changes. During the 1950–62 period, population grew annually at about 1% in Europe and at perhaps 1.5% in the United States; more relevant, the work forces grew by .9% and 1.1% (Denison, 1963, p. 52). But the scale change that produces economies of scale is the scale of the *economy*, much of which would have occurred even if the population were stationary. Therefore, we must calculate the economies of scale due just to the growth in population (labor force). This may be done by considering the proportion of the total growth in the economy due to increase in labor force. Denison estimated that increase in labor force accounted for 33% of the total observed increase in the scale of the United States economy, and 18% in Northwest Europe. These estimates imply an elasticity of perhaps .1 for the United States, and about .18 for Northwest Europe. That is, a rate of increase of 1% in population (labor force) would be expected to produce a continuing increase of .1% in production due to increases in efficiency in the United States, and about .18% in Northwest Europe.[5]

Thirlwall (1971, p. 16) estimated a similar elasticity with a cross-sectional regression of Denison's data in this form:

$$\begin{pmatrix} \text{Rate of change in} \\ \text{productivity} \end{pmatrix} = a + b \begin{pmatrix} \text{Rate of change of} \\ \text{labor force} \end{pmatrix}$$

He obtained the relatively high coefficient of .274, but it was not very significant statistically ($t = 1.2$); hence, not much weight should be given to his findings.

These magnitudes may seem small at first. But it should be remembered that the elasticity of advances in *knowledge* with respect to population is considerably higher than that of economies of scale, as we shall see in

---

[4] This causes economies of scale to appear both because of the nature of the technology involved in the production of consumer durables, as well as because of their relative prices and the technical matter of their differential impact when prices are weighted in different countries' prices. For discussion of this complex matter, see Denison, p. 235 ff.

[5] The calculation is:

$$\frac{33\% \times .36\%}{1.1\%} = .1 \text{ for the United States}$$

and

$$\frac{18\% \times .93\%}{.9\%} = .18 \text{ for Northwest Europe}$$

the next section, because advances in knowledge—holding education constant—can be attributed entirely to the growth in people rather than to the growth of the economy as a whole. And the rate of growth of the former is much less than the rate of growth of the latter, implying higher elasticities, *ceteris paribus*.

Hagen (1953) studied the correlates of the incremental capital-output ratio. A lower ratio implies that an economy can obtain more output per unit of investment, which is an advantage. Hagen found that in eight MDC's, "the relationship between the rate of increase in the working force and ICOR [incremental capital-output ratio] is striking." That is, a faster-growing work force seems to cause investment to be more profitable, which is an economy of faster growth. Hagen offers this explanation: "A rapidly increasing labor force absolves a country from penalty for almost all mistakes in investment."[6]

Diseconomies Due to Congestion

Recently, economists have begun to speculate that increased population also causes important diseconomies of scale, especially from congestion. Each person is said to impose costs on other people by decreasing the space in which the other person can move around, and by each person depositing his waste (e.g., soot) on other people. Therefore, *ceteris paribus* the more other people there are, the less space each person has and the more pollution he suffers from. These effects would be expected to be felt both in decreased ease and joy of living, and in higher prices due to higher costs of production caused by congestion costs.

Economic evidence of such congestion effects is, however, not obvious or easy to come by. The only explicit study of the matter is that of Nordhaus and Tobin. Their method was to *assume* that the higher wages which people receive in larger cities, holding education and several other variables constant, is a measure of the disamenity of larger cities. By regressing median income on relevant variables, they estimate that 8% of national income may be considered to be the "value" of such urban disamenities, with an elasticity of .06 for income with respect to population size and density taken together (1972, pp. 50 and 54). But interpreting the income differential as a measure of urban disamenities seems unsound to me. The Nordhaus-Tobin regressions do not allow for dif-

---

[6] On the other hand, Hagen finds some evidence (though scanty) that abundance of natural resources in the form of land makes investment more profitable. This implies that population *density* has a negative economic effect through efficiency in investment, whereas population *growth* has a positive effect, which is almost a contradiction. But the density effect is much weaker than the growth effect in Hagen's data. More work deserves to be done along this line.

ferences in skill and talent, over and above differences in education, exercised by people in similar occupations in different-size places. Common observation suggests that the best advertising copy-writers in New York and Chicago are much more skilled and talented than the best people in that job in small towns; the best ones in the small towns go to the big cities, which explains why some advertising men in New York and Chicago, but none in Champaign or Springfield, make $100,000 or $200,000 per year. Similarly, the best doctors tend to practice in bigger cities: this is why patients with difficult ailments are more likely to be sent there. It is also true of entertainers and of many other occupations that the level of skill is much higher in bigger places. And the fact that there are higher incomes in *some* occupations probably raises income levels in other service occupations because of the positive income elasticity of demand. This in turn is likely to affect wages in other occupations. This fact of higher skills and talents in many occupations in bigger cities, with its derivative effects, would seem to me to explain more of the income differentials by size of city than do the disamenities of larger places— though direct inquiry into the matter would seem very worthwhile.

If there really are important congestion costs in bigger cities, one would expect them to be reflected in the markets for goods, for example in the standard-of-living data for different size cities. Figure 4–3 plots Bureau of Labor Statistics (BLS) costs of living on a moderate budget in three of the nation's four main regions (the cost of living in the South is lowest across the board). No strong relationship between size of city and cost of living is apparent. And from a study of the BLS cost-of-living indices for four geographical regions Sheffer (1970) concludes that "the overall impression that one may obtain from the above analysis is that, by and large, no significant relationship exists between population size of SMSA [Standard Metropolitan Statistical Area], and the consumer expenditure necessary for a given standard of living." Alonzo and Fajans (1970) calculated that there is a "slight" positive association between city size and the BLS budgets. But they find that much of this association is due to the fact that the BLS budgets contain higher-quality items in bigger places, where incomes are higher. (Income rises considerably faster with city size than does the BLS cost of living.) This, in turn, is due to higher expenditure aspirations and expectations of people in larger cities. Alonso and Fajans conclude that "it is not more expensive to live in larger urban areas . . . The common belief that bigger places are more costly appears the result of higher expectations rather than higher prices" (p. 3). Haworth and Rasmussen (1973) found a positive relationship between city size and cost of living when they omitted per-capita income from the analysis: "'In the high budget . . . for each additional million additional popula-

71

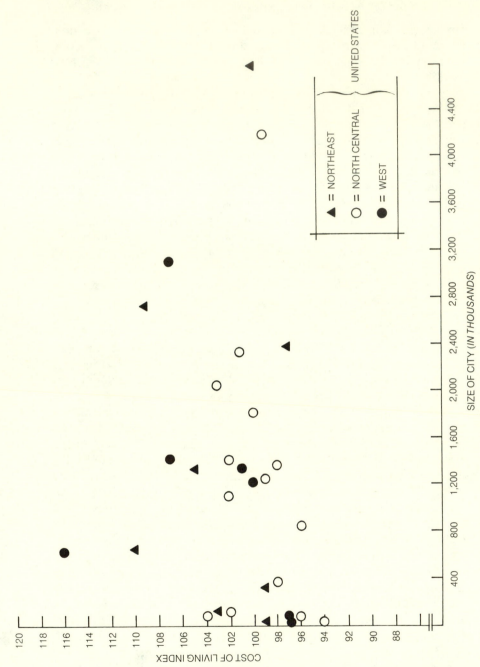

FIGURE 4–3 RELATIONSHIP OF CITY SIZE IN THE UNITED STATES TO COST OF LIVING, 1969

SOURCE: Bureau of Labor Statistics, *Handbook of Labor Statistics 1969*, Bulletin no. 1630, July 1969.

tion the cost of living goes up by . . . one per cent,' and less in moderate and low budgets (no effect in latter)." But the magnitude of their finding is so small in economic terms that it is equivalent to no effect.

Perhaps the most general and best test of whether an even denser population would increase or decrease people's individual welfare is by observing which levels of density people *choose*, taking together all the conditions of life in various places. That is, do more people move to the biggest cities or to smaller cities? (This test lumps together the welfare of people or workers and also of employers, because it includes the wages "paid by employers and their location choices.) There are several possible measurements that might be appropriate, but none seems to show that more people are choosing smaller cities in preference to larger ones (Bogue, 1953; Zitter, 1970; Berry, 1972)."[7]

All in all, there seems no strong evidence of diseconomies of scale in production even in the most densely settled areas of the MDC's. Rather, the evidence seems to point to significant economies of production scales, which will be handled as part of the overall impact of population size upon productivity in the MDC simulation model in Chapter 6.

ADVANCE IN KNOWLEDGE AS A FUNCTION OF POPULATION GROWTH

Technological Advance

An example to start with: a larger population makes it more possible for a country to raise enough taxes and manpower for huge knowledge-creating projects like areospace missions to the moon. Sweden's per-capita income is higher than that of the U.S.S.R., but if the latter were the size of the former it probably could not mount a moon shot.

It cannot be emphasized too strongly that "technological advance" does not mean "science," and scientific geniuses are just one part of the knowledge process. Much of technological advance comes from people who are neither well educated nor well paid—the dispatcher who develops a slightly better way of deploying the taxis in his ten-taxi fleet, the shipper who discovers that garbage cans make excellent cheap containers for many items, the supermarket manager who finds a way to display more merchandise in a given space, the supermarket clerk who finds a quicker way to stamp the prices on cans, the market researcher in the supermarket

---

[7] Middle-size SMSA's *may* be growing at a faster *rate* than the biggest SMSA's. But even if this is indeed occurring, this would not necessarily indicate that middle-size SMSA's are more attractive—that is, attractive to more people—than bigger SMSA's, unlike the logic of Stigler's "survivorship" test in industrial organization.

chain who experiments and finds more efficient and cheaper means of advertising the store's prices and sale items, and so on. Kuznets emphasizes the importance of this sort of technological advance (lectures in Jerusalem, 1970–71) and I agree. On this view, it makes straightforward sense that a larger labor force brings about faster technological advance in the MDC world, *ceteris paribus*.

As with economies of scale, technological advance cannot be cleanly separated from other elements of economic growth. But the attempts that have been made to isolate its effect are interesting nevertheless.

Let us begin with Denison's assessment:

> I have estimated that in the 1929–57 period the advance of knowledge, as distinguished from changes in the lag, contributed .58 percentage points to the measured growth rate of national product. This is equivalent to saying that the average level of knowledge relevant to measured production increased .58 per cent a year. . . .
>
> These increases are much smaller than the increases in the population of the United States, of advanced nations as a whole, or of the world. Maintenance of a constant rate of increase in knowledge therefore implies a declining per capita contribution to knowledge, whichever of the three population bases is used. In fact, it is highly unlikely that in the past the increase in the annual increment to knowledge relevant to measured production has even approached the population increase. It is perfectly obvious that it has fallen far short of the increase in scientists, engineers, or college or high-school graduates. If this were not so, the past growth rate of national product would have been sharply accelerating.
>
> This fact might mean that advances in knowledge are increasingly difficult to achieve as the level of knowledge advances, requiring a steady increase in inputs to maintain the same rate of advance. Alternatively, it can be interpreted to indicate that the pursuit of knowledge is subject to very sharply decreasing returns to scale; that the main determinant is the time required for one advance to lead to another, and that multiplying the number of individuals involved can by no means achieve a proportional contraction of the time span. The latter interpretation conforms to the conclusion reached by numerous observers of research projects, and particularly so with respect to the more basic or radical advances. (1962, p. 237.)

On the other hand, Kelley (1971) examined Higgs' (1971) data on inventions[8] from 1870 to 1920 and found that the elasticity of inventions with

---

[8] Although informal technological development by nonprofessional knowledge creators surely is of great importance, its quantity is hard to measure independently. It is for lack of such data that we turn to information on professional knowledge-creators.

respect to population size was more than unity, even when urbanization is controlled. Kelley implies that it is unlikely that education or another variable accounts for the apparent relationship. And he finds some indication that the elasticity has declined somewhat over time. But please notice that an elasticity of unity for knowledge with respect to population growth is very high, and an elasticity of *much less* than unity is quite compatible with a rise in population having an over-all *positive* effect on per-worker income. (The over-all effect depends on the size of the negative effects from other sources—which alone must be far below unity, as we shall see—and on the extent of other positive effects.) But partial elasticities cannot be interpreted well. Only an examination of the complete system can give an answer to the effect of population growth on per-worker income. That is the aim of the simulation model described in Chapter 6.[9]

Studies of the relationship of country size to scientific output indicate that, with per-capita income held constant, the quantity of scientific output is *proportional* to the size of the country (Price, 1972). That is, doubling the labor force implies doubling the rate of scientific output, *ceteris paribus*.[10,11]

---

[9] Implicit in the previous discussion is that the genetic potential for knowledge creation is, on the average, the same among people in larger and smaller populations. That is, it is assumed that a larger population is not larger just because the *least gifted* people are having more children; if in fact it were true that the difference in growth is made up only of those who will not contribute to knowledge, the total stock of potential knowledge-producers might be no higher with the larger population than with the smaller. But in the United States, most children are born to the middle class, and it is variations in the middle-class birth rate that have largely accounted for the post-World War II variations in the aggregate birth rate. Hence, the assumption about equal average genetic potential in various size populations seems reasonable in the United States context. Nevertheless, the possibility that the genetic intellectual potential might be relatively less on average with the bigger population is allowed for, at least to some extent, in the simulation models in the next chapter where education is a negative function of population growth rate.

[10] Of course, one cannot directly deduce from this evidence that if the number of people were doubled in the MDC world as a whole, scientific output would double. If there were no national or cultural or spatial barriers to knowledge, one would expect to find scientific output proportional to the labor force in each place *even if* additional labor force were highly redundant and produced much less than the proportional increment. But there are, in fact, important barriers to the free flow of knowledge and persons from place to place, as well as differences in the kind of scientific knowledge needed in various places. Hence, the scientific establishments in various countries are self-contained to at least some degree. And the fact that output is nevertheless proportional to labor-force inputs suggests that additional labor force might well contribute proportionally to output.

[11] The data presented in this chapter have shown that *exogenous* technological advance will be higher where there are more people. But technological advance may also be caused by the increased demand that stems from more people. Data seems to be nonexistent, and therefore this bit of history seems relevant:

The effect of population increase on the production and dissemination of agricultural knowledge is shown by Slicher van Bath (1963) over the sixteenth to nineteenth centuries. Before and after the hundred years from 1550 to 1650, population grew relatively rapidly,

Some writers, even eminent ones, have questioned whether more people imply more ideas and technological development. But is there anyone who would bet on Sweden or Holland, against Great Britain and the U.S.S.R., producing the great discoveries that will make nuclear fusion practical? (I have omitted the United States because of its higher per-capita income.)

Quantity and Quality of Education

Another possible negative effect on knowledge due to population growth is a reduction in the amount of education children receive. Human capital as well as physical capital is crucial in the productivity of an economy. And people might not provide (or authorities might not demand) enough additional tax revenues to maintain the equivalent level of schooling. If so, the larger population, with its larger *proportion* of children, might lead to less education on the average, and less potential to advance knowledge *in total* than the smaller population.

The conventional theory of population growth's effect upon the amount of education per child is straightforward Malthus: A fixed educational budget of money and resources divided among more students implies less resources per student on the average. This theory also yields the quantitative prediction that the elasticity of the impact would be -1; that is, a 1% increase in children should cause about a 1% decrease in education per student.

But as we know from a host of evidence, people and institutions often respond to population growth by altering apparently fixed conditions. For example, in agriculture more children cause increased labor input by the parents (see Chapter 9). And when there are additional profitable opportunities for investment, economic theory tells us that people will shift some resources from consumption to investment; additional children constitute such an additional opportunity for profitable investment. Therefore, we must allow for possible responses contrary to the simple Malthusian pie-sharing theory.

---

but it did not grow much from 1650 to 1750. "In the principal west European countries in the sixteenth century there was a flourishing literature on farming. . . . [But] there was no agricultural literature of importance between 1650 and 1750: what did come from the press was mostly reprints of older works" (1963, pp. 205 and 219). After 1750 there again developed a literature on agriculture, including scientific experimentation, by such men as Arthur Young and Von Thunen (p. 239). It seems reasonable to generalize this effect to modern MDC's, though it would be hard to demonstrate that an increase in population increases the *total* of knowledge rather than shifting attention to fields where population pressure is felt most acutely.

Also relevant is Shmookler's (1965) demonstration that industrial demand can have a major influence on the extent of invention in various industries.

There is no way of knowing from theory alone which of the two effects will dominate. Therefore we cannot know a priori whether the impact of population growth will approach the elasticity of unity that Malthusian theorizing suggests it will, or whether the elasticity will approach zero and complete offsetting the Malthusian effect by the induced-response effect; we must turn to empirical data.

A study across states of the determinants of United States expenditures on public education by McMahon (1970) yielded a coefficient for the effect of children aged 5–17 as a percent of the population that implies an elasticity[12] of .82 for expenditures with respect to the dependency rate; that is, if there is any negative effect of population growth on educational level, it is slight. The regression coefficients in a study by Miner (1963) imply *no* negative effect of the proportion of children under 18 on total expenditures per pupil.[13] After extensive survey of the literature, Miner concluded that his results are representative of and consistent with the literature. Those studies suggest that the best available estimate, given the present state of the art, is that the elasticity of educational expenditure with respect to the number of children is close to or equal to 1.0. Of course a nation-wide change in fertility may have different effects than do differences among states, but this cannot be judged from available data, because *local* expenditures per child are lower where the proportion of dependents is higher, state and federal funds making up the slack. This mechanism might not work to allow for the effect of higher state-wide or nation-wide dependency ratios that come with faster *nation-wide* population growth, but this is a matter for speculation.

On the other hand, Lindert (forthcoming, Chapter 7) plotted the course of educational expenditures from 1840 to 1972 in the United States. He finds a reduction in the upward trend (though still a continuation in growth) starting in 1950, about the same time that children began to be a rising share of the population after having been a declining share of the population in earlier years. Though this is hardly proof that fertility reduces educational expenditures per child, it is at least suggestive. Stronger negative evidence comes from Tolley and Olson (1971). In a

---

[12] The estimate is based on a cross-section of U.S. states in 1958. The regression coefficient is .155; the mean of children/total population and the mean of (education/disposable personal income) in 1966 were, respectively, 25.5% and 4.8%. Time-series estimates for 1946–68 are also given by McMahon; they cover a wider range than the cross-section estimate, but they are less appropriate because of the likely downward bias in a short time-series when the effects are lagged (Aigner and Simon, 1970). I appreciate a useful conversa- with Walter McMahon about his article and the literature on the topic.

[13] This result is taken from Miner's regressions using all school systems in the sample (p. 98). The regressions using school systems *within* individual states show negative coefficients, but this clearly is because per-capita income—an important determinant of school expenditures—is not allowed for in the within-individual-state regressions, whereas it is allowed for in the all-school-systems regressions.

TABLE 4-1

THE EFFECT OF POPULATION INCREASE ON SCHOOLING IN MDC'S

Dependent variable	Regressions using crude birth rate		Regressions using dependency rate		Number of countries
	Elasticity from logarithmic regression	Elasticity from linear regression	Elasticity from logarithmic regression	Elasticity from linear regression	
Primary school attendance	−.01	−.007	−.07	−.07	19
Secondary school attendance	−.67*	−.57	−.82†	−.72	20
Tertiary school attendance	.28	.20	.82*	.67	20
Expenditures on schooling per child in dollars	−.45	−.32	−.26	.05	20

SOURCE: Pilarski and Simon, 1975.

NOTE: Elasticities and standardized regression coefficients for schooling as the dependent variable in regressions with either the crude birth rate or the dependency burden along with per-capita income, median education, life expectancy, and socialist-non-socialist as the independent variables in a sample of MDC countries.

*Significant at 10% level.

†Significant at 5% level.

careful simultaneous-equations estimation of educational expenditures and income across the states, they found that expenditures per pupil has an elasticity of −.47 with respect to pupils per employee.

A cross-section of MDC nations was examined by Pilarski and Simon (1975).[14] Regressions were run of the following form:

Percent attending specified level of schooling (e.g., primary) =
$\qquad$ f (Birth rate or dependency rate; other variables);

and

Expenditures on schooling = f (Birth rate or dependency rate; other variables).

In Table 4–1 we see that both the crude birth rate and the fertility ratio have a substantial negative effect on expenditures per child and upon secondary enrollment, though not on primary or post-secondary enrollment. The effect on expenditures is nowhere near as great as simple Malthusian theory would suggest, however. More than half of the extra effort is made that would be necessary to keep expenditures per child at the same levels as if fertility were lower. And even the negative effect on expenditures that the data suggest is cast into question by the lack of statistical significance and by the fact that in a parallel linear regression the signs of fertility are positive rather than negative. But on balance, the data do suggest some negative effect of fertility on expenditures per child in MDC's.

In summary, the evidence in MDC's suggests that faster population growth has at least some negative effect on education per child, but the effect does not seem to be large.

Do Some Groups of Children Make a Negative Contribution?

Chapters 3–6 discuss children as if they are a homogeneous lot, making equal contributions to the society. The reader may wonder, however, whether some classes of children—particularly the poor—may be a drain upon the economy even if most children make a positive contribution. There seems to be no evidence for this view, however. The research of Jones and Smith, should be relevant even though it pertains to New Commonwealth immigrants into England rather than to new births.

[Though] the income per head of members of New Commonwealth households is less than that of the indigenous population . . . the proportion of income saved—representing resources generated by the

[14] I am grateful to Adam Pilarski for allowing me to use these results of our unpublished joint work.

New Commonwealth labour force but made available for contributions to an increase in the capital stock—is higher than the average for the total population . . .

They have tended to arrive at times when, and gone to places where, industrial capital has afforded jobs for which there were no indigenous takers. . . .

Their demands per head on the social services are significantly below the national average. . . .

Immigration did much to allow these aspirations for higher living standards to be realised. Certainly it seems improbable that, as some have feared, immigration has restrained indigenous living standards below the level which, in its absence, they might have attained. Among other evidence which points to this conclusion, special mention should be made of those sections of the study that indicate demands on the social services below those of the indigenous population, and an impact on the housing market which may well have helped, marginally, to raise the standards at which the indigenous population, on average, lives (1970, pp. 122, 123, 134, 161).

The data presented in this chapter should be qualified by the observation that they pertain to "Western" MDC's and Japan. They may not be relevant to "socialist" countries. As Kuznets says,

Any relation between demographic trends and economic growth that might be derived from the experience of these non-controlled, non-authoritarian developed countries—that is the preponderant part of our known experience—may be invalid or irrelevant to a highly centralized system in which some groups of the population were subject to compulsory pressures and all population to fairly tight control in their roles in production and consumption. And, given the recent emergence of the U.S.S.R. type of social organization with its changing trends, our direct tested knowledge of its patterns of response, of relations within it between population trends and economic growth, are hardly adequate to permit us to dispense with analysis of wider and longer ranges of modern growth experience (1965, p. 24).

Other Demographic Variables

The discussion in this chapter, and the model constructed in Chapter 6, deal only with the impact of one demographic variable—total fertility—upon the MDC economy. But there are other demographic variables that could affect the standard of living, including the following: (1) The age at which women bear children can differ greatly. The length of time between generations of blacks in the United States is much less than that of whites, largely because blacks have children at younger ages. (2) The spacing between children can affect both the birth rate and the amount of time women are out of the labor force. (3) The year-to-year changes in mortality now taking place are not great. But there could occur in the future a significant lengthening of life. It would matter very much whether the lengthening takes place after the working years, or whether the working years are prolonged, also. (4) Choice of child's sex by parents could affect the sex composition of the work force, as well as subsequently influencing the birth rate. (5) Immigration and emigration affect the economy quite differently from fertility, both because migrants are largely of labor-force years and because they have different educational backgrounds than the rest of the labor force. (5) Though it does not show up in statistics concerning population growth, internal migration has a very large influence on the economy. Internal migration almost always represents an improved allocation of productive resources, as noted above.

Some day a model may be developed which will be able to account for these other demographic variables in addition to fertility.

Summary (Chapters 3 and 4)

The history of the more-developed countries since the Industrial Revolution does not support the simple Malthusian model. A negative relationship between population growth and economic growth is not seen in anecdotal history or in time-series over the past hundred years or in contemporary cross-sections. Data shown in Chapter 3 suggest that there is no simple relationship between population growth and economic growth.

Various explanations of this discrepancy have been offered. The most general and most appealing explanation scientifically is the nexus of economies of scale, creation and adaptation of additional new knowledge by additional people, and the creation of new resources from new knowledge. Therefore the model constructed in Chapter 6 builds on this fundamental element of economic progress which has previously been left out of population models.

Chapter 3 next reviews the data on the key micro-economic variables to be entered into the MDC model. These include the effect of children upon saving (rather indeterminate) and the effect of additional children on the amount of labor-force work done by the mother and father (of less importance than usually supposed). Then Chapter 4 discusses the main macro-economic positive effects of population growth—economies of scale (substantial), and the evidence on the effect of population size and growth upon advances in knowledge (difficult but not impossible to quantify).

CHAPTER 5

Natural Resources, Pollution, and Population Growth in MDC's

GENERAL THEORY AND DATA

THIS CHAPTER restates a fundamental idea developed most fully by economists at Resources for the Future (RFF) (see especially Barnett and Morse, 1963), put here in the context of population growth. But despite thorough development of this idea over almost two decades, most of the public and even some very competent economists are not fully aware of it—probably because of its paradoxical non-common-sense counterintuitive nature.

The essence of the idea is as follows: It is common practice to forecast the future status of a natural resource by (1) estimating the known physical quantity of the resource in or on the earth, (2) extrapolating the future rate of use from the current use rate, and (3) subtracting the estimate of use in (2) from the physical "inventory" in (1). The RFF argues that this procedure is unsound and misleading. The two main reasons are: (1) The physical quantity of a resource in the earth, *no matter how closely defined,* is not known at any time, because resources are only sought and found as they are needed; an example is the *increase* over time in the known supplies of oil, as shown in Table 5–1. (2) More important, even if they were known, the physical quantities of particular closely defined natural resources would not be economically meaningful, because of the economy's capacity to develop additional ways to meet its needs, e.g., using plastic instead of wood and metal, the developing of ways of exploiting low grades of ores previously thought not usable, and the developing of atomic power. This is *not* a matter of staving off

TABLE 5–1
CRUDE PETROLEUM: U.S. PRODUCTION AND PROVED RESERVES, 1927–67
(IN MILLIONS OF BARRELS)

Year	Production	Proved reserves
1927	901	10,500
1937	1279	15,506
1947	1857	21,488
1957	2617	30,300
1967	3216	31,377

SOURCE: Brandis, 1972, p. 594.

82

disaster by digging deeper and deeper into some "reservoir," at greater and greater "ultimate" cost, and using ever-poorer resources.

[T]he increasing scarcity of particular resources fosters discovery or development of alternative resources, not only equal in economic quality but often superior to those replaced. Few components of the earth's crust, including farm land, are so specific as to defy economic replacement, or so resistant to technological advance as to be incapable of eventually yielding extractive products at constant or declining cost. When coal, petroleum, hydroelectric power, and the atomic nucleus replace wood, peat, and dung as sources of energy; when aluminum yields its secrets to technology and is made to exist, as never before, in the form of metal; when the iron in taconite, once held there inseparably, becomes competitive with that in traditional ores—when all this happens, can we say that we have been forced to shift from resources of higher to those of lower economic quality?

We think not; the contrary is true. And we doubt that it is proper, in long-term, empirical growth analysis, to ask what would have happened to the economic quality of natural resources in the absence of technological progress. For the technological progress that has occurred was a necessary condition for the growth that has occurred, and if the former is ruled out the latter cannot appropriately be taken as a given fact. The strength of the demand-pull on the resource base, therefore, and the resources that would have been used in the absence of progress are not meaningfully determinate" (Barnett and Morse, 1963, pp. 10–11).

Thus the concept of an existing "inventory" of natural resources is operationally misleading; physical measurements do not provide useful operational definitions to use as the basis for forecasting future supply situations.[1]

The RFF writers argue that the most appropriate *economic* measure of scarcity is the *relative price* of a natural resource. And the relative prices of most natural resources have not been rising over the past 100 years despite the reduction in cost of so many other products due to increased efficiency in producing them; this may be seen in Figure 5–1. Another concept of scarcity is the labor cost per unit of output. This shows an even more striking picture in Figure 5–2. Labor cost measured in man days or hours per unit of *output* has declined, despite that labor

---

[1] A frequent response to this argument is "But surely *something* is finite. The earth itself offers a finite limit, even if nothing else does." But why should a fixed boundary be drawn even around the earth? We use energy from the sun. We have begun to explore the moon and bring back pieces of it. Why should not the boundary of our resources continue to recede as it has receded in the past?

83

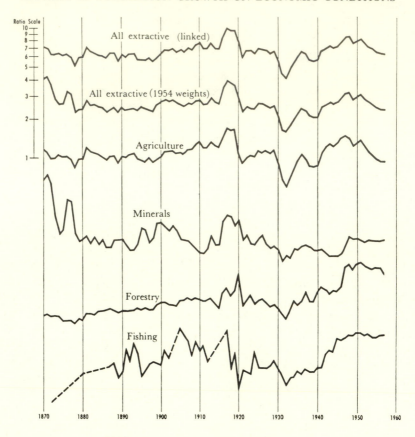

Note: Solid lines connect points in annual series; dashed lines connect points over a year apart.

FIGURE 5–1 TRENDS IN UNIT PRICES OF EXTRACTING PRODUCTS RELATIVE
TO NON-EXTRACTIVE PRODUCTS IN THE UNITED STATES, 1870–1957
SOURCE: Barnett and Morse, 1963, p. 210.

costs per unit of *labor* have risen markedly over time. These data suggest
the counter-intuitive conclusion that even as we use coal and oil and
iron and other natural resources, they are becoming *less scarce*. Yet
this is indeed the appropriate economic way of viewing the situation.

The sharp rise of crude oil prices in the 1970's does not contradict the
RFF point of view. The price rise is clearly due to the cartel action of
the oil-producing countries' association, OPEC. The cost of production
has not risen at all, being somewhere between 100 and 200 times the
selling price of crude (a cost of perhaps 5–10 cents per barrel, in com-

84

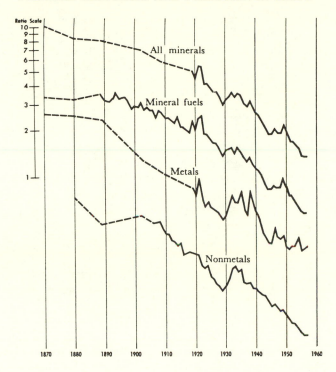

Note: Solid lines connect points in annual series; dashed lines connect points over a year apart.

FIGURE 5–2   U.S. MINERALS: LABOR COSTS PER UNIT OF
OUTPUT, 1870–1957
SOURCE: Barnett and Morse, 1963, p. 181.

parison to a selling price of somewhere around $10 per barrel)[2]; the price rise is therefore quite clearly the result of politics and cartel use of monopoly power. As of the date of writing, the press reports that:

In the face of a world-wide oil surplus, Saudi Arabia and several other OPEC nations have cut their oil production by 10 percent this month in order to prop up oil prices. Industry sources attribute the

[2] Between September 1970 and September 1974, Kuwait's tax revenues rose from $.80 per barrel to $9.60 per barrel—while the cost of *production* remained at $.06 per barrel (Yaari, 1974). The *International Economic Report of the President* (United States Government Printing Office, February, 1974) gives the production cost of Persian Gulf Crude as ten cents per barrel. Before the OPEC cartel got into action, oil prices had been *declining* relative to other commodities. The price of Iranian oil fell from $2.17 in 1947 to $1.79 in 1959 (Shah of Iran, 1974).

85

decision to cut production to ARAMCO, owned jointly by Saudi Arabia, Exxon, Texaco, Mobil and Standard Oil of California. ARAMCO officials, however, blamed "weather conditions" for the slash (*Near East Report*, Aug. 28, 1974, p. 188).

and

O.P.E.C.'s decision also served as a needed reminder that oil prices these days are set not by free-market economics but by politics, particularly in the Middle East. Economics would dictate a cut at this time instead of a disguised increase in oil prices. World demand has been held down because, after the quadrupling of prices by O.P.E.C. in the past year, consuming nations cannot afford to buy as much oil as they would like and the crude shortages of last winter have given way to a surplus (*Time*, Sept. 23, 1974, p. 52).

and

Growing oil glut . . . Sagging Western demand for oil has forced OPEC members to cut production sharply to maintain the current high price of crude (*Newsweek*, March 3, 1975, p. 31).

A recent study using the "sophisticated" technique of input-output analysis confirms the RFF conclusions for more recent years. Fisher (1971) and colleagues analyzed the trend of prices since 1953 in the United States: ". . . the cost of raw materials . . . is projected to decline in relation to the average" of all prices, while the cost of services is projected to rise relatively. "Energy prices are projected to decline most" (p. 21).

(There are always some people who respond to such figures by saying that they do not reflect what happened last year or last week, and that the long-term trends no longer hold. There is no way of proving such statements wrong. But it is a safe guess from the *history of analyses* that extrapolations from the recent past that run against previous long-run trends are more often wrong than are extrapolations of the long-term trends. It would be interesting to empirically examine various forecasts to test this proposition.)

At first most people do not feel comfortable with the Barnett-Morse position. To explicate the matter we must go to the philosophy of scientific definitions. Many people have in their minds the "actual" deposits of natural resources; their implicit definition of the potential supply of oil is the amount that someone would record if he conducted an exhaustive survey of all the earth's contents, and this supply is apparently fixed. But such a definition is thoroughly unoperational because such a survey is impossible even in principle. The operational supply is either that which is known today, or that which we may forecast as being known in the near future, or that which we estimate will be sought and found under varying conditions of demand. These latter notions of supply are decidedly not fixed, but rather are variable, and are the ones relevant for policy decisions.[3]

The above argument applies a fortiori to land, which is not exhausted with use (more details below).

Nordhaus and Tobin have recently deepened our understanding of the matter. They first experimented with a variety of three-factor (labor, capital, natural resources) production functions to find those that seemed to best explain changes in the national product over time. Using a "best fit" function, they estimated the elasticity of substitution between (1) natural resources and (2) a composite of labor and physical capital, regressing the ratio of the distributive shares on a function of the ratio of the inputs. The result was interpreted as an "elasticity of substitution between neo-classical factors and resources of about 2 . . ." (1972, pp. 63–70). Also consistent with the observed facts is that technological change is natural-resource-saving relative to other factors of production. Whether this or a high elasticity of substitution is the more important influence, however, Nordhaus and Tobin concluded that if "the past is any guide for the future, there seems to be little reason to worry about the exhaustion of resources which the market already treats as economic goods." (Of course some goods may not now be treated as economic, and therefore may have inappropriate prices placed on them. This will be touched on shortly under the heading of pollution.)

Two Historical Examples

Coal and Timber

The histories of the first two important natural resources that caused worry about depletion—coal and timber—are very instructive. Take coal first: In 1865, W. Stanley Jevons, one of the last century's truly great social scientists, wrote a careful comprehensive book that predicted that England's industry would soon grind to a halt due to exhaustion of England's coal. ". . . It will appear that there is no reasonable prospect of any relief from a future want of the main agent of industry" he wrote (1865, p. xiv), ". . . we cannot long continue our present rate of

---

[3] It may help the reader if I explore further some physical facts. By one test a pool of oil may be quite exhausted if a pump produces no oil. But if the price of oil rises high enough and technology advances enough, much additional oil can be retrieved by forcing water into the exhausted pool. But this in turn will not take out the oil that is in the rocks, which must wait for another technique. And so on! So how can one even imagine a single estimate of *the* supply of oil?

progress. The first check for our growing prosperity, however, must render our population excessive" (1865, p. xvi). Figure 5–3 shows the frontispiece from Jevons' book "shewing the impossibility of a long continuance of that progress."

Because of the perceived future need for coal, and because of the potential profit in meeting that need, prospectors searched out new deposits of coal, inventors developed better ways to get coal out of the earth, and transportation men developed cheaper ways to move the coal. At present, the proven U.S. reserves of coal are enough to supply a level of use far higher than at present for many hundreds of years into the future.[4] And the use of coal is even being subsidized in some countries[5] even though coal's labor cost per unit of output has been *falling* continuously (Barnett and Morse, 1963, p. 181) because the cost of *other* fuels has dropped even more. This suggests that *not enough* coal was mined in the past, rather than the future being unfairly exploited in earlier years.

The case of timber was studied by Olson in *The Myth of Depletion* (1971). In 1905 President Roosevelt said, "A timber famine is inevitable," a statement which culminated national worry, that began as early as 1860. There was special concern over such woods as hickory. But despite heavy use of wood since then, the picture is quite different by now. A "glut of low grades of factory lumber exists . . . a lack of market opportunities continues to set severe limitations on improvement of state and national forests . . . [By 1951] hickory trees were taking over the eastern hardwood forest . . . In spite of expanded uses of timber for pulp and paper, we are [in 1971] probably growing more cubic feet of wood annually than we were in 1910" (Olson, 1971, p. 2). A study of the years since 1953 reveals that the price of wood has fallen sharply relative to the prices of other products. (The price actually remained constant in current dollars despite inflation; Fisher, 1971).

The confounding of predictions and the shift from apparently impending "famine" to actual glut was not fortuitous, but rather occurred *in response* to the perceived need. One response was that timber was purposely grown, but interestingly enough that was not the major adjustment. More important were "behavioral responses to the threat of depletion and . . . the most important were made by the major industrial consumers of wood, not by forest owners, managers, or lumber

---

[4] Even if the U.S. rate of use of coal should rise to six or eight times the present rate of use, the presently estimated reserves would last for at least four hundred years (Hubbert, 1969, p. 205).

[5] Hans Brems informed me that the use of coal is required on German railroads despite its higher cost than oil.

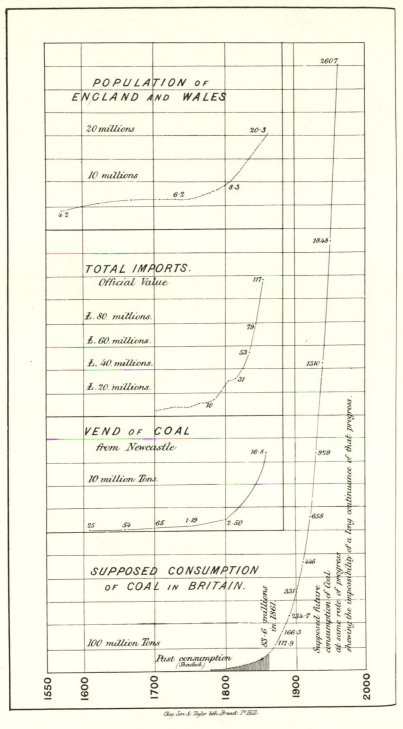

FIGURE 5–3   SUPPOSED FUTURE COAL CONSUMPTION, ENGLAND AND WALES, 1865
SOURCE: Reproduced from Jevons, 1865, frontispiece.

producers. These critical responses took the form of investments in research, specifically research in the use of wood and its substitutes.

"Technological change in other sectors of the economy also helped make possible adjustments in the timber market. The effects on the forest products industries of a half century of technical improvements in transportation and business organization were dramatically positive, and wholly unexpected" (Olson, 1971, p. 3).

We see these behavioral changes in our homes—plastic bags substituted for paper bags, newsprint made thinner (and yet stronger) as in "airmail editions" of overseas newspapers, and so on. Certainly, the fears of the past about running out of wood and coal have been quite wrong, and there is no reason to believe that the trends of history are suddenly reversing their direction in this decade.

One reason that the paradoxical nature of resource creation is hard to understand is that the analogy of the family and its resource endowment is not immediately relevant. If one thinks of a family on a desert island with a limited supply of pencils and paper, then more people on the island will lead to pencil-and-paper scarcity sooner than otherwise. But for a society as a whole, there is practically no resource which is not either growable (such as trees for paper) or substitutable for—except energy. And the supply of energy should present no problem, as will be discussed shortly.

It may be helpful to point out that there is no *logical* reason why natural resources are not available in infinite supply. It is often argued that because a perfect physical audit of the earth would show finite and limited quantities of everything, sooner or later we must run out of something. The point will be made below that with energy any other resource can be made. But there is another logical possibility: An increasing rate of recycling. No more iron would ever be needed than is used in present structures if the rate of recycling were infinitely fast. And there is no *logical* reason why the rate of recycling should not increase as much as the rate of use. To illustrate, consider a metal jug that one rubs to obtain the services of any genii. If only the one jug exists, and there are two families at opposite ends of the earth, each of them could obtain the genii very infrequently. But if the earth were populated densely, the cup could be passed rapidly from hand to hand, and *all* families might have a chance at obtaining the recycled jug and genii more often than with less dense population. So it could be with iron or whatever.

Even in the "short" run—say, to the end of the twentieth century—the rate of population growth is not likely to affect very much the supply or cost of raw materials in the United States, according to an RFF study (Ridker, 1973).

90

Is Land Different?

Even land, which seems to many people to be a special kind of resource, is subject to the processes of human creation just as are other natural resources. Though the stock of usable land *seems* fixed at any moment in time, the stock is constantly being increased—at a rapid rate in many cases—by clearing or reclamation of waste land,[6] as will be discussed in Chapter 11.

Also land is constantly being substituted for by multiplication of the number of crops per year on each unit of land, and by increased yield per crop with better farm methods and with chemical fertilizer. And last, but not least, land is created anew where there is no land. Much of Holland originally belonged as much to the sea as to the land. "According to strict geographical determinism, one would expect to find there nothing but a fever-ridden delta and lagoons, the undisputed domain of sea fowl and migratory birds. Instead, we find a prosperous and densely-peopled country, with in fact the highest densities of population in Europe" Wagnet, 1968, p. vi). The land of Holland, much of it, has been made by dyking and drainage. "This is essentially a triumph of human will; it is the imprint of civilization on the landscape" (Wagnet, p. 85). A hundred years ago someone said of the Netherlands, "This land is not soil: it is the flesh and blood and sweat of men" (Wagnet, p. 85).

Holland was mostly created by muscle power. But our potential for creating new land has increased as our knowledge and machinery and new power sources have developed. In the future, the potential for creating new land will be even greater, as we will be able to put what are now mountains where there is now water, as we learn new techniques of changing the nature of soils, and as we learn how to desalinate and transport fresh water to arid areas.

In its natural state, the land along the Columbia River in eastern Washington and Oregon is a forbidding expanse of shifting sand, sagebrush and Russian thistle, and only the hardiest of farmers or ranchers would try to wrest a living from it. The region is so desolate that the Navy uses some of the land as a bombing range. But for all this, the mid-Columbia region is one of the most thriving new agricultural areas in the world. Thanks to a remarkable new system of irrigation, the desert along the river is blooming: Its fields are lush with bumper crops of potatoes, corn, alfalfa, and beans. Corporate farmers, including such

---

[6] During periods of depopulation, the process is reversed, and land is lost to forest or water. This happened after the fall of the Roman Empire in Italy and in the Middle Ages in Europe, as a result of wars in Holland, New England, and elsewhere.

unlikely newcomers as the Boeing Co., are scrambling for every acre of land they can get.

"It's a goddam gold rush," sums up Glenn C. Lee, publisher of the Pasco (Wash.) Tri-City Herald . . .

The Columbia River reclamation actually started about five years ago, but it has been vastly speeded up by the agricultural boom. And it was made possible in the first place by the perfection of a fascinating new bit of farm technology called pivot irrigation . . .

Conventional flood irrigation wouldn't work along the Columbia; the water quickly drained through the sand. With pivot irrigation, the water is pumped from the river to the center of a round field a half-mile in diameter. A giant arm of 6-inch pipe a quarter-of-a-mile long pivots around the center of the field like the hand of a clock, making one revolution every 12 hours. The arm is supported 10 feet off the ground by ten towers; each tower rolls along on two rubber-tired wheels driven by electric motors. Sprinklers along the length of the pipe shower the ground continuously through the long growing season, dropping the equivalent of 60 inches of rain annually on the land compared with the natural fall of only 7 inches a year. The segmented irrigation pipe can even move up and down the slopes of rolling land.

Since much of the land is almost pure sand, it must be continuously fertilized, and here too the sprinkler system is used by feeding the appropriate nutrients into the water (*Newsweek*, May 20, 1974, p. 83).

Assuredly, the supply of land is not fixed in any meaningful way. Land is a resource like all the others. And its supply does not pose a threat of a special kind. (See Chapter 11 for more on this subject in the context of LDC's.)

People, when thinking about the effects of population growth also worry about the availability of recreational land and wilderness. On the face of it, it seems obvious that a larger number of people implies less recreational land and the disappearance of wilderness. But as with similar intuitively obvious statements about resources, this one is not right.

What matters is the *availability* to the potential user of recreational land and wilderness. Because of the increased means of transportation and the increased level of income to which population growth has contributed over the centuries, the average person in an MDC now has far greater *access* to recreational land and wilderness than in any earlier time. The average American has greater access to resort areas now than a king did 200 or 1,000 years ago, because of fast, safe transportation.

To put it in economist's terms,[7] the cost of a day in the wilderness has steadily gone down, and the income to pay for it has gone up, due in part to population growth. And there is no reason to see a change in this trend relationship in the future. (On the other hand, the *value* of a day in the wilderness may have gone down over time as the number of people sharing it has gone up. This tempers the positive conclusion.)

Even the *absolute* quantity of unsettled land is going *up* in the United States, as people move to the city. Succeeding censuses show that rural areas are less and less densely settled, and more counties have a net *loss* of population than have a net gain.

So the availability of land should not be seen as an argument against population growth.

Energy

Recently there has been much concern about impending energy shortages. The beginning of this chapter documented how energy shortages have frightened even the most intelligent of analysts for centuries. But the fears have not materialized because of man's capacity to create new energy resources. The most recent source of concern, an oil shortage, was shown to be the result of cartel and political power rather than rising costs of extraction. Furthermore, the cost of oil substitutes are not so high as to disrupt Western economies—a rise "ranging between 1.1 percent a year for electricity and 3.5 percent a year for transportation . . . We should not be haunted by the specter of the affluent society grinding to a halt for lack of energy resources" (Nordhaus, cited in *Brookings Bulletin*, Vol. 11, No. 1, Winter 1974, pp. 3–4). The consensus of energy experts is that "The world is not confronted by an imminent physical shortage of energy, nor—if they act wisely—need consumers of energy face the prospect of continuously rising prices" (*Brookings Bulletin*, Vol. 11, No. 2, Spring 1974, p. 5).

Energy may be thought of as the master resource, because energy enables one material to be converted into another. As natural scientists continue to learn more about the transformation of materials from one form to another with the aid of energy, this will be even more the case. Our knowledge of, and ability to execute, such transformations renders it less likely that any single material can constitute a bottleneck while other materials are plentiful.

Advances in fundamental science have made it possible to take advantage of the uniformity of energy/matter—a uniformity that

[7] Martin Spechler suggested that the argument be put this way.

makes it feasible, without preassignable limit, to escape the quantitative constraints imposed by the character of the earth's crust. A limit may exist, but it can be neither defined nor specified in economic terms. Flexibility, not rigidity, characterizes the relationship of modern man to the physical universe in which he lives. Nature imposes particular scarcities, not an inescapable general scarcity. Man is therefore able, and free, to choose among an indefinitely large number of alternatives. There is no reason to believe that these alternatives will eventually reduce to one that entails increasing cost—that it must sometime prove impossible to escape diminishing quantitative returns. Science, by making the resource base more homogeneous, erases the restrictions once thought to reside in the lack of homogeneity" (Barnett and Morse, 1963, p. 11).

Hence, if the cost of energy is low enough, all other resources can be made plentiful. For example, it is mostly the cost of energy that makes water desalinization too expensive for general use; reduction in energy cost would make possible water desalinization and irrigated farming in many areas now deserts. If energy were sufficiently cheap so that transportation could be cheaper, sweet water could be moved to arid areas far inland. Low energy costs would enable people to create enormous quantities of useful land. Also, if energy costs were low enough, all kinds of raw materials could be mined from the sea.

The main barrier to cheaper energy in very large quantities seems to be know-how. Nobel-winner Bethe sees it this way:

> Finally there is the possibility of generating power from fusion of heavy hydrogen rather than from fission. The nuclear physics of this is simple and well known. But it has so far proved impossible to contain deuterium long enough at high temperature to make power extraction possible. It will probably take a long time for this problem to be solved, meaning perhaps 20, perhaps 100 years. Ultimately I believe it will be solved, and we evidently are in no hurry to solve it because there is a great deal of uranium fuel available. One should not expect that fusion power will be cheaper than fission power; it is quite likely that it will be more expensive, because more complicated apparatus will be required for its extraction. However once it is developed, power requirements will be filled essentially forever. There are enormous amounts of heavy hydrogen in sea water. If I assume an electric power capacity of 100 billion kw, 100 times what I assumed [earlier] then the heavy hydrogen supply of the world will be sufficient to give us power for one billion years (1969, p. 92).

All told, the future supply of energy, and the effect of population growth upon it, should not be cause for concern. And perhaps population

94

growth, with its consequent additional demand and additional contributions to knowledge, will on balance have a positive effect on the supply and cost of energy rather than exacerbating it.

Food

The production of that very special resource, food, is taken up in the context of LDC's (for MDC's the matter requires no additional discussion) in Chapters 8, 9, 11, and the Appendix to Chapter 9. There the likelihood of population growth leading to increased food supplies is discussed in considerable micro-economic detail, including historical data. Therefore only a few additional comments are needed here.

On the one side we have frightening forecasts. The UN Economic and Social Commission for Asia and the Pacific forecasts "500 million starvation deaths in Asia between 1980 and 2025" (Associated Press, Feb. 12, 1975). And some see in such estimates the warrant for such policies as "triage—letting the least fit die in order to save the more robust victims of hunger" (*Newsweek*, Nov. 11, 1974, p. 16).

On the other side are the facts about past food-production performance. The over-all trend (even in recent years) has been an *increase* in food produced per person, even in LDC's; this may be seen in Figure 5–4 for the years 1956–1969. Johnson (1974) in an authoritative recent review (the President's Invited Lecture to the American Statistical Association) said:

"The available evidence indicates that the increase of the food supply has at least matched the growth of population in the developing countries, taken as a group, for the past four decades. This has been a period of very rapid population growth in the developing countries . . . . Thus the recent achievement in expanding food supplies in the developing countries has been a significant one—food supply has at least kept up with population growth during a period of unparalleled increase in population . . . .

"While there are undoubtedly exceptions, there is evidence that there has been a long term gradual improvement in per capita food consumption over the past two centuries" (Johnson, 1974, p. 91).[8]

The increase in food supplies is also in keeping with the trend in the incidence of famines: "An important change in the food situation that has occurred since World War II has been the dramatic decline in the

---

[8] "Adolph Weber . . . compared the per capita caloric intake in 1971 [for virtually all countries] with the French per capita calorie consumption of 1780. In 1780 France was one of the leading world powers—economically, socially, culturally, militarily. All countries of the world had by 1971 surpassed the French per capita caloric consumption of 1780. . . . He did note, however, that only a third of the world's population had surpassed the 1780 French per capita consumption of livestock products" (Johnson, 1973, pp. 4–5).

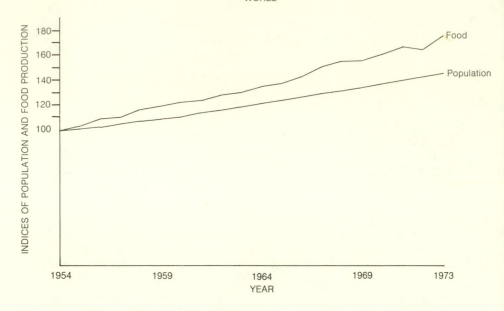

WORLD

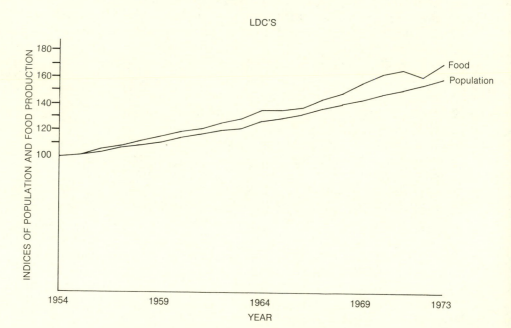

FIGURE 5–4   FOOD AND POPULATION TRENDS IN LDC's, 1954–73
SOURCE: *Annual Report to the Congress for Fiscal Year 1970*, p. 13.

incidence of famine. There is fairly firm evidence that at least 20 million deaths were caused by famine in the last quarter of the 19th century. While there have been some deaths due to famine in the third quarter of the 20th century, it is highly unlikely that the famine caused deaths equal a tenth of the period 75 years earlier.

"There has not been a major famine, such as visited China and India in the past, during the past quarter century. There have been some near misses, such as in India in 1965–66, and the current sad situation in Africa should not be ignored because a relatively small population is involved. But the food supply has been far more secure for poor people during the past quarter century than at any other comparable period in the last two or three centuries. I should add that I do not attribute the diminished incidence of famine as much to improved food supplies as I do to improvements in communication and transportation, but whatever the reasons we have witnessed an improvement of great significance . . . .

. . . [T]he percentage of the world's population who find themselves subject to actual famine conditions is probably lower now than at any time in the past" (Johnson, 1973, pp. 6–7).

The increase in food supplies over time is not incompatible with increases in food prices. A major cause of the price rises has been increases in world incomes and the increased demand for *better* foods such as meat (which requires much grain to produce).

The very latest news suggests that there has been no break in the long-term trends. As of this writing, the future prices in commodity markets indicate that traders—whose survival depends on obtaining the latest information and assessing it correctly—are "extremely bearish . . . [expecting] larger and better crops around the world . . . feeling that commodities are headed back to pre-1970 price levels" (*Champaign-Urbana News Gazette*, May 12, 1974, p. 46). "World wheat markets seem to settle down after 2 hectic years . . . prices decline as supplies of most varieties rise . . . the Agriculture Department's Foreign Agricultural Service think supplies will be ample: 'Responding to rising world demand and strong price incentives, the world's output of grains in fiscal 1974–75 could approach (one) billion tons for the first time in history'" (*Wall Street Journal*, April 5, 1974, p. 1).

The Key Resource: Human Imagination

In the earlier section on energy it became clear that the only constraint upon the capacity to enjoy unlimited energy at acceptable prices or lower is knowledge. The same is true for other natural resources. And the source of knowledge is the human mind. Ultimately, then, it seems that the key constraint is human imagination and the exercise of educated skills. This is why an increase of human beings constitutes an addition to the crucial stock of resources along with causing additional consumption of resources.

This general point of view does not assert that there cannot be shortages, or even disasters. Indeed, history shows some catastrophic shortages, such as the land exhaustion that destroyed the Mayan community, and the contemporary outlook is not completely optimistic: Shortages of such goods as space and pure air are possible in 1970's-type economies. Though technology and other resources exist to resolve these shortages, and though the difficulty may lie in social and institutional and political factors, shortages can and do occur.

Perhaps the key point with respect to the relationship between natural resources and population growth is that the development of new methods that prevent scarcity is *not fortuitous*. The situation is *not* one of a "race" between two independent competitors—technology and development, on the one hand, population increase and economic growth on the other. To a large extent new methods are invented and developed *in response to* the signals of impending scarcity. In the private sector the response is to a perceived opportunity to make a profit out of the impending situation.[9] Like other market mechanisms, this response mechanism is reasonably reliable. Of course, there is always the possibility that the mechanism may not act fast enough to keep prices of natural resources from rising because of scarcities. But in the past the trend has been the other way, toward lower prices in most cases, as was seen in Figure 5–1. And with the passage of time, the ability of MDC economies to respond to signals of impending scarcity has increased, which suggests that response should be even faster and stronger in the future than in the past.

Resources and Future Generations

Some people have worried unnecessarily that use of resources now is at the expense of future generations. The matter is easiest to understand where the relative prices of natural resources can be expected to be the

---

[9] "Over the first 20 postwar years, a majority of important decision-influencing people at one time or another forecast coming famines in [many] products. The world then progressively created unsaleable and unprofitable surpluses in every one of them: temperate foodstuffs after 1947; raw materials after 1951; "manufactured goods that could conceivably ever be sold to the United States and bridge the dollar gap" after about 1954; fuels (especially coal after 1945, and oil after Suez); orthodoxly trained university students (especially from the science faculties) after 1960. Less important people in this period at one time or another forecast "limitless opportunities" for durable consumer goods, other leisure products, computers, advertising agencies, go-go business conglomerates, and media for international equity investment by the small man. The market system therefore proceeded to create smaller but rather unprofitable surpluses in each of these" (*The Economist*, Jan. 22, 1972, p. v).

same or lower in the next generations—as seems reasonable for most natural resources in the light of their price histories. Such a situation implies that the next generations will be faced by no greater economic scarcity than we are, but rather will have just as large supplies to tap, despite contemporary use of resources. If the economic situation were different than it is—if technology were constant and prices of resources would therefore be higher in the future than now, indicating greater scarcity then than now—it might be appropriate to make ethical judgments that would differ from the results of the market discount-rate effects. But this is not necessary or appropriate.

> [W]hile the use of ethical principles to mediate the competing claims of different generations would have clear relevance in a Ricardian world, where today's depletion curtails tomorrow's production, it has little if any relevance in a progressive world, where efforts to serve the interests of the present also serve those of the future. If those now living devote themselves to improving society's productive power, and also its capacity to reach decisions concerning the use of that power that will increasingly benefit themselves and their children, the value of the social heritage will grow continually. To increase current real income, physical capital is accumulated. To satisfy his curiosity, man adds to society's intellectual capital. To enrich its own life, each generation strives to improve the health and education of its children, thereby augmenting society's human capital. And, in consequence of efforts to improve society's functioning as a productive enterprise, economic institutions and standards are rendered more effective. By devoting itself to improving the lot of the living, therefore, each generation, whether recognizing a future-oriented obligation to do so or not, transmits a more productive world to those who follow (Barnett and Morse, 1963, p. 249).

And since we can expect future generations to be richer than we are, no matter what we in practice do about resources, saving resources for future generations is like asking the relatively poor to make gifts to the relatively rich.

Resources, Ethics, and LDC s

Nor is there likely to be need for ethical judgments superseding market decisions in the matter of MDC's buying raw materials from LDC's. The idea that the rich countries are "raping" the poor countries and "pirating" their bauxite, copper, and oil does not rest on a solid intellectual foundation. Those resources have no value at all for home use in a country with no industry. When sold to an industrial country, the

99

resources provide revenue that can aid in development—and, in fact, may represent the LDC's very best chance of development.[10] Nor are contemporary LDC people benefiting at the expense of future generations when they sell natural resources, whether development of the LDC takes place or not. "Saving" the materials for the LDC's future runs the grave risk that the resources will drop in relative value in the future, just as coal has become less valuable in the past century; a country that hoarded its coal starting 100 years ago would be a loser on all counts.

It is also relevant that the United States exports large amounts of primary products that LDC's need—especially food. The primary products that the LDC's produce enable them to trade for the MDC's primary products, an exchange from which both parties gain. Of course, nothing in this paragraph suggests that the prices at which MDC's buy these resources from LDC's are "fair" prices. The price is indeed an ethical matter—but one which is likely to be resolved by the hard facts of supply, demand, market power, and political power.

Summary Concerning Natural Resources

All in all, there seems to be no reason to believe that national resources should be treated in a manner different from other physical capital when considering the economic effect of different rates of population growth. There is no reason to believe that the relatively larger use of national resources that would occur with a relatively larger population would have any special deleterious effects upon the economy at present or in the future.

POLLUTION AND THE ENVIRONMENT

The Background of Pollution

A discussion of natural resources is not complete without mention of environmental pollution, because the two phenomena are the opposite sides of the same coin: Sooty air is undesired pollution; it may also be thought of as the absence of the desired resource of pure air. The key difference between the two topics is that the supply of the goods we call "natural resources" is largely in the hands of the private sector,

---

[10] "Many of those Indonesians who took to the streets only eight months ago to protest alleged Japanese exploitation of their natural resources are now beginning to complain that the Japanese are not exploiting them enough. Because of setbacks in their won economy, Japanese importing companies have had to cut their monthly purchases of 760,000 cubic yards of Indonesian timber by as much as 40%. As a result, Indonesian lumber prices have dropped some 60% and the Indonesia Timber Corp. claims that 30 firms have already gone bankrupt, causing widespread unemployment in such timber-dependent areas as Kalimantan" (*Newsweek*, Sept. 30, 1974, p. 52).

100

where there is strong self-interest profit motivation for suppliers to provide consumers with what they want. A deal is made through the market, and people tend to get what they are willing to pay in. In contrast, the goods we call "absence of environmental pollution" are largely under the control of the public sector, where the political mechanism which adjusts supply and demand is far less automatic and—for better or for worse—seldom uses a pricing system which would arrive at the same result as would a free market. Another difference is that natural resource transactions are mostly limited in impact to the buyer and the seller, whereas one man's pollution is "external" and may touch everybody else. This difference may be more apparent than real, however. One man's demand for natural resources affects the price that all men pay, at least in the short run; and conversely, the price that one man must pay depends upon the demand of all other men for the resource. Much the same would be the case for pollution if there were a well-adjusted system by which people had to pay for the privilege of polluting. But such a price system for regulating pollution is not so easy to achieve, and hence the situations of resources and pollution do differ in how "external" they are.

Sound discussion requires that we think about the *many* possible pollutions rather than just about a single general pollution. Many pollutions have lessened over time in many places (e.g., filth in the streets in the United States, buffalo dung in the streams of the Midwest, soot in the air and lack of fish in the rivers of England,[11] organic impurities in foods in MDC's, and so on). Other pollutions have worsened, for example, gasoline fumes in the air, noise in many places, and atomic wastes. The long-run course of others is unknown, for example, crime in the streets. It is not possible here or elsewhere to consider, one at a time, all the past, present, and future pollutions, because their number is as large as the ecologist's imagination. But to summarize the direction of such a varied collection of factors is difficult and can be misleading.

If one has to choose a single measure of the state of pollution, the most plausible measure is life expectancy. The expected length of a newborn's life has increased greatly in the past centuries, and is still

[11] "British rivers . . . have been polluted for a century while in America they began to grow foul only a couple of decades ago. . . . The Thames has been without fish for a century. But by 1968 some 40 different varieties had come back to the river" (Friendly, 1970). "Now to be seen [in London] are birds and plants long unsighted here. . . . The appearance of long-absent birds is measured by one claim that 138 species are currently identified in London, compared with less than half that number 10 years ago. . . . Gone are the killer smogs. . . . Even fog itself—a sometimes romanticized but often ominous aspect of life in London over the centuries—is becoming increasingly a thing of the past. Londoners . . . are breathing air cleaner than it has been for a century . . . effects of air pollution on bronchial patients is diminishing . . . visibility is better, too . . . on an average winter day . . . about 4 miles, compared with 1.4 miles in 1958" (*U.S. News and World Report,*).

increasing rapidly in many LDC's. Hence, the sum of the health-related "pollutions" (using that term in its widest sense) has been diminishing. (On the other hand, very recent data for the United States suggest a possible reversal in life expectancy in the United States.)

But—in an advanced technological society there is always the possibility that a *totally new* form of pollution will emerge and finish us all before we can do anything about it. Though the prospects of a general catastrophe to the human race grew less year by year from the time of the Black Death forward, the risk may have begun to increase in this century and in recent decades—from atomic bombs or from unknown but powerful pollution. The present risk of catastrophe cannot be known except in the future with hindsight. There is no counterpart to this explosive unknown in the context of scarcity of natural resources, and there is no answer to this threat except to note that life with perfect security is not possible—and would not be meaningful.

In general, there may be little basis for saying that the pollution situation has recently been getting better. But there is (in my judgment) even *less* basis for saying that things have been getting worse. It *is* clear, however, that there has been an increase in *concern* about pollution in the past decade. Herfindahl and Kneese wisely note that "the present concern with environmental quality may stem as much or more from increased demands [for a clean environment] as deterioration in supply" (1965, p. 3). But the *cause* of the concern does not matter; what does matter is the fact that people actively want a purer environment.

It is also reasonably clear that advanced economies have considerable power to purify their environments.

> The meager evidence . . . does not indicate that degradation of all aspects of the physical environment is continuous and inexorable. Serious deterioration in some aspects of environmental quality did take place between say, 1840 and 1940, but because in the process other values were created it is difficult to determine whether it was excessive. By most measures the quality of air and water deteriorated, sometimes severely. Wild areas were brought under development, and their beauty frequently was impaired or destroyed. Game populations diminished rapidly, and in many cases ugly and congested cities were created.
>
> Since 1940, however, the quality of the environment has in some respects markedly improved. Rivers have been cleaned of their grossest floating materials; cities have substantially reduced the particulate matter in their atmosphere; some of the worse slums have been eliminated; public health, at least so far as infectious diseases are concerned,

has been greatly improved; much land has been returned to a wild state, and many important varieties of wildlife have been encouraged to increase spectacularly (Herfindahl and Kneese, 1965, p. 2).

And the key element in purification is well known. England's top anti-pollution bureaucrat, Lord Kennel, stated it: "'. . . with rare and usually quickly solved exceptions, there is no contaminating factor in the environment, including noise, that defies a technical solution. All it takes is money'" (Friendly, 1970). In other words, purification requires the will to devote the necessary part of a nation's present output and energy to do the job.

Long used for recreational purposes, Lake Washington [18-mile-long body of fresh water bordered by Seattle on its western shore and a number of smaller communities on its eastern side] began to deteriorate badly soon after World War II when ten newly built waste-treatment plants began dumping some 20 millions gallons of treated effluents into its water every day.

Algae thrived on the phosphorus and nitrogen in the sewage discharge, and each time more of the burgeoning aquatic plants died, so did a little bit of the lake—in the form of oxygen lost in decomposition. The lake became cloudy and malodorous, and the fish died along with the algae.

Alarmed, the state legislature in 1958 created a new authority—the Municipality of Metropolitan Seattle—and charged it with sewage disposal for the Seattle area. With the support of local residents, Metro, as the agency soon became known, built a $121 million integrated system that funnels all of the area's effluents far out into Puget Sound. In that way, the wastes are dissipated by tidal action.

Starting in 1963, the system was far enough along for the plants that had been dumping their nutritive wastes into the lake to begin, one by one, to divert their output into the new system and Puget Sound. The results were obvious in the clearer, cleaner water and the return of fish populations. "When the phosphorus levels fell off, so did the algae blooms," says one zoologist, "and so did the pollution." What Lake Washington demonstrates, of course, is that pollution is not irreversible—provided the citizenry is really determined to reclaim the environment, and willing to pay for past years of neglect (*Newsweek*, November 16, 1970, p. 67).

The pollution of our living space by trash and discarded goods, especially junk autos, is a particularly interesting case. Not only is this problem very amenable to solution by the expenditure of resources for clean-up, but it also illustrates how *resource scarcity is decreasing*. Iron supplies and steel-making processes have now gotten to the point of cheapness at which junked cars are no longer worth the recycling. The old cars—if they could be stored out of sight—could be thought of as a newly created reservoir of "raw" materials for the future. In this important sense, iron is not being used but only stored in a different form for future use, until prices rise and/or better methods of salvage are developed. Much the same is true with many other discarded materials. But to repeat, unlike market-produced-and-mediated goods, the amount of pollutants produced and the price of polluting are not automatically regulated by public demand, either by ballot vote or by dollar voting. And there are strong private interests that militate against remedial actions. The outcome of a pollution process, therefore, will largely depend on the social will and the political process.

Population Growth and Pollution

Now we must ask how various rates of population growth would affect the amount of pollution? The total amounts of most kinds of potential pollutants depend upon the *total scale of industry* in an economy. This scale may be roughly gauged by the country's GNP (except that beyond some per-capita income, the proportion of industrial products in GNP begins to decline as the proportion of services increases). Some writers have deduced from this that there is only a slight relationship between population growth and total pollution, arguing that pollution in the United States grows at a putative 9% a year, while population grows at perhaps 1% per year.

This point of view receives support from the facts that (a) in Australia's rather affluent cities there is much pollution despite low population density in Australia, and (b) the communist countries fall afoul of pollution when industrial production goes up, just as do capitalist countries.

In Russia, a huge chemical plant was built right beside a beloved tourist attraction: Yasnaya Polanya, Leo Tolstoy's gracious country estate. Unmonitored fumes are poisoning Tolstoy's forests of oak and pine, and powerless conservationists can only wince. With equal indifference, the Soviet pulp and paper industry has settled on the shores of Lake Baikal. No matter how fully the effluents are treated, they still defile the world's purest waters.

The level of the Caspian Sea has dropped 8½ ft. since 1929, mainly because dams and irrigation projects along the Volga and Ural rivers divert incoming water. As a result, Russia's caviar output has decreased; one-third of the sturgeons' spawning grounds are high and dry. Meanwhile, most municipalities lack adequate sewage treatment plants, carbon monoxide chokes the plateau towns of Armenia, and smog shrouds the metallurgical centers of Magnitogorsk, Alma-Ata and Chelyabinsk (*Time*, Nov. 30, 1970, p. 44).

The slight relationship between population growth and pollution may be seen quantitatively in Figure 5–5. The solid rectangles show the

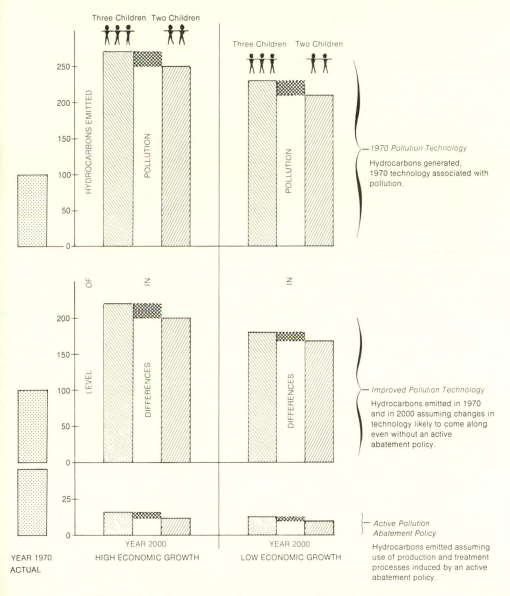

FIGURE 5–5   POPULATION, POLLUTION, AND ECONOMIC GROWTH

differences in emitted hydrocarbon pollution between the two-child and the three-child family projections for the year 2000, within the high-economic-growth and low-economic-growth projections. These differences are obviously small compared to the differences within projections between various pollution treatment policies (A, B, and C), and even small compared to the differences between the high and the low economic-growth conditions. The President's Commission on Population Growth's "general conclusions are similar for other pollutants" to these conclusions about hydrocarbons (Ridker, 1972, p. 25).

That GNP growth has more influence on pollution than does population growth may be true for a very short period—say, one or ten or thirty years—before the additional children under discussion join the labor force. In the long run, however, the total output will be more-or-less *proportional to the labor force* (as discussed in detail in the next chapter). Hence, a population twice as big implies about twice as much total pollution, *ceteris paribus*. If the increased population results in a proportional increase in population density, each person would be exposed to twice as much pollution, *ceteris paribus*.

But it is not reasonable to assume *ceteris paribus*. When pollution increases, political forces arise to fight pollution. The end result of this process, once begun, *may* be *less* pollution than if the situation had not been so bad at first—*or* on the other hand, nothing may happen except a much worse level of pollution than otherwise. The outcome simply cannot be known in advance; there seems to be nothing in economic logic or political history that can help us predict with confidence whether the end result of the larger population and of the initially higher pollution would be a situation that would be better or worse than if the population had not grown so large.

SUMMARY

In a book on population growth, neither natural resources nor pollution are central topics. Increases in resource consumption and environmental pollution are influenced far more over time by increases in per-head consumption than by increases in the number of heads. Furthermore, natural resources compose a very small and ever-decreasing proportion of total production—and hence are not an important added cost of added people.[12] Therefore, the effect on natural resources and pollu-

[12] "The gross value of extractive output relative to value of national product has declined substantially and steadily from 1870 to the present. In 1870, the extractive share was nearly 50 per cent. By the turn of the century, it had fallen to 32 per cent; and, by 1919, to 23 23 per cent. In 1957, the figure was 13 per cent, and still trending downward" (Barnett and Morse, 1963, p. 220).

tion is not an important consideration when weighing up the effect of additional people in MDC's.

The argument is made and documented that natural resources *grow in response* to increased demand from increased population as well as from economic activity generally. Though paradoxical, supplies of natural resources may be expected to *increase* indefinitely, and the long-run resource outlook is good. The ultimate constraint upon resource availability is human imagination, and hence population growth can augment resources in the long run by increasing knowledge.

CHAPTER 6

The Effect of Population on Per-Worker
Income in MDC's: A Simulation

INTRODUCTION

MORE BIRTHS are commonly thought to mean a lower standard of living, both in the short run and in the long run. The root of the argument is first-edition capital-dilution Malthus: Adding people who must work and live with the original fixed supply of land and capital implies less product available for each person. *The Limits to Growth* simulation (Meadows et al., 1972) only expands this argument with a complex and sophisticated method.

If, however, one adds to the simple neo-classical model another fundamental fact of the economic growth of nations—the increase in productivity due to additional people's inventive and adaptive capacities—one arrives at a very different result.

This chapter constructs and experiments with a simulation model of the effect of population growth on per-worker output in MDC's. This model is outlined in Figure 6–1. It embodies not only the standard classical and neo-classical capital effects but also the effects of knowledge advance, economies of scale, and natural resource use. The latter elements have been omitted from population models in the past, but they are crucial to a balanced understanding of the problem. Chapters 3, 4, and 5 analyzed the available data and provided rough estimates of the parameters for use in the models constructed in this chapter.

The various models given in this chapter are intended to be illustrative and suggestive, and do not purport to represent either the United States or any other single country or the developed world as a whole. The central finding results from adding a single element—the effect of population size upon productivity—to a simple conventional model, within what seem to the writer to be reasonable ranges of the basic parameters. But though it is true that one can immediately deduce from the input arguments the main *directional* conclusion—that at some point in the future, per-worker output may begin to be greater with a higher population growth rate—the simulation is needed to tell *when if ever* the effect becomes positive under various assumed conditions. One cannot know from examination of the model's structure alone whether this will be in 30 or 300 or 3,000 years. The results of the simulation suggest that the answer is between 30 and 80 years.

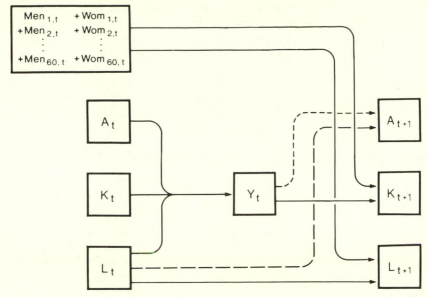

Note: The line with long dashes from L_t to A_{t+1} represents the feed-back effect in the Residual model, whereas the line with the short dashes from Y_t to A_{t-1} represents the feedback effect in the Ver-doorn model.

FIGURE 6–1 SCHEMATIC OF MDC MODELS WITHOUT EDUCATION

The result that population growth's effect becomes positive after 30–80 years is arrived at with two separate but related approaches. The aim of both models is to estimate quantitatively the interaction and ultimate net effects of the negative and positive impacts of population growth. Both models embody—in addition to the conventional economic considerations including the effects of dependency and labor-force participation— the impact of additional people upon technological advance through the creation of knowledge and through the economies of larger scale, working together with the natural-resources effect.

One of the models embodies this knowledge-and-scale effect directly by way of the assumption that the observed "residual" in studies of economic growth—the over-all growth of productivity due to technological advance—is a function of the labor force and the creativity found therein at all levels. The "Residual model" approach makes sense a priori, but the empirical evidence for it is only vague. Therefore, a second model is constructed that takes advantage of Verdoorn's empirical law that productivity goes up as the square root of total output. This "Verdoorn model" is an indirect way of getting at the same effect as does the Residual

109

model. Total output is a function of the size of the labor force, and Verdoorn's law may be thought of as a proxy for the relationship of labor force to productivity and technological advance. Or if one prefers, one may think of it simply as a net estimate of returns to scale.

It is encouraging that the Residual model and the Verdoorn model give similar results. This strengthens belief in the reasonableness of both models and in the general result they jointly yield. The over-all finding is that within 30 to 80 years, the initial negative effect of another birth upon per-worker output is displaced by a positive effect that rapidly increases in magnitude as the person's legacy of productivity advance accumulates. The length of the time required for the effect to become positive depends upon the parameters one decides are most reasonable.

This chapter may be viewed as an attempt to quantify[1] Kuznets' masterful paper (1960). In the formal approach used here, many of the influences discussed by Kuznets and by Chapters 3 and 4 are necessarily left out. Also, this chapter is not an empirical study, but rather is a theoretical exercise which uses the simulation technique instead of analytic methods. This has the disadvantage of less generality than analytic methods, because the results hold only for the specific sets of parameters on which the models are run, and apply only by analogy to other sets of parameters within the ranges of the simulated sets. Unlike analytic methods, no results are proven to hold for all cases consistent with the basic assumptions. On the other hand, the simulation method has the advantage of allowing one to theorize about a much richer and more realistic model than analytic methods allow, and with more specificity.

The context of the chapter is near-full employment. The time horizon— perhaps 50 or 150 years—is sufficiently short so that possible major changes in the natural-resources situation may be disregarded, but sufficiently long so that delayed effects of knowledge can come to play their role.[2] Also, it is crucial to note that though the terms of reference are to the United States, it would be most appropriate to conduct this analysis for the developed world as a whole, because of the scientific and technological inter-dependence among the MDC's. This point of view skirts the possibility that one country might decide to take a ride on the coattails of technological advance created by other countries.[3]

---

[1] ". . . we have no tested, or even approximate, empirical coefficients with which to weight the various positive and negative aspects of population growth" (Kuznets, 1960, p. 339).

[2] Einstein lowered per-capita income for the years during his childhood. Even in his scientific manhood the results of his research may have had no beneficial impact. But starting perhaps 80 years after Einstein's birth, and continuing thereafter, his birth caused great economic gain.

[3] Some individual countries might indeed reason this way. The extent to which all knowledge requires local research, development, and experience for satisfactory adaptation may easily be underestimated, however.

The purposes of the chapter are these: (1) to understand in the history of industrial nations the influences of population growth on income through changes in capital, scale and knowledge; and (2) to consider what the future course of output per worker might be with higher or lower birth rates.

The dependent variable is output (or income) *per worker*,[4] and not output or consumption per capita (or per-consumer-equivalent).

In the long run the two measures are much the same. In the short run an increase in population through an increase in fertility necessarily implies a drop in consumption per capita even if output per worker remains the same, because the total number of workers remains the same while the number of people increases (a point discussed at greater length in the Appendix to Chapter 10). In the household, income is then spread among more people. And when population grows faster there is greater public consumption of education and other child-raising services,[5] which implies larger taxes and less resources available for private consumption and saving.

But in the long run, measures of consumption per capita and output per worker will give much the same result, and the focus here is on the long run. Furthermore, lower per-person consumption need not mean lower total utility. In fact, depending on one's social welfare function, the same total consumption spread among more people might be seen as yielding higher total utility.

THE FEEDBACK MODELS

Kuznets (1960) suggested that an additional person's contribution to knowledge might lead him to have a net positive effect upon the standard of living. But Kuznets did not quantify the argument or compare the likely effect of the additional knowledge against the classical capital-diluting effects of population growth. Such quantification, leading to an estimate of how long it takes for the effect to become positive (if ever), is the aim of the models used here.

Except for the feedback effect to allow for the influence of population growth or output growth upon productivity, the models are quite unexceptional: a Cobb-Douglas production function, allowances for the effects of the rate of dependency upon saving and labor-force participation, and a simple demographic model in which all persons enter the labor force at 21 and work until they die at age 60. The effect of population growth upon education is a bit less standard, and several variants are used. But

---

[4] It is *not* assumed here that per-capita income is the appropriate measure of welfare; in Chapter 19, I argue that it is not. But per-capita income is *one* of the arguments in almost everyone's welfare function.

[5] The investment aspect of education will be treated later.

those details may be left for later. This section takes up the central feed-back elements of the two alternate models.

Notation

A_t = level of the economy's productive efficiency as of year t

ART = complex of natural resources, economies of scale, and technological knowledge

EFF_t = the effective labor force; the number of workers weighted by their education

K_t = stock of capital

L_t = number of people in the labor force

$MEN(i)_{j,t}$ = number of males of age j alive as of year t in demographic structure i

$POP(i)_t$ = total population in year t in demographic structure i

R_t = natural resources available for use

S_t = total resources spent on physical investment and education

XED_t = expenditure on education

$WOM(i)_{j,t}$ = number of females of age j alive as of year t in demographic structure i

Y_t = the aggregate output

e_L = elasticity of labor force with respect to children born

e_s = elasticity of the saving ratio, s, with respect to number of children

s_t = the proportion of saving to output

w = ratio of children age 20 and under to adults ages 21–60

α = exponent of capital in Cobb-Douglas production function

β = exponent of labor in Cobb-Douglass production function

The Residual Model

The Residual model derives an estimate of the effect of population growth upon the indissoluble complex[6] of knowledge creation, natural

---

[6] To disentangle the three ART factors from each other seems hopeless. Rather they must be treated together as a complex, and doing so is a main methodological feature of this study. To illustrate why they must be treated together, consider natural resources first. Natural resources might be thought of as a third factor of production

$$Y_t = AK^\alpha L^\beta R^\gamma$$

and it would seem reasonable that R_t is a negative function of output in previous years, perhaps the sum of the previous output

resources, and economies of scale—hereafter referred to with the acronym "ART complex"—from the "residual" found in studies that attempt to explain U.S. economic growth. The residual is the unexplained portion of economic growth left after inputs of capital and labor have been accounted for; it is commonly associated with technological advance.

The Residual model assumes that the size of the residual is a function of the size of the labor force. In this formulation the residual is positively influenced by population growth, which is a quantitative expression of Kuznets' qualitative assertion. In the context of the Cobb-Douglas production function, the residual may be seen as changes in technological level, A. The problem about whether the increases in capital (and labor) should or do reflect improvements due to increased knowledge is critical here, but we shall merely look the problem in the face and then pass rapidly on.

The ART element is introduced as follows. The amount of change in A is assumed to be a function of the entire labor force. But an increase in the knowledge component of ART does not result in an instantaneous increase in productivity; rather, the effect of much knowledge is substantially lagged. The extent of the lag in the application of knowledge

$$R_t = f\left(\sum_{t=0}^{t} Y_t\right).$$

The last equation is consistent with the static physical point of view that natural resources such as coal and oil must diminish over time. But the definition of resources by the amounts that are "really" in the earth is not operational and hence meaningless. What is relevant is that the economically meaningful *available* resources have mostly *not* decreased over time, as Barnett and Morse (1963) have shown. This increase in available resources is a function of increasing knowledge, e.g., new ways to prospect for and retrieve oil, new plastic materials to substitute for metals, and improved forestry techniques. Seen this way, natural resources are not different from physical capital. We may therefore think about the stock of available resources at time t as part of the capital factor, and the future course of the stock of natural resources will be affected by saving and by increase in knowledge in the same way as conventionally-defined physical capital.

Considering economies of scale and technological knowledge, now: The two factors conceptually could be separated. One may imagine an experiment in which every other person and installation in the United States would be removed, holding the stock of knowledge constant, to see the effect upon output per worker. But such an experiment is not feasible, and the growth of scale and of knowledge have been so collinear in the past that it is not possible to separate them statistically. For this reason, and also because of their inseparability in the production process, we must treat them together. Kuznets emphasized this inseparability (in conversation). And Fellner uses a framework in which "economies of scale . . . become merged with 'progress'" (1970, p. 9).

Denison's attempt (1967) to get at the effect of scale is useful but does not resolve this difficulty, I believe. In passing, one might note that his estimate of the rate of advance of knowledge alone is "much smaller than the increases in the population . . . , [which] implies a declining per capita contribution to knowledge" (1962, p. 237). In the context of this paper, it should be remembered that such advance in knowledge is only one of the sources of contribution to the ART complex.

113

is an important empirical question concerning which I know of no evidence (though it would seem that the length of the lag is decreasing). Let us suppose that the present mean of the lag distribution for the ART complex as a whole, for an average cross-section of workers, is 5 years. This means that the first increment to the productivity residual can be dated at 5 years after the incremental workers enter the labor force, with an *additional* increment to productivity in each of the following 40 years until 5 years after they retire. The equation for the change in A in the main approach is as follows:

$$\frac{A_t - A_{t-1}}{A_{t-1}} = bL_{t-5}, \quad \text{or} \quad A_t = A_{t-1} + bA_{t-1}L_{t-5}, \quad (6\text{--}1a)$$

where b is chosen so that $A_{t=1} = (1 + x)A_{t=0}$ in the basic demographic structure, and x is the parameter[7] relating the size of the labor force to the increase in the ART complex, that is, A. When x is set at .01, a stationary labor force in period $t = -5$ would produce a .01 increase in $A_{t=0}$. If the labor force is growing at a rate of Δ per year, the labor force in year $t = -5$ causes $A_{t=0}$ to be $(1 + \Delta)(.01)A_{t=-1}$. That is, in the context of this model, the increase in A from year to year is proportional to the size of the labor force. This mechanism is calibrated so that the labor force at time $t = -5$ in structure BASE produces an x increase in A_t in year $t = 0$, where x is whichever of .01, .015 or .02 is being tried in that run. The point to notice here is that the ART additions from an increment of workers, knowledge and economies of scale are *cumulative and nondepreciating*, as is the stock of productive know-how.

One source for an estimate of the growth in per-worker output due to the increase in knowledge and scale, including the effect of natural resources, is Denison (1967), who estimated the effect of elements roughly comparable to ART. For the period 1950–62 for the United States, Denison estimated yearly growth of .76% for "advances in knowledge" (which excludes the effect of education on the labor force), and .30% for "economies of scale" (1967, p. 298), for a total just over 1%. For Northwest Europe he estimated .76% for "advances in knowledge," .56% for "changes in the lag in the application of knowledge, general efficiency, and errors and omissions," and .41% for "economies of scale" (pp. 287, 300), for a total of something over 1.5%. Solow's estimate for the United States for the 40 years from 1909 to 1949 is about 1.5% per year (1957, p. 316). Solow also adduces, though "not really comparable," an estimate of .75% per year from 1869 to 1948 by Valavanis-Vail, and Schmookler's estimate for 1904–13 to 1929–38 which (though including agriculture) was of similar size to Solow's estimate.

---

[7] If no lag were involved, b would equal x.

If a larger labor force causes a faster rate of productivity change, one would expect to see this reflected in observed changes in the rate of productivity advance over time in the United States. In fact, Solow concludes that the yearly rate of change of A went from 1% to 2% over the 20 years from the (median of the) first half of his study period to the (median of the) second half of his period (1957, p. 320). Fellner, using Kendrick's data, arrived at these rates of productivity increase over time (using two methods of calculation): 1900–29: 1.8% (or 1.5%); 1929–48: 2.3% (or 2.0%); 1948–66: 2.8% (or 2.3% and 2.6% for the two subperiods within 1948–66; 1970, pp. 11–12). These data are consistent with the assumption that the rate of increase of productivity is indeed higher when population is larger—though other factors could explain part of the rate of increase, of course.

The model will be run with estimates of 1.0%, 1.5%, and 2.0%. Most of the reported results will pertain to the "conservative" estimate of 1.5%, roughly the average for the twentieth century which is well below the rate observed for the most recent period.

The reader may not feel comfortable with this method of estimating the feedback effect of the ART complex. But to just ignore the effect altogether is not a reasonable alternative. To leave out the effect is to implicitly estimate that the effect is zero (which is what all the classical models do). But certainly there is overwhelming evidence that the effect is not zero, though its size is difficult to estimate. Hence, it would seem that the appropriate argument is about how to estimate it, and which estimates to use, rather than whether to include the effect at all.

The reader may object that advances in knowledge have not been linked solidly to population at a micro-economic level. True. But where else but from people's minds, past and present, can advances in knowledge come from, holding the quantity of capital constant? Physical capital alone cannot generate advances in knowledge, though it may serve as a basis of ideas to people. All the advances-in-knowledge concepts that Denison mentions are related to people: "Knowledge concerning the physical properties of things, and of how to make, combine, or use them in a physical sense" (p. 280); "managerial knowledge" (p. 280); "organized research" (p. 287). As noted earlier, it is possible that there are interactions among people such that the quantity of advance in knowledge is not a simple linear function of the number of people, but the evidence does *not* show that any such interaction is *less* than a simple linear function.

It may be useful to show some static partial computations to illustrate the main forces operating. Assume that in the year $t = 1$, *and only in that year*, the cohort of workers aged 21 is larger than in the base demographic structure, and hence the work force as a whole is larger than it would otherwise have been. Assume also that the exponent of labor $\beta = \frac{2}{3}$ in the Cobb-Douglas production function, and the base yearly increment due to gains in knowledge is 1%. If one calculates separately the drop in per-worker product from the capital-dilution effect, and the rise in output due to the ART effect as in equation (1), in year $t = 5$—the first year in which this cohort's ART contribution to A is felt—the downward push from the former effect is 32 times the upward push from the latter effect. But in the second year, $t = 6$, the drop from the capital effect is only 16 times the rise from the ART effect, because the incremental workers have now contributed *two* ART increments to A. In the third year the ratio is 32 to 3. In less than 32 years the two effects would be roughly equal, and product per worker would be about what it would have been if the incremental workers had not entered the work force. From then on, product per worker is higher than it would otherwise have been.

This static model allows us to understand the mechanism by which faster population growth may overcome the drag of capital dilution. But a full dynamic simulation with reasonable parameters is necessary to tell us whether the net effect really *is* likely to become positive. Perhaps more important, the dynamic simulation is needed to indicate the *length of time* the process is likely to take.

Now we turn from the Residual model to an entirely different way of getting at the same question, the Verdoorn model.

The Verdoorn Model

Verdoorn[8] found that in a sample of industries over the periods 1870 to 1914 and 1914 to 1930, productivity rose as the square root of total output. Other sorts of evidence consistent with this "law," were discussed in Chapter 4.

Verdoorn's law provides another approach to our subject. Additional workers certainly are not the only cause of increased outputs. But over any period longer than the business cycle, the size of the labor force is a major influence upon total output. And if one holds constant the capital endowment and the original level of technological practice in a *ceteris paribus* analysis, then population size is the *only* influence upon total output. Therefore, it is reasonable to think of Verdoorn's law as a proxy for the labor force-productivity change relationship; that is, output itself does not change productivity, but rather the people engaged in producing that output change productivity (and in fact, Verdoorn explains his law as caused by learning; Clark, 1957, p. 357). One may, of course, also think of Verdoorn's law simply as an empirical estimate of economies of scale without specifying a behavioral mechanism. Either interpretation is consistent with the work here.

---

[8] Verdoorn published his findings in *L'Industria*, No. 1, 1949, pp. 45–46. I have been unable to obtain a copy of that publication, and hence I rely on the reports by Balassa (1961) and Clark (1957; 1967).

In the Verdoorn model, the Equation 6-1b is used where Equation 6-1a is used in the Residual model:

$$\frac{A_t - A_{t-1}}{A_{t-1}} = b\sqrt{bY_{t-1}} \quad \text{or} \quad A_t = A_{t-1} + bA_{t-1}\sqrt{Y_{t-1}} \quad (6\text{-}1b)$$

where b is chosen so as to provide the desired initial rate of productivity change in the base population, for example, 1%, 1.5%, or 2%.

"Learning by doing" accounts for part of the effect of the rate of output upon productivity. The increased efficiency of production within firms and industries as experience accumulates has been well documented in many industries, starting with the air-frame industry in the 1930's (for bibliography see Arrow, 1962). But intra-industry learning is only one of the many productivity-increasing mechanisms that are at work as over-all output increases. In addition, each industry benefits by the advances in other industries. But the latter effect does not appear in the sort of industry studies done by Verdoorn, Rostas (1948), Paige and Bombach (1959), and the subsequent tradition. Therefore, such intra-industry estimates may understate the economy-wide effect.

One might wonder whether it is proper to extend Verdoorn's law from individual industries to an economy as a whole. One might also question whether the observed relationship shows an influence of new-discovery-caused increases in productivity on total output rather than the converse. But at least one of the main sorts of data used by Verdoorn and by Clark to support Verdoorn's law—the Rostas and the Paige and Bombach data on two countries at two points in time, all compared to one country at the earlier date—is reasonably free of both of these problems; both countries have the same access to new knowledge, so exogenous discoveries are not likely to account for the observed relationship. The fact that new basic discoveries do not account for the observed relationship also allays worry that Verdoorn's law at the level of industries only reflects a shift in resources among the industries in response to new opportunities. Hence, aggregation does not seem to run the danger of a composition fallacy. Another reason not to believe that productivity is responsible for the output differences in these data is Schmookler's (1962) demonstration that, to an important degree, advances in knowledge are induced by demand rather than the relationship running mainly from productivity to output via prices.

OTHER ELEMENTS OF THE MODELS

The Demographic Structures

The population and labor-force structures to be compared, shown in Figure 6-2, are as follows: The comparison base, structure "BASE," has an exo-

117

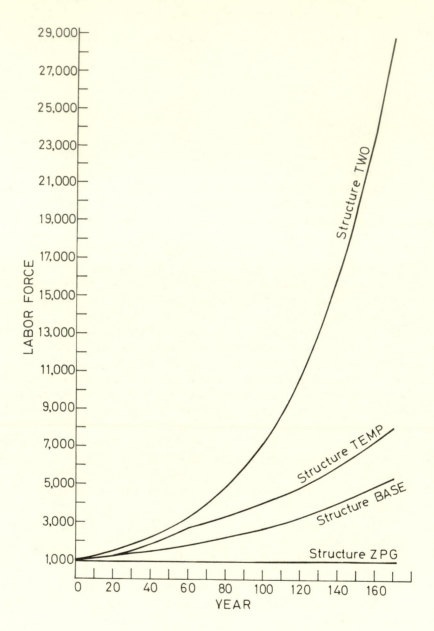

FIGURE 6–2   LABOR FORCES IN VARIOUS YEARS IN VARIOUS
DEMOGRAPHIC STRUCTURES: THE BROAD PICTURE

genous 1% growth in the birth-rate each year, that is, $\text{WOM(BASE)}_{1,t} = 1.01\text{WOM(BASE)}_{1,t-1}$, and $\text{MEN(BASE)}_{1,t} = 1.01\text{MEN(BASE)}_{1,t-1}$, starting in year $t = -60$. In this and in all other population structures infants live until they enter the labor force at age 21, and also through the end of their labor-force service at age 60, that is, $\text{MEN}_{1,t} = \text{MEN}_{21,t+20} = \text{MEN}_{60,t+59}$, and the same for females. The number of males and females of each age are equal in this and in all other structures. (All children are assumed born on January 1, and up until the end of their first year the cohort is labeled MEN_1 and WOM_1. Adults are assumed not to matter economically after age 60.)

The population in year $t = 0$ in structure BASE is

$$\begin{aligned}
\text{POP(BASE)}_{t=0} = {} & \text{MEN(BASE)}_{60,t=0} + \text{WOM(BASE)}_{60,t=0} \\
& + \text{MEN(BASE)}_{59,t=0} + \text{WOM(BASE)}_{59,t=0} \cdots \\
& + \text{MEN(BASE)}_{1,t=0} + \text{WOM(BASE)}_{1,t=0} \\
= {} & \text{MEN(BASE)}_{60,t=0} + \text{WOM(BASE)}_{60,t=0} \\
& + (1.01)\,\text{MEN(BASE)}_{60,t=0} \\
& + (1.01)\,\text{WOM(BASE)}_{60,t=0} \\
& + (1.01)^2\,\text{MEN(BASE)}_{60,t=0} \\
& + (1.01)^2\,\text{WOM(BASE)}_{60,t=0} \cdots \\
& + (1.01)^{59}\,\text{MEN(BASE)}_{60,t=0} \\
& + (1.01)^{59}\,\text{WOM(BASE)}_{60,t=0}
\end{aligned}$$

(6–2)

In structure BASE, in which births increase 1% per year, half the women are assumed to work. The labor force L at time $t = 0$ is then

$$L(\text{BASE})_{t=0} = \sum_{j=21}^{j=60} \text{MEN(BASE)}_{j,t=0} + .5 \sum_{j=21}^{j=60} \text{WOM(BASE)}_{j,t=0}$$

In structure "TEMP" the population is "temporarily" augmented by a 50% increment in the birth rate in just a single year, $t = 1$, that is, $\text{MEN(TEMP)}_{1,t=1} = 1.51\,\text{MEN(TEMP)}_{1,t=0} = 1.51\,\text{MEN(BASE)}_{1,t=0}$. All other cohorts remain the same as in structure BASE. Hence for the 40 years from $t = 21$ to $t = 60$ there is in structure TEMP a single cohort that is roughly 50% larger than its next-aged cohorts, and the labor force is larger by that many workers for the 40-year period. This may be seen in Figure 6–3, which shows the fine detail from Figure 6–2 for the first thirty years after $t = 0$.

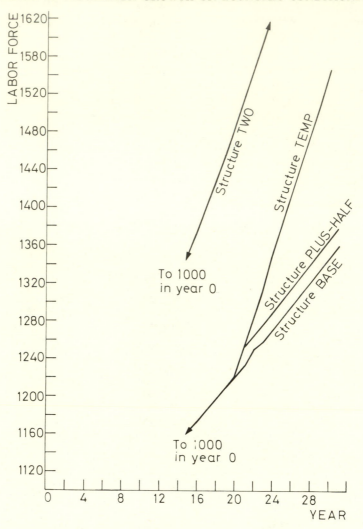

FIGURE 6–3 DETAILS OF LABOR FORCES IN EARLY YEARS IN
VARIOUS DEMOGRAPHIC STRUCTURES

In structure "PLUS-HALF" the birth-rate is incremented by 50% over structure BASE in year $t = 1$, but unlike structure TEMP, the bulge continues in each successive year. That is, in structure PLUS-HALF, $MEN(PLUS\text{-}HALF)_{1,t=1}$, and $MEN(PLUS\text{-}HALF)_{1,t=3} = 1.01$ $MEN(PLUS\text{-}HALF)_{1,t=2}$, and so on. Hence all cohorts from $t = 1$ onward are more than 50% bigger in structure PLUS-HALF than in structure BASE.

It is worth noting that after an adjustment period the dependency ratio, w, is again the same in structure PLUS-HALF as in structure BASE.

In structure "TWO" the birth-rate rises by 2% a year instead of the 1% in structure BASE, that is, $\text{MEN(TWO)}_{1,t+k} = 1.02\ \text{MEN(TWO)}_{1,t+k-1}$.

In structure "ZPG" the birth rate is the same in every year, a "stationary" population with zero population growth.

The simplicity of this model stems largely from the fact that the total amount of labor supplied is fixed exogenously, as seems reasonable in an MDC, rather than depending upon income and tastes. This is unlike the LDC situation to be seen later, where the total amount of hours worked is endogenous to the system even when the potential labor force is fixed exogenously; in LDC's the amount of agricultural work supplied is a function of death and sickness rates, and—even more importantly— of tastes influenced by family size and prices of industrial goods. This means that the entire demand side of the system need not be dealt with at all in MDC's, though it must be surely be dealt with in LDC's.

The Production and Saving-Investment Function

The general framework is a Cobb-Douglas function such as

$$Y_t = A_t K_t^{\alpha} L_t^{\beta}, \tag{6-4}$$

where $\alpha = .33$ and $\beta = .67$.

This aggregate production function is a major simplification of the two-sector agriculture-and-industry general model described in Chapter 2. The simplification to one sector is reasonable because agriculture is a small part—perhaps only a tenth or a twentieth—of the total economy of the developed world. This enables us to avoid the complexity of the allocation of labor to the two sectors, and also explains why we need not deal with endogenous variations of work hours by agriculturalists as a function of family size, prices of industrial goods, and other influences.

Next comes the net investment function, which for simplicity is a proportion of each year's income where $s = .06$

$$K_{t+1} = K_t + sY_t. \tag{6-5}$$

The Effect Through the Supply of Parents' Labor

Incremental babies will cause some women to be out of the labor force who would otherwise work outside the home. From studies of U.S. census data based on work by Bowen and Finegan (1969), Cain (1966), and Sweet (1970) together with the assumption that each woman will have at least one child, I have calculated that an incremental child results in a total decrease of .45 of a woman's work year, spread over the two years after the child is born. On the other hand, by my calculations from the

121

1960 U.S. census, an incremental child causes a total increase in .10 of a man-work-year by fathers, spread over 25 years (details in Chapter 3).

In those simulations runs in which the labor force is to be adjusted for the effect of children on the supply of labor,

$$L_t = \sum_{j=21}^{60} \text{MEN}_{j,t} + .0025\,(\text{MEN}_{1,t} + \text{WOM}_{1,t}) + .0025\,(\text{MEN}_{2,t}$$

$$+ \text{WOM}_{2,t}) + \cdots + .0025\,(\text{MEN}_{25,t} + \text{WOM}_{25,t})$$

$$+ .5 \sum_{j=21}^{60} \text{WOM}_{j,t} - .22\,(\text{MEN}_{1,t} + \text{WOM}_{1,t})$$

$$- .22\,(\text{MEN}_{2,t} + \text{WOM}_{2,t}). \tag{6-6}$$

The effect of incremental children on the parents' labor supply will be shown in the comparisons of structures TEMP and PLUS-HALF to structure BASE; in these cases all conditions are the same up to time $t = 0$, and different thereafter as the numbers of births differ. But there seems to be no way to compare the labor-force effect of additional children in stable populations with different rates of growth, that is, structure-TWO versus structure BASE.

Surprisingly, however, the effect of incremental children on the parents' labor supply turns out not to be important in sensitivity analyses. This can be seen in even an unrealistically high upper-limit estimate of the effect of incremental children on the economy through the parents' labor-force. If the birth-rate is a low 25 per 1,000 and there are a low 400 employed workers per 1,000, a *doubling* in the birth rate would only mean a drop in the labor-force to $(400 - .45 \times 25) = 389$, or about 3%, using an estimate of .45 worker-years lost per incremental child. Total output would drop even less, maybe 2%. Physical saving might then go down by, say, $(.12 \times .02) = .0024$ of total output. The cumulative effect on output would be very small as a result of even such an improbably large change in an MDC's birth rate over a decade.

The Effect through Changes in Private Saving of Physical Capital

Several kinds of evidence, discussed in the previous chapters, are relevant for an estimate of the effect of the number of children on private saving. These include family budgets, cross-sections of nations, and time-series evidence. One may find support for an estimate higher than -1.0, or as low as 0, for the elasticity of the proportion of income saved with respect to a proportional change in family size. Separate simulation runs were therefore made with elasticities of -1, $-.5$, and 0, though most runs reported here use $-.5$. The ratio,

$$w = \frac{\sum_{j=1}^{20} (WOM_{j,t} + MEN_{j,t})}{\sum_{j=21}^{60} (WOM_{j,t} + MEN_{j,t})},$$

is computed for each year in each case. For structure BASE it is .67 for each year, and is referred to as $\hat{w}$. In other structures the saving ratio for each year is then calculated as

$$s_t = \hat{s}\left[1 + e_s\left(\frac{\hat{w} - w_t}{\hat{w}}\right)\right], \qquad (6\text{--}7)$$

where $\hat{s}$ is the proportion of income saved in structure BASE, and e_s is the elasticity of saving with respect to children.

The Effects of Schooling

Schooling is the only social expenditure considered here. Two aspects of education are relevant. First, more children mean higher expenditures on education, which may cut into investment on physical capital as well as reducing consumption. Second, if incremental expenditures on schooling are less than proportional to the number of incremental children and if there are no economies of scale in education, an increased number of children will cause a lower average quality of the work force in future years.

The bases for the estimate of the effect of children on public schooling costs are as follows: (1) Expenditure on education is 4.6% of U.S. national income (Harbison and Myers, 1964, p. 41); (2) A quarter of the population is in school, 18.4% of the population being in the 5–14 age group (*ibid.*); (3) In 1968, $623 per year was spent by public schools per student year (*Statistical Abstract*, 1969, p. 102); (4) $6,856 average year-round male earnings in 1966 (*Statistical Abstract, 1969*, p. 233). This estimate excludes foregone earnings, on-the-job training costs, etc.; (5) A high-side inclusive estimate of U.S. education plus training costs is 12.9% of adjusted GNP, by Machlup (Harbison and Myers, 1964, p. 28n). How much of children's education expenditures should be considered as *consumption* is a matter not considered here. On the basis of these data, the base expenditure on education is assumed to be 6% of gross national product.

The responsiveness of educational expenditures to increases in the number of children is also important. As discussed in Chapter 4, based on the studies of Miner (1963) and McMahon (1970) for the states in the

123

United States, I have calculated that the elasticity (the index of proportionality) is not far from unity, and perhaps equal to unity. That is, an increase in population in the United States can be expected not to reduce the level of education per child, if these data are appropriate. (On the other hand, no data known to me provide the basis for any estimate of the effect of educational expenditures upon investment in physical capital. The best that can be done, therefore, is to try out several possibilities in the simulation.)

Education is treated in several ways. In the basic no-education variant, education is ignored completely, and investment in physical capital[9] is 6% of output each year in all the demographic variations. In variant B, the level of education as measured by expenditures per child per year of school age is fixed and rising at 1% per year, because the annual increase in average school-leaving age has been of this general magnitude in the last half century in the United States. In the base year (and also for all other years in structure BASE) expenditure on education, $XED_{t=0}$, is 6%. In all years, the total expenditure in physical investment plus education is

$$S_t = XED_t + (K_t - K_{t-1}). \qquad (6-8)$$

That is, an increase in education expenditure implies a decrease in physical investment. In each year after $t = 0$ the expenditure on education is made a function of the number of children.[10]

$$XED_t = MEN_{j=6}q_{k=6} + MEN_{j=7,t}q_{k=7} \ldots MEN_{j=20,t}q_{k=20}, \qquad (6-9)$$

where the relationships among the expenditures for various school years, q_k, are fixed according to a crude schedule, for example, grade $1 = 1$, grade $2 = 1.125 \ldots$ grade $9 = 8 \ldots$. The effective labor represented by a worker in any year in variant B is the square root of the total amount spent on his schooling during his youth.[11] The effective labor force in any year, EFF_t, is the sum of the persons of labor-force age weighted by their effective labor values

$$EFF_t = \sum_{j=21}^{j=60} MEN_{j,t} \sum_{k=6}^{k=20} (q_{j,k})^{1/2}, \qquad (6-10)$$

where the subscript k refers to the various years in the past when the cohort received its education.

---

[9] The corresponding initial capital-output ratio is 3. Runs were also made with a savings rate of .12 and a capital output ratio of 4, with much the same results.

[10] Showing only males in equation (6–9) is shorthand for showing both male and female children.

[11] See Denison (1969) for relationships between years of schooling and earnings, the latter a proxy for individual productivity.

In variant C, the level of education is not fixed exogenously. Rather, the total amount spent on education is made a function of the dependency ratio weighted by the relative school-year cost in each cohort.

$$
\mathrm{XED}_t = \frac{\displaystyle\sum_{j=6}^{j=20} \mathrm{MEN(i)}_{j,t}q_k}{\displaystyle\sum_{j=21}^{j=60} \mathrm{MEN(i)}_{j,t}} \Bigg/ \frac{\displaystyle\sum_{j=6}^{j=20} \mathrm{MEN(BASE)}_{j,t}q_k}{\displaystyle\sum_{j=21}^{j=60} \mathrm{MEN(BASE)}_{j,t}}, \qquad (6\text{--}11)
$$

where i refers to a demographic structure other than BASE. This model suggests that the standard of education falls if the number of children rises.

A more refined model would change the proportions over time of each cohort getting education and working. But such modification would not be likely to affect the particular sorts of conclusions this chapter is intended to provide.

The effect on *saving* of the social spending for education and other children's services is most unclear. To my knowledge, there is no basis on which to estimate either the elasticity of spending on schools with respect to population growth, or the extent to which the incremental expenditures on schools substitute for other social investment without causing new tax levies. I shall therefore simply assume that the three private saving elasticities being tried will bracket the elasticity that includes social as well as individual saving.

In variants B and C the labor-force argument in the production function is replaced by the effective labor force

$$
Y_t = A_t K_t^{\alpha}(\mathrm{EFF})_t^{\beta} \qquad (6\text{--}12)
$$

The Effect through the Increments to the Labor Force

Now let us move ahead to the time when the incremental children enter the work force. If the capital stock does not receive an increment proportionally as large as the increment to the work force—or, a fortiori, if the capital stock is even smaller than otherwise due to a reduction in saving—then per-worker output will be lower than otherwise.[12] This is the fundamental Malthusian element.

The model begins in each case with $L_{t=0} = 1$ and $K_{t=0} = 1$. $A_{t=0}$ is started at $\frac{1}{3}$. Separate runs were made with the savings elasticity at

---

[12] If the family and society save enough extra so that average capital per worker would be the same with or without the increment of children, as may be the case with the Hutterites, per-worker income would be the same after the incremental workers entered the work force. But this must occur at a cost of lower per-consumer consumption prior to the years of labor force entrance.

−1.0, −.5, and 0, and both with and without the adjustment for the parents' labor-force effect.

RESULTS

The results for the five demographic structures with the Residual model and the no-education variant are shown in Table 6–1a; the corresponding results for the Verdoorn model are shown in Table 6–1b. Summarized selected results from no-education variant and education variants B, and C are shown in Table 6–2. The rates of growth from period to period will not be shown for other than the basic models; these "absolute" results were quite unrealistic for the other models because they were run with the same Cobb-Douglas exponents and other parameters as were used in the basic model, and more realistic models would require that these parameters be different when education is handled differently. But the *relative* values among the demographic structures are meaningful, and are shown as percentages of the 1%-growth demographic structure BASE. Also, only the runs with the "conservative" estimates of the ART effect (1.5% per year) will be shown. Runs with more realistically higher estimates show population growth in an even more favorable light.

1. The most important outcome is that under every set of conditions, demographic structures PLUS-HALF and TWO with more rapid population growth come to have higher per-worker income than structure BASE in less than 80 years, even with a base rate of change of A of 1%. And in every run, structure TWO, which reaches a labor force (in millions, say) of 23,769 in year $t = 160$ from the starting point of 1,000 in year $t = 0$, has a higher per-worker income than structure PLUS-HALF, which reaches a total labor force of 7,346 in $t = 160$. (For comparison, the labor force for structure BASE in year 160 is 4,913. And the zero population growth structure (ZPG) holds its advantage over the BASE structure only about as long as BASE holds its advantage over faster population growth.

In many runs the higher fertility structures overtake the BASE structure's per-worker output after only 30 years—which is only about 10 years after the entrance of the first additional children into the labor force.

These results may be compared with the results from classical growth theory where there is no feedback effect; as seen in the first block in Table 6–2, lower population growth has higher output per worker in the classical model. It is true that the long run—30–80 years—is a long way off, and therefore of less importance than the short run. But we should remember that our long run will be someone else's short run, just as our short run was someone else's long run. Some measure of unselfishness should impel us to keep this in mind as we make our decisions about population policy.

Furthermore, the short-run economic differences between the various demographic structures are small by any absolute measure. And as Leibenstein (1972, p. 64) noted, the differences are *relatively* small compared to "other variables which are subject to governmental policies, actions, and influences. The economic implications of the differences between the United States and the Japanese saving rate are much greater than the differences between the demographic structures. A modest decrease in the unemployment rate could more than offset any likely short-run drop in per-worker income due to higher fertility." Leibenstein thinks that even an improved consumer information program and elimination of agricultural price supports could substantially offset higher fertility. So even the short-run negative impact of higher fertility in these models is not of major economic proportions absolutely or relatively.

The mainspring that produces higher per-worker income with higher population is, of course, the element that makes the rate of change in the productivity coefficient A a function of the number of persons in the work force or of total output. One might argue that the basic yearly rate of productivity increase would, in the foreseeable future, be even less than .01, or negative. But one certainly finds no basis in conventional studies of growth of national production using the GNP concept for a belief that productivity will cease to increase.

The higher the base rate of productivity change, the greater must be the relative final advantage of the cases of faster population growth, and the sooner the high population growth structures overtake the BASE structure. In Table 6–1a and Figure 6–4 of the no-educational Residual model, which has the $A_{t=1}/A_{t=0}$ equal to 1.015 and elasticity of savings of -0.5, structure PLUS-HALF overtakes structure BASE at period 50 and structure TWO does so between periods 30 and 40, whereas the overtaking time for $A_{t=1}/A_{t=0} = 1.01$ is between periods 70 for both structures PLUS-HALF and TWO. For $A_{t=1}/A_{t=0} = 1.02$ the overtaking period is even shorter than for $A_{t=1}/A_{t=0} = 1.015$.

2. The dependency effect of incremental children on savings can have substantial impact on the results in structure TWO. In the no-education model with $s = .12$ and $K/Y = 3$ (results not shown), by year 160 the comparison of the -1.0 savings elasticity with the zero elasticity shows ratios of approximately $4:5$ for the final results, that is, the end result for a structure TWO run is lower by one-fifth when the savings elasticity is -1.0 rather than 0. The -0.5 elasticity produced results roughly in between the zero elasticity and the -1.0 elasticity. But the effect of dependency is quite small relative to the differences in Y/L between structure TWO and structure BASE. For structure PLUS-HALF, the savings effect is *very* small. The savings effect is even less when $s = .06$, as may be expected. All in all, the dependency effect is not of major consequence in the results from these models.

127

TABLE 6–1a

OUTPUT PER WORKER IN RESIDUAL MODEL: INITIAL CAPITAL-OUTPUT RATIO OF 3, INITIAL PHYSICAL SAVINGS RATE OF .06, LABOR FORCE NOT ADJUSTED FOR EFFECT OF DEPENDENTS, SAVING ELASTICITY OF .50

Base rate of productivity change (% A)	Demographic structure	0	10	20	30	40	50	60	70	80	90	100	110	120	130	140	150	160	170
1.010	BASE*	100	114	135	162	192	234	294	375	495	672	945	1374	2088	3321	5559	9849	18594	
1.010	TEMP	100	114	135	162	189	234	294	381	501	681	954	1389	2112	3357	5622	9963	18804	
1.010	PLUS-HALF	100	114	132	147	177	222	300	441	672	1074	1803	3207	6078	12348	27099			
1.010	TWO	100	111	126	150	189	252	357	555	963	1911	4479	12837						
1.010	ZPG	100	120	141	165	195	231	270	318	372	435	510	498	696	813	948	1104	1287	1500
1.015	BASE	100	120	150	192	249	336	571	684	1035	1654	2754	4890	9255	18804				
1.015	TEMP	100	120	150	192	249	339	577	696	1053	1671	2802	4971	9411	19122				
1.015	PLUS-HALF	100	120	147	177	234	336	528	927	1749	3546	7791	18684						
1.015	TWO	100	117	144	189	264	408	702	1386	3246	9345								
1.015	ZPG	100	126	156	195	243	306	381	477	597	747	933	1164	1458	1821	2277	2847	3558	4449
1.020	BASE	100	129	168	231	330	489	762	1257	2202	4110	8250	17916						
1.020	TEMP	100	129	168	231	330	495	774	1284	2250	4203	8436	18315						
1.020	PLUS-HALF	100	129	165	216	312	504	930	1983	4650	12036								
1.020	TWO	100	123	165	237	372	669	1401	3540	11256									
1.020	ZPG	100	132	174	231	306	405	540	720	963	1287	1725	2313	3102	4164	5589	7509	10089	1356

* In BASE population growth is one percent per year, in TWO it is two percent per year, and in ZPG population is stationary. Population structures TEMP and PLUS-HALF are explained in the text.

TABLE 6–1b
OUTPUT PER WORKER IN VERDOORN MODEL: OTHERWISE SIMILAR TO TABLE 1a

Base rate of productivity change (% A)	Demographic structure	0	10	20	30	40	50	60	70	80	90	100	110	120	130
1.010	BASE*	100	114	135	159	195	246	324	453	687	1188	2598	9717		
1.010	TEMP	100	114	135	159	195	246	324	456	693	1200	2637	9984		
1.010	PLUS-HALF	100	114	132	150	177	225	306	465	801	1719	6006			
1.010	TWO	100	111	126	147	177	228	315	486	909	2511	23505			
1.010	ZPG	100	120	144	174	213	267	339	441	597	843	1263	2073	3939	9822
1.015	BASE	100	120	153	201	279	420	726	1593	6042					
1.015	TEMP	100	120	153	198	276	420	732	1623	6228					
1.015	PLUS-HALF	100	120	150	186	255	393	750	2133	18234					
1.015	TWO	100	117	141	186	261	420	858	2979						
1.015	ZPG	100	126	162	213	294	423	654	1119	2292	6681				
1.020	BASE	100	129	174	255	423	855	2655							
1.020	TEMP	100	129	174	255	423	861	2715							
1.020	PLUS-HALF	100	129	171	237	378	840	3465							
1.020	TWO	100	123	165	240	417	990	5583							
1.020	ZPG	100	132	186	270	429	765	1695	5949						

*In BASE population growth is one percent per year, in TWO it is two percent per year, and in ZPG population is stationary. Population structures TEMP and PLUS-HALF are explained in the text.

TABLE 6–2
SUMMARY OF RESULTS OF SELECTED MODELS*

Model and variant	Demographic structure	$t = 0$	$t = 20$	$t = 40$	$t = 80$	$t = 160$	Year of crossing
No-feedback model, $\Delta A = 1.015A$	TEMP	1.000	1.000	1.000	1.000	1.000	—
	PLUS-HALF	1.000	1.000	.892	.900	.953	—
	TWO	1.000	.943	.865	.800	.775	—
	ZPG	1.000	1.086	1.135	1.225	1.525	—
Residual model, no-education variant, $\Delta A = 1.01A$	TEMP	1.000	1.000	0.984	1.012	1.013	—
	PLUS-HALF	1.000	0.978	0.922	1.358	—	50–60
	TWO	1.000	0.933	0.984	1.945	—	40–50
	ZPG	1.000	1.044	1.016	0.752	0.069	(40–50)‡
Residual model, no-education variant, $\Delta A = 1.015A$	TEMP	1.000	1.000	1.000	1.017	—	—
	PLUS-NAME	1.000	0.980	0.940	1.690	—	50
	TWO	1.000	0.960	1.060	3.136	—	30–40
	ZPG	1.000	1.040	0.976	0.577	—	(30–40)
Residual model, no-education variant, $\Delta A = 1.02A$	TEMP	1.000	1.000	1.000	1.022	—	—
	PLUS-HALF	1.000	0.982	0.945	2.112	—	40–50
	TWO	1.000	0.982	1.127	5.112	—	20–30
	ZPG	1.000	1.036	0.927	0.437	—	(30)
Verdoorn model, no-education variant, $\Delta A = 1.015A$	TEMP	1.000	1.000	0.989	1.031	—	50
	PLUS-HALF	1.000	0.980	0.914	3.018	—	50–60
	TWO	1.000	0.922	0.935	—	—	50
	ZPG	1.000	1.059	1.054	0.379	—	(50–60)
Residual model, no-education variant, sq. rt. function $A_t = A_{t-1} + bA_{t-1}\sqrt{L_{t-5}}$ $\Delta A = 1.015A$	TEMP	1.000	1.000	1.000	1.009	1.007	—
	PLUS-HALF	1.000	0.980	0.909	1.133	—	60–70
	TWO	1.000	0.939	0.948	1.261	—	50–60
	ZPG	1.000	1.061	1.052	0.881	0.250	(50–60)

Model description	Structure					Crossing years[‡]
Verdoorn model, no-education variant, half the rate of change in basic model, ΔA = 1.015A	TEMP	1.000	1.000	1.000	1.008	—	70–80
	PLUS-HALF	1.000	0.976	0.911	1.040	—	70–80
	TWO	1.000	0.929	0.893	1.048	—	70–80
	ZPG	1.000	1.071	1.107	1.008	—	(80–90)
Residual model, level of education fixed exogenously and expenditures on education a function of number of children, $S_t = S_t^K + S_t^L = .12$. Initial ΔA = 1.051A	TEMP	1.000	0.956	1.013	1.033	—	20–30
	PLUS-HALF	1.000	0.750	0.723	2.451	—	50–60
	TWO	1.000	0.941	1.088	—	—	30–40
	ZPG	1.000	1.015	0.906	0.346	—	20–30
Verdoorn model, same education variant as line above, ΔA = 1.015A	TEMP	1.000	0.950	1.000	—	—	40
	PLUS-HALF	1.000	0.733	0.624	—	—	—
	TWO	1.000	0.900	0.856	—	—	50–60
	ZPG	1.000	1.033	1.040	—	—	(40–50)
Residual model, level of education an inverse function of dependency ratio weighted by relative school-year cost, initial ΔA = 1.015A	TEMP	1.000	0.985	1.006	1.034	—	30
	PLUS-HALF	1.000	0.838	0.748	2.412	—	50–60
	TWO	1.000	0.897	0.975	—	—	40–50
	ZPG	1.000	1.044	0.981	0.395	—	(30–40)
Verdoorn model, otherwise same as line above ΔA = 1.015A	TEMP	1.000	0.986	0.993	—	—	40–50
	PLUS-HALF	1.000	0.822	0.608	—	—	—
	TWO	1.000	0.863	0.757	—	—	—
	ZPG	1.000	1.082	1.075	—	—	(40–50)

* In all runs, initial Y/K = 3, initial $S_{t=1}^K = (K_{t=1} - K_{t=0}) = .06Y_t$, and elasticity of saving $(e_s) = .50$. The results shown are per-worker incomes in other demographic structures as a proportion of Y/L in structure BASE in the same year.

† Dashes indicate that the values of the numerator or the denominator became very large, but that the trend observed in the last two entry years is continued.

‡ Crossing years shown in parentheses indicate that the crossing was from above BASE to below BASE. Other crossings are from below to above.

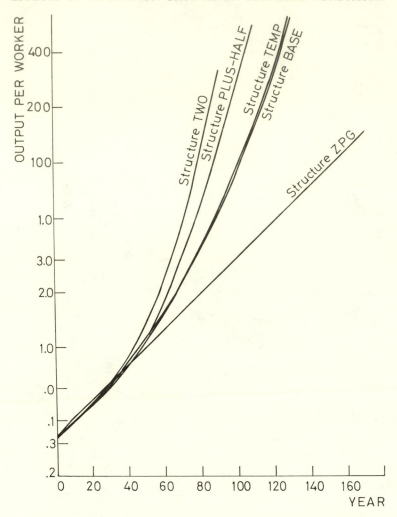

FIGURE 6–4   OUTPUT PER WORKER WITH VARIOUS RATES OF
POPULATION GROWTH

3. With respect to the labor-force adjustment: The effect through the parents' labor supply of incremental children after the first child is quite insignificant, just as preliminary calculations had suggested it would be. In no case was the relationship between structures BASE and PLUS-HALF as much as a quarter of a percent different in year 160 between the runs that were and were not adjusted for the parents' labor-force effect.

132

4. The time required for Y/L in structures PLUS-HALF and TWO to overtake Y/L in structure BASE is generally longer in models where expenditures on education affect physical saving, even where education positively influences both EFF_t and A_t. But this is not invariably true, especially for structure TWO where the labor force always has a younger average age and hence *may* have a higher average education than in structure BASE, because of the secular growth in education.

DISCUSSION OF RESULTS

1. Some may question the framework of this chapter on the grounds that the past rate of increase in knowledge, economies of scale, and productivity may not continue in the future. Perhaps. But even if so, this formulation should add to our understanding of the growth of population and per-worker income in the past history of the United States and Western Europe. And for at least a short period in the future, it does not seem unreasonable to project the long-term trend of the past. Further into the future we must bring other arguments to bear to help us decide whether the growth of productivity will be faster or slower than in the past. The same criticism may also be made about natural resources in the future, with the same response.

2. The physical capital-output ratio is falling over time in the United States due to the shift to tertiary activities and the discovery of better ways to make capital equipment. But on the other hand, the social cost of schooling will rise in the future. On balance, one does not know whether the social cost of an incremental labor-force entrant will fall or rise in the future relative to his earnings.

3. The difference in effects of population increase in LDC's and MDC's comes out sharply in this analysis. Productivity per worker does not grow much from year to year in many LDC's, and hence the effect of the feedback is correspondingly small. This implies that an increase in workers will not increase productivity per worker much in LDC's. This conclusion is made even stronger by the fact that a considerable portion of the increase in knowledge operative in LDC productivity increase occurs outside any LDC, and is rather independent of the size of the LDC work force.

4. The dependent variable in this model is output per worker *measured in conventional national-income terms*. If such amenities as space and purity of the environment that are a function of total population are negative and were included in the measurement, the results might be different. A calculation that includes them might show a lower "adjusted income" or welfare measure per person for a large population that would

133

otherwise have a higher income per person measured in conventional terms. If such disamenities are really substantial, the results of this chapter would be biased in favor of the larger population. But no convincing measurement of the over-all effect of population density has yet been developed. An authoritative recent survey of studies of such *partial* measures of welfare as longevity of life, crime rate, mental illness rates, recreational facilities, number of fires, ease of travel, and so on, concludes that higher population density is not the unalloyed evil it is commonly thought to be (Hawley, 1972). Different densities and different city sizes have different advantages and disadvantages.

A related matter is leisure, the amount and value of which can make an enormous difference in a measure of welfare. As income per person rises, people work fewer hours and enjoy more leisure (Kindleberger, 1865; Denison, 1967, Chapter 6; Nordhaus and Tobin, 1972). This implies that the gap between the outputs per worker yielded by any two demographic structures is smaller than otherwise shown, and the amount of time required for convergence or crossing would therefore be shorter. This would tend to reinforce the main point of this chapter—that even if faster population-growth structures start out behind in output per worker, they will catch up with and overtake lower population-growth structures.

5. No distinction has been made between market-induced and market-autonomous productivity increases for the following reasons: (1) The variation explained by economic incentives that induce innovation is much greater within a given industry than within a society as a whole; (2) The reward structure has more influence on whether an inventor works on airplanes instead of railroads than it does on whether he innovates or does not innovate at all, it would seem; (3) The incentives are endogenous, and hence are most easily treated as innards of the black box that is considered here only in its over-all shape and behavior.

6. The simulated models of the MDC sector discussed in this chapter are quite simple compared to the general model outlined in Chapter 2, and compared to the model for LDC's to be discussed in coming chapters. (This is why the MDC sector is treated in only four chapters whereas the LDC's require seven chapters.) The main simplifications are these: (1) The entire economy is viewed as a single industrial sector; (2) The effect of population growth is essentially a scale effect, including the increase in knowledge. Such scale effects do not require fundamental changes in people's behavior. For example, there are no changes in the trade-off of leisure for goods, or people becoming market oriented, or increasing control of fertility. This is *not* to say that there are no directly population-induced behavior changes in MDC's; such effects, both positive and negative, do indeed exist, for example, moving to less-crowded areas to avoid congestion, and the invention and development of the skyscraper. But

primarily the response to population growth in MDC's is "more of the same," rather than fundamental transformations to quite different behavior as occur in LDC's. Such transformations in LDC's are much more complex, and it is the absence of this complexity that enables the MDC model to be so streamlined.

7. Models such as those set forth in this chapter would have had absolutely no chance of being accepted by readers 10 or 20 years ago, because of the pre-eminence of physical capital in the thinking of economists. But with the recognition in recent years of the fundamental importance of knowledge, education and of the quality of the labor force in the productive process, models that allow for the effect of population growth on technology and human capital should not be uncongenial to readers.

8. Though this and the previous chapter deal only with MDC's, the reader may wonder whether MDC population growth has negative effects upon LDC's even when the effects of additional fertility are positive for the MDC's themselves. This question can be answered with an unequivocal "No." As discussed in Chapter 5, the effect through increased demand, use and prices of natural resources is clearly positive. (A person who sympathizes with the LDC's and doubts the value to them of trading their natural resources should ask himself if any LDC would be better off if the MDC's decided to buy no oil, coffee, and so forth from LDC's.) And the LDC's clearly should benefit from the additional knowledge and technological advance which higher population growth is bound to produce in MDC's.

9. The speed of the onset of the positive effect of an additional child is understated in the results because the impact of an additional child on the parents' work supply surely is much more positive than is shown in the model.

10. As you question the conclusions in this chapter, check with your intuition whether you think that the United States and other countries would be better off today if there had been half as many people in the United States in 1830 or 1880 or 1930 as there actually were. Our ancestors had positive effects upon us through the knowledge they created and the economies of scale they willed us, and if there were fewer of those ancestors the legacy would have been smaller. It is worth keeping this in mind when speculating about whether life today would be better if there were fewer people alive *today*.

But the MDC and LDC models go beyond "human capital" as a commodity that is essentially plastic and inert as is physical capital. These models really reflect the feedback of people *as people*, responding to their needs with physical and mental efforts up to and including the creative spark. Imagination and creativity are not concepts commonly found in

135

economic models, nor are they ever above the surface here. But let us recognize their importance unself-consciously, and be willing to give them their due.

SUMMARY

Increases in productivity as a result of increased scale and of knowledge caused by increases in population were added to a simple classical model of an MDC, using two quite separate models. One model uses the residual to estimate the feedback from the labor-force size to productivity; the second model uses Verdoorn's law to estimate the feedback effect of total output on productivity.

Under assumptions about the parameters that I trust are reasonable, demographic structures with larger rates of population growth, after initially falling behind in per-capita income, usually overtake structures with lower rates of population growth in 30–80 years, and the shorter end of this period is implied by recent rates of change of productivity. That is, though an increment of population initially has a negative effect upon economic welfare, after some decades the effect has become positive. This outcome is a step toward quantifying Kuznets' reasoning about the role of people as creators of knowledge in modern growth.

CHAPTER 7

The Effect of Population Growth on
LDC Economies and Their Development:
The Model in General

INTRODUCTION

THIS IS THE first of seven chapters that discuss the effect of population growth in LDC's upon their economic development. In this chapter the formal model is sketched in a general way. Chapters 9–12 then discuss which parameters would be appropriate to insert into the model to see the effects of population growth under different sets of circumstances. Chapter 13 gives the details of the model and performs a numerical simulation to learn the over-all outcomes of the model under different sets of assumptions.

Consider what the model must do: (1) The model must allow for the fact—observed in China and in India over a period of many hundreds of years before this century—that when population grew, the output of the society grew too (though somewhat afterward) eventually reaching the same per-capita level as before the spurt of population. But during long periods when population did *not* grow, the level of living also did not grow, but rather stayed the same. The simplest Malthusian model, in which production-increasing inventions appear independently from time to time, does not fit this basic chunk of history. (2) The model must reconcile and make sense of the apparently contradictory assertions that (a) population growth was good for England's economy in the eighteenth and nineteenth centuries (Deane and Cole, 1964; Habakkuk, 1963; Eversley, 1965, 1967;[1] Mathias, 1969); but (b) population growth has short-run ill effects for India at present (Coale and Hoover, 1958). No simple model resolves this apparent contradiction. (3) Most generally, the model must provide reasonable assertions about the shorter-run and longer-run economic consequences of different rates of population growth in various sets of specific conditions, including such questions as: (a) Are there some periods during the development process when population growth is more beneficial than at other periods? (b) Is the effect of population increase monotonic or is it curvilinear? (It is sometimes asserted

---

[1] Eversley writes: ". . . population growth at this time (1750–80) was 'right'—neither so small as to cause shortages of labour, or of demand for goods and services, nor so large as to reduce real wages, creates labour surpluses and destroy the basis of demand" (1967, p. 249).

that fast population growth is detrimental, but slow growth would be better than none.) (c) How does the effect of population increase depend on particular conditions within an economy and society?

There is a surprising dearth of literature with the same general aim as this model. The work of Fei and Ranis (1964) does not seem helpful here because their assumption of zero marginal productivity in agriculture leads in the opposite direction from the aim of the work undertaken here. Jorgensen's model (1961; 1967) is provocative but lacks an investment function in agriculture, and other mechanisms necessary for understanding the effect of population growth on industrialization. Kelley's exploration (1968) of the effect of additional children in increasing the demand for food and hence retarding industrialization is valuable and constitutes one of the main elements of the analysis given here, but by itself it is not enough. The Kelley-Williamson-Cheatham model (1972) is closer to the needs of this study, but their economy does not resolve its central questions by the work-leisure decision, as is necessary here. (Also they have not concentrated on the role of population growth.)

Simulations focused on the effect of population growth in the tradition of Coale and Hoover (1958)—including that of Hoover and Perlman (1966); Barlow (1967), who was first to include in the model a production function, which was a glaring omission in Coale and Hoover; and Enke (1970)—are in the background of this study. But aside from capital dilution, those studies lack the main response mechanisms built into the model constructed here, and those additional response mechanisms lead to results quite different from the results of studies in the Coale-Hoover tradition. Yotopolos and Lau (1974) also attempt to build the leisure-output choice into a development model, but in a quite-different fashion and for different ends. I have not found other works from which to depart. The *Limits to Growth* model of Forrester and his associates is not useful for a number of reasons, as reviewers of it are almost unanimously agreed. One reason is that "It's behavioral-scientific content is virtually zero" (Shubik, 1971). A related reason is that an alteration by Boyd (1972) of the *Limits of Growth* parameters to equally reasonable a priori values produces quite opposite results than arrived at by Forrester (1971).

At this time in the mid-1970's when academic opinion so generally agrees that population growth is bad for LDC's, an inquiry into whether and where this is indeed true requires some justification. Here are some relevant observations: First, as mentioned above there is the *historical* fact that population grew at an unprecedented rate during the period of Europe's economic development from 1650 onward. And population growth was necessary and useful for England. Second, Habakkuk points out that "There is no lack of possible mechanisms by which an increase in population could in principle have . . . favorable repercussions on income" (1963. p. 614). Third, recent research has shown that some of the relevant mechanisms actually *do* operate, e.g., Boserup (1965), Mendels (1971), deVries (1971), Chenery (1960), plus the evidence on economies of scale in MDC's which is reviewed in Chapter 4, and the material in Chapters 9–12. Fourth and most important, the scanty empirical evidence on the over-all relationship between contemporary population growth and economic growth certainly does not reveal a consistent pattern.

As seen in Chapter 3, there is no significance correlation in the historical series of population growth and economic growth over the past century or half century in those countries now regarded as developed. Easterlin (1967), Kuznets (1967), Conlisk and Huddle (1969), Chesnais and Sauvy (1973), and Thirlwall (1971) have all arrayed LDC countries by their recent population growth rates[2] and their economic growth rates, to examine for a relationship between the two. (a) Easterlin's data are given in Table 7–1. " It is clear from the table that there is little evidence of any significant association, positive or negative, between the income and population growth rates" (1967). (b) Kuznets compiled data on 21 countries in Asia and Africa, and 19 countries in Latin America. In the separate samples, and in the 40 countries together, there is *not* a significant negative correlation between population growth and growth of per-capita product

TABLE 7–1

FREQUENCY DISTRIBUTION OF DEVELOPING NATIONS BY GROWTH RATE OF REAL PER-CAPITA INCOME CROSS–CLASSIFIED BY GROWTH RATE OF POPULATION, 1957–1958 TO 1963–1964

Rate of population growth (% per year)		Rate of growth of real per-capita income (% per year)						
	Total	Less than zero	0 to 0.9	1.0 to 1.9	2.0 to 2.9	3.0 to 3.9	4.0 to 4.9	5.0 and over
Total	37	3	4	12	12	2	2	2
3.5 and over	2	1	0	0	0	0	1	0
3.0–3.4	10	0	2	3	4	0	1	0
2.5–2.9	11	1	2	5	1	1	0	1
2.0–2.4	8	0	0	3	5	0	0	0
1.5–1.9	4	1	0	0	2	1	0	0
Less than 1.5	2	0	0	1	0	0	0	1

SOURCE: Easterlin, 1967, p. 106.

NOTES: The countries included are non-Communist ones in Africa, Asia, and Latin America (except for Israel, Japan, and the Union of South Africa) with populations of around two million or more, for which data were available. In a few cases data for one of the two variables were not available for the specified period, and the nearest overlapping period was used.

[2] There do not exist data on enough LDC countries for long periods to permit long-run time-series inquiry. See Kuznets (1971, pp. 30–31).

(see Table 7–2); the correlations are actually positive though very weak. (c) Chesnais and Sauvy (1973) analyzed the relationship between demographic and economic growth in the 1960's for various samples of up to 76 LDC's and found non-significant correlations (mostly slightly positive). (d) Conlisk and Huddle (1969) regressed the growth rate on the savings rate and the rate of population growth, over roughly 1950–63 across 25 LDC's. The coefficient of population growth was .692, suggesting that an increment of population will, ceteris paribus, have a slight negative effect on growth. (e) Thirlwall (1971) regressed the percent change in output on the percent change in population over 1950–66 in 32 countries, and obtained a coefficient just below unity, .907. (f) Hagen plotted the rate of growth of per capita income as a function of population density. As seen in Figure 7–1, higher density is not associated with lower growth except perhaps at the very highest densities, and low densities clearly are associated with low economic growth.

These overlapping empirical studies certainly do *not* show that fast population growth in LDC's increases per-capita income. But they certainly do imply that one should not confidently assert that population growth *decreases* economic growth in LDC's.[3] Of course, such simple aggregated data covering short periods, with the Communist countries excluded and with many other statistical shortcomings, could not in any case support such a causal assertion, even if the data were much more consistent than they are.

A key difference between previous work and the LDC model to be constructed here is the inclusion of the effects of population growth upon the productive process through channels other than the dilution of capital. The MDC model in Chapter 6 also has this as its distinguishing feature. But whereas in the MDC model the effect is mostly on the rate of technological advance, in the LDC model the effect is largely through changes in people's willingness to do more work (plus economies of scale together with increased social infrastructure, and demand-induced industrial investment).

The Pre-Industrial Agricultural Economy and the Agricultural Sector

Let us begin the analysis at the time when the industrial sector of a country is very small, and hence may be temporarily disregarded. Output in the

---

[3] It is interesting that in spite of their data, both Kuznets and Easterlin believe that lower population growth rates than at present would be good for the economic development of LDC's. But the data serve to keep us in some doubt, and they suggest the necessity of coming to a much more solid understanding of the situation before confidently making policy prescriptions.

TABLE 7–2
ANNUAL RATES OF GROWTH OF POPULATION AND TOTAL AND PER-CAPITA PRODUCT, NON-COMMUNIST COUNTRIES IN ASIA, AFRICA, AND LATIN AMERICA POST-WORLD WAR II PERIOD (MOSTLY FROM THE EARLY 1950's TO 1964)

	Groups	Population	Per-capita product	Total product
	Asia and Africa (excluding Israel and South Africa)			
7.	1–4	1.81	2.17	4.02
8.	5–8	2.25	2.91	5.23
9.	9–13	2.76	1.28	4.07
10.	14–17	3.05	2.34	5.46
11.	18–21	3.43	2.67	6.19
12.	Average, 21 countries	2.66	2.23	4.95
	Latin America			
13.	1–4	1.56	2.51	4.12
14.	5–8	2.30	0.94	3.26
15.	9–12	2.84	3.24	6.17
16.	12–15	3.05	1.60	4.70
17.	16–19	3.40	2.66	6.15
18.	Average, 19 countries	2.61	2.20	4.86

SOURCE: Kuznets, 1967, p. 191.

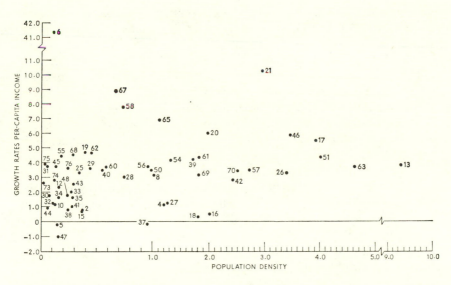

FIGURE 7–1   ECONOMIC GROWTH RATES RELATED TO POPULATION DENSITY, 1960–65

SOURCE: Reproduced from Hagen, 1975, p. 189.

agricultural sector is assumed to be some interactive function of labor in man-hours, land improvements plus other private physical capital considered together, social capital, and the technological knowledge available. This production function is given symbolically in Equation 7–1. The function f_1 has diminishing returns to scale because the total area that may be used for agriculture is fixed in the short run. It is intended to include switches in technique as more labor is used at a given level of capital; the technology for these switches is assumed to be already available (a matter to be discussed at length in Chapter 8.) The shape of the function may well be different for different historical situations, for example, eighteenth century England compared to twentieth century India.[4]

$$Q_{F,t} = f_1(M_{F,t}; K_{F,t}; J_t; A_{F,t}) \qquad (7\text{--}1)$$

where $Q_{F,t}$ = agricultural output in year t, *not* including any saving and investment in agriculture

$\quad\ A_{F,t}$ = the technological know-how in use in agriculture at time t in the country being analyzed

$\quad\ J_t$ = social capital, i.e., infra-structure together with economies of scale

$\quad\ K_{F,t}$ = privately owned agricultural capital

$\quad\ M_{F,t}$ = the total number of man-hours worked in agriculture per year.

The subscript G will later be used to designate industrial activities, in contradistinction to the subscript F which indicates the agricultural sector.

It is clear that if technology (A) and capital (K) and infrastructure (J) were to remain unchanged while population increased, output per head would fall permanently unless increases in man-hours of labor (M) took up all the slack. Population has increased many-fold over time in many LDC's and output per head did *not* fall permanently, and increases in man-hours did not account for all the increase in product. It is therefore crucial to inquire whether A and/or K increase, and the process by which the increases come about.

One possibility is that all or part of the possible increases in A and K are caused by independent inventions which immediately cause an increase in A, and which then lead to increases in K. This is the original Malthusian model. But independent invention cannot account for *all* the gains in productivity: If A or K grow independently of population growth, then income per head would grow when population is stationary—which is

---

[4] All the equations discussed in this chapter are specified in econometric detail in Chapter 13.

contradicted by the historical examples of India and China. Therefore, it seems reasonable that K or A or both should be made functions of population size or growth, as well as perhaps being functions of time as a proxy for the independent inventions that might occur over time, and other factors. Such changes will be detailed in Chapter 8.

Agricultural investment in this context includes land clearance, local irrigation, and construction of improved tools, the inputs of which are mostly off-season labor by the farmers. If such agricultural investment ΔK_F is to be influenced by population growth, it seems reasonable to make it a function of some "target" income[5] together with actual income. Subsistence income might be taken as the target income, but there are several arguments against this choice. First, "subsistence" is not easy to define, even in a given agricultural society. Second, a system with subsistence as a target income would always be somewhat *below* subsistence because the reaction to population growth cannot be instantaneous. Third, even the poorest farmers probably aim at some income level a bit higher than what they obtain in normal times. Therefore, ΔK will be made a function of the *gap* between the income aspiration and the actual income, where the aspired-to income level is defined operationally as a function of the income in the 5 best years among the previous 25 or 50,[6] or alternatively, as a proportional function of the change in capital necessary to produce a capital-output ratio equal to the initial ratio.

Technology, too, changes as population increases, as is emphasized by the "population push" hypothesis developed by Boserup (see Chapter 8). This endogenous aspect of technological change will be allowed for in the shape of the production-possibility frontier, which embodies all the technologies available and which the "population push" hypothesis assumes are already known. Technology is also affected *somewhat* by the passage of time; hence a term for time is probably appropriate, the rate depending on the date in history, as shown in equation 7–2. In a peasant economy, the level of technology in agriculture is not likely to be very sensitive to the agricultural laborer's wage, but this factor will become important later in the industrializing economy.

$$A_{F,t+1} = f_2(A_t). \qquad (7-2)$$

[5] Conceptually this is much the same as a choice between leisure and long-run output. But that would be a more complex—though more explanatory—way of viewing the matter.

[6] This model may seem, and is, thoroughly "psychological." But note that it is no more psychological than, say, Modigliani's early "ratchet" consumption function (1949) which has a formal and substantive similarity to the investment function used here. It is also no more psychological than Keynes' "fundamental psychological law" of the consumption function. And the classical work-leisure function is a map of a psychological assumption as is the mean-variance investment function. So the "psychological" quality of this assumption should not be grounds for objection by economists.

The effect on agricultural investment of an income-aspiration "gap" may be different in different circumstances:[7] "A given growth of population was likely to have more effect in stimulating investment and invention and less effect in depressing per capita incomes when it occurred in areas where land was abundant and/or land-saving techniques were available. And that where additional land was no longer available and the possibilities of land-saving improvements exhausted the reverse effect was more likely" (Habakkuk, 1963, p. 616).

Contemporary income aspirations are certainly different than in the past; people now aspire for more than they ever had; people aspire for *growth*. The rate of investment also should be a function of the amount of social capital, which facilitates private investment. Cultural factors surely affect agricultural investment, too, but in an economic model such as this one, it is not useful to enter them.

Investment in agriculture probably is also affected by the relative prices as perceived by the peasant (in contrast to the in-city prices) of industrial and agricultural goods; better terms of trade are likely to induce higher investment and production; in the pre-industrial period of isolation of the agricultural sector, the relative price of industrial goods may be thought

---

[7] "1. The probability of a strong reaction is greater if the population increase comes as a sudden shock. A community may not feel impelled to 'make a stand' when population increases and declines in living standards are slow, just as workers will sometimes experience greater difficulty in maintaining their real wages in the face of creeping inflation than when prices rise a good 20% a year. For this reason, the dramatic decline in mortality rates and the consequent massive increase in numbers that is taking place today in underdeveloped areas holds greater promise of a vigorous reaction than the far slower increases of previous epochs.

"2. A population increase is likely to be more action-stimulating if it is combined with urbanization and therefore leads to obvious needs and pressures for more overhead facilities, such as housing, schools, and public utilities.

"3. Again, the reaction may be facilitated if population growth takes place in underdeveloped countries which as a result of the increase in numbers pass minimum production thresholds in a number of important industries, as compared to more populous countries where these thresholds have long been passed or to much smaller countries where they remain far away.

"4. The reaction may be easier to accomplish if the increase affects primarily the upper classes of society, or at least the upper classes along with the lower classes, for the need to provide for one's children is in this case more likely to take the form of increased entrepreneurial activity.

"5. Finally, the closer a country actually is to the rigid assumptions of the neo-Malthusian models . . . i.e., the more fully and perfectly its resources are already utilized, the less room there is for any reactions outside of the most direct ones—namely, birth control and postponement of marriage. Precisely because of the assumption of fixed resources, this reaction to population pressures has virtually monopolized the attention of demographers. From our point of view, the 'preventive checks' are only one of the many forms which the reaction mechanism can take. Under present conditions, in fact, it is in many countries more difficult to visualize population pressures resulting in effective birth control measures than in improvements of agricultural techniques and in stepped-up capital formation in industry and public utilities" (Hirschman, 1958, p. 180.)

of as very high. An agricultural wage economy is affected by agricultural wages; the higher the agricultural wage, the more likely is capital investment to substitute for labor in a market-agriculture situation. (But neither prices nor wages will actually enter into the model used here.) The agricultural investment function also should explicitly take account of physical depreciation, which is slow in farm capital compared to industrial capital.

$$K_{G,t+1} - K_{G,t} = f_3\left[\left(\frac{\left(\frac{\hat{Y}}{C}\right) - \frac{Y_t}{C_t}}{\left(\frac{\hat{Y}}{C}\right)}\right), \frac{P_F}{P_G}, W_{F,t}, d\right]$$

where $\left(\dfrac{\hat{Y}}{C}\right)$ = aspired-to income per-consumer equivalent

$\left(\dfrac{Y_t}{C_t}\right)$ = per-consumer income in year t

P = price level

W = wage level

d = the rate of depreciation

The agricultural investment function is likely to be affected by population density in two opposite ways. On the one hand, increased density in previous years would have resulted in improved transport and other social infrastructures that make added investment easier, and that make increased investment more profitable to the extent that the agricultural product goes to the market. On the other hand, an increase in farm workers per unit of land means there is less new land to open up and fewer other unexploited opportunities such as irrigation. In accord with Chayanov (1966), and with general contemporary economic opinion, the model will assume that the latter effect of population density predominates.

The agricultural investment function and the agricultural production function have the unusual property that no conservation equation connects them, because in peasant agriculture investment is mostly *not* a withheld part of total population. Nor is the labor devoted to crop production in sharp competition with the labor devoted to clearing new fields, irrigation works, and so forth; the investment labor and the crop labor usually take place in different seasons. Hence, there seems to be no compelling reason to think of them as alternative uses of the same total output and the same total labor supply. At some point in the development process, agricultural investment will begin to use market goods

145

heavily, and at such a moment the investment equation given here would no longer be appropriate.

Next we must consider the role of social capital, including such infrastructure as roads, irrigation facilities, and markets. But the role of social capital is very unclear. For example, does it mostly increase current production by speeding the crop to market and reducing crop spoilage, does it mostly act as a substitute for or adjunct to private capital, or does it facilitate additional private investment? The same amount of effort will produce more private capital when the farmer has the benefit of more social capital. Better roads and communications and central irrigation systems make easier his construction of his own irrigation system, improve his ability to use new water-fertilizer-seed systems, and so forth. The answer probably is that infrastructure does each of these things and others, to an important degree. In the simulation the effect of infrastructure will be entered as a *multiplier* of the agricultural production function.

The *quantity* of social capital will be indexed by the population density in earlier years, which would create such social capital; this is justified in Chapter 12

$$J_t = f_4 \text{ (population density in previous 50 years).} \qquad (7\text{--}4)$$

The function f_4 will be concave downward.

Now let us turn to the demand-for-goods function, which is really the same as the supply-of-labor function here. Demand may be thought of as a set of social indifference curves[8] each showing various combinations of leisure (or work) and output. The shapes of these indifference curves may be expected to be influenced by the number of consumer equivalents in the society, the number of adult-male-worker-equivalent persons in the economy, the level of income aspiration, the terms of trade (not actually used in the simulation here), and the size of family. It is operationally simplest to think of such a function as representing each worker head-of-household, multiplied by the number of workers, as in Equation 7–5:

$$D_t = L_t \left[f_5 \left(\frac{C_t}{L_t}, \frac{Y_t}{C_t}, \frac{P_F}{P_G} \right) \right] \qquad (7\text{--}5)$$

where D_t = the set of indifference curves
L_t = the number of male-equivalent workers available.

---

[8] This function is intended to represent community behavior, just as does the production function shown in Equation 7–1. But there would seem to be no conceptual difficulty in building up this aggregate function from the indifference curves of individual families using, for example, the number of consumer-equivalents in the family as the analogy to number of consumer-equivalents in the society.

In other words, we assume that if there are more children in agricultural families, the father and other working members of the family will as a consequence work harder to produce more food and other goods. The question is, *how much* more work will be supplied. (Many sorts of responses to additional children *other than* more work are possible, ranging from infanticide to making up the whole "deficit" with more work.) Chapter 9 describes those various possibilities, and the appendix to it discusses which responses are likely in the case example of village India.

The numbers of persons of various ages eligible for work in any year are functions of births and deaths in earlier years. The birth rate is the policy variable, to be manipulated in order to observe the various results.[9] But the death rate is endogenous to the system, a function of income, as in Equation 7–6.

$$E_{j,t} = f_6\left(\frac{Y}{L}\right) \quad \text{or} \quad = f_6\left(\frac{Y}{\text{POP}}\right). \tag{7–6}$$

where $E_{j,t}$ = age-specific death rate

Health is just as important as death. The work capacity of the persons of each age available for work in any year depends upon their health, and health is a function of per-capita income, as in Equation 7–7.

$$\text{EFF}_t = f_7\left(L_t, \frac{Y_t}{C_t}\right), \tag{7–7}$$

where EFF is the effective labor force.

The number of women available to work in each cohort also is affected somewhat by the number of children they have.

People's productive capacity is importantly influenced by their educational level, which is the most quantifiable aspect of their mental equipment. Different countries at the same income level may devote different amounts of resources to education, however, and the bases of these decisions would be most difficult to model. Hence, the educational level may be thought of as a function of per-capita income in prior years. A somewhat less attractive alternative is to treat investment in education as part of the total investment in *all* capital, which may be operationalized by using a higher capital-output ratio than if only physical capital were being considered. For simplicity, however, the effect of education is omitted from the present models.

---

[9] For descriptive purposes, in some simulation trials fertility is made endogeneous by making it a function of time plus the gap between desired and actual income, the parameters depending on the particular society.

Let us pause to inquire how the quantity produced and consumed would be determined in a purely agricultural economy. (This leads into the more general problem of the two-sector economy whose output-determination mechanism will be discussed shortly). The agricultural production function for *any single growing season* in a pre-industrial economy is given by equation 1, assuming K_t is determined by the results of the previous growing season. The determination of the total amount that will be produced for consumption may then be found by the utility-maximizing tangency of the indifference curves with the production function,[10] as in Equation 7–8

$$Q_{F,t} = D_{F,t} \qquad\qquad (7\text{–}8)$$

where $Q_{F,t}$ and $D_{F,t}$ are the optimizing values. The optimizing solution is illustrated in Figure 7–2, where point V shows the tangency of the production function and the highest achievable indifference curve.

The equilibrating mechanism in this model is not "profit maximization" in the sense used by T. Schultz (1964, 1965). The price of leisure to farmers cannot easily (if at all) be independently assessed, and hence the profit-maximization notion makes no sense here. The evidence amply shows that the amount of labor supplied is very variable in peasant economies, and depends on all kinds of conditions. For India, Nair shows anecdotally that men work less as their incomes rise.

> In these prosperous and rich districts of southern Mysore . . . a new social pattern of work and sonsumption [has become general]. Previously, as among all rural communities in which both men and women work in the fields, men always left the house earlier while the women stayed back to cook. The wife then carried the meal to the farm and stayed on to work with the husband for the rest of the day. Early in the morning, before leaving, the man generally ate cold rice or *ragi* porridge kept over from the previous night. He got a hot meal only for supper. But then he was poor. Now he has more money. *So not only does he himself work less*—he employs more labour—but he wants good hot meals with the additional luxury of coffee in between. Coffee has become the fashion. Women, however, have no share in it. Nor has their share of the burden or work in the field or in the house been lightened. The men frankly admit to the charge. (1962, p. 55, italics added.)

---

[10] This is really a composite of *several* production functions—one for each type of agricultural practice. The shift from one practice to another is the point emphasized by Boserup; and it was analyzed by Mellor (1966, p. 172). The chosen combination of production and work is where the highest indifference curve touches *some* production function. See Chapter 8.

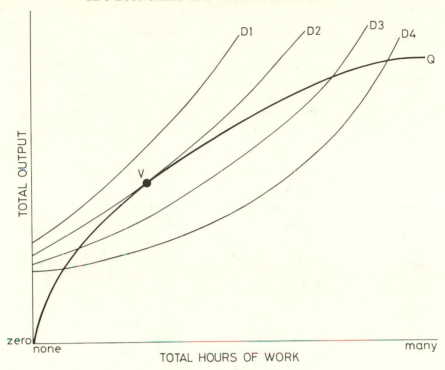

FIGURE 7–2   THE WORK-LEISURE TRADE-OFF AND THE DETERMINATION OF OUTPUT

Boserup's (1965) historical-anthropological survey shows many examples of the variability of farmer labor as a function of economic situations, and especially of population growth. But the overwhelming statistical proof for peasant agriculture is in Chayanov's summary (1923–66) of dozens of Russian field surveys. (Proof for industrial work hours was shown in Chapter 3.)

The theory of the phenomenon is well established, too. Long ago Malthus noted that if it were not for population increase, no "motive . . . would be sufficiently strong, to overcome the acknowledged indolence of man, and make him proceed in the cultivation of the soil" (1803, p. 491). Chayanov (1923–1966) worked out the formal utility theory very well, as did Mellor (1963) and Sen (1966). I think it is fair to say that any model of the agricultural sector (or of industrialization) which treats the supply of self-employed labor hours as fixed rather than as a function of tastes and external conditions must go astray.[11] The necessity of treating the amount

[11] But see Hymer and Resnick, who claim that the "shift from inferior methods of home production to superior methods based on specialization and exchange" is more important than "the replacement of leisure or idleness by work" (1969, p. 503.)

149

of labor supplied as variable in response to needs and tastes is why the LDC model is more complex than the MDC model given earlier.[12]

The model sketched above seems to fit the case of agricultural China for the five hundred years prior to the middle of the twentieth century (Perkins, 1969). In the model, per-capita income keeps up with population growth in the long run, as Perkins says it did in China (1969, p. 32). But during long periods when population growth was low or nil there was no growth in production. The lack of economic growth when there is no population growth implies that in the absence of population growth net savings are zero and there is no change in the productivity coefficient.[13] But unless the yearly per-worker input of labor in China rose to take up the slack when population grew—and Perkins suggests that increased labor input did not account for all the rise in total production—then when population grew, investment or productivity or both must have changed.

Indeed, Perkins found that much of the rise in production came from an increase in land cultivation, construction of water-control systems, and improved seeds.[14] The first two of those changes may be considered to be net investment. But the improved water-control systems also resulted in changes in the type of technology used by farmers, especially changes in the number and type of crops planted each year; this is not new knowledge, however, but rather a shift in technology of the sort that is built into the composite production function under discussion here. In contrast, an improvement in seed varieties is new knowledge and perhaps largely exogenous—a "Malthusian" sort of invention, as will be discussed in Chapter 8. But this sort of technological improvement was relatively unimportant in Chinese history. An important element in the Chinese history was the absence of industrial goods to tempt people to work harder for the means of payment, both because world technology did not yet know how to produce industrial goods in quantity and because of the absence of well-developed local markets and an internal trading system.

In summary, a drop below the accustomed subsistence level seems to provide motivation to work harder, invest more, and apply newer labor-using techniques. This is the "population push" motivation emphasized

---

[12] Tastes for work differ, of course, among individuals and groups. Myrdal notes: "Idleness and low labor efficiency depend upon institutions, custom and tradition, attitudes toward work and leisure—including taboos and inhibitions related to status and to the participation of women in work. Moreover, the relevant attitudes are set in a framework of institutions, and the relationship between attitudes and institutions is mutually reinforcing" (1968, pp. 999–100). The model in Chapter 13 will be run with different labor-responsiveness parameters for different groups of people.

[13] It seems plausible to assume no savings and no change in productivity rather than assuming one positive and the other negative.

[14] Perkins estimated the shares of labor, land, and technological progress in the rise in production from 1400 to 1967 (Appendix to Chapters III and IV). But that estimation does not provide a *behavioral* explanation of the phenomenon, which is the aim of this chapter.

by Boserup (1965). But the mechanism cannot and does not work instantaneously, and hence the level of living may fall below subsistence for a time after a rise in population, as happened repeatedly in China. All in all, the above model seems to give a reasonably good *qualitative* account of population growth in a pre-industrial economy. A quantitative description requires numerical simulation of the sort that is carried out in Chapter 13.

THE INDUSTRIAL SECTOR AND INDUSTRIALIZATION

Now to proceed to the two-sector industrializing economy. At some point in history, something happens to a country that begins the process of industrialization. Perhaps it is a regime that demands high taxes, forcing the peasants to produce more than before, or an autonomous increase in the efficiency of agriculture. Perhaps it is the rise of industrial technology, or a change in the political system, for example, to or from colonialism. More likely—and more appropriate to this model—is an improvement in domestic or international transportation and communications that effectively lowers the price of industrial goods to the peasant. This improvement may be due to accumulation of economic infrastructure—especially transportation and markets—for which increase in population density is likely to have been the autonomous factor.[15] No matter what the initial stimulus, increases in rural productivity and in the aspiration for industrial goods will surely be fundamental aspects of the industrialization process.[16]

Assume for the moment that the initiating element is foreign traders opening up the rural market, offering textiles and other desired industrial goods at prices peasants can pay. This will influence the rate of agricultural saving, as shown in Equation 7–3. Output then increases because of the larger stock of capital used in agricultural production, as shown in

[15] North and Thomas (1970) also emphasize population increase as the key initiating element for a growth process, but in their theory the effect is through increased food prices which stimulate agriculture.

[16] Ricardo stated the importance of increases in aspirations for economic development: "The friends of humanity cannot but wish that in all countries the labouring classes should have a taste for comforts and enjoyments, and that they should be stimulated by all legal means in their exertions to procure them. There cannot be a better security against a super-abundant population. In those countries where the labouring classes have the fewest wants, and are contented with the cheapest food, the people are exposed to the greatest vicissitudes and miseries. They have no place of refuge from calamity; they cannot seek safety in a lower station; they are already so low that they can fall no lower" (Ricardo, 1963, p. 49). D. Freedman's study of Taiwan has shown that families with a relatively high desire for ownership of modern durables tend to save more and are innovative. (She did *not* find "a consistent relationship . . . between repeated work effort and consumption of modern objects," but "it cannot be determined whether the mixed relationship . . . is due to deficiencies in the measures of work effort or other factors" (1970, pp. 45, 46).

Equation 7–1. Over time this increases the desired income level and hence savings even more. Such a process would continue until it reaches a new higher level of equilibrium, determined by the production function and the new set of indifference curves. So far we are discussing nothing more than a shock to the old system with a consequent re-adjustment.

The interesting dynamics begin when a *domestic* industrial sector starts up, either substituting for foreign imports as in the case of present-day LDC's, or an autonomous development as in the case of England. Such a domestic industrial sector uses workers drawn from the agricultural sector.

The central question the economy must answer at each moment during the process of industrialization is the proportion of workers who will work in agriculture and in industry. Before approaching that question, the structure of the industrial sector must be set forth. (The agricultural sector remains as described for the pre-industrial period.) Equation 7–9 shows the industrial production function:

$$Q_{G,t} = f_9(A_{G,t}, K_{G,t}, M_{G,t}, J_t) \qquad (7–9)$$

Industrial output as written here includes any output that will be used for *industrial* investment. This is conventional, unlike the agricultural case where additional investment comes from additional labor input in the off-season rather then from diverted outputs.[17]

Industrial investment is a function of industrial output, prices, profits, and changes in these quantities. There also must be a mechanism whereby an increase in the labor force will increase the return on capital, and hence will increase investment.[18] On the other hand, an increase in labor force will decrease wages, *ceteris paribus*, which should reduce the stimulus to replace men with machines; the *net* outcome of the effect through wage changes is not clear. More predictable is a reduction in public-sector industrial investment due to the increased dependency ratio that accompanies higher fertility. In some countries, at some times, public-sector investment constitutes a major part of total industrial investment. The

[17] Data at the industry level showing considerable economies of scale in manufacturing in MDC's were shown in Chapter 4; it is not unreasonable to expect a similar effect in manufacturing in LDC's. Keesing and Sherk (1971) have confirmed and extended the findings of several writers that the export-import ratio of manufactured products—a reasonable proxy for manufacturing efficiency—is positively influenced by both population density and country size in a sample of LDC's. Myrdal (1969, pp. 1189, 1191) suggests that there are increasing returns to scale in LDC industry at any given moment due to increased capacity of labor and plant. But that phenomenon is not the one referred to here, being necessarily a short-run phenomenon, and it probably did not apply to England in the eighteenth century. The economies of scale referred to here come from indivisibilities in plant and equipment, and from increased knowledge due to greater experience.

[18] Stanley Engerman and Nathaniel Leff emphasized this point to me.

extent of that public investment is likely to be affected by the need for nonindustrial investment such as schools, health, and housing which in turn is affected by the population growth rate. This is one of the key elements in the Coale-Hoover model of India and Mexico.

Perhaps most important, the response to a small or moderate increase in money sales or profits will be a relatively larger proportional increase in industrial investment, that is, an increase considerably greater than would be required to produce that much increase in output with the same technology and proportionally increased labor. This is due to Schumpeterian producer and investor optimism caused by an increase in business volume, and to an accelerator effect in capital goods industries. But investment is likely to be some diminishing function of increased output, especially the immediate (first year) investment, because there are physical and psychological constraints on increases in investment at any one time. This is consistent with the widely held view regarding both contemporary LDC's and England in the eighteenth century that a moderate amount of population growth—for example, 1% per year—would be beneficial, while fast population growth—for example, 3% per year—would be harmful.

The investment function is summarized in equation 7–10:

$$\Delta K_{G,t} = f_{10}\left(\Delta Q_{G,t},\ W_{G,t},\ \frac{P_G}{P_F},\ \frac{L_t}{C_t}\right) \tag{7--10}$$

The accelerator function used here, and the aspirations functions used in the agricultural sector, cannot be embraced by a neo-classical theoretical framework. It may be, or it *mat not* be, that an investment function which depends on the expected rate of return explains industrial investment behavior better than an accelerator function; the evidence is not clear. But because of the nonmonetary nature of the model constructed here—in common with all existing models focusing on the effect of population growth in LDC's—a neo-classical function could not be used. Furthermore, the various realistic behavioral assumptions built into the industrial sector of this model would not sit easily in a neo-classical framework. For example, investment must depend *only* on the expected rate of return in a neo-classical framework. A neo-classical framework would be quite inadequate to handle the agricultural sector here, plus other crucial aspects of the model as a whole.

Change in industrial technological practice is likely to be a function of the wage rate, exogenous changes indexed by time, the average income level, and changes in the total size of the industrial sector:

$$\Delta A_{G,t+1} = f_{11}\left(W_{G,t},\ t,\ \frac{Y_t}{L_t},\ \Delta Q_{G,t}\right). \tag{7--11}$$

Total output (or what is much the same thing, total labor-force size) also has an important effect upon the level of productivity through economies of scale. For conceptual and pragmatic reasons, the effect of the over-all size of the economy on productivity is handled together with the effect on infrastructure with the scale term J, while the *changes* in the output influence A in the model.

Chenery's (1960) estimate of the effects of scale in LDC's is especially appropriate for the meaning of J in the industrial sector. Such change in technological practice accounted for a large part of England's growth and industrialization. Particularly important, her technological lead in the world enabled her to continue her success with her exports.[19] Demand increase certainly is one crucial element. Through such mechanisms as investment-induced invention, learning by doing, on-the-job training, emergence of new entrepreneurs, and so forth, the increase in demand undoubtedly caused a big rise in productivity per worker in England during the industrial revolution. If the increase in population did indeed have an over-all beneficial effect, it was probably due to these demand-induced effects, rather than to the avoided "lack of labor" that Deane (1967) speaks of.[20] Investment, learning, and technological change must respond to increased demand in a lagged rather than instantaneous fashion. The benefits of increased demand and of the related phenomenon of improvements in infrastructure such as roads and market systems are seen only after a long time, but their importance in economic development is clearly enormous.

SOLVING THE MODEL

Now we are in a position to tackle the labor-and-output determination for a country which is already in the process of industrializing. Let us first consider a single period, for example, the period in which agricultural and industrial employment decisions are implicitly made together just before a given agricultural season begins. The capital in agriculture and industry is fixed for the decision period, as are the amounts of potential labor and the state of technological know-how. One may construct a function expressing all possible combinations of (1) leisure, (2) agricultural goods, and (3) industrial goods that can be produced with that fixed capital and technology. One may also array a set of indifference surfaces, each of which shows those sets of the two sorts of goods and leisure

---

[19] Eversley, however, disputes that exports were as important in England's industrialization as asserted by Deane, John, and "most of the Cambridge economists and historians" (1967, p. 271).

[20] Certainly, the demand for goods may be thought of as mostly preceding the demand for labor in almost any economic causal chain.

among which the community as a whole can be said to be indifferent. The point of tangency between the production function and the highest indifference surface determines the amounts of leisure and goods that will be produced. This is a three-dimensional generalization of Figure 7–2.

This solution determines the number of hours of work supplied in agriculture and industry, as well as the prices (in hours of work) of agricultural and industrial goods; these are the marginal amounts of output per unit of labor at the "equilibrium" point. This determination refers to a closed economy; an open economy will be taken up shortly. This general solution must be simplified in any actual numerical simulation. One likely simplification is to make industrial output an exogenously fixed function of total output at each level of per-capita output, a reflection of observed income elasticities for agricultural and industrial goods.

To review, for the short run the proportion of the labor force that will be working in industry at any given point in time is determined by: (1) tastes for the two kinds of goods and for leisure, as influenced by family size, among other forces; (2) the amount of capital in agriculture and industry; (3) the type and level of technological practices in use in agriculture; (4) the level of technological know-how in industry. The more productive is industry, the lower the prices of goods, and the more willing farmers will be to trade leisure for industrial goods, thereby freeing others to work in industry.[21]

In the longer run the model is also determined by being made fully recursive. Capital, technology, productivity per worker, wages, and the aspiration level of agricultural workers are endogenously determined by lagged-value equations. Hence the course of industrialization over time is determined. Only changes in population growth and some aspects of taste are exogenous, as are the parameters.

This model shows that, as has been recognized by many writers, the course of development depends upon both demand and supply factors. More than that, the model emphasizes that the supply and demand factors in the two sectors are interrelated, including the crucial influence of the supply of industrial goods upon the supply of agricultural labor. This brings out sharply that there are no simple explanations of industrialization or short-cut methods of achieving it.

INDUSTRIALIZATION IN AN OPEN ECONOMY

Opening up a new foreign export market may be seen as causing a new aggregate "attainment" function. That is, with its previous endowment

---

[21] As the economy develops, the amount of labor expended can be increasingly regarded as being fixed, as more of the labor force is in industry where the individual has less discretion about how many hours to work.

of resources, and given the possibility of trade with another country, "our" country can attain combinations of goods that were not available with its domestic attainment (production) function. The total value of the "open" attainment function, measured in the domestic prices prevailing before the opening up of the new trade, will be greater at some labor inputs than was the "isolated" attainment function. Given the tastes of the other country for goods and leisure, the total system may then be considered to be determined, though the terms of trade are endogenous. The tangency of the new combined attainment function and the highest indifference curve fixes the amount of labor supplied in total, as well as the labor in each sector and other endogenous values. Whether the result is more or less labor supplied than if the foreign market does not exist probably depends on (1) how the foreign market changes the domestic production function, and (2) tastes for agricultural and industrial goods and for leisure.

Summary of Model

The course of industrialization and economic growth can be summed up as follows. Increases in productivity per worker in *both* the industrial and agricultural sectors are necessary. Among the important ingredients of an increase in industrial productivity are increases in investment and economies of scale. These in turn are caused by increases in demand. Increases in demand for industrial goods are highly dependent on increases in agricultural productivity, or else there is no "surplus." Important in causing the increases in agricultural productivity are increases in the amount of work supplied per worker in the agricultural sector and increases in investments. The impetus to both of these (including the willingness to take bigger risks) depends heavily on the aspirations of agriculturalists, which are a function of what farmers can buy with their agricultural produce, which, in turn, depends upon the industrial productivity level, as well as upon communications and transportation. Thus, increases in agricultural and industrial productivity are interdependent.

An additional child is likely to increase the amount of work supplied by his parents. But at the same time he alters the shape of their indifference functions among industrial goods, food, and leisure. The net result will probably be less demand for industrial goods, especially in relatively poor countries, which will slow down the industrialization process.

After he enters the work force, the additional person may have a positive effect upon total and industrial demand. If the increase in *total* demand over the entire life cycle of an incremental person is large enough, and if the accelerator and other investment effects, plus economies-of-scale effects, are great enough, an incremental person can have a net positive effect upon the proportion of the work force in industry. But if the parameters are not appropriate for it, the proportion of people working in industry will be less than otherwise.

The key element in the determination of this model is a choice between leisure and the two classes of goods, industrial and agricultural. Though this element need not appear in models of MDC's, it is crucial for the agricultural sector of LDC's. This is precisely the opposite of assuming that the marginal product of additional labor is zero, à la W. Lewis and Fei-Ranis (1967) (though the marginal product of additional persons might be less than their consumption in this model). A key difference between this and the Fei-Ranis model is thereby revealed. In their model, an exogenous increase in productivity gives the push to growth, which clearly does not explain the case of China. In this model, increases in productivity are endogenous to an important degree, though exogenously caused increases in productivity may perhaps be important also, of course.

The model suggests that the "lack of labor" explanation for population growth's putative beneficial effect in England is muddled at best, and may be just plain wrong. It also emphasizes the importance of an increase in industrial productivity per worker in the industrialization process, one reason being that the amount of labor supplied per worker is less variable in industry than in agriculture.

Now we proceed to Chapters 8–12 which discuss the estimation of some of the important parameters of the model.

CHAPTER 8

Change in Agricultural Techniques: The Population-Push and Invention-Pull Theories of Economic-Demographic History Reconciled

INTRODUCTION

THIS CHAPTER begins estimation of the key parameters of the general LDC model sketched out in Chapter 7; discusses the invention and adoption of innovations, especially in agriculture; and more specifically, inquires into the historical evidence for the proposition that changes in technological practice have come about simply and directly by independent invention or instead by a more complex process in which population pressure has been an instrumental force. In the context of the algebraic general model outlined in Chapter 7, this chapter discusses the extent to which changes in agricultural technological practice have come about by (1) exogenous changes in the technological coefficient A_F—which would be captured operationally by a time trend along with sharply diminishing returns in the production function; or instead by (2) shifts in practice among already-known technologies—which would be represented by a production function with less sharply diminishing returns, and not by time trend.

There are at least two ways in which population growth may affect the type of productive techniques that individuals and groups use. One effect is the impact of additional people on the stock of knowledge; this technological effect is at the heart of the model of the more-developed world discussed earlier. A second effect is the adoption of practices for which the knowledge has earlier been discovered but which require additional labor in the production process; to the extent that population growth affects technological practice in the peasant-agricultural sector of LDC's, it is likely to be this sort of phenomenon. The task of this chapter (and also of Chapters 9 and 11) is essentially to assess how sensitive agricultural productive techniques in LDC's are with respect to population growth.

History should be able to tell us something about the effect of population growth on technological change. And we should be able to glean some insights into our cultural history from the ethnology of peoples at less-developed economic levels. The question to be asked of history may be phrased as follows: Would the changes that occurred in productive practice have come about with less pressure from population growth? Or more generally, what was the causal role of population growth in economic growth?

Since Malthus, the established theory of demographic-economic history has been what will be called the "invention-pull" hypothesis in this chapter. It suggests that from time to time inventions appear, independently of population growth, which increase productive capacity and provide subsistence to more people. Population then increases to use this new capacity until all the productive potential has been exhausted. According to the Malthusian hypothesis, then, the history of population growth is only the reflection of the history of autonomous invention.

In 1965 Boserup published a lengthy statement of another point of view, here called the "population push" hypothesis. That hypothesis asserts that though production-increasing inventions may occur independently of the prior rate of population growth, the *adoption* of "new" knowledge depends upon population growth. Hence in the population-push hypothesis, population growth is necessary for there to be a change in productive techniques.[1] Whereas the Malthusian invention-pull hypothesis is a single-influence explanation of history, the population-push hypothesis sees two forces at work: (1) independent invention occurring sometime prior to its adoption; and (2) population growth leading to adoption of previously unused existing knowledge. The causes of the inventions are not central in either hypothesis. The two hypotheses imply very different judgments about population growth. The invention-pull hypothesis sees nothing good or necessary about population growth, either in past history or (by implication) in the future. But the population-push hypothesis views population growth as necessary, though not sufficient, for economic growth.

The first aim of this chapter is to explicate the invention-pull and population-push hypotheses and the economic mechanisms that presumably underlie them, to aid in the examination of their claims to explain economic-demographic history. The most important finding is that the apparent conflict between the hypotheses is illusory. The conflict results

---

[1] The kernel of this idea may be found in Von Thunen's explanation of differences in farming methods in Europe in his classic economic analysis of the interrelationships of agricultural method and location (1826–1966). The economic elements of the analysis, along with a wealth of supporting data for the peasant economy of Russia, are given quite explicitly by Chayanov (1925–66). The hypothesis was used frequently by Gourou (1966) in his geographic analysis of primitive agriculture in the tropics, by Slicher van Bath (1963) in his history of agriculture in Europe from 500 to 1850, and probably by other writers of whom I am not aware. It was Boserup's contribution, however, to have developed the idea at length. She applied it to the long course of pre-industrial and is most responsible for the idea getting some attention. Clark also has developed this idea broadly, and promulgated it (1967; 1969).

from failure to distinguish between the types of inventions to which each of the two hypotheses does and does not apply. Put crudely, both hypotheses make micro-economic sense if (1) the invention-pull hypothesis is restricted to inventions that are purely labor-saving relative to established practice; and (2) the population-push hypothesis is restricted to inventions that have no labor-saving advantages at the time of invention but can produce *higher* levels of output with relatively less labor per unit of output (though absolutely more labor per person) than the existing technology; hence such inventions come to be used later on as population grows. Rather than being substitute hypotheses, the two hypotheses constitute *complementary* explanations of complementary elements. Taken together in this way, they constitute a more general and more satisfying explanation of demographic-economic history in subsistence-agriculture situations than does either hypothesis alone.

The argument can also be phrased another way: Any invention increases the choices available to the farmer. But inventions can be of two sorts: (1) Compared to the technology in use at present, the invention may produce the same output with the same amount of land and with less labor (a better calendar is an example); or (2) Though the invention will not produce more output with the same labor and land than the presently used alternative technology, at the *higher* rates of output that would be necessary at a higher population density the invention will produce more output than the alternative method with given amounts of labor and land (an example is multiple cropping when shifting agriculture is being practiced and where output is still plentiful). An invention must do one *or* the other, or it is not useful (capital requirements aside).

If an invention is of the sort that produces the same output with less labor and no additional capital, it lowers the price of output in terms of labor, and a sensible farmer will adopt the invention immediately. That is, the lower cost of output in terms of labor input makes immediate adoption economically sensible. This also increases the total "capacity," and population is likely to grow in response to the invention and its adoption. But if the invention will only produce more output with the same amount of labor as the old technology *after population and the demand for food has grown* and made land and output more scarce relative to labor, then it does not make sense to adopt the invention *until* population has grown to that point at which the adoption is sensible. Whereas in the previous case the invention and its adoption "pulls" population growth, in this case population growth eventually "pushes" the adoption of the invention that was discovered earlier.

The second aim of this chapter is to examine some historical and anthropological examples of economic-demographic growth in order to determine for each of the examples whether one hypothesis or the other seems to fit best. Enough examples are found in which each hypothesis fits to suggest that both processes are important in history and economic development. This confirms the theoretical analysis.

The original purpose of this chapter was to explore the technological-change parameters of the general population-growth model for LDC's. But the inquiry also attempts to explicate the invention-pull and population-push theories in such a manner that their claims as explanations of history may better be examined. To this end, the theories are first analyzed in terms of basic micro-economic constructs. Next, a variety of historical examples are adduced to see how well the two contending hypotheses explain what happened. The inquiry does not, however, attempt to determine which of the two theories is the more correct one, or even to judge which is the more important. In fact, the chapter concludes that the two theories tend to be *complementary explanations of complementary forces,* rather than being in essential conflict. As for its contemporary relevance, the chapter concludes that *in the presence* of unused technological knowledge, population pressure can affect the rate of adoption of one major class of inventions: those inventions that do not immediately reduce the costs of the output being produced at the time of invention. Given that at a particular time in an LDC there does exist knowledge of a large body of techniques that might be used (with some adaptation), there is reason to believe that increased population pressure can make for technological change. But the chapter can offer no suggestion about just how sensitive the response is or how delayed it will be. Such estimates must be derived by other methods as discussed in Chapter 9.

The chapter is concerned only with those possibilities that eventuate in economic change. Ignored here are all those possible sequences of events beginning with population growth which *do not* result in economic change. This is very different from the policy-oriented question which asks the *likelihood* that population growth will be followed by economic change in particular circumstances.[2]

The chapter does not discuss the issue of induced innovation, because the cause of original invention is not a part of either the invention-pull or population-push hypothesis; that is, invention is exogenous to both. Rather, both hypotheses concern the outcome of invention.

Boserup (1965) considered the issue in the framework of subsistence agriculture, as did Malthus, and the focus of this chapter is therefore limited to subsistence agriculture, though at least Clark (1967) extends the same argument to the full sweep of human history.

---

[2] "for every case where there has been some degree of successful adaptation, one can undoubtedly cite others where people have failed to adapt and there has been considerable deterioration in the natural habitat" (Van de Walle, quoting Wilde, 1972, p. 120).

INVENTION PULL: THE MALTHUSIAN EXPLANATION OF POPULATION GROWTH

Though the invention-pull theory is labeled "Malthusian," it is *not* explicit in Malthus' *Essay on Population* (1798). It is, however, the explicit line of thought of most writers on the subject, of which Childe (1937) and Cipolla (1962) may serve as representatives. Crudely stated now, the argument begins with a society that is somewhat above the subsistence level. Population expands until it reaches the subsistence limits of the technology in use. Then sometime thereafter population size becomes stationary—by mortality alone in the narrow Malthusian view which shall be discussed here, or by mortality and/or birth control in the wider Malthusian view which is closer to Malthus' later editions. Someone then makes a discovery which permits more food to be produced on the same land area, and a shift to the new technology then takes place. Population expands again until it reaches the subsistence limit of the newer technology, and so forth. If a society is observed to be at a position above subsistence, it is assumed in this theory to be in a transitory state on the way to the stationary equilibrium at subsistence-level. The process is shown in Figure 8–1: a direct causal line from an autonomous invention to a change in the food situation, to a decrease in mortality, to an increase in population, the process continuing until the new food constraint is reached. Technological change is assumed to have social and economic causes apart from the growth of population itself.

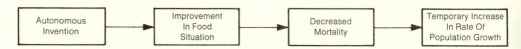

FIGURE 8–1   INVENTION-PULL MALTHUSIAN PROCESS

Let us first analyze the basic Malthusian process from the standpoint of an idealized head-of-household provider who has rights to the produce of a given piece of land.[3] The agriculturalist can choose between different amounts of product and leisure. If population increases so that he has less land to work with, he will have to work harder than before. That is, the price of his leisure in terms of output is higher than before, so he trades more leisure for output. But nevertheless he obtains less output than before.[4]

---

[3] The description of early agriculture tenure systems is not accurate, but the abstraction should not cause trouble here.

[4] I will be happy to send interested readers a version of this chapter that contains geometrical and numerical demonstrations of the micro-economic analysis given here in words.

According to the invention-pull hypothesis, an invention suddenly appears at some time. This invention increases the output that can be attained at all or some labor inputs. This technological change enables the farmer to obtain the same output with less labor than previously, or he could obtain more output with the same labor as before. Hence the invention makes possible further increase in population, and growth then proceeds in the fashion of the "magnificent dynamics."

According to the invention-pull hypothesis, population expansion comes to a halt through increased mortality when the "carrying capacity" of the land is reached with the known method of farming. (One may think of the limit of carrying capacity roughly as the point at which the average level of output is at subsistence, and where not much additional output can be produced even if large amounts of additional work is done.) Then at some later time after the population becomes stationary, again someone discovers a "better" form of agricultural production, the people begin to practice the new technique, and the population begins to expand once more.

The invention-pull hypothesis assumes that an invention will begin to be adopted "immediately" after the invention is made,[5] no matter whether the population is close to or far from that level of subsistence at which further population growth must cease. Therefore, we must now consider the characteristics of an invention whose adoption would begin immediately. One class of examples includes inventions that will yield the *same amount of output for less labor* than does the established practice, assuming no change in the amount of land or other capital—for example, replacement of the wooden plow with the iron plow, the stone axe with the iron axe,[6] and the substitution of one shape of digging stick, sickle, or scythe with another and faster-operating shape, inventions classified as "mechanical" by Heady (1949), all of whose effects are to reduce the amount of labor required to produce a given quantity of food. There would be no point in increasing the total amount of output in most circumstances, because total calorie consumption is reasonably inelastic.[7]

---

[5] Please note that invention-pull hypothesis assumes only that diffusion *begins* immediately. Diffusion will take time to *complete*, of course, as learning takes place, and uncertainty and risk are reduced.

[6] "The Amerindians in the Amazon basin used to burn the trunks little by little so as not to use their wretched stone axes more than necessary. Hence, the arrival of iron implements with the Europeans caused a considerable technical revolution. 'A very few strokes of the steel axe were enough to modify the conditions of labour, to increase the area felled, and double and even treble the harvests.' Hence, after the discovery of America there was among the Indians a thirst for iron as great as that felt by Europeans for gold" (Gourou, 1966, p. 32, with quotation by A. Métraux, "Le caractère de la conquête jésuitique," *Acta Americana*, Jan.–March 1943, pp. 69–82.)

[7] The invention-pull and population-push theorists generally ignore shifts in food quality, so that will also be done here. This assumption, however, runs some risk of invalidating the entire issue.

There would not be any point in adopting an innovation that would increase the amount of output per unit of land unless one could reduce the amount of land in use and thereby get the same amount of output with less labor.

Another relevant class includes inventions that yield *greater* output with the *same* labor per acre. Such inventions make it possible *either* to enjoy greater output with the same labor *or* to cut back on capital and labor and have the same output as before. An example is a better calendar. This second class of inventions may be found among either the "biological" or the "mechanical-biological" categories of Heady (1949). (The difference between the two classes in this context is that an innovation which increases productivity with the same land and labor can produce more food per capita, and hence increases potential population. An innovation that only reduces labor and does not increase output cannot provide for more people, but only gives more leisure.)

Both classes of inventions mentioned above may be regarded as "labor saving" because they produce the same or more output with less or the same amount of labor (assuming a fixed amount of the major capital element, land) than does the technology currently in use,[8] and therefore they will be adopted immediately after invention. And the second class of inventions in turn provides the basis for further population growth.

It is an important part of the intellectual history of the invention-pull hypothesis that the kind of inventions to which it refers has generally not been made clear.

In summary, then, the Malthusian invention-pull hypothesis accurately describes economic-demographic history in cases where an invention occurs that produces the same output with less labor compared to the technology in use.

THE POPULATION-PUSH HYPOTHESIS

Next we consider the "population-push" hypothesis. The key idea is that at a given moment an agricultural people knows a method of obtaining higher yields from their lands than given by the methods they use. But the higher-yield method demands more work, and will *not* produce the *same* output with less labor. The new method therefore is not used. But a later increase of population then pushes people to adopt the new methods even though they require more work. In other words, population growth

---

[8] Please notice that such statements as "labor saving" are comparisons relative to the agricultural technology *then in use*. To be labor-saving, capital using, etc., is not an inherent property of an invention, but rather refers to the *difference* between a given invention and existing practice. Lack of recognition of this relativity has sometimes flawed discussions of technological advance.

makes labor less scarce relative to land, and output is more scarce relative to labor. Therefore a shift to the more labor-intensive method then occurs. For comparison with Figure 8–1, the population-push hypothesis is schematized in Figure 8–2.

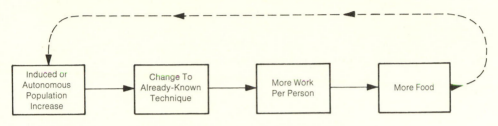

FIGURE 8–2   POPULATION-PUSH PROCESS

There are two population-push mechanisms that can bring about the shift to the new methods. In the first mechanism, less land is available to each family because of the *increased number of families*. This reduces the output of the average family with a given amount of labor, and this makes it sensible to shift to a method yielding relatively more output at a higher labor input.

The second population-push mechanism refers to an increase in the size of the representative family, assuming the same size plot of land. If there are 6 rather than 4 consumer equivalents in the family, it is reasonable to assume that the desired output will rise. Therefore, it is sensible to shift to the method that will produce the *greater* amount of output with relatively less additional labor.

The population-push hypothesis implicitly suggests that population growth puts *both* of the above mechanisms into operation. And both work in the same direction to induce a shift to previously known but previously unused production methods.

The analysis assumes that there is physical capacity for harder work in some or most cases. And there is evidence to believe that this is so among "primitive" peoples. Among the Hadza in Tanzania "Over the year as a whole probably an average of less than two hours a day is spent obtaining food . . ." (Woodburn, 1968, p. 54). The "Kung Bushmen of Dobe (Botswana), despite their harsh environment, devote from twelve to nineteen hours a week to getting food" (R. B. Lee. 1968, p. 37). And the Australian aborigines of Arnhem Land average less than four hours a day in getting food (Sahlins, 1968, pp. 86–87, quoting McCarthy and McArthur, 1960). Some observers (e.g., Thomsen, 1969, p. 180) believe that the state of health in LDC's makes impossible any more work than is now done, especially in the tropics. But Gourou's examples from Congo-Leopoldville are convincing to me.[9] There the Zande men work many fewer hours than do the Zande women, though both sexes are equally nourished.[10] And the Lélé men spend a great deal of energy in hunting, though they obtain very little food from it. Both groups are underfed and badly nourished. But both groups have plenty of land. Apparently the men just are not willing to do agricultural work, leaving it to the women (1966, pp. 84–85).

To explicate the population-push hypothesis in a more aggregated manner, let us start with a hunting and/or food-collecting group of 10 people on 800 square kilometers of land.[11] This is ample to support them with a minimum of labor, say 2 hours work by each person on 250 days a year. (In arctic and desert regions food gathering is much more laborious, of course.) With a group as small as 10 people the workings of chance necessarily make for some variation in population size over time, leading either to the disappearance of the small family group or to its increase. If population rises toward 40 people the group will find it harder to make a living because game does not increase with the population size. Prob-

---

[9] "A study of the Zande area in the Wele region of Congo-Leopoldville in 1959–61 showed that the menfold devoted 19 per cent of their working time to agriculture, and the women 27 per cent. These diverse observations are in a way encouraging, because they confirm not only that if the men worked as hard as the women the food situation would be much improved, but also that the men's state of health would not hinder them from supplementing the labour force, for the women, who work much harder, are in no better (or worse) health than the men. . . ." [T]he Lélé tribe in the north of the Kasai district of Congo-Léopoldville . . . are underfed and badly nourished, but not for want of space, for the density of population is no more than four to the square kilometre, nor because of soil poverty. The real reasons are: first, that the men take no interest in agriculture of animal-rearing, but only in hunting, which yields almost nothing; and secondly, that the women, who do all the agricultural work, are very conservative in their methods, and are rigidly bound by customs that restrict their activity. Amongst these are the observance by the Lele of a three-day week, with every third day being one of rest; and whether Christian or not, they rest on Sundays; and they always take a holiday after the visit of any important person.

"The following sequence occurred during a week in September at the time of planting.

"*Sunday:* (fortunate—or unfortunate?—coincidence of the Christian Sunday with the day of rest in the three-day week).

"*Monday:* women work in fields.

"*Tuesday:* day of rest to mark departure the day before of an important visitor.

"*Wednesday:* day of rest in the three-day week.

"*Thursday:* there was too much rain for working.

"*Friday:* a holiday in honour of the agronomist who left the day before.

"*Saturday:* rest day in the three-day week; and then.

Sunday again!" (Gourou, 1966, pp. 84–85).

[10] It is apparently the rule in Africa that women work more hours on the farm than do men. Even more noteworthy are the small number of hours worked by the men in both Africa and Asia while outside labor is hired to increase output (Boserup, 1970, pp. 21 and 25).

[11] Illustrative numbers abstracted from various examples given by Clark and Haswell (1967, pp. 26–27 and 47) and Kroeber (1948, pp. 389–390). Somewhat higher population densities for hunting and fishing, and for "pastoral and forestry," are given by Wiechel (cited by Jefferson cited by Hawley, *Human Ecology*, 1950, p. 151).

ably, game decreases as hunting is intensified. The workers now need to work 4 to 8 hours a day instead of only 2 hours a day, to kill or collect the same amount of food per person as before. If the population then grows even more, it will be difficult or impossible to make a living by hunting and collecting, no matter how hard the people work.

According to the population-push hypothesis, what now happens is that the group begins to farm a bit. The 40 people could get more food from 4 hours farming per person than from 4 hours hunting and collecting. Please remember that the population-push hypothesis assumes that the group already has the technological knowledge necessary for this primitive agriculture long before it shifts to the new technique. The shift from one food-getting method to another need not be sudden or all at once, but rather, is likely to be gradual as is consistent with the basic economic logic implicit in the production function. The 40 people could minimize the time required to get the basic food ration by employing both methods at once—at least until population grew much larger. This is consistent with the observation that in many primitive communities the women farm while the men hunt (Clark and Haswell, 1967, p. 27).

As population on this 800 square kilometer trace expands to 200 people, according to the population-push hypothesis all work would be primitive agriculture and none would be hunting. Then population expands to 800 people, which nears the limit for this type of simple farming (even if animals have been tamed and kept in pasture.) The population-push analysis suggests that in the course of the expansion to 800 people agricultural technique shifts again, this time to slash-and-burn agriculture. With short work days, slash-and-burn agriculture produces less food than the more primitive agriculture. But if the 800 people work somewhat harder, they can get a *full* ration of food with less effort using slash-and-burn long-fallow agriculture than using a more primitive system. So—assuming, as the population-push writers do, that people already know about the method—people will now gradually shift to slash-and-burn agriculture. The shift to slash-and-burn will be completed as population expands to, say, 6,000 people on the 800 kilometer tract. Then, as population grows even more, there will be a shift to 3-course agriculture. These successive shifts from one type of agricultural system to the next, each system demanding more labor per worker and a shorter fallow period than the one before and each shift caused by growth in population, are the heart of the population-push hypothesis.

Now let us restate the characteristics of the kinds of inventions that might not be adopted until some time after their discovery and as a result of a population push. These inventions will not be labor-saving relative to the technology in use, because there is every reason for the adoption of labor-saving inventions to begin *immediately* after discovery. Instead they will be inventions that meet the need of producing *more output as population grows* and which require *more labor*—the latter being the reason that their adoption did not begin immediately upon invention. All of these inventions will be among those classified as "biological" by Heady (1949). The most important examples of such inventions are short-fallow and multi-cropping systems, all of which require more careful farming and more hours of labor per unit of output than do long-fallow systems. Some of the new seed varieties (e.g., rice that requires the laborious Japanese method of wet-farming) are related examples.

ANALYTIC COMPARISON OF THE TWO HYPOTHESES

To recapitulate, the Malthusian invention-pull hypothesis is a reasonable description of the process that begins with exogenous inventions that are immediately "labor-saving" and "profitable." Such an invention can be one that "dominates" previous technology in the sense of using less labor for each and every level of output, or it can be an invention that uses less labor at the present level of output though it uses more labor than previous technology at lower output levels. It is probable that such inventions will be adopted immediately, and because they produce more output at the same amount of labor as before, they lead to further population growth.

The population-push hypothesis, in turn, is a good description of the place in economic-demographic history of inventions that produce the same output with less labor, or more output with the same labor, but *at higher labor and output levels* than are in effect at the time of invention. That is, in the population-push hypothesis the key technological discoveries are *not* more "profitable" than the old technology at the time of invention, but rather are less desirable at the time of invention. The new invention becomes desirable later on, after population density has increased and total food "needs" have increased, according to the population-push hypothesis.

This brief analysis of the difference between the hypotheses focuses on (1) the properties of the key inventions and (2) people's "needs" for food and leisure at the time of the inventions. Now, we know that some inventions are labor-saving at all output levels (e.g., a better calendar and implements such as bronze and iron sickles and scythes; see Curwen and Hatt 1953, especially p. 94). We also know that other inventions require much more labor than would ever be used with previous technology though the new inventions also can produce much more output per unit of land, for example wet-farming and double-cropping. The two hypotheses do not conflict with each other. Hence, they should not be seen as competitive explanations of pre-modern agricultural development, but

168

rather as complementary. Both types of inventions have been important in history, which implies that both the invention-pull and the population-push mechanisms have operated in history.

As to the relative importance of the two mechanisms in history, there is at least one fact indicating that *both* were important: Even after much change in technology and after much population growth, the amount of work done on yearly crops by individual farmers in densely populated places is *not* higher by a different order of magnitude than in sparsely populated places. In both situations farmers work most of the daylight hours during the harvest season and much less during most of the year. This suggests that invention pull was not the complete explanation; if it were, all inventions would be labor-saving and the work done would have become *less* as agriculture advanced. On the other hand, the amount of work per farmer has not *increased* enormously, suggesting that population push is not the whole story either, because the technological changes it describes require *more* labor than before. Thus, *both* mechanisms must have complemented each other.

A word about more advanced agriculture: Neither of the two hypotheses describes the development of modern annual-crop and multi-crop agriculture in which output per farmer *rises*. The invention-pull point of view must be that there was an acceleration in the rate of exogenous inventions such as the internal combustion engine and many of the other components of farm machinery. But an increased rate of exogenous inventions has no logical connection with the invention-pull hypothesis. On their side, population-push theorists point to social and psychological changes that occur as people progress to more advanced agriculture. More economical social organizations with more division of labor evolve as people live closer together. Roads are built. Most important to Boserup and Clark, however, is that changes in individual psychology take place, people becoming more willing to work hard over sustained periods. Together with the other social changes, this is the engine that eventually brings about a "take-off" far beyond subsistence and near-subsistence living, in their view. But these changes are not inventions, or if they are inventions, there is no lag between invention and utilization. These changes are induced, just as in the United States new seed varieties are induced by market forces and by purposeful foundation or government research stimulated by foreseen needs. Of course there is a lag between the invention of the tractor and its use in India, but that is of the same nature as the delay between the invention of the fork-lift truck and its use in warehouses in India. The point is that after the passage from mostly-subsistence to mostly-market agriculture, neither the invention-pull hypothesis nor the population-push hypothesis has much to say that is distinctive and useful.

The foregoing analytic discussion may be sufficient to make the argument advanced in this chapter. Nevertheless, it seems worthwhile to examine some historical cases to provide some relevant concrete evidence. This will be done in the next section.

SOME HISTORICAL AND ANTHROPOLOGICAL EVIDENCE

Early Biblical Period

Genesis makes very clear that the shift from food-collecting to tilling the soil was perceived as an increase in labor-intensivity. "Behold, I have given you every herb yielding seed, which is upon the face of all the earth, and every tree, in which is the fruit of a tree yielding seed—to you it shall be for food" (Genesis 1:29). But then: ". . . cursed is the ground for thy sake; in toil shalt thou eat of it all the days of thy life. Thorns also and thistles shalt it bring to thee; and thou shalt eat the herb of the field. In the sweat of thy face shalt thou eat bread, till thou return until the ground" (Genesis 3:17–3:19). According to the Bible, the technological shift in the Garden of Eden was caused not by population growth but by sin. Aside from that, however, the description is that of von Thunen (1966), Gourou (1965), Slicher van Bath (1963), and Boserup (1965).

The rest of the story in Genesis may be prototypical, at least for people in hot, dry, countries. If the tribe flourishes rather than being overcome by mortality, there come to be a few more members of the family and tribe than before, and the people then use a somewhat larger area of land for pasture, hunting, and gathering, all without a major decrease in product per person. Probably there is some gain in efficiency from their cooperative efforts in hunting and defense.

But if there come to be enough people in the tribe so that at the edges of their area the land is less bountiful, "personal income" will fall. When this happens the tribe will probably split, as with Abraham and Lot;[12] one group will move to different grounds. The group that moves is likely to have poorer prospects than the group which remains, and the movers will certainly incur a cost in moving. Hence the overall level of per-capita income apparently falls over the last part of this population expansion, or at least people will have to work harder on poorer hunting and collecting areas to sustain the same standard of living.

Over-all judgment: The Biblical period is consistent with the population-push mechanism.

---

[12] Malthus also adduced this example (1803, p. 65).

Other Hunting-and-Gathering Groups

A crucial element of the population-push hypothesis is that there is pre-knowledge of techniques that will increase aggregate output from the given land area. But there are at least some situations where such techniques are clearly not known to hunters and gatherers. One such situation was that of the Netsilik Eskimos in the 1920's and 1930's, whose situation "did not leave the Netsilik with much leisure" (Balikci, 1968, p. 82). Life was very hard for the Netsilik by any material test. This does not fit the population-push hypothesis.

And before agriculture was invented no one knew about it. Of course it is conceivable that in all societies agriculture was discovered before it was needed, but this hardly seems likely. The control of plant reproduction is nowhere near so obvious that anyone who could benefit from it would automatically know about it.

> All cultivated plants have been derived from wild varieties, and the first step in cultivating them consists in taking the seeds of the wild plants, sowing them in suitable soil, and by care and attention promoting their growth . . . It may seem incredible to us that for countless thousands of years it never occurred to man to take this simple first step, but the very fact that he did not do so for so long emphasizes the magnitude of the discovery that eventually led him to take it (Curwen and Hatt, 1953, p. 15).

But the knowledge of agriculture was certainly available to *some* pre-agricultural groups *before* their population was pressing on its limits, and the knowledge came to be used as population grew.[13] The knowledge of agriculture has been shown to have diffused from one or a few discovery points in Eurasia—though also independently in the Americas, etc. Hence, some groups are likely to have learned of agriculture while they still had plenty of land on which to hunt and gather. It should not surprise us, therefore, that some or most hunting-and-collecting tribes live a comparatively easy life, as suggested in the examples adduced earlier.

Over-all judgment: Some instances of hunting-and-gathering groups illustrate the invention-pull mechanism, and others illustrate the population-push mechanism.

---

[13] Malthus read the history of Scandinavia after population increases in exactly this "anti-Malthusian" way: "The nations of the north were slowly and reluctantly compelled to confine themselves within their natural limits and to exchange their pastoral manners and with them the peculiar facilities of plunder and emigration, which they afforded for the patient, laborous and slow returns of trade and agriculture" (1803, pp. 80–81).

Slash-and-Burn Agriculture

Slash-and-burn agriculture uses land more intensively than does collecting or hunting, but sill not very intensively by standards of developed agricultural sectors today. As done today in the tropics, "the first trees are felled with axes, and when dry the vegetation is burnt; after the drop harvest the parch lies fallow and the forest regains control until it is once more burnt" (Gourou, 1966, p. 31). The plot is then farmed for 1, 2, or 3 years in succession, and then the land lies fallow for up to 30 years but sometimes as little as two or three years. ". . . Between eight and twelve years are necessary to get a good cover of woody vegetation" (Gourou, 1966, p. 38). Meantime, the agriculturalists work other land. The important point here is that a large area is needed to supply food for a group of people—up to 30 times as much as is cultivated in a single year.

Whether in earlier times practitioners of slash-and-burn agriculture generally knew of more "advanced" methods we cannot know for sure. But there is no reason to doubt that *present-day* slash-and-burn agriculturalists know about other techniques, as shown by the fact that the two systems coexist in some places (Gourou, 1966, pp. 107–108). The reason agriculturalists still prefer to continue using the slash-and-burn technique, according to Gourou (1966, p. 52), Clark and Haswell (1967, Chapter VII), and Boserup (1965, pp. 44–48), is that, for the quantities of food produced on the available land, slash-and-burn agriculturalists work fewer hours than if they were to use more intensive methods (at least, up to machine methods) to produce the same amount of food. Also there is much evidence that when population density increases, people shift from slash-and-burn to more intensive shorter-fallow agriculture. One of the most persuasive pieces of evidence is that when population density *decreases*—perhaps due to an increase in tribal safety on low lands, an event exogenous to population growth—the process reverses and people go "back" to less-intensive longer-fallow methods (Gourou, 1966, p. 107; Boserup, 1965, pp. 62–63).

Data on population and farming intensity among the Kikuyu in the Central Province of Kenya confirm the anecdotal reports and show clearly that higher population density is associated with less shifting cultivation and more settled farming; see Table 8–1.

Other persuasive evidence comes from anthropological restudies. When one observes a society at only a single point in time, or over a very long sweep of history, one cannot be sure that it is not the change in agriculture technique that is the leading force, with population growth only following. But if one observes a society at a point in time, notes an increase in population taking place, and then observes a generation later that a shift in agricultural technology occurred, this argues strongly that

TABLE 8–1
POPULATION DENSITY AND LAND USAGE, CENTRAL
PROVINCE OF KENYA, 1954

| District | Population per square mile | % land under various forms of cultivation | |
		Settled agriculture	Shifting cultivation
Kiambu	860	91.5	8.5
Nyeri	596	93.7	6.3
Fort Hall	499	89.7	10.3
Embu	351	68.3	31.7
Meru	236	66.7	33.3

SOURCE: Barber, 1970.

it was population growth that was the cause of the change in technique rather than the reverse—especially when the farmers tell the observer exactly these motivations for the change in method. Chan Kom, a village in Yucatan, Mexico, was studied by Redfield and Rojas in 1931, and again by Redfield in 1948. Population increased from about 250 people to about 445 during those 17 years. In 1931, there was unappropriated land available for anyone to farm (1934, p. 42). But by 1948 the situation had changed.

So long as there remained to the south an unpopulated territory, it was possible to take care of the increasing numbers of people by the making of new settlements on that frontier. The people of a village would go farther and farther from their home community to find good land . . . the lands available to the village yield less than they did twenty-five years ago . . . as land becomes scarcer, it is planted again in a shorter interval after its last abandonment to bush . . .

The average size of milpas [maize plots] is surely smaller now . . . about one-half as large as they used to plant . . .

Four or five of the men have begun the development of such small tracts by planting fruit trees, tomatoes, beans, and other small crops, by building cattle corrals, establishing poultry on the tract, and, in a few cases, by digging wells . . . .

The people see the population press upon the resources. So far as they speculate as to remedies, they turn to the possibility of increasing resources. Don Eus sees a hope in diversified agriculture (Redfield, 1957, pp. 54, 55, 57, 171, 172).

The changes in Chan Kom fit the population-push mechanism very well.

Another restudied village is Tepoztlan, in the Mexican State of Morelos. The picture one gets from the study in 1926–27 (Redfield, 1930) and restudy in 1943–48 (O. Lewis, 1951) is somewhat different but essentially consistent with that of Chan Kom. Unlike Chan Kom in which only slash-and-burn agriculture was practiced, in Tepoztlan as of 1930 both slash-and-burn agriculture *and* no-fallow plow agriculture were practiced. In the former technique a hole is made with a dibble or hoe for each seed; in the latter the ground is broken with a plow pulled by oxen, and the seeds are dropped into the furrow and then covered with the foot. Slash-and-burn requires much more land, but it *also* requires much more labor per unit of output—at least in Tepoztlan in the 1940's. Plow culture requires more capital in the form of oxen and plow. Plow agriculture began in Mexico only after the Spanish came; before that the plow was unknown. After the Spanish came there was also a *massive depopulation* of Mexico generally, and of Tepoztlan specifically (O. Lewis, 1951, pp. 26–30). Therefore farmers must have adopted plow agriculture *not* because of increasing pressure of population on land, but simply because with the innovation one could get more output with less labor, even though using much less land. This conclusion is consistent with the existence of much unfarmed land in Mexico even until the recent very fast population growth. Hence, the shift after the Spanish came to a system of no-fallow plow agriculture is not consistent with the population-push view of history, but rather fits the invention-pull hypothesis quite well.

In the years between the Redfield and Lewis studies of Tepoztlan, population grew rapidly (O. Lewis, 1951, p. 148). People responded with *an increase in slash-and-burn agriculture* in fields far away from the town, which contradicts the specific assertions of Gourou (1966) and Boserup (1965) about the sequence of shifts in technique. But it is also true that the daily trip to the milpa requires many hours back and forth; this trip increases the labor input so that it must be much greater per unit of output than in plow agriculture, and in this respect the shift fits the population-push hypothesis. Tepoztlan is also consistent with the population-push hypothesis in that knowledge of several techniques is available, and the agriculturalists choose that technique which maximizes their utility from production and leisure, given the land available to them and the indifference curves that reflect the number of children that they have.

Over-all judgment: Most slash-and-burn agricultural situations fit the population-push argument, but some fit the invention-pull mechanism.

Polynesian Short-Fallow Agriculture

Taro is the staple crop on the isolated Polynesian island of Tikopia, which Firth studied in 1928–29 and again in 1952. As of 1952 the Tiokopians were worried about the press of population upon food resources because of population growth. "The taro resources of the people might possibly be increased by adopting a technique of irrigation and conservation . . . . But this would require . . . specific instruction by an external agency" (Firth, 1939–1965, p. 50).

Firth implies that the Tikopians really do not know of a technological alternative that, even with increased labor, would expand their food supply greatly. Instead they look to birth control and suicide-migration by canoe to adjust population and food resources.

The physical isolation of this island is obviously a key element in its lack of alternatives, both for technological change and for migration.

Over-all judgment: Tikopia's situation fits the Malthusian invention-pull hypothesis better than it fits the population-push hypothesis, in the sense that an increase in population cannot be handled by a shift to an already-known invention that will increase output though requiring more labor.

Shifts in Fallow Periods and Crop Rotations in Europe

The relevant highlights of the history of European farming from 500 to 1850 are as follows. Population reached its nadir, 19.3 million, near the beginning of the period (Clark, 1967, p. 64). From then on the secular population growth was continuous, though not without major fluctuations around the trend. For the most part, then, we may associate changes in farming methods in the Middle Ages with increasing population.

A key change was from 2-course to 3-field rotation methods. In the former, "land was tilled or left fallow in alternate years." In the latter, ". . . winter corn (wheat or rye) was sown the first year, spring corn (barley or oats) the second, and in the third year the ground lay fallow" (Slicher van Bath, 1963, p. 59). The 3-course method increases total output per unit of land because more land is in production each year.

Slicher van Bath asserts that "it was nearly always at a time of increasing population that there was a changeover from two- to three-course rotation, for instance, in England in the thirteenth century . . . (1963, p. 60). And in some places where it fitted farmers' needs, "both systems were running concurrently, or being alternated according to the crop: wheat in the three-course rotation and rye in the two course." (Slicher van Bath, 1963, p. 60).[14] Boserup generalizes from this that "virtually all of the

[14] From, say, 1550 in Europe the pattern suggests that changes in agricultural technology were the result of changes in the nexus of prices and population density. The knowledge necessary for the changes was in existence long before, much of it in the Roman period when population density was higher; the methods were not new inventions at that time: "The high price of arable farm produce made it worth while to manure the land more richly. . . . In England and some parts of France, in the sixteenth century, marl and lime were put on the

methods introduced in this period had been known before-hand" and awaited adoption until population density grew sufficiently (1965, p. 38).

Chayanov[15] (1925–66) explored in great analytic depth and factual detail the workings of the push of population and consumer wants upon the behavior of Russian family-farmers at the turn of the century.[16] Chayanov investigated the "annual labor expenditure" of all the workers taken together on each farm, and found that the chief determinant, given any set of "production conditions," was "the pressure of family consumer demands on the workers" (p. 76), that is, the number of consumers in the family.[17] "This forcing up of labor intensity, buying increased annual agricultural income at the price of reducing labor unit payment, is achieved either by an intensification of work methods or by using more labor-intensive crops and jobs" (p. 113). It cannot be emphasized too strongly that Chayanov's conclusions are based, not on casual observation, but on the extremely detailed careful surveys of Russian agriculture that were made around the turn of the century by skilled, dedicated statisticians—surveys which still constitute perhaps the best available source of data on matters such as this. And though Chayanov's data, with a few notable exceptions, cover a single period, it is reasonable to assume that the cross-sectional differences recapitulate the changes over time as population density increased on the Russian peasant farm.[18]

Von Thunen described with wonderful precision the Belgian and Mecklenburg systems of cultivation, and clearly showed how the difference in techniques used was related to population density (1966, pp. 85 ff). But details will be omitted because this segment of history belongs more to market than to subsistence agriculture.

---

land for the first time since the Roman period and the thirteenth century. (Slicher van Bath, 1963, p. 205). . . .

"The old monotony of cereal-growing in the countryside was broken down, and crops of other kinds began to take up more of the fields. The systems they esteemed so new, dated, in fact, back to the Middle Ages; the seventeenth and eighteenth centuries had brought them nothing different in principle. It was the great expansion of these systems that was revolutionary" (*ibid*, pp. 243–44).

[15] I am indebted to James Millar for bringing Chayanov's extraordinary book to my attention.

[16] These farms averaged 20–50% of their income in money and the rest in subsistence in the various areas Chayanov studied (1925–66, p. 121). This probably makes them as much "subsistence" farms as most of those in Asia today.

[17] The pressure of population apparently worked its influence less directly, too, "In most parts of Europe . . . there were strong institutional obstacles to the introduction of the new techniques which were removed only under the pressure of population" (Habakkuk, 1963, p. 612).

[18] The above-cited data on European population-push adoption of labor-using innovations goes hand in hand with the well-documented population-pushed increases in investment in land reclamation, drainage, and irrigation discussed in the nonmonetized investment section of Chapter 11.

But population-pushed changes in crop rotation and related work methods do not constitute the entire story of European agriculture from the Middle Ages.[19] The development of the heavy plow and of horse-power to replace oxenpower were, according to some historians, equally important with the 3-course rotation in the agricultural revolution. The heavy plow required iron for its blade, and the horse required both iron for horseshoes and the new chest-harnesses that were being perfected at that time. General use of both the heavy plow and the horse had to wait upon the increased supplies of iron that occurred in Europe at the beginning of the Middle Ages. When it became available, these innovations—together with the new harnessing and the 3-course rotation—enabled European farmers to work profitably with the heavy soils of more northern lands than had previously been cultivated.

According to White (1962, Chapter 2), the inventive knowledge underlying the availability of iron and the adoption of the heavy plow, new harness methods, and horsepower were *not* available before the Middle Ages, in direct opposition to Boserup's (1965) assumption. White further asserts that the 3-field system was *also* invented in the Middle Ages. He cites the fact the "Charlemagne himself thought . . . the new pattern . . . as something so new and significant that he felt impelled to rename the months in terms of it" (1962, p. 69). White's account is very much one of new inventions pulling upward the size of the population, especially in Germany and Scandinavia (1962, p. 54), rather than of population pushing adoption of previously-known methods.

New crops are still other exogenous technological advances which did *not* have to wait on further population increase in Europe for adoption. "The earliest type of technical change that came to modify medieval agriculture in Europe was in the introduction of new crops. Some of these changes were the pre-condition for changes of other kinds" (Dovring, 1965, p. 631). The potato had the most dramatic impact.

> . . . [O]n a pathetically small patch of ground one could grow in potatoes from two to four times as much food as one could in terms of wheat or other grains, enough indeed to feed a family of more than average size . . . It was introduced [into Ireland] about the year 1600 and before the end of the seventeeth century had been generally adopted by the peasantry. By the end of the eighteenth century the common man was eating little else . . . . The unspeakable poverty of the country should, it would seem, have militated against any considerable population increase. Yet the population did increase from 3,200,000 in 1754

---

[19] This following section is based on White (1962, Chapter 2). I am grateful to Larry Neal for bringing it to my attention.

to 8,175,000 in 1846, not counting some 1,750,000 who emigrated before the great potato famine of 1845–1847.

It was perfectly obvious to contemporaries, as it is to modern scholars, that this Irish population could exist only because of the potato. Poverty-stricken though it might be, the Irish peasantry was noteworthy for its fine physique. Clearly people were doing very well physiologically on their potato fare. Young people rented an acre or less for a potato patch. On the strength of this they married young and had large families" (Langer, 1968, pp. 11, 15).

Though Langer emphasizes the effect of potato cultivation[20] in increasing fertility, other writers (e.g., McKeown and Brown, 1955) emphasize the potato's effect in reducing mortality, especially infant mortality due to malnutrition. Whichever is correct, there is little dispute that the "invention" of the potato and its diffusion throughout Ireland caused population to increase more than it would have otherwise.[21]

---

[20] In England, increasing population led to the adoption of turnip husbandry and the accompanying creation of new wheat lands. "Under turnip husbandry the great sandy wastes in Norfolk were transformed into some of the best wheat land in England and the promoters of the reform are said to have, in effect, added a province to their country. The new methods spread very slowly in the first part of the [eighteenth] century but rapidly in the latter part, a remarkable fact when the notorious conservatism of those engaged in agriculture is remembered. The rapidly growing population provided the necessary stimulus; in the North, the agriculturists found new and lucrative markets springing up at their doors, in the South, London continued to grow in size and wealth. In both cases canals made easier the transport of agricultural products" (Buer, 1926, p. 70).

[21] Though mostly qualitative, Connell's history of the potato in Ireland is a satisfactory demonstration that the potato increased output on given land input with no increase in labor, and hence had a neat Malthusian invention-pull effect: ". . . the history of the potato in Ireland shows that it was of quite fundamental importance in *permitting and encouraging the rapid growth of population* in the sixty or seventy years before the Famine. It permitted the growth of population because, in early eighteenth-century Ireland, population had been pressing on resources: any substantial expansion of population implied a parallel expansion of the means of subsistence, and in large measure it was in an abundance of potatoes that the increasing number of people found its sustenance . . . .

"It is not difficult to see how the potato lifted the restraints to the growth of population. When people had been living largely on grain, the substitution of the potato allowed their land to support at least twice as many people as before: when, as with the Irish before their general dependence on the potato, pastoral products had bulked large in the popular dietary, at least a quadrupling of the density of population became possible. At the same time, land which to a pastoral or grain-producing community had been of next to no economic importance became capable of yielding satisfactory crops of potatoes, and of allowing, therefore, a further measure of population-increase . . . .

"It was not only through the substitution of the potato for the traditional crops that its influence was felt in relaxing the limits to population growth. There is evidence that, in the fifty and more years before the Famine, the potato itself was undergoing a process of substitution. Increasingly the traditional varieties were losing ground before new and more prolific types, which allowed a further increase in the density of the population of the areas where they were grown . . . .

"The potato provided not only a prerequisite for the growth of population; it provided also a mechanism; it not only permitted, but encouraged increase. As potatoes were sub-

Over-all judgment: There were some innovations and events during the Middle Ages in Europe that apparently illustrate the invention-pull mechanism, and others that apparently illustrate the population-push mechanism. The relative importance of these innovations and the dates of their inventions are subject to scholarly dispute, however. Therefore, an over-all judgment is difficult to form—perhaps because more is known about this situation than about other situations discussed here.

Traditional Agriculture in China[22]

Over almost 600 years from 1368 to 1957 the population of China increased from 65–80 million to 647 millions. But per person consumption did not decline secularly over this period, and perhaps rose. No fundamental shifts in mechanical technology took place.[23] Some new crops were introduced, but none had a revolutionary effect. Opening up new lands accommodated the largest part of the population growth.[24] Exten-

---

stituted for the traditional foodstuffs, a family's subsistence could be found from a diminished section of its holding. There tended to appear on every tenancy a margin of land that was needed neither to provide the peasant's subsistence, nor the landlord's customary rent. The tendency of landlordism was to force up rent until this margin had to be entirely assimilated with the section of the holding . . ." (Connell, 1950, pp. 159–60).

[22] This section is drawn from Perkins (1968, particularly Chapters 1 and 9). I appreciate Peter Schran's bibliographical advice on this topic.

[23] ". . . In China there were few improvements in 'best' technique in the six-century period [from 1368 to 1957] and little apparent spread of that 'best' technique from 'advanced' to 'backward' regions. The major innovations that did appear in the post-fourteenth-century period had to do with improved seeds and new crops from the Americas. Improved seed varieties were being discovered in China and brought in from abroad throughout these six centuries and in previous centuries as well. These seeds raised yields, reduced crop fluctuations, and contributed to the increase in double cropping. But there was no general movement of improved varieties from 'advanced' to 'backward' regions. If anything, the trend was in the opposite direction" (Perkins, 1969, p. 186).

Ho gives a slightly different emphasis: ". . . It is partially true that for centuries there has been no technological revolution in Chinese agriculture, evidenced by the fact that the same kind of agricultural implements have been used by Chinese peasants of certain areas for centuries. Yet such a generalization requires qualification. During the Ming period there were significant improvements in agricultural implements, particularly in various kinds of water-pumps" (Ho, Ping-Ti, 1959, p. 169).

[24] But this expansion of cultivated area was interrelated with the introduction of new types of crops, which is a technological change.

"In the absence of major technological inventions the nature of the crops has done more than anything else to push the agricultural frontier further away from the low plains, basins, and valleys to the more arid hilly and mountainous regions and has accounted for an enormous increase in national food production" (Ho, Ping-Ti, 1959, p. 169).

"Early-ripening rice aided the conquest of relatively well-watered hills. American food plants have enabled the Chinese, historically a plain and valley folk, to use dry hills and mountains and sandy loams too light for rice and other native cereal crops. There is evidence that the dry hills and mountains of the Yangóze region and north China were still largely virgin about 1700. Since then they have gradually been turned into maize and sweet potato farms. In fact, during the last two centuries, when rice culture was gradually approaching

sion of water-control systems and double cropping contributed less, and both of these methods had been well known before 1368. These facts are more consistent with the population-push mechanism than with the in-vention-pull mechanism.

Chinese history raises a puzzle. If the Chinese farmers were apparently able to increase total production under the pressure of more people, why did they not raise production *even faster?* One possible answer is that the parallel trends of production and population are just a coincidence. But this coincidence seems unlikely because the methods of raising production were known. Nor can one satisfactorily explain the relationship by the increase in labor alone, as Perkins shows (1968, pp. 79–84); such an explanation would require that there are no *ceteris paribus* diminishing returns in agriculture, which there clearly are.

The most likely explanation why per-person consumption did not rise even faster, I judge, is that the Chinese farmers preferred not to trade more work for more output. This choice may (or may not) have been heavily influenced by the absence of consumer goods which would whet their desires. In any case, however, the outcome fits the population-push hypothesis.

The extent of change in the individual Chinese farmer's behavior as a result of "population pressure" may seem from the statistics greater than it actually was, because it was surely the young families just starting out who supplied much of the energy. If Chinese life was like Irish life in the eighteenth and early nineteenth centuries (Connell, 1965, pp. 428–29) it was the young just-married men and women who cleared uncultivated lands and settled there. The increase in output required of a mature father was much less than proportional to the number of persons in his nuclear family, especially after the children grew up.[25]

---

its limit and encountering the law of diminishing returns, the various dryland food crops introduced from America have contributed the most to the increase in national food pro-duction and have made possible a continual growth of population" (*ibid.*, p. 184).

Population pressure was apparently necessary in bringing about this shift. For example, "Mai Chu, governor general of Hupei and Hunan, 1727–1733, stated in a memorial that wheat was not grown extensively in Hupei, excepting in two northern prefectures. But after the serious flood of 1727 the peasants in low-land Hupei, under the persuasion of the pro-vincial government, began to grow wheat widely" (*ibid.*, p. 180).

"The repeated Sung exhortations, however, could not prevail over climatic and topo-graphical factors; neither could they force the majority of rice farmers to adopt a more labor-intensive system of double-cropping in a period when land was still comparatively plentiful in the inland Yangtze region" (*ibid.*, p. 178).

[25] The history of Chinese agriculture after the Communist regime gained complete con-trol is a slightly different story. Certainly, food production increased greatly, to the point of continued self-sufficiency, except for the disastrous "Great Leap Forward" episode, cul-minating in ten consecutive "bumper harvests" (Schran, 1969; *Kwang Ming Daily*, in *Kayhan International*, Teheran, Jan. 30, 1970, p. 2). The increase in agricultural produc-

Over-all judgment : The last six centuries of Chinese history suggest that the arrival of new knowledge—especially of seeds—was important. But population pressure was necessary for the innovations to be adopted.

Summary and Conclusion

Two apparently conflicting hypotheses—the invention-pull hypothesis and the population-push hypothesis—have been offered as explanations of demographic-economic growth in near-subsistence agricultural situations. The invention-pull hypothesis asserts that the diffusion of new methods begins immediately after invention occurs, and that the diffusion makes possible additional population growth which then takes place. The population-push hypothesis asserts that a pool of unused agricultural knowledge is available in each period, but that each more productive method requires more labor per worker. An increase in population is therefore necessary to force the adoption of the more productive methods, according to the population-push hypothesis. The population-push hypothesis sees population growth in a much more favorable light than does the Malthusian invention-pull hypothesis.

This chapter first demonstrates analytically that the invention-pull hypothesis refers only to inventions that are labor-saving relative to the methods in use. The population-push hypothesis refers only to inventions that are output-increasing but require more labor than is expended with the methods in use at the time of the new invention. Once this distinction is made, the two hypotheses are seen to be complementary rather than mutually exclusive.

The second part of the chapter reviews some historical and anthropological cases of economic-demographic change as they are relevant to the two hypotheses. Some cases are found which are well described by the invention-pull hypothesis, others by the population-push hypothesis. That is, some important inventions—such as the potato—have been immediately labor-saving, and therefore adoption began immediately after invention. Others—such as slash-and-burn agriculture—have been mostly output-increasing but require additional labor relative to the methods in use at the time of invention, and their adoption has awaited further population growth which requires additional output. This review confirms that both the invention-pull and population-push hypotheses have an important place in explaining economic-demographic history.

---

tion was accomplished without major technological change (though with a considerable increase in the use of fertilizer), and certainly not because of new discoveries, but rather due to a social reorganization which caused an increase in the amount of work done by agriculturalists. This certainly is consistent with the population-push hypothesis.

181

Neither hypothesis, however, explains original inventions themselves, and neither describes the development of modern business farming.

From the standpoint of the human *future*, the thrust of the chapter seems quite positive. Considerable basic knowledge already exists from which the LDC's can either draw directly when their needs and wishes (influenced by population growth or other forces) change so that the new practices are desirable, or which they can adapt for local use.[26] Institutional and communication blocks may stand in the way, of course, even if there is no lack of basic knowledge. But if enough people are motivated, institutions can and do change. The situation is at least subject to human control; this is the reassuring point.

[26] Soybean agriculture in India is an example. The same seeds and products used in Illinois cannot be used successfully in India. But soybean scientists know *how to learn* which changes are necessary to make a successful transfer.

CHAPTER 9

Behavior Change, Amount of Work,
and Population Increase
in LDC Agriculture

INTRODUCTION

THE EXTENT to which population growth is a *necessary* condition for changes in agricultural practice in LDC's, in contrast to new-practice adoption independent of population growth, was discussed in Chapter 8. In this chapter we must consider the extent to which population increase is a *sufficient* condition for technological shifts, in conjunction with increased inputs of labor. That is, we will take up the influence of additional children upon the amount of productive work that farmer-parents do, and the techniques that they use. The conclusion is that the effect is substantial: Agricultural families do respond to the needs of additional children by changing methods, working harder and producing more.

Technological shifts in agriculture involve *behavioral* changes rather than changes in the allocation of given quantities of capital and labor. Farmers must then work harder (at least for a while), in new ways. This inquiry therefore is an investigation of the *likelihood* that population growth will cause changes in *economic behavior* that increase or decrease agricultural growth in the short run or long run. That is, we want to know how likely it is that having additional children will cause farmers to work harder, create more agricultural capital, and change their farming methods. In formal terms, we want to know (1) how an increase in children affects the shape of indifference curves between leisure and output during the growing season, and (2) the size of the response coefficient governing the increase in investment as per-consumer income falls as a result of an increase in consumers. The former will be discussed in this chapter, and the latter will be left for Chapter 10.

Quantitative estimates of the parameters are necessary as inputs to any model that will produce a quantitative (or even qualitative) understanding of the population-industrialization nexus. But the parameters of behavioral changes will be very different in different situations, for example, Japanese and Indian peasants may respond very differently to shortfalls from desired income. This chapter builds a general and mostly non-quantitative framework for quantitative analysis of any particular situation. Then the Appendix to Chapter 9 will examine a case study of village India to which other situations can then be modified.

The paradigm of this chapter is quite different than that of the previous chapter on population history. Chapter 8 examined situations where change in productive practices *did* occur and asked what caused the changes, whether population growth or independent invention. That is, the view of Chapter 8 is *ex post change in productive practices*. In contrast, this chapter asks whether or not there *will be* changes in productive practices if population growth occurs. That is, the point of view of this chapter (and the next one) is *ex ante population growth*.

To make this point in different words: The previous chapter considered only those cases in which economic change occurred, and distinguished two types: (1) those cases in which population growth could be considered to be the cause, and (2) those cases in which new discoveries could be considered to be the cause. Now we consider *all* the possible outcomes of population growth including (1) changes in productive practices, and (2) the many other possible responses which are inconsistent with changes in productive practices, such as an increase in the death rate.

The time period must constantly be kept in mind. The effects of a given extra child may be quite opposite in the shorter and longer runs. The birth of an additional baby immediately lowers the per-capita income of his family, if only by arithmetic. The baby may, or may not, cause its father to work sufficiently harder on the farm so that the family's standard of living will not drop much, but its mother almost certainly will work less in the fields, for a while anyway. Thus, the baby's short-run impact is most likely negative. Each year its father may improve the land a bit more than he otherwise would, however, and the land handed on to the children and subsequent generations will then be richer than otherwise. This increase in productivity of the land may or may not be enough to offset the increased number of children who claim part of the farm. And as one looks further into the future, the economic impact of the additional baby born today is even more uncertain. So to repeat, the long-run and short-run effects can be quite the opposite of each other. Understanding the *net* effects of the additional child in the short and long runs requires the simulation in Chapter 13.

This chapter is limited to the agricultural sector because individual farmers have more freedom to choose to vary their productive practices than do most urban workers. Furthermore, farmers are quantitatively very important in LDC's.

The first and longest part of the chapter lists and discusses the various possible responses to fertility increase. The most detailed discussion is of the response of working harder, both on the current crop and on agricultural investment, because this is the response that must be estimated directly; some quantitative estimates are given. The last part of the chapter lists possible influences on the choice of responses by individuals and groups.

THE POSSIBLE RESPONSES TO ADDITIONAL PEOPLE

We shall now review some of the possible outcomes of an increase in births.[1] The inquiry is at two levels of aggregation and complexity. At one level we ask the consequences of the birth of a single incremental child who might otherwise not have been born—perhaps a child who was conceived without explicit intention by the parents. At a higher level of complexity, the effects of a higher-than-otherwise birth rate for a village or agricultural sector, rather than just for a given family, are discussed next. The distinction is made for analytic purposes only.

As the possible responses to an increment of people in an LDC agricultural sector are discussed one by one, it should be remembered that the likeliest response of a society (and perhaps of individual families, too) would be composed of *several* of these possibilities rather than just one. The descriptions are separated for analytic convenience only.

In short, the objective is to learn the likelihood that an increase in population will lead to a change in productive practices.

Change in Productive Practices and Labor Expended in Cropping

INTRODUCTION

As a result of the birth of the "additional" child and of his consumption needs, the farmer may work harder.[2] Additional labor may be put into the current crop, including such activities as more weeding and irrigation and more careful planting and harvesting, and into agricultural investment, especially clearing more land; Chinese terracing is a vivid example. Or the farmer may opt for a combination of more current-crop work and new investment, such as altering his farming practices in ways that require additional labor invested in developing the land and also in the seasonal work itself. An important example is a shift to irrigation. Constructing the irrigation system—even just the feeder channels from the main irrigation system to one's own land—requires much labor. And irrigated crops tend to use more labor per unit of output, though total output over the year is greater.

Such technological shifts constitute the process described earlier as the "population-push" hypothesis. Malthus believed in its operation. "I do not see what motive [other than population increase] there would be, sufficiently strong, to overcome the acknowledged indolence of man, and make him proceed in the cultivation of the soil" (1803, p. 491).

---

[1] The discussion of Slicher van Bath (1963, p. 13) runs along somewhat similar lines.

[2] Some have thought that in situations of extreme poverty leisure has little value to unemployed or underemployed people. But Clark and Haswell (1967, p. 128) and Clark (1969) point out that even in such situations it will take a wage at least twice as great as the cost of subsistence to get such a person to give up his leisure and work instead.

185

Massive documentation of shifts to labor-intensive methods under the pressure of population is given by Boserup (1965). Chapter 8 gives historical and contemporary qualitative documentation; no more such examples are needed in this chapter to show that this phenomenon really does occur in many places and times. It is clear that people do sometimes increase the time spent on their crops in response to increased perceived need. What one really needs to know is *how great* the response is or will be in a particular situation. That is, *quantitative* estimates are needed. But estimating the increased-labor response, either in terms of labor or in terms of output, is most problematic as of now. This is certainly one of the "softest"—perhaps *the* most questionable—of the elements in any reasonable model of the LDC industrialization.[3]

OPPORTUNITIES FOR MORE WORK

Before we turn to data on the actual relationship of number of children to the amount of work done by the parents, let us be clear that even in apparently-crowded lands there is *opportunity* for people to increase the work input productively, as in Mexico (see p. 173). And Table 9–1 shows that in Taiwan the labor input *per worker* increased substantially from 1911–15 to 1961–65 (the total work days in column 2 grew faster than the number of workers in column 1). Though the cultivated area rose less than 30% in column 3, the increased labor, in conjunction with increases in capital and such inputs as fertilizer, led to a 331% increase in total output in column 4.

In Africa, Clark says that only "the need for weeding sets a limit to the amount of land which can be cultivated" (1969a, p. 4). And with respect to China, almost every foreign observer in the nineteenth and early twentieth century concluded that China was so densely populated that there was no opportunity for increase in agricultural population. Yet under the post-1949 Communist regime which induced people to work more days, "the average annual increase in population is about 2 per cent while that of grain is nearly 4 per cent" (*Ta Kung Pao*, April 19, 1973, p. 10). And this increase in output occurred without major technological change. Obviously the opportunity to obtain additional output with additional effort is present even in the most densely settled countries.

---

[3] It is interesting, though not comforting, that there is a similar lack of knowledge about the related phenomenon of total-output response to agricultural price changes, a subject on which considerable attention has been focused. "All inferences concerning the contribution of price incentives to aggregate agricultural output rest on a very weak empirical foundation at the present time," concluded the President's blue-ribbon panel in 1967 (United States, 1967, Vol. 2, p. 529). (One cannot learn about the *aggregate* response from the studies of changes in output of *particular crops* with respect to price changes.)

TABLE 9–1

MAJOR INPUTS INTO TAIWANESE AGRICULTURE, 1911–70

INDEXES (1911–15 = 100)

	Agricultural workers	Labor input	Cultivated area	Output index
1911–15	100.0	100.0	100.0	100.0
1916–20	97.3	111.6	105.6	115.2
1921–25	97.5	118.1	109.6	134.1
1926–30	102.8	125.8	115.9	165.6
1931–35	111.3	138.9	118.5	202.6
1936–40	119.0	144.6	123.7	229.4
1946–50	126.9	141.4	123.2	178.7
1951–55	135.0	178.7	126.2	269.9
1956–60	140.0	198.4	126.5	337.1
1961–65	144.8	200.0 (est.)	128.3	431.1
1966–70	149.0	not available	130.6	546.7

SOURCE: Mueller, 1973; originally from T. H. Lee and T. H. Sun, "Agricultural Development and Population Trends in Taiwan Area," paper presented at the seminar on Effects of Agricultural Innovation on Population Trends, Manila, February, 1972, pp. 22–24; S. C. Hsieh and T. H. Lee, *Agricultural Development and Its Contribution to Economic Growth in Taiwan*, Joint Commission on Rural Reconstruction, Taiwan, 1966, pp. 19 and 24.

RESPONSE OF WORK TO CHANGED CIRCUMSTANCES

Generally, people change the amount of work they do in response to changes in their needs, opportunities, and economic circumstances. Evidence concerning the general effect of family size on hours worked in MDC's was shown in Chapter 3. Now here is some evidence on the relationship of work to economic circumstances in LDC's. (Evidence on the relationship of family size to work done will be explored in detail below.)

1. In Taiwan, there is a connection between people's aspirations and the labor-force participation of both men and women. "Couples who want modern goods and services are industrious. The data suggest that the wives of wage and salary earners (the modern and rapidly growing segment of the labor force) are more likely to be in the labor force if the couple has a high level of wants. The data also show a high incidence of extra jobs among aspiring couples" (D. Freedman, 1972b, pp. 25–26).

2. Since 1850 in the United States, the rise in per-capita income has been closely associated with the fall in the agricultural work week as shown in Table 9–2 and Figure 9–1, in a fashion similar to the relationship shown for the industrial work-week data shown in Chapter 3.

TABLE 9–2

LENGTH OF AVERAGE WORK WEEK IN AGRICULTURE
IN THE UNITED STATES, 1850–1960

Year	Hours of work
1850	72.0
1860	71.0
1870	70.0
1880	69.0
1890	68.0
1900	67.0
1910	65.0
1920	60.0
1930	55.0
1940	54.6
1941	53.2
1942	55.3
1943	58.5
1944	54.4
1945	50.6
1946	50.0
1947	48.8
1948	48.5
1949	48.1
1950	47.2
1951	47.9
1952	47.4
1953	47.9
1954	47.0
1955	46.5
1956	44.9
1957	44.2
1958	43.7
1959	43.8
1960	44.0

SOURCE: De Grazia, 1962, Table 1.

3. Across a sample of LDC's and MDC's, the level of income is closely associated with the weekly work week in industry, as seen in Figure 3–3.

4. The number of days worked by the average Chinese peasant increased from 119 in 1950 to 189 in 1959 (Schran, 1969). And output per capita also increased, from perhaps 217 kg/head in 1952 to 273 kg/head in 1965 (Swami and Burki, 1970, p. 62), with further increases to 1971 as China reaped its "tenth consecutive bumper harvest" (*Kwang Ming Daily*, quoted in *Kayhan International*, Jan. 30, 1972, p. 2).

DATA ON THE FAMILY SIZE-AGRICULTURAL WORK RELATIONSHIP

Now we proceed to data that bear directly on the relationship of family size to agricultural work. By far the largest body of relevant data comes from pre-revolution Russian farm surveys dating back to the nineteenth

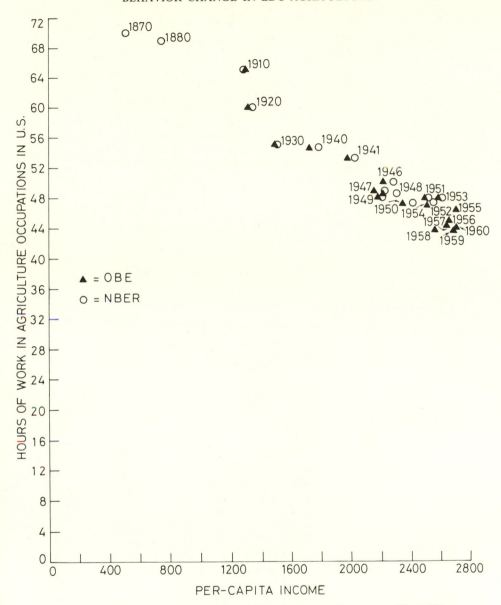

FIGURE 9–1   THE RELATIONSHIP OF PER-CAPITA INCOME TO LENGTH OF WORK WEEK IN
AGRICULTURE OCCUPATIONS IN THE UNITED STATES, 1870–1960

SOURCE: Work Week, De Grazia, 1962, Table 1; per-capita income, *Historical Statistics of the U.S.*

century, as presented and analyzed by Chayanov (1966). Though they
may seem to be old, there is no reason to believe that they are out-of-date
or unreliable. The survey methods used were far ahead of their time, and
seem to contain no glaring flaws that would invalidate them.

Chayanov first arrays the working days per year per worker on 25 farms in a single county, in which the range is from 78 to 216 days (1966, p. 77). Then he shows Table 9–3 in which the ratio of consumers to workers clearly is related strongly to the working days per worker. A graph of these four values suggests that the amount of labor supplied goes up even faster than the number of dependents. Of course, the scheme of measurement shown in Table 9–3 is inferior to a count of total hours worked *outside the house*, which would allow for the effect of dependents on women's work. Also it would be better to allow for the intensity of work at different men's and women's ages. But the relationship still might be of the sort shown in Table 9–3.

TABLE 9–3
EFFECT OF DEPENDENCY UPON LENGTH OF AGRICULTURAL WORK YEAR BEFORE THE RUSSIAN REVOLUTION

Consumers per worker	Worker's output (rubles)	Working days per worker
1.01–1.20	131.9	98.8
1.21–1.40	151.5	102.3
1.41–1.60	218.8	157.2
1.61–∞	283.4	161.3

SOURCE: Chayanov, 1966, p. 78.

We must inquire further, however, to see whether this relationship should be taken at face value. One possibility is that if a couple owns relatively much land they will (1) have relatively many children, *and* (2) spend a relatively high total number of days at work. This possibility would seem to be confirmed by Table 9–4 which is subclassified by land held and which shows a lower elasticity of output with respect to dependents than does Table 9–3 except for families holding more than 3.0

TABLE 9–4
THE RELATIONSHIP OF WORKER'S OUTPUT TO CONSUMER/WORKER (C/W) RATIO AND AMOUNT OF LAND HELD, RUSSIA

Arable per worker (desyatinas)	Worker's output (rubles)			Consumer's personal budget (rubles)		
	C/W ratio			C/W ratio		
	1.00–1.30	1.31–1.60	1.61–∞	1.00–1.30	1.31–1.60	1.61–∞
0.0–2.0	76.4	106.3	107.8	71.1	75.2	71.8
2.1–3.0	103.5	125.8	136.6	85.1	87.8	72.7
3.1–∞	105.1	128.6	175.8	86.3	85.9	88.7

SOURCE: Chayanov, 1966, p. 79.

desyatinas of land.[4] But Chayanov argues that this qualification is not very meaningful because the family *expands its land holdings by renting more land* as the consumer-worker ratio increases. This effect is indeed seen in Table 9–5. Chayanov also showed data on the considerable variation over 30 years in the amount of sown area on an individual farm, which he interpreted as confirming that "the connection between family size and size of agricultural activity should be understood as a dependence of area of land for use on family size rather than conversely" (1966, p. 68). In countries where families cannot so easily get more land, "the area of land for use [loses] its ability to be a *measure* of the volume of economic activity" (p. 69). But in that case, the family finds other means (e.g., fertilizer) to enable increased labor input to produce greater output. It is reasonable to accept that the relationship between number of children and amount of work is as shown by Chayanov.

TABLE 9–5
LAND RENTED (DESYATINAS) AND CONSUMER/WORKER (C/W)
RATIO, RUSSIA

Own arable per worker (desyatinas)	Land rented (desyatinas)		
	Consumers per worker		
	1.00–1.30	1.31–1.60	1.61–∞
0.1–2.0	0.50	0.73	1.19
2.1–3.0	0.08	0.56	0.50
3.1–∞	0.10	0.41	0.65
Average	0.23	0.57	0.79
Average consumer/ worker ratio	1.15	1.45	1.75

SOURCE: Chayanov, 1966, p. 111.

Table 9–4 is an important waystation in analyzing other Chayanov data which give output per worker but *not* the number of working days per worker. One may not interpret a positive relationship between the consumer/worker ratio and worker *output* as simply running causally from the former to the latter, because of the simultaneous effect of income on family size, as discussed in considerable length in Part II of this book.[5]

---

[4] The data for Tables 9–1 and 9–2 come from different places, hence they should not be expected to jibe arithmetically.

[5] Chayanov inquires into the effect of income on fertility. For lack of better data, he finds that the proportion of total family size represented by children 6 or under—who are clearly not producers—is *not* larger on large farms than on small farms (1966, p. 65). This test, however, has various flaws and is far from conclusive; and such studies as that of Stys (1957) for Polish farms (see Chapter 16) suggest that there is at least *some causal* relationship running from amount of land to fertility. Chayanov concedes that the relationship is likely to be stronger (1) where the farm family is closer to subsistence, and (2) where it is harder to obtain any additional land (1966, pp. 64–65).

191

Data on the relationship between workdays supplied and fertility therefore are particularly valuable, because they are less likely to be affected by a man's endowment of land and skill than is the relationship between income and fertility. If we assume that there is *no* relationship between workdays and land endowment, then the data on the workdays-dependency ratio can be used to adjust data on the worker output-dependency ratio so as to yield additional estimates of the relationship between workdays and dependency ratio. The rate of increase of output per worker with higher consumer/worker ratios is about twice as much as the rate of increase of workdays. Hence we may try to adjust other output-dependency ratios by such a factor. Table 9–5 shows output and estimated workerdays for four other counties ("uezd's").[6] I computed the elasticity of worker output with respect to the consumer-worker (c/w) ratio by using the data for the groups with the smallest and largest ratios (using a consumer-worker value of 1.8 for the open interval). Then I divided the results in half to make the adjustment discussed above. The results are .96, .28, .62, and .45 for the 4 counties. The midpoint between .62 and .45—say, .53—is the elasticity that I settled upon as an estimate of the increase in work per additional consumer in early twentieth-century Russian conditions. That is, an increase of 20% in the number of consumers may be expected to produce 10% more work.

TABLE 9–6

EFFECT OF CONSUMERS PER WORKER ON WORKER'S OUTPUT, RUSSIA

	Number of consumers per worker (C/W ratio), and worker's output in rubles				
Starobel'sk uezd, Khar'kov guberniya c/w ratio	1.00–1.15	1.16–1.30	1.31–1.45	1.46–1.60	1.61–∞
Worker's "output" (rubles)	68.1	99.0	118.3	128.9	156.4
Novgorod guberniya c/w ratio	1.00–1.25	1.26–1.50	1.51–∞		
Worker's "output" (rubles)	91.56	106.95	122.64		
Vologda uezd, Vologda guberniya c/w ratio	1.01–1.15	1.16–1.30	1.31–1.45	1.46–1.60	1.61–∞
Worker's "output" (rubles)	63.9	79.1	84.4	91.7	117.9
Vel'sk uezd, Volgoda guberniya c/w ratio	1.01–1.15	1.16–1.30	1.31–1.45	1.46–1.60	1.61–∞
Worker's "output" (rubles)	59.2	61.2	76.1	79.5	95.5

SOURCE: Chayanov, 1966, p. 78.

[6] Chayanov (1966, p. 77, fn) shows data for a Hamburg, Germany study in which output per worker rises much less with increases in the consumer-worker ratio than does the Russian data. But the German data may well be for urban workers; Chayanov does not say.

The increase in *work* caused by an increase in consumers must overstate the consequent increase in *output* because of diminishing returns to the partially fixed factor, land. Unfortunately, I could not find a way to squeeze from Chayanov's data an estimate of the relationship of output per worker to number of working days, holding farm size constant. But Paglin presents relevant data for Indian farms, shown in Figure 9–2. ("Input" is a satisfactory proxy for labor, because the proportion of labor to "input" is much the same on all sizes of farms in the Indian sample.) From his fitted curve $Y = -276.3 + 223.1 \log X$, where Y is output per acre in rupees and X is input per acre in rupees (including imputed wages), one may estimate that the elasticity of output with respect to labor input is about .6, which also would not seem unreasonable for countries where farms are bigger.

If we now combine the Chayanov and Paglin functions, we find that output per acre (in money) responds to additional consumer-weighted

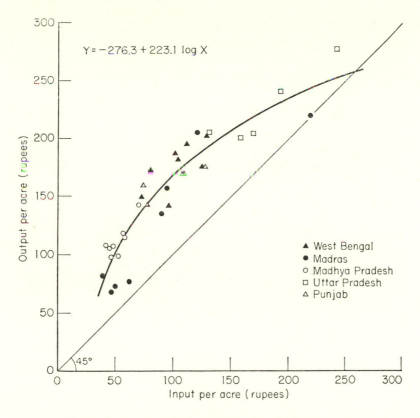

FIGURE 9–2   INPUT-OUTPUT FUNCTION IN INDIAN AGRICULTURE.
SOURCE: Reproduced from Paglin, 1965, p. 820.

193

dependents with an elasticity of $.6 \times .53 \approx .32$. That is, for each 10% increase in number of consumer-equivalent dependents, output is estimated to expand immediately by 3.2%. Of course, this estimate does not take into account the delayed effect on productivity of additional investment due to increased family size (see Chapter 10). The data used above are a peculiar mix with various possible defects. But the likely defects do not seem worrisome enough to completely invalidate the estimate.

Another (and much newer) piece of evidence comes from Yotopoulos' and Lau's careful estimate (1974) of the labor-supply function from Indian data. For our purposes, their regression held constant demand, prices, wage rates, debts, and so on, the elasticity of labor supply, and especially the number of workers in the household. After all the other factors are allowed for, the elasticity of labor supply with respect to the total number of household family members is a huge 1.12 when their entire model is estimated simultaneously. (The elasticity in a labor supply regression estimated by itself is .67.)

Perhaps the strongest evidence concerning the relationship of dependents to agricultural work per worker comes from Scully's careful study (1962) of 38 Irish farms.[7] He held constant the farm size, soil type, costs per acre, and density of livestock, and examined the effect of number of children[8] separately upon (1) gross output per acre (total money sales), and (2) family income per acre (gross output less costs other than family labor). The results are that an increase of one child (in the mean family with 4.8 children) leads to an increase in pounds sterling of $1.133/23.7 = 4.8\%$ in gross output per acre, and of $.996/15.2 = 6.5\%$ family income per acre. If one assumes that young children are on the average equal to half an adult consumer-equivalent—certainly on the high side—then a two-parent family with 5.8 rather than 4.8 children has 4.8 rather than 4.4 consumer-equivalents, an increase of $.5/4.4 = 11\%$. The relevant elasticity of work supplied with respect to number of consumers may be estimated as $\dfrac{.048}{.11} \simeq .4$ or $\dfrac{.065}{.11} \simeq .6$.

All things considered, the elasticities derived from the vastly different Chayanov data on Russia, the Yotopoulos-Lau data on India, and the Scully study of Ireland jibe quite well. This greatly increases confidence that we may have some reasonable idea of the response of extra work, and of the resulting effect on output, to an increase in the number of children—an elasticity of output of somewhere between .3 and 1.2. This

---

[7] I am grateful to Chester Baker for bringing this valuable study to my attention.

[8] On only 9 of the farms were there children of ages where they contributed any work at all to the farm, and hence the number of workers "has had little influence on the results of the analysis" (Scully, 1962, p. 121).

will be used in the model to estimate the effect on people's tastes for leisure versus output.

Increased Rural Investment

Farmers can increase production by working to improve their lands, as well as by working harder on their crops. Such land improvement, much of which is nonmonetized agricultural investment, is commonly omitted from macro-economic discussion, though it is very clear that such investment is crucial. The magnitude of the investment response in agriculture will be discussed separately in Chapter 11. And the over-all effect of increased labor on current-season work and in investment may be seen only in the context of an over-all model, as in Chapter 13.

Prevention of Subsequent Births in the Absence of
Production-Increasing Know-How

If in year *t* an accidental birth occurs, the family may respond by avoiding a birth in some year after *t* that they otherwise planned. (If the parents had planned to have *no* more children, this response would be impossible.) Aside from the slight advance in time, the sequence of events—one birth causing the absence of another—has no net economic effect. The subsequent child may be prevented by abstinence, contraception, abortion, or infanticide; from the point of view of economics, the method makes no difference.

This sequence of events *may* occur because the parents think their food supply is inelastic—that is, because they do not know of ways of increasing the production of food. This is the situation Malthus had in mind when he wrote about the "check of moral restraint." At the societal level, an increase in births may also trigger a group decision to reduce subsequent births, by custom, taboo, or law as has taken place in various societies such as the Tikopia (Firth, 1965; see Chapter 16 for more details).

Prevention of Births in Preference to Change in
Production Practices and Effort

In the preceding paragraph above it is assumed that people *do not know* ways to increase food production. But people may know ways to increase food production but recognize that such ways would require further work and/or a change from valued ways of life (e.g., settling down in one place rather than wandering from place to place).[9] They may therefore choose

---

[9] Mead reports that for many societies there is a "positive value which the traditional way of life holds for many of the people. Where this is paramount, change is either resisted or, if accepted, it is kept along the fringes. Changes which increase income, and are introduced in the interest of an improvement in living-standards, are rendered ineffective by this attitude" (1955, p. 185).

to prevent further births instead. Many hunting and gathering groups are said to fit this description.

Direct Rise in Death Rate in Absence of Production-Increasing Know-How

Another possibility in a subsistence society is that the birth of an extra child means one more child death than otherwise because of lack of knowledge of how to increase production. In any society parents are likely to be able to make *some* adjustment in food production to respond to the increased size of family—by either finding a little more land or working a little harder to squeeze out a bit more crops using existing technology. But at some point, they may just run out of know-how to exploit. Know-how does not travel instantaneously; any teacher is too well aware of that. Diffusion studies at both the micro- and macro-level show that the passage of information and practice take time, sometimes agonizingly long. And the tens of millions of malnourished children (to the point of Kwashiorkor and death) in Africa shows that the spread of know-how and the concomitant processes does not always keep up with population growth in the short run. (In the long run the two quantities cannot diverge, but this does not imply that know-how necessarily increases. Population growth might be checked instead.)

A long-range perspective is important for understanding the mechanism of a rise in the death rate. An extra child is not likely to mean a compensatory death immediately. It may, however, result in a somewhat lower level of nutrition for all the family, thereby increasing somewhat the toll taken by endemic or epidemic disease. Furthermore, when a bad crop year comes famine may kill more people than otherwise, perhaps making up in full for the extra child. This is the reality of Malthus' "positive check."

> The great toll of life taken by the epidemics of the fourteenth and fifteenth centuries was a result of the marked growth of population which took place between 1150 and 1300 . . . . The steadily increasing overpopulation in the thirteenth century must have led to malnutrition or shortage of wholesome food. The high mortality from the Black Death and the other fourteenth-century epidemics can only be explained as the result of prolonged undernourishment" (Slicher van Bath, 1963, p. 89).

Rise in Death Rate in Preference to Changing Productive Practices and Effort

People *may* know of more productive methods and choose not to use them even when the alternative is more precarious living, closer to the

196

edge of nonsubsistence.[10] There is more than one possible reason for the refusal to change their behavior. People may not want to make changes in their traditional way of life; this view has been held by some anthropologists (e.g., Mead, 1954), but I think this explanation has been over-worked. Another possibility is that the people are willing to take bigger risks of a bad harvest and starvation rather than (1) work harder on a more diversified crop base, or (2) use more labor-intensive techniques to raise a bigger crop that would offer a larger margin of safety.[11]

How can one guess the relative importance in history of (1) the "positive" check of a death rise,[12] either in the absence or presence of production-increasing know-how, and (2) the check of "moral restraint"? Obviously the two forces interact; one of the reasons for practicing restraint is to avoid more death. Perhaps the best example of the death-rise check operating straightforwardly is the history of the Mayas (Gourou, 1966, p. 58). After population increased, the Mayas apparently farmed the

[10] The statistics on hunger and malnutrition are much quoted but little documented. M. Bennett investigated the topics. "Constantly one encounters maps and tabulations suggesting, when not explicitly stating, that the inhabitants of a great many countries of the world are hungry all the time. Lord John Boyd-Orr, writing in 1950, expressed the idea concisely: 'A lifetime of malnutrition and actual hunger is the lot of at least two-thirds of mankind.' . . .

"Lord Boyd-Orr served as the first Director of the FAO of the United Nations . . . . Today's widely current, heart-rending picture of world hunger seems in the main to have been outlined initially by the FAO and subsequently reproduced in many quarters. . . . One wonders. Can it really be true that for five years the Portuguese were 14 per cent short of calories required to maintain weight or physical activity, Brazilians 12 per cent short, Filipinos 14 per cent, Peruvians 27 per cent, Japanese 6 per cent, Tanganyikans 18 per cent, Indians 13 per cent, and so on? . . .

"I think not. There are too many probabilities of error in the reckonings and in the interpretations as well. Who really knows of Brazil that per capita consumption there in 1934–38 was really 2,150 calories as against 2,450 required, when the FAO itself had once (in 1949) estimated the consumption as 2,552 calories? Who observed and statistically documented a large fraction of the Mexican population then behaving lethargically as so many Germans did during the turnip year 1916/17, or losing heavily in body weight? Who observed and documented this in India or Portugal or Tanganyika or Venezuela or any of the other countries? . . . Above all, who can say that the FAO's new basis of calculating caloric 'requirements' of a population really takes account of entirely normal national variations in degree of physical activity? . . . Even in thinking of Oriental countries, I do not find it possible to believe that on the one hand there could have been, as seems the fact, a rising degree of urbanization and wider and wider resort to fully polished rice, and on the other hand trend decline in per capita ingestion of total food calories; for that would mean, other things equal, a population choosing to throw away digestible food and growing hungrier year by year" (1954, pp. 189, 197, 245).

Though Bennett's evaluation was written more than two decades ago, it is apparently still descriptive and accurate, see Poleman (1975).

[11] I know that I am being vague when I talk about "they" and "the people," leaving unclear whether I am referring to individual or social decisions—the latter being what Mairas calls "social strategies," (1973, pp. 66–83). Later I will be more precise about this.

[12] Ohlin's discussion (1970) of this matter is interesting. His central point is that "demographic history must shade into the general history of economic development" (p. 8).

land harder but in the same old way, shortening the fallow period. This led to exhaustion of the soil, falling yields, and eventually depopulation. The death rate must have been high at some periods during Mayan history. Petersen says, "The normal death rate of the great civilizations of Asia . . . may be said to contain a constant famine factor" (1969, p. 387).

The history of Europe is more ambiguous. It is hard to know whether the death rate would have been lower if the birth rate had been lower. Clearly there were famines and pestilence that substantially reduced population during certain periods:

> As late as the middle of the nineteenth century, European populations were subject to frequent famines. Lack of transportation made each small locality dependent upon its own harvest, and a crop failure resulted in famine even though within relatively short distances the harvests were normal. In western Europe alone, 450 more or less localized famines were recorded from 1000 to 1855. During the eighteenth century, France, the richest country on the Continent, suffered repeated periods of severe scarcity. At least nine severe harvest failures were recorded in the Scandinavian countries between 1740 and 1800, each resulting in a substantial rise of the death rate. In Norway, the death rate in 1741 was more than three times as high as in 1736–1740; about one person out of fifteen in the whole population perished in that year. The main cause was the acute crop failure which visited all the northern European countries in 1740–1742. In Sweden, during the severe famine of 1773, the death rate rose to 52.5 per thousand population . . . in years with poor harvests the crude death rate in these countries was about 2 points above the average, whereas in years of good harvests it was some 2 points below the average" (United Nations, 1953, p. 51).

And Ohlin concludes that "some direct and much indirect evidence confirms the view that there was a significant rise [in mortality] in the seventeenth century 'following the major surge' in population in Western Europe in the sixteenth century" (1970, p. 7).

On the other hand, one view has it that ". . . in Europe—ancient, medieval, or modern—actual famines have been relatively less frequent and less severe than in Asia . . . on the scale of world history, Europe's food shortages have always been relatively puny" (Petersen, 1969, p. 387).[13] But compare: "To what extent there was a chronic insufficiency of food is not clear. Ogburn is of the opinion that between famines the

[13] Others have estimated, however that Asia's food situation was generally better than Europe's until the seventeenth century or later. For a general discussion see United Nations (1973, pp. 143–44).

population may have been fairly well fed. On the other hand, it is entirely possible that some groups were always exposed to chronic insufficiency of food" (United Nations, 1953, p. 51). So the relative severity of famines and pestilences might have been just as great if the populations had been somewhat smaller.

Another possible form of death response is war. ". . . In 1851 the world's greatest civil war, the Taiping Rebellion, broke out. It lasted fourteen years and affected nearly all provinces of China Proper, but most of all the densely populated central and lower Yangtze regions. Although the factors contributing to the rebellion were many, there can be little doubt that the pressure of population was one of the most basic" (Ho, Ping-Ti, 1959, p. 274). Such a Malthusian judgment is most difficult to support or refute, of course.

Famine does *not* prove, however, that more births cause more deaths, or that there is "overpopulation." A famine can occur in a society that has plenty of land and that plants a crop which, given even a minimally good yield, will be more than sufficient to provide for all its needs, as was the case in Europe as described above. Even today lack of transportation facilities is the main obstacle to over-coming famine, as in Bangladesh after the India-Pakistan war, and as in the Sahel.[14]

A scoeity will grow enough food so that a normal harvest will just satisfy demand plus a bit more, perhaps. There will never be a large surplus: that would just be a waste, because of lack of storage.[15] Data detailing the decline in famines may be found in Chapter 5, pages 95–97.

A Shift to Crops with Different Nutritional Values

In some situations an increase in population may lead to a family or societal choice between calorie scarcity and decreased nutritional value

[14] "The food itself was not a problem—in fact, almost 600,000 tons were pledged by various donors (in particular, the United States and the European Economic Community) by January of this year. But the food is useless unless it can be shipped to northern areas where the hungry people are.

Roads are few in the Sahel. When they exist, they are simple dirt tracks that are covered by drifting sand in the dry season and washed away by the rains. On the average, a Land-Rover can cover 100 miles a day. The normal life of a truck, in these conditions, with few servicing facilities, is about 1,000 hours. There are also four old and frail railroads that go from the ports on the coast up to the southern part of the marginal zone" (*New York Times Magazine*, June 9, 1974, p. 42).

[15] "In 1930 every man and grown boy in the village [Chan Kom in Mexico], except one, planted and harvested corn. In 1931 the amount of land planted diminished by almost one-third, and five men did not make milpa at all. This was because the price of corn fell after the harvest of 1930;[1] therefore the people did not sell their surplus corn, and so reduced the amount of planting for the following year. Four of the men who did not plant at all lived on their accumulated stores of maize" (Redfield and Rojas, 1934, p. 52).

"[The] modern Maya, devoting 190 days a year to the production of maize from a 10-acre plot, produces twice as much maize as is required by a family of five and has 175 days available for other activities (Digby, 1949, p. 16)."

199

in the diet. People may opt for the shift to crops with more calories but lower nutritional values. Slicher van Bath argues that a shift over several generations from protein to starchy products induced prolonged malnutrition that opened the door to the Black Death and other epidemics of the fourteenth century (1963, p. 84). And the Tikopia faced this choice very explicitly, both as families and as a society: "At present coco-nut provides the Tikopia with their principal supply of vegetable oils and vegetable proteins; to increase by a large amount their consumption of carbohydrate might quite likely have deleterious effects" (Firth, 1965, p. 50). This shift to poorer foods has indeed been the response to population growth in many places.

The spread of manioc (cassava) must be viewed with some disquiet, for the cassava flour is particularly poor in proteins, as indeed it is in fat and in mineral matter as well. When cassava is substituted for a cereal or for yams or taro, the greater richness of these foods in protein, fat and minerals is lost; famines may have been avoided, but deficiency diseases multiply rapidly. However, the progress of cassava has also some advantages. The plant will grow on any soil, and accommodates itself to any tropical rainfall regine; the yield is enormous in favourable conditions and quite large even in poor conditions. Cassava requires less labour than cereals, yams or taro; its leaves are a useful vegetable, and the plant can be left in the ground, thus dispensing with the labour of building grain stores. It is easy to understand why cassava, which was introduced into Africa in the sixteenth century, has so appealed to the Africans (Gourou, 1966, pp. 80–81).

The result may be Kwashiorkor or other nutrition-deficiency diseases.

Migration

The "extra" child may leave the place where he was born and migrate to another area or to the city. The likelihood that he will do so depends heavily on such factors as the prevailing inheritance system (e.g., older son gets all), whether he is from a landless family, and the opportunities elsewhere.

Migration caused by population increase may be a grim prospect, as Handlin (1951) described it in Europe in the nineteenth century. But the long-run results may be positive (e.g., the development of the United States). This response is at the boundary of the peasant agricultural sector that this chapter focuses on. The more modernized is the society, the more relevant is this response.

New Invention

A longer-run possibility is that extra children will eventually cause more inventions than otherwise because of the greater "need," which, in turn, may force people to work harder and to *invent new ways to reduce work*. (In paradise no one would have an incentive to invent anything.)

Factors That Influence Choice of Response to Increased Fertility

The goal of this chapter has been to forecast the effect *on a given subsistence-agricultural society* that will result from an incremental child— or more narrowly to assess the likelihood that *a change in productive practices* will result from the growth in population. There are many possible responses, and therefore we must now briefly consider some of the factors that influence the probabilities of various responses, and especially the factors that bear upon the likelihood of a shift to new productive practices.

In one respect, the decision to change one's productive behavior is an aspect of the diffusion of innovations. But in this situation the existence of the new technology is assumed to be known, and the new element is population pressure; in the usual case of diffusion, the new element in the situation is the introduction of the knowledge to the group. Another distinction between this inquiry and the literature on diffusion of innovations is that most of the innovation literature has focused on differences in adoption speed *among individuals within a given group*, and hence most of the explanatory variables are individual characteristics. The focus here is on differences *between groups*, because the between-group variation is greater than the within-group variation (e.g., almost everyone in a given Japanese village will use the Japanese method of rice transplantation, whereas in a given Indian village almost no one will). This is not to say that individual characteristics do not matter—they do (e.g., *some* individual must have the characteristics to be the first to do something. But we wish to inquire why in some groups that first individual will begin and other individuals will follow him, whereas in other groups nothing happens. The analysis is in this respect similar to the study of the quantity of entrepreneurship, an individual matter which occurs in qualitatively different amounts in some groups than in others. There is also, however, an important difference between the subject under present discussion, and the study of entrepreneurship: Choice of agricultural techniques is ultimately a group matter; most of the members of a group will come to

201

act similarly in agriculture. In contrast, the entrepreneur acts exceptionally. Therefore we must be interested in the *proportions* of the group that think and act in one way or another (e.g., the proportion that have indifference curves tipped strongly toward work rather than leisure, instead of the opposite).

Also in contrast to the standard diffusion literature—as Griliches (1959) argued against his critics from that tradition—the decision may be a purely rational calculation of family benefits and family costs, including the cost of foregoing leisure for work. Of course the framework of values and tastes within which the farmer decides is influenced by his particular society and particular personality. But these particular factors may not weigh very heavily relative to more universal tastes and values, including the way tastes and values shift as a result of an increase in family size.

At this time, we cannot do better than classify the relevant factors that influence a shift in farming practices. We are not in a position to state whether any particular combination of factors would cause the shift to take place or not. This suggests that one should go to a purely empirical approach of predicting future adoption on the basis of the past record of adoption. Such an empirical approach may be helpful in some situation, but it will not work in all cases. Hence, study of the underlying factors may be worthwhile, and may provide a basis for prediction if one has sufficient knowledge of a given situation.

A List of Factors Affecting a Shift in Farming
Practices as a Result of an Increase in Births

A. Economic factors (c.f., Schultz, 1964, esp. p. 28; 1965, Chapter III):
   1. Differences in labor and physical inputs between the new process and the old; differences in output per units of inputs.
   2. Farmer's present income.
   3. Capital required for the new process. (This may not be crucial in many cases.) Wealth and liquidity of farm families; this strongly affects attitude toward risk (related to average size of farm).
   4. Perceived riskiness of new process.
   5. Land-tenure system.
   6. Existence of off-farm work opportunities.
B. Knowledge factors.
   1. How well-known the new process is (e.g., how much first-hand and second-hand experience the farmer has with it).
   2. Availability of extension services in providing more knowledge.

C. Personal, psychological, and social factors.
   1. Valuation of leisure.
   2. Physical health.
   3. General attitude toward change.
   4. Past record of success and failure in innovation.
   5. Education.
   6. Customs, taboos, political and social institutions.
   7. The congeries of "personality variables" (see Rogers and Stanfield, 1968, pp. 241–42).
   8. Last, but perhaps first in importance, are people's aspirations (see p. 187 above).

Summary

People *may* change the amount or type of work that they do in response to the increased "need" caused by additional children. A quantitative estimate of the elasticity of current-season agriculture work with respect to additional children was presented in this chapter. The response in agricultural investment will be discussed in Chapter 11. The general topic needs much more quantitative research, but at least some guidelines for a numerical model have been suggested.

Case Study of the Sensitivity
of Agricultural Productive Behavior
to Increase in Farm Population
in Village India

INTRODUCTION

HOW FAST will agriculturalists respond to an increase in population? With what speed will they add land and improve it, and how quickly will they increase their yearly labor input? At present the basis for a general estimation of this set of parameters is somewhere between flimsy and non-existent. One thing is sure however: The relevant parameters must differ from situation to situation. Schumpeter noted: "Sometimes an increase in population actually has no other effect than that predicted by classical theory—a fall in per-capita real income; but at other times, it may have an energizing effect that induces new developments with the result that per capita real income rises" (1947, p. 149). There is variation because the human spirit is a crucial element in the process under discussion, as is the social will;[1] both are variables in a fundamental sense. The human spirit is capable of incredible variability in response, and the consequent variation has enormous effect on the world.

The review of history in Chapter 8 shows that even if population growth is a necessary condition for agricultural change in subsistence-agriculture sectors, it is not a sufficient condition. That is, the speed of adjustment of agricultural labor input and of work methods with respect to increases in population often has not been rapid "enough." Too often population has grown by an increment, and then there was a disaster which returned the group to original size or even smaller. Primitive tribes offer many examples; so does Europe during the Dark and Middle Ages, the Black Death period being one of the most dramatic examples. But in other times and places the results were happier. The implication is that particular cases must be examined individually, and further evidence is necessary

[1] How else besides the human spirit and the social will does one explain a small group of enthusiasts in a town of 30,000 people (Northbrook, Illinois) producing large numbers of Olympic ice skaters and medal winners, culminating in 1972 in one of its girls winning gold and silver medals, and another winning gold and bronze medals? (*Champaign-Urbana Courier*, February 13, 1972, p. 17.) How can one doubt that the unused capacity for achievement is everywhere enormous, and that under some conditions people will mobilize themselves to exploit this capacity to remarkable effect?

204

to help us decide whether in a given place at a given time the positive effect of a population increment upon agricultural production behavior will be fast enough to offset its negative effects.

A numerical model such as Chapter 13 requires numerical parameter estimates, however. And if one knows something about a specific situation, the estimates for the particular situation should be somewhat better than general estimates. Therefore, this appendix tries to get specific, with a specific guesstimate for a specific locale—village India.

The results of the work described in this appendix are thin and frustrating—for both writer and reader. On the basis of the flimsy data, I conclude that the propensity of the Indian peasant to respond with more work to the needs caused by population growth is probably less than elsewhere—but this propensity undoubtedly varies among Indian communities. The main aim of the exercise is not to suggest how the estimation might be done, but how difficult it is. A prudent reader without special interest in the matter may well omit reading this appendix.

Methods of Estimation

Just how does one make a reasonable forecast of the necessary sort? Boserup believes that history provides a sound basis for forecasts of the effect of 1975-type population growth. But clearly some of the relevant conditions differ from those in the past. For example, the modern reservoir of available technological knowledge such as new seeds and fertilizer, of which many LDC areas have yet to avail themselves, is larger than in the past. Of course such technology is not always quickly or cheaply adapted to new areas, but modern communications and research techniques can make such technological knowledge available to more people more quickly than in earlier years. Change, therefore, probably will occur faster in the future. Also consumer goods are relatively cheaper now than in previous decades and centuries, and farmers are more aware of them, which must have a powerful stimulating effect on farmers' behavior.

Less favorable to the contemporary case is the fast speed of population growth compared to that of earlier periods. The likelihood that production practices will change fast enough to feed the new mouths depends on how fast the population is growing. If the population grows 30% over 10 years rather than 30% over 500 years, it is harder to maintain the same standard of living, *ceteris paribus*. If the increment in population arrives gradually, the proportion of people in the labor force will remain much the same, and the method of production will not have to change as much to accommodate the increase in population. But if population grows 30% in 10 years, none of the children born during that period will work much during that period, and the method of production (and/or the amount of

205

work per person per year) will have to change very much to take up the slack. For this reason if for no other, the sort of historical evidence offered by Boserup (1965) is not completely relevant.

It is also clear that the speed of response may differ greatly even among apparently similar groups.[2] Contiguous villages in India sometimes differ greatly in their choice of occupation and life-style, as Nair (1962) has vividly shown.[3] Therefore a forecast for one place based on the results observed elsewhere is treacherous.

The only sound methodological strategy for situation-specific estimates is general wisdom—putting together and assessing a composite from whatever we may learn from history, anthropology, agricultural econometric studies, statistical surveys of the area in question, and—perhaps most important—first-hand interviews and observation of the area in question. The gravest danger is being blinded to facts by theoretical beliefs held before the facts are observed. The next gravest danger is believing the answer given by a man who practices only one profession— be he agronomist, historian, population biologist, economist, village,

---

[2] "Compare the differences in attitude toward irrigation of the peasants in Coimbatore in Madras, Raichur in Mysore, Kurnool in Andhra, Gaya in Bihar, Edna Kalaska in the Punjab and Kaira in Gujerat. Compare also the differences of the three communities of Pradhanatikara, Budelpali and Champaparda, all within the one district of Sambalpur in Orissa, in their response to the Kirakud irrigation project. These differences were not due to variations in administrative efficiency in distributing the water, or to differences in material resources or in the educational equipment of the peasants. They had much deeper roots in traditional beliefs and attitudes, such as those to work, to surplus production, and to diet. . . .

"It is not only in their attitude to manual work that the peasant communities differ. There are significant differences also in respect of other traits and aptitudes, such as thrift, industry, mobility and readiness to exploit economic opportunity . . ." (Nair, 1962, pp. 191–192).

[3] "In Ratnagiri is another interesting example of two communities living side by side for generations but not learning from each other. Here the Muslim fishermen of the Daldi community, for example, are far more prosperous than the local Hindu fishermen, because for one thing, Daldis have bigger boats and superior equipment by way of nets, hooks and line than the Hindus. The Hindus' boats are only one-man *tonies*, they fish mainly in the creek and use only hook and line with small hooks. Second, the Daldis also trade in fish, retail and wholesale. Thirdly, the Daldis alone salt the fish. The Hindu fishermen on the other hand, do not salt or cure the fish, with the result that whatever they catch they must sell fresh, the same day. What they are unable to sell in the local market by sundown, they dispose of at any price, or just throw the fish in the gutter. But they will not salt it because it is not the custom or tradition with them to do so. Daldis, in fact, buy wholesale from the Hindu fishermen at low prices, and then salt the fish and sell it far into the hinterland at a handsome profit. Yet the Hindu and Muslim villages are side by side.

"The difference in incomes between the Daldis and Hindus is reflected clearly in the appearance of their villages. Mikriwada, a Daldi village, for example, has many *pucca* houses, tiled roofs, furniture inside. Their women are well-dressed and wear a certain amount of gold jewelry. The children also are properly clothed and most of them are attending school.

"In the village of Mirya, on the other hand, where all fishermen are Hindus of Bhandari community, the huts are small, with mud walls and thatched roofs. The people are poorly dressed, and the children are naked, under-fed, and thin and pale. The whole atmosphere is one of depression and severe poverty" (Nair, 1962, p. 162).

worker, administrator—when he tells you what will happen to agricultural production as a result of population growth.

CASE STUDY OF VILLAGE INDIA

Village India has been chosen for attention because India is important, and because more is known about India than about many other countries. (The exhaustive review of the facts and literature by Myrdal in *Asian Drama*, 1968, is particularly helpful.) A study of a society such as China whose likely response to population growth is different from India's would be a valuable and dramatic comparison. But statistical facts about China are lacking, most of our information being impressionistic. We do know, however, that China has gone from a famine-ridden under-nourished country in the 1930's to an adequately fed country today even though its population has "exploded." China much more than doubled grain production from 108 million tons in 1949 to 250 million tons in 1973 (*Newsweek*, October 14, 1974, p. 20), impressing all the Western agricultural experts including those whose ideology would have suggested Communist failure. And most of this increase in production is due to more hard, disciplined work using traditionally known farming methods. The head of the team of American agricultural experts who visited China in 1974, Wortman, said: "[China] is one country in the world that I am going to worry less about whether it will be fed. . . . They have cut off the rhetoric and they have gone to work" (*ibid*, p. 65).

It must be emphasized that this case study of India does not attempt to *forecast* the future of Indian agriculture. Rather, the point of the discussion is to ask how the course of events would be affected by a higher or lower birth rate.

Let us consider a representative Indian farmer—either a land-owner or a tenant farmer—in the years immediately following the birth of an "additional" child. We want to know if, given the present social-political-economic system, the additional child will cause the farmer to work harder and perhaps also change to a technology new to him. (Merely putting in more hours with the old technology (e.g., doing more weeding) will not maintain his standard of living indefinitely.) There are four questions here: (1) Will the farmer's willingness to trade leisure for more output increase in such a manner that he will work more than otherwise?[4] (2) Is there other technology available that will yield additional output with additional work? (3) Does the farmer know about this technology? (4) Will his evaluation of risk and the costs of change make the new technology attractive?

---

[4] More formally, will his indifference curves shift? The work represented in the leisure-output indifference curves is here intended to include both current-crop season work *and* work on improving the farm.

A Hypothetical Survey Method

In principle, one could get answers to the above questions by asking a sample of Indian farmers what they would do if they had one more child than they now have. This has not been done. Nor would it be easy to elicit meaningful answers to such a question. Therefore, we must proceed to less direct methods.

Historical Evidence

India's population was "virtually stationary" during the 2,000 years prior to 1600 at perhaps 100 million people, about the same as Europe's population at that time. If anything, it "declined rather than increased" over that period. Sustained population growth began in India about 1600, but growth was slow until perhaps the middle of the nineteenth century, when much more rapid population growth began. After 1600 and well into the twentieth century, Europe's population, however, grew much more rapidly after 1600 than did India's. (K. Davis, 1951, pp. 24–25).

Despite the increase in population after 1600, "crops and ways of growing them were very much the same in Akbar's time (1556–1605) as they still are today over wide sections of India. . . . Agricultural implements and techniques did not change significantly between Akbar's time and the early twentieth century" (B. Moore, 1966, pp. 330–331). Agricultural methods continued the same despite population pressure; even in good times people were not really well fed, and when the rains were poor, massive famines occurred (*ibid.*, pp. 330–331, 407–408).

India's agricultural techniques failed to change *despite* the fact that more productive (per unit of land) techniques were known. For example, "The advantages of transplanting rice were known, at least in some areas, in the early part of the nineteenth century and very likely earlier" (*ibid.*, p. 331). But the Indian farmers either did not adopt the more intensive techniques, or practiced them badly: "[O]n the banks of the Ganges it was common practice . . . to sow large quantities of seed broadcast on dry earth without previous preparation of the soil . . . . Throughout Buchanan's reports [for the years 1809–10] there runs the same theme of inefficient cultivation and low productivity that occurs in the earlier French accounts of the situation under the Moguls" (*ibid.*, p. 332).[5] And ". . . cultivation remained poor over wide areas of the country after land had become scarce" (*ibid.*, p. 333). This is quite at variance with the European experience, where techniques changed rapidly during the last four centuries.

---

[5] There have been reports of situations where the broadcast method produces *higher* output with less labor than does seed insertion, though I do not understand why it should be so.

As to output: As of the end of World War II and shortly thereafter

... [s]ince the 1890's total output of all crops has risen, but unimpressively; total output of food crops has fallen off; and per capita output of both food crops and all crops has declined impressively. The trend in agricultural output over the last sixty years may be characterized as stagnation. ... As of 1953, however, we remain without reliable or comparable national income estimates for any phase of India's economic development. ... In default of precise data, recent writers on Indian economic development have put forward two different opinions. Some hold that ... per capita income has been rising; others, that it has not been rising. There is a third logical possibility, that per capita income has been *declining*. Until knowledge of India's economy and its evolution comes to rest on a more solid foundation, it would seem premature to rule out this third possibility (Thorner and Thorner, 1962, pp. 102, 105, 122).

Sometime after World War II, production of food per-consumer equivalent began to increase. According to Bhatia (1967, p. 341) the daily supplies of calories per capita rose from 1,700 in 1948–49 to 2,040 in 1961–62 (the latter including imports, however). The rise is now accelerating, a rate of growth of output in the Punjab of 4.5% per year for 1951–64 (1.8% per year of productivity gain) versus 1.1% (0.6%) per year for 1907–1946 (Herdt, 1970, p. 519); the corresponding figures for India as a whole are between 2.50% and 2.75% from 1952–53 to 1964–65, versus 0.11% from 1907–46 (Herdt, correspondence, November 29, 1972). For the period 1951–1971 total production of food grains rose 86% and per capita production rose 16% (Revelle, 1974, p. 170).

Another measure of economic welfare is the trend of famines. Bhatia tells us that there was an "alarming increase in the frequency of visitations of these calamities in this country [India] over a span of 49 years, from 1860 to 1908" (1967, p. v).[6] But in recent years there have been no famines of the old sort, partly because of food imports from the United States but more because of changes in transportation and other conditions in India.

All in all, Indian history since 1600 does not seem basically different from Chinese history until the Communist regime took over, though population is much less dense in India than in China. For purposes here, the high points of the Indian history are these:

Until recently, output responded to population growth slowly and without vigor. Even with the relatively low rates of population growth in the past two millennia, output per head has not yet (or has just now)

---

[6] It should be noted that Bhatia (1967) attributes the increase in famine not only to the increase in population but to changes in wages, terms of trade, taxes, and other commercial variables.

caught up with what it was a long time ago. During the past several hundred years, the rate of agricultural response in India has certainly been slower than in Europe, though perhaps no slower than in China, and in the first half of the twentieth century it was much slower than in Japan. The rate of response of output almost surely was sufficiently sluggish so that the death rate was higher than it might have been with a higher rate of response. And without doubt, increases in population did not spark a process of *more*-than-proportional response, i.e., economic development.[7]

The historical evidence is not a sufficient basis for a forecast of present-day Indian response to population growth because (1) population is now growing at a faster rate than in the past; (2) village India is now in closer touch with the rest of the world; (3) it now has a larger reservoir of technological possibilities; (4) transportation and communications have improved; (5) and other countries have demonstrated the possibility of economic development; this demonstration has led parts of India to aspire to economic development, also; (6) knowledge and availability of consumer goods are another new force working in villages; (7) India is now politically independent; (8) there are other possible stimuli for economic growth than population growth, and the increase in total productivity may have begun *despite* population growth rather than *because* of it. Thus, one cannot simply extrapolate the past relationship of population and output growth to India's future.

Evidence from Double-Cropping

According to Boserup's (1965) formulation of the population-push hypothesis, Indian farmers should resort to double cropping if they choose to increase output. Of course, double cropping is easiest where there is a community irrigation scheme; the individual farmer cannot himself create a whole regional water-control system in response to new incentives affecting him, nor may even a village be able to do so. But in many places in India farmers can irrigate their fields from their own open wells. So double-cropping may be possible even without community irrigation projects. Furthermore, there are parts of India where—apparently for reasons of personal preference—irrigation water is not used by the farmers even though it is available and even free (Nair, 1962, pp. 46–49).

---

[7] The development of the exciting new wheat and rice varieties by the Rockefeller teams and others in the middle of the twentieth century are, however, proof positive that the *fear* of population increase *can* spur invention. That is, the seed inventions themselves may be seen as a response to population increase. The *adoption* of them by Indian farmers occurs both for the invention-pull reason of dominating the existing technology (see Chapter 8) *and* because of the greater demand for output both in the market and for subsistence in the farm sector.

As of the mid-1950's, there was not very much more double-cropping on the smallest Indian farms than on the biggest farms (Paglin, 1965, p. 818).[8] This suggests that greater availability of labor and greater "need" for food are not likely to increase double-cropping very quickly.[9] But India began to increase the quantity of irrigated land rather rapidly at the beginning of the 1950's—from 44 million to 55 million acres from 1949–50 to 1960–61 (out of total areas of 245 million and 279 million acres; Lele and Mellor, 1964, p. 20).[10]

Present-Day Density of Population and the Potential for Expansion

The amount of *good* farm land per person is much greater in India than in China or Japan. In India in the mid-50's there were 240 people per 100 hectares of *cultivated* land, compared to 560 in China and 1,620 in Japan (Myrdal, 1968, pp. 426 427). The density of population relative to cultivated land is about the same in India as it is in Europe (Myrdal, 1968, p. 416). This indicates plenty of potential for expansion of output using well-tried technology.

Indian villages that are closer to cities have (1) larger populations and (2) more modern agricultural techniques (especially irrigation systems and the use of chemical fertilizers) than villages further away (Adelman and Dalton, 1971). This implies that there is indeed the possibility of change in response to *some* stimuli, though the relevant element in this particular comparison is probably accessibility to agricultural and consumer-goods markets, rather than population increase.

These are some of the ways in which additional labor can increase output: (1) more care and attention to such routine farm chores as weeding; (2) irrigation work, and subsequent double-cropping; and (3) new technology, such as the new seed varieties.[11] There is also vast scope for

---

[8] But at least one close statistical observer of the Indian agricultural scene says that "the intensity of irrigation is higher on small farms and [I] believe that double cropping is more prevalent as well" (Herdt, correspondence, November 29, 1972).

[9] Buck's data for China are consistent with the finding for India that size of farm is not strongly related to extent of double-cropping (1937, p. 274). The extent of double-cropping did increase substantially from the 1930's to 1957, but Perkins (1969, pp. 45–46) attributes this to central-government pressure in the 1950's to overcome "innate conservatism or the lack of demand from outside for surplus rice [that] had inhibited [double-cropping's] development in the past" (p. 46). He observes that the increase in double-cropping was not caused by increased population density; rather, the rate of population increase in the areas where double-cropping increased most either had low or no population increase during the period.

[10] I am grateful to Robert W. Herdt for this and related references.

[11] "The new . . . practices required by the Green Revolution require a lot of additional labor. They call for careful seedbed preparation. They require the application of fertilizer selectively and well.

"They take exhaustive weeding or the weeds will soak up the fertilizer. They require the careful application of pesticides. In some instances, double, triple, and even quadruple cropping will take place.

"All of this demands increased use of labour . . ." (Freeman, 1969, pp. 27–28).

labor-intensive cooperative efforts such as village access roads. But voluntary cooperative efforts are apparently rare among Indian villagers (though probably not as rare as among Sicilians; see Banfield, 1958). For example, in village after village one sees not one common well with a rim around it, though this simple device can reduce the intestinal diseases that so afflict Indians. There is a vast *potential* for improvement with increased labor and cooperation.

The Institutional Framework of Incentives to Work in Village India

How does the existing social framework affect the quantity of work and output in Indian villages as compared to other possible institutional frameworks? Does the existing framework make for resistance to change? For these questions to make sense, it must first be shown that the marginal product of additional labor is not zero. The argument seems to have been settled decisively in favor of there being positive marginal returns to additional labor in India and elsewhere; see e.g., Lau and Yotopoulos (1971) and Myrdal (1968, pp. 1007–1113; pp. 2041–61; and, esp. pp. 2050–54). With respect to India, the most conclusive evidence of the possible increase in output with additional labor input is the relatively low yield per acre compared to other countries, despite the excellent natural fertility of India.

Moore believes that it is "institutional factors that may explain India's low productivity . . ." (1966, p. 398). "The organization of labor in the Indian peasant community . . . helps to explain the relatively low level of civilization . . . and to have inhibited both changes in the division of labor and its intensive application to a specific task" (pp. 333–334). Referring to the famine[12] of 1943 he says: ". . . fundamentally, the famine was a product of the structure of Indian society" (p. 407). And Myrdal concludes as follows:

> . . . The institutional mold in which agriculture has been cast is highly inimical to improvements in productivity based on a fuller utilization of labor. The tenancy system—particularly in its sharecropping aspect—is doubly iniquitous. Not only does it tend to give command over the agricultural "surplus" to a group of landowners who, for the most part, are not disposed to provide resources that might increase the productivity of the land, but it also erodes the initiative of those who actually perform farm work (1968, p. 1092).

The main practices to which Myrdal and Moore refer are the rental system by which the land-owner gets a proportion of the crop rather than

---

[12] Herdt wrote me, however, that "Most students believe that [the 1943 famine] was . . . atypical for the 20th century" (November 29, 1972).

a flat rent,[13] the lack of clear ownership of the land by those who cultivate it, the fragmentation of land-holdings, and the caste social value of not working with one's own hands.[14]

Various other subtle institutional arrangements can also affect production. For example, Epstein observed that though the farmers in Wangala village were enterprising in response to new opportunities in raising sugar cane, in rice production "not a single farmer has attempted to use the Japanese Method" (1962, p. 63) though the farmers understand its advantages. The explanation apparently lies in the institutionalized pay arrangements between farmers and the groups of women who do the transplanting and weeding. The women would not do the harder Japanese-method work at the old rate of pay, and farmers "are bound by the customary rates of pay in the village and cannot offer higher pay even if they are prepared to do so" (1962, p. 64). Writers are not, however, unanimous on the *importance* of institutional factors in affecting production as this observation by T. W. Schultz (1964) shows: ". . . a basis for distinguishing between traditional and other types of agriculture . . . is *not* to be found in the differences in particular institutional arrangements, for example, in whether farms are under resident or absentee ownership, whether they are small or large, whether they are private or public enterprises, and whether the production is for home consumption or for sale" (1964, p. 29, italics added).

Indian institutional factors may in the future change in such ways as to allow or cause increased productivity. Moore believes that the market has begun to penetrate Indian society in such a manner as to open the door for change. And Epstein showed in great detail how, under the pressure of irrigation coming into the area of India she studied, ". . . some aspects of social structure changed while others remained the same, and . . . some aspects of culture changed while others persisted" (1962, p. 312). For example, some hereditary relationships between castes broke up or changed. Some joint family ties broke up, the father-son relationship was altered, and wives became less obedient. Some values about the economic aspects of life changed. But the labor role of women did not change.

[13] Cheung (1968) has recently adduced theoretical reasons, however, why the share-cropping system is not uneconomic in the large.

[14] The difference between Indian and American values on the status of manual labor may be illuminated by the following example: My wife called a local employment agency for a woman to clean our house. The woman who first called and then came to work was a qualified teacher and the wife of a full professor at our university. She was earning extra money for a European trip. When I told the story to the Indian research assistant who works with me, he refused to believe that this had happened. Of course, the event was *unusual*. But it did and could happen in America, though not in India.

Individual Tastes for Work, Leisure, and Consumption

In any culture, and within any institutional framework, an individual has some discretion about how to divide his time between work and leisure. His tastes may have been formed by his culture, but they come to have some "functional autonomy" in Allport's term (i.e., the tastes come to have some independent existence of their own). These tastes affect productivity, and the likely effect of more children upon work and productivity depends upon these tastes (and also by the possibility of their change).

Myrdal sifted the relevant evidence and concluded that Indians work much less than do other peoples in similar circumstances, for example, the Thais (1968, pp. 1085–1087). Fewer members of the Indian farm family work, the work year has fewer days in it, the working day is shorter, and hours of work are relatively unstrenuous. Gandhi and Nehru stressed those facts. Nair vividly describes the point of view of Indian farmers, and concludes: "After talking to the peasants all over the country . . . I came to the conclusion that the problem of material resources is only one of several factors that must be taken into consideration and to which any programme designed to raise farm yields must be adjusted. And it is not always the most important. A community's attitude to work can be a more decisive determinant for raising productivity in Indian agriculture than material resources, or for that matter even technology. What is more, this attitude to work, as we have seen, differs widely between regions and communities" (1962, p. 190).

But qualified observers are not unanimous on the issue. T. W. Schultz refers particularly to India: "It does not follow that people who belong to a class or caste which does farm work have a penchant for being idle. It could be that the preferences and motives for working are essentially the same for a wide array of agricultural communities. If so, traditional agriculture is not a consequence of particular farm people having preferences of loafers but what appears to be loafing is a consequence of the low marginal productivity of labor" (1964, p. 27). But "low" marginal productivity of labor is not defined by Schultz, and what is low to an Indian may not be low to a Japanese or Chinese; Japanese farmers are apparently willing to do work for an extra pound of rice that Indian farmers will not do (Paglin, 1965, p. 825). This implies that the reservation price of leisure is higher in India than in Japan—even though income per worker is lower in India than in Japan. (The higher *market* price of rice in Japan is not relevant if we assume subsistence has higher priority than market goods.) Furthermore, Nair (1962) shows that what is too low in one Indian village is not low enough to keep a neighboring village from working. Hence, I do not think Schultz argues convincingly that the Indian's particular tastes for work and leisure do not matter.

It seems to me that much of the argument denying different propensities to work in various places—especially the position of Schultz—stems from the attempt to ram the peasant farmer's economic decision-making into the model of the money-profit-maximizing firm. Chayanov's classic book (1925/1966) should have destroyed this approach once and for all, substituting instead the broader (and therefore less powerful) framework of leisure-output utility-maximization, as outlined in Chapter 8.

After a close anthropological-economic study of two neighboring Indian villages, Epstein concluded: "[E]vents which occurred in Wangala and Dalena during the past 25 years [demonstrate] that villagers were not slow to react to new economic opportunities. In fact they were no slower than farmers the whole world over . . . Both Wangala and Dalena villagers accommodated themselves relatively quickly to the new economic environment created by irrigation in the area" (1962, p. 311). (But Epstein goes beyond her data when she says Indian villagers react as fast as villagers in other countries.)

CONCLUSION

The first conclusion of this appendix is that estimating the additional work that farmers will do in response to population growth is exceedingly difficult. As to the particular case examined here of the Indian farmer's propensity to work in response to increases in population? I judge that the average Indian—given his health and cultural background—will respond somewhat less quickly to population growth than will farmers in most other countries. I also judge that there is important variation among communities in India in this propensity. All told, it seems to me at present the indifference curves of the trade-offs between income and leisure are different in India than in other places, yielding a *ceteris paribus* "solution" with more leisure and less output for any size population. In the longer run, however, there may be major changes in the psychological and social structure of the Indian village which would lead to a different conclusion.[15]

---

[15] More generally, I think it is safe to say that the effect of population growth upon India as a whole in the medium and long run surely will depend upon the extent of structural change in India—how much alteration there is in the social and economic arrangements. The importance of such social change in economic history is clear to economic historians such as Kuznets, Hicks, and Clark; to Marxists such as Dandekar and Boserup; and to such eclectic observers as Myrdal. It is also clear to sociologists. Only economic allocation theorists do not see the problem this way, because economic theory has no categories for structural change.

CHAPTER 10

The Effect of Additional
Children on Nonfarm Physical and
Human Capital in LDC's

INTRODUCTION

CHAPTER 7 sketched the general LDC model, and Chapter 9 investigated the effect of additional children upon current-season agricultural work as an input to the simulation model run in Chapter 13. Now we come to saving.

Population growth affects the amount that people save and invest, and the way that the society invests these resources. Even if savings and investment were not influenced by the population growth rate, and the total amount of productive capital were therefore the same as otherwise, there would be less capital *per worker* because there are more workers with a high population growth rate. The capital dilution would then affect the output and income per worker. Therefore, estimating the size of the over-all effect of population growth on physical and human capital per worker in LDC's for use as input to the LDC simulation model is the task of this and the following two chapters.

The division of the discussion in Chapters 10–12 is not neat. Some of the subtopics are structurally intertwined with each other, and the data and previous studies do not follow an ideal division. Ideally, one would like to know the total values of investments in such categories as (1) agriculture, (2) industry, (3) housing and school facilities, and (4) social infrastructure that may be expected in conjunction with different rates of fertility or population growth. But neither the raw data nor the results of most of the important relevant studies correspond to these quantities. First, the national statistics do not include nonmonetized investment, which can be a very important part of agricultural and infrastructure investment in LDC's. Second, the data used in cross-sectional studies of these matters are proportions of national output. This implicitly suggests that *total* output would be the same with various population growth rates, which need not be the case. Third, the available data and studies often aggregate all categories of investment (though with the omissions and defects indicated above), and one cannot determine what are the effects of population growth on the different categories, although the effects may be quite different.

216

The materials will be presented as follows. This chapter presents studies which refer mostly to aggregate monetized physical and human investment. This usually includes most public and private industrial and urban investment, as well as part of agricultural and infrastructure investment. The literature on the subject is relatively well developed, and hence, this chapter is mostly a summary of prior studies. The following chapter discusses the effect on rural investment, a large part of which is nonmonetized and hence not included in the aggregate studies in this chapter. Chapter 12 discusses the effect on social infrastructure capital, some of which is covered by this chapter.

Empirical Partial Estimates and Calculations of the Effect of Fertility on Saving and Investment

Cross-national comparisons are one source of empirical information about the effect of increased fertility on saving. The main empirical estimate is that of Leff (1969). Across a sample of aggregate data for 47 under-developed countries, holding constant per-capita income and its rate of growth, Leff found an elasticity of -1.3 for per-capita saving with respect to the child-dependency ratio (-1.2 for savings as a proportion of national income), which transforms to elasticities of about $-.56$ and $-.51$ with respect to population growth rates (for the method, see Chapter 11, fn 19). Saving in Leff's study includes *all* the outlays that governments report as "gross domestic investment," which means that "demographic investment" in housing and public facilities used by the additional population are included.

Leff's regression method implies that the difference in dependency *causes* a difference in saving. But it is not unlikely that some third factor might influence both savings and fertility, and hence account for the association between the two. Such a factor might be a relatively short time-period in people's reckonings, or high uncertainty about important future events, or lack of work and investment opportunities, or a whole institutional, social, psychological complex usually called "traditionalism." McClelland's (1961) "need for achievement" variable, which is apparently related to economic development over time and across nations, may be a variable of this sort. But without direct evidence with respect to savings and fertility, perhaps the best course in constructing a quantitative model of LDC population growth is to note the possibility of specification error in Leff's estimates, and to try a range of values that includes his estimate.

Another kind of cross-national information comes from Thirlwall's

217

cross-section study of (only) nine LDC's. Thirlwall's regression yielded $\frac{\Delta K}{K} = 6.005 + .449\left(\frac{\Delta POP}{POP}\right)$, where total population is Thirlwall's proxy for changes in the labor force (but in this context it may also be thought of as a proxy for changes in the nonlabor force dependents). Thirlwall concludes from this regression that "There is no support for the view that population growth and the rate of capital accumulation are inversely related in less developed countries" (1971, p. 16). But such a regression, even in the context of the other regressions. Thirlwall ran with capital, labor and total productivity, is extraordinarily hard to interpret, especially with respect to the effect of dependents on saving. An increase in population this year clearly stems arithmetically from births this year. But the birth rate this year is highly correlated with the birth rate in earlier years and hence to growth in the labor force this year. So the positive increase in capital this year as a function of the increase in the population increase this year could be consistent with a positive effect of an increase in the labor force *and* a *negative* but smaller effect of the increase in the number of dependents.

Because his regression did not include some variables relevant to the question under discussion, and because of the smallness of the sample, Thirlwall's result should not be given much weight in this context, but it does at least call Leff's result into question.

Intracountry household budget surveys are another basis for estimating the effect of population growth on savings rates. Kelley (1971) studied the relationship of the savings rate to family size among a sample of workers in the United States in 1889. The context was much more akin to the LDC world today than to the MDC world today.[1] He found that the savings rate (savings ÷ income) of households with two children was higher than households with *less* than two children, and much higher than households with *more* than two children, as may be seen in Table 10–1.

For Taiwanese families that have been married ten years or more, D. Freedman (1972) found that—holding income and education constant—smaller families were more likely to have accumulated some savings since marriage. The percentages were 48%, 41%, 40%, and 31% for families size 0–2, 3, 4, and 5+ respectively.

---

[1] Mean *family* income in current dollars was $603—assuming a family of, say, 5 or 6— which meant that their income was well below the 1887–1891 per-capita U.S. income at that time. The latter was 1/9 of real per-capita income in 1967. (United States, Department of Commerce, *Historical Statistics of the U.S.*, 1960, p. 139). This means that the average family income of Kelley's sample was much less than 10% of average family income in the United States today.

TABLE 10–1

EFFECT OF FAMILY SIZE ON SAVINGS RATES OF
U.S. WORKER FAMILIES IN 1889 (RENTERS OF HOMES)

| | Number of children | | | | | | |
	0	1	2	3	4	5	6+
Calculating with mean income of sample							
Savings rates (S/Y) in %	7.91	7.91	11.73	6.94	3.11	1.65	2.65
Index	100	100	148	90	39	21	33
Calculating with mean income of families with no children							
Savings rates (S/Y) in %	4.46	4.46	8.28	3.68	−.34	−1.80	−.80
Index	100	100	186	82	−8	−40	−18

SOURCE: Kelley, 1971, p. 39.

Taken together, the Leff (1969), Freedman (1972), and Kelley (1971) results suggest that in families that already have some children, additional children reduce the *proportion* of savings to income. (Qualifications to this conclusion have been discussed in Chapter 3. Perhaps the most important qualification here is that the additional child may lead to more work and more output, which is consistent with a lower *proportion* saved but the same or higher *total* saving.)

Dynamic Simulations of the Effect on Capital

Now let us proceed to the over-all effects on capital per worker that are calculated from the Coale-Hoover (1958) and Enke *et al.* (1970) models. (The light these models throw on capital formation is their primary usefulness, I believe. A criticism of their more general implications will be offered shortly, on page 235.) The reader who is acquainted with this literature may skip without loss to page 223, where begins discussion of how these capital-effects simulation models may be used in the general LDC model.

The starting point for any LDC model must be the appropriate demographic structure—or more precisely, the several mortality structures for various fertility assumptions. That is, it is necessary to know how many deaths will take place at each age for each cohort in order to estimate the number of people of each age that will be available for work at each year in the future. It is reasonable to think that the mortality schedules in LDC's should depend upon earlier fertility rates, especially in the long run. This is unfortunately not the case in the models that will be described here, but the omission may not be too serious. A more serious omission from these models may be the absence of an allowance for the different states of health, and hence for differences in ability and desire to work hard, under different birth-rate schedules.

The explorations of Coale and Hoover were mostly confined to 2 patterns of birth rates in India: a continued high level of births somewhere between 43.2 and 40.0 per 1,000; and a 50% linear decline in birth rate from 43.2 to 23.4 per 1,000, over a 25 year period 1956–81 (1958, p. 38). This pattern of gradual decline is more realistic than assuming that one birth rate would suddenly be 50% of the other starting at time $t = 0$, because birth rates fall only slowly. But the gradual decline is not neat analytically, and makes it harder for us to derive general analytic conclusions. Hence I also undertook an experiment with the Coale-Hoover model assuming an immediate drop to 50% of the birth rate at time $t = 0$, and also another experiment with an immediate drop to 25% of the birth rate at $t = 0$.

The Enke et al. model worked with a "no decline" level of 44 births per 1,000 in the idealized country of "Developa," a "slow decline" regime which dropped from 44 to 36 in 30 years, and an "accelerated decline" regime which dropped from 44 to 26 in 30 years. The age-specific birth rates for the "high" and "low" fertility ends of the "accelerated decline" regime in Developa are illustrative of the inner workings of their fertility schedule in Table 10–2.

TABLE 10–2
BIRTH RATES FOR "DEVELOPA" (PER 1,000 FEMALES)

Age	Schedule 1 (high)	Schedule 2 (low)	Ratio of low to high
15–19	111	35	0.32
20–24	295	180	0.61
25–29	304	181	0.60
30–34	248	114	0.46
35–39	183	59	0.32
40–44	81	20	0.25
45–49	20	18	0.90

SOURCE: Enke et al., 1970, p. 36.

As to mortality, Coale and Hoover made an extensive study of the likely future mortality regimes in India (as viewed from the early 1950's) and constructed two alternative life tables—one at 200 and the other at 250 deaths per 1,000 live births as of the 1951 origin date. The Enke et al. model used standard U.N. (1963) and Coale-Demeny (1966) life tables.

220

Now for the economics of the models.[2] The starting point of the LDC capital-effect model is a production function that shows how output is related to the factors of production. Output is a function of labor and capital, indicated by Equation 10–1

$$Y_t = f_1(A_t, L_t, K_t). \qquad (10\text{–}1)$$

In most of their work, Coale and Hoover made output a function of only technology and capital, assuming that the labor force would be much the same no matter which fertility variant would occur, because in a period as short as their basic 30-year period—which was the main focus of their study—differences in births have little effect on labor force. That is, capital—modified by the expected trend of technological advance—was the only factor considered to affect total productivity. I have, however, added labor force by converting their model into the standard Cobb-Douglas form, and these results will later be presented along with the Coale-Hoover basic results. Enke *et al.* also use the standard Cobb-Douglas form.[3]

In LDC's it makes sense to think of the two main sectors of the economy separately. Coale and Hoover treated the economy as a whole, however, rather than breaking it into agricultural and industrial sectors, as also did Enke *et al.*

The amount of capital in existence at any one time, $t + 1$, is a function of the amount of capital at time t plus the *net* saving in period t, assuming all savings are invested. This identity may be written

$$K_{t+1} = K_t + S_t. \qquad (10\text{–}2)$$

The important question is what determines the amount of saving and investment. It is clear that absolute saving can be greater if the total product is larger. But just *how* saving depends upon the total product and on other factors in the economy, such as family size and level of living, is both very important in reality and in determining what happens in a model, as well as very difficult to determine empirically. In the Coale-Hoover model, the amount of investment is a negative function of per-capita income as well as a positive function of total income. That is, investment is not a constant proportion of the output, in their model; investment depends on output but also depends upon the number of

---

[2] A complete description of the Coale and Hoover (1958) model and its inputs requires their entire book, though the model itself is described mostly in their Chapter 17 and is summarized algebraically on page 282.

[3] Other functions, such as the CES function used by Kelley et al. (1972), may be more appropriate for failure work in this area.

people among whom the output is divided (Equation 10–3). Their formula was

$$K_t - K_{t-1} = C_t \left[\frac{(K_t - K_{t-1})}{C_0} + a \left(\frac{Y_t}{C_t} - \frac{Y_0}{C_0} \right) \right], \qquad (10\text{–}3)$$

where $(K_t - K_{t-1})$ = total investment, and magnitudes with zero subscripts indicate the base value. The coefficient a was set equal to .30 in most Coale-Hoover runs (.25 and .35 in some runs). At the 20-year point in the Coale-Hoover model, for example, this means that 9% fewer consumer-equivalents in their "low" fertility version caused 11.4% higher total investment,[4] an elasticity of -1.3 which is of the same order of Leff's empirical estimate.

Enke *et al.* also assumed an investment function dependent on GNP and the number of adult consumers. Their equation (1970, pp. 26, 52) is

$$(K_t - K_{t-1}) = Y_t - .80\,Y_t - \$30\,C_t. \qquad (10\text{–}4)$$

At the $200 per-capita starting-point of the Enke *et al.* model, this formula translates into a 3% drop in investment for a 1% increase in nonproductive consumer equivalents, considerably higher than Leff's estimate or the Coale-Hoover assumption.[5]

Another important issue concerning the capital effects of population change is how much of savings will go into various *kinds* of investment. A crucial distinction is between investment to bring up children, and investment in physical capital that will produce goods in the short-run. Coale and Hoover elaborated the important matter of public saving and the extent to which public expenditures are allocated to existing or new population. First, they distinguished between "welfare-type" public expenditures and "direct-growth-type" public expenditures. The former include public expenditures on housing, education, and other social services, and the latter on public investment—roads, factories, and so forth—that promote production reasonably quickly. In their model, the direct-growth public investments plus private investment add to the total direct-growth investment in the society. Then they distinguished between the welfare-type outlays needed for the *existing* population, and those outlays necessary for the *additions* to the population. In their view, "10 times as much [public expenditure on welfare needs] is required to make initial provision for an added person as is thereafter required

---

[4] Calculated from their example, 1958, p. 271.

[5] It should be noted that the concepts used by Coale-Hoover and Enke et al. are net investment, though the data used by Leff and Thirlwall are for gross investment. Physical depreciation is an important factor because the rate is different in different sorts of capital (industrial, agricultural, infra-structure), and it is independent of the birth rate. Hence it would be best to deal with separate gross-investment and physical-depreciation magnitudes.

each year for [public expenditures on welfare needs by] one person" (1958, p. 266). By drawing large amounts of public expenditures into welfare needs, additional people therefore have a strong negative effect on public direct-growth investment in their model. Given that publicly controlled saving was estimated by them to be almost a third of total (monetized) saving in India (1958, p. 156), the effect of additional people on total direct-growth investment is obviously substantial in their model. By the end of their 30-year period, at which time the low-fertility regime finally reaches low fertility, direct-developmental expenditures are 14.7% of national income for the low-fertility projection as compared to 10.4% for the high-fertility projection. (The former represents an even larger total investment relative to the latter, because total national income in the Coale-Hoover model is higher for the low-fertility projection than for the high fertility projection.) In elasticity terms, the effect on "direct-growth-type" investments, net of all "demographic investments," is as follows: The 9% fewer consumer-equivalents result in a 22.5% higher "direct-growth-type" investment, an elasticity of -2.5. For a country which fits the Coale-Hoover structural assumptions, the above estimates can be used to estimate the effect of additional population by way of public investment. This estimate should not be much affected by the omission of a labor term from their production function.

The Effect through Capital on Output Per Worker

The previous sections of this chapter have discussed the effect of population growth upon investment and capital. But capital and investment are ultimately of interest only insofar as capital affects output.

It is the central point of this set of chapters that basing one's thinking upon physical capital alone—or even physical capital plus human capital in the labor force—is a serious error in thinking of LDC economic development. Therefore, I am quite unsure about whether it is useful or detrimental to present the Coale-Hoover and Enke *et al.* results concerning the effects of population growth upon output. There are two reasons for doing so: (1) As short-run models, the results can be illuminating, though this may lead to a wrong conclusion about the long run; and (2) The results may throw light on the *partial* effect on output of capital alone—though it may be that such a separation from noncapital effects is misleading. In any case, this tradition has historical importance in economic demography, and hence presentation of their results seems appropriate.

One must immediately face the question about which measure to use. Clearly *output per consumer* is not relevant, because an addition of a child immediately makes a difference in that measure even though there

223

is no change in the economy as a *productive* system—and it is indeed as a productive system that one ought to view the economy when discussing economic development. Nor is the change in *total output* very meaningful. India's total output is higher than Norway's, but by common agreement Norway is far more developed than is India. The best measure, it seems to me, is *output per worker*. To assess output per worker, a production function including both labor and capital is necessary. I have therefore expanded the Coale-Hoover structure a bit to include a Cobb-Douglas function[6] with $\alpha = .5$ and $\beta = .5$.[7] We may also inspect the Enke *et al.* model in this connection. To repeat a warning, the capital-effect estimates generated by these models are not the appropriate *overall* capital-effect inputs to the more general model, because the more general model must also embody nonmonetized investment and other capital effects left out of the Coale-Hoover and Enke *et al.* models. On the other hand, the Coale-Hoover examination of monetized capital effects is probably more detailed than one would build into a more general model.

The Enke *et al.* results are seen in Table 10–3. Over 30 years, output per worker in the labor force would rise $\left(\dfrac{991 - 553}{553}\right) = 79\%$ for the continued-high-fertility regime (column 1), whereas it would rise 96% for the declining-fertility regime (column 3). The assumptions underlying these estimates include the assumption that some workers are unemployed. If one computes the output per *employed* worker—assuming that there really would be no measurable unemployment, or at least no changes in it over time—the rises in output per employed worker for the

---

[6] Coale and Hoover made a supplementary study of a longer-run model using a Cobb-Douglas function (1958, Chapter 22), but their analysis only began at the end of the first 30-year period. Few results were given. Hence, it seemed wiser to start from the beginning of the period with this line of thinking.

[7] The new production-function equation was

$$Y_{t+2.5} = Y_t + \left(\frac{2.5\text{GRO}}{\text{COR}}\right)^{.5} [a(L_{t+2.5} - L_t)]^{.5}$$

where

$$a = \frac{(2.5G/\text{COR})_{t=0}}{(L_{t+2.5} - L_t)_{t=0}}, \text{ a factor to adjust the model at the starting point}$$

GRO = Coale and Hoover's "equivalent growth outlays"
COR = roughly the capital-output ratio. See the Coale-Hoover definition
      on their page 283.

It should be noted that this formula may not be used in any year in which the labor-force declines in size.

224

TABLE 10–3
OUTPUT PER POTENTIAL WORKER AND
PER EMPLOYED WORKER IN "DEVELOPA"

Year	Continued high fertility model		Declining fertility model	
	Output per potential worker (1)	Output per employed worker (2)	Output per potential worker (3)	Output per employed worker (4)
1970	553	651	553	651
1975	589	695	590	695
1980	643	744	646	744
1985	711	803	719	805
1990	791	877	814	889
1995	884	969	933	999
2000	991	1081	1078	1140

SOURCE: Enke *et al.*, 1970, pp. 83 and 93.

two fertility regimes (columns 2 and 4) would be 66% and 75% respectively. The ratio of the advantage of the declining-fertility regime over the continued-high-fertility regime is 1078/991 ($= 1.09/1$) for the computation that includes the effect of unemployment. Assuming no unemployment, the ratio is 1140/1081 ($= 1.05/1$).

For the Coale-Hoover model[8] the results are as seen in the "continuing high" and "declining" fertility columns (1) and (2) of Table 10–4. Over a 30-year period, the rise in per-worker output for the declining-fertility regime is $\left(\dfrac{1.25 - .70}{.70}\right) = 79\%$, and for the continued-high-fertility regime it is 40%. The advantage of the declining-fertility regime over the continued-high-fertility regime is 1.25/.98 ($= 1.28/1$). Though the absolute income and output rise is somewhat faster in the Enke *et al.* model than in the Coale-Hoover model, due to the quite different models and parameters, the relative advantage of the declining-fertility variant after 30 years is not very different in the two models.

The difference in output per worker between the high and low fertility models may be thought of as the gap that would have to be made up by factors omitted from the Coale-Hoover and Enke *et al.* models, or by higher saving with high fertility, if population growth were not to have deleterious effects on economic development.

These are some additional results that I derived from modifications of the Coale-Hoover model (for which Enke *et al.* did not publish comparable estimates):

[8] The results come from their model expanded with a Cobb-Douglas function with $\alpha = .5$ and $\beta = .5$, but for the first thirty-year period the results are similar to their model without labor as a factor of production.

225

1. The original Coale-Hoover model[9] was run with additional fertility variants, and extending the results for a total of 55 years. The results are shown in columns 3–5 of Table 10–4. A fertility regime in which fertility was immediately halved in the first period—unrealistic but interesting analytically—shows a much greater per-worker advantage over the continued-high-fertility regime than does the Coale-Hoover declining-fertility regime. In the first 30 years, the rise in per-worker output for the immediate-halving regime is 203%, an advantage over the high-fertility regime of 2.12/.98 (= 2.16/1). By the end of the 55-year period, the advantage of the immediate-halving regime over the continued-high-fertility regime is a ridiculous 8.8/.94 (= 9.36/1). For fertility regimes in which fertility immediately falls to a *quarter* of the original high fertility, and to *zero births*, respectively, the advantages after 55 years are even more ridiculous—respectively, 21.8/.94 (= 23.2/1) and 117/.94 (= 124/1).

It is quite clear that these results for a 55-year period are silly, most especially for immediate quartering of the birth rate, and for zero births. This *argumentum ad absurdum* shows that the apparently most-desirable result apparently would occur in a situation where there is *no one at all* under 55 years of age, and hence practically no one to produce the society's output for the very large number of elderly dependents. Of course this calculation does an injustice to the Coale-Hoover model, because one should not ask a model to perform beyond the situation it was designed to model. But this exercise does emphasize that the results of Coale and Hoover stem mainly from the arithmetic fact of reducing the denominator in the output/worker (or output/consumer-equivalent) ratio, rather than from changes in the economic structure.

2. If one does *not* assume with Coale and Hoover that saving will be a function of per-capita income in addition to being a function of total income, but instead assumes that saving is a function of total income alone—which many observers regard as more plausible—the negative effect of population growth upon capital is smaller. That is, the advantage in output per worker of the declining-fertility regime over the continued-high-fertility regime is less with a proportional saving function than where saving is made a function of per-capita income, as may be seen in Table 10–5. When one simply compares the 30-year results for the two, the difference seems small: an advantage of 1.52/1.29 (= 1.18/1) for the declining-low-fertility variant with the proportional saving function (from columns 3 and 4) rather than 1.24/.98 (= 1.26/1) with the Coale-Hoover saving function (columns 1 and 2). But the difference in the saving

[9] The high-fertility and low-(declining)-fertility results differ slightly from Coale and Hoover's because of various computer approximations.

TABLE 10-4
TOTAL OUTPUT AND OUTPUT PER WORKER IN THE ORIGINAL
COALE-HOOVER MODEL WITH TIME AND DEMOGRAPHIC EXTENSIONS

Year	Continuing high fertility: Total output ÷ labor force = output per worker (Y/L) (1)	Declining to low fertility Y ÷ L = Y/L (2)	Immediate halving of fertility Y ÷ L = Y/L (3)	Immediate quartering of fertility Y ÷ L = Y/L (4)	Zero fertility Y ÷ L = Y/L (5)
1956	108/154 = .70	108/154 = .70	108/154 = .70	108/154 = .70	108/154 = .70
1961	127/167 = .76	128/167 = .77	130/167 = .78	132/167 = .79	134/167 = .80
1966	150/183 = .82	151/183 = .82	160/183 = .875	165/183 = .90	171/183 = .94
1971	177/203 = .87	181/203 = .89	200/186 = 1.08	213/177 = 1.2	228/168 = 1.36
1976	208/228 = .91	218/226 = .96	254/190 = 1.34	279/171 = 1.63	309/152 = 2.02
1981	243/256 = .95	266/247 = 1.08	326/195 = 1.68	370/165 = 2.25	422/135 = 3.14
1986	283/288 = .98	330/265 = 1.25	423/199 = 2.12	495/154 = 3.20	579/117 = 4.95
1991	327/326 = 1.0	414/281 = 1.46	554/201 = 2.75	666/145 = 4.60	794/101 = 7.9
1996	372/407 = .92	523/293 = 1.78	729/203 = 3.60	895/140 = 6.40	1085/85 = 12.8
2001	414/420 = .98	665/305 = 2.18	961/198 = 4.86	1200/125 = 9.6	1477/66 = 22.3
2006	471/482 = .98	850/314 = 2.70	1271/195 = 6.5	1614/111 = 14.5	2001/45 = 44.5
2011	519/552 = .94	1093/322 = 3.38	1676/191 = 8.8	2158/99 = 21.8	2691/23 = 117.0

UNITS: Total output in billions of rupees.
Labor force in millions of men.
Output per worker in thousands of rupees per year.

NOTE: Upper left hand block shows range of original Coale-Hoover model.

TABLE 10–5

TOTAL OUTPUT AND OUTPUT PER WORKER IN THE ORIGINAL
COALE-HOOVER MODEL WITH DIFFERENT SAVINGS FUNCTIONS

| | S = f(Y, Y/C) (Coale-Hoover model) | | S = f(Y) | |
	Continuing high fertility $Y \div L = Y/L$	Declining to low fertility $Y \div L = Y/L$	Continuing high fertility $Y \div L = Y/L$	Declining to low fertility $Y \div L = Y/L$
	(1)	(2)	(3)	(4)
1956	108/154 = .70	108/154 = .70	108/154 = .70	108/154 = .70
1961	127/167 = .76	128/167 = .77	128/167 = .77	128/167 = .77
1966	150/183 = .82	151/183 = .82	155/183 = .85	155/183 = .85
1971	177/203 = .87	181/203 = .89	190/203 = .94	192/203 = .95
1976	208/228 = .92	218/226 = .96	236/228 = 1.04	242/226 = 1.07
1981	243/256 = .98	266/247 = 1.08	295/256 = 1.15	310/247 = 1.25
1986	283/288 = .98	330/265 = 1.24	371/288 = 1.29	402/265 = 1.52

UNITS: See Table 10–4.

function matters more when we look at growth rates. For the Coale-Hoover saving function the comparison is between $\left(\dfrac{.98 - .70}{.70}\right) = 40\%$ and $\left(\dfrac{1.24 - .70}{.70}\right) = 77\%$ for the two fertility structures, whereas with saving a function only of income the comparison is between

$$\left(\frac{1.29 - .70}{.70}\right) = 84\% \text{ and } \left(\frac{1.52 - .70}{.70}\right) = 113\%.$$

That is, the difference in fertility structure matters less with a proportional saving function than with the Coale-Hoover saving function. Therefore, the Coale-Hoover conclusions are weakened somewhat by this alteration in the savings function.

The appendix to this chapter contains a more general criticism of the Coale-Hoover model and others in its tradition, especially concerning the conclusions about per-capita income drawn from such models.

In ending this section, it must be emphasized again that the estimates of the effect of fertility on capital pertain *only* to the monetized sector, and should therefore be applied mainly to the industrial sector in a two-sector model. The appropriate estimate might be that of Leff, plus a range of estimates above and below his central value.

228

THE IMPORTANCE OF INVESTMENT IN HUMAN CAPITAL:
KUZNETS' APPROACH

The Theoretical Importance of Investment in Education and Human Capital

Another sort of approach to monetized investment and population growth is that of Kuznets (1967). Unlike Coale and Hoover, he does not run a model with two or more rates of population growth as inputs to see what happens to the rate of growth of national income. Instead Kuznets starts by *hypothesizing* a rate of growth of national income, and he asks what amounts of investment are *necessary* to produce such a rate of income growth with various rates of population growth. A major advantage of this method is that it can be done easily with pencil and paper, because it does not ask about the *cumulative* effects of the population growth over long periods of time but rather about the amount of investment required in any given year to prevent any deficit in reaching the income-growth goal under given rates of population growth.

If one considers that only *physical* investments in machinery and construction are required, then Kuznets' reckoning may be seen in Table 10–6. The top two lines show the assumed rates of growth of population and per-capita product[10] for the four cases Kuznets considers. When

TABLE 10–6
EFFECTS OF RISE IN RATE OF POPULATION GROWTH ON
CAPITAL REQUIREMENTS AND PER-CAPITA CONSUMPTION

Case	(1)	(2)	(3)	(4)
1. Assumed rate of growth of population, % per year	1.0	3.0	1.0	3.0
2. Assumed rate of growth of per capita product, % per year	2.0	2.0	0.1	0.1
3. Rate of growth of total net product, % per year (from lines 1 and 2)	3.02	5.06	1.101	3.103
4. Net capital investment required as % of net product (Incremental net capital–output ratio, ICOR, assumed to be 3.0)	9.06	15.18	3.303	9.309
5. Government consumption as % of net product (assumed)	10.0	10.0	10.0	10.0
6. Private consumer expenditures as % of net product (100 minus lines 4 and 5)	80.94	74.82	86.70	80.69
7. Consumption per equivalent, consumer unit	60.54	50.85	64.83	54.82

SOURCE: Kuznets, 1967, p. 175.

[10] Again we find the use of per-capita rather than per-worker quantities. The usage may be less misleading when talking of growth rates as Kuznets does, however, rather than different income levels as in Coale and Hoover.

one looks at line 6, it appears that only a fairly *small* difference in consumer expenditure—the difference going into investment—would be required to attain any given level of income growth if population growth is higher (say, 3% yearly) rather than lower (say, 1%). The range of national product going into consumption is only from 75% to 87%. This is very tantalizing. It seems as if only a tiny extra effort is required, only a reduction in consumption from say 81% to 75% at an economic growth rate of 2%, to accommodate a population rising at 3% instead of at 1% (see columns 1 and 2). It seems as if just a small turn on the lever can have a big effect. Or to put it another way, if one can only spend just a small fraction less out of consumption—say, 75% instead of 81%—one can apparently increase the rate of development from 0.1% to 2% yearly, even with a 3% rate of population growth (see columns 2 and 4).

But there is a basic fallacy in this model. As Kuznets then points out, *investment in physical capital is not enough.* To develop, a country must also invest in the *education and health* of its citizens, because health and education are necessary in order that the physical capital be used efficiently. (The importance of such investment in "human capital" is a lesson only relearned in the 1950's and 1960's after long years of neglect since Adam Smith emphasized its importance.) A larger population requires much larger expenditures to attain given levels of health and education. When one now considers this more comprehensive concept of investment, the difference in investment needed to attain a given level of income growth is no longer so small. This may be seen in Table 10–7, where data are shown for five values of the capital/output ratio (which Kuznets purposely does not specify as net or gross, 1967, p. 180). The concept of capital *includes* education, health, and related services, which makes the capital/output ratio much higher than one is accustomed to seeing. (The ratios over 10 are quite high even by this wider definition, however, and are given for analytic insights only.) Lines 5 and 6 in Table 10–7 show that for capital/output ratios of 5 (quite plausible) or above, the reduction in per-capita consumption required to "finance" population growth of 3% rather than 1% is now upward of 20%, and it is much higher with higher capital/output ratios.

That is, when education and health are included as part of the society's total capital, a *large* difference in per-capita consumption would be required to "make up" the difference between population growth rates of 3% and 1% if growth of per-capita product is to be the same in both cases. Much the same effect would be seen if one ran the Coale-Hoover model with and without the social welfare expenditures, which are an important part of their model as it stands.

TABLE 10–7

EFFECTS OF RISE IN RATE OF POPULATION GROWTH, OR OF GROWTH IN
PER-CAPITA PRODUCT ON PER-UNIT CONSUMPTION,
DIFFERENT VALUES OF CAPITAL-OUTPUT RATIO

Assumptions: (1) income per capita = 100; (2) government consumption
(excl. all implicit capital) = 5% of total product

Case	Values of incremental C/O ratio				
	2.5 (1)	5.0 (2)	10.0 (3)	15.0 (4)	20.0 (5)
Consumption per-equivalent consumer unit					
Growth of per-capita product = 2.0%					
1. Population growth = 1%	65.38	59.74	48.45	37.16	25.87
2. Population growth = 3%	55.97	47.37	30.17	12.98	−4.21
Growth of per-capita product = 0.1%					
3. Population growth = 1%	68.97	66.91	62.80	58.68	54.56
4. Population growth = 3%	59.29	54.02	43.47	32.93	22.39
% reduction in consumption per-consumer unit					
associated with rise in population rate of growth					
5. Growth in per-capita product = 2% (lines 1 and 2)	14.4	20.7	37.7	65.1	116.3
6. Growth in per-capita product = 0.1% (lines 3 and 4)	14.0	19.3	30.8	43.9	59.0

SOURCE: Kuznets, 1967, p. 180.

Most LDC societies cannot readily choose among levels of investment. Rather, LDC societies are pretty much stuck with the consequences
of a rate of population growth, given a *particular* rate of saving and investment. Saving and investment cannot easily be manipulated by a
society simply to "make up" for larger population growth. That is, the
rate of investment is really *not* a *decision variable* in this context, whereas
one can at least hope that the rate of population growth *is* a decision
variable and can be changed if a society (or the directors of a society)
should so decide. Kuznets' approach is of analytic interest, nevertheless.
It makes clear that if the capital effect of additional population is not to
be a drag upon economic development, considerable additional effort
would be required:

Obviously the high rates of population increase, and a rapid acceleration like that of the recent decade or two, resulting from continuing
high or even slightly rising birth rates and sharply declining death
rates, aggravate the already difficult problems of growth. Channeling
more resources into capital formation, broadly defined, is an additional
organizational task that would increase the burden of the already
overtaxed machinery of the existing economic, political and social
institutions in underdeveloped areas (Kuznets, 1967, p. 189).

231

On the other hand, Kuznets emphasizes that the capital effect is by no means the whole problem, and hence alleviation of the monetized-capital effect by population control or other means cannot approach a complete solution.

And yet, if the preceding discussion correctly describes the balance of factors with respect to the *aggregate* supply of goods per capita, a higher rate of population increase, although an *additional* problem, would probably not be as great an obstacle as the failure to exploit the potential due to delays in adjusting social and political institutions. . . . The core of the problem seems to lie in the inadequate internal social and political institutions, including some with a dominant economic content, which fail to provide the auspices for effective, sustained exploitation of the advantages of economic backwardness, and which are not easily modified. . . . The implications of this position for the evaluation of population policies should not be misunderstood. Unquestionably, strenuous efforts at reducing the birth rate in the underdeveloped countries are fully warranted, if they do not constitute a large drain upon economic and organizational resources that would otherwise be used advantageously to raise per capita product and indirectly induce a more rational long-term family planning process in a different and farther-going fashion. After all, even the partial reduction of additions to what is otherwise a heavy burden is all to the good. But other inferences may put policies aimed at direct population control within a better perspective and prevent placing undue hopes on their effects (Kuznets, 1967, p. 189).

The Effects of Population Growth upon the Quantity of Education and the Investment in Human Capital[11]

The previous section made clear the importance of investing in human capital, and the magnitude of the effort needed to provide any given level of education with higher rather than lower population growth. This section considers just how various levels of population growth really do affect the level of education in LDC's.

The theory of the effect of population growth upon investment in human capital—that is, investment in education—was discussed in Chapter 4, pages 76–79; the result is a theoretical stand-off. Therefore, an empirical investigation was made (Pilarski and Simon, 1975) of a sample of LDC nations, of the same nature as the MDC study described in Chapter 4.

---

[11] This section is part of a larger project done jointly with Adam Pilarski. I appreciate his permission to discuss the work here.

TABLE 10–8
THE EFFECT OF POPULATION INCREASE ON SCHOOLING IN LDC's

Dependent variable	Regressions using crude birth rate		Regressions using dependency rate		Number of countries
	Elasticity from logarithmic regression	Elasticity from linear regression	Elasticity from logarithmic regression	Elasticity from linear regression	
Primary school attendance	.27	.16	.16	.13	47
Secondary school attendance	−.40	−1.26	−.81*	−1.61	46
Tertiary school attendance	.09	−.43	−.33	−.33	43
Expenditure on schooling per child in dollars	−.08	−.36	.16	−.30	44

SOURCE: Pilarski and Simon, 1975.
NOTE: Table shows elasticities for schooling as the dependent variable in regressions with either the crude birth rate or the dependency burden as the independent variable along with per-capita income, median education, life expectancy, and socialist-non-socialist in a sample of LDC countries.
* Significant at 10% level.

The results may be seen in Table 10–8. In brief, higher birth rates and higher dependency burdens do not seem to have a statistically or economically significant negative effect upon the level of *primary* schooling. But there is a significant negative effect upon *secondary* schooling (also observed by Anker, 1974, in a sample of 76 countries with per capita incomes of less than $1000 in 1969). With respect to schooling expenditures per child, the elasticity is between 0 and −.36. Though this effect could be important, it is much less than the negative effect to be expected if the full Malthusian effect were taking place (which would be an elasticity of −1.0). Countries are apparently making up most of the expenditures needed to maintain a *ceteris paribus* schooling level (though where the funds are coming from is unknown and perhaps have important effects elsewhere in the economy).

Summary

The chapter first reviews several approaches to the estimation of the effect of the rate of population growth and the dependency burden upon the rate of saving in physical capital in LDC's. These approaches include empirical cross-sections of countries and of households within countries, and simulations and calculations of the likely effects of population growth on the capital stock given various sets of assumptions. The most plausible estimates would seem to be that for each per cent increase in dependency burden the rate of saving would decline by something less than 1%—perhaps as little as half a per cent or perhaps not at all. (In elasticity terms, a range from 0 to −1 seems plausible.)

The chapter then discusses the place of investment in human capital in economic development, and the effect of population growth upon such investments. When education expenditures are taken into account, the additional investment necessary to provide for higher rates of population growth is much larger than investment in physical capital alone, and requires much greater sacrifice of consumption if levels of investment and output per worker are not to fall. But the empirical results of a cross-section of LDC's suggests that countries do, in fact, find ways to "make up for" much of the effect of higher population growth upon investment in human capital. The level of primary education seems affected positively if at all by the rate of population growth, the proportion of students in secondary school is negatively affected, and the expenditure on schooling per child is negatively but not drastically affected.

An appendix critically reviews the Coale-Hoover model and results as not being relevant to the understanding of population growth's effect on economic development.

Criticism of the
Coale-Hoover Results[12]

THIS APPENDIX offers some criticism of the Coale-Hoover model and
its central result. (The criticism also applies to other work following in
the same tradition as Coale and Hoover: Enke *et al.*, 1970, Hoover and
Perlman, 1966, and Barlow, 1969. It should be understood, however,
that I judge the Coale-Hoover book to have been a major leap forward
in the understanding of the effects of population growth in LDC's—a
well-thought-out, excellently executed study, it has provoked other
important work. The fact that almost 20 years after publication this
reappraisal and criticism still seem appropriate is itself a tribute to
their work.

My central criticism of Coale and Hoover is that, even though the
title of their book is *Population Growth and Economic Development*, and
though most of the descriptive material in the book is very much about
economic development, the central empirical findings they offer—their
Table 37, which is reproduced here as Table 10–9 and which has been
so widely quoted—has practically nothing to do with economic development. One reason is that *income per consumer-equivalent* is not the rele-

TABLE 10–9

INCOME PER CONSUMER IN COALE AND HOOVER'S PROJECTION 1
(1956 = 100)

	1956	1961	1966	1971	1976	1981	1986
Continued high fertility	100	107	114	120	126	132	138
Declining to low fertility	100	108	117	128	143	165	195

SOURCE: Coale and Hoover, 1958, p. 272.

[12] Myrdal (1968, Appendix 7), gives a more technical and wide-ranging criticism (though
also acknowledging the authors' "pioneering effort"). He argues that the apparent stability
of their main conclusion across various alterations in assumed conditions is an artifact
resulting from (1) a too narrow range of conditions investigated and (2) their practice of
varying only one variable at a time. He also says that "it would be more plausible to make
savings depend on total income than on both total income and income per head" which
would "greatly reduce the superiority of the [Coale-Hoover] low-fertility projection over
the high-fertility one" (1968, pp. 2073, 2074). In general he feels that "Their conclusions do
not add to our knowledge since they are contained in the questionable simplifications of
their premises" (p. 2075).

235

vant measure of economic development. It is *output per worker* that tells the state of a country's economic development. Another reason why Table 10–9 is not relevant to economic development is that the projected differences in income per consumer over 30 years are not due to differences in the *productive* economy under the various fertility regimes. Rather, they stem almost completely from differences in the numbers of pre-labor-force-age persons added to the society, as the authors themselves note: "The inauspicious showing of the high-fertility case in terms of improvement in levels of living is traceable entirely to the accelerated growth in the number of consumers that high fertility produces" (Coale and Hoover, 1958, p. 275).

The results could not be otherwise in a period as short as 30 years, which is why Coale and Hoover omit labor from their production function. But this also means that the effect obtained by the addition of more consumers has nothing to do with *economic development*, which is a concept related to *production*. The Coale-Hoover estimates do give an answer about the *distributive* effect of adding more consumers, and surely a society wants to know the distributive effect when it is considering population policies. But the complexity and detail of the Coale-Hoover model was not necessary to make this point. Malthus stated it quite clearly in a few sentences: An increase in population "increases the number of people before the means of subsistence are increased. The food therefore which before supported eleven millions, must now be divided among eleven millions and a half. The poor consequently must live much worse, and many of them be reduced to severe distress" (1803, p. 12).

Malthus' simple point is the heart of the main numerical results given by Coale and Hoover and quoted everywhere. Perhaps if those estimates had not been preceded by a long book full of sound and valuable information on India, and if the estimates had not emanated from a simulation model which seems economic in content, the estimates might not have been interpreted as a statement about economic development. But they were and are so interpreted, which is obfuscating rather than enlightening.

Coale and Hoover were well aware of the criticisms raised here. And in their longer-run 55-year analysis they added the labor force into the production function. That part of their work comes closer to the substance of economic development. But even the results of that section are reported on an income-per-consumer basis rather than an output-per-worker basis (though in the long run the two measures approach each other).

It might be suggested that Coale-Hoover-type models may be reasonably satisfactory for an assessment of the *very short-run effects of a short-*

run variation in population size, perhaps over 20 years. If an LDC government wishes to assess the effects over the next 20 years of a one-time increment (or decrement) of population, Coale-Hoover-type models might offer satisfactory answers. But seldom will it be appropriate to ask so narrow a question. Rather, a government generally wants to know about the effect on the entire development process, of which the first 20-year period is only the introduction. And it is quite likely that population increase has effects on productive behavior *other than through changes in capital*, which will first begin to show up more than 20 or 30 years later.

As discussed in Chapters 8–13, there also are long-run demographic effects: A country cannot choose that its population during a single year, or during a single 20-year period, will be one size or another, *ceteris paribus*. Rather, higher population now implies a bigger population 50 years from now. Therefore, it will seldom be meaningful to view a model in the isolation of a short period. And the long run is obviously *not* simply a series of short-run models strung end to end, at least when assessing the economics of population growth. Hence, for almost all purposes the monetized-capital-effects models of the Coale-Hoover type should be considered too partial for long-run assessment, but rather as useful for yielding crucial inputs to more general models.

To repeat, the contribution of Coale and Hoover was enormous— marshalling raw data for subsequent analysis, supplying input to other studies (e.g., the welfare-outlay effect discussed in this chapter) and focusing attention on the *possibility* of learning about the effects of population growth on economic development with numerical simulations of the economy. But their main numerical result about the relationship of fertility rates to per-consumer income reveals nothing by itself about the relationship of fertility to economic development.

CHAPTER 11

The Effect of Population Growth on
Agricultural Investment in LDC's

INTRODUCTION

THE EFFECT of population growth on the nonagricultural capital stock was discussed in Chapter 10. This chapter attempts, to estimate the effect of population growth on agricultural investment.

The importance of agricultural investment in population history was clear to Malthus, who described Germans in Roman times thus:

> ... when the return of famine severely admonished them of the insufficiency of their scanty resources, they accused the sterility of a country which refused to supply the multitude of its inhabitants; but instead of clearing their forests, draining their swamps, and rendering their soil fit to support an extended population, they found it more congenial to their martial habits and impatient dispositions, to go "in quest of 'food, of plunder, or of glory," into other countries (1803, p. 78).

Farm investment is, if anything, more important in the modern world than in the ancient world. The key idea is that *land is man-made*, just as are other inputs to farm production.

> An important way in which farming is very similar to other industries, though it is widely presumed to be different, is that the productive capacity of a farm is largely man-made. It is a cumulative result of what has been done to the land in the past and is largely the result of investment.
>
> Farms, of course, commence with an initial productive capacity provided by exposure to solar energy, rainfall, and plant-food nutrients naturally present in the soil. The ceiling which these set for production, however, is wholly inadequate for progress in agriculture. The more progressive agriculture becomes, the smaller is its dependency on the natural endowments for achieving total productive capacity of the farm and the greater the proportion of these imports that is man-made, the result of investment (United States, White House, 1967, Vol. I, p. 64).

Evidence that the amount of capital formation in subsistence agricultural can vary greatly depending on people's motivations is found in China. The amount of labor by the average peasant rose 59% from 1950 to 1959—from 119 days yearly to 189 days. "Increase in employment served to increase efforts at subsistence capital formation" (Schran, 1969, pp. 75, 78).

Models of population and economic growth (e.g., Coale and Hoover, 1958) commonly assume that *ceteris paribus*, higher fertility means lower aggregate saving. The available data apparently support this assumption, notably that of Leff (1969). Leff's study has little bearing, however, upon the relationship of population growth to *agricultural* investment in less-developed countries (LDC's), because much agricultural investment is nonmonetized, and the national accounting data used by Leff refer only to monetized investment. Furthermore, much of the agricultural investment that is paid for in money is omitted from many national accounts. Both of these omissions are shown by the capital/output ratios suggested for agriculture by the published national accounts of India and other LDC's, for example, 1.5 (Manne in Tinbergen, 1967, Appendix E) and 0.9 (Reddaway in Myint, 1964, p. 97). In contrast, the survey data for all LDC's now and in earlier years show that the capital/output ratio at contemporary valuations is actually upward of 4 (see page 257).

Given that agricultural output represents perhaps half of a poor LDC's total product, and given that (contrary to the common opinion) the rate of investment in LDC agriculture is quite respectable compared to the industrial sector,[1] if population growth has a *positive* effect on saving in agriculture, the effect might be great enough to rival any negative effect outside of agriculture. For this reason, as well as because of the intrinsic importance of the agricultural sector, the effect of population growth upon agricultural investment needs to be known if sound policy decisions about population growth are to be made.

This chapter demonstrates that population growth has a large positive effect upon agricultural saving. This effect may be of the same general magnitude, but in the opposing direction, as the observed negative effect of population growth on monetized capital formation in LDC's.

SOME THEORY

The aim of this chapter is to understand why investment takes place or does not take place when population grows. Therefore, it is necessary to have some theoretical basis for inferring a rate of investment from a particular set of empirical data.

An increase in family size affects a subsistence farmer much as an increase in the demand function affects a firm with some monopoly power. For a firm, the increased price at which the firm can sell any given amount of output will generally lead to an increase in output. Similarly, an in-

[1] See page 259 below.

239

crease in family size may be expected to affect the farmer's indifference curves in such manner that he is willing to pay a higher "price" in terms of his own labor for increased output, and he responds to this increase in his own demand with increased labor. This theory has been described more fully in Chapters 7 and 8.

A firm has a variety of ways of increasing output, including various combinations of increased labor and capital. That is, additional capital and labor are substitutes for each other in production, and the profit-maximizing firm will choose that combination that maximizes its long-run profits. Similarly, a subsistence farmer has a choice of how to produce additional output over time. He can increase his labor each year on the current season's crop, with more careful farming or by shifting to more labor-intensive crops and methods. Or, he can also invest in such additional capital as new land,[2] land irrigation, farm buildings, or additional equipment and animals. (Boserup, 1965, gave relatively little attention to the role of investment, and hence she concluded that population growth and additional output would necessarily lead to *more* work per person on current crops).

Over a long period of time, say, 700 years in China, one can assume that total output will roughly keep pace with total population; that is, one can

---

[2] Perhaps it is necessary to say a word about whether land should indeed be considered capital in this context. The argument against this approach is that land is a natural endowment, and the returns to it are a rent to the descendants (natural or financial) of the man who simply affixed his mark to it. But this argument simply will not work. First, if the land were simply used and used, it would soon be useless for agriculture. Land must constantly be maintained, and this maintenance is gross investment. Second, when it was originally claimed, the land had to be cleared and made useful for agriculture. And as we know from contemporary land-clearing projects in Siberia, Brazil, Africa, and elsewhere, the cost of land clearance is not far from the market value of comparable land presently in use—as one may expect. Costs per acre (2.471 acres equal one hectare) among a sample of land-development projects were: Guatemala, $32 and $91; Nigeria, $118; Sudan, $218; Ceylon, $307; Morocco, $307; United States, $612; Kenya, $973. (United States, White House, 1967, Vol. II, p. 436). The weighted average of a world sample of projects in settled areas was $400 per acre (*ibid.*, p. 461). More recently, a considerably lower estimate has been made by the FAO: "to add 5–7 million hectares to food production would cost between $137 and $312 per hectare" (United Nations, 1974, pp. 64–67, quoted in United States Department of Agriculture, 1974, p. 59). For irrigation alone, on presently cultivated lands in India, the estimate is $250–$300 per acre (*ibid.*, p. 450). The weighted average cost for a variety of world projects was $325 per acre, and omitting one large project it was $581 per acre (*ibid.*, p. 461). And third, though some land may be cheaper to clear than others (e.g., the U.S. Midwest was cheaper than the Brazilian jungle) even the cheapest-to-clear land was far from the "free gift" that some historians speak of. The costs of disease, danger from Indians, isolation, lack of markets, and so forth, were very substantial. Proof is found in eighteenth-century New England where people remained even though population grew to the point at which it was considered "overcrowded" and land prices rose (Lockridge, 1968), because the perceived cost of opening the new land was greater. Additional evidence is the relationship of the cost of purchasing underdeveloped land to the cost of readying it for farming. In the 18th century a representative 40-acre field cost $50, but fencing, clearing and cabin-building cost $250 (Lebergott, 1964, p. 141).

assume more-or-less-constant per-consumer-equivalent consumption of food in the long run in a subsistence society, with dips below subsistence at some times, and perhaps slight rises to "luxury" foods such as meat at other times.

We wish to know the role of investment—as distinguished from increases in work hours, technology, and so forth—in this increase in *total* product. Knowledge of two parameters of investment are necessary for our understanding, and later for a numerical model: (1) the *proportion* of increase in capital to the total increase in inputs; and (2) the *speed* with which the investment response occurs. That is, an increment of births, which may be thought of for empirical purposes as a percentage increase in population, occurs in year t. It will then have some effect on investment in each of the following years. The observed event, the investment in a single period, may be written as the following function:

$$\left(\frac{K_{F,t+1} - K_{F,t}}{K_{F,t}}\right) = a_0\left(\frac{POP_{t+1} - POP_t}{POP_t}\right) + a_1\left(\frac{POP_t - POP_{t-1}}{POP_{t-1}}\right)$$

$$+ a_2\left(\frac{POP_{t-1} - POP_{t-2}}{POP_{t-2}}\right)\ldots \quad (11\text{--}1)$$

where K is capital and POP is total population. If the growth process is steady over time, the total investment caused by a given year's population increment is equal to the *sum* of the a coefficients in the above process. Furthermore, if the process is steady, this sum of coefficients may be estimated by the proportional change in investment divided by the proportional change in population over a given period of time. On the assumption that output per-consumer-equivalent remains the same over time, this sum of coefficients, which almost surely will be less than unity, stands for the proportion of the total product accounted for by investment. For example, if:

$$\left(\frac{K_1 - K_0}{K_0}\middle/ \frac{POP_1 - POP_0}{POP_0}\right) = .7, \quad (11\text{--}2)$$

this suggests that 70% of the increase in production caused by population increase was accounted for by increases in farm capital; the rest presumably is accounted for by increases in labor per worker, technology changes, and other factors.

We have been talking of time-series data. In contrast, cross-section data represent "fully adjusted" observations. That is, the *state* of a cross-sectionally observed capital-investment level at time t encompasses the effect of all past population growth (except for the influence of the last few years, which have not yet played out their effects). If the growth process has been reasonably constant over a period of years, the relationship at a given moment between the two state variables—for which population density per unit of area, and capital stock per unit of area are the likely proxies—may be viewed as the sum of the lagged effects upon investment of a change in population.[3]

The second parameter to be estimated is the *lag structure* of the coefficients $a_0, a_1, a_2 \ldots$ (if one assumes a geometric process, one may think of this structure as the decay rate). But if one is observing a process that is rather steady over the observed time period, as the rate of population growth is likely to be over the 20 or 50 years for which data are available, then the lag structure cannot be estimated from time-series data. We can guess that if much of the investment is deferred until the "additional" child grows up and clears his own land, the lag could be quite long. Farm survey data are the only hope to provide estimates of this lag structure.

Now let us consider the factors which influence whether the farmer chooses to invest or to supply more current labor to increase production. These factors must be similar to the factors which influence how a firm makes an investment decision: (1) the relative prices of capital and current-season labor; and (2) the farmer's time-preferences for consumption (i.e., the subjective discount rate). More specifically, where it is relatively easy to obtain and cultivate new land, or to build an irrigation system, more investment will be undertaken than where there is no unused land and where irrigation systems are very costly in time. In the latter case, the farmer will spend more time on his current crop and farm more carefully, and he will use more fertilizer.

There is also a difference between industrial investment and peasant investment: It is in the nature of decisions about private and public industrial and urban investment that they are mostly *allocative* decisions about saving, that is, choices between investment and consumption. In contrast, decisions about nonmonetized agricultural investment are often choices between work and leisure.

Another matter: Over a long period of time, say, 500 years, investment's share of responsibility for increased output is likely to be lower than over a shorter period of time, say, 5 or 20 years, because the longer the period, the bigger the share for which new technological knowledge will account. Thus, the share accounted for by technological change over the period in question must be estimated and taken out of the analysis before the share accounted for by investment can be estimated.

---

[3] If the variables are measured logarithmically, this magnitude is the long-run elasticity. The nature of such cross-section and time-series data when there is a lagged effect is discussed in Grunfeld (1961), Malinvaud (1966), or Aigner and Simon (1970).

MEASUREMENT DIFFICULTIES

It is usual to study investment functions with data generated by national income accounts. But this method is not feasible in the study of agricultural investment in LDC's. One reason is that one cannot assume that savings become investment, because in some countries much of the saving in the agricultural sector is not transformed into productive investment. In a town in India, S. Simon found that

> [C]onsiderable investment was made in jewelry. Sixty-four Landowner Class families, or 88 percent of all the Landowner Class families in the village, reported how much they held in gold jewelry. A total of Rs. 358,600 was reported as the current value of the gold jewelry which they held—an average of about Rs. 5,600 per reporting Landowner Class family. The value of the gold per family, however, ranged all the way from a few hundred to many thousands of rupees. These data suggest that the value of total holdings of jewelry in Senapur is nearly equal to a year's total income for the village. The funds invested in jewelry appear rather high for the income levels reported by the villagers, even though the flow of funds into jewelry appears to be declining (1968, p. 334).

Another obstacle to the use of national income accounts for the study of agricultural investment is that much of the investment does not originate from saving as a holdback of consumption. Rather, much agricultural investment has always come from *additional* labor by the farmer himself during the off-season[4] when he is not engaged in crop work. For example, in Rapitok parish in New Britain, "men of working age invest one-quarter of their man-power per year in the formation of new agricultural assets such as cocoa and coconut trees. This is a long-term agricultural investment . . ." (Epstein, 1965, p. 177).

Partly for these two reasons—saving does not necessarily imply investment, and investment does not necessarily imply saving in LDC agriculture—the estimates of agricultural investment found in national income accounts have often used misleading techniques of estimation. According to Hooley (1967), a frequent technique is to include as agricultural investment only the *imported equipment*, which constitutes a very tiny proportion of total real agricultural investment. (This estimation method

---

[4] The mechanism of off-season non-monetized investment work is still important in MDC's, as this quote from a farmers' column in an Illinois newspaper shows: "It's a waiting game. While the corn is maturing and bean pods are filling, it's time to get a lot of other odds and ends out of the way. Like mowing the fence rows, painting the cribs or installing draining tile. Or maybe vacationing" (September 3, 1971. *Champaign-Urbana Courier*, p. 21).

excludes all land reclamation and improvement, which constitute by far the largest part of agricultural investment.) As a result:

> [I]n the conventional estimates of capital resources and of capital formation in underdeveloped countries, the results of the expenditure of time, effort and money in the creation, extension, improvement and upkeep of agricultural holdings are often disregarded. This seems to be the common practice in dealing both with holdings producing for the subsistence sector and local markets and with those producing cash crops for export markets. This omission is serious. . . . Disregard of investment of effort and resources by individual cultivators in agricultural capital must in these societies give gravely misleading statistical results (Bauer and Yamey, 1957, pp. 29–30).[5]

It is therefore necessary to resort to methods other than the analysis of national income accounts to understand the effect of population growth on the stock of capital in LDC agriculture.[6]

---

[5] Bauer and Yamey offer this additional interesting observation: "The millions of acres [in Africa and Asia] of smallholdings under rubber, cocoa, kola nuts, cotton, rice, groundnuts and millet are obvious examples of investments (large-scale in total) made by peasants in the expectation of profitable rèturns which often occur only several seasons later or extend over a number of seasons. The failure to include this form of investment in estimates of capital formation is no doubt partly responsible for the erroneous notion that the indigenous population of underdeveloped countries, such as the African peasant or the Malay smallholder, are unable and unwilling to take a long view in economic matters" (1957, p. 30).

[6] One may think of turning to valuation of the stock of capital to estimate investment. But such an estimate—especially in the case of land—flows from the value of output. This will lead to circular reasoning unless very special and very sophisticated data are available— and they are not. "[T]he statistical and conceptual difficulties of attempting to isolate and measure capital-forming activities in agriculture, and particularly in agriculture producing crops for local consumption, are likely to discourage even those observers who are aware of the importance of investment in peasant holdings. One example of the difficulties may be mentioned. Very different results would be obtained if one valued, say, the cocoa acreage in the Gold Coast, the rubber smallholdings in Sumatra, or the padi fields of South-east Asia on the basis of the cost of establishing the holdings rather than on the basis of the discounted value of the net returns yielded by the investment. Moreover, either basis involves the computer in estimates: in the former case the main element of cost may not be money outlays but opportunities for more immediate returns or for leisure forgone; in the latter case the usual estimates of physical yields, future prices and discount rates have to be made" (Bauer and Yamey, 1957, p. 30). One might appraise the value of the nonmonetized investment at the change in market price of the land, though the interest rate as used for discounting by potential investors is probably too low by most tests. The need for an interest rate is obviated, however, if the contributions to output in each future period are accurately appraised for each type of capital. Such appraisal requires only that one estimate (1) the effect of the added investment on output in the immediate period, and (2) the rate of physical depreciation. This shall be done in the model used here.

There is also another conceptual difficulty. Obviously, land clearing is capital widening of the most fundamental sort, the productive techniques to be used in the newly cleared land will be the same as in previously cultivated land. But are the acts of the building and using an irrigation system only an increase in capital or are they a shift in technology? The question is not well resolved in this book—or elsewhere.

In principle, farm-labor surveys should provide the basis for estimates, especially Chayanov's (1926/1966) unique survey data on farmer expenditures in labor and cash. But it turns out to be extremely difficult to estimate the farmer's investment from examination of the inputs. One crucial problem is that much labor and material are expended on gray-area activities such as livestock maintenance. Is this investment? Probably, yes. But what about holdbacks of seed from consumption? Clearly, this is saving and investment in the most fundamental sense, but it is not "reproducible capital" or "producer's goods," in the usual sense of these terms. Even if one made clear which categories he is interested in—construction and repairs of land improvements and buildings, say—it would be difficult to estimate the amounts of time spent on these activities from any but the most painstaking labor survey, the existence of which I am unaware. Furthermore, much farm investment is in spurts. The most important is the concentrated effort made in clearing new land; this is difficult to catch in a survey. Still, some surveys have made useful attempts at measuring total rural investment. What no survey (to my knowledge) has yet given results for, however, is the relationship between *family size* and investment.

ESTIMATES OF THE RESPONSE SENSITIVITY

Two lines of evidence will be considered, the historical evidence, and cross-sectional data on irrigation, in that order.

Historical Data on Investment and Population Growth[7]

IRELAND

In the late eighteenth century and the first half of the nineteenth century in Ireland—a period of very rapid population growth—the peasants invested great amounts of labor in new lands, even though they did not own the land.

> Every new holding marked out in mountain or bog made possible the creation of a new family. . . . The state, for all the advice of government committees and private investigators, played no significant part in works of drainage and clearance until the time of the Famine. The landlords, with outstanding exceptions, were hardly more active. The main agent of reclamation was the peasant himself. In spite of the immense discouragement of tenurial relationships which increased rent in proportion—or more than in proportion—to the increase in the value of his holding, he steadily added an acre or two a year to his

[7] The illustrations given here are by no means a systematic survey of available material. In the future I hope to survey this subject more thoroughly.

cultivated area; or his sons established themselves on land hitherto unused. The peasant and his children were driven to such arduous and unrewarding work by the two forces which give their distinctive character to many of the institutions of the Irish countryside—the pressure of population and the landlords' demand for ever-increasing rents" (Connell, 1965, pp. 430–31).

Evidence for the rapidity of Irish land clearance is shown in Table 11–1. Over the decade 1841–51 the amount of cultivated land increased by 10%, though even in the previous decade—at the height of the population increase *before* the famine starting in 1845—population only increased from 7,767,000 to 8,175,000, a decadal rate of 5.3% (Connell, 1965, p. 423). This suggests that rural investment was enough to account for all— and even more—of the increase in total food product required by population growth during those years.[8]

CHINA

From 1400 to 1957 the cultivated acreage in China expanded fourfold-plus from 25 million hectares to 112 million hectares (Perkins, 1969, p. 240). This increase in cultivated land apparently accounted for more than half of the increase in grain output that sustained the living standard of the eightfold-plus increase in population over the same period. Investment in water-control systems and tarracing accounted for much of the rest of the increase in output. "Only a small share of the rise in yields can be explained by improvements in the 'traditional' technology" (Perkins, 1969, p. 77). In this context, where the "rural technology in China was nearly stagnant after 1400" (*ibid.*), growth in output had to be accomplished with increases in capital and/or labor-per-person, and it is clear that additional investment was very largely, if not almost completely

---

[8] The land-clearance data are limited to those shown because others are not available, and not because those shown are unusual. "There is a strong presumption that reclamation at so considerable a rate as that suggested by Table [11-1] in a decade which was dominated by the Famine implies at least a proportionate amount in the preceding years. It is most unlikely that there was as much reclamation in the five years after 1845 as in the preceding five (when the forces shaping rural economy differed little from those of the twenties and thirties). It is true that an act of 1847 was the first to give any serious state encouragement to works of drainage, but by 1850 only 74,000 acres had been reclaimed with state assistance out of the 1,338,281 acres that had been added to the cultivated area between 1841 and 1851. The Famine ruthlessly thinned the population and robbed the colonizing movement of much of the force it had derived from the pressure of population. When starvation was most universal, it can hardly be supposed that the peasants had either the resources or the initiative to drain mountain and bog as never before. And, moreover, when death and emigration caused neighbours to vacate their holdings it is unlikely that the need to clear fresh land seemed as urgent as in former years" (Connell, 1950, p. 48).

TABLE 11–1
AREAS OF AGRICULTURAL AND WASTE LAND IN THE PROVINCES OF IRELAND, 1841 AND 1851

County	Agricultural land				Waste land			
	1841		1851		1841		1851	
	Acres (in thousands)	Percentage of total area	Acres (in thousands)	Percentage of total area	Acres (in thousands)	Percentage of total area	Acres (in thousands)	Percentage of total area
Leinster	3,961	81.23	4,038	82.80	732	15.00	666	13.66
Munster	3,875	63.89	4,310	71.08	1,893	31.22	1,485	24.48
Ulster	3,408	62.23	3,994	72.95	1,764	32.22	1,199	21.89
Connaught	2,221	50.57	2,460	56.01	1,906	43.39	1,674	38.12
Ireland	13,464	64.71	14,803	71.14	6,296	30.25	5,024	24.14

SOURCE: Connell, 1950, p. 47.

responsible.[9,10] Furthermore, this capital formation seems to have been *caused by* population growth in the case of China. This process continues into the present. As an explanation of the last of the ten years of good harvests the Chinese had enjoyed as of 1971, the New China News Agency said that the Chinese people "worked hard at irrigation, drainage and fertilizer production last year and this should show good results in 1972 provided the weather holds up."[11]

EUROPE

In the previous examples the investment was largely direct and non-monetized. The same mechanism can also operate in market-agricultural sectors of LDC's, though in a bit more complex manner, through the increased market demand for food caused by the rise in population. Slicher van Bath (1963, pp. 195–239) documents the close relationship between population, food prices, and land reclamation in Europe from 1500 to 1900; when population grew at a fast rate, food prices were high, and land creation increased. "The higher cereal prices after 1756 stimulated agricultural development. . . . Around Poitiers the area of reclaimed land was usually either 30 to 35 acres or about 2 hectares. In the former case the reclamation was the work of a day-labourer for a whole winter, in the latter that of a farmer with a team of oxen" (Slicher van Bath, 1963, p. 231). Data for the Netherlands are shown in Figure 11–1; when food prices went up (a concomitant of population increase) investment in land went up sharply.

---

[9] Unfortunately Perkins does not provide much evidence on how much the labor input *per person* changed over time.

[10] The lands that were brought into cultivation lay fallow because there were not enough farmers to cultivate them. Farmers are quite limited in their capacities to cultivate land. The picture of Chinese population growth as a progressive subdivision of farms to uneconomically small units is thereby shown to be wrong, as an example after the Taiping rebellion shows. Ho quotes Richthofen (1871) approvingly:

"'It is an interesting subject of speculation for the national economist, to trace the causes of the exceedingly slow rate at which the country is recovering its productive power. While there was formerly overpopulation, a few individuals are now masters of the soil, and new comers can purchase, at 1,000 cash (80 cents) a *mow*, as much as they like of the same ground which was worth, formerly, 40,000 cash a *mow* . . . yet the area put under cultivation is increasing at an incredibly slow rate. It appears, indeed, that a Chinese is capable of cultivating only a certain number of square yards of ground to every head of the population, and cannot overstep that limit with impunity.'"

"Richthofen was right: the repopulation of many lower Yangtze localities was indeed a very slow and gradual process. The inability of the average farmer to cultivate more than two or three acres of rice paddies was one reason, but there were other factors too. After a long period of neglect, the land required major reclamation" (P. Ho, pp. 243–44).

[11] I regret offering such reporting as evidence, but it seems more than mere casual opinion in this case.

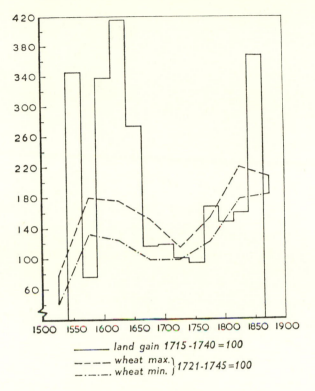

_____ land gain 1715-1740 = 100

_ _ _ _ wheat max. }
_._._. wheat min. } 1721-1745 = 100

FIGURE 11–1   INDICES OF LAND GAINED IN NETHERLANDS BY POLDERS COMPARED
TO THE PRICE INDICES OF WHEAT, 1525–1875
SOURCE: Reproduced from Slicher van Bath, 1963, p. 201.

DeVries concludes from such data that "the glory of the Dutch cities in
the seventeenth century owed much to the responsive and adoptive capacity of the rural society . . . Backward linkages stimulated investment in
drainage improvements, established a commerce in fertilizer and fodder
. . . Equally impressive was the much increased level of drainage and
dyke maintenance taxes paid by the farmers themselves in order to improve soil quality" (1971, pp. 266–68).

For Sweden, Gemery shows the interesting picture in Table 11–2. The
increase in total population apparently caused enough of an increase in
grain acreage to accommodate the additional people. (There was only
a 3% increase in yield per acre per decade.) This increase in acreage was
created by the additional work of an agricultural labor force that did not
increase much in size (due to emigration, migration to the city, earlier
fertility and mortality, and so forth). Not only did the agricultural labor
force bring enough new land into production to feed the additional people,

249

TABLE 11–2

RELATIONSHIP OF POPULATION GROWTH TO AGRICULTURE IN
SWEDEN IN THE NINETEENTH CENTURY

Period	% rate of natural increase per decade (1)	% change in grain acres cultivated per decade (2)	% change of agricultural labor force per decade (3)	% change in total grain production per decade (4)	% change in grain production per capita per decade (5)	% change in output per agricultural worker per decade (6)
1800–50	8.3	10	4.5	15.0	7.7	9
1850–1900	11.5	9	0.3	14.6	7.5	15

SOURCE: Gemery, no date.

but output per capita *rose* (see column 6)—and it would show an even faster rise if we calculated in terms of consumer equivalents rather than total persons.

INDIA

In the Indian village of Senapur, studied in 1954 by Hopper and in 1964 by S. Simon, the agricultural class increased their agricultural income considerably over the period. And: "The increase in agricultural income derives primarily from the greater amount of acreage that is cultivated. The Noniyas, traditionally an earth-working class, have in the past reclaimed large areas of previously worthless, saline land through extremely laborious methods" (S. Simon, 1968, p. 313).

Data for land improvement in India from 1949–50 to 1960–61 are shown in Table 11–3. Not only did irrigated land increase in quantity, but the total area of *all* cultivated land increased about 10% over that period, and about 20% from 1951–1971 (Revelle, 1974, p. 170).

TABLE 11–3
GROSS AREA UNDER FOODGRAINS, INDIA, 1949–50 TO 1960–61

Year	Unirrigated area	Irrigated area	Total area
		(millions of acres)	
1949–50	201	44	245
1950–51	195	45	240
1951–52	194	46	240
1952–53	205	47	252
1953–54	220	49	269
1954–55	215	52	267
1955–56	223	50	273
1956–57	225	50	275
1957–58	216	51	267
1958–59	227	53	280
1959–60	228	54	282
1960–61	224	55	279

SOURCE: Lele and Mellor, 1964, p. 20.

TAIWAN

The excellent data from Taiwan in Table 11–4 show how land creation and improvement responded to population growth. During the period from 1900 to 1930 much new land was developed, along with an increase in the amount of irrigated land. From 1930 to 1960 when there was little new land to develop, more land was irrigated. (At the same time, the crop

251

TABLE 11–4
LAND INPUT AND UTILIZATION IN TAIWAN, 1905–60

Year	Total acres	Paddy field	Dry land	Crop area	Multiple cropping index
1905	624,501	304,908	319,593	685,987	109.8
1910	674,100	332,372	341,728	731,431	108.5
1915	700,080	343,087	356,993	812,226	116.0
1920	749,419	367,177	382,242	829,797	110.7
1925	775,488	373,629	401,839	925,009	119.3
1930	812,116	396,670	415,446	976,396	120.2
1935	831,003	478,689	352,314	1,090,174	131.2
1940	860,439	529,610	330,829	1,117,371	129.9
1945	816,017	504,709	311,308	867,819	106.4
1950	870,633	530,236	340,397	1,441,956	165.6
1955	873,002	532,688	340,314	1,466,909	168.0
1960	869,223	528,580	343,643	1,557,227	179.2

SOURCE: Y. Ho, 1966, pp. 50–51.

area was increased by multiple cropping, and the use of fertilizers allowed total productivity to continue rising at a very rapid rate.)

OTHER COUNTRIES

Data for Japan, given by Ohkawa *et al.* (1970, pp. 11, 18, 22; quoted by Mueller, 1973) show that arable land increased steadily from 1877 until World War II, even though the number of agricultural workers was decreasing steadily. The amounts of livestock, trees, and equipment rose at increasingly fast rates. These increases in agricultural capital must have been caused by the increase in Japanese population together with the increase in the level of income in Japan.

In Burma, the amount of land in cultivation rose at an astonishing rate starting in the middle of the nineteenth century. The cultivated area in acres was *fifteen times* as great in 1922–23 as in 1852–53 (Furnivall, 1957, p. 48). Over the same period population increased by a factor of almost five (Andrus, 1948, p. 245). In addition to the increase of population, the opening of the Suez Canal enabled Burma to trade its rice with Europe. Both these forces gave Burmese farmers an incentive to reclaim land, and they did so with extraordinary rapidity—until World War II, when millions of acres were overrun by jungle.

A review of recent Asian experience impresses one with the extent to which increases in output continue to be accounted for by increases in land inputs, even in the most densely populated countries of the region. During the last decade increases in area planted accounted for roughly one-fourth of the growth of rice output in Japan, for one-third of the growth in India, and for the entire increase in rice output in the Philippines (Ruttan, 1969, p. 356.)

KUMAR'S STATISTICAL ANALYSIS

Using data for as many countries as were available, Kumar investigated the relationship between population density and the extent to which rural land is cultivated or lies fallow. He found a strong relationship: the higher the population density, the higher the proportion of land that is cultivated (1973, p. 218).

SUMMARY OF HISTORICAL DATA

In summary, what do these historical data show? They show that in LDC's increased investment in land accounts for most of the long-run increase in agricultural output, and agricultural output in the long run kept up with population increase. (This implies that, putting aside the extra labor involved in the investment itself, the end-result of the population-growth process does not necessarily cause present-day cultivators to work a great deal harder on crops than their ancestors did.)

One might wonder whether the increase in land investment was really *caused by* the population growth. This argument might have some validity in recent decades. But this objection clearly does not apply to China's long history; in its nonmarket economy, there was no motive for increasing food production other than an increase in size in one's family or village.

International Cross-sectional Data on Irrigation[12]

It is reasonable to think of the building of an irrigation system as a response to two conditions: (1) increased demand for food over the previous period; and (2) new land sufficiently scarce so that the cost of clearing it is higher than the cost of building an irrigation system to produce the same amount of additional output. High population density per acre of cultivated land would seem to indicate the presence of condition (2); if there were more easily-cultivated land available, people would clear it and the density would be lower. The comparison of two countries with different population densities may be seen as a proxy for changes in the same country at two stages of population increase. Therefore, the relationship between (1) population density per acre of cultivated land, and (2) the proportion of the cultivated land that people have irrigated, may be taken as a measure of the effect of population increase on the amount of investment in irrigation.

---

[12] This section gives the highlights of a study reported in detail in Simon (1975).

The necessary data were collected by the President's Commission on the World Food Problem (United States, The White House, 1967, Vol. 11, pp. 441–42). The population data are estimates for 1965. The data on irrigated and cultivated areas are a mixed bag from publications in various years in the 1950's and 1960's.

The simplest approach is the linear regression of the proportion[13] of cultivated land that is irrigated (IRR/CUL) with respect to the population per unit of cultivated land (POP/CUL),

$$\left(\frac{\text{Irrigated land}}{\text{Cultivated land}}\right) = a + b\left(\frac{\text{Population}}{\text{Cultivated land}}\right), \quad \text{or} \quad (11\text{–}3)$$

$$\text{IRR/CUL} = a + b_1(\text{POP/CUL})$$

The logic of the independent variable is that POP/CUL is a better measure of population density with respect to agricultural production than is population/total land (POP/LND); when considering agricultural production it is reasonable to remove from the comparison of the various countries uncultivable mountain or desert land.

The results of this simple regression for the 48 countries in the pooled sample, for the 18 Asian countries alone, and for the 19 South American countries alone, are shown in lines 1–3 of Table 11–5. In the pooled sample the independent variable has a t ratio of 4.3, and explains 29% of the variance ($r = .54$). The separate Asian and South American samples have coefficients of the same general order as each other and as the sample as a whole, which lends support to the meaningfulness of the several relationships. Population density clearly increases the extent of irrigation.

A second approach is to characterize the variables as logarithms,

$$\log(\text{IRR/CUL}) = a + b_1 \log(\text{POP/CUL}). \quad (11\text{–}4)$$

The unstandardized regression coefficients may be interpreted as elasticities; the elasticity for the pooled sample is 2.72, and the separate Asian and South America estimates are a bit lower (lines 4–6 in the table).

Additional regressions with geographical dummies, cultivated land as a proportion of total land, per-capita income, and so forth (shown in Simon, 1975) increase the proportion of the variance explained but leave the size of the coefficient of population density much the same as in the simple regressions shown in Table 11–5. These regressions are unanimous

---

[13] There would seem to be no problem of spurious correlation here. "The question of spurious correlation quite obviously does not arise when the hypothesis to be tested has initially been formulated in terms of ratios . . ." (Kuh and Meyer, 1955, p. 401). The relationship of interest here is the effect of population *density* to the *proportion* of irrigated land, for which the ratios in the regression are the appropriate proxies.

TABLE 11–5
THE EFFECT OF POPULATION DENSITY UPON EXTENT OF IRRIGATION

Row number (1)	Equation (1)	Sample (2)	Size (3)	Dependent variable (4)	POP/CUL (5)	log POP/CUL (6)	R
		All countries					
1	11-3	pooled	48	I/C	.54 = beta coefficient 8.33 = regression coefficient 4.33 = t ratio		.54
2	11-3	Asia	18	I/C	.65 6.06 3.43		.65
3	11-3	S. Amer.	19	I/C	.33 4.76 1.45		.33
4	11-4	Pooled	48	log I/C		.47 = beta coefficient 2.72 = regression coefficient which is an elasticity 3.62 = t ratio	.47
5	11-4	Asia	18	log I/C		.56 2.08 2.73	.56
6	11-4	S. Amer.	19	log I/C		.38 1.99 1.68	.38

NOTE: The top number in each cell is the standardized regression coefficient (beta). The middle number is the unstandardized regression coefficient, which may be interpreted as an elasticity for the log regressions. The bottom number is the t ratio.

in showing that population density affects the building of irrigation systems in an important way.

The reader may question whether causality also runs from investments in irrigation to population density. Indeed, in some cases governments have undertaken large-scale irrigation projects in barren areas, and population settlement has followed. But such government irrigation projects are for the purpose of domestic resettlement. They influence population distribution (i.e., population densities in various parts of a country). But given the reasonable assumption that the irrigation project does not affect national fertility or international migration, density for the country *as a whole* is not affected by such a project. Hence we may dismiss the possibility that these data show causality running from irrigation to density. This strengthens the case for believing that the data reflect causality running from population density to irrigation intensity.

The Economic Meaning of the Irrigation Results

It should be interesting to translate the statistical estimates into economic magnitudes. Let us take as our best estimate for the effect of POP/CUL the regression coefficient in Equation 11–4, which may be interpreted directly as an elasticity; it is 2.7 for the sample as a whole (line 4). Given that in the average country in the sample 18.4% of cultivated land is irrigated, an increase in population density of 1% would produce an increase of $(.01 \times 2.7 \times .184) = .5\%$ in the stock of irrigated land, or a population-growth elasticity of .5. And given that irrigated land can increase output per acre by a factor of 2 or more, it is apparent that this mechanism can have a very important role in adjusting food supply to population increase—perhaps taking up the whole slack in a representative country in our sample. When considering the over-all quantitative impact of POP/CUL upon IRR/CUL, it should be remembered that measurement error in POP/CUL biases the coefficient downward. Therefore, the effect is surely greater than the coefficients suggest. And it is reasonable that population density also has a positive effect on other aspects of agricultural capital formation such as land clearing, which increases the expected total response.

RELATIVE SIZE EFFECTS OF POPULATION GROWTH ON AGRICULTURAL AND NONAGRICULTURAL INVESTMENT

It is illuminating to consider the importance of the effect of population growth upon agricultural investment relative to the effect on other investment, though such a calculation is neither needed nor used in the model to be described in Chapter 13. First, the *stock* of agricultural capital is a very large part of total capital in most LDC's. For the Philippines, a

typical LDC country in this respect, Hooley (1967) made the direct estimate that half of the society's capital is in land. Indirect confirmation
comes from the combination of two facts: (1) In a typical LDC, agriculture accounts for close to half the total product; and (2) The capital/output
(K/Y) ratio is higher in agriculture than in nonagriculture sectors. This
latter fact (surprising to some) may be shown true as follows: In China in
1921–25, the K/Y ratio in Chinese dollars for the average farm acre
(excluding livestock and supplies) was $1736/$376 = 4.6 (Buck, 1930,
pp. 65–66). For land alone, it was $1374/$376 = 3.7. In Orissa, India,
1958–59, the average investment per acre[14] was Rs. 535, and in land alone,
it was Rs. 474, whereas output there was Rs. 125 per acre, a K/Y of 4.3
(Government of India, Orissa, 1958–59, pp. 25 and 29). In the Punjab,
1955–56, the value of land averaged Rs. 840 per acre, where the value of
output per acre was 193, giving a K/Y of about 4.3 (Government of India,
Punjab, 1955–56, pp. 28 and 56). In Andhra Pradesh in 1959–60, the K/Y
ratio (land plus all other capital) was 6.4 (Government of India, 1968,
p. 174). In the years 1910–16, the ratio of land value to output ranged
from 3.05 to 3.56 in Australia, Canada, France, Russia, Switzerland,
and the United States (Clark, 1957, p. 637), countries in which land was
surely a smaller proportion of total capital than in India or China.

Thus, the K/Y ratio in agriculture everywhere is upwards from 4,
whereas for a country like India, the K/Y ratio *outside* agriculture is
between 2 and 3 (Manne, 1964, in Tinbergen, 1967, Appendix E). These
K/Y ratios are *not* being offered here to indicate anything about the investment behavior of people in earlier times, because the present land prices
do not represent the opportunity costs when the land was "built." Rather,
the K/Y ratios indicate the importance and present value of land relative
to other capital in LDC's.

Turning from the *stock* of agricultural capital to *changes* in it, (i.e.,
investment), it should be noted that gross investment over time can be

[14] The make-up of agricultural investment in India is shown by Mellor as follows:

THE COMPOSITION OF INVESTMENT, TYPICAL FARMS IN VARIOUS STATES IN INDIA

Form of assets	Punjab	Madras	West Bengal	Bombay
	(per cent of total)			
Land	80	68	85	73
Buildings	4	7	8	3
Wells	2	17	—	10
Farm Equipment	3	2	1	4
Livestock	11	6	6	10
Total of above	100	100	100	100

SOURCE: Mellor *et al.*, 1968, p. 312.

smaller in agriculture than in other sectors. Yet agricultural capital can still be as large or larger than nonagricultural capital, because physical depreciation of investments in land improvement is far slower than in industrial equipment, especially if upkeep is properly figured.[15] Whereas an average rate of physical depreciation for industrial capital may be 5% per year (Enke, 1963, p. 46), it is much less in agricultural capital.

The national income data on savings partially include agricultural investment; the extent of this overlap must first be considered. The private sector of agricultural investment is overwhelmingly the larger in most LDC countries, with the exception of China. ". . . Even in so development-conscious a country as India, about two-thirds of total investment in productive capital applied to agriculture is provided for by private individuals, and only about one-third by public sources" (Hoselitz, 1964, pp. 353–54). And usually, only one small part of the private-sector agricultural capital is included in national-income accounts: the agricultural equipment which is imported into the country (Hooley,[16] 1967; Rozenthal, 1970). This is confirmed by the K/Y ratios usually given for agriculture, values such as 1.5 (Manne, 1964, in Tingbergen, 1967) and 0.9 (Reddaway, 1939, in Myint, 1964, p. 97). But such low K/Y estimates for agriculture are ridiculous, as we have seen earlier. It is clear that in these K/Y ratios computed from savings in national-income account, "capital" excludes land and includes only implements and equipment, and usually only the imported material. Hence, we may assume that less than 25% of private-sector agricultural investment is included in the national-savings account. Public investment in agriculture will also appear in the national-income accounts, and will be reflected in Leff's (1969) estimates. So perhaps half of total agricultural investment will appear in the national-income account of India, and probably less in other countries.[17]

Now about the amount of investment in LDC agriculture. First we must dispel a myth. The over-all proportion of investment to output in agriculture is certainly *not much smaller* than in the nonagricultural private sector, and perhaps larger. This may be seen in Indian farm surveys. After reviewing the evidence from surveys of Indian agriculture where it

---

[15] A truck or a soap plant or an electric power station has a far shorter life than does an irrigation system. Stone dams built by the Nabateans in Israel's Negev almost 2,000 years ago are still used by the Bedouin (who themselves build only mud dams). Roman roads are still in use. Underground irrigation ghanats in Iran still carry water a thousand or more years after construction. And stone-clearing from a field continues to yield returns literally indefinitely.

[16] I am grateful to Nathaniel Leff for bringing Hooley's work to my attention.

[17] Hoselitz compares sample data to central statistical organizational data and finds that "the estimate by the Central Statistical Organization is less than half" the estimate from the survey data (1964, p. 350).

is common to assume that people are too poor to save anything, Hoselitz summarizes that "additions to productive capital invested in agriculture amount to more than 8% of total (including non-cash) income," and if durable goods such as housing are included, "total investment . . . may be assumed to reach a magnitude of 10% or even 12% of total income" (1964, p. 357). During the same years, net fixed monetized investment in India was approximately 6–7% (Coale and Hoover, 1958, p. 149), with gross investment a somewhat higher percentage. Total output in agriculture was roughly equal to total output outside agriculture in those years (Coale and Hoover, 1958, p. 85; Mitra, 1969). On the basis of the above considerations, agricultural investment not included in national-income accounts may be half or more the size of total savings recorded in national-income investment in LDC's. If total agricultural and nonagricultural investments are equal, total agricultural investment will be about ⅔ as big as investment shown in the national-income accounts. Agricultural investment not shown in national-income accounts will be ⅓ the size of national-income savings.[18]

Leff's estimates imply that a 1% increase in population produces a .56% decrease in national-income savings.[19] But as was seen earlier, the elasticities estimated for agricultural-investment data are higher than Leff's (1969) figure in all the observed cases, and in the opposite direction. So if net investment in agriculture is, say, ⅔ as large as national-income savings, then the over-all quantitative effect of population growth on *total* savings may be either positive or negative; the agricultural sector has a higher elasticity but is smaller in size than investment included in the national-income accounts.

It would not be wise to further refine the estimates made above in order to say whether the effect on agricultural investment is higher or lower

---

[18] These idealized relationships are schematized in the following table:

PERCENTAGES OF TOTAL INVESTMENT

	Recorded on national-income accounts	Not recorded in national-income accounts	
Agriculture	25%	25%	50%
Nonagriculture	50%	—	50%
	75%	25%	100%

[19] The elasticity of savings with respect to child dependents, who constitute 40–46% (say 43%) of the populations in his LDC's, is −1.3. A 1% increase in dependents implies a .43% increase in population. Hence, a 1% increase in population produces −1.3 × .43% = .56% decrease in nonagricultural savings.

259

than is the national-income-accounts saving effect estimated by Leff.[20] The data used here have many shortcomings. And Leff's data and regression specification are open to many sorts of questions also. These data do suggest, however, that the two effects are of somewhat the same order of magnitude and in opposite directions. The net effect of population growth on total investment in LDC's may be either negative or positive or a trade-off. Much additional research is necessary before it is possible to determine whether the over-all effect of population growth on saving is positive or negative. Until then, it is an open question.

SUMMARY

The data adduced in this chapter show that LDC investment in agriculture is large. It is large relative to saving outside agriculture and in terms of the amount of work done in agricultural investment compared to current-season crop work, though most of this agricultural investment does not show up in national-income accounts. The very poorest farmers, too, improve their land and increase their farm-capital savings.

Furthermore, as the theory given in the chapter suggests is the case, the amount of saving in agriculture is shown to be influenced by family size and the rate of population growth; more children lead to higher saving and investment. This is seen in historical data relating population growth to agricultural investment. It is also seen in data on investment in irrigation systems as related to population density.

[20] One might wish to make a separate calculation of the response in irrigation to the national-income-account saving response to population growth. We want to know the proportional increase in *total* capital caused by a 1% increase in population and a .48% increase in irrigated land. If the stock of irrigated land is counted as a 3-for-1 against non-irrigated land, its total value is 3 × .18 = 54%. Nonirrigated land was priced at Rs. 500 per acre, and irrigated land at Rs. 1500 per acre, in 1955 in one of the Indian villages Epstein studied (Epstein, 1962, p. 90). In the other village she studied the ratio was 4 to 1 rather than 3 to 1 (*ibid.*, p. 215). An increase of .5% in irrigated land is therefore a .54 × .5% = 27% increase in the total stock of agricultural capital for a 1% increase in population. This much increase by itself suggests only .27/.56 = 48% of the negative effect estimated by Leff (1964). But the C/O ratio in agriculture is perhaps twice as high as outside agriculture, which would make this effect almost equal to the negative effect Leff found. Furthermore, the estimate that only as much *new* land is cleared, acre for acre, as is irrigated, is certainly too low even now, as Lele and Mellor (1964) showed for India; from 1949–50 to 1960–61 irrigated land increased by 11 million acres, but total acreage increased by 34 million acres (1964, p. 20). Consideration of the associated capital formation in buildings and equipment would push even higher the estimated agricultural investment response to population growth. Throughout history—which current data mostly still reflect—irrigation was not an important response to population growth. (As of 1880, only about 20 million acres were under irrigation, compared to 380 million acres now [United States, The White House, 1967, Vol. II, p. 440].) This implies that our data must understate the marginal effect on irrigation, as irrigation is now relatively more important than in the past. Hence, these data support the belief that the positive effect of population growth on agricultural saving outweighs the negative effect on saving elsewhere in the economy.

A minimum estimate of the positive influence of population growth upon saving may be seen in the irrigation-saving data (minimum because irrigation is only part of farm saving). The elasticity of the irrigated area with respect to population density on cultivated land is .5. It is difficult to compare this positive effect with the negative effect, as observed by Leff (1969), of population growth on monetized savings. The data presented here, however, do suggest that the two effects are somewhat of the same order of magnitude and in opposite directions. The net effect of population growth on *total* investment in LDC's may be either negative or positive or a trade-off. But clearly its effect upon *agricultural* investment is positive.

261

CHAPTER 12

The Effect of Population Growth on
Social Capital and Economies of Scale

INTRODUCTION

THE CAPITAL discussed in previous chapters has mainly been the sort of productive goods that enter quite directly into the production of consumer goods—especially land, agricultural buildings and implements, factories, and factory equipment.[1] This chapter discusses infrastructure social capital, which affects production indirectly but powerfully. "Infrastructure" here means *all* the physical, and *some* social, conditions which (1) aid the other factors of production—land, labor, equipment, knowledge—to produce more effectively, and (2) are themselves variable in the course of human events, being the products of society. This definition is framed to include such items as a road, a pestilence-free water supply, and a village organization, but excludes the sunshine. As discussed in Chapter 7, infrastructure may best be thought of as itself a factor of production in this context.

Social capital is a main element in economies of scale. But economies of scale also include the effects of increased market size, division of labor, and the other forces discussed in Chapter 2 (see pages 35–37). The best over-all estimate of economies of scale in LDC's is that of Chenery (1960), which applies only to the manufacturing sector. He estimated that the elasticity of output with respect to population size is .20. That will be the central value of the parameter used in the model to allow for the effect of population growth on productivity due to increased social capital and other economies-of-scale effects in the agricultural and industrial sectors of the typical LDC. (The interested reader should consult the extensive material on economies of scale in MDC's in Chapter 4, pages 63–70, because the phenomenon has many points of similarity in LDC's and MDC's.)

This chapter concentrates on transportation as a key element of infrastructure, and then discusses health more briefly. It shows that higher population density has a strong positive effect upon the presence and cost of transportation, and upon health conditions.

---

[1] Though schooling and housing and public facilities affect production only indirectly through the productive quality of people, these sorts of capital were included in the data and models in Chapter 10 on nonagricultural capital.

THE IMPORTANCE OF TRANSPORTATION

If there is a single key element in economic development other than culture and institutions and psychological make-up, that single key element is transportation together with communication. Transportation obviously includes roads and railways and airlines which transfer agricultural and industrial outputs and inputs as well as persons and messages. It also includes irrigation and electrical systems which transport inputs of water and power. There is abundant testimony by the best students of contemporary and historical economic development that "the one sure generalization about the underdeveloped countries is that investment in transport and communications is a vital factor" (Hawkins, in Wilson, *et al.*, 1966, p. 2).

There are many reasons why transportation is so important in economic development. The increased ability of farmers and businesses to sell in organized markets, and to deliver and obtain delivery at reasonable cost, is of course fundamental.[2] Some historical examples of how poor transportation presents a barrier to development follow:

1. In early nineteenth-century United States, farm products could be transported only where there were natural waterways. As for overland transport, "the cost of transportation was so high that even if corn had cost nothing to produce, it could not have been marketed twenty miles from where it was grown. It was cheaper to move a ton of iron across the Atlantic than to carry it ten miles through Pennsylvania" (Owen, 1964, p. 23). The Erie Canal reduced freight rates from New York City to the Great Lakes from $100 to $15 per ton (Owen, 1964, p. 24).

> We are so accustomed to today's high communication and easy transport that it is difficult to imagine the crudities with which elements in the productive process then meshed—or the resultant discontinuities that brought immense capital gains to some, but unemployment (hence, reduced incomes) to many others. Since provisions in the Galena silver mines were generally imported in the 1830's, an accident that kept the steamboat from arriving at St. Louis would make prices "rise frequently one or two hundred percent" (Lebergott, 1964, p. 143).

2. In eighteenth-century France "food would not normally be transported more than 15 km. from its place of origin" (Clark and Haswell, 1967, p. 179). Inability to transport food from farm to large markets

---

[2] Adam Smith stated: "Good roads, canals and navigable rivers, by diminishing the expense of carriage, put the remote parts of the country more nearly upon a level with those in the neighborhood of the town. They are upon that account the *greatest of all improvements* [italics added] . . . they break down monopolies . . . they open new markets . . ." (quoted by Zimmerman, 1965, p. 113).

could be seen in the great difference between at-the-farm prices and market prices.

3. In Europe the following general situation prevailed.

Of all the agencies at work [in Europe] in the process of improving food supplies, the most important was the change in the pattern of communications, allied with the emergence of a national food market. If the food producers invested capital to increase production, it was not as a long-term speculation, but in response to clearly defined market stimuli: higher prices or the possibility of selling more without depressing prices induced them to rationalize field systems and tenancies, improve buildings and drainage, experiment with new crops and livestock. *Such a response was dependent on communications.* In England, river, coastal and canal navigations played the most important role in this process. The same appears to be true of the Rhine/Ruhr district, the Belgian coalfields, and the American heavy industrial areas, all of these starting the process of urban concentration before the days of the railways which finally solved the food problem and gave fresh impetus both to industrialization and agricultural change. In Sweden the process of reducing mortality in bad harvest periods has been related to the reduction in isolation and the disappearance of local subsistence economies (Eversley, 1965, p. 61, italics added).

4. In "mid-nineteenth century Ghana, which was at that time almost entirely out of contact with world commerce . . . a ton of maize in Ghana cost 112 pence [1.2 English pounds] at a time when its world price was about 7 pounds . . . [In] Basutoland . . . in 1839 sorghum was selling at 1 shilling/bushel, and at 6 or 7 times that price in Carlsberg, 200 miles away" (Clark and Haswell, 1967, p. 180).

5. "In Thailand, partially used jungle land was transformed into highly productive, prosperous farms along the hundred-mile course of the Friendship Highway [see Figure 12–1]. Travel time was reduced from eleven hours on the old road to three on the new. The production of sugar cane, vegetables, bananas, and other fruits more than tripled in three years and Thailand began to export corn to Japan.

"In Boliva, the highway from Cochambamba to Santa Cruz reduced travel time in the rainy season from several weeks to fifteen hours and provided a link between the country's food supplies and its consumers. Until then, the price of Bolivian rice was 50 percent higher than imported rice simply because the cost of domestic transport was high. The highway has largely eliminated the need for imports.

"In Costa Rica, before the Inter-American Highway was constructed, driving beef cattle from grazing lands to San José customarily resulted in a 40 percent loss of weight, and imports were necessary to satisfy

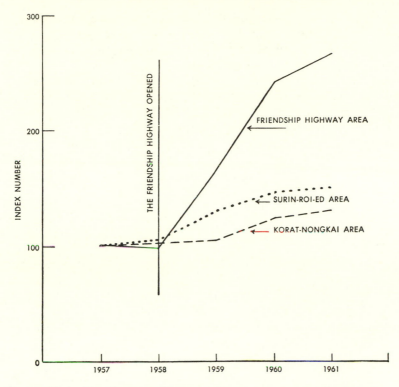

FIGURE 12–1   THE EFFECT OF HIGHWAY CONSTRUCTION UPON PRODUCTION
OF UPLAND CROPS AND VEGETABLES

SOURCE: Reproduced from Wisit Kasiraksa, "Economic Effects of the Friendship Highway,"
Unpublished Master's thesis (SEATO Graduate School of Engineering, Bangkok, 1963),
p. 48, as shown in Wilson *et al.*, 1966, p. 131.

domestic market demand for beef. With an all-weather highway, it be-
came possible to deliver cattle by truck-trailer units overnight and Costa
Rica has become self-sufficient in meat" (United States, The White
House, 1967, Vol. II, p. 573.)

6. In India, "road conditions in Uttar Pradesh (India) are an important
factor in the lack of tubewalls, shortages of fertilizer, backward agricultural techniques, and failure to produce more renumerative crops for
market. All these conditions reflect the difficult supply lines to town
centers that provide both a market and a source of inputs and technical
help" (Owen, 1965, p. 58).

7. A 15-mile farm-to-market road linking seven Indian villages, which
had previously had no transportation facilities available to them, had
these results: "It was Chano's family . . . who showed us the road's

265

importance. Unhulled rice in jungle villages was selling for about $1.50 for 83 pounds. Rice taken 12 miles in bullock carts on the new road to the only real town in the district, Jagdalpur (population about 15,000), brought twice as much" (Chapelle and Chapelle, 1956).

The comparative costs of the kinds of transportation that are possible under various conditions make clear why the availability of various forms of transportation can have such a big effect on merchandise prices and on quantities transported. The enormous advantage of water (canal) travel compared to overland travel in England about 1790 is seen in Table 12–1. And representative costs of various methods are shown by Clark and Haswell in Table 12–2. The most expensive form of transportation is

TABLE 12–1

TRANSPORTATION COSTS PER TON BY LAND AND WATER IN
ENGLAND ABOUT 1790

Route	By land	By water	By water as a % of by land
Liverpool-Wolverhampton	£5.0	£1.5	25.0
Birmingham-Gainsborough	3.18	1.0	25.6
Manchester-Potteries	2.15	0.15	27.2
Birmingham-Liverpool	5.0	1.10	30.0
Liverpool-Stourport	5.0	1.10	30.0
Manchester-Stourport	4.13	1.10	32.2
Manchester-Birmingham	4.0	1.10	37.5
Chester-Wolverhampton	3.10	1.15	50.0
Chester-Birmingham	3.10	2.0	57.1

SOURCE: Zimmerman, 1965, p. 113.

TABLE 12–2

TRANSPORT COSTS IN DEVELOPING COUNTRIES
(expressed as kilograms grain equivalent/ton-kilometer transported)

	Maximum	Median	Minimum
Porterage	12.4 (East Africa)	8.6	4.6 (China)
Wheelbarrow			3.2 (China)
Pack animals	11.6 (East Africa, donkey)	4.1	1.9 (Middle East, camel)
Wagons	16.4 (18th century, England, milk collection)	3.4	1.6 (U.S.A. 1800)
Boats	5.8 (Ghana 1900)	1.0	0.2 (China 11th century)
Steam boats		0.5	
Railways	1.4 (Australia 1850s)	0.45	0.1 (Chile 1937)
Motor vehicles	12.5 (Basutoland)*	1.0	0.15 (Thailand)

SOURCE: Clark and Haswell, 1967, p. 189.
*This figure hardly seems meaningful.

sixteen-or-more times as expensive as the price of the least expensive type.

Transportation is also important in the flow of *information* about all kinds of things—technical agricultural know-how, birth control, health services, modernizing ideas, and so forth. It makes an enormous difference if a particular village in India can be reached with a truck, a jeep or even a bicycle, rather than just by a bullock for whom the trip to the city is out of the question. Most villages in countries like India and Iran cannot easily be reached by motor transportation. When transportation is improved, radical changes of many kinds occur, as in Senapur, India.

Senapur has actually experienced a revolution in transportation. Compared to even a few years ago, the ease of traveling a distance has been greatly increased, and the time and cost have been greatly reduced. The major factor in this change has been the rapid growth in the frequency of bus service. Frequent, cheap bus service has had a vast impact on the market system and consumption patterns of the villagers and has perhaps further facilitated the movement to nonfarm jobs . . . In 1964, no one in Senapur owned either a four- or a two-wheeled motor vehicle. Bicycles and, for some purposes, bullock carts are the major means of transportation for local travel . . . Better transportation facilities, better-developed markets nearby, and increased income have all affected trading and consumption patterns in Senapur. Better-quality food, more variety in the diet, and availability of such items as soap, combs, hair oil, sunglasses, and toothpaste contribute to the feeling among inhabitants in the village that they are well off compared to their position a few decades ago. In addition, they feel stronger ties to the urban centers from which these products come (S. Simon, 1968, pp. 302, 319).

It is also clear that there is very great room for improvement in transportation systems, especially local rural transportation, in LDC's. This may be seen by comparison of countries with well-developed agriculture to those countries where agriculture is less developed.

In agriculturally advanced Western countries, there are from 3 to 4 miles of farm-to-market roads per square mile of cultivated land. The mileage is smaller in grain-producing areas where fields are large and higher where farms are smaller and the topography difficult. In Britain, France, Japan and the United States, the average is about 4 and in Taiwan and Denmark it is closer to 3. In India there is only about 0.7 of a mile of road per square mile of cultivated land. In Malaya it is about 0.8 mile and in the Philippines about 1 mile. None of the developing countries that are most dependent on agriculture has sufficient rural access roads (United States, The White House, 1967, Vol. II, p. 582).

The situation in India is particularly acute. If a farmer lives more than 1.5 miles from an all-weather road, he will not use chemical fertilizer and other marketed supplies which cannot be transported to him (Owen, 1964, p. 52). Table 12–3 shows that ¾ of India's farms are farther than 1.5 miles from an all-weather road, and Table 12–4 shows that more than ⅓ of the villages in the State of Maharastra have no approach road at all to serve them.

Lack of transportation facilities not only hampers the Indian farmer's ability to *sell* his product, but also prevents him from buying the inputs, especially fertilizer, that he needs for modern agriculture: "Lack of information about fertilizer is not a significant bottleneck to its use. The more serious constraint on expansion of fertilizer consumption has been

TABLE 12–3

DISTRIBUTION OF INDIAN VILLAGES BY DISTANCE
FROM AN ALL-WEATHER ROAD

Distance	% of villages
Within village	10.9
Up to 1.5 miles	18.2
Between 1.5 and 3.5 miles	20.7
Between 3.5 and 5.5 miles	12.3
Between 5.5 and 10.5 miles	15.9
Between 10.5 and 20 miles	9.6
More than 20 miles	7.8
Information not available	4.6
Total	100.0

SOURCE: Owen, 1964, p. 52. Data are based on a survey undertaken in 1959 by the Ministry of Community Development, Government of India.

TABLE 12–4

VILLAGES WITHOUT ACCESS TO ROADS IN THE
STATE OF MAHARASHTRA, 1966

Category	Number of villages
Villages reporting	34,361
Villages not on main roads	26,947
Villages without approach roads	13,899
Villages connected by cart tracks	11,222
Villages connected by foot tracks	2,231
Villages connected by rivers or other waterways	446

SOURCE: Owen, 1964, p. 56; originally from Government of Maharashtra, Finance Department, *Report on Regional Transport Survey of Maharashtra State* (Bombay, 1966), Vol. I, Pt. II: "Appendices," Tables 6 and 8.

the frequent failure of transportation and marketing network to provide adequate fertilizer supplies at the time when they are needed to support the production cycle" (Mitra, 1969).

THE EFFECT OF POPULATION GROWTH ON TRANSPORTATION SYSTEMS

Clearly there is an intimate inter-connection between population density and the system of transporting goods, people, and information. The causal connection goes in both directions. On the one side, a dense population makes a transportation system both more necessary and more economical. Twice as many people in a small village implies that twice as many people will use a wagon path if it is built, and also implies twice as many hands with which to build the wagon path; the latter is true both of self-help nonmonetized projects and of centrally organized monetized (or forced labor) projects which use local labor. For example, in Europe and England "the growth of population—or more strictly the attainment of a certain density of population—made it worthwhile to improve and create transport facilities" (Habakkuk, 1963, p. 615). On the other side, a better transportation system brings an increased population (e.g., Wilson *et al.*, 1966), and probably leads to higher birth rates because of a higher standard of living. Furthermore, the existence of transportation connections means that a village's death rate is likely to be lower because it is less likely to be devastated by famine and starvation, as is shown by the history of India in the past 100 years.[3]

The interconnected nexus of transportation, communication, population, and modernity of practices is indicated by a factor analysis of Indian village characteristics:

Villages which score high on Factor 1 have relatively large populations stratified into many castes. They use more modern agricultural techniques and sell a high proportion of their output to nearby, easily accessible towns. They are also more aware of national legislation concerning untouchability and have better educational facilities, more school-age children in school, and a higher incidence of literacy. By

---

[3] A new and sad page in that history was being entered as the first draft of this chapter was being written. A newspaper advertisement for Bangladesh Relief carried this headline: "Tons of food, enough for several weeks, lie in the harbors . . . but few bridges and trucks exist to carry it inland. . . . Getting food grain through the shambles of a transportation system to people who need food is the problem" (*New York Times*, April 9, 1972, p. 5E).

And as the last draft is being finished in the summer of 1974, still another horrible page of this story is being entered. In the Sahelian area of Africa there is grave famine, starvation of people and cattle, and vast suffering because the governments failed to plan ahead of time and cooperate in providing the transportation of food even in the face of clear warnings and the provision of the necessary supplies by the United Nations and contributing nations.

contrast, the villages which score low on Factor 1 have small populations and few castes, use traditional agricultural techniques, produce principally for their own consumption rather than for market sale, *are distant from towns and cities, and have poor access (or none at all) to modern means of transport.* They are also less aware of national social legislation, have fewer educational facilities and are less educated. Theirs is a profile of traditional economic and cultural isolation and self-sufficiency and reflects the absence of integrative interactions with the larger economy and society.

The composition of Factor 1, therefore, suggests that it represents the extent of economic and social modernization at the village level (Adelman *et al.*, 1971, p. 570, italics added).

A quantitative estimate of the effect of population growth on transportation is necessary both for general understanding and for input to a numerical model. Glover and Simon (1975) have attacked this question with a cross-national study of the effect of road density upon population density. The general model[4] is

$$\frac{RDS}{LND} = f\left(\frac{POP}{LND}, \frac{Y}{POP}\right) \tag{12-1}$$

where RDS = miles of roads
       LND = square miles of land
       POP = population
and   Y = national income.
Later, PVD = miles of paved roads
       TOT = total miles of all roads
and i = country index.

The first method is a linear regression in a cross-section of 113 nations in 1968:

$$\left(\frac{TOT_{i,1968}}{LND_{i,1968}}\right) = -.119 + \underset{\substack{(t = .613) \\ (beta = .613)}}{.0025} \left(\frac{POP_{i,1968}}{LND_{i,1968}}\right) \tag{12-2}$$

$$+ \underset{\substack{(t = 7.4) \\ (beta = .422)}}{.0003} \left(\frac{Y_{i,1968}}{POP_{i,1968}}\right), R^2 = .65. \tag{12-2}$$

---

[4] Regressions would seem to be relatively little affected by causal effects running from transportation to population density, because better roads are not likely to influence migration from country to country, *ceteris paribus*.

270

The same relationship was also run in double-logarithmic form. The data are plotted in Figure 12–2 for each of the 5 quintiles of per-capita income (a device to hold income roughly constant). The relationship between population density and road density is clearly very strong. The log-log regression produces convenient estimates of elasticities as follows:

$$\log\left(\frac{TOT_{i,1969}}{LND_{i,1969}}\right) = -.380 + \underset{\substack{(t\,=\,18.1)\\(\text{beta}\,=\,.704)}}{.726\log} \left(\frac{POP_{i,1969}}{LND_{i,1969}}\right)$$

$$+ \underset{\substack{(t\,=\,12.4)\\(\text{beta}\,=\,.483)}}{.657\log} \left(\frac{Y_{i,1969}}{POP_{i,1969}}\right), R^2 = .83. \quad (12\text{–}3)$$

These results seem impressive. The R^2 of .83 is exceptionally high for cross-national regressions, especially in view of the fact that only two independent variables are used; an R^2 this high suggests that one need not search further for additional independent variables to explain the varia-

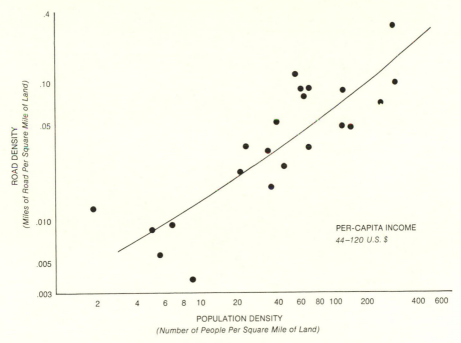

FIGURE 12–2   RELATIONSHIP BETWEEN POPULATION DENSITY AND ROAD DENSITY
FOR PER-CAPITA INCOME QUINTILES

SOURCE: Reproduced from Glover and Simon, 1975, p. 457.

271

FIGURE 12–2 (Continued)

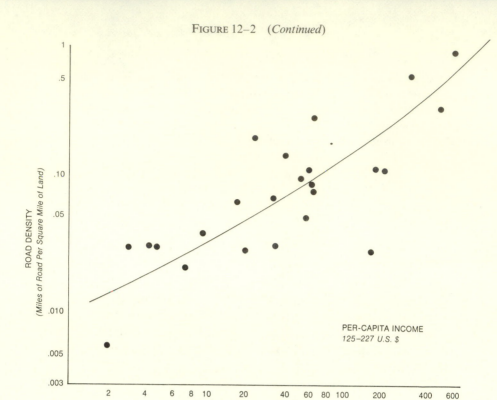

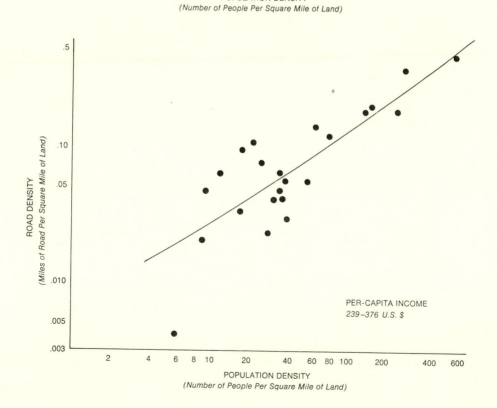

FIGURE 12–2 (*Continued*)

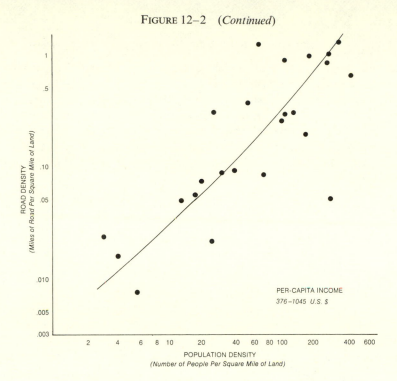

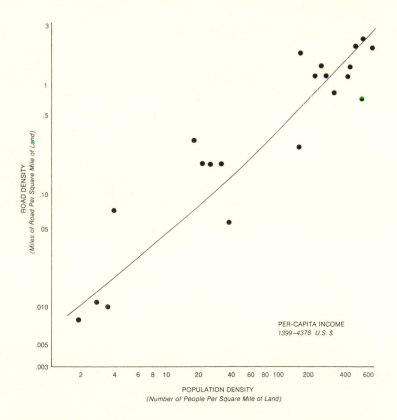

tion in the dependent variables. The elasticity of .73 of road density with respect to population density—that is, a 1% increase in population causes a .73% increase in road density, or as population doubles, roads increase 1.5 times—indicates that the relationship is very meaningful in economic terms. And the "real" relationship must be even higher because the estimate is biased downward because of measurement error. This regression may serve as the basis for estimates of the effect of population growth upon road density.

A cross-sectional sample of the countries' experiences over time was also run. The regression was

$$\left(\frac{TOT_{i,1969} - TOT_{i,1957}}{TOT_{i,1957}}\right)$$

$$= .066 + \underset{\substack{(t = 3.9) \\ (\text{beta} = .448)}}{.985} \left(\frac{POP_{i,1969} - POP_{i,1957}}{POP_{i,1957}}\right)$$

$$+ \underset{\substack{(t = 1.3) \\ (\text{beta} = .151)}}{.0006} \left(\frac{Y_{i,1969} - Y_{i,1957}}{Y_{i,1957}}\right), R^2 = .22. \tag{12-4}$$

This method is inherently free of many of the trend problems and other defects of simple time-series regressions (J. Simon, 1966), and multicollinearity is observed to be very low (.04). The coefficients in this regression may be read immediately as elasticities. Population density shows a very significant elasticity of almost unity, while per-capita incomes effect is small and not significant.

The main cross-sectional regression using *paved roads* is as follows:

$$\log\left(\frac{PVD_{i,1968}}{LND_{i,1968}}\right) = -6.431$$

$$+ \underset{\substack{(t = 21.9) \\ (\text{beta} = .714)}}{1.166} + \log\left(\frac{POP_{i,1968}}{LND_{i,1968}}\right)$$

$$+ \underset{\substack{(t = 15.7) \\ (\text{beta} = .509)}}{1.095} \left(\frac{Y_{i,1968}}{POP_{i,1968}}\right), R^2 = .88 \tag{12-5}$$

The R^2 of .88 in the log-log relationship—an unusually large proportion of variance explained in a cross-sectional study with low collinearity

($r = .197$) and only two variables—gives the impression that this is the whole story. The elasticities in the paved-roads regressions are even higher than in the total-roads regressions. This makes sense, because there is an increase in the *quality* as well as in the quantity of a country's roads as income increases. This is reflected in an increased proportion of total roads that are paved, which is consistent with the higher elasticities in the paved-roads regressions.[5]

In sum, population density seems to have a significant and strong effect on total road density—an elasticity of .7 or higher. The effect on paved-roads construction is even stronger—an elasticity higher than unity. These relationships *can* be interpreted causally because there is not much migration among countries, our units of observation. The results imply that an increase in population has a very positive effect on a country's infrastructure, on the reasonable assumption that increased congestion does not negate all the benefits of the additional facilities.

OTHER EFFECTS OF POPULATION ON SOCIAL CAPITAL

Increased population density can also have many other sorts of productivity-affecting impacts which are exceedingly subtle or indirect, but yet very important. For example, local government becomes better organized as population increases (Stevenson, 1968); such government improves the possibility of community projects and of the sort of stability that encourages economic activity. A major effect is the impact upon health, especially malaria.

Malaria is the most widespread of tropical diseases. Though it occurs in certain temperate regions, its main spheres of action are in the hot, wet belt. It attacks (or did until recently) something like one-third of the human race, but in practice all the inhabitants of the hot, wet belt may be considered to be more or less infected. Malaria weakens those whom it attacks, for the bouts of fever sap their physical strength and make them unfit for sustained effort. Hence agriculture does not receive all the care it needs, and the food supply is thereby affected. In this way a vicious circle is formed. Weakened by insufficient nourishment, the system offers small resistance to infection and cannot provide the effort required to produce an adequate supply of food. The malarial patient knows quite well that a bout of fever may be the unpleasant reward for hard work. . . . Undoubtedly, malaria is largely responsible for the

---

[5] A possible contributing reason is that the data for paved roads are likely to be more accurate than the data for total roads.

poor health, small numbers, and absence of enthusiasm for work of tropical peoples. . . .

In the pre-scientific age, men kept the most serious infectious diseases in check by organizing the total occupation of the land, thus eliminating the breeding places of the mosquito. Such occupation demanded a high density of population and a complete control of land use, and hence the interdependence of a highly organized agricultural system (itself a function of soil quality, reliable climate and a certain degree of technical competence), a dense population and an advanced political organization. . . . It is also difficult to improve sanitation and health in sparsely peopled areas; anti-malarial campaigns stand but small chance of lasting success, whilst the tsetse fly finds such areas very much to its liking, for it is impossible for a population of ten or a dozen persons to the square mile to keep down the vegetation to a level unfavourable to this insect (Gourou, 1966, pp. 8, 9, 14, 98).

The data on Ceylon in Table 12–5 support Gourou's argument, showing that low population is associated with a high incidence of malaria. Of course one might wonder whether population was low in non-malarious areas because people moved away from malaria. But the history of Ceylon suggests otherwise (Gourou, 1966, p. 10). Also it has been suggested that the decline of the Roman Empire was in large part due to the spread of malaria after political upheaval and decreased population density interfered with the maintenance of the drainage system (Gourou, 1966, p. 10).

Looking to examples of improvement rather than retrogression, now, the history of England was heavily affected by the decline of malaria induced by population growth. "Westminster was paved in 1762 and the City in 1766, 'Fleet ditch was then first covered in and the streets

TABLE 12–5

POPULATION, AREA, AND POPULATION DENSITY OF DISTRICTS OF CEYLON (SRILANKA) GROUPED BY THE ENDEMICITY OF MALARIA IN THE DISTRICTS*

Endemicity of malaria	Spleen rates* (%)	Population[†]		Area		Population density per square mile
		Number	%	Square miles	%	
Not endemic	0–9	4,142,889	62	5,113	20	810
Moderately endemic	10–24	1,207,569	18	5,271	21	229
Highly endemic	25–49	994,495	15	8,460	33	118
Hyperendemic	50–74	312,466	5	6,489	26	48

SOURCE: Frederiksen, 1968, in Heer, 1968, p. 70.
*Average of surveys in 1939 and 1941.
[†] 1946 census.

paved with large stones,' and the marshes near London were drained about the same time. To this cause Lind ascribed the extinction of acute malaria in the Metropolis. A writer in 1781 said, 'Very few die now of Ague in London'" (Buer, 1968, p. 219).

The economic development of the United States also reveals the influence of malaria, and the effect of increased population on malaria incidence. ". . . A mighty influence buoying up wages paid to the men building canals during the 1820's and 1830's was the danger of yellow fever and malaria. Built through marsh and swamps (in many instances) to reduce construction problems, the canals were known as killers . . . As the country was settled, the marshy land where malaria was bred was filled in. Buildings covered the waste spaces where animal vectors could survive. . ." (Lebergott, 1964, p. 250).

Though it is reasonably clear that increased population density may have a positive effect on rural infrastructure in LDC's, this section does not even come within reaching distance of a quantitative estimate of the over-all effect. In the meantime, the elasticity estimated earlier for the response of roads to population size may be taken as a proxy for the effect on all social capital.[6] More generally, Chenery's (1960) estimate may be taken as the basis for the estimation of the effects of population size on economies of scale including social capital, an elasticity of .20.

Summary

This chapter discusses the effect of population size on crucial elements of social infrastructure—especially the transportation and communication networks, and the level of public health. An increase in population size has a strong and salutary influence on these crucial elements. With respect to the road network—which is indispensable for marketing agricultural produce and hence for agricultural and over-all development, it was shown that the amount of roads per unit of area is roughly proportional to the population density, which suggests a great benefit of higher population density. In the context of the LDC model to be presented later, however, the effect of population size on social infrastructure will be subsumed under over-all economies of scale as estimated by Chenery (1960) to increase productivity by about one-fifth of one percent for each percent of increase of population size (an elasticity of .20).

---

[6] Barlow (1967) built a simulation model of the effect of malaria eradication in Ceylon which suggests negative long-run economic results because of the increase in population resulting from the eradication, though positive short-run results were positive. But Barlow's model does not embrace such effects of improved health as a greater propensity to work, more mental energy, higher expectations about one's children's life expectancy (and hence lower fertility), and so forth. I believe that if these important elements were taken account of, malaria eradication would be seen to have long-run positive economic results.

CHAPTER 13

Simulations of the Effect
of Population Growth on the Economic
Development of LDC's

INTRODUCTION

THE GENERAL model proposed for the study of the effect of population growth on the development and industrialization of LDC's was outlined and argued in Chapter 7; the reader should refer to that chapter for discussion of any general points not covered in this chapter. Then Chapters 8–12 studied the empirical bases for the various parameters and relationships that enter into the model. This chapter puts it all together. Various specifications of the model are simulated, and the rate of economic development is then investigated under different assumptions about population growth.

To recapitulate, there is a fundamental contradiction in economic knowledge concerning the effect of population growth in LDC's. On the one hand, the main conventional theoretical elements suggest that more population retards the growth of output per worker.[1] The overwhelmingly important element in the conventional theory is Malthusian diminishing returns to labor as the stock of capital (including land) does not increase in the same proportion as does labor. Another important theoretical element is the dependency effect, which suggests that saving is more difficult for households when there are more children, and that higher fertility causes social investment funds to be diverted away from industrial production. Combined together in simulation models (e.g., Coale and Hoover, 1958; Enke and Zind, 1969), these conventional elements suggest that relatively high fertility and positive population growth have a negative effect upon output per worker (and an even more negative effect upon income per-consumer equivalent, because the proportion of consumer equivalents to workers is higher when fertility is higher).

But the empirical data discussed in Chapters 3 and 7 do not support this a priori reasoning. When the theory and the data do not agree, either (or both) may need re-examination. This chapter re-examines the theory.

---

[1] Output per worker or output per-worker hour, and not income per person or income per-consumer equivalent, is the appropriate measure of the productive power of an economy. And productive power rather than the quantity of consumption would seem to be the underlying concept in economic development. Hence output per worker (Y/L) is the measure of performance used throughout this chapter.

A model is constructed that includes the elements of the standard models but also embodies other elements discussed in the qualitative literature as being important: demand effects upon investment (emphasized by the historians of England); the work-leisure choice,[2] and variations in work activity as a function of differences in needs and standard of living, and economies of scale.[3] The model also embodies elements recognized elsewhere in the development literature as important: intersectoral shifts in labor (e.g., Chenery, 1960), depreciation (e.g., Enke, 1963), and land building (e.g., Slicher van Bath, 1963). All these elements are discussed in Chapters 8–12.

The model solves by utility maximization—finding the highest current leisure-output indifference curve that touches the current production function. This solution determines the allocation of labor to the agricultural and industrial sectors, and the outputs of the two sectors. (The solution embodies empirically observed elasticities of demand and allocations of output at different income levels in LDC's.)

Using a variety of parameters, the simulation indicates that *moderate* population growth produces considerably better economic performance in the long run (120 to 180 years) than does a slower-growing population, though in the shorter run (60 years), the slower-growing population performs slightly better. A *declining* population does very badly in the long run. And in the experiments with the "best" estimates of the parameters for a representative Asian LDC (the "base run"), moderate population growth (doubling over 50 years) has better long-run performance than either fast population growth (doubling over 35 years or less) or slow population growth (doubling over about 2,000 years).

Experiments with one variable at a time reveal that the difference between these results and previous theoretical studies is produced by the *combination* of the novel elements—the leisure-output work decision, economies of scale, the accelerator investment function, and depreciation; no one factor is predominant. Perhaps the most important result is that within the range of positive population growth, different parameters lead to different positive rates of population growth as "optimum." This means that no simple qualitative theory of population growth can be very helpful, and that a more complex quantitatively-based theory is necessary.

The various parametric specifications are intended to capture the key elements of such circumstances as China in the seven centuries prior to World War II, eighteenth-century England, contemporary India, and contemporary countries growing faster than India. Sensitivity analyses

---

[2] See Chapters 8–12; also Tussing (1969) quoted in Kelley, Williamson and Cheetham, 1972, writing on Japan; and Myrdal 1968, Chapter 22.

[3] See Chapter 12, above.

279

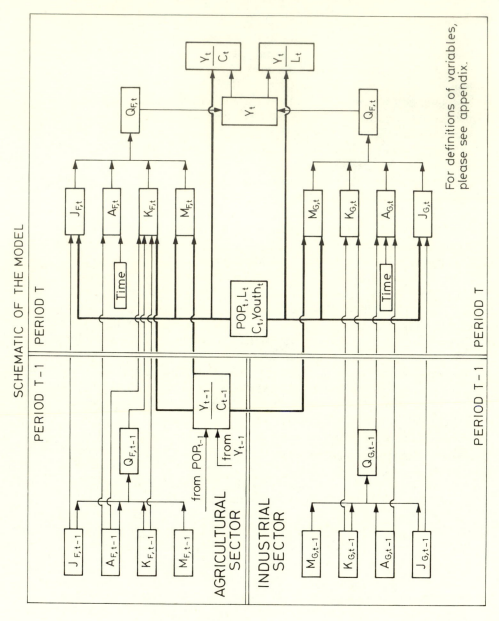

SCHEMATIC OF THE MODEL

For definitions of variables, please see appendix.

FIGURE 13–1 SCHEMATIC OF THE LDC MODEL

are carried out to determine which parameters the model seems to be more and less sensitive to. Two sets of birth-rate structures are used in the experiments. The structures in the first set are all income responsive, but they differ in two respects: (1) the speed with which fertility falls as a function of income; and (2) whether or not there is an initial rise in fertility with the initial rise in income. The other three fertility structures are various constant proportions of births to women in the child-bearing cohorts, ranging from very low to very high fertility ratios.

The chapter first specifies the form of each equation in the system, and indicates the bases for the range of estimates used in the various experiments. Then the results of the various experiments are presented, along with the conclusions that the results seem to warrant.

THE MODEL

This description of the model skims quickly over the aspects that are common to such models, and dwells on the novel ones. Additional reasoning behind the specification, and data underlying the parameters, is found in Chapters 7–12. The model is sketched in Figure 13–1.

Output (Q_F) in the agricultural sector (denoted by F for "farm") is made a Cobb-Douglas function of land plus other physical capital together (K_F), labor in man-hours (M_F), social capital (J), and the level of agricultural productive efficiency at that point in history (A_F):

$$Q_{F,t} = A_{F,t} K_{F,t}^{\alpha} M_{F,t}^{\beta} J_t \tag{13–1}$$

The exponents α and β in the base run are .5 and .5, respectively; the conclusions are not different with other reasonable exponents, however.

Social overhead capital, which is treated together with economies of scale,[4] is made a function of total labor force (L_t):

$$\frac{J_{t+1} - J_t}{J_t} = a_{112}\left(\frac{L_t - L_{t-1}}{L_{t-1}}\right) \tag{13–2}$$

---

[4] Social capital is treated together with economies of scale because the two factors cannot well be separated. The J term stands for such items as better road networks that accompany higher population, (Glover and Simon, 1975) efficiencies in production that accompany larger markets, improved government organization (Stevenson, 1968), and better health services and malaria eradication that go along with higher population density in agricultural areas.

The parameter a_{112} is .20 in the base run[5] (Chenery, 1960). Runs are also made with elasticities of .40 and of 0 to see the importance of the scale parameter.

Agricultural investment[6] is made a function of the "gap" between the *aspired-to* ("desired") amount of farm capital and the *actual* amount of farm capital:

$$\frac{K_{F,t+1} - K_{F,t}}{K_{F,t}} = a_{1140} \text{GAP}_t - a_{1141}. \tag{13-3}$$

The aspired-to level of farm capital is made a multiplicand of farm capital and technological efficiency, and is set at four times the output; all over the world the value of agricultural capital is very close to four times as large as the value of a year's gross output (Buck, 1930; Clark, 1957; Gov. of India, various years) so apparently that is a goal that is aspired to (and reached).

$$\text{GAP}_t = \frac{Q_{F,t} - A_{F,t}K_{F,t}}{A_{F,t}K_{F,t}}, \tag{13-4}$$

where $A_{F,t}$ is initially set at .25[7] and $K_{F,t}$ is initially set at $4 Q_{F,t=0}$.

The farmer is assumed to make up some proportion of the gap in each year: 25% is the proportion in the base run. That is, the coefficient a_{1140} in equation (13-3) is set at .25 in the base run, and takes other values in other runs. The term a_{1141} stands for depreciation[8] and is set at .01 in the base run; it is varied in other runs.

The agricultural investment function and the agricultural production function together have the unusual property that no conservation equation connects them. That is, investment and production for current consumption do not trade off within total production, because in peasant

[5] One may well argue that total output is the best measure of J. But I have opted for measuring J in terms of the labor force because the only solid estimate of economies of scale in the manufacturing sector (Chenery, 1960) uses the closely related total-population measure: "If income level is held constant, however, population may be taken as an indicator of the net effect of market size" (p. 645). Given that the parameter used in the base runs in this study is derived from Chenery, it seems reasonable to use a measurement concept similar to his.

It would be interesting to try some runs with J defined on output in each sector. But it seems likely that this change would only intensify the results given here because output is more volatile than the labor force.

[6] Agricultural investment in this context includes land clearance, local irrigation, and construction of tools. The input of such investments is mostly off-season labor by farmers.

[7] More specifically, $A_{F,t}$ and $K_{F,t}$ are initially set to allow for the 4 to 1 capital output ratio in agriculture.

[8] The response functions for investment and technology in both sectors are constrained to be nonnegative. Depreciation can, however, cause net investment to be negative on balance and does so in some trials.

agriculture investment is mostly *not* a matter of part of total production being withheld from consumption as it is in industrial investment. The labor devoted to crop production is mostly not in competition with the labor devoted to clearing new fields, irrigation works, and so forth; rather, the two activities take place in different seasons.

The absence of conservation is part-and-parcel of the model not being constructed as a closed resource system equilibrated by rational economic behavior on the part of producers and wage-earners. Rather the system is an open set of equations, each chosen pragmatically for its representation of a relevant aspect of a dynamic production-consumption system; the marginal products of labor and capital, therefore, do not remain equal in the agricultural and industrial sector. This approach is less aesthetic from the standpoint of economic theory than is a neo-classical economic-development model such as that of Kelley et al. (1972). But there are two justifications for this choice. First, an attempt to construct this model in neo-classical terms would face fundamental theoretical problems such as the valuation of land and other agricultural capital that was formed hundreds of years earlier (an income-stream approach being circular here). And a neo-classical model embodying a work-leisure choice by workers would require breaking new ground in that direction (though see Sen, 1966; Yotopolous and Lau, 1973). Second the appropriate comparison of this model and its results is to such models as Coale-Hoover (1958), Enke et al. (1969), and perhaps *Limits to Growth* (Meadows et al., 1972), which also are not neo-classical. That is, the appropriate and fair comparison is to other models whose primary aims are similar—to assess the effects of different rates of population growth on the rate of economic development—rather than to models which aim to accomplish other purposes.[9]

The gain-in-technological-knowledge function in agriculture is made to depend only on time, as seems appropriate in most LDC agriculture. (Switches in technique of the sort emphasized by Boserup, 1965, are embodied in the production function.)

$$A_{F,t+1} = a_{115}A_{F,t} \qquad (13\text{–}5)$$

with $a_{115} = 1.005$ in the base run, and other values in other runs.

The labor-supply function will be described later in the context of the integrated two-sector model.

---

[9] It should be noted that though the neo-classical sort of "sacrifice"—the choice between investment and consumption—is not found in this model, the model does embody the choice of "sacrificing" labor for more agricultural investment and especially for more current production. This latter choice, in turn, is left out of the neo-classical models. So, on balance, this model would seem to need little apology on this score.

Now for the industrial sector (denoted by the subscript G). The industrial production function is

$$Q_{G,t} = A_{G,t} K_{G,t}^{\gamma} M_{G,t}^{\epsilon} J_t \qquad (13\text{–}6)$$

Exponents are $\gamma = .4$ and $\epsilon = .6$ in the base run.

Technological change in industry is a function of both time and the change in output:

$$A_{G,t+1} = A_{G,t} + a_{1170} A_{G,t} + a_{1171} \log_{10}\left(\frac{Q_{G,t} - Q_{G,t-1}}{Q_{G,t}}\right) A_{G,t}$$

$$\left(\frac{Q_{G,t} - Q_{G,t-1}}{Q_{G,t}}\right) \geq 0 \qquad (13\text{–}7)$$

where a_{1170} is .005 and a_{1171} is .002, respectively, in the base runs.

Industrial investment is made to depend upon the change in industrial output. It also depends upon the burden of youth dependency. And there is a deduction for depreciation:

$$K_{G,t+1} = K_{G,t} + a_{1181}\left[\log_{10}\left(\frac{Q_{G,t} - Q_{G,t-1}}{Q_{G,t}}\right)\right]$$

$$\times\, (1 - a_{1182}\, \text{YOUTH}_t)(K_{G,t}) - a_{1183} K_{G,t} \qquad (13\text{–}8)$$

$$\left(\frac{Q_{G,t} - Q_{G,t-1}}{Q_{G,t}}\right) \geq 0$$

where $a_{1181} = .0275$, $a_{1182} = .50$ and $a_{1183} = .025$, in the base run (other values in other runs). That is, the amount of investment that would otherwise take place is modified downward by the youth dependency burden.[10] The depreciation parameter implying a 40-year life for equip-

---

[10] More specifically, the absolute amount of youth dependency is calculated in this context in the same manner as Leff (1969), in order to make the parameter consistent with his estimate:

$$\frac{\sum_{i=1}^{14}(\text{MEN}_i + \text{WOM}_i)}{\sum_{i=15}^{64}(\text{MEN}_i + \text{WOM}_i)}$$

The dependency burden for any year, YOUTH_t, is computed as a difference between that year's burden and the base year's burden:

$$\text{YOUTH}_t = \frac{\left[\dfrac{\sum_{i=1}^{14}(\text{MEN}_i + \text{WOM}_i)_t}{\sum_{i=15}^{64}(\text{MEN}_i + \text{WOM}_i)_t}\right] - \left[\dfrac{\sum_{i=1}^{14}(\text{MEN}_i + \text{WOM}_i)\,\text{base year}}{\sum_{i=15}^{64}(\text{MEN}_i + \text{WOM}_i)\,\text{base year}}\right]}{\left[\dfrac{\sum_{i=1}^{14}(\text{MEN}_i + \text{WOM}_i)\,\text{base year}}{\sum_{i=15}^{64}(\text{MEN}_i + \text{WOM}_i)\,\text{base year}}\right]}$$

ment is almost surely too small; a 20-year life is probably closer to the truth in LDC's (Kuznets, 1966, Table 5–5), and some estimates have put depreciation much faster even than this in some places (Fei and Ranis, 1964, quoted in Kelley and Williamson, 1971).

Equation 13–8 is a mixed-bag operational summary of the savings and investment effects, especially with respect to industrial output. It is assumed that an increase in output makes producers desire to increase their capital, and that they therefore save and invest to realize that desire. The youth-dependency effect is assumed to result from decreased private savings, and investment is assumed to equal savings and hence is reduced by increased dependency.

If an "additional" child's parents choose to spend money on educating him rather than in investing that sum in their farm or shop, the choice will show up as a decrease in national saving because of the way national accounts are kept. The same is true in the government sector; a shift from investment in infrastructure or industry into schooling will show up as a decrease in monetized saving, because most public educational expenses are salaries on current account. Therefore, the adjustment of the savings rate for the youth-dependency effect allows for the cost of the investment in human capital in outfitting additional children for the labor force. This implicitly assumes that average new entrants to the labor force have the same skills as average old entrants, which seems *not* to be true. But allowing for this is beyond the scope of this simulation.

A device to combine the agricultural and industrial sectors is necessary to complete the supply side and construct an aggregate production function.[11] This is done here by fixing the relative sizes of the outputs of the two sectors in any given period as a function of the per-consumer-equivalent income (Y/C) in the previous period.[12] That is, at a lagged Y/C of $75, total output is set at 35% industrial output plus 65% agricultural

---

The value $-.50$ for a_{1182} is roughly equal to Leff's estimate, and is used in the base run. Values of zero and -1.0 are also used in other runs.

[11] Theoretically, it is conceivable to develop this model with the three mutually competing outputs of agriculture, industry, and leisure. But this would present great problems both in making it intuitively satisfactory and in developing methods of calculation.

[12] C_t = consumer equivalents = $.11 (\text{MEN}_1 + \text{WOM}_1) + .14 \left[\sum_1^4 \text{MEN} + \sum_1^4 \text{WOM} \right] +$

$.39 \left[\sum_5^{14} \text{MEN} + \sum_5^{14} \text{WOM} \right] + .90 \left[\sum_{15}^{24} \text{MEN} + \sum_{15}^{24} \text{WOM} \right] + 1.0 \left[\sum_{25}^{99} \text{MEN} + \sum_{25}^{99} \text{WOM} \right].$

This calculation of consumer equivalents is based on the weights of Kleiman (1967) and others for the amount of consumption of people and various ages in LDC's. The appropriate weights change in the course of economic development. But the lack of such an adjustment here is not likely to make a major difference in the simulation.

output. At a Y/C of \$1,000, output is set at 90% industrial output plus 10% agricultural output. These divisions roughly correspond to the facts for LDC's and MDC's in the world today, and reflect observed income elasticities for the two types of goods. Between these two points the interpolation is linear:

$$\frac{Q_{G,t}}{Q_{F,t} + Q_{G,t}} = .35 + \left[\frac{\left(\frac{Y_{t-1}}{C_{t-1}}\right) - \$75}{\$1000 - \$75}\right](.90 - .35). \quad (13\text{--}9)$$

This function does more than allow for the Engel-effect difference in proportions of agricultural and industrial consumption at different levels of development, however. It also allows for the effect of different dependency ratios on output, as follows: An additional baby born in a given family does not immediately alter total output, but it does immediately lower the income per-consumer-equivalent, hence immediately producing an increase in the proportion of total output that is agricultural.

The accounting identity for the aggregate production function is:

$$Y_t = Q_{F,t} + Q_{G,t} = A_{F,t}K_{F,t}^{\alpha}M_{F,t}^{\beta}J_{F,t} + A_{G,t}K_{G,t}^{\gamma}M_{G,t}^{\epsilon}J_{G,t} \quad (13\text{--}10)$$

Given that for any amount of Y_t the amounts of $Q_{F,t}$ and $Q_{G,t}$ are fixed, there is a single-valued amount of Y_t that will be produced for any given input of labor hours, M. (All the other terms in the production functions are predetermined.) Hence, the community (in the model) can choose without further complication between just the two goods, leisure and output.

The demand side is a set of tastes for various mixes of leisure and output (i.e., a set of indifference curves). The indifference curves are constructed for a "representative" worker, and are then summed over the number of workers. Each indifference curve is semi-logarithmic to reflect the almost universal observation in psychology that proportional differences are felt to be equal-size differences. This functional form also is commonly assumed by economists (on the basis of intuition and casual empiricism) in discussions of the marginal utility of money, taxes, and so forth. Sensitivity experiments have not been done with other functional forms of the indifference curves, but such experiments are no easy matter computationally.

Each indifference curve in Figure 7–2 at a given time t is equivalent to a straight line drawn on a semilogarithmic graph, as shown in Figure 13–2. The horizontal axis measures work effort from 0% to 100% of possible yearly man hours[13] (actually 0 to 1.0 for the variable Z). Each indifference

---

[13] For data on the variation in hours worked per week in industry in countries with different income levels, see Denison (1967), Kreps (1967), Moore (1971), and Winston (1966). Evidence that consumption aspirations affect work effort is shown in Taiwan by D. Freed-

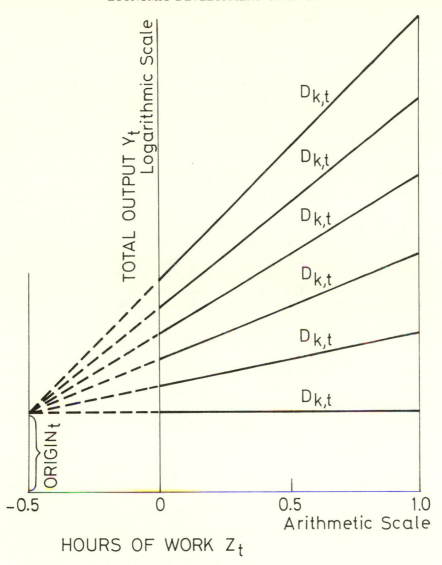

FIGURE 13–2   THE WORK-LEISURE TRADE-OFF ON A SEMI-LOGARITHMIC SCALE

man (1972b). The higher the aspiration index—a composite of the respondent's plans and desires for the purchase of consumer durables—the more likely the wives of wage-and-salary workers are to be employed. The proportion ranges from 25% to 33% over the aspiration index. Taiwanese families with "modern" consumption patterns are also likely to save more (D. Freedman, 1970).

curve $D_{k,t}$ (k is the index of a particular curve within the set D_t at time t) is formed as follows:

$$D_{k,t} = \text{ORIGIN}_t + b_k \ (\text{antilog}_e Z_t), \tag{13–11}$$

where b_k is the slope that characterizes any one indifference curve $D_{k,t}$ within the set of indifference curves D_t at time t. Each indifference function $D_{k,t}$ runs through a point whose coordinate on the horizontal axis is equal to $-.5Z$ in most runs. Only values $0 < Z < 1.0$ are allowed, to reflect the fact that no one can work less than zero hours or more than his maximum.

The other coordinate for the point of departure for each $D_{k,t}$ in the set D_t at time t is, on the vertical axis, the height of ORIGIN, which depends upon (1) dependency as measured by the ratio of consumer equivalents to workers; the larger the number of dependents, the more the worker "needs" goods, and the more work he will trade for output, *ceteris paribus;* (2) the aspirations function RELASP, which rises less than proportionally with real income, in accordance with such studies as those of Fuchs and Landsberger (1973) and Centers and Cantril (1936); (3) the "standard of living (STD$_t$)"; the basis for the standard of living is actual income, but the standard of living is assumed to change less rapidly than actual income.

$$\text{ORIGIN}_t = (\text{RELASP}_t)(\text{STD}_t)\left(\frac{C_t}{L_t}\right) \tag{13–12}$$

A change in ORIGIN via a change in any of its elements causes a shift from one to another *set* of indifference curves, D.

The elements in equation (13–12) are:

$$\text{STD}_t = \frac{Y_{t-1}}{C_{t-1}} \text{ subject to} \tag{13–13}$$

$$(1 - a_{1193})\text{STD}_{t-1} \le \text{STD}_t \le (1 + a_{1193})\text{STD}_{t-1}.$$

The constraint on equation (13–13) ensures that the standard of living does not rise or fall at a precipitous rate; its movement is less volatile than that of real income. This reflects the behavior of the consumption function over business cycles, changing less rapidly than income. The constraint parameter a_{1193} is .015 in the base run.

The RELASP aspirations function varies inversely with income, linearly over the range of income $75–$1,000.

$$\text{RELASP}_t = a_{141} - a_{142}\left(\frac{Y_{t-1}}{C_{t-1}} - \$75/\$925\right) \tag{13–14}$$

a_{141} is .4 and a_{142} is .2 in the base run.

Next the labor-force function:

$$L_t = \text{labor force} = \sum_{i=15}^{64} \text{MEN}_i + .5 \sum_{i=15}^{64} \text{WOM}_i. \qquad (13\text{–}15)$$

The labor force counts each man aged 15–64 as a male-equivalent worker, and each woman as half a male-equivalent worker. (This assumes she spends at least half her time working in the home, work which is outside the scope of our model.) The consumer-equivalent function was defined earlier.

The system is solved by finding the value of Z which corresponds to the point of tangency of (1) the aggregate production function (Equation 13–10), and (2) the highest $D_{k,t}$ among the set of indifference curves D_t (Equation 13–11), that touches the production function (see Figure 7–1). This solution simultaneously fixes the amount of output and the total labor input in man-hours.[14] Formally,

$$L_t D_{k,t} = Y_t \text{ at the point of solution.} \qquad (13\text{–}16)$$

All the other elements in the production function and the indifference curves are predetermined by the prior year's values, and hence are constants in the numerical solution. Actually, the solution is obtained by an iterative convergence program. The values so obtained check well with analytic solutions obtained for the special cases where they could be found.

The initial age distribution of the population is in every case that of India in the 1950's as estimated by Coale and Hoover (1958). The numbers of persons of various ages eligible for work in any year are functions of births and deaths in earlier years. The death rate is a function of the prior period's income.[15] For each cohort in each period, the death rate is a logarithmic interpolation between the mortality schedules for India and Sweden, setting $75 and $1,000 per capita as the endpoints of the interpolation.

The fertility functions—in the form of the general fertility ratio (births/women 15–44) which is initially .142—are the control variable in the model. Three functions depend upon per-consumer-equivalent income. The function called "fast falling fertility response to increasing income" declines with an elasticity of 1.0 as income rises. The function called

---

[14] There is no independent allowance for the negative effect of fertility on female work outside the home. Nor is unemployment treated separately. Rather, both of these effects are subsumed by the over-all work-leisure relationship in the indifference curves. Future work might well include these factors in a more explicit fashion.

[15] Krishnamurty (1966) estimated that for India over the period 1922–60, the elasticity of the death rate per 1,000 population was about -2 with respect to real per-capita income, allowing for trend. The elasticities would surely be greater at the lower ages, smaller at the higher ages. (The elasticities surely would be weaker at ranges of income higher than India's, of course).

"slowly falling fertility response to increasing income" declines with an elasticity of .5. "Rising then fast falling fertility response to increasing income" has fertility rise with income at first, and then fertility falls with an elasticity of 1.0. The effects of these functions can be gauged best by the number of consumer-equivalents in various years as seen in Table 12–1. But the population size varies from run to run because fertility and mortality are functions of income, and income is a different function of fertility in runs with different economic parameters.

There is also a fertility structure called "thousand births" with 1,000 births each year, the starting point of the systems in all runs. And there is a structure with a constant ratio of births to women aged 15–44 which is roughly equivalent to a crude birth rate (CBR) of about 32, called "constant high." The structure "constant very high" has a birth/woman ratio equivalent to a CBR of 42. And in some runs there are structures with CBR's of 25 ("constant moderate") and 37.

The Findings

1. Using those parameters that seem most descriptive of LDC's today, the very high birth-rate structures and the very-low birth-rate structures both result in lower long-run per-worker outputs (hereafter referred to as "economic performance") than do birth-rate structures in between. It will surprise no one in this decade that very high birth rates are not best. But the outcome that very substantial birth-rate structures produce higher incomes in the long run than do low birth rates runs very much against the conventional wisdom. The same result appears with quite different levels of the various parameters.

More specifically, columns 4–6 in Table 13–1 show the per-worker output in various years for the six experimental birth-rate structures described earlier, whose population sizes in various years in consumer equivalents are shown in columns 1–3 of Table 13–1 (or row 1 of Table 13–2). These data are plotted in Figures 13–3 and 13–4. In the earliest years the very-low-fertility populations have slightly better economic performance. But with time, the very-low-fertility and very-high-fertility populations fall well behind the moderate-fertility population. Much the same result appears in runs with a wide variety of parameters subject to the discussion to follow. Data for per-consumer-equivalent results are plotted in Figures 13–5 and 13–6 for those who find that measure useful.

The difference between these results and those obtained by Coale and Hoover (1958) and the more recent work in that tradition such as that by Tempo is due to the inclusion in this model of several factors omitted from the Coale-Hoover model: (1) the capacity of people to vary their work input in response to their varying income aspirations and family-

TABLE 13–1
RESULTS OF BASE RUN IN LDC MODEL BY YEAR*

Year Fertility structure	Consumer equivalents (C) in tens of thousands of consumer equivalents			Output per worker (Y/L) in constant dollars			Index of labor utilized (Z)			Output per consumer equivalent (Y/C) in constant dollars		
	60 (1)	120 (2)	180 (3)	60 (4)	120 (5)	180 (6)	60 (7)	120 (8)	180 (9)	60 (10)	120 (11)	180 (12)
Fast-falling fertility response to increasing income	36	34	28	443	552	472	.54	.53	.60	277	339	289
Rising then fast falling response	53	105	104	438	715	915	.54	.46	.43	272	448	554
Slow-falling response	46	78	111	442	696	1076	.54	.46	.37	275	431	661
Thousand births	39	45	48	446	641	949	.54	.47	.40	279	394	546
Constant moderate 25 ratio	41	73	152	438	680	1058	.54	.46	.37	271	419	648
Constant high 32 ratio	57	158	512	438	692	1025	.53	.47	.40	270	424	625
Constant 37 ratio	73	283	1242	432	666	926	.54	.49	.44	265	405	562
Constant very high 42 ratio	93	477	2723	423	622	812	.55	.52	.48	257	375	489

NOTE: $C_{t=0} = 24,605$ $Y_{t=0}/L_{t=0} = 217$ $Z_{t=0} = .530$
*For a summary of the parameters, see Table 13–2, row 1.

TABLE 13–2

OUTPUT PER WORKER (Y/L) AND ACTUAL WORK AS PROPORTION OF POTENTIAL WORK (Z) WITH VARIOUS PARAMETERS

A. PARAMETERS

	Economies of scale a_{112} (1)	Dependency industrial saving a_{1182} (2)	Agricultural investment response a_{1140} (3)	Agricultural depreciation a_{1141} (4)	Industrial investment response a_{1181} (5)	Industrial depreciation a_{1183} (6)	Agricultural technological change—time a_{115} (7)	Industrial technological change—time a_{1170} (8)	Industrial technological change response a_{1171} (9)	Aspiration origin proportion a_{141} (10)	Constraint on living-standard change a_{1193} (11)
1. Base run	.20	.5	.25	.01	.0275	.025	1.005	.005	.002	.4	.015
2. Fixed work hours	.20	.5	.25	.01	.0275	.025	1.005	.005	.002	.4	.015
3. No economies of scale	.00	.5	.25	.01	.0275	.025	1.005	.005	.002	.4	.015
4. No economies, extra depreciation	.00	.5	.25	.015	.0275	.037	1.005	.005	.002	.4	.015
5. No economies, extra depreciation, extra investment	.00	.5	.25	.015	.035	.037	1.005	.005	.002	.4	.015
6. Double economies of scale	.40	.5	.25	.01	.0275	.025	1.005	.005	.002	.4	.015
7. Low growth	.20	.5	.25	.005	.020	.012	1.0025	.0025	.001	.4	.015
8. No dependency	.20	.0	.25	.01	.0275	.025	1.005	.005	.002	.4	.015
9. No economies, no dependency	.00	.0	.25	.01	.0275	.025	1.005	.005	.002	.4	.015
10. England	.30	.5	.5	.01	.0275	.025	1.005	.001	.002	.5	.015
11. India	.10	.5	.1	.01	.020	.025	1.005	.005	.001	.3	.0075
12. England with regular aspirations	.30	.5	.5	.01	.0275	.025	1.005	.001	.002	.4	.015
13. India with regular aspirations	.10	.5	.10	.01	.020	.025	1.005	.005	.001	.4	.0075
14. England with regular economies	.20	.5	.5	.01	.0275	.025	1.005	.001	.002	.5	.015
15. India with regular economies	.20	.5	.1	.01	.020	.025	1.005	.005	.001	.3	.0075

B. Results

	Results with endogenous fertility structures								Results with externally fixed fertility structures							
	Fast-falling fertility response to income		Rising then fast falling		Slow-falling response		Thousand births		Moderate constant child/woman ratio (25)		High constant child/woman ratio (32)		Constant 37 ratio		Very high constant ratio (42)	
	Y/L (12)	Z (13)	Y/L (14)	Z (15)	Y/L (16)	Z (17)	Y/L (18)	Z (19)	Y/L (20)	Z (21)	Y/L (22)	Z (23)	Y/L (24)	Z (25)	Y/L (26)	Z (27)
1*	472	.60	915	.43	1,096	.37	949	.40	1,058	.37	1,025	.40	916	.44	812	.48
2	—	—	—	—	—	—	1,666	.41	1,189	.41	1,047	.41	888	.41	730	.41
3	561	.54	623	.47	675	.45	711	.45	669	.45	567	.49	—	—	300	.59
4	182	.85	365	.63	402	.61	163	.89	412	.61	357	.64	291	.69	232	.73
5	332	.70	565	.50	617	.48	415	.63	616	.47	524	.51	434	.57	347	.62
6	431	.63	788	.49	1,486	.31	1,149	.36	1,455	.31	1,497	.31	1,534	.311	1,435	.33
7	480	.56	742	.47	717	.46	579	.49	698	.46	717	.48	407	.51	605	.55
8	400	.66	824	.46	963	.40	741	.46	977	.39	1,091	.38	1,124	.38	1,129	.39
9	456	.61	617	.47	637	.47	610	.50	631	.47	585	.48	541	.50	498	.52
10	287	1.0	620	.90	851	.62	367	1.0	917	.58	922	.59	—	—	792	.70
11	388	.39	364	.39	379	.39	307	.41	390	.38	358	.39	—	—	265	.42
12	286	.75	691	.54	813	.47	334	.72	829	.46	854	.47	—	—	719	.53
13	368	.68	466	.59	497	.57	349	.69	502	.56	450	.60	389	.64	329	.69
14	270	1.00	641	.85	760	.69	334	1.0	787	.66	756	.71	685	.78	604	.89
15	432	.39	481	.39	489	.38	347	.41	467	.38	474	.39	436	.40	384	.42

SOURCE: See text.

NOTE: Output per worker (Y/L) and actual work as a proportion of potential work (Z) in year 180 under various assumed conditions.

* See description in panel A above.

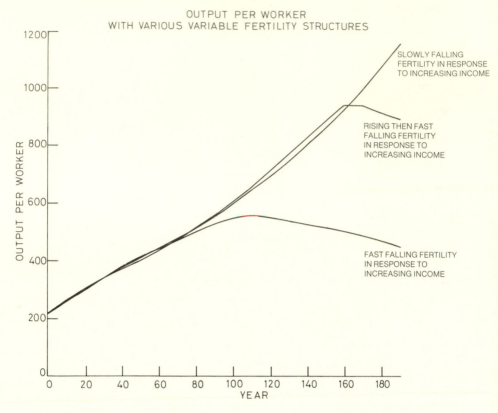

OUTPUT PER WORKER
WITH VARIOUS VARIABLE FERTILITY STRUCTURES

FIGURE 13–3 OUTPUT PER WORKER WITH VARIOUS VARIABLE FERTILITY STRUCTURES

size needs; (2) an economies-of-scale social-capital factor; (3) an industrial investment function (and an industrial technology function) responsive to differences in demand (output); and (4) an agricultural savings function responsive to the agricultural capital/output ratio. These factors together, at apparently reasonable parameter settings, are enough to offset the capital-dilution diminishing returns effect as well as the effect of dependency on saving found in the Coale-Hoover and Tempo models.

The model surely contains some specifications and parameter estimates that are overly favorable to population growth. But there are also specification and parameter estimates that are overly favorable to slow or no population growth. Examples of the latter are: (1) Low depreciation (and the accompanying investment function) turns out to be favorable to relatively low population growth. And the industrial-depreciation parameters used are almost surely too low, which therefore makes the conclu-

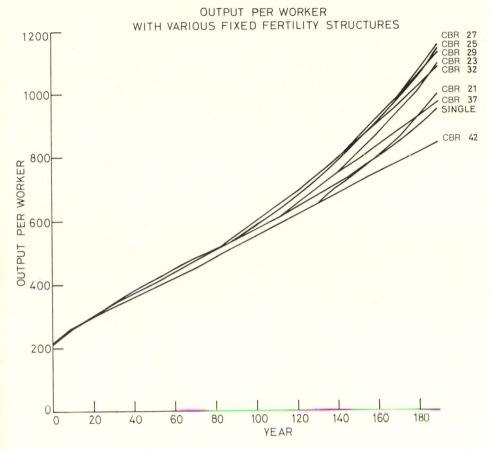

FIGURE 13–4   OUTPUT PER WORKER WITH VARIOUS FIXED FERTILITY STRUCTURES

sions drawn from the simulation even stronger, a fortiori. (2) Making allowance for the effect of the rise in skills over time of the new labor-force entrants would tend to work *against* the negative dependency burden and be favorable to population growth, but this effect is not included in the model.

2. In the base-parameter run the moderate-fertility populations enjoy more leisure in the long run than do the low-fertility and high-fertility populations. This may be seen in columns 7–9 of Table 13–1.

3. In many runs with a variety of parameters (columns 19, 21, and 23 in Table 13–2), over quite a wide range of moderate to high birth rates, the effect of fertility upon income is *not* spectacularly large—seldom as much as 25% even after 180 years (though the difference between low

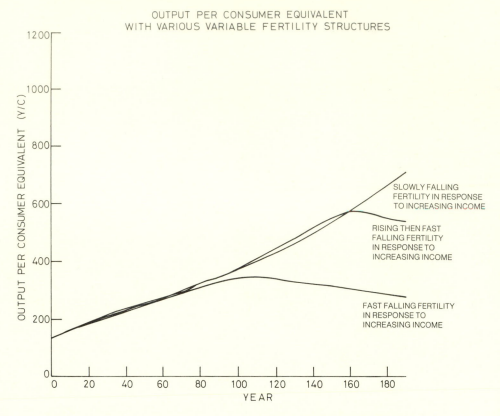

FIGURE 13–5   OUTPUT PER CONSUMER EQUIVALENT WITH VARIOUS VARIABLE
FERTILITY STRUCTURES

and moderate birth rates is great). This is extremely surprising at first thought. But this is what Kuznets expects:

> . . . given the political and social context, it does not follow that the high birth rates in the underdeveloped countries, per se, are a major cause of the low per capita income; nor does it follow that a reduction of these birth rates, without a change in the political and social context (if this is possible), will raise per capita product or accelerate its rate of growth. We stress the point that the source of the association between demographic patterns and per capita product is a common set of political and social institutions and other factors behind both to indicate that any direct causal relations between the demographic movements and economic growth may be quite limited; and that we cannot easily interpret the association for policy purposes as assurance

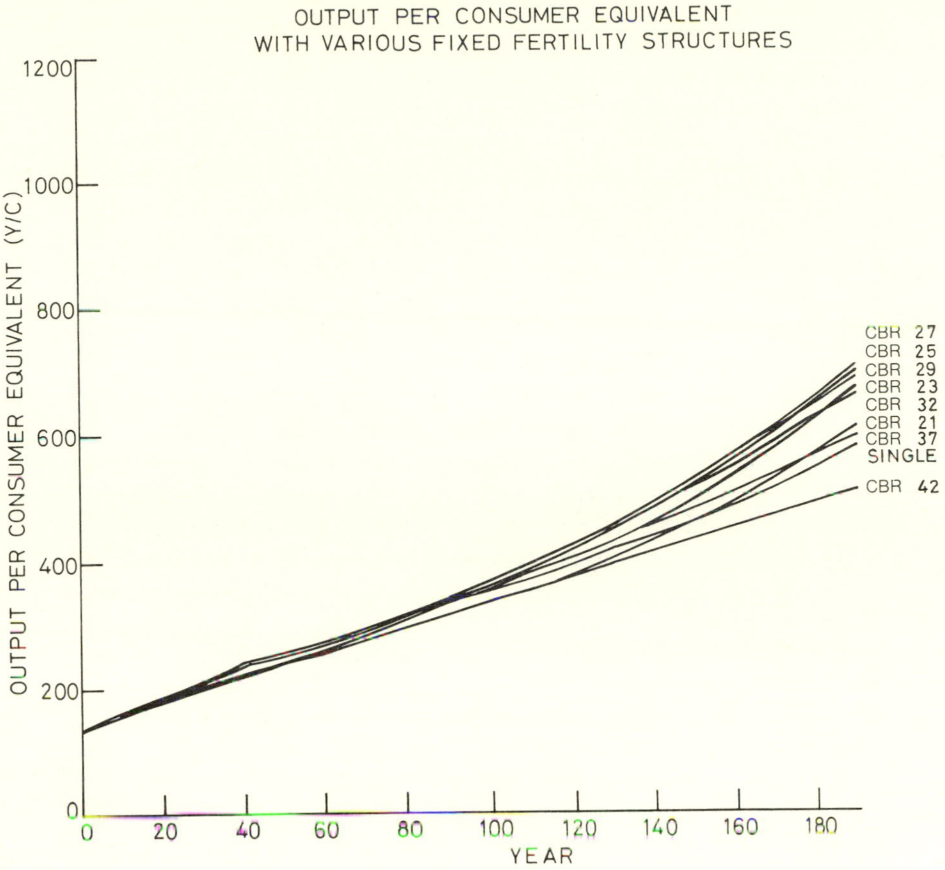

OUTPUT PER CONSUMER EQUIVALENT
WITH VARIOUS FIXED FERTILITY STRUCTURES

FIGURE 13–6   OUTPUT PER CONSUMER EQUIVALENT WITH VARIOUS FIXED
FERTILITY STRUCTURES

that a modification of one of the variables would necessarily change
the other and in the directions indicated by the association (1965, p. 29).

Still, this phenomenon demands some explanation. And an explanation seems within this system, as will be seen in the results to be described
presently.

4. One important element offsetting the capital-dilution effect is the
difference in work done per year under the different birth-rate structures,
as may be seen in columns 7–9 of Table 13–1. In year 120, the average
worker works at 52% of capacity in the highest birth-rate variation, and
at 47% in the next-highest birth variant. This difference of 5/47 or roughly

297

10% goes a long way to make up for less capital per worker in the higher fertility variants. In the industrial sector this also has an important effect on investment. (In the agricultural sector, population growth and increased output immediately cause a parallel increase in agricultural investment.) Other factors that help account for the lack of difference in economic performance among the moderate to high birth rates will be discussed below.

The effect of the variations in work supplied in response to aspirations and perceived need in the base run may be seen with the aid of a run where the work supplied per worker is held constant in all the birth-rate variations, other parameters being the same as in the base run. The results are shown in row 2 of Table 13–2.

5. It is of fundamental importance that economic performance apparently is not a monotonic (inverse) function of fertility. An important element in this finding is the economies-of-scale variable J. Its importance is shown by the fact that when the parameter is set so that there is no increase in social capital as a function of labor-force size, rather than the Chenery estimate used in the base run, there is almost (but not quite) a monotonic (inverse) relationship between birth rate and economic performance, as seen in row 3 of Table 13–2.

The economies-of-scale social-capital factor is not the sole factor or even the dominant factor, however, in the inferior performance of the low-fertility structures relative to the moderate-fertility structures. This may be seen in the inferior performance of the lowest endogenous birth-rate structure even with no economies of scale ("fast falling" in column 12 in row 3 in Table 13–2). And in various other runs with zero economies of scale, the relationship is also not monotonic. When, for example, depreciation is made higher than usual the low constant-fertility-ratio population does much better in the first 60 years than does the moderately high constant-fertility-ratio population, but in the long run higher fertility does much better (row 4 in Table 13–2). The same is true when investment is made more responsive to output than usual; the low constant-fertility-ratio structure has eventually declining economic performance, though higher fertility-ratio variations do not (row 5 in Table 13–2).

When the economies-of-scale effect is twice as great as in the base run, the highest fertility structures have better economic performance than any of the populations with lower birth rates (row 6 in Table 13–2).

6. The determinants of physical investment are crucial in this model as in all other economic models.[16] It is a fundamental difference between

---

[16] This would be somewhat less true if the effectiveness of labor were made a function of past income, to represent changes in the quantity of education and in its technological level. But educational investment would be very positively correlated with physical investment, despite its less cumulative nature. Therefore, the latter alone may be thought of as a not-too-bad proxy for both physical and educational investment.

this and Coale-Hoover-type models that gross industrial investment depends here upon demand, as measured by the change in last year's industrial output less the prior year's output, rather than being a proportional function of absolute output. This reflects the universal fact that investment is responsive to business prospects. It also reflects the historians' recent consensus that demand was a key factor in England's economic development. And the empirical literature on investment in MDC's emphasizes the influence of changes in output on investment. The concept of the accelerator provides theoretical foundation for this function. Hence, it seems that there is every reason to make the investment function in this model a function of changes in output.

Though this result may seem surprising at first, it is reasonable that a relatively small difference in industrial output should have a large effect on industrial investment. Investors are likely to project a present-period decline (or increase) in output into a future trend. Because investment is undertaken with an eye to several periods in the future rather than just one period, the expected trend has a cumulative effect far beyond the output results of a single year.

Inclusion of depreciation explicitly—rather than working with a net investment function—has an important enriching effect upon the model which allows interesting and realistic results to emerge. It is depreciation that brings about a decline in incomes when economic stagnation sets in; without allowance for depreciation, income would remain much the same in such stationary conditions. Such declines in economies are actually observed both secularly and cyclically, and it is a benefit that the model shows them. Long-run secular declines are mostly found among the lowest birth-rate trials, and the cause is the failure of output to rise. An example of such a decline is seen in the performance of the lowest income-responsive birth-rate structure (row 7 in Table 13–2), which describes a run with "lower growth" parameters, all the parameters being set at values that seem more appropriate to an LDC in the nineteenth or eig.. teenth century rather than in the twentieth.

Another example of the importance of the depreciation function is seen in two runs with no economies of scale that differ in the depreciation parameters (rows 3 and 4 in Table 13–2). Where depreciation is faster, the constant-moderate-fertility-ratio structure has better economic performance than the constant-low-fertility-ratio structure. Where depreciation is slower, the constant-low-fertility structure does better. (The explanation is that a bigger labor force increases output and hence increases investment, which is relatively more important when depreciation is faster.)

These results suggest a population "trap"—though a very different sort than the Malthusian trap elaborated by Nelson (1956) and Leibenstein (1954). The nature of this trap is that if population growth declines too fast as a function of increasing income, total output fails to rise enough to stimulate investment. Depreciation is then greater than investment, and income falls. In the model this results in a return to higher fertility and another cycle, though this may not be plausible historically. If—as is more plausible historically—fertility continues to be low, economic performance would continue to decline toward a low-level plateau.

7. The dependency effect of children upon industrial investment has considerable impact on the results. A trial without such a dependency effect shows a monotonically positive relationship of fertility to income (row 8 in Table 13–2), whereas otherwise the relationship is curvilinear as seen in the base run (row 1 in Table 13–2). Removing the dependency effect has the opposite effect from removing the economies-of-scale from the base run (row 3 in Table 13–2). And there is probably much more doubt about the fact and size of the dependency effect than about the economies-of-scale effect. This suggests that models such as Coale-Hoover and Enke et al., which embody a dependency effect but not an economies-of-scale effect are seriously biased against population growth for this reason alone, even if for no other.

Removing both the economies-of-scale and the dependency effects cancels out (row 9 versus row 1 of Table 13–2), though the relative strengths of the dependency and economies-of-scale effects are influenced by the rate of growth produced by the other parameters.

8. The advantage of moderate birth rates over low birth rates generally appears only after quite a while, say, 75–100 years. This is another reason why the results found here differ from those of the Coale-Hoover and Tempo models, in which the time horizon is only 25–30 years (55 years in the Coale-Hoover minor extension), whereas the time horizon here is 180 years (longer in some cases). This points up the grave danger in the study of population of using short-horizon models whose effects take a long time to begin and much longer to cumulate.

9. In an attempt to understand the difference in the common judgments about the effect of population growth in eighteenth-century England and twentieth-century India (and other contemporary LDC's), separate sets of economic parameters (but 1950's Indian demographic parameters) were constituted judgmentally to picture the two situations. The main differences are in the functions for economies of scale, agricultural investment response, industrial investment, industrial technology, the maximum increase in aspirations from year to year, and the extent of increase in aspirations as a function of income. The specifics are found in the coefficients in rows 10 and 11 in Table 13–2. The results indicate that high population growth up to very high fertility is indeed very beneficial for economic performance with the parameters chosen to represent England in the eighteenth century. And very slow population growth is slightly (and

only slightly) better for India than is moderate growth—and zero growth is worse than either. If these sets of parameters represent eighteenth-century England and twentieth-century India, the different judgments about the effects of population growth on income in the two situations may be considered reconciled.

Though income per capita and output per worker grow more slowly with Indian parameters than with eighteenth-century English parameters, the simulated Indian population benefits from a much larger quantity of leisure—due to the lower income aspirations set into the Indian model. A run in which the same aspirations function is given to both situations markedly reduces the leisure differential. But the output-per-worker differential is reduced much less, though substantially (rows 12 and 13 in Table 13–2).

The reader may wonder how important the economies-of-scale parameter is in the comparison of twentieth-century India and eighteenth-century England. The previously described sets of parameters were therefore run with the same economies-of-scale parameters as in the base run. The results are shown in rows 14 and 15 in Table 13–2.

The model and its outcome also suggest that the concept of "lack of labor," which population growth is said by economic historians to have remedied in industrializing England, is neither useful nor logical.

10. Several sensitivity experiments were made with the fundamental economic parameters of the system that have no strong theoretical tie to the effect of fertility. These separate experimental variations in the base run include: (1) Cobb-Douglas exponents of .4 and .6 instead of .5 and .5 in the agricultural production function, and (2) various capital-output ratios in industry and agriculture. The insensitivity of the basic findings to these experiments is encouraging. It increases confidence that the basic model is not flawed in a fundamental structural fashion, and suggests that the factors chosen as population-sensitive are indeed more important in this context than are the other structural factors.

Another reason for confidence in the model and its results is that the *absolute* size of the per-worker results is very different with different sets of parameters, but the relative results are much the same, as seen in the various runs in Table 13–2.

11. The differences in economic performance in the *early* years seem small in all runs, much smaller than the sorts of differences in performance one finds in the Coale-Hoover model. One of the larger differences is between $239 and $210 in "India" in year 60 for the low-constant-fertility-ratio and the highest-constant-fertility-ratio, and even this small difference is large compared to the results of other models. (And by year 180, the low-fertility structure comes to have relatively poor economic performance.)

301

This model yields no direct answers to policy questions. Any population-policy decision must employ a discount factor to commensurate the effects in various periods of the future. The range of plausible choices of the discount factor is very wide indeed, from an almost equal weighing of present and future generations' welfare to discount factors making quite unimportant everything which will happen more than 15–20 years in the future. The results of this long-run model should be relevant to policy discussions which do not heavily discount the future. In any case, the main thrust of the model is analytic rather than policy-making.

Nevertheless, it is natural to ask about the "optimum" fertility structure. Only a small subset of the large number of possible fertility structures has been tried, of course, but they would seem to sample the important possibilities. The generalization may be hazarded that *some* population growth is beneficial in the long run in all the circumstances examined. The "best" rate of growth in terms of long-run output per worker (or income per-consumer-equivalent) is relatively slow growth under some reasonable sets of conditions—a doubling in perhaps 90 years—whereas with some other sets of conditions the doubling time for the best economic performance is considerably shorter. The differences in economic performance between the "best" fertility structure and a wide range of other moderate-to-fairly-high rates of growth are, however, relatively small by any measure—most especially by comparison to the difference between the economic performances of positive population growth and negative population growth.

Though within the wide range of moderate-to-fairly-high population growth economic performance does not vary much and the advantage sometimes is with higher and sometimes with lower growth, populations with lower (but not declining) fertility almost always have somewhat more leisure—an important economic property of any system. (Populations with no growth or with a decline in population size do worse in both respects.)

12. Perhaps the most important result in the simulation experiment is that it shows that there are *some* reasonable sets of conditions under which fairly high fertility shows better economic performance at some times than does low fertility, while there are also other reasonable sets of conditions under which the opposite is true. There are even sets of conditions well within the bounds of possibility under which extremely high fertility offers the highest income per capita and output per worker in the long run. That is, the results depend upon the choice of parameters within the range that seem quite acceptable. This implies that any analytic model of population which concludes that any one fertility structure is unconditionally better than another must be wrong—either because that model's construction is too simple, or for some other reasons.

The sole exception to this rule of nongenerality is fertility so low as to be below replacement. Such a fertility structure does poorly under every set of conditions simulated here, largely because a reasonable increase in total demand is necessary to produce enough investment to overcome the drag of depreciation.

13. Perhaps the most important methodological contribution of this model is that it bridges the literary historical studies that bring in all the key variables, and the quantitative simulations that lack key variables. By so doing this model should focus attention on these omitted key variables so as to see how they quantitatively affect the overall outcome.

EVALUATION OF MODEL AND FINDINGS

Though the method used here is computer simulation, this model is of a theoretical nature—just as are analytical models.[17] Both types of models have in common the problem of evaluation and validation. Best of all would be to fit the theoretical outputs to empirical data of the same nature —in this case, year-to-year movements of an economy of the sort being modeled. Development models such as those of Fei-Ranis (1964), and Kelley et al. (1972), have done that. But this is not possible here, just as it is not possible with other population models such as Coale-Hoover. The main reason is that the aim of these models is to compare the results of population growth structures that have *not* existed. In such a situation, one may evaluate the validity of a model on two criteria : (1) the theoretical and empirical reasonableness of the model's structure, and (2) how well the over-all results fit the range of empirical experience. Let us test the model against these two criteria in that order.

1. First, the model includes all the main accepted elements that are found in other LDC population-growth models—such as diminishing returns, and the effect of dependency. Second, it also includes other elements that are generally agreed to be important in qualitative discussions but are omitted from previous models: demand and its effect on investment, the shift of labor from agriculture to industry, the leisure-output choice, and the effect of aspirations. Third, the model substitutes an accelerator investment function for the constant-proportion-of-output function found in Coale-Hoover and other work in that tradition; an accelerator function has all the weight of economic theory and empirical findings behind it. Taken together, these three aspects of this model's construction should make it more convincing than previous models— having all their good features and a lot more. The reasonableness of the wide range of parameters must be judged by each reader.

[17] The advantages and disadvantages of computer-simulated theoretical models versus analytical theoretical models are well known, and need not be discussed here.

2. The results of this model agree better with the historical and cross-sectional data than do previous models.

On the basis of this combination test, this model and its results should be more acceptable than Coale-Hoover and its descendants.

DISCUSSION

1. The model is constructed entirely in real terms. Prices of goods and money have no part in the model. There are at least two reasons for proceeding in this way. First, constructing the model in money terms would have added very greatly to its complexity. Such added complexity would not contribute much to this model, and it might obscure and interfere with the representation of some key aspects of the model (e.g., the farmer's investment of his own labor in his land). Furthermore, attempting to represent the production function in value terms rather than in real terms would have come up directly against some fundamental problems in capital theory (see, e.g., Solow, 1957; Hicks, 1974). Constructing the model in real terms leads to unequal marginal products of labor in the agricultural and industrial sectors after a while, but that seems to be inevitable in a growth model of this sort.

2. The model does not take into account the *distribution* of income, either as a result of different population-growth structures or as a further influence upon economic growth. Of course no growth model is better in this respect. But more important for purposes here, there is no a priori reason to think that income distribution would be affected differently by one or another population-growth structure, so it is reasonable to leave it out of account here. (But see Lindert, forthcoming.)

3. Though the model explicitly deals with the total volume of employment by means of the work-output mechanism, forced unemployment is not dealt with. This might be an important omission if higher population growth really results in higher forced unemployment. But despite the universal belief that this is the case, there is no evidence for it. Skimpy evidence from a study by Blandy (1974) and a preliminary study by Pilarski and Simon (1974) suggests that population growth may *not* have a pronounced negative effect, if any, on the proportion of people unemployed.

SUMMARY

A model is constructed that includes the elements of the standard LDC models, but that also includes other important elements discussed in the literature: demand effects upon investment (emphasized by the historians of England), the work-leisure choice, variations in work activity as a function of differences in needs and standard of living, and economies-of-scale, intersectoral shifts in labor, depreciation, and land building. The model solves by utility maximization, that is, finding the highest current leisure-output indifference curve that touches the current production function. The allocation of labor to the agricultural and industrial sectors, and the outputs of the two sectors, are found as a function of observed elasticities of demand and allocations of output at different income levels in LDC's.

Using a variety of parameters, the simulation indicates that *positive* population growth produces considerably better economic performance in the long run (120 to 180 years) than does a *stationary* population, though in the short run (60 years), the stationary population performs slightly better. (And of course the burden upon families and public facilities is greater in the short run with positive growth than with a stationary population). A *declining* population does very badly in the long run. In the experiments with the "best" estimates of the parameters for a representative Asian LDC (the "base run") moderate population growth (doubling over 50 years) performs better in the long run than either fast population growth (doubling over 35 years) or slow population growth (doubling over about 200 years). Experiments with one variable at a time reveal that the difference between these results and previous theoretical studies is produced by the *combination* of the novel elements—the leisure-output work decision, economies-of-scale, the accelerator investment function, and depreciation; no one factor is predominant. Perhaps the most important result is that within the range of positive population growth, different parameters lead to different rates of population growth as "optimum." This means that no simple qualitative theory of population growth can be very helpful, and a richer quantitative model such as this one is necessary.

SUMMARY OF MAIN STRUCTURAL EQUATIONS

$Q_{F,t} = A_{F,t} K_F^{\alpha} M_F^{\beta} J_t$ Agricultural production function

$$\left[\frac{J_{t+1} - J_t}{J_t} \right] = a_{112} \left[\frac{L_t - L_{t-1}}{L_{t-1}} \right] \quad \text{Economies of scale}$$

$$\frac{K_{F,t+1} - K_{F,t}}{K_{F,t}} = a_{1140} \text{GAP}_t - a_{1141} \quad \text{Agricultural saving}$$

$$\text{GAP}_t = \frac{Q_{F,t} - a_{113} A_{F,t} K_{F,t}}{a_{113} A_{F,t} K_{F,t}} \quad \text{Agricultural capital aspirations function}$$

$A_{F,t} = a_{115} A_{F,t}$ Agricultural productivity

$Q_{G,t} = A_{G,t} K_{G,t}^{\gamma} M_{G,t}^{\epsilon} J_t$ Industrial production function

$$A_{G,t+1} = A_{G,t} + a_{1170} A_G + a_{1171} \log_{10}\left[\frac{Q_{G,t} - Q_{G,t-1}}{Q_{G,t}}\right] A_{G,t}$$

Industrial productivity

$$\left(\frac{Q_{G,t} - Q_{G,t-1}}{Q_{G,t}}\right) \geq 0$$

$$K_{G,t+1} = K_{G,t} + A_{1181}\left[\log_{10}\left(\frac{Q_{G,t} - Q_{G,t-1}}{Q_{G,t}}\right)\right]$$

$$\times (1 - a_{1182} \text{YOUTH}_t)(K_{G,t}) - a_{1183} K_G \quad \text{Industrial saving}$$

$$\left(\frac{Q_{G,t} - Q_{G,t-1}}{Q_{G,t}}\right) \geq 0$$

$$\frac{Q_{G,t}}{Q_{G,t} + Q_{F,t}} = .35 + \left[\frac{\left(\dfrac{Y_{t-1}}{C_{t-1}}\right) - \$75}{\$1000 - \$75}\right](.90 - .35) \quad \begin{array}{l}\text{Allocation of output} \\ \text{between sectors}\end{array}$$

$Y_t = Q_{F,t} + Q_{G,t}$ Total production identity

$D_{k,t} = \text{ORIGIN}_t + b_{k,t}(\text{antilog } Z_t)$

$\text{ORIGIN}_t = (\text{RELASP}_t)(\text{STD}_t)\left(\dfrac{C_t}{L_t}\right)$

$\text{STD}_t = \dfrac{Y_{t-1}}{C_{t-1}}$ subject to

$(1 - a_{1193})\text{STD}_{t-1} \leq \text{STD}_t \leq (1 + a_{1193})\text{STD}_{t-1}$

Household demand function and its components

$$\text{RELASP}_t = q_{141} - a_{142}\left(\frac{\dfrac{Y_{t-1}}{C_{t-1}} - \$75}{\$925}\right)$$

$L_t D_t = Y_t$ Aggregate demand equals aggregate production

$\text{Mortality}_t = f\left(\log \dfrac{Y_{t-1}}{C_{t-1}}\right)$

$L_t = \text{MEN}_t + .5 \text{WOM}_t$ aged 15–64   Labor force

Fertility = various endogenous and exogenous functions.

306

PART II

The Effects of Economic Conditions on Fertility

INTRODUCTION

PART I of the book analyzed the effects of population growth upon the economies of nations. Part II turns to the converse relationship, the effects of economic variables upon modern-day population growth's main control element—fertility. This topic is treated in much greater detail in a separate monograph (Simon, 1974) from which much of Chapters 14–17 is drawn.

Chapter 14 introduces the topic, and discusses basic concepts such as the appropriate measurements of income and fertility, and the extent of rationality in fertility decisions. Then Chapter 15 presents data and conclusions about the short-run and long-run fertility effects of income changes in MDC's. Chapter 16 does the same for LDC's. Chapter 17 then discusses possible uses of income as a variable to alter fertility. The main control-variable possibilities are (1) income redistribution, which is not likely to be feasible or effective, and (2) money incentives, which probably could be effective in some situations if the incentives are sufficiently large.

309

CHAPTER 14

The Effect of Income on Fertility:
Basic Theory and Concepts

INTRODUCTION

THERE ARE two main reasons to be interested in the effect of income—its level and its changes—upon fertility: (1) to forecast what will happen to fertility in any country as its income and economic conditions change, and (2) to evaluate income as a possible social control variable. The first includes such illustrative questions as: What pattern will fertility follow in a poor African or South American country as the country develops? What will happen to fertility in rich industrialized countries as their economies continue to change? The second aim includes such questions as: Is economic development, with its consequent rise in income levels, an effective instrument for lowering fertility? Can income redistribution influence fertility patterns? Are incentive payments in money or kind an effective way of inducing people to have fewer or more children, if one or the other is desired?

This chapter begins with a brief review of the theory of income's effect upon fertility. Then the appropriate concept of income is discussed. Next comes discussion of the crucial distinction between the short-run partial effect of income upon fertility and the long-run total effects. Last, there is discussion of two factors that affect income's relationship to fertility: the extent of rationality in childbearing decisions, and the influence of the joint family system upon childbearing in LDC's.

Chapter 14 and its appendix also resolve the paradox that the simple cross-sectional relationship of income to fertility is usually negative while the time-series relationship over the business cycle is positive. This is seen to be a statistical artifact due to the facts that cross-sectional relationships embody the long-run indirect effects of income via education and other fertility-reducing variables, whereas in time-series analysis these effects wash out, leaving only the positive direct effect of income to appear.

The Theory of the Effect of Income on Fertility in Brief

Compiled in Figure 14–1 are a set of factors useful in understanding the effect of income on fertility. Change in economic conditions is the central exogenous variable here. One might argue that a congeries of psychological and sociological conditions commonly called "the beginning of modernization" precedes and causes changes in income level. Perhaps so.

310

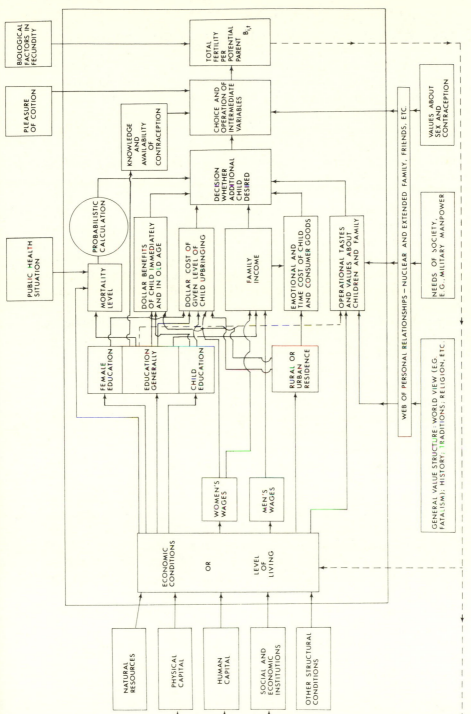

FIGURE 14-1 The Relationships between Income and Fertility

But for the purposes of this analysis it matters not whether it is change in technology or politics or markets or other conditions that is a "first cause." What matters here is that once the growth process is in motion, changes in economic conditions cause further changes in technology, social organization, and other conditions, which then feed back on the level of living. Hence it can be meaningful for a study to focus on the level-of-living variable and its effects on fertility.

The economic theory of the effect of income on fertility has usually concentrated on the micro-economic family-decision-making aspects. The theory has gone through several stages.

The first stage was simply to *assume* that a child is a good like most consumer goods. As income rises people buy more of most goods, and it was assumed they would then have more babies too. Early theorists also assumed, however, that a rise in income affects tastes and values in such manner as to reduce the number of children people want. In the Dumont-Banks variation (Banks, 1954) a rise in average income was said to increase individuals' aspirations for social advancement, which may be thought of as an increased desire for other goods which compete with children for family resources. This would act to reduce the number of children people would have. In this theoretical tradition, as in some subsequent stages of economic theorizing, a rise in income has effects on fertility in both directions, with no way of determining in advance which force will dominate. Hence there can be no purely theoretical prediction of the over-all effect on fertility.

Next came the idea that with a change in family income come changes in (1) the economic benefits from a child in terms of the child's expected contribution to the family economy, and (2) the costs of a child in terms of the family's expected expenditures in raising the child. This view was spelled out most fully for LDC's by Leibenstein (1957).

Then Becker (1960) formalized the notion of the demand for children as "consumption" goods. He distinguished between two dimensions of a family's fertility decisions, the "quantity" (number) of children a family "purchases" and the "quality" (e.g., education) per child it decides to purchase. Central to Becker's argument was that economic analysis of fertility should proceed on the assumption that tastes and values are unchanged by income changes. Becker's is very much a micro-economic and short-run theory; it does not take up such matters as increases in education that result from increased average income.

Next came Mincer's (1963) focus on the woman's work decision, emphasizing that children represent an opportunity cost in foregone wages because additional children reduce the capacity of women to work in the market.

312

Recently, there has been considerable sophisticated formal theoretical exploration by Ben-Porath (1972), De Tray (1970), Michael (1970), and Willis (1973) of the wider place of an additional child in the family's time budget as well as in the income budget, time and money being related in a manner analyzed by Becker (1965). Another aspect of this work tradition is a shift from thinking of commodities being consumed to thinking of the services—including "child services"—yielded to consumers by the objects of the expenditures of time and money. Perhaps the most provocative theoretical outcome of this "household-utility-maximization" school has been the conclusion that an increase in income might immediately be translated into a decrease in fertility by way of an increase in the purchase of other goods whose enjoyment requires time and hence competes with the time the family might spend with children.

Because the elaborated economic theory tells of income-produced forces that act on fertility in opposite directions, pure economic theory by itself cannot predict whether the effect of additional national or individual income will on balance be lower or higher fertility. If one also makes limiting assumptions appropriate to a particular situation, however, one can deduce the direction of the effect of income on fertility. The value of this theorizing is that it directs attention to the search for operational proxies for some of the various influences mentioned in the theory, in order to measure whether they behave as expected.

The Definition of Income

The term "income" requires immediate attention. Two related income concepts are used here: (1) The income of the individual earner or of the individual family is the appropriate concept when one focuses the analysis micro-economically on the individual, either theoretically or empirically. (2) Average national income (per-capita income) concept is both more aggregate and more general than is individual income. It refers to the economic conditions prevailing in a given country at a given time, and it is a social policy variable appropriate for aggregate macro-economic social analysis. For example, when one talks of the effect of economic development or of business cycles upon fertility, it is average income that is usually being referred to. "Economic condition" is a slightly more general term than "average income"; it includes other measures such as production and unemployment, in addition to average income.

It would be best if we could define income as the "lifetime" or "permanent" income of the family. But unfortunately, such data are very rare, and therefore most analyses of family behavior work with the current year's income. This leads to an important understatement of the strength

313

of the short-run relationship between income and fertility. Some analyses employ ingenious devices to get around this problem, but most cannot.

Husband's income is generally a more useful income variable than family income, because family income (especially wife's income and children's income) is more affected by the number of children than is husband's income, and hence the effect of family income on fertility is less clear than that of husband's income because of simultaneous causation.

DISTINCTION BETWEEN SHORT-RUN PARTIAL EFFECTS AND LONG-RUN TOTAL EFFECTS OF INCOME ON FERTILITY[1]

The influences on family fertility decisions that originally stem from changes in national income may be classified conveniently into two groups. One group consists of the forces that *immediately* flow from changes in the family's current income opportunities. These forces directly affect the family's time and money resources. They include an increase in the husband's earnings (assuming he continues to work the same amount of time each year), and increase in other goods that the family buys from its increased income, changes in the wife's earning opportunities as well as in her felt need to earn income because of the increase in husband's earnings, and so forth. These effects, which can take place in a period as short as a year or two and hence are here labeled "short-run," have been the special focus of economic theorizing about fertility decision in MDC's, though these forces can be expected to be important in LDCs, too. When important structural forces are held constant these forces can, for the most part, be captured empirically by a single variable for husband's income.

The other group of forces triggered off by a change in national income are those that affect the structural aspects of people's life situations. Important examples include increases in education, population shifts from country to city, and improved health. Partly because these effects are structural, they take a relatively long time to operate. An increase in children's education, for example, affects time and money resources only after 10–20 years. Such forces are referred to as "long-run" and "total." No single variable comes close to capturing all of them empirically.

This distinction between the short-run and the long-run effects of income on fertility reconciles the apparent contradiction between the observed negative relationship usually observed in simple cross-sectional analyses, and the positive relationship observed in time-series analysis. Higher family income a decade or so earlier leads to more education and

[1] This section develops ideas set forth in J. Simon (1969b).

other fertility-reducing effects in the present. But higher education in earlier years is correlated with higher income now. So it is reasonable that cross-sections—which embody long-run effects—indicate a negative relationship because of the lagged (indirect) effect of income in earlier years. In short time-series, education and other indirect effects of income are held reasonably constant, and hence they wash out; the positive short-run direct effect of income can therefore show itself in short time-series analyses. Informal explanations of this phenomenon may be found in Heer (1966) and Easterlin (1969); a formal demonstration (taken from Simon, 1969b) is in the appendix to this chapter.

CHILDBEARING AND RATIONAL DECISION-MAKING

The factors shown in Figure 14–1—especially income—can affect fertility only if rational self-conscious thought affects the course of sexual passion. Therefore we must briefly ponder the extent to which reason and reasoning are at work in the actions of individual people in various societies, at different periods in their histories. To put the matter bluntly, we must inquire into the notion that poor people in poor countries tend to breed without thought, foresight, or conscious control.[2] (We shall not, however, inquire into "collective rationality." To judge whether a community acts rationally one must know what its goals are and whether given behavior will attain those goals—both of which concepts are far beyond the scope of this chapter.)

For most couples in most parts of the world, marriage is antecedent to births. It is therefore clearly relevant to a judgment about the amount of reasoning involved in "breeding" that marriages are, in most "primitive" societies, contracted after a great deal of careful thought, especially with reference to the economic effects of the marriage. Arensberg's description

---

[2] A related idea about poor uneducated people's feelings and regard for children is often held by the well educated. Anthony Lewis makes the point with a sad incident at the time of Biafra's break-up: "Coming down the road from Okigwi, we were stopped at an army roadblock a few miles from Owerri. As always, there were refugees hoping for a lift. But this time there seemed to be something special about one family, not just pathetic but urgent. The soldiers asked us to take them. The mother, very pregnant, fell to her knees at the side of the car and prayed for a ride. She and her husband and the two tiny children got in. The father told what had happened. Ten minutes before, a huge new police truck had pulled up at the roadblock. The driver agreed to let the family aboard. The father lifted their few belongings over the high side of the truck and put his 5-year-old son in. Then, as he reached down for the next child, the truck roared away. 'I shout, I scream, I wave, but the driver just goes on. . . .' In the confusion, no one could be found who had seen a big blue truck go by. We tried the police station. . . . Now the mother, who had been sobbing, broke into strangled cries, her head going from side to side. 'I finish. I finish,' she wailed. I thought about the white experts in Africa who assure us that children do not mean the same thing to Africans as to us" (1970, p. 26).

315

of a match being made in rural Ireland makes clear the importance of economic factors:

"The young lady's father asks the speaker what fortune do he want. He asks him the place of how many cows, sheep, and horses is it? He asks what makings of a garden are in it; is there plenty of water or spring wells? Is it far in from the road, he won't take it. Backward places don't grow big fortunes. And he asks, too, is it near a chapel and the school or near town?"

The Inagh countryman could pause here; he had summarized a very long and important negotiation.

"Well," he went on, getting to the heart of the matter, "if it is a nice place, near the road, and the place of eight cows, they are sure to ask £350 fortune. Then the young lady's father offers £250. Then maybe the boy's father throws off £50. If the young lad's father still has £250 on it, the speaker divides the £50 between them. So now it's £275. Then the young man says he is not willing to marry without £300—but if she's a nice girl and a good housekeeper, he'll think of it. So there's another drink by the young man, and then another by the young lady's father, and so on with every second drink till they're near drunk. The speaker gets plenty and has a good day" (1968, pp. 107–108).

Economic conditions acting through rational self-conscious control are also seen to affect the marriage decision in a vignette recorded by Banfield in a Southern Italian town that then was "as poor as any place in the western world" (Banfield, 1958, p. 45). The young man whose account is given had a total yearly cash and computed income for his four-person family of $482 as of 1955, not much higher than the income of a peasant family in India. Banfield described the courtship and marriage decision.

In 1935 I was old enough to marry. My sisters wanted me to take a wife because they had no time to do services for me.

At that time there was a law that anyone who was 25 years old and not married had to pay a "celibacy" tax of 125 lire. That amount was much, if we recall that to earn it you had to work 25 days. I thought it over and finally decided to marry.

My present wife was at that time working with relatives of my employer. Once I stopped her and asked her to marry me, and she liked the idea too, but I had to tell it before her father. He was happy to accept me, and we talked about what she had to bring as dowry and what I had to do.

He asked me to bring my mother to call so that everything would be fine. The next time I brought my mother, and we had a nice feast.

When I wanted to meet my financee I had to ask the boss' permission.

In 1937 I asked the girl and her family to hasten the marriage before I was 25 years old. The father told me that she was not ready with the dowry. I asked him if at least we couldn't have the civil ceremony on February 6, 1938, two months late, so that I had to pay the tax for that year.

Once my mother and I went to Addo to visit my father-in-law in order to discuss and establish definitely what they were going to give us [in the dowry]. My mother wanted everything to be conveyed through a notary. My father-in-law gave us one tomolo of land and my mother gave the little house, but she reserved for herself the right to use it. Everything was written on official taxstamp paper by the notary. As soon as my wife was ready with the dowry the church marriage was set for August 25, 1938 (Banfield, 1958, pp. 111–12).

The effect of the harvest on nuptuality in Sweden in the eighteenth century, a backward agricultural country (but one that happened to have good vital statistics), is further evidence that people's sexual behavior is sensibly responsive to objective circumstances. When the harvest was poor, people did not marry, as Figure 14–2 shows. Birth rates were also responsive to the harvest, as will be seen later. Even unmarried fertility was affected by objective economic conditions.

As to reason and thought about fertility *after* marriage, even among the most "primitive" and "backward" of people fertility is subject to some

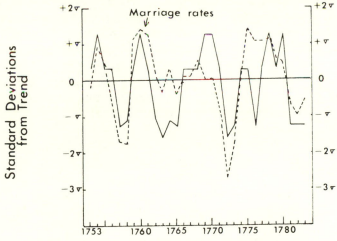

FIGURE 14–2   CYCLES OF HARVEST INDEX AND MARRIAGE RATES, SWEDEN, 1752–83
SOURCE: Reproduced from Thomas, 1941, p. 82.

317

degree of both personal social control. For a single example, here is Firth's summary of the situation on the Polynesian island of Tikopia:

Strong social conventions enforce celibacy upon some people and cause others to limit the number of their offspring" (1939, pp. 36–37). . . . the motive of a married pair is the avoidance of the extra economic liability which a child brings. In this small but flourishing community there is a conscious recognition of the need for correlating the size of population with that of the available land. Consequently it is from this point of view that limitation of families is mainly practiced. The position is expressed very clearly by the people themselves. Here is a typical statement: Families by Tikopia custom are made corresponding to orchards in the woods. If children are produced in plenty, then they go and steal because their orchards are few. So families in our land are not made large in truth; they are made small. If the family groups are large and they go and steal, they eat from the orchards, and if this goes on they kill each other (1936, p. 491).

After an extensive study of the anthropological literature, Carr-Saunders concluded, "The evidence so far adduced shows that the mechanism whereby numbers may be kept near to the desirable level is everywhere present" (1922, p. 230), the particular mechanisms being "prolonged abstention from intercourse, abortion, and infanticide" (p. 214). And as a result of a study of "data on 200 societies from all over the world . . . from tropic to artic . . . from sea level to altitudes of more than 10,000 feet . . .," Ford concluded that "both abortion and infanticide are universally known. . . . It is extremely common . . . to find a taboo on sexual intercourse during the period when the mother is nursing. . . . In nearly every instance, the justification for this abstinence is the prevention of conception . . ." (1952, p. 773). He also found instances of many kinds of contraceptive practices. Some are "clearly magical." Others "are relatively effective mechanical devices [for example] inserting a pad of bark cloth or a rag in the vagina. . . . Attempts to flush out the seminal fluid with water after intercourse . . ." (*ibid.*, pp. 765–66).

Physical evidence to confirm the anthropologists' findings about customs and norms comes from actual fertility itself; in practically no observed society (except, paradoxically, the very modern Hutterites and a few other groups) does fertility seem to come anywhere near to women's total fecundity. And in many very "primitive" societies fertility is quite low. Krzywicki ransacked the anthropological accounts to obtain estimates of the number of children born and raised in hundreds of tribes and groups. Table 14–1 shows the averages among various tribes in various parts of the world. And despite the fact that "Every one of the [individual tribal estimates], taken apart from the others, is open to

TABLE 14–1
FERTILITY IN SOME PRE-MODERN SOCIETIES IN THE PAST

Race	Number of children born		Number of children left to be reared, or actually reared
Australians	4.8–5.0		2.7–3.2
Other savage [sic] peoples		2.5–3.5	
Eskimo and Northern people		2.1–2.8	
North American Indians		3.0–4.0	
African Negroes	3.7–4.3		2.8–3.3
	(3.1–3.8)		(2.4–3.0)

SOURCE: Krzywicki, 1934, p. 217.

serious doubt. . . . They mutually confirm each other by the unanimity of their purport: all unanimously indicate that, at the lower stages of culture, the number of (living) children is smaller than that to which pre-War European conditions have accustomed us" (1934, p. 216).

A more recent surveyor of the anthropological evidence reached somewhat different conclusions from those of Carr-Saunders and Krzywicki, however:

Of 61 societies 35 have been rated as high, 16 as low, and 10 are very low on the [fertility] scale used in this study. These results do not agree with Carr-Saunders (1922, p. 98) and Krzywicki's (1934, p. 256) findings that the fertility levels of "primitive" societies are generally quite low. . . . The data used in evaluating the fertility levels of these societies are not very satisfactory, but they are better than those used by Carr-Saunders and Krzywicki.

On the other hand, it is not correct to assume that all non-industrial societies have uniformly high fertility. The statement by Davis and Blake (1956, p. 1), "A striking feature of underdeveloped areas is that virtually all of them exhibit a much higher fertility than do urban-industrial societies," seems to be too strong. The range of the value of total maternity ratio in my selection is 2.6–10.4 . . . (Nag, 1962, p. 142).

Nag's classification of "high," "low," and "very low" was an over-all judgment based on several measures of fertility. The figures corresponding to this classification for children ever born to women at the end of child-bearing ("total maternity ratio") were: 5.5, 3.01–5.5, and 2–3 respectively.

Now for some evidence that *income* matters in people's *thinking* about fertility. For MDC's, some students of population, and especially some sociologists (e.g., Blake, 1966; 1967) doubt that income level affects attitudes about fertility. Let us therefore begin with some impressionistic evidence that at least *some* people's fertility behavior—and hence *neces-*

sarily the fertility behavior of the population as an aggregate—is affected by economic considerations.

> GRENOBLE, France—a 29-year-old grade school teacher gave birth yesterday to quintuplets, three boys and two girls. . . . The children's grandfather, a tailor, said, "This certainly creates a lot of problems and you can't say it's really a joyous event because you've got to think about raising these little wolves" (*Champaign-Urbana Courier*, Jan. 20, 1971, p. 1).

Rainwater (1965) interviewed 409 Americans about "family design." In what the author offered as representative interviews with three pairs of husbands and wives, *all* interviewees mentioned economic factors prominently, though many other sorts of other factors were also salient in the interviews, of course.

> *Husband 1:* Would you prefer two or four children? I guess two because you can give two more than four. You can send them to college. The average family could not give four very much. . . . Two is all we can support adequately.
> *Wife 1:* Two, but if I had loads of money I would want loads of kids. . . . If I had lots of money, enough for full-time help, and plenty of room I would like half-a-dozen or more.
> *Husband 2:* I think two is ideal for the average American family based on an average income of $5,000. I don't see how they could properly provide for more children. Personally I'd take a dozen if I could afford them. I wanted four when we got married, or as many as the family income could support. . . .
> *Wife 3:* I think three is ideal because I feel this is all most people are equipped to raise, to give a good education and send them through college (Rainwater, 1965, pp. 162–73).

Rainwater summarized the entire sample:

> Looking at the total pattern of rationales for large and small families, we can abstract one central norm: one shouldn't have more children than one can support, *but one should have as many children as one can afford* (Rainwater, 1965, p. 150).

Next let us review the more systematic verbal data, beginning with questions about the family size considered "ideal" in various hypothetical economic circumstances. Whelpton et al. (1966) gathered data on this matter in their 1960 U.S. sample:

> The average number of children considered ideal is more than twice as large for a high-income family as for a low-income family [Table 13–2].

Several things should be noted about these answers, however. The interviews did not define high and low incomes, and the terms undoubtedly meant different things to many wives. . . . Some wives may have given different replies to these two questions simply because they thought it was expected of them. Nevertheless, *the results do suggest that most wives believe income ought to be an important consideration in determining ideal family size* (pp. 35–36, italics added).

This method holds tastes constant because each question was asked of *each* respondent; it is the responses "within" respondents, as a function of hypothetical income, which are being measured in Table 14–2.

TABLE 14–2
AVERAGE NUMBER OF CHILDREN CONSIDERED IDEAL
IN THE UNITED STATES

Type of reply	All respondents	White	Nonwhite
	For the average American family		
Minimum number	3.4	3.4	3.6
Maximum number	3.5	3.5	3.8
	For a high income family		
Minimum number	4.7	4.7	5.0
Maximum number	4.9	4.9	5.2
	For a low income family		
Minimum number	2.1	2.1	2.1
Maximum number	2.2	2.2	2.3

SOURCE: Whelpton *et al.*, 1966, p. 35.

Another glimpse into the effect of income on fertility is given by wives' statements about why they are not expecting to have a larger family than they are in fact expecting. The *first* reason given by more than a majority of a sample of U.S. wives was economic, as shown in Table 14–3.

(There may not, however, be a connection between what people say about their fertility decisions and their actual fertility. Arnold and Fawcett (1973) report very big differences between urban lower-class Filipinos in Hawaii as compared to Japanese and Caucasians in Hawaii in perceived democratic, psychological, and social benefits and costs of children. But there is *not* an actual fertility difference among the groups.)

Hypothetical questions are another approach. That is, if actual behavior cannot yet be observed, people's *conjectures* about their own behavior may provide some guidance. In Israel, when a random sample of the population was asked if they would have had more children than they actually bore if their apartment had been one room bigger than it actually was, 18% answered "Yes, for sure," 12% answered "Maybe,"

321

TABLE 14–3
REASONS FOR NOT EXPECTING A LARGER FAMILY IN THE UNITED STATES

First reason	All respondents	White	Nonwhite
Number of wives	2,684	2,414	270
Percent:			
Total	100	100	100
Subfecundity	18	17	22
All other reasons	82	83	78
Economic reasons	44	45	36
Would cost too much, couldn't afford more, etc.	22	22	22
Couldn't support more at desired standard of living	6	7	3
Couldn't educate more	5	6	3
Low income, insecure job, part-time work, unemployment	3	4	2
Other economic reasons	7	7	5
Poor health (parents and/or children); pregnancy unpleasant, or dangerous to wife or baby	8	8	6
Hard to "care" or "have time" for more	8	7	10
This is a "nice" number, number wife and/or husband wants; no more needed for happiness of family, etc.	5	5	7
Other reasons, don't know	14	14	14
Not ascertained	4	4	5

SOURCE: Whelpton et al., 1966, p. 55.

19% answered "I don't think so," and 51% answered "No, for sure." And when asked about the effect of a 20% higher income on their past or future childbearing, even more people indicated that there would have been an effect on their family size: 20% "Yes, for sure," 16% "Maybe," 19% "I don't think so," and 45% "No, for sure." The corresponding figures for future behavior of families where the wives are still in the child-bearing ages were 17%, 20%, 12%, and 44% (7% not believing or making plans about children; Peled, 1969, pp. 92–94).

In brief, despite the fact that income in MDC's is more than sufficient to provide the means of bare subsistence for many more children than the average family chooses to have, in response to questions of various sorts people *say* that their incomes constrain their family size.

In LDC's, now, evidence that incomes and economic circumstances are important in poor people's thinking about fertility is found in answer to questions about disadvantages and advantages of large families in Africa. Table 14–4 shows Caldwell's summary of various surveys in various parts of Africa. The top two lines in the table reveal that economic motivations are indeed important.

TABLE 14–4

STATED DISADVANTAGES OF A LARGER FAMILY
TROPICAL AFRICA, 1963–68

	Ghana								Nigeria						Kenya		
					Rural households							Pro-vincial urban female (Ife)	Pro-vincial urban female (Oyo)	Pro-vincial urban female (Ibadan)			
	Urban female(a)	Urban elite male	Female urban elite	Rural female(a)	Total	(1)	(2)	(3)	Urban female (1964)	Urban male	Urban female (1968)				Urban male	Urban female	Rural female
Total	100	103(g)	125(g)	100	107(g)	112(g)	102(g)	106(g)	100	192(g)	168(g)	100	100	100	100	100	100
Economic burden (a) general	32	16	31	36	45	50	55	38	38(e)	54	44	10	10	5			
(b) for adequate upbringing (especially education)(b)	12	66	64	8	12	7	7	17	26	68	54	81(c)	81(c)	93(c)	84	87	75
Family problems (noise, difficult to look after)(d)	34	17	23	38	34	34	27	37	19	36	27	5	6	0	9	9	9
Childbirth strain	6	(e)	(e)	8	2	0	0	3	(e)	5	10	0	0	0	(e)	(e)	(e)
Other responses	0	0	0	0	0	0	0	0	2	9	7	(f)	(f)	(f)	1	0	1
Nothing bad	(f)	0	4	(f)	14	20	13	11	13	19	22	(f)	(f)	(f)	5	3	11
No response	16(f)	4	3	10(f)	0	1	0	0	2	1	4	4(f)	3(f)	2(f)	1	1	4

SOURCE: Caldwell, 1968a, p. 603.

NOTES:

(a) Responses to questions about reasons for wanting a small family.

(b) Includes problems of feeding and care.

(c) "Adequate upbringing" apparently so defined as to cover some responses appearing in "general" in other surveys.

(d) Includes responses suggesting children more likely to become delinquent, and other people more likely to regard parents as irresponsible.

(e) Not coded but may be included in "Other responses."

(f) "No response" would include "Nothing bad."

(g) Adds to over 100 because of multiple responses.

Perhaps typical among the studies summarized by Caldwell is that of Heisel for Kenya

> Thirty-eight percent of the responses . . . to this question, which requests the respondent to find something good in having a large number of children . . . [refer] to some aspect of the economic advantages of many children . . . another 38 percent denied the premise of the question, that there is, in fact, something valuable in having many children, and took the position that there is nothing good at all.
>
> It is not necessary to look for the reason for this rejection. The next question in the interview was: "What is the worst thing about having many children?" Here, there was no difficulty for the great majority of respondents in accepting the premise of the question. Seventy-five percent answered that economic strain (school fees, food, clothing, and so forth) is introduced into the family when there are many children. . . .
>
> The central theme of the responses to these two questions is that children may be economically useful, but that a big family is expensive and may not be an advantage at all. There is a strongly marked tendency to see children in an economic rather than a psychological or a social context. All other considerations relevant to family size—the psychological or social benefits of a large or small number of children, risks to the mother's health, fear of infant or child mortality—occur with nearly insignificant frequency (1968b, pp. 634–35).

The central point of Heisel's observations for the short run is that LDC people do indeed think about economic circumstances in relationship to fertility.

On balance, this preliminary evidence—which the rest of Part II seems to confirm—shows that in all societies people do indeed give much thought to sex, marriage, and childbearing. To repeat, fertility is everywhere clearly subject to at least some rational control, though the degree to which achieved family size matches people's family-size desires varies somewhat from group to group. Families in some countries plan family size more carefully and are better able to carry such plans to fruition than are families in other countries, because of differences in available contraceptive technology, infant mortality, and intracouple communication patterns. But there is certainly strong evidence that people think rationally about fertility, and hence other objective forces influence fertility behavior to a significant degree, everywhere and always. Therefore it can be useful to explore the extent and the nature of the effect, which task is the subject of Part II of the book.

SUMMARY

Rational thinking affects fertility all over the world. Hence, income constraints can be seen to influence people's thinking about fertility. This is the basis for the examination of the empirical relationship of income to fertility in the next two chapters.

It is necessary to distinguish between the short-run direct effect of income on fertility (which is generally positive in MDC's and LDC's) and the long-run effect through income's effect on education, industrialization, rural-urban residence, and other fertility-affecting variables, whose effects are on balance negative in LDC's.

The apparent paradox that the simple cross-sectional relationship of income to fertility is usually negative, while the time-series relationship over the business cycle is positive, is a statistical artifact. It arises because cross-sectional relationships embody the long-run indirect effects of income via education and other fertility-reducing variables, whereas in time-series analysis these effects wash out, leaving only the positive direct effect of income to appear.

325

A Formal Reconciliation of the
Contradiction between Time-Series and
Cross-Section Evidence on
Income and Fertility[1]

Over the course of the business cycle the relationship between income and fertility is positive, whereas most unconditional cross-sectional studies show a negative relationship.

This appendix will show there is no real statistical contradiction between the various types of evidence. Rather, the various estimation techniques yield different images of fertility behavior because they take pictures in different ways. All of the images are seen to be consonant as soon as we look beyond some statistical artifacts.

For simplicity let us make fertility a function only of (i) income and (ii) all other factors lumped together into "modernization."

$$B = f(Y, \text{MOD}). \qquad (14\text{–}1)$$

where

$$B_{i,t} = \text{Births (one or zero) in family } i \text{ in year } t;$$
$$Y_{i,t} = \text{Income of family } i \text{ in year } t;$$
$$\text{MOD}_{i,t} = \text{Modernization state of family } i \text{ in year } t.$$

No hypothesis need be made about the direction of the effect of modernization, though the direct effect of income is here assumed to be positive.

Lagged as well as current entries are made for each independent variable, and a linear form is adopted for simplicity. It is the lagged arguments that unravel the paradox.

$$B_{i,t} = b_{i,0}Y_{i,t} + b_{i,1}Y_{i,t-1} \ldots b_{i,45}Y_{i,t-45} \pm c_{i,5}\text{MOD}_{i,t-5}$$
$$\pm c_{i,6}\text{MOD}_{i,t-6} \cdots \pm c_{i,45}\text{MOD}_{i,t-45}, \qquad (14\text{–}2)$$

Individual subscripts are shown in Equation (14–2) for each coefficient. We shall henceforth drop them and work with coefficients that are some pooled community analogies to the individual coefficients.

The modernization terms run from $t - 5$ backward to suggest that the effect of modernization variables is primarily during the pre-adult taste-formative years.

---

[1] From J. Simon (1969b). Exactly the same sort of analysis explains the apparent paradox between cross-sectional and time-series analyses of suicide (J. Simon, 1968b) and in the consumption function (J. Simon and Aigner, 1970).

Modernization is a positive function of income:

$$\text{MOD}_{t-k} = mY_{t-k}. \tag{14-3}$$

Substituting we get

$$B_t = b_0 Y_t + b_1 Y_{t-1} \ldots b_{45} Y_{t-45} \pm c_5 m Y_{t-5} \ldots \pm c_{45} m Y_{t-45}. \tag{14-4}$$

We now see that in Equation (14–4) *the total effect of income can be positive or negative*, depending upon the relative weights of the various coefficients.

The key point is that, given the same model above and a given set of coefficients, a cross-section and a time series may well show different relationships between B_t and Y_t. This breaks open the apparent paradox, as we shall see.

Take the cross-section first. Assume that the specified cross-section model is, as is conventional, $B_t = bY_t$. Elsewhere (Grunfeld, 1961; Malinvaud, 1966; Aigner and Simon, 1970) it is shown rigorously that

$$\hat{b} = b_0 + r_{Y_t Y_{t-1}} b_1 + r_{Y_t Y_{t-2}} b_2 \ldots r_{Y_t Y_{t-45}}$$
$$\pm r_{Y_t Y_{t-5}} c_{t-5} m \pm r_{Y_t Y_{t-6}} c_{t-6} m \ldots r_{Y_t Y_{t-45}} m \tag{14-5}$$

where $\hat{b}$ is the observed coefficient in the contemporaneous cross-section. the b_{t-k}, c_{t-k}, and m are the "true" coefficients, and the $r_{Y_t Y_{t-k}}$ are the correlation coefficients between the incomes of individuals in one period and their incomes in another period. This means that the extent to which $\hat{b}$, the estimated mean coefficient, differs from b_0, the "true" mean coefficient for the *current period*, is a function only of the relative sizes of the coefficients, and of the correlations between the sets of independent variables in each pair of two periods. If the correlations are high, as they always are in income from period to period, and if the lagged effect is substantial, then $\hat{b}$ can differ greatly from b_0. It can be seen intuitively that if $r = 1$, $\hat{b}$ equals the sum of all the b_k and $c_k m$. And that sum might well be negative if the $c_k m$ are large relative to the b_k, and if the lags are strong. Hence a cross-section of this model can yield a negative $\hat{b}$.

This analysis certainly does not *require* cross-section relationships to be negative; in fact, it may cast further light on some reported positive cross-section results, especially those among homogeneous rural samples, as discussed in Chapter 16. Spengler, among others, has explained such results by recourse to the internal similarity of the samples: "family size often tends to be positively associated within groups that are otherwise homogeneous" (1952, p. 10). But homogeneous samples necessarily have relatively low period-to-period income correlations, and hence the positive relationship is *forced*, in the sense that the omitted past variables are washed out by the way the sample is constituted. Hence these homogeneous sample results are not at all inconsistent with the model put forward above.

Now consider a time-series regression analysis over the course of the business cycle. By definition, the fluctuations in income over the cycle are large relative to the secular change. While $r'_{Y_t Y_{t-1}}$ might be fairly high (letting the prime stand for the time-series case) the $r'_{Y_t Y_{t-k}}$ for periods further back—which are the periods of taste formation by the modernization variables—will be low and there will be both negative and positive cases, effectively cancelling the effect of those lagged variables. Therefore, there will be little specification bias if a time-series regression is run on the usual specification:

$$B_t = b' Y_t. \tag{14–6}$$

That is, $\hat{b}'$ will not differ much from the true b_0. Given that the effect of modernization is largely in the past, the effect of modernization cancels out in such an analysis, and the observed relationship is the positive one between $b_{i,t}$ and $Y_{i,t}$ in the micro-model.

The last aspect of the reconciliation refers to long-run secular time series, which are observed to be negative over the course of development. In such long series, unlike short series over business cycles, the $r'_{Y_t Y_{t-k}}$ will be positive and quite high, because the year-to-year fluctuations are small relative to the long secular trend. Therefore, if a graph is simply plotted as in Equation (14–6), the specification error can cause the relationship to be negative just as in the cross-section, if the $c_k m$ are relatively large and if the time-lag is considerable.

This appendix shows that with the same factor catalogue one can understand why cross-section and time-series analyses of the relationship of birth rate to income can lead to different results if some or all of the analyses are carried out with insufficient time specification. It must be emphasized, however, that Equation (14–2) should *not* be interpreted as a hypothesis about fertility behavior or as a useful explanation of fertility, but only as a simple possibility to show how paradoxes can arise.

CHAPTER 15

The Short-Run and
Long-Run Effects of Income
on Fertility in MDC's

INTRODUCTION

THE PREVIOUS chapter showed that people's economic situation influences their thinking about fertility, and that thinking affects fertility. This chapter and the following ones review the quantitative facts about the income-fertility relationship. This chapter deals with MDC's, and Chapter 16 deals with LDC's. This chapter finds that the short-run effect of income on total fertility is mildly positive, though not enough so to make this effect an important planning consideration for the MDC economy. At the more detailed level of individual parities, income has a *positive* effect in inducing *low-parity* families to have additional children, but it has a *negative* effect in inducing *high-parity* families to have fewer children. Hence, a rise in income can be seen as an important factor in bringing about a "convergence" to family sizes of two to four children in MDC's. In the long run the effect of income on fertility is rather indeterminate because of the conflicting forces of the husband's income and the wife's opportunity-cost effects, as well as other income-induced effects including the "cost" of children.

SHORT-RUN EFFECTS OF INCOME ON FERTILITY IN MDC's

Time-Series Evidence on the Short-Run Effect in MDC's

BUSINESS CYCLES

The time-span of the ordinary business cycle is so short—say, 3–7 years—that people's education, tastes, and attitudes—that is, the noneconomic forces shown in Figure 14–1—do not change. Therefore, it is reasonable to assume that changes in fertility over the business cycle are caused by changes in income. Hence business-cycle evidence is particularly relevant for the study of the short-run direct effect of income.

The income-fertility relationship is strongly positive over the business cycle. Study after study has brought in this conclusion, before and after Yule (1906) and D. Thomas (1925)[1] and including many countries.

---

[1] D. Thomas has provided a valuable history of early work on the relationship of marriage and fertility to both harvest and business cycles (1925, Chapter II).

329

Figure 15–1 shows the relationship of business conditions to *marriage* rates in Sweden during 1865–1913 (in standardized deviations); the relationship of *birth* rates to business cycles is almost as close during 1921–43 (see Figure 15–2). And there was a close relationship between fertility and employment (as a proxy for income) in Germany between the two World Wars, adjusted for secular trend.

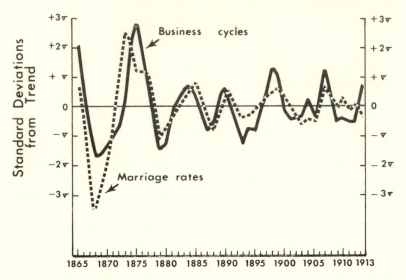

FIGURE 15–1   BUSINESS CYCLES AND CYCLES OF MARRIAGE RATES, SWEDEN, 1865–1913
SOURCE: Reproduced from Thomas, 1941, p. 16.

For the United States over 1920–1958, the correlation coefficients between the indices and trend deviates are mostly very high (Kirk, 1960). Galbraith and Thomas (1956) disaggregated United States births by birth order and obtained the close relationship of deviations from trends shown in Figure 15–3 Kirk figured that "economic conditions control about one-half of the annual variance of fertility from its trend . . . half of the control operates through nuptiality and the other half is exercised directly on fertility" (1960, pp. 253–254). Silver (1965), who did a careful analysis of the relationship of business cycles to births and marriages in the United States over a long period, found that "Fluctuations in real per capita gross national product explained 31 percent of the residual variance of the birth rate 1871–1961; over approximately the same period this variable explained 51 percent of the residual variance in marriages" (pp. 254–255).

Ben-Porath (1971; 1973) studied the economic conditions-fertility relationship for Israel. His techniques included disaggregation by social

330

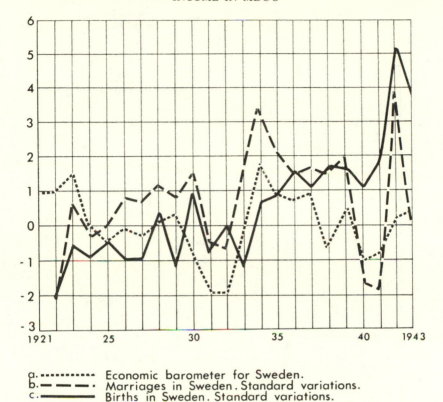

a. ············ Economic barometer for Sweden.
b. ── ── ── · Marriages in Sweden. Standard variations.
c. ━━━━━━ Births in Sweden. Standard variations.

FIGURE 15–2   BUSINESS CYCLES AND FERTILITY, SWEDEN, 1922–43
SOURCE: Reproduced from Hyrrenius, 1946, pp. 17–18.

group, examination of various measures of income and unemployment, examination of both yearly and quarterly data, and the study of various lagged relationships. Over the periods 1950–51 to 1959–60 and 1960–61 to 1968–69, unemployment explained 64% and 54% of the variance, respectively, for the total Jewish population using first differences.

These findings about the extent of the variance explained are interesting. But more useful for some purposes is a quantitative statement of the *elasticity:* "On the average over the whole period studied a trend deviation of 4 percent in personal income produced a trend variation of only 1 percent in fertility," i.e., an elasticity of .25 (Kirk, 1960, p. 254). For the period 1920–57, Becker calculated United States average "cyclical" income elasticities as a bit more than .50 for first births and a bit less than .50 for higher order births; these were the average changes in fertility from trough to peak and peak to trough, as a function of the proportional

331

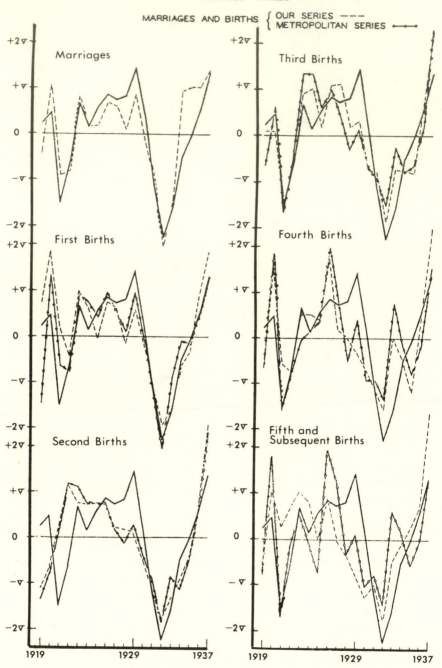

FIGURE 15–3 RELATIONSHIP BETWEEN BUSINESS CYCLES AND MARRIAGES AND
BIRTHS (ONE YEAR'S LAG) OF VARIOUS ORDERS, UNITED STATES, 1919–37
SOURCE: Reproduced from Galbraith and Thomas, 1941, p. 192.

change in income. Silver estimated that "the response of births is in the range of 20%–30% of the corresponding change in national income." For all Jews in Israel, Ben-Porath found an elasticity of .43 for fertility with respect to real per capita GNP over 1960–69. In quarterly data over 1965–70, the elasticity was about .20.

Wilkinson (1973) studied the excellent Swedish data over the period 1870–1965. He found short-run and long-run elasticities of fertility with respect to children for the periods 1870–1910, 1911–40, and 1941–65, to be, respectively, .08 and .13; .24 and .33; 1.00 and 2.04.

There are three important qualifications to the estimates of Kirk, Becker, Silver, Ben-Porath and Wilkinson about the effect of income changes on fertility. First, the estimates apply only to changes (1) from year to year, (2) over the length of a business cycle, and (3) in a developed country. It would be most unwarranted to use these estimates as a basis for predicting what would happen if, say, there were a change in income distribution, or if the income variation were to take place over a cycle longer than the business cycle (the case to be discussed next), or if income were to be raised permanently. These estimates may reasonably only be used to predict what will happen to the birth rate *over a business cycle*, and for no other predicted situation—though these estimates may also help us understand the general income-fertility mechanism.

A second important qualification to the business-cycle estimates is that they refer to the differences in births at various points in the business cycle, and they do *not* directly indicate the effect of these changes on the birth rate for the business cycle as a whole. That is, the estimates reflect *shifts in timing* of births from one year to another, *along with* long-run fertility effects. If a drop of 4% in income below trend in a given year leads to births being 1% or 2% lower in the following year—say, 1,000 births less in a given country—than would otherwise be the case, this does not mean that 10 years later the population will be smaller by 1,000 people than if income in the year in question had not dropped 4% below trend. Rather, some of the births will be *postponed* to subsequent years with no ultimate effect upon the size of their families. This is seen most clearly by looking at marriage data. The marriage rate is strongly affected by the business cycle, as seen, for example, in Figure 15–3, and by the correlation of .67 between marriage rates and business cycles in Britain during 1854–1913 (D. Thomas, 1927, p. 93). But judging by the high proportion of people that ultimately marry, it is pretty clear that the business cycle has much less effect on whether people ultimately marry than on whether they marry in a year of low or high income. And birth rates are strongly affected by marriage rates. Hence at least part of the effect of business cycles on births must be a shift rather than a permanent additon or subtraction or births. The fact that the fertility-income relationship grades from strongest to weakest as one looks in Figure 15–3 from marriage to low parities to high parities lends empirical support to the idea that much of the observed effect over the business cycle is timing, because marriage and low parity births happen to almost everyone at some time during their lives.

A third and perhaps the most important qualification to the business-cycle studies is that the *magnitude* of the fertility variations which they explain is not very great. The differences between fertility at the high points and the low points of business cycles have generally been small compared to the long-run fall from pre-industrial high fertility to MDC low fertility, and they have even been small relative to fertility differences over the long cycles to be discussed shortly. And fertility differences of the magnitude observed over the business cycle, lasting for only the few years of a business cycle, could not have any meaningful effect on the economy. The following calculation shows that changes in birth rate of the size observed over the business cycle could not cause a change in business activity large enough to show up immediately in business activity. Assume an impossibly large, sudden jump from an MDC birth rate of 15 per 1,000 to a birth rate of 30 per 1,000. Assume also that a baby has the very high consumption "needs" of .5 of an adult consumer, and that his parents respond by increasing their total consumption in such a way that their expenditure per-consumer-equivalent stays the same rather than falling, by means of a decrease in savings of that full amount. Even under these extreme conditions, total consumption would rise by only $(.030 - .015)(.5) = .0075$, less than 1%. A change in consumption of this size is far too small to show up amidst the much greater changes from other causes taking place over the business cycle. (This also implies that the effect running from business activity to birth rates is likely to be the more important cause of the relationship between the two variables over the business cycle.) Over longer cycles the effect of a higher birth rate has time to add up to a more substantial effect, but even over longer cycles it seems to me that it would be difficult to find the effect statistically. Hence, we should not hope for much light to be thrown on the effect of fertility increase on savings and investment from time-series data.

LONG SWINGS

If one now considers a slightly longer period, such as the long (Kuznets) swings of 5–30 years, *most* of the factors shown in Figure 14–1 probably will not change enough over the period to matter much, and the direct partial income effect may still be assumed to dominate. In his study of long swings, Easterlin successfully used various statistical expedients to cause many anomalies to disappear. In particular, the sharp birth-rate decrease in the 1930's, the baby boom of the 1950's, and the recent fertility decline can all be seen as sensible continuations of past history, modified by contemporary economic conditions. Some of these analyses may be seen in Figure 15–4.

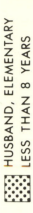
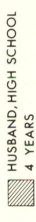
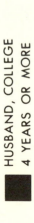

HUSBAND, COLLEGE
4 YEARS OR MORE

HUSBAND, HIGH SCHOOL
4 YEARS

HUSBAND, ELEMENTARY
LESS THAN 8 YEARS

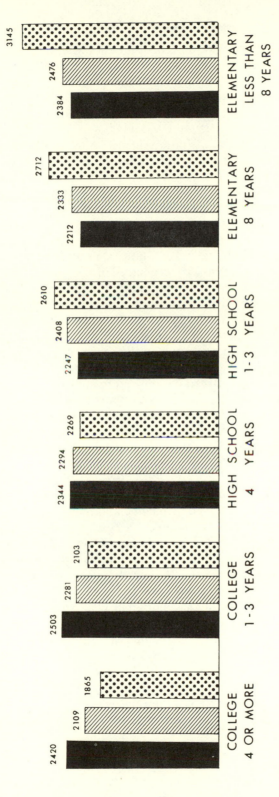

SCHOOLING OF WIFE (YEARS)

FIGURE 15–4   LEVEL AND RATE OF CHANGE OF URBAN WHITE FERTILITY RATIO (U.F.R.),
AND UNEMPLOYMENT OF CIVILIAN LABOR FORCE (U.), UNITED STATES, 1885–1958

SOURCE: Reproduced from Kiser *et al.*, 1968, p. 167.

Though Easterlin's work on Kuznets cycles after 1885 suggests that economic condition explains much of the *deviations from the trend* in fertility—as measured by decadal and quinquennial percentage changes in the urban native-white fertility ratio—his results clearly do *not* suggest that the trend itself may be explained by such economic changes. Just the opposite. "If one considers the estimates for urban fertility from only 1895–99 to 1925–29, there is little evidence at all of systematic change (Easterlin, 1968a, p. 88). This clearly indicates that forces other than economic conditions must have been strongly at work to oppose the direct income effect during this period, because income rose greatly over this period. This matter will be considered in more detail when long-run effects are taken up later.

The sort of effect Easterlin found is not limited to the United States. Silver (1966, p. 315) found that "The timing and magnitudes of the cyclical responses of births and marriages in the United Kingdom are very similar to those in the United States . . . the cyclical (Kuznets or ordinary) response of births in Japan is similar to that prevailing in the Western countries" for 1855–1959 in the U.K., and 1878–1959 in Japan.

The relationships Easterlin found may reflect causality running from the birth rate to economic activity as well as the converse. The possibility of this effect is greater in a long-swings study than in a business-cycle study because, as noted earlier, it is difficult to imagine new births having much effect on business activity in very short periods of time, whereas births may indeed have an effect on long swings in economic activity. An answer to this reservation must await finer-grained studies using more powerful techniques on fuller and better data.

Cross-Section Evidence on the Short-Run Effect in MDC's

A cross-section by income of a population has bound up in it many long-run variables that are affected by income and that are themselves influences on fertility. That is, a cross-section holds at one point in time the entire story of Figure 14–1. Higher income leads to, for example, more contraceptive knowledge which in turn reduces fertility. The net effect of all these relationships may theoretically yield a negative *or* positive unconditional relationship between income and fertility. But in almost every country until now the unconditional relationship has been negative; higher income is associated cross-sectionally with lower fertility. This pattern may be seen for the United States in Table 15–1. Though the relationship is less negative in cohorts that have more recently ended or nearly ended childbearing, the effect is still clear and large.

These unconditional cross-section data have led to the belief that in the short run children are not a "normal good," and that a short-run rise in income leads to a decrease in fertility. In response, researchers

336

TABLE 15–1

OVER-ALL U.S. CROSS-SECTIONAL INCOME-FERTILITY RELATIONSHIP
(income of husband in 1959—number of children ever born per
1,000 white women, age 15 and over, married and husband present,
by age of woman, for the United States, 1960)

| | Age of woman in 1959 | | | |
Income of husband in 1959	50 and over	45–49	40–44	35–39
None	3,108	2,785	2,860	2,905
$1 to $1,999 or less	3,281	2,949	3,066	3,097
$2,000 to $2,999	2,745	2,754	2,901	2,947
$3,000 to $3,999	2,542	2,558	2,680	2,755
$4,000 to $4,999	2,400	2,380	2,523	2,619
$5,000 to $6,999	2,175	2,234	2,439	2,576
$7,000 to $9,999	1,973	2,125	2,407	2,583
$10,000 to $14,999	1,844	2,097	2,415	2,601
$15,000 and over	1,875	2,156	2,482	2,733

SOURCE: U.S. Department of Commerce, 1964, p. 181.

have estimated short-run effect of income with *all* other relevant variables held constant. This tactic cannot be carried out fully, for reasons given elsewhere (Simon, 1974a, Appendix B.) But a partial use of this tactic shows that in many relevant circumstances the short-run effect of a rise in income would be an increase in fertility. A first approximation is to increase the homogeneity of the subgroups by finely cross-classifying by such fertility-affecting variables as age of wife, age at marriage, color, husband's occupation and profession, and residence area; the partial effect of income is seen to be positive. Consider as a crude index of the effect of income on fertility for women married at ages 22 or over: the ratio of the numbers of children born to women in the $7,000–9,000 and the $2,000–3,999 husband's income classes. Of the 90 cells for the United States in 1959 for which there are data, only 10 do not show higher fertility for the higher income group. And there is only 1 instance in which both age cells within the same occupation-education-residence categories fail to show higher fertility with higher income, suggesting that sampling error may account for some or all of the reversals. (The data for women married at age 21 or earlier do not show such positive effect, however.)

Going a bit deeper into the cross-sectional income and fertility data reveals even stronger evidence of the positive partial effect of income. For example, there is a remarkably consistent positive relationship between income and the proportion of U.S. couples having *at least one* child, among white women married at age 22 or over in urban areas in Table 15–2. Childlessness is not a perfect substitute variable for fertility, by any means, but it is certainly an important component of fertility, and

337

TABLE 15–2
PERCENT OF CHILDLESS WHITE WIVES, BY INCOME,
URBANIZED AREAS, UNITED STATES, (age 45–54, married at age 22+)

Husband's income in 1959	Professional, technical and kindred workers	Managers, officials and proprietors, except farmers	Clerical, sales and kindred workers	Craftsmen, foremen, and kindred workers	Operatives and kindred workers	Service workers, including private household	Laborers, except farm and mine	Farmers, farm managers, farm laborers, and farm foremen
No high school								
$1 to $1,999 or loss	—	39.3	38.1	43.9	32.3	41.3	33.2	Insufficient data
$2,000 to $3,999	—	31.2	32.7	27.1	28.2	32.9	27.7	
$4,000 to $6,999	29.0	23.2	27.1	25.0	24.1	26.7	24.8	
$7,000 to $9,999	32.9	20.6	23.0	21.1	17.8	21.0	16.1	
$10,000 and over	16.9	21.8	23.1	20.9	29.1	—	—	
High school								
$1 to $1,999 or loss	39.4	28.9	39.6	34.4	31.0	35.2	25.4	
$2,000 to $3,999	46.5	30.8	34.1	29.4	30.6	33.8	29.2	
$4,000 to $6,999	30.1	27.1	26.4	23.6	24.0	25.2	18.1	
$7,000 to $9,999	23.9	22.2	22.7	20.3	19.1	17.9	—	
$10,000 and over	17.8	20.7	22.9	20.1	20.4	17.9	—	
College								
$1 to $1,999 or loss	25.0	30.3	29.8	—	—	—	—	
$2,000 to $3,999	31.6	26.0	36.0	36.9	33.4	43.8	28.8	
$4,000 to $6,999	25.9	25.3	27.1	28.2	21.8	25.6	—	
$7,000 to $9,999	24.6	20.3	23.9	23.0	20.0	24.6	—	
$10,000 and over	16.2	16.7	18.3	14.5	10.8	—	—	

Source: U.S. Department of Commerce, 1964, p. 181.

hence relevant in this connection. (On the other hand, data subclassified in ways shown in Table 15–2 do *not* show such clear effects for women married at age 21 or earlier. One might guess that if knowledge of contraception were also held constant, the positive relationship might clearly appear, however.)

The one clear, obvious, and immediate conclusion is that the relationships embodied in cross-section data are far from obvious and clear. We must, therefore, go much deeper in an attempt to understand.

A strong positive direct income effect has also been found in some industrialized countries other than the United States. Glass's recent data for Germany (1969), Rosenberg's for New Zealand (1971), and Edin and Hutchinson's earlier data for Sweden (1935) show this clearly.

Holding education and 1920 income constant, Edin and Hutchinson found that favorable changes in income during 1920–1930 were associated with higher fertility in the first 10 years of marriage of Stockholm families, as compared to families with unfavorable changes in income. The same sort of effect was shown for the United States by Freedman and Coombs (1966b); the more positive the family's income change (a proxy for income expectations) between their first and third interviews, the more children the family had between the first and third interviews, and the more children it expected as of the third interview, holding current income and religion constant.

In one of the first and neatest multivariate analyses, Mincer (1963) used the 1950 BLS Survey data to show that when the wife's earnings and the husband's education are held constant, the relationship of husband's income to fertility is positive. And in a multivariate study of the 1967 U.S. Survey of Economic Opportunity data, Smith (1973) found that family (not husband's!) income is positively associated with fertility for both whites and blacks (though there is a weak *negative* effect of net worth of fertility).

The importance of these family cross-section results is *not* that they themselves generally show a positive partial income effect. Furthermore, the *size* of the observed effect is without any meaning at all, except perhaps as a lower limit to the effect. What is important is that the partial income effects gets progressively *more* positive as the samples are made more homogeneous by the device of successively fine classification. For example, for all white women 35–39 years old in the United States, the ratio of numbers of children ever born for families with husband's income $7,000–$9,999 to $2,000–2,999 is 2,583 ÷ 2,947 = .80 (Table 15–2). (For $7,000–$9,999 to $3,000–$3,999 it is 2,583 ÷ 2,755 = .93). An even grosser classification lumping women of all ages and colors together would undoubtedly produce ratios even further below unity. But now if we move to one more degree of fineness, classifying by residence areas, the ratios for $7,000–$9,999 to $2,000–$2,999, and $7,000–$9,999 to $3,000–$3,999 respectively, white women 35–39 years old are: urbanized, 2,509 ÷ 2,494 = 1.01 and 2,509 ÷ 2,420 = 1.04; other urban, 2,618 ÷ 2,863 = .91 and 2,518 ÷ 2,701 = .93; rural non-farm, 2,755 ÷ 3,207 = .86 and 2,755 ÷ 3,002 = .92; rural farm, 3,166 ÷ 3,277 = .97 and 3,166 ÷ 3,286 = .96 (all data from U.S. Department of Commerce, 1964, Table 37). And further classifying by husband's occupation and education raises the ratio considerably above unity.

A similar result emerges when the data are standardized by the multivariate methods of Cho et al. (1970) rather than by subclassification. Table 15–3 (the ratios of fertility for given groups to the average fertility for the U.S.) shows that the effect of income on fertility is much less negative when standardized for wife's age than when not so standardized, and still less negative (more positive) when also standardized for wife's education.

TABLE 15–3
NATIVE WHITE FERTILITY IN THE UNITED STATES
(own children under age 5 per 1,000 married women with husband present; standardized for age and education; ratio to national average)

Income of husband	Unstandardized	Age standardized	Age education standardized
Under $1,000	0.81	0.87	0.86
$1,000	0.93	0.86	0.86
$2,000	1.05	0.92	0.92
$3,000	1.07	0.94	0.94
$4,000	1.07	0.96	0.97
$5,000	1.06	1.01	1.02
$7,000	0.99	1.06	1.06
$10,000	0.87	1.09	1.07
$15,000 and over	0.75	1.10	1.05

SOURCE: Bogue, 1969, p. 717.

The observed income-fertility relationship in household cross-sections must be strongly understated because of the "permanent-income" effect, i.e., current income is not a very good proxy for expected income here. Gardner (1973) circumvented the permanent-income difficulty by using *consumption* expenditure (including imputed values for housing and durables) as a measure of income. In a sample of rural North Carolina women, the coefficient of the long-run income proxy is positive, and considerably *more* positive than the coefficient for current money income.

340

This suggests both that the effect of income on fertility is positive in this rural sample, and that the permanent-income effect is of some importance in income-fertility studies.

The permanent-income effect can be largely avoided by using average values for geographical areas, because the average income *differential* among the areas should be much the same from year to year. This eliminates the year-to-year variation in incomes of individual families which biases downward the observed income-fertility relationship. Cain and Weininger (1972) worked with a cross-section of the largest (over 250,000 population) standard U.S. metropolitan areas, and regressed children ever born on male income, female wage rate, female education, and region. (Other variables were also used in the various models.) In the 1960 Census data, the income elasticities for white age groups were around .2 to .3. This implies that between $8,000 and $12,000 of additional income would bring about an increase of 1 child per family.

COMPLEX DIRECT EFFECTS OF INCOME

Recently a provocative but hard-to-interpret result was obtained by Sanderson and Willis (1971). Using the 1-in-1,000 U.S. 1960 Census tape, and working with cell means of about 100 socio-economic groups in each of three age groups, they show that at higher levels of women's education and husband's income, an increase in husband's income will indeed produce an increase in children, but at *low* levels of women's education and husband's income an increase in husband's income produces a *decrease* in fertility.

Willis and Sanderson's theoretical explanation of this result is as follows: Increased income provides the wife with more "household goods" to use and enjoy, and (assuming her education is too low to give her a reasonably good opportunity to find a well-paying job) she will tend to spend more time using these household goods, which might include, for example, the capacity to travel and be out in society. This competes with the time she might otherwise spend with the children. That is, the additional goods that the wife can buy with higher income raise the value to her of the time she might otherwise spend with an additional child, and the opportunity cost of an additional child is thereby made higher.

An alternative explanation of the Sanderson-Willis finding is that it reflects income elasticities of different signs with respect to *different birth orders*—a finding that is reported in the next sub-section. A positive income elasticity with respect to the first children and a negative income elasticity with respect to later children will produce the results Willis and Sanderson showed.

Ben-Porath (1972; 1973) tested the Sanderson-Willis hypothesis on an Israeli household survey, and also found negative coefficients for husband's income (and for women's potential earnings, as estimated by women's education weighted by average earnings for that income level) and a positive interaction term. These results are consistent with the Sanderson-Willis hypothesis. But Ben-Porath speculated that the observed results might also be caused by the U-shaped association of fertility with women's education which is frequently seen in the raw data. He tested this hypothesis by adding a variable for the *square* of the woman's potential earnings. This variable does at least as well as the Sanderson-Willis type interaction term in an otherwise similar regression, and almost eliminates the influence of the interaction term when both are included *together*. Both these results give weight to Ben-Porath's hypothesis versus Sanderson and Willis'. The coefficients of husband's earnings remain negative in the curvilinear regressions, but much *less* negative than in regressions with the interaction term.

The Effect of Income on Successive Birth Orders

The cross-sectional studies that have been discussed so far have all used total-children-ever-born as the dependent variable. It is an implicit assumption of such studies that the effect of income on the family having an additional child is the same for all birth orders, i.e., the same for the sixth child as for the first. But this may well not be the case, as is shown by the gross data in Table 15–4. The simple relationship of income to total-children-ever-born is negative whereas the relationship to whether the family has *any* children or none is positive, i.e., lower-income families are less likely to have *any* children than better-off families. This suggests that the relationship to income may well be different for the different birth orders.

TABLE 15–4

FERTILITY OF WHITE WOMEN IN THE UNITED STATES, AGE 45–49
(married and husband present in 1959)

Income of husband	Number of women with one or more children, per 1,000 women	Number of women with no children per 1,000 women	Children ever born per 1,000 women
None	808	192	2,785
$1 to $1,999 or loss	814	186	2,949
$2,000 to $2,999	827	173	2,754
$3,000 to $3,999	829	171	2,558
$4,000 to $4,999	830	170	2,380
$5,000 to $6,999	836	164	2,234
$7,000 to $9,999	842	158	2,125
$10,000 to $14,999	842	158	2,097
$15,000 and over	858	142	2,156

SOURCE: U.S. Bureau of the Census, 1964, p. 181, 182.

To examine this matter, I finely subclassified the 1-in-1,000 1960 U.S. Census sample by various demographic characteristics, and then applied discriminant analysis within each cell with more than ten observations. The dependent variable in each run is a dichotomous yes-no variable. The two categories in each birth-order variation are whether the wife has n children, or more than n children. In the first of the six birth-order variations the two categories contain wives with no children, and those with 1 or more children, respectively; this variation is designated as the $n = 0$ run. In the second ($n = 1$) variation the categories are 1 child, and 2 or more children. There are 6 variations, the $n = 5$ variation having wives with 5 children in one category, 6 or more children in the other. The discriminant function finds those values of the independent variables that most effectively separate the observations into the two dependent-variable categories.

The independent variable of interest here is husband's income; some other factors are included in the discriminant function to hold them constant. The units of observation are women, ages 35–54, with husbands present. The observations are then subclassified by race, degree of urbanization of residence place, husband's occupation, and wife's age.

The most reliable estimation for the effect of a given variable in the group of runs in a given variation is the ratio of the coefficients that are positive to those that are negative. For example, in the $n = 0$ variation reported in row 1 of Table 15–5 the income coefficients in 199 cells were positive, while 96 were negative. (Zero coefficients were not counted.) The ratio $(199/96) = 2.07$ is an index of the direction of income's effect in that variation, to be compared with $160/118 = 1.36$ for the $n = 1$ variation in that set of runs, and so forth, as seen in Table 15–5. A coeffi-

TABLE 15–5

EFFECT OF HUSBAND'S INCOME ON VARIOUS BIRTH ORDERS

Fertility categories in dependent variable

0, ≥1	1, ≥2	2, ≥3	3, ≥4	4, ≥5	5, ≥6
2.01	1.36	1.03	.82	.78	1.16
($N = 295$)	($N = 278$)	($N = 246$)	($N = 189$)	($N = 107$)	($N = 67$)

NOTE: The ratio of positive income coefficients to negative income coefficients among discriminant functions of the form: dichotomous fertility category $= f$ (husband's income, education of wife, education of husband, wife's age). The variables of cell subclassification are: race, urbanity, wife's education, husband's education, husband's occupation, wife's age.

Compare across the rows. Numbers greater than unity indicate a *positive* relationship between husband's income and fertility, on the average; numbers less than unity show a negative association. The sample size, N, shows the number of sub-groups with more than ten observations in which the regression coefficients were non-zero.

343

cient greater than unity implies a positive effect, and a coefficient smaller than unity implies a negative effect.

The effect of husband's income on various birth orders may be seen by looking across the rows in Table 15–5. Higher husband's income is *positively* associated with the family having at least one child rather than none. The relationship then moves smoothly from positive to negative as one looks to the higher birth orders up to the sixth birth in row 1 and the fifth birth in row 2.

The association between the husband's income and the probability of having children becomes negative in the neighborhood of the third or fourth child. That is, though a larger income *increases* the probability that the family will have more children when they have no children or 1, it *decreases* the probability that they will have additional children when they already have as many as 3, 4, or more. The finding is generally confirmed by the findings for Sweden reported by Bernhardt (1972), Namboodiri (1974), and Seiver (1974).

An implication of this finding is that *ceteris paribus*, a rise in income contributes to an explanation of the "convergence" of Americans to families with 2–4 children, and away from families with fewer or more than 2–4 children, as income has risen secularly in the United States during the 1900's and before. The mechanism can be seen as follows: Assume a group of people distributed among tendencies to have completed families of 0, 1, 2, 3, 4, 5 . . . . An increase in income for each of the families increases the likelihood that those who would have 0 children will have 1 child instead, or 2 instead of 1. At the other end of the distribution, the data observed here suggests that those who would have, say, 4 children *ex ante*, will have 3 instead. That is, the increase in income changes some "no's" to "yes's" for the small families and some "yes's" to "no's" for the large families. The over-all effect is a narrowed distribution of families by total children. This is consistent with the observed fact that poor people are disproportionately represented at *both* ends of the total-completed-family size distribution. Simply increasing the income of some of the poorer people will cause some to leave both ends of the distribution and to obtain a family size nearer the center of the distribution.

LONG-RUN EFFECTS OF INCOME ON
FERTILITY CHANGES IN MDC'S

Assume a situation in which infant mortality approaches 10 per 1,000, knowledge of contraceptive methods is almost 100%, and farm residence is at a level so low that even a large proportional decline in the remaining farm population could have only a small effect on aggregate fertility. Also assume a time-horizon long enough so that norms and values can change in response to other forces in the society, and hence are not an independent factor. Starting from this point, the main *economic* forces that may act upon fertility in the long run are (1) the direct effect of income levels on men's wages, (2) the direct effect on women's wages, (3) the indirect effect of income on men's education and opportunity cost, (4) the indirect effect on the education of women and the opportunity cost of their foregone employment, and (5) changes in the "costs" of raising children.

Before beginning the discussion of the long-run effect of income on fertility in MDC's it should be noted that the variance in number of children among families is small—relative to the variance in earlier years in present-day MDC's, and relative to the variance within present-day LDC's. For example, fully 58% of the families in the United States with wives age 35–44 in 1960 had 2–4 children. The implication of this small variance is that differences in conditions (including income) with MDC's do not have massive effects on fertility. On the other hand, there is a fertility spread among nations that is *not* related to income (Kuznets, 1968, p. 26). Together, these facts suggest that the long-run effects of changes in income on fertility are not likely to be large.

Theory alone provides no basis for guessing whether the direct effects on wages, or the indirect partial effects through education and the cost of children and perhaps tastes, will dominate. The net outcome will depend partly on how elastic is the average expenditure on children with respect to income, and how much discretion parents have in choosing to spend more or less on children.

In the absence of theoretical guidance, we must turn to data. The relevant empirical evidence yields two impressions: (1) lack of strong unconditional correlation between income and fertility cross-sectionally in MDC's; and (2) decrease or lack of change in fertility over time despite long-run increase in income in MDC's. Consider first the lack of correlation cross-sectionally. Casual inspection reveals that many extremely rich people in the United States have 2 or 3 or 4 children, while the much poorer Hutterites average 12 children. And recent sophisticated multivariate analyses (e.g., Michael, 1970; Willis and Sanderson, 1970) still leave a great proportion of the fertility variation among families unexplained by income and income-related variables.

Now consider the *aggregate* birth rates for countries that meet our initial starting conditions of low mortality, low farm population, and high knowledge of contraception, e.g., United States, United Kingdom, Canada, Western Europe, Scandinavia. Among these the cross-sectional relationship of average income to fertility is not strong, if it exists at all, though the range of income is considerable. After inspecting this evidence Kuznets concluded: "Clearly, there are substantial international birth rate differentials, *not* associated with per capita product (and probably any measure of economic performance)." He cited such phenomena as that "in general, birth rates in the high income countries overseas are distinctly higher than in the older countries in Europe with equally high incomes: For the $400–699 and $1,100 and more groups, the rates for Europe are 18.1 and 15.7 per 1,000, and those for the Americas and Oceania are about 24.5" (Kuznets, 1968, p. 26). On the other hand, the spread among countries has been narrowing in the past decade.

Long-run time-series in MDC's also suggest unresponsiveness of fertility to long-run economic changes. Easterlin (1961) notes that the most important group (quantitatively) in American fertility is increasingly the urban native-born (white) population, and he found "substantial stability" in the fertility ratio for this group from 1895–99 to 1925–29. Kiser (1970) found, however, continuous decline among wives who completed their fertility from the turn of the century until 1950—and especially among wives and men in urban-concentrated occupations. Income was rising throughout this period, so there may well have been a tradeoff between the direct effect of income on men's earnings, and the indirect effect through education of women and consequent changes in their opportunity costs.

The Individual Components of the Long-Run Indirect Effect of Income

THE SHORT-RUN DIRECT EFFECT OF INCOME

The paucity of evidence on the overall relationship throws us back on available evidence about the supposed components, and the direct effect of income is one such component. The first section of this chapter on the short-run in MDC's suggests that the direct partial income effect is positive. It is less clear, however, just *how strong* is the short-run effect of income. The time-series data suggest a fairly strong temporal effect, but postponement of births from worse to better years could account for a major part of the effect. The cross-section data suggest a weaker income effect, even when several variables are held constant.

WIFE'S EDUCATION

Concerning now the indirect effect of income through education and the wife's opportunity costs: American data show that holding husband's education constant, wives with more education generally have lower fertility (e.g., Ruggles and Ruggles, 1960, Table 3, pp. 172–73, and Table A–1, pp. 194–95). And using 1950 BLS survey data, Mincer (1963) found a strong and large effect of the wife's full-time earnings upon fertility,

346

among women who worked full time. And in grouped Israeli census data Ben-Porath (1970; 1973) shows that, holding husband's education constant, fertility declines with more women's education. In 1963 survey data he also found a negative effect of women's education on fertility, holding husband's earnings constant.

Unfortunately for economic reasoning, or at least for *simple* economic reasoning, not all the data on the effect of women's education on fertility are consistent with the notion that the labor-force opportunity cost is the dominant mechanism. A hint of this is in Ben-Porath's finding that in Israel the main fertility differential is between women with no education and those with *even a little* education, additional education making relatively little difference.

In the U.S. data in Figure 15–5 one also sees that the biggest effect of white women's education is at the lower levels of women's education. And the effect interacts with husband's education; additional education for low-education women only reduces fertility significantly when the husband also has low education. Additional education for white women who have more-than-average education and whose husbands have college educations actually *raises* fertility. And for *black* women the effect on fertility of additional education is *negative* for women with less than eight years of education (Smith, 1973, p. 55). All this calls into question a purely opportunity-cost explanation of the effect of women's education.

HUSBAND'S EDUCATION

Figure 15–5 shows that at low women's education levels, more education for the husband is associated with lower fertility. But when the wife has much education, more education for the husband is associated with *higher* fertility. This mixed effect does not help us estimate the long-run effect of income through husband's education.

COSTS OF CHILDREN IN THE LONG-RUN

The "costs" or "price" of children clearly are important. But just as clearly, Michael and Lazear (1971) are right that "neither the magnitude of the price of a child nor the own-price demand elasticity is, as yet, well documented empirically" (1971, p. 22).

TASTES

For many years people have speculated that income may alter tastes for children, either absolutely or relative to other goods, in such manner that additional income leads to fewer children in the long run. Lindert's careful work (forthcoming) seems to show that there is indeed such an

347

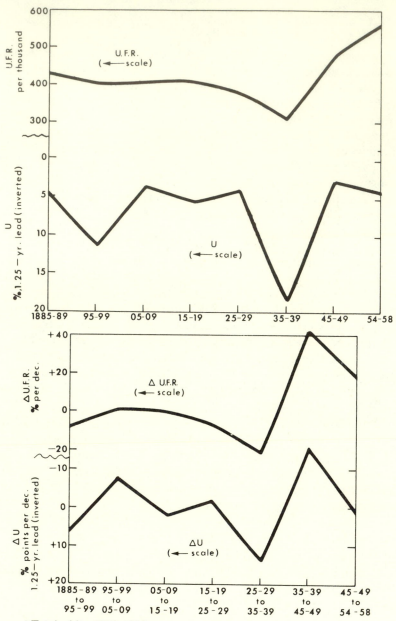

^a Total white, 1925–1929 on.

Notes

The unemployment scale is inverted.

The unemployment scale is dated 1.25 years before the actual data because of the lagged relationship between economic conditions and births.

The lower scale in the lower graph is percentage changes from decade to decade.

FIGURE 15–5   NUMBER OF CHILDREN EVER BORN PER 1,000 WHITE WOMEN, AGE 35–44, MARRIED AND HUSBAND PRESENT BY YEARS OF SCHOOL COMPLETED BY WIFE AND HUSBAND: URBANIZED UNITED STATES, 1960

SOURCE: Reproduced from Easterlin, 1968, p. 102.

effect. Income in prior decades has a strong negative effect on American fertility over and beyond changes through education and the cost of children.[2]

Taken together, this evidence confirms that prior income as well as current income influences fertility, and prior income explains much in the over-all fertility pattern.

The Far Future in MDC's

If average income continues to grow, and if the relative cost of children does not increase greatly, then it is possible—though by no means certain—that income and fertility will become increasingly separated.

One may imagine an income level so Rockefeller-high that additional income will not affect family size. But family size at such high incomes might still be of the same order as in average U.S. families today; the family size of the highest income people today is not particularly high.

One may, however, take the view—implicit in Easterlin's work (1973)—that people's income aspirations are rising, and may be expected to continue to rise. And people whose income is lower than their expectations—or lower than that of people within their ken such as their parents—may then continue to adjust their fertility in relationship to their perceived income situation. If so, fertility may continue to be affected by fluctuations over time and by the shape of the income distribution. Only the distant future will tell the answer to these speculations, however.

SUMMARY

First let us review the short-run direct effects of income on fertility in MDC's beginning with the time-series data. In the short run during which parents' aspirations and tastes and backgrounds can be considered to be fixed, aggregate time-series data show that changes in personal income and unemployment have a clear same-direction effect on fluctuations in fertility. Over the business cycle, perhaps a quarter or half of the variation around the long-term fertility trend may be explained by variations in economic conditions; for each one-percent change in per person income or unemployment, there is a .25% or .50% change in fertility in the same direction. Marriages and first births are more sensitive to income variations than are higher order births.

Some or even most of the variation in fertility over the business cycle may be explained by *shifts in parental timing*, however. It is clear that almost all of the variation in marriage rates over the business cycle is

---

[2] The importance of prior income and its possible taste-altering effect in MDC fertility was stressed in Simon (1969b). See pages 314–315 above, and the appendix to Chapter 14.

indeed due to shifts in timing, because most people do eventually get married. The variations in fertility itself are more complex. And though work on the topic is now going on, no research technique has yet been developed which provides a satisfactory answer about the extent to which the business cycle affects completed-family size and timing. Hopefully such a technique will soon be developed.

Over the longer (5–30 years) economic swings in MDC's, income explains a considerable amount of the fertility variation around the long-run trend. But the long-run downward trend over the industrialization period still dominates the last century's history in the United States and other MDC's.

Next we summarize what is known about short-run income effects from cross-section data: Comparisons of fertility rates among different income groups at a single point in time—census data are the most common source—tell relatively less about the short-run "pure" partial direct effect of the income than about the longer-run effects. No matter how finely one may subclassify the population or specify the regression—by race, occupation, education, and so forth—the different income groups within a sub-classification are likely to differ in characteristics other than their incomes that are *systematically related* to their incomes. Therefore, the fertility differences associated with income in the cross-section may be caused by the income differences *or* by the systematically related variables. Another phenomenon that obscures the relationship in cross-section data between income and fertility is that the income recorded by the census refers only to a period much shorter than the individual's lifetime, usually a year. But income received in earlier years, and perhaps the income stream the couple expects to receive in future years, affects the couple's fertility decisions. Because past and future income are very imperfectly related to the short-period income recorded by the census, error is introduced. It would be an important advance in income-and-fertility studies if the researchers were to obtain data on people's past and expected future incomes.

Whereas without any or much subclassification, the relationship of income to fertility is sometimes weakly positive and sometimes negative, within *very* detailed sub-classifications the relationship is almost invariably positive. This positive relationship concurs with the time-series and verbal-behavior evidence that if people with *given* tastes and backgrounds are given additional income, they will have more children. The *quantitative* relationship between income and fertility should not be estimated from cross-sectional census data, however.

Cross-section data indicate rather conclusively that lower order births are more responsive to income changes than are higher order births, a

350

finding that jibes with the business-cycle evidence. These findings call into question the meaning of the income coefficient in studies done with total-children-ever-born as the dependent variable.

To summarize the entire section on short-run effects in MDC's: As I read the evidence taken altogether, there is strong reason to believe that fertility in MDC's will exhibit a positive relationship to income and employment over business cycles and over somewhat longer swings in economic activity. The facts that (1) fertility is not strongly higher for higher income groups than lower income groups in general cross-section data, and (2) poorer paid occupations frequently have higher fertility than better paid occupations, do not contradict the assertion that the *ceteris paribus* partial direct income effect is positive and important in the short run. This is because education and occupation and other determinants of overall income level and tastes are not subject to short-run change.

Next we proceed to summarize the overall *long-run effect* over their lifetime of an increment of income obtained by families who are *now* at present-day income levels in the United States and other MDC's where urbanization is high and child mortality low. From the studies on the short-run effect mentioned earlier, we infer that the partial direct effect of income is to raise fertility by increasing the family's power to afford children. But in the long run a rise in income has many other sorts of effects upon people, some of which then influence fertility either upward *or* downward. Some of these effects are strong and unambiguous, while others are subtle and complicated. It is these other effects that come into the total longer run analysis.

The clearest indirect effect of income is by way of women's education. Increased parental income causes more education for a girl, and more earning power for her as a woman. This in turn implies that more salary must be foregone if she takes time out to have another child. As theory suggests, additional education is strongly associated with fewer children in most segments of MDC society. At the very highest education levels, however, the effect reverses. And among the highest husband's-income families, women's education does not matter much, because very few of the wives of the highest income men work outside the home.

It is also clear that increased average income for the society increases people's access to contraception and abortion, which reduces the number of high-parity families. We do not know, however, the relative importance of the direct income effect that makes it easier for people to purchase contraception and abortion, and the indirect effect through education and changes in tastes. And at some not-too-distant time in countries like Sweden and the United States, access to contraception will be sufficiently

351

general that additional income cannot matter much—just as the urban revolution is now sufficiently complete so that increased income cannot continue to raise urbanity and thereby decrease fertility.

Income increases may also have many other effects upon people's actual and perceived economic situations that may affect fertility in complicated ways. For example, children are not homogeneous, and people have at least some discretion about how much they will choose to spend on an additional child (e.g., whether or not to pay for his education through graduate school). This discretion complicates the decision about whether to have additional children, because a couple can pick different combinations of numbers of children and expenditures on each of them. Rises in income affect both (1) the prices of goods and services involved in raising children, and (2) the tastes and beliefs of parents about how much they want to spend and feel they ought to spend. It is, therefore, theoretically possible that a rise in income will have the direct effect of *lowering* the number of children people "purchase," but no evidence has been shown for such an effect.

Some other possible subtle effects of income rises in MDC's include these: (1) A rise in income enables one to purchase some goods and services that require time for enjoyment (e.g., snowmobiles and trips abroad). The desire to enjoy these time-using purchases may conflict with the time-demands of children. (2) An income rise is likely to affect both the Smiths *and* the Joneses. The Smiths may therefore feel *relatively* no better off when both their incomes rise, and they may feel the need to keep up with the Joneses in their expenditures on the children as well as on other things, and hence they may feel no better off and no more disposed to have more children than before the income rise. Little is now known about this phenomenon. And if relative income is important in fertility behavior, it implies that alterations in the income *distribution* would affect the fertility of sub-groups and probably of the society as a whole. Research on this matter also is lacking. (3) Increases in income, and associated rises in education and communications and mobility, may alter the structure of people's *tastes* for children versus other expenditures in ways other than those mentioned up until now.

Perhaps it is best to end this chapter on MDC fertility with a cautionary note: The variance in fertility among families and over time in MDC's is relatively small, at least as compared to LDC's, which leaves relatively little for economic variables to explain. And of the existing variance, existing income differences do not explain very much.

CHAPTER 16

The Short-Run and
Long-Run Effects of Income
on Fertility in LDC's

INTRODUCTION

THE PREVIOUS chapter discussed the effects of income on fertility in MDC's. This chapter discusses the effects of income on fertility in LDC's. The first part of the chapter finds that the short-run effect of an income increase is to raise fertility, especially in very-low-income groups. More important is the main finding of the second part of the chapter: The long-run total effect of increased income and economic development, together with the related modernization nexus, is to *reduce* fertility from high pre-modern to low industrialized-country levels.

This effect combines with the results reported in Chapter 13 concerning the effect of population growth on the economic level in LDC's, to disprove Malthus' contention for LDC's that population rises to the limit of subsistence.

EVIDENCE ON THE SHORT-RUN EFFECT OF INCOME ON
FERTILITY IN LDC's

Time-Series Evidence

Let us begin with some time-series data. Apparently fertility did increase at the beginning of the economic development of the European countries. The same effect has been observed in the LDC's in the twentieth century. "While the data are not so good as to give decisive evidence, it seems very likely that natality has risen over the past generation—certainly in the West Indies, very likely in tropical America, and probably in a number of countries of Africa and Asia" (Kirk, 1969, p. 79). A thorough cross-sectional study of the Phillippines by Encarnacion (1974) is consistent with such a rise in fertility as the incomes of the poorest people increase.

Such rises may partly result from physical factors such as a reduction in venereal disease or from income-induced changes in customs and patterns of life, such as shortened lactation periods, or the rises may be caused by improvements in nutrition. They may also partly result, however, from very direct income effects, as a close observer of an Indian village reports:

353

In the early 1950s, conditions were distinctly unfavorable. The large influx of refugees from Pakistan was accompanied by severe disruption of economic and social stability. We were repeatedly told by village leaders on the panchayat, or elected village council, that important as all of their other problems were, "the biggest problem is that there are just too many of us." By the end of the study period in 1960, a remarkable change had occurred. With the introduction of more irrigation canals and with rural electrification from the Bhakra Nangal Dam, and with better roads to transport produce to market: improved seed and other benefits of community development, and especially because there were increasing employment opportunities for Punjabi boys in the cities, a general feeling of optimism had developed. A common response of the same village leaders now was, "Why should we limit our families? India needs all the Punjabis she can get." During this transitional period an important reason for the failure of education in family planning was the favorable pace of economic development. Children were no longer a handicap (Taylor, 1965, pp. 482–83).

For eighteenth-century Sweden, which was very much an LDC at that time, Figure 16–1 shows all the relevant rates—harvest, death, marriage, and birth. They are strong evidence of the short-run direct effect of income on family-size decisions.

In a study of eighteenth-century Flanders, Mendels (1970) found that the marriage rate in agricultural areas moved directly with the prices of rye, implying that a rise in farm income caused more marriages. In cities where the linen trade was important, the marriage rate moved together with the ratio of rye prices to linen prices. This suggests that lower rye prices and higher linen prices (both of which imply higher income to people in the linen trade) produced more marriages.

R. Lee (1971) considered the long-run trends of population size, mortality, and real wages in England during 1250–1750. He formulated a simultaneous equation model in which fertility is a function of the real wage, the real wage is a function of population size, and population size is a function of fertility and mortality, with mortality being an exogenous variable. The resulting estimate for the elasticity of fertility with respect to the real wage is a substantial .4.

Family Cross-Sectional Evidence

For subsistence-farming rural societies the best study is that of Stys (1957) for rural Poland in 1948. Table 16–1 shows that, for all those age groups of women that had reached 45 at the time of the study, fertility was higher for women who lived on bigger farms. There are variations in

354

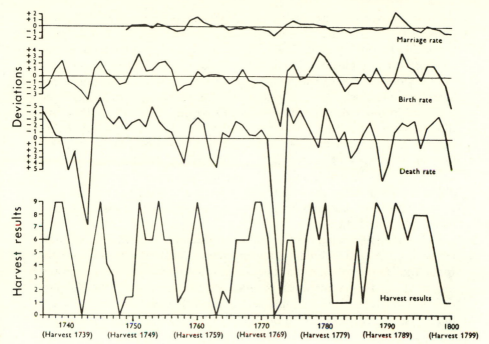

FIGURE 16–1   HARVEST RESULTS AND DEVIATIONS OF MARRIAGE, BIRTH, AND DEATH RATES FROM
THEIR RESPECTIVE TRENDS, SWEDEN, 1735–1800
SOURCE: Reproduced from Gille, 1949, p. 45.

TABLE 16–1
CHILDREN BORN BY POLISH PEASANT MOTHERS OF DIFFERENT AGES

Mother born in	Land-less	\multicolumn{10}{c}{Farms by size in hectares}									
		0–0.5	0.5–1	1–2	2–3	3–4	4–5	5–7	7–10	10–15	Over 15
	\multicolumn{11}{c}{Average numbers of children born}									
1855–80	3.89	5.46	5.30	6.10	6.57	6.40	7.54	7.83	9.08	9.00	10.00
1881–85	3.50	3.50	4.94	5.38	5.84	7.23	7.30	8.09	8.17	6.00	—
1886–90	6.00	3.55	3.75	5.15	5.39	6.26	6.00	6.67	7.00	9.80	—
1891–94	4.33	4.31	5.16	4.43	4.83	4.81	6.12	5.56	5.40	7.00	—
1895–97	2.00	4.28	3.74	4.54	4.77	5.29	4.53	5.00	3.75	5.50	—
1898–1900	4.50	3.71	3.20	3.49	4.07	4.57	4.84	3.88	7.17	6.50	—
1901–1902	—	4.40	2.85	3.80	4.02	4.27	4.60	5.14	4.75	7.50	—
1903–1904	4.00	3.64	2.94	3.42	3.72	3.72	3.64	2.67	4.40	—	—

SOURCE: Stys, 1957, p. 140.

the data, to be sure, but Stys's least-squares-regression analysis showed positive slopes for each age group. The detailed data for Polish farm women born during 1855–1880, shown in Table 16-2, are especially valuable for our purposes. First consider line 10, which indicates that during those years between the first and last child fertility was much the same for all farm-size groups, and in fact was almost as high as has been observed in the highest-fertility societies known. This suggests that fertility was not controlled during that time-span, and that physical health was excellent. Line 3 shows that the poorer the prospective couple, the later the marriage—an economic check on fertility. Furthermore, poorer couples ceased having children at earlier mothers' ages (line 5), and physical infirmity was not a likely cause. A comparison of lines 10 and 11 show that a later start and an earlier stop to fertility in poorer families had a substantial effect.

Chayanov (1966) suggested a reason to question the meaning of such a relationship, and offered supporting data. Farmers may increase by rental the amount of land that they farm when their family size requires more output. This factor was more likely to be important in the Russian or Polish context of the late nineteenth and early twentieth century than in Asia, however, especially at present.

As in MDC's, refined analysis introducing additional variables to account for the long-run effect of income can reveal a mixed or positive effect of current income on fertility instead of the negative effect seen in simple regressions. This has most recently been seen in Taiwanese data, where income-class means adjusted with Multiple Classification Analysis are positively related to fertility, "ideal" number of children, and contraceptive use, whereas the relationship of unadjusted income to fertility and "ideal" number of children is negative (MacDonald and Mueller, 1975). In other studies such as that of Snyder (1974) in urban Sierra Leone, the partial relationship is still negative. But it can be said with some confidence that after other relevant and measurable variables are allowed for, the short-run effect of income on fertility in LDC's is neither strongly negative nor strongly positive though Kleinman (1973) found that in rural India (Gujarat) "The resource variable set accounts for 44 percent of the variance of general fertility."

Geographical Country Cross-Section Studies

Geographical country cross-sections tell us little about the "pure" direct effect of income because fuller specification and better data would almost surely make the sign of the coefficient more positive. Specification is particularly difficult in the study of income and fertility because the variables stand at different stages of causation with respect to the dependent

TABLE 16-2

FERTILITY OF POLISH MOTHERS BORN, 1855–80

	Land-less	\multicolumn{8}{c}{Size of peasant farms in hectares}							
		0–0.5	0.5–1	1–2	2–3	3–4	4–5	5–7	7+
1. Number of mothers	9	13	23	47	53	10	13	18	15
2. Average year of birth	1872	1875	1875	1876	1875	1875	1873	1875	1874
3. Average age at marriage (years)	31	25	25	25	24	23	23	22	20
4. Average period of actual fertility (years)	9	15	15	17	18	19	19	20	23
5. Average age of mother at birth of her last child	40	40	40	42	41	42	42	42	43
6. Average number of children born	3.9	5.8	5.3	6.1	6.6	6.4	7.5	7.8	8.1
7. Average number of children deceased	1.00	1.31	1.22	1.21	1.57	1.00	2.08	1.55	1.2
8. Average number of children surviving	2.9	4.1	4.1	4.9	5.0	5.4	5.5	6.3	8.0
9. Child mortality per 1,000	257	239	230	199	238	156	275	200	127
10. Average number of children born per year of potential fertility, from marriage to age 45	0.28	0.27	0.26	0.30	0.31	0.29	0.34	0.35	0.37
11. Average number of children born per year of actual fertility	0.43	0.36	0.34	0.35	0.37	0.33	0.40	0.39	0.40

SOURCE: Stys, 1957, p. 139; after Davis, 1963, p. 357.

variable (e.g., average income is itself a variable in the regression as well as a fundamental cause of change in other regression variables such as education). Hence, though regressions such as these can be very useful for informing us about the partial effects of other variables such as infant mortality and urban-rural residence, we should not look to them for information about the direct partial effect of income.

Another important difficulty with the cross-national and intra-national geographic regression studies is that while the regressions are linear, the key underlying relationship may well be curvilinear; it may well be that fertility rises and then falls as income rises in LDC's (for example, a study of 24 LDC's, Iyoha, 1973). If so, it may be inappropriate to lump together LDC's at the very lowest per-capita income levels with higher income countries.

Yasuba (1961) conducted a study of the United States in the nineteenth century—a period in which it qualifies as an LDC—both cross-sectionally and over time. He worked with the amount of easily accessible land, which certainly is related to income prospects in a rural society. In those states where there was more accessible land per family, the birth rate was higher. And as the amount of accessible land diminished over time, so did the birth rate. These results continue to appear after such factors as land quality, urbanization, and average income are allowed for (see also McInnis, 1972).

Population Trap Models

The short-run direct effect of income rises in LDC's has primary theoretical interest in the context of the so-called "low-level equilibrium trap." Leibenstein's trap model (1957, pp. 170–173) is a rigorous contemporary statement of Malthus' doctrine. The key idea is that under some LDC conditions, as income rises population will rise just as much in response. For example, in Leibenstein's model a 2% increase in total income immediately induces a 2% increase in population. This response would leave per-capita income unchanged, and hence block the growth of economic development. In Leibenstein's model the rise in population may be due to—in various unspecified proportions—a decrease in the death rate as well as an increase in the birth rate. In Nelson's trap model (1956), the entire effect is through the death rate.

But in the twentieth century, a very large part of the observed drop in death rates in LDC's seems to have occurred independently of rises in income. That is, much of the increase in population growth that is accounted for by a drop in the death rate is not caused by a rise in income (e.g., the expectation of life at birth is now in the sixties in Albania, Ceylon, Costa Rica, Cuba, Dominican Republic, El Salvador, Guyana, Hong

Kong, Jamaica, Korea, Malaysia, Mexico, Panama, Philippines, Portugal, Taiwan, Venezuela, and in some other countries where birth rates are still high and where per-capita income is far below the level of Europe or North America). Kuznets observes that, historically, "economically significant rises in per capita income were not followed invariably by significant and perceptible declines in birth rates ... death rates may remain stable for decades, while per capita income rises, or declines sharply while per capita income barely moves as they did recently in many underdeveloped countries" (1965, pp. 8–9).

After a reasonably short series of such decreases in mortality, a plateau must be reached at which further major reductions are unlikely. This means that if a rise in income is to cause a fully counterbalancing growth in population, it must be *fertility* that responds positively to the rise in income. If mortality does not take up any of the effect, then the elasticity of fertility with respect to income must be +33! For example, if the birth rate were 30 per 1,000, and if a 1% income increase were to come along and induce a 1% incremental increase in population, the birth rate would have to rise to about 40 per 1,000 to accomplish the offset. This would mean a 33% increase in the birth rate in response to the 1% population growth rate. Needless to say, there is no evidence of a short-run income elasticity anywhere near this high. Hence, the idea of a population "trap" is not relevant to LDC reality.

Evidence on the Long-Run Indirect Effect of Income on Fertility in LDC's

The cross-sectional data in Figure 16–2 show that there is a clear and strong long-run negative relationship between income and fertility across the range of LDC's and beyond. These data trace out what is called the *demographic transition*. The history of present-day MDC's also makes it clear that falls in mortality, falls in fertility and rises in income (which we call "economic development") go together, after the initial rise in fertility, as seen in Figure 16–3 for Sweden. And there is enough vital-statistics evidence in hand from countries that have more recently begun the economic-development process that a decline in fertility is already happening or may soon be expected in those countries. Statements about people's family-size desires jibe with the vital-statistics evidence. These fertility declines occur despite the high-fertility value systems with which LDC's enter into economic development. Such value systems apparently change in the face of the new needs and opportunities presented by economic development, though the change may be sufficiently slow so that the fertility response to economic development is slower than it otherwise would be.

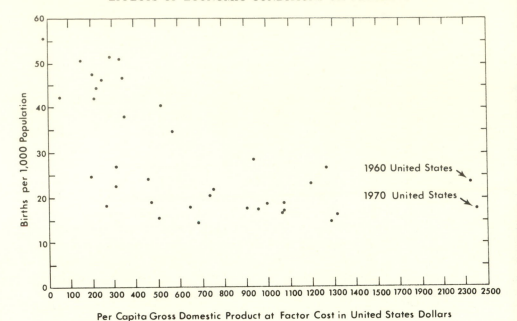

FIGURE 16–2   PER-CAPITA INCOME AND CRUDE BIRTH RATES, WORLD, 1960
SOURCE: Bogue, 1969, p. 85 and *Population Index*, various issues.

This long-run fall in fertility as economic development proceeds and as income rises, is the most important fact in the economics of fertility. This fact flies directly in the face of Malthus' assumptions (but not against his hopes!), and in the face of assumptions of many contemporary model-builders as well. And this fact, together with the finding about the long-run effects of population growth upon economic level in Chapters 7–12 and culminating in the model in Chapter 13, enables us to conclude that population growth does not counteract economic growth in the long-run, as Malthus supposed it does.

But just *how* does increased income reduce fertility as economic development takes place? In fact, is income really the causal force? The linkages between income rise and fertility decline are much less clear than is the observed over-all empirical relationship. Income rise and economic development imply such changes as increases in education, shifts from rural to city employment and living, increases in child health and life expectancy, and increased availability of contraceptive technology. Each of these phenomena is by itself related to lower fertility. But one cannot easily analyze this complex into separate parts for two reasons: (1) All of these correlates of rises in income are closely associated statistically, which makes it impossible to learn their separate effects by statistical analysis. (2) These forces are all interacting constituent parts of

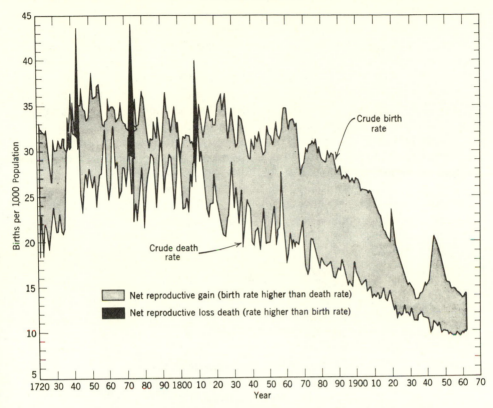

FIGURE 16–3   CRUDE BIRTH AND DEATH RATES, SWEDEN, 1720–1962
SOURCE: Bogue, 1969, p. 59.

economic development, all linked together and working hand in hand. Hence it is not even sensible to try to separate their effects.

The relationships between fertility and some of the intermediate variables are not directly economic or income-related (e.g., a drop in infant mortality probably reduces fertility because people's basic desires for children can then be met with fewer births). And an increase in contraceptive knowledge and availability increases people's abilities to achieve the family sizes they desire. But other of the variables clearly are income-related. An increase in education for women increases the foregone wages if they choose not to work in order to have more children. A move from farm to city reduces the earnings of children that adults can count upon,[1]

---

[1] Kasarda's cross-sectional study (1971) of a wide variety of countries showed that—as economic theory suggests—better market opportunities for children to work increase fertility, and better market opportunities for women to work reduce fertility. (Furthermore, he shows that these are intervening variables that explain the relationships of urbanization, industrialization and education to fertility.)

361

while raising the out-of-pocket costs for children. Some studies have demonstrated the negative effect on fertility of felt economic burden and the positive effect of felt economic benefits (e.g., an unusually careful study by Anker, 1973, pp. 172 and 193; see also Mueller, 1975 and Repetto, 1975). And by raising standards of education, the whole of the economic-development process raises the amounts many parents aspire to spend on their children's education. The best statement would seem to be that income is indeed a causal force in long-run fertility decline, but operating through a variety of other factors such as increased education, decreased mortality, improved health, and so forth. In my 1974 monograph I discuss these factors at length. But it comes down to saying that it is the entire nexus of forces which we call economic development—of which income increase is both an indicator and a driving force—that causes fertility to fall in the long run as economic development takes place (see Oechsli and Kirk, 1975).

Summary

To summarize the evidence on the partial direct short-run effect of a rise in average income in LDC's: The immediate effect of an income rise at the beginning of a secular rise in income in a traditional subsistence-agriculture setting is to increase fertility. This is the "classical" case in economic theory of the effect of income on fertility, tastes in the short run remaining unchanged while people find they can afford to raise more children. This effect may be expected in contemporary LDC's just as it was found secularly in Western Europe and confirmed by the cyclical harvest fluctuations in Scandinavia in the eighteenth century.

The cross-sectional evidence seems consistent with this proposition: Before the agricultural sector is much affected by modernization, the education and outlook of richer and poorer farmers may be much the same. Therefore, the relationship of family size and income or wealth (usually measured by size of farm) may be interpreted as showing the direct partial effect of income. Such cross-sections in both Europe and Asia mostly show that richer peasants have more children. There is, however, some evidence that such empirical relationships are at least partly due to the pressure of more children stimulating farmers to acquire more land for cultivation, but the relative importance of this latter factor is not known.

The short-run effect is not likely to be important of itself from a policy point of view in LDC's, unless there should be exogenously caused very large transfer payments of the sort to be discussed immediately as "incentive payments." The above discussion, then, should be viewed mostly as an exercise relevant to our general understanding of fertility behavior, and perhaps as an argument against worries about trap effects.

Malthus thought that when income rises for some reason, fertility rises in response sufficiently to wipe out the income gain. But the sum of the evidence suggests that the likely rise in fertility in direct response to a rise in income is at most a very tiny fraction of what would be required to offset a growth in income in LDC's. And the long-run effect of economic development and income rises in LDC's is to reduce high fertility to low MDC fertility levels. This long-run effect combines with the effects of population growth upon economic development described in Chapters 7–12 and then in the model in Chapter 13 to demonstrate that Malthus was wrong: Population does not rise in response to an increase in subsistence in such a manner as to prevent economic growth.

In short, the effect of additional income in LDC's may be thought of as (1) nonlinear, rising with the first income increase for the poorest countries, and falling with additional increases, and (2) rising in the short run but falling in the long run.

363

CHAPTER 17

Incentives and Income Redistribution
as Devices to Alter Fertility

INTRODUCTION

THE PRECEDING three chapters have described the unconditional relationship between income and fertility. This chapter takes up the *conditional* economics of fertility change; that is, the effectiveness of incentive payments in getting people to alter their fertility, to have either more or fewer children according to a country's desire, as well as the likely effectiveness of income distributions for altering fertility.

The chapter concludes that large money incentives might have an important effect, but the amounts would have to be considerably larger than any society has deemed reasonable until now. It also concludes that income redistribution undertaken for other purposes could reduce fertility in LDC's. General income redistribution is not likely to be a policy tool used to influence fertility, however. Redistribution of access to education might be effective though the effects would not appear for one or two decades.

The chapter begins with income redistribution, and then moves on to incentives.

THE EFFECTS OF INCOME REDISTRIBUTIONS ON LDC FERTILITY

Recently several writers (e.g., Kocher, 1973; Rich, 1973) have suggested that fertility is lower where the income distribution is more equal, *ceteris paribus*.[1] They imply that LDC countries ought to consider income redistribution *in order to* reduce fertility (in addition to whatever other effects it might have). Their discussions and most of this section focus on LDC's, though some aspects apply to MDC's, too.

Before considering whether income distribution of some sort is a feasible policy tool for influencing fertility, let us consider the theory and the facts of the relationship of income distribution to fertility.

The Theory

The theory is simple. There are two ways in which income distribution might affect fertility.

---

[1] Jim B. Marshall of the State Department also had the idea to study the effect of income distribution on fertility, and he commissioned me to do a feasibility study of the subject. Much of this section is drawn from the report of that study.

364

There may be a relative income effect. That is, a family's fertility may be a function of the neighbors' income as well as the family's own. D. Freedman (1963) presented some evidence for the operation of such a relative effect in a MDC context. But no data exist for LDC's, where the matter of income distribution is more relevant for fertility. It should be noted that if there is a relative income effect it is likely to be related to the income distribution *within occupations or areas* rather than to the income distribution of the nation as a whole; in fact, Freedman's data refer to the distribution within occupations.

Income redistribution also changes the *absolute* incomes of the affected people. Therefore, an income redistribution may influence fertility through the absolute relationship of income to fertility. It seems to me that this absolute effect is likely to be more important than a relative income effect.

Evidence About the Relationship of Income Distribution to Fertility

As to the facts, Kocher and Rich offered anecdotal comparisons apparently showing that narrower income distributions are associated with lower fertility.

> [T]he per capita income in Taiwan was approximately $246, or similar to that of the Philippines, which was $235. There was, however, a considerable discrepancy between the distributions of income in the two countries. The highest 10 per cent of the population in the Philippines was significantly wealthier than the same group in Taiwan, but the lowest 20 per cent was more than twice as well off in Taiwan. Moreover, there also is evidence that in Taiwan, income distribution has improved markedly over time, whereas in the Philippines it has become more and more concentrated among the wealthiest 20 per cent of the population. These two factors help to explain why a much greater share of the population appears to have reached the socio-economic level conducive to reduced fertility in Taiwan than in the Philippines. Comparisons similar to that between Taiwan and the Philippines can also be made between Barbados, Argentina, South Korea, Singapore, Uruguay, Cuba, Costa Rica, or China on the one hand, and Venezuela, Mexico, Brazil, and many of the other Latin American countries on the other. (Rich, 1973, p. 24.)

Rich also calculates that the correlation between LDC birth rates and the per-capita incomes of the poorest 60% of populations is stronger ($R^2 = .64$) than between the birth rate and the over-all per-capita income ($R^2 = -.46$).

But what we would like to know is just *how different* the birth rate would be in a country if its income distribution were different. To that

365

end, the following statistical procedure was used on the same data Rich used.[2]

1. Plot each country on a graph showing the mean income of the lowest-income 60% of the population as a function of the mean income of the country as a whole, as shown in Figure 17–1. The mean income of the lowest-income 60% relative to the over-all mean income is used here as a proxy for income distribution. At each level of over-all mean income on the horizontal axis, the country that is highest on the vertical axis in Figure 17–1 has the narrowest income distribution.

2. Draw a "curve" through the highest observations on Figure 17–1. This envelope connects the countries with the narrowest income distributions. The strategy is to determine the fertility of the countries on this envelope, and then to ask what the fertility of other countries would be *if* their income distributions were the same as the countries on the envelope at the same level of overall mean income.

3. Plot only the countries on the envelope curve in Figure 17–1 on Figure 17–2 that shows the crude birth rate as a function of the mean income of the country.

4. Draw an eyeball-least-squares line through the observations in Figure 17–2. This estimates fertility as a function of per-capita income for the countries with the narrowest income distributions.

5. On a replica of Figure 17–2 plot *all* the countries now, as seen in Figure 17–3. We can now compare the fertility of countries not on the income-distribution envelope to the fertility of countries on the envelope. The plot shows that countries that are not on the envelope generally have higher fertility than is indicated by the envelope curve. The vertical distance between the countries not on the envelope curve, and the envelope curve itself, estimates how much lower their fertility would be if their income distribution were as indicated by the envelope curve.

Figure 17–3 clearly indicates that a narrower income distribution is associated with lower fertility, and the fertility effect is not trivial in magnitude.

Another approach to this matter is that of Repetto (1974) whose work is more sophisticated and proceeds with a better and fuller data set than Rich. Repetto regressed the gross reproduction ratio, and separately, a measure similar to the general fertility rate, on income per capita, newspapers per capita, and the income distribution as measured by the Gini coefficient. The elasticities of fertility with respect to income distribution are 0.39 and 0.47 for the two fertility measures, respectively. To the extent that the relationship is causal, these estimates suggest that a 10% change in the income distribution measure is associated with a 3.9% change and

---

[2] I am grateful to William Rich for making these data available to me.

366

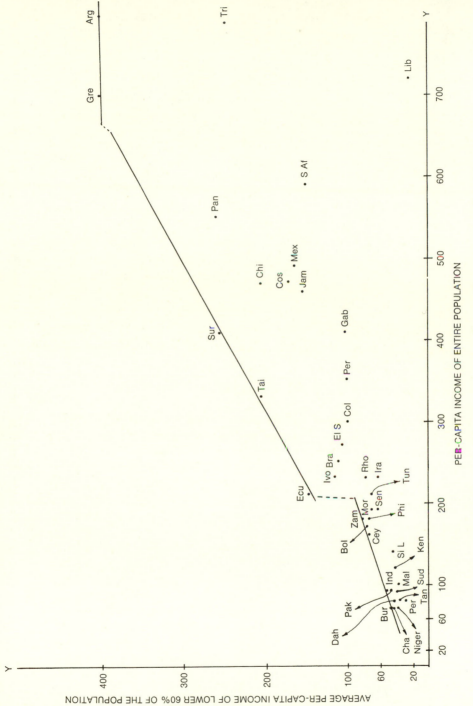

FIGURE 17–1 THE RELATIONSHIP OF INCOME DISTRIBUTION TO INCOME

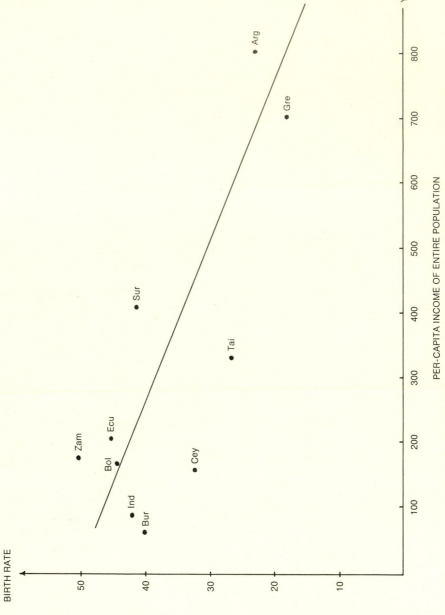

FIGURE 17–2 BIRTH RATE BY AVERAGE INCOME, COUNTRIES WITH NARROW INCOME DISTRIBUTION

BIRTH RATE

PER-CAPITA INCOME OF ENTIRE POPULATION

FIGURE 17-3 BIRTH RATE BY AVERAGE INCOME, SHOWING EFFECT OF INCOME DISTRIBUTION

a 4.7% change in fertility, respectively. It is important and impressive that the elasticities appear to be even higher than those just cited when Repetto takes account of the effects of fertility on income distribution as well as on the converse, with a simultaneous equation estimation method. This reinforces our belief that the estimated effect of income distribution upon fertility is indeed causal. On the other hand, the absolute effect of a 10% change in income distribution (a large change) is not great in terms of a country's fertility—a reduction of only 0.21 in the gross reproduction ratio.

So the data suggest that an aggregate income redistribution might reduce LDC fertility. But, nevertheless, it does not make sense to think of a country undertaking an aggregate redistribution *for the purpose of* reducing fertility, for at least two reasons: First, redistribution may be undertaken for social justice, diminution of economic power blocs, increased agricultural productivity, general economic and social invigoration, increased savings, or other. But it is not likely that a country will redistribute in order to reduce fertility.

Second and more important, "income redistribution" does not describe a concrete policy that a government might undertake. Rather, a government may seek to alter the distribution of income with land reform, educational redistribution, alteration in the terms of trade, or other of the sorts of policies to be discussed shortly. And different policies that might alter the over-all distribution in the same direction may well have quite different effects upon fertility in the short and/or long run. For example, a land redistribution scheme might have very different fertility effects than an increase in the progression of the money income tax. Therefore, it is necessary to inquire about the effect on fertility of each of the concrete possible specific redistributions that an LDC might undertake, rather than discussing income redistribution in the aggregate.

Not only are these specific redistribution policies sharper and more meaningful than aggregate income redistribution from a scientific point of view, but also they are capable of enough variation in a reasonably short length of time to exert a meaningful effect on fertility. That is, a land redistribution may really alter the distribution of land ownership in 10 years. But the income distribution for a country as a whole is likely to be much more glacial; one important reason is that the distribution of education and skills cannot rapidly be altered, and the distribution of income is heavily influenced by their distribution.

Still another reason for specificity in discussing income distribution is that policy-makers actually discuss policies for income redistribution at this more specific level rather than in general.

Here are some of the considerations that must be applied to each sort of income redistribution policy under discussion:

370

1. Each ex ante income class must have its fertility response estimated separately. The *sizes* of the income classes must be assessed. And then the *aggregate* fertility effect of the policy may be estimated.

2. The short-run fertility effects of income change, before education and tastes have a chance to change, must be evaluated apart from the longer-run effects which are caused by the changes in those background factors.

3. The purely economic effects of income redistribution through the family budget, both directly on fertility and indirectly through such intermediate variables as education, must be considered separately from such noneconomic variables as a sense of national elan or increases in social mobility that may accompany a redistributive policy. Such distinctions need not be made if the study is empirical at an aggregate level; one then does not care *which* intermediate variables are responsible for the internal changes. But if the information is to be obtained from more analytic techniques, at a lower level of aggregation, then such problems must indeed be considered.

Fertility Effects of Some Redistribution Policies

Let us now consider some specific income-redistribution mechanisms that a country might undertake partly with an eye to affecting fertility.

LAND REFORM

In a land-reform redistribution, the smaller land-holders, and perhaps the landless, have their holdings (and hence their wealth and income) increased, while the larger owners lose land and wealth. Some possible examples may be found in the history of nineteenth-century Europe, in twentieth-century India, Mexico, Colombia, the White Revolution in Iran in 1963, and the Agrarian Reform in Egypt in 1952. In principle, examinations of fertility before and after these reforms would tell about their effects upon fertility.

There is probably no feasible way at present to empirically relate historical land reforms to fertility. We may, however, try to estimate the effect of such a land reform by analysis. We can probably ignore the effects on the people who *lose* land. Those who lose land are relatively few and rich. For example, in Egypt, where only about 10% of the land was expropriated in 1952, more than 1/3 belonged to "the King and other members of the royal family" (Warriner, 1957, p. 34). Land-owners could retain up to 300 acres (giving 50 acres to each of 2 children), which is still an enormous farm in a country where 72% of the land owners had 1 acre or less, 22% had 1–5 acres, and 0.1% (2,100 owners) had 200 acres or more (*ibid.*, p. 24). Furthermore, the expropriated owners received bonds in compensation for land they had taken away from them. To the extent that the Egyptian reform is typical—and it probably is, in this respect—there will be no significant aggregate fertility effect on those who *lose* in the redistribution.

The gainers from the redistribution are likely to include both the landless families and the smallest land-holders. Let us assume that the rural sector will continue in much the same way as in the past, with a slow rate of change in modernization occurring—which would seem to be a good assumption in the case of India (though probably not for China). On that assumption, the effect of income redistribution would simply be a shift in the *numbers* of families in the different farm-size and fertility categories. But the people *within* each category would be the same sorts of people observed in contemporary surveys. And the gist of these surveys is that families with larger holdings have more children (see Chapter 16).

These facts suggest the conclusion that the initial impact of a land redistribution policy in a poor LDC is likely to cause an *increase* in fertility in the short run, because many more peasants will have their land-holdings increased than will have them decreased.[3]

The longer run is another story, of course. To the extent that the increase in income causes increases in education, mobility, urbanization, and the process of modernization generally, the long-run effect of the land reform's increase in income to the small land-holders will be to *reduce* their fertility (see Chapter 16). But for this to happen the land reform must really lead into economic development. Hence, the land reform is far from a sure-fire quick-acting policy tool for reducing fertility.

REDISTRIBUTION OF ACCESS TO EDUCATION

This sort of redistribution has apparently happened in many parts of Asia and Africa in the last two decades. Direct evidence on the effects of redistributions of educational access are not available, however, so we must make inferences based on existing educational differentials.

Increased parental education in LDC's reduces parents' fertility. This is clear from both the cross-national and intra-country cross-sections. In fact, the relationship between education and fertility is stronger and

---

[3] Of course this inference assumes that there is no *relative* wealth effect involved (i.e., it assumes that the operative factor is not whether a man is *relatively* well-off, but rather what his *absolute* wealth is). If such a relative wealth effect *is* in fact the main determinant of fertility differentials by income, then the land redistribution would not be expected to change aggregate fertility. But the observed fact that the first surge of increased income tends to raise fertility in the aggregate in LDC's makes me doubt that relative income is such a strong factor here, and hence I would expect an increase in fertility to follow immediately upon land reform.

more consistent over the observed ranges than is the relationship of fertility to any other single variable[4] (J. Simon, 1974, Chapter 4).

Even more relevant for redistribution, however, is that an increase of an added year of education has more of a (negative) effect on fertility at low educational levels than at higher education levels (e.g., Ben-Porath, 1973). This implies that a transfer in the direction of education equality will reduce *aggregate* fertility, and the magnitude of the effect is likely to be large.[5]

REDISTRIBUTION OF MEDICAL CARE

In LDC's—and MDC's, too—medical services are concentrated in urban areas and are disproportionately available to people who are better-off economically. A government might choose to redistribute access to health care. (China has done so.) One immediate result would be to reduce infant mortality, to raise life expectancy at all ages, and increase total population, because the returns to health care surely are a decreasing function of the amount of health care, and hence more equal distribution raises total health output. The impacts on fertility would seem to be downward, judging from the results of Knodel (1968), Schultz (1968; 1970), Schultz and DaVanzo (1973), and Ben-Porath (1974).

REDISTRIBUTION OF JOB OPPORTUNITIES

A government might attempt to increase job opportunities to the poorest people at the expense of those better off, as India has done in favor of the untouchables. But the number of jobs that a government might re-

---

[4] The *nature* of the causal connection from education to fertility is more complex. The woman's opportunity-cost effect is clear, but there is no apparently strong direct reason other than contraceptive education why an increase in *father's* education should decrease family fertility. It may be that the effect of education on the parents' fertility is through their children. If educational facilities are available parents may choose to invest their purchasing power (and loss of children's labor) in more education for fewer children. This may be a good economic choice for the parents, as Caldwell (1965) found in Ghana. And for Colombia and Taiwan, T. P. Schultz found that "the enrollment rate is powerfully inversely associated with fertility" (1969b, p. 23).

[5] It should be noted that some countries have decided on the wisdom of a policy of purposefully *non*equalized access to education, for example, Tanzania: "Instead of expanding the number of standard I classes (first grade), the government decided to increase rapidly the number of classes at standards V–VII (grades 5–7) so that every child entering primary school could receive a full seven years of education. In supporting this position, Nyere argued as follows: "We have made this decision because we believe it is better that money should be spent on providing one child with a 7-year education which may help him or her to become a useful member of society, rather than divide the same amount of money and staff between two children, neither of whom is likely to get any permanent benefit'" (Harbison, 1973, pp. 58 and 59, quoting United Republic of Tanzania, *Second Five-Year Plan for Economic and Social Development* [Dar es Salaam, Government Printing office, 1969], Vol. I, p. xii).

distribute in an LDC is unlikely to be large enough to have much effect on aggregate fertility.

A traditional method of changing the income distribution in the MDC's is by taxing a higher proportion of the incomes of the rich than of the poor. But the dispersion of family sizes in MDC's is now too small for any likely income redistribution to have any observable effect on aggregate fertility.

With respect to LDC's, based on the sort of evidence adduced on land reform I would deduce a mild increase in fertility at the very outset, but as the added income leads into the cumulative process of modernization (assuming it does), fertility would be expected to be lower than prior to the income redistribution. Myrdal notes that taxation redistributions have not been successfully executed or even attempted with vigor. This may well be because most poor LDC's do not possess the pre-conditions for effective progressive income taxation (1968, 2098–103). Much of the product is not monetized. The institutions cannot enforce tax collection and prevent corruption. And the social will is not consistent with sharp taxation of incomes.

There would seem to be no practical way to empirically assess the effects of such a taxation redistribution on fertility in LDC's at present.

Such a policy seems to have been undertaken by the Soviet Union in the 1920's, though whether the terms of trade were really influenced is open to some doubt. The effect of this sort of redistribution toward (or away from) agriculture is to reduce (increase) the real incomes of farmers, assuming that the government's share does not change. An equal change would seem to have less effect on a city-dweller, however, than on a farm family, because the urban family is already exposed to much of the force of modernization, and his fertility is already lower than in the farm family (Kuznets, 1974; but see W. Robinson, 1963). Hence one might expect, if the redistribution affects equal numbers of people with equal incomes in the two sectors, that the farm sector would show more fertility change than the city sector, i.e., the rise in farm income in the short run would result in a bigger rise in fertility than the fertility drop in the city. But in the longer run one would expect a bigger *drop* in fertility in the farm sector than the rise, if any that would occur in the urban sector following on a redistribution of consumption.

The government may influence the distribution of incomes with its public-investment budget. For example, the government may decide to invest in infrastructure or industry in the West rather than the East of a country; this raises incomes in the West relative to those in the East, and if the former were initially lower, the income distribution is therefore equalized; the government may tilt the budget toward (or away from) labor-intensive industries and practices, or investments may be oriented toward (or away from) industries and occupations which would employ more women; and so forth.

Each of these redistributions of public investment will have main effects similar to redistributions discussed earlier in this section.

Whose Fertility Will Be Altered?

So far the discussion has not distinguished among additional children. But any policy that affects fertility must consider *which kind of* babies will be born in larger or smaller quantities. From the economic planning point of view (though not so easily from an ethical point of view) it matters whether an Edison or Einstein or Ghandi will get born, or whether the additional child will be a person who never leaves his village. This matter might be considered when income-redistribution policies are considered, though the issue is one of values.

SUMMARY

The aggregate evidence suggests that income redistribution might have a very substantial effect upon fertility. But the fertility-reducing effect would come through indirect effects of additional income such as education and urbanization. And such indirect effects must lag at least a decade behind the income redistribution.

Redistribution toward equalization of access to education is likely to be the most effective and most attractive fertility-reducing sort of redistribution. (In addition, it is likely to be relatively effective in equalizing the income distribution.) Land reform may increase aggregate fertility in the short run.

CONDITIONAL INCOME TRANSFERS—INCENTIVE BONUSES AND TAXES[6]

Introduction

This section deals with money and other payments that are made *if* a couple has a particular number of children. That is, the incentives that are the subject of this section are made *conditional upon* having or not

---

[6] Pohlman (1971) is a useful review of this subject and its background. See especially Chapter 6 on some Indian evidence. Gillespie (n.d.) is also valuable. Rogers (1972) reviews past and future field research on incentives.

For more theoretical discussion, see Chapter 20, and Enke (1960a, 1960b; 1961a; 1961b; 1962; 1963; Chapter 20, 1966); Demeny (1965); J. Simon (1968).

having children of given parities. These transfers are income redistributions, but they have a quite different behavioral meaning than do unconditional income redistributions in which the transfers take place independent of the number of children the couple has. It is quite clear that a payment to a family if they do not have a third child, say, is more likely to have a strong anti-natalist effect than is the same size transfer that does not depend on having or not having the third child.

The situations in MDC's and LDC's with respect to natality-incentive payments are sufficiently different so that it is reasonable to discuss them separately.

Incentives can be given in cash or kind, and either to raise or to lower fertility. Different modes of giving can have different sorts of effects. Whether incentives are economically beneficial and socially desirable in a given situation depends upon both the *effects* of the fertility change, and the philosophical *values* which one brings to bear in judging the worth of additional human lives. One special question about incentives, however, is which criterion to use in judging how high a level of incentive may be ethically acceptable in cases where the average income might be benefited by even *very* high incentives. Enke (1960a and 1960b) has proposed the interesting criterion that the limit to incentive payments should be that level at which even the family which *does not* reduce its fertility, and hence does not receive incentive payments but only pays taxes to finance them, should benefit enough by the *indirect* benefits of the incentive plan, so that, on the balance of the indirect positive effects and the direct costs of the transfer payment from it to families that do reduce fertility, this family should be *no worse off* than without an incentive plan—while other families would be better off, of course. This matter arises especially in the context of an *anti*-natalist incentive plan.

Another ethical matter special to incentives turns upon *whom* an incentive plan's impact falls. This problem arises especially in the context of a *pro*-natalist incentive plan. Do parents—who themselves receive the payments—benefit at the expense of the children, thereby inducing more children than will be brought up well? This problem can be affected by the *form* of the payments (i.e., payments in kind for child use rather than money payments). If milk and children's shoes are given to parents, the children may be expected to receive all the benefits of the payments, whereas money payments may go partly into beer for the parents as well as into milk for the children.

Chapters 15 and 16 show that a short-run increase in money income induces an increase in fertility in MDC's and in LDC's, too. Therefore, fertility incentives *must* have *some* effect on fertility. *Some* family must be at the margin of indifference about having more or fewer children than they have. The sole question, then, is *how much* of an effect an incentive

376

program will have. The effect of the incentive will depend upon its average size, and upon its size relative to income for particular income classes.

Fertility Incentive Payments in MDC's

In the past, MDC's have employed incentives to *raise* fertility. The likely pro-natality mechanisms are bonuses for children, or child payments, or income tax deductions for children. Incentives might, however, also be used to reduce fertility in MDC's. The most likely anti-natality mechanisms would be child taxes or the requirement to pay for the education of children after the second, third, or whatever.

The only sound basis for a response estimate would be studies of actual programs. But useful data are practically nonexistent. Kirk (1942/1956) found that the effect of the Nazi experiment is blurred: ". . . a major part of the Nazi successes on the demographic front must have been the result of re-employment, as opposed to the more spectacular appeals of race and 'folk' on the one hand, and specific inducement to child-bearing on the other." And Petersen said of the Dutch experience: "Whether the cumulative effect of these [pro-natality] measures is to keep Dutch fertility high cannot be shown one way or another—first because the determinants of fertility are very imperfectly understood; secondly because in any case it would probably be impossible to isolate the effect of these measures. Actually, however, no one doubts their effect . . ." (1955/1956). Glass reviewed the pre-World War II experience in France and Belgium. He found that the data would not suffice to support a conclusion (1940, p. 181), partly because governments "persistently tried to buy babies at bargain prices" (p. 371). Schorr (1965/1970) recently reviewed the results of income allowances in Canada and France after World War II. In Canada the changes caused by other factors are so great as to swamp any possible effect of the allowance payments' that began in 1945; this may be seen in Figure 17–4, which shows similar major movements in the U.S. and Canadian birth rates. And for France, Schorr also finds that one cannot reach any solid conclusion about the effect of the 1945 increase in family allowances.

In sum, family-allowance and birth-incentive programs undertaken earlier by various countries provide no solid ground for quantitative estimates of the possible effect of incentive programs.

Eastern European countries have recently undertaken programs of very substantial child payments, according to Berent (1970); they have been increasing up to the time of writing (McIntyre, 1974). In Bulgaria, for example, as of 1973 for the third child alone the family receives three months wages. Soon it should be possible to analyze the effects of such payments. In passing, it is interesting to notice that though these payments

377

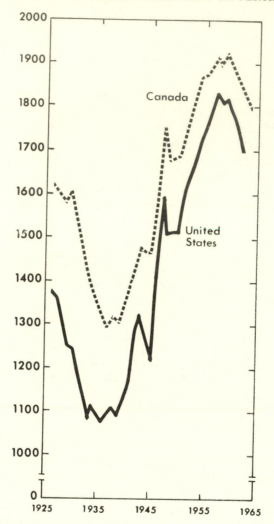

FIGURE 17–4   GROSS REPRODUCTION RATES,
UNITED STATES AND CANADA, 1925–61
SOURCE: Schorr, 1965, p. 443.

are called "family allowances," the relatively high payments for second and third children in Bulgaria and Hungary rather than higher-parity children indicate a social policy designed to elicit more children of lower rather than higher birth orders.

For the United States, R. Simon and I (1974) have studied the effects of incentives with a survey using hypothetical questions. The basic question was as follows (with appropriate changes for (1) families that were planning to have more children, (2) for "projective" questions about other people's behavior, and (3) for incentives to have children rather than not have them):

Now let's talk about your family. You said you do not plan to have any more children. If the government were to give you a payment of $50 a month for each child beyond the second until the child is 18 years old—that is, $600 per year for each child after the second until the child is 18 years old—do you think that you would have a bigger family than you now have? To make this a little clearer, under this scheme if you had three children the government would pay you $50 each month, if you had four children the government would pay you $100 each month, and so on. If the government had such a plan, do you think you would have more than you do?

The results shown in Table 17–1 and Figures 17–5a–d suggest that money incentives could have a significant effect in inducing people to have more or fewer children, especially people with low incomes. Money incentives would seem to be more effective for *reducing* family size than for *increasing* the number of children a family would have. And people are more likely to say that their neighbors will respond to money incentives than that they themselves will respond. That is, the projective questions indicate a greater responsiveness to incentive payments, especially in the upward direction, than do the direct questions. One may only guess whether the "truth" is closer to the results of the direct or to the projective question.

To summarize what we know about the likely effects of incentive payments to raise births in MDC's: We have little solid knowledge. The experiences of MDC's that have tried to raise fertility by child-allowance programs provide almost no guidance about the efficiency of such programs; the payments have been sufficiently small relative to other income changes so that, in the absence of a controlled-experimental design, the possible effects cannot be detected. A questionnaire shows that people in the United States *say* that they and their neighbors would have different-size families, larger or smaller, in response to relatively large financial incentives to do so. But hard evidence will continue to be lacking until some country conducts a controlled experiment (which would raise difficult ethical questions about the propriety of conducting such research). It is reasonable to guess, however, that in MDC's incentives would have to be very substantial in size relative to income for there to be even a chance that they would have a significant effect.

FERTILITY INCENTIVE PAYMENTS IN LDC'S

The short-run effect of incentive payments to reduce fertility in LDC's is of considerable interest at present because of the possible role of this device in LDC population programs. Earlier it was noted that little is

TABLE 17–1

PERCENTAGES OF RESPONDENTS WHO SAY THEY WOULD HAVE MORE OR FEWER CHILDREN: DIRECT AND PROJECTIVE QUESTIONS

Amount of payment per month per child	Direct form of question				Projective form of question			
	Nat'l	Nat'l	Illinois	Nat'l	Nat'l	Nat'l	Illinois	Nat'l
				% say they would have more children				
$25	$7_{(10)}$	—	—	—	$26_{(36)}$	—	—	—
$50	$9_{(13)}$	$14_{(18)}$	$5_{(10)}$	—	$34_{(47)}$	$27_{(36)}$	$15_{(33)}$	—
$75	—	—	—	$12_{(17)}$	—	—	—	$32_{(43)}$
$100	$15_{(21)}$	$18_{(24)}$	$7_{(15)}$	—	$53_{(74)}$	$47_{(61)}$	$28_{(60)}$	—
$150	—	—	—	$19_{(26)}$	—	—	—	$51_{(69)}$
$200	—	$22_{(29)}$	$10_{(22)}$	—	—	$57_{(76)}$	$39_{(84)}$	—
$300	—	—	—	$26_{(36)}$	—	—	—	$62_{(83)}$
				% say they would have fewer children*				
$25	$33_{(39)}$	—	—	—	$46_{(54)}$	—	—	—
$50	$43_{(51)}$	$38_{(39)}$	$35_{(49)}$	—	$60_{(70)}$	$45_{(53)}$	$68_{(119)}$	—
$75	—	—	—	$33_{(43)}$	—	—	—	$50_{(57)}$
$100	$53_{(61)}$	$42_{(55)}$	$41_{(59)}$	—	$69_{(81)}$	$66_{(78)}$	$76_{(133)}$	—
$150	—	—	—	$50_{(57)}$	—	—	—	$63_{(72)}$
$200	—	$45_{(59)}$	$44_{(61)}$	—	—	$73_{(86)}$	$79_{(139)}$	—
$300	—	—	—	$53_{(61)}$	—	—	—	$68_{(77)}$

NOTE: The upper number in a cell indicates the proportion of people in the subsample who say they would change their fertility behavior in response to that particular money incentive (or a smaller one). The lower number in parentheses gives the absolute number of people giving that positive answer.

The four subsamples in the table includes the single Illinois subsample and the three groups within the national sample that were given different incentive schedules.

* Responses are based on families that have 3 or more children.

SOURCE: R. Simon and J. Simon, 1974–75.

known about the likely effects of pro-natal incentives in MDC's. Our uncertainty about the effect of anti-natal incentives in LDC's is equally great or greater, because even less evidence is available. Some LDC's have initiated programs to use what they call "incentives" to promote programs of sterilization and contraceptive usage. In most cases, however, the emphasis has been on paying "promoters" and medical personnel to recruit acceptors, rather than incentives to contraceptive acceptors themselves (Gillespie, n.d.).

Anecdotal evidence suggests that small pay-offs to acceptors such as time off from work can boost the sterilization rate in India (Repetto,

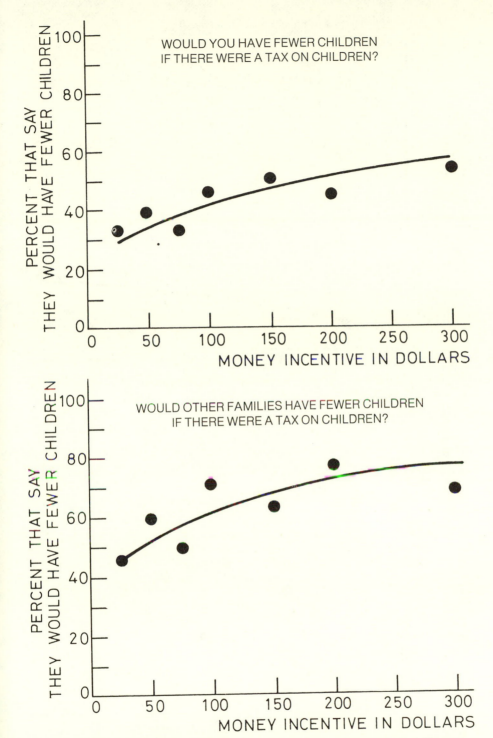

FIGURE 17–5   PROPORTIONS OF PEOPLE WHO WOULD HAVE MORE OR FEWER CHILDREN
IN RESPONSE TO MONEY INCENTIVES IN THE UNITED STATES

SOURCE: Table 17–1.

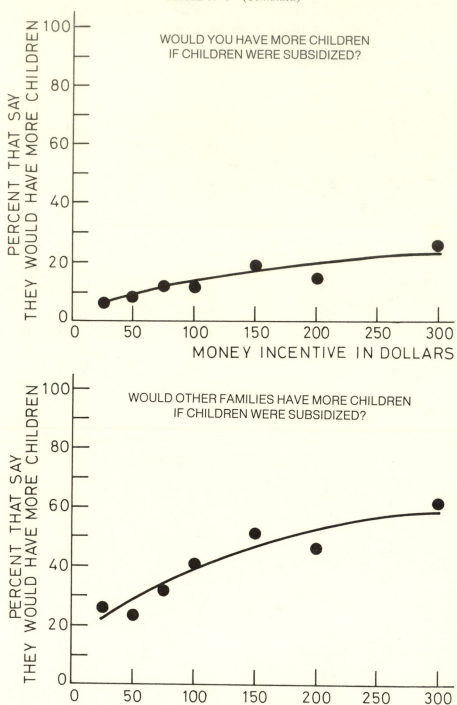

FIGURE 17–5 *(Continued)*

1968, p. 9). (But of course a high level of official and public interest in family planning could account for *both* the activity in incentive programs *and* high rates of sterilization in a given state.) More impressive evidence comes from several vasectomy campaigns in Ernakulam District in India in 1970 and 1971 (Rogers, 1972), and in 1971–72 (*Population Chronicle*, July 1972). Payments of 86 and 114 rupees ($11.45 and $15.20) to acceptors, and of 10 rupees ($1.33) to promoters, produced large jumps in the numbers of vasectomies performed as compared to previous periods when incentives to acceptors were 21 rupees ($2.80) and 2 rupees ($.27) to promoters, as seen in Figure 17–6. There is no doubt that the increased incentives were the major cause, over and above the special promotion and atmosphere.

Starting in September 1967 a total of 3,988 workers in four Tata factories in India were offered incentives of 210–220 rupees (about $27). A total of 3,872 workers in 5 other nearby factories were offered small incentives of 10–20 rupees ($1.25–$2.50) (3 factories) and 35–65 rupees ($4.37–$6.85) (2 factories). For the lowest-paid Tata workers, the incentive of 210–220 rupees represented well more than a month's pay. Figure 17–7 would seem to indicate that the incentives had a sizable effect. But by the end of the observation period the *relative* effect is much smaller

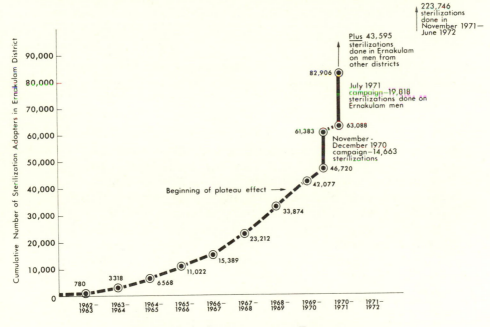

FIGURE 17–6   STERILIZATIONS IN ERNAKULAM
SOURCE: Adapted from Rogers, 1972, and *Population Chronicle*, July 1972.

383

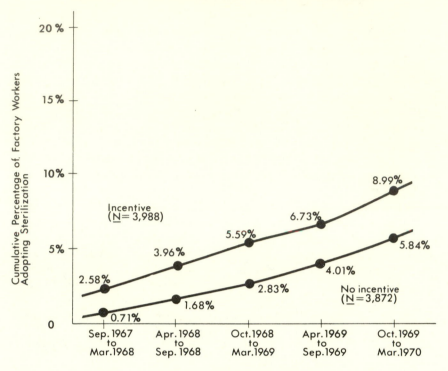

FIGURE 17–7   INCENTIVES AND STERILIZATIONS IN ERNAKULAM

SOURCE: Rogers, 1971; originally from Research and Marketing Services (1970), *A Study on the Evaluation of the Effectiveness of the Tata Incentive Programme for Sterilization*, unpublished report, Bombay, 1970, p. 27.

than at the beginning. The difference between the high-incentive and low-incentive programs is only a little over 3% of all workers by the end of the observation period, and it is not increasing rapidly. This suggests that this incentive only induced a total of about 3% of all men to be sterilized, not very large in relationship to any population policy, though this figure has to be translated into nonbirths to be meaningful.[7]

It should be noted that the incentives offered for sterilization in the Tata study were not large relative to those being discussed in the theoretical and policy literature; the latter might amount to a sum as large as the "high" incentive in the experiment being given to the family *every year*

[7] Ronald Ridker has kindly provided the information that the results from the three areas differed greatly, and the data described in Figures 17–7 and 17–8 combine data from the three areas. In one area the incentives had a strong positive effect, in another it was insignificant, and in the third apparently negative. These results were not investigated by the original research organization, and it has not been possible for others to get access to the raw data. These results, together with other facts, suggest lack of care in the analyses which might vitiate it altogether.

rather than just once. It should also be noted that I have no detailed information about this study; the observed effect might be considerably smaller *or* bigger than the "actual" effect.

As one would expect, the 210–20 rupee incentive had its strongest effect upon the poorer workers. Figure 17–8 shows that 10.6% of the poorest workers accepted sterilization in the high-incentive program, as compared to 3.3% in the lowest income class, the difference representing 7.3% of the total workers in the poorest group. This proportion of the workers in the lowest income group—which also have the most children on the average—might be important for population policy purposes.

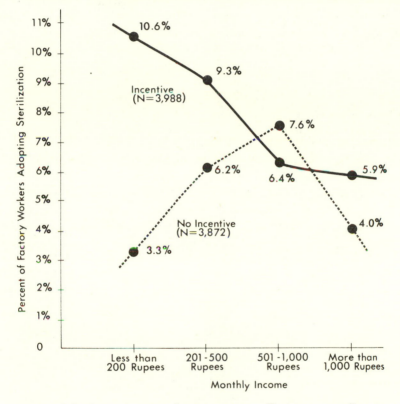

FIGURE 17–8   INCENTIVES AND STERILIZATIONS IN ERNAKULAM BY INCOME

SOURCE: Rogers, 1971; originally from Research and Marketing Services (1970), *A Study on the Evaluation of the Effectiveness of the Tata Incentive Programme for Sterilization*, unpublished report, Bombay, 1970, pp. 30–31.

In brief, in India small incentives to couples (10–30 rupees, about $1.33–$4.00) have some effect. Incentives of $10–$27 have had sizable effects. The over-all magnitude of the response to incentives this size probably is not large enough to have a substantial effect on India's birth rate, but the appropriate reckonings are still to be done. Payments of this size are far smaller than are many judgments of the size of the *benefits* of averting the births. Whether *really* large incentives—of the order of, say, $25 for *each year* that fertile couples do not produce a child—would have a major effect is still quite unknown. A conclusive answer about the effects of incentives in LDC's will not be available until a well-controlled experiment[8] with varying levels of incentives is actually carried out and completed.

In Taiwan, a certificate for children's education that "can total U.S. $385 after fourteen years for couples with two or fewer children or U.S. $192 for couples with three children" was offered in a rural township starting in 1971. As of a year after the beginning of the program, administrators had the impression that the offer had affected fertility, but lack of scientific controls makes quantitative evaluation impossible (Wang and Chen, 1973).

Nonmonetary Incentives

Governmental policy with respect to housing may be an important in-kind influence upon fertility. The price of living space surely has an important effect upon a family's decision to have more or fewer children, especially for apartment dwellers. By making living space more or less expensive relative to other goods, therefore, the government can push fertility down or up. Such a policy may be implemented administratively by taxes (or subsidies) on land and on the components of building construction, or by influencing the rate at which money is loaned for home purchases, or by changes in the price of government-owned housing where this is an important factor. Where government housing is important, the government may influence fertility by making the family's apartment size contingent on its family size.

Some evidence on the importance of the influence of housing upon fertility comes from experience in a Columbian housing project (Felson and Solaun, 1967). Families who received apartments subsequently had lower fertility than families that received houses which could be enlarged by the families, though the houses were originally no larger than the apartments. Additional evidence comes from Israel, where in a survey almost half the parents said that they might have had more children if their apartment had been larger (Peled, 1969).

Unintended Incentives

The discussion so far has referred to policies that are explicitly related to the number of children. But in all countries there are various social

---

[8] An experiment on the Indian tea estates may yield better data. Favorable results have been reported (Chacko, 1975), but the decline in observed fertility may be largely or completely due to the public-health and mortality-decline components of the overall program.

and economic policies that are related to family size and that may act as incentives to have more or fewer children, though they are not so intended and labeled. An example is the provision in the income-tax law of the U.S. that allows a $750 deduction for each dependent. This works in a pro-natalist direction, though it is not likely to be very important for many Americans. (If a family is poor, the tax deduction does not reduce their taxes much because they pay at a low rate; if they are rich, the total saving is small relative to their total income.)

More important is the cost of public schooling, much of which is free in the sense that the parents pay the same amount of taxes no matter how many children they have. If parents had to pay the full cost of public schooling for their children, the sum might be great enough to influence fertility downward to a significant degree. Numerous surveys in poor and rich countries have shown that the cost of education is an important consideration to parents when deciding how many children to have. Laws that provide additional public education or otherwise subsidize education can have a pronatal effect. This poses a real dilemma for countries that wish to reduce population growth: Education is crucial for economic development, but increasing the availability of education by lowering its price to families may increase fertility. I have heard informally that some countries have tried to get around this by subsidizing education only for children up to three or four. But such a policy raises additional ethical problems. In any case there seems to be no evidence on the *strength* of the effect of education subsidies in any country.

On the other hand, legislation that requires children to attend school can have the same effect as (and often goes together with) child labor laws. Such policies can reduce the economic value to parents of additional children. The only national experience of this sort that has been studied is the English experience in the nineteenth century, and the results of the research (Branson, 1968; West, 1968; Becker, 1960) seem to be inconclusive as to whether the effect of the compulsory schooling and child-labor laws was significant. (Many parents were already sending their children to school voluntarily at the time the laws were passed.)

The law of inheritance may affect fertility unintendedly. This idea dates back to Malthus, who attributed the difference in fertility in France and England to differences in their laws of inheritance. But present notions of equity suggest that no country will opt for a change to a less-equal inheritance system as a way of reducing fertility, even if it were thought to be important. Hence, the matter can be mostly ignored in this context.

Social security laws may have an unintended effect upon fertility by reducing old people's dependence upon their children's support, and thereby lessening the economic value of children. But in most MDC's the parents rely little on children's support (a sharp shift in this direction has occurred even in Japan after World War II). And in most LDC's a major social-security program is beyond their financial capacity. Hence social-security legislation decisions are not likely to affect fertility decisions very much.

SUMMARY AND CONCLUSIONS

Income redistribution could affect fertility significantly. The qualifications are: (1) The fertility-reducing effects would probably come about only after a decade or more; and (2) Governments are not likely to undertake redistributions just to reduce fertility. But the time-span is not long compared to other "structural" socio-economic changes which may be fundamental in fertility determination. And even if governments may not undertake redistribution for fertility reduction alone, the added factor that redistribution could influence fertility significantly might make redistributions more likely. Furthermore, some particular sorts of redistributional policies are likely to be more effective than others. For example, redistribution which increases access to education among poorer people may be expected to reduce fertility directly by way of the education, and indirectly by way of the economic development which education speeds.

Concerning the likely effects of incentive payments to raise births in MDC's: The experience of MDC's that have tried to raise fertility by child-allowance programs provides almost no guidance about the efficiency of such programs; the payments have been sufficiently small relative to other income changes so that, in the absence of a controlled experimental design, the possible effects cannot be detected. Questionnaire study shows that people in the U.S. *say* that they and their neighbors would have different-size families, larger or smaller, in response to relatively large financial incentives to do so. But hard evidence will continue to be lacking until some country conducts a controlled experiment, and such research would raise difficult ethical questions. It is reasonable to *guess*, however, that incentives would have to be very substantial in size relative to income for there to be even a chance that they would have a significant effect.

With respect to LDC's, the evidence is even more scanty. Incentive programs might have a major effect in places and among people whose life conditions make it reasonable for them to choose lower fertility. (See Chapter 22 for a classification of conditions within which one may expect various responses to birth-control campaigns.) But lack of well-controlled experiments in various conditions still keeps us ignorant of just how effective incentives might be.

PART III

Economic Decisions about
Population Growth

INTRODUCTION

THE FIRST TWO parts of the book were "positive" economics. That is, they attempted to describe relationships and to make conditional statements about the expected level of the dependent variable (economic conditions in Part I, and fertility in Part II) in the presence of particular background conditions and given values of the independent variables (fertility, and economic conditions, in Parts I and II, respectively.)

Part III turns to "normative" economics. It discusses methods of deciding which population policy is best, given certain assumptions. Chapter 18 analyzes whether additional children have positive or negative economic value under various sets of conditions. It concludes that the welfare judgment about additional children depends very much on the economic model and the value-judgment assumptions one uses. Hence, *general* welfare judgments about population growth *cannot be made scientifically*.

Chapter 19 discusses the welfare criterion most commonly used in normative studies of the economics of population, the per-capita-income criterion. Beyond a limited range of application of this criterion, it does not correspond to the basic values of most people, either in the sentiments people express or in the revealed-preference behavior of communities with respect to population growth. Hence the per-capita-income criterion is quite defective.

Chapter 20 asks how, on the assumption that per-capita income *is* the appropriate criterion, an LDC may best put an economic value upon one more or one less birth. The aim is to evaluate the benefits of a lower birth rate in an LDC that might be achieved by various sorts of family-planning campaigns or incentives plans. The chapter shows how the usual partial-analysis methods are fallacious, and presents a general macro-economic analysis. The macro-economic analysis reaches somewhat *higher* estimates of the value of an avoided birth than do the partial-analysis methods.

Chapter 21 offers a cost-benefit framework that combines the results of Chapters 19 and 20 with data on the cost of family-planning campaigns in LDC's. The end point of Chapter 21 is a system for making business-like national decisions about family-planning policies—given, of course, that there is a consensus in the country that economic development is the relevant goal and that per-capita income is its measure.

Chapter 22 takes up the marketing economics of birth control. It suggests a market-segmentation scheme to aid in making decisions about birth-control sales campaigns, and discusses how such a scheme may be implemented.

Finally, Chapter 23 summarizes the various chapters of the book and presents their highlights. Over and beyond the summary, it combines the material of Part III with Parts I and II into a general assessment of population growth. Chapter 23 is affected by the values and tastes of this writer, but—as argued in Chapter 18—*any* assessment and judgment of population growth necessarily is influenced by the beliefs and values of the person making the judgment. Chapter 24 offers some speculations. And the Appendix refutes some popular objections to the conclusions reached by this book.

The Welfare Economics of Fertility

INTRODUCTION

IS AN additional child good or bad from an economic point of view? The search for a logically satisfying answer to this question inexorably drives one beyond facts and toward that rather esoteric branch of ethical philosophy called "welfare economics." This chapter therefore is particularly technical in its analysis, and the reader may well choose to skip it if he is not especially interested in welfare economics, or he is willing to accept on intuitive grounds the chapter's central proposition: Whether additional children are calculated to bring positive or negative economic effects depends on (1) one's values about human life now and in the future, and (2) one's economic analysis of the effects of population growth on the streams of future output and expenditures. (The analyses of the effects are given in Chapters 3–13.)

Analyses of the welfare economics of population growth generally make one or more of the following assumptions: (1) The criterion of social welfare at a given moment is per-capita (or per-consumer) income (e.g., Enke, 1966). (2) The effect of a given individual upon society is limited to his own impact during his own lifetime (e.g., Mirrlees, 1972). (3) Welfare is assessed at a single given moment, or at the same rate along a growth path, or without distinguishing between the various periods of the additional child's life cycle (e.g., Phelps, 1968). Most of the older literature makes *all* of these assumptions (see Gottlieb, 1945/1956). This chapter shows that a judgment about the magnitude and even the *direction* of the welfare effect of an added child depends upon each of these assumptions.[1] That is, changing one or more assumptions to other reasonable

---

[1] To put it another way, this general question is not one to which welfare-economics techniques can give any general answer. In this context the question of whether people should have more or less children is similar to the question of whether grocery stores should expand. One would never expect or try to deduce a general answer from welfare economics on the latter question; there are just too many if's and but's. Furthermore, the larger the number of if's and but's, the less possible it is to provide a general answer, or even manageably few answers, from welfare economics. This is unlike the question about whether a price ceiling on wheat is a good thing; with only a few if's and value assumptions, the economist can produce a general answer to such a question.

This is not to say that the economist is useless in the case of food-store expansion or family-size decisions. He has two useful functions: First, he can sit with the decision-makers in a *particular* situation, determine which way all the if's and but's go in that particular situation, and help reach a situation-specific decision. Second, he can list the considerations that are relevant and must be decided explicitly in *any* specific situation (e.g., the discount factor). But where there are many conditions that affect the answer, the welfare economist cannot produce a sound general answer about the better policy.

assumptions often shifts the conclusion about the welfare effect from positive to negative or vice versa. Therefore, the aim of the chapter is to map out the welfare effect of additional children under many different sets of assumptions.

From this welter of possible conclusions one can draw an important irrefutable conclusion: Analysis of the effect of population growth is complex and tenuous: it is *not* straightforward and clear-cut as it is too often presented in newspapers, television and professional journals by both laymen and academics; any judgment is contingent on one's values and assumptions.

I do not mean to suggest that the various contradictory assumptions and values that will enter the discussion are morally indistinguishable. But it is not within the competence of economists or demographers to judge their relative morality. That must be left to the community, perhaps with guidance from philosophers who are now busily arguing these ethical-moral questions (e.g., Narveson, 1967, 1973; Stearns, 1972; Brandt, 1972). It is important that these values and assumptions be made explicit so that the community can properly evaluate the arguments presented for community choice.

To illustrate the complete dependence of welfare-economics conclusions about population growth upon the very different assumptions that people might make, consider these examples: (1) To a Daniel Boone, the resource of nature, untouched by humans and without the presence of another person, is of sufficient value that maximization of his welfare function requires that *no other people at all* be in that part of the world. No further analysis is needed to deduce a policy of no children (and no adults except D. Boone). (2) To some people with special religious or military interests, the absolute number of bodies is itself the only "resource" that matters, and not how well they live. This value requires at least enough economic analysis to decide how the largest total numbers of people may be supported at various times in the future. But aside from that, the optimum number is the largest possible number, given such a value.

The term "welfare" as used in this chapter refers to whether a given society is judged to be made better off or worse off on balance by a given action. That is, if one concludes that an additional child makes society worse off (or better off) under a given set of conditions, he is judging that there is a negative (or positive) welfare effect of the additional child.

The term "utility" refers here to the satisfaction that an individual gains from his life. The term is used in the original Benthamite-Utilitarian-Pigovian sense, referring to happiness rather than to choice, the latter being the meaning of utility in contemporary economics. With the exception of the parents of the additional child—whose utility *is* assumed to be affected by the number of children they have—utility is assumed to be a function only of the individual's own level of income (consumption). If an individual's utility were seen to be influenced one way or another by the number of siblings and the size of the community (aside from their effect on his income), the analysis would be even more complex and less determinate—which would only reinforce the central point of this chapter.

The strategy of the chapter is to disaggregate the problem in two directions. The first disaggregation is *over time:* Instead of asking for a single time-discounted value that summarizes whether welfare is higher or lower considering all of the future periods together, welfare judgments will be discussed for a few separate segments of the future: (a) the added individual's childhood; (b) his adulthood; and (c) after the individual's death. Summary measures will also be considered critically.

The second kind of disaggregation is *by groups.* Instead of only a single criterion of welfare for the community as a whole, judgments will be made about (a) the individual's welfare; (b) the welfare of his parents; (c) the welfare of all *other* persons excluding the added individual; and (d) some over-all assessments.

The chapter begins with the simplest situation, that in which the individual has no negative or positive effects external to his own family, and leaves no negative or positive inheritance of any kind to future generations. This situation (with the single complication that the additional child already has siblings) is briefly summarized in Table 18–1. Then the chapter moves on to situations where there are externalities during his life, and then to situations where there are continuing external effects after his death. The situations are analyzed with various welfare functions, under various assumptions about the directions of the externalities.

The results of the analyses are summarized in Table 18–2. The text explains how only a few of the results in Table 18–2 are obtained. Once the reader is satisfied that there are at least *some* results with opposite signs in Table 18–2, further study of it is not necessary. The material in the table should be considered as data on which the general conclusion of the chapter is based. The main point of Table 18–2, and of the chapter as a whole, is that the welfare effects of an additional person are very mixed and are largely indeterminate; the judgments must depend upon the particular economic conditions, the economic and value assumptions, and the choice of welfare criteria. The aim is to refute all analyses which purport to arrive at firm scientific conclusions about the welfare effect of population growth without noting the sensitivity of those conclusions to different welfare criteria and to the differing ramifications of additional people in various economic situations.

The strategy of the chapter is like that of the mathematician who constructs counterexamples to show that a generalization does not hold. But in economics the counterexamples should be reasonable ones rather than

TABLE 18–1

WELFARE EFFECTS OF AN ADDITIONAL CHILD IN A SIMPLE
AGRICULTURAL SITUATION, ACCORDING TO SOME DIFFERENT CRITERIA
(conditions: subsistence agriculture, no externalities beyond
the family, child has older siblings
[excerpts from column b in Table 18–2])

The welfare criterion and the time period in the life cycle of the additional child	Welfare effect
In childhood	
1. Utility to parents	Positive welfare effect
4. Utility to older siblings	Negative welfare effect
6. Sum of utility of children in family if each utility function is concave and positive	Positive welfare effect
7. Sum of utility of children in family if shape of utility function is *not* assumed positive and concave	Indeterminate
8. Average utility of children in family	Negative welfare effect
9. Average utility of family including parents (parental utility including non-income-related utility from children)	Indeterminate
13. Per-capita income (average utility) of community as whole	Negative welfare effect
14. Sum of utility of community as a whole if each utility function is assumed positive and concave	Positive welfare effect
15. Sum of utility of community as a whole if utility can be negative	Indeterminate
In Adulthood	
21. Sum of utility of older siblings	Negative welfare effect
23. Per-capita income (average utility) of all children in family	Negative welfare effect
25. Sum of utility of all family's children if utility functions are assumed positive and concave	Positive welfare effect

SOURCE: This table is drawn from Table 18–2, which shows a large variety of such situations and criteria. Row numbers correspond to those in Table 18–2; the welfare effects are excerpts from column b.

NOTE: The aim of this table is to show that the judgment about the welfare effect of an additional child in a simple situation (with the complication of siblings) depends upon the criterion chosen.

396

mere logical possibilities. Therefore, only criteria and situations that have some plausibility and social meaning are shown in Table 18–2, and these are only a sample of those that might be examined.

Different countries have different needs, even at the same level of economic development. Singapore feels an urgent need to *reduce* fertility, and Rumania feels the need to *increase* fertility. Everything said here should be understood to be subject to the special economic needs of each country, which may suggest a very different course of action than does the general discussion.

No Externalities beyond the Family during or after the Additional Child's Life

During His Childhood: No Siblings

We begin with the simplest situation worth considering: the kind of subsistence-agricultural community in which a child has practically no economic effects external to his family during or after his childhood, and in which there are until now no children in the family. This case is not very far from the real situation of the large proportion of India's people who live in villages. Social expenditures per child are small, and most of any additional children will remain in the village and work on the family farm. Even in such a simple situation one can arrive at a variety of welfare conclusions about the addition of a child to the community depending upon one's assumptions. Here are three such welfare-judgment possibilities:

1. If an additional *first* child in a family has no effects external to the family during its childhood, then the welfare of all *other* persons in the society is unaffected by his birth—by assumption.[2] However, by definition the welfare of his parents is increased by the occurrence of an event the parents desire.[3]

---

[2] Here and elsewhere in this chapter it is assumed that children are brought into life because their parents desire them, and that no more children are born than parents want. Evidence about the reasonableness of this assumption is given in Chapter 14. Also, the monetary and psychic costs of controlling fertility are ignored here, as are noneconomic welfare benefits such as the value of liberty.

[3] A lengthy matter that may be passed over by all except the most demanding reader: In a full formal treatment it is necessary to distinguish between the utility that the parents get *from the utility the children get from consuming resources*, and the utility of the children to the parents *for the parents' own sake*. The distinction might be phrased as the difference between the parent's utility from the parent's "consumption" of the child, and the parent's utility from the child's own consumption. For example, a father takes pleasure in his newborn son, it would seem, not because he believes that the child now enjoys life, but for the father's own sake. On the other hand, it is clear that parents can feel happy because they believe that the children are happy, for example, the sensation the parent feels as the child eats a piece of cake. "I feel happy for you" is the expression we use to describe this situation.

Many writers on population problems choose to restrict the discussion to the effects on the welfare of those living now. If the welfare judgment is limited to the welfare of only those now living, the Pareto-optimum test immediately tells us that if, in this simplest situation, parents choose to have a child when they have none, the result is higher welfare, by the following simple reasoning: The parents are better off (by our definition of the situation), the rest of the community is no worse off (by our definition of the situation), and therefore the over-all welfare increases.

2. Now let us bring the welfare of the added child himself into the discussion. The judgment about the welfare of the *child himself* depends upon one's assumption about the human utility function, together with the facts of the case. According to the assumption made by Meade (1955), Dasgupta (1969), Ehrlich (1968), and others, the welfare of a very poor child can be *negative* (Table 18–2 column a, line 3). But of course one can just as reasonably assume that the child's welfare is neutral or positive when he is very young. (Later, after he is old enough to make his own choices, we can argue about his welfare in a different fashion, as will be discussed later.) But no matter what one assumes about the value of life, by the test of *per-capita income*, *general* welfare *falls* during this childhood period, because the same amount of product (assuming no increase in labor by the parents) is divided among more people (column a, line 13, Table 18–2).

The reader may not immediately find meaning in the idea of imputing welfare or a utility function to a person who does not now exist.[4] But this concept is really not very different from other concepts in common use,

---

I shall assume that the utility a parent gets from the utility the child derives from consumption of the income the child uses is *less* than the child's own utility from that consumption. This need not be true a priori, of course. A parent might believe very strongly in the value and importance and joy of life, and hence bring a child into the world despite the fact that the parent himself does not expect to get any personal pleasure from beholding the child, but on the contrary, expects the child to be only a burden to the parent. If in fact that child also gets little joy from his life, one could imagine that the child's positive utility is less than the parent's negative utility from the child, giving a net negative balance. But it seems reasonable that a parent generally gets less utility from a child's consumption of resources than does the child himself, which justifies this assumption. I am painfully aware that this distinction is vague, perhaps impossible to measure sensibly, and at least bordering on the metaphysical. But one cannot get around such a distinction unless one wishes to assume that the parent's utility from the child is all his own pleasure of the senses in "consuming" the child, rather than "indirect" utility derived from the child's pleasure in life. And if one does wish to so assume, all conclusions of this paper are the same as otherwise, and are arrived at even more directly.

[4] Catholics may note a similarity between the treatment here and that of their church, in that there is no sharp distinction between the rights of the born and the unborn, including those who might or might not be born in the future. And why should there be a logical distinction for our purposes here, except that the death of an infant usually causes more grief than the expiration of a fetus, which in turn usually causes more grief than a nonpregnancy?

implicit and explicit. To buy insurance or a supply of diapers before a baby is born is to act as if one can now affect the future welfare of an unborn person. And nature-conservation programs are largely aimed at the welfare of unborn future generations. More abstractly, sending money to a foreign charity is to try to improve the welfare of a person of whose existence you do not know specifically; this is operationally much the same as giving charity to a person you do not know because he has not yet been born. As a last example, all economic growth theory assumes welfare horizons far beyond the lifetime of present generations. All in all, the objection that the welfare of unborn people cannot be taken into account does not stand up, in my judgment (see p. 504).

3. If one uses as a welfare criterion the *sum* of individual utilities, general welfare *rises* if the additional child's utility is positive.[5] The same conclusion can be reached by a more economic and powerful approach, that of an expanded Pareto optimum (an idea also suggested by D. Friedman, 1972): If a person whose utility is positive is *added* to the society, and if none of the existing people thereby have their positions altered for the worse, it is reasonable that this represents an increase in the society's utility. (The application of this criterion is unique to the very simple case under discussion, however; even the existence of brothers or sisters makes the criterion inapplicable without further assumptions, as we shall see.)

A curious implication of the analysis for this simple situation is the following: Parents have *fewer* children than would maximize the total utility of the community. The reasoning is as follows:[6] The parent continues to have children until he is at his own margin, indifferent between the birth and nonbirth of another child as is the rest of the community in this simple situation. But at this margin an additional child would himself

---

[5] This is the welfare function which is implied by the Biblical "Be fruitful and multiply" and by the Utilitarian "The greatest good for the greatest number." "Assuming, then, that the average happiness of human beings is a positive quantity, it seems clear that, supposing the average happiness enjoyed remains undiminished, Utilitarianism directs us to make the number enjoying it as great as possible. But if we foresee as possible that an increase in numbers will be accompanied by a decrease in average happiness or *vice versa*, . . . it would follow that, if the additional population enjoy on the whole positive happiness, we ought to weigh the amount of happiness gained by the extra number against the amount lost by the remainder. So that, strictly conceived, the point up to which, on Utilitarian principles, population ought to be encouraged to increase, is not that at which average happiness is the greatest possible,—as appears to be often assumed by political economists of the school of Malthus—but that at which the product formed by multiplying the number of persons living into the amount of average happiness reaches its maximum" (Sidgwick, 1901, pp. 415–16). Malthus, who had direct links to the Utilitarian tradition, saw "the end [purpose] of nature in the peopling of the earth" (1803, p. 492).

[6] The grounds used here to reach this conclusion are quite different than the grounds on which Phelps (1969) reached a somewhat similar conclusion from a welfare function that would maximize the utility of the parental generation. His grounds were essentially a Berry-Soligo-type international-trade argument plus consideration of savings ratios.

Assumptions about

	Peasant agriculture, no labor force entry, no externalities beyond the family.	Same as column a, but with older siblings.	Labor force entry, but no other externalities, all markets perfect. No end-of-life savings, no creation of knowledge or economies of scale.	Same as column c, except end-of-life *savings positive* but *less than* rate of population growth contributed by individual and his children.	Same as c, except *savings equal* to contribution to population growth rate.	Same as c, except *savings greater than* contribution to population growth rate.
	a	b	c	d	e	f
In Childhood						
1. Utility to parents of additional person	+ directly by assumption	+	+	+	+	+
2. Additional person's own utility (assumed positive)	+ directly by assumption	+	+	+	+	+
3. Additional person's own utility (function not assumed positive or concave)	⑦ depends on family's income	±	±	±	±	±
4. Older siblings' utility (positive concave function assumed)	NA	⊖	−	−	−	−
5. All children in his family including him, consumption per child	NA	−	−	−	−	−
6. All children in his family including him, sum of utilities, function assumed concave and positive	NA	⊕	+	+	+	+
7. All children in his family including him, sum of utilities, his utility not assumed positive or negative	NA	⊕	±	±	±	±
8. Average utility of children in family	−	−	−	−	−	−
9. Average utility of family including parents (parental utility including non-income-related utility from children)	±	±	±	±	±	±
10. Other persons in community (i.e. beyond the family), per-capita income	= directly by assumption	=	=	=	=	=
11. Same as line 8, sum of utilities, positive concave function assumed	= directly by assumption	=	=	=	=	=
12. Same as line 8, sum of utilities, concave function not assumed	= directly by assumption	=	=	=	=	=
13. Community as a whole including the additional person and his family, per-capita income	⊖	−	−	−	−	−
14. Community as a whole including the additional person and his family, sum of utilities, positive concave function	+	⊕	+	+	+	+

400

Various Factual Assumptions and Value Judgments

the economic situation

g	h	i	j	k	l	m	n	o	p
Schooling and child-service externalities, but paid for by parents. Otherwise same as c.	Same as g with respect to externalities. Same as d otherwise.	Same as g with respect to externalities. Same as e otherwise.	Same as g with respect to externalities. Same as f otherwise.	Same as g but externalities *not* paid for.	Same as h but externalities *not* paid for.	Same as i but externalities *not* paid for.	Same as j but externalities *not* paid for.	Same as l (negative childhood externalities, positive savings but less than rate of population growth), and positive contribution to knowledge and economies of scale effect during adulthood.	Same as n (negative childhood externalities, savings greater than rate of population growth), and positive contribution to knowledge and economies of scale effect during adulthood.
↑ Same as column 3 ↑	↑ Same as column 4 ↑	↑ Same as column 5 ↑	↑ Same as column 6 ↑	+	+	+	+	+	+
				+	+	+	+	+	+
				±	±	±	±	±	±
				−	−	−	−	−	−
				−	−	−	−	−	−
				+	+	+	+	+	+
				±	±	±	±	±	±
				± −	± −	± −	± −	± −	± −
				−	−	−	−	−	−
				−	−	−	−	−	−
				−	−	−	−	−	−
				−	−	−	−	−	−
				⊕	⊕	⊕	⊕	±	±

401

(*Continued on next page*)

Assumptions about

	Peasant agriculture, no labor force entry, no externalities beyond the family.	Same as column a, but with older siblings.	Labor force entry, but no other externalities, all markets perfect. No end-of-life savings, no creation of knowledge or economies of scale.	Same as column c, except end-of-life *savings positive but less than* rate of population growth contributed by individual and his children.	Same as c, except *savings equal* to contribution to population growth rate.	Same as c, except *savings greater than* contribution to population growth rate.
	a	b	c	d	e	f
15. Community as a whole including the additional person and his family, sum of utilities, no assumed constraint on function	⊕	±	±	±	±	±
16. Community as a whole including the additional person and his family, expanded Pareto criterion, assuming positive and concave functions	+	±	+	+	+	+
				└─── aside from siblings ───┘		
17. Utility of parents of added person	+	+	+	+	+	+
18. Utility of parents of added person, cumulatively through childhood	+	+	+	+	+	+
19. Added person himself, utility assumed positive, cumulatively through childhood	+	+	+	+	+	+
20. Added person himself, utility not assumed positive or concave, cumulatively through childhood	±	±	±	±	±	±

In adulthood

	a	b	c	d	e	f
21. Older siblings, total utility, concave positive functions assumed	NA	⊖	−	−	−	−
22. Older siblings, total utility, concave positive functions, cumulatively through childhood and adulthood	NA	−	−	−	−	−
23. All family's children including him, per-capita income	NA	⊖	−	−	−	−
24. All family's children including him, per-capita income, cumulatively	NA	−	−	−	−	−
25. All family's children including him, sum of utilities, assuming concave and positive functions	NA	⊕	+	+	+	+
26. All family's children including him, sum of utilities, assuming concave and positive functions, cumulatively	NA	+	+	+	+	+
27. All family's children, sum of utilities with no assumptions about utility function	NA	±	±	±	±	±
28. All family's children, sum of utilities with no assumptions about utility function, cumulatively	NA	±	±	±	±	±
29. All workers in same occupation, per-capita income	=	=	⊖	−	−	−
30. All workers in same occupation, per-capita income, cumulatively	=	=	−	−	−	−

the economic situation

Schooling and child-service externalities, but paid for by parents. Otherwise same as c.	Same as g with respect to externalities. Same as d otherwise.	Same as g with respect to externalities. Same as e otherwise.	Same as g with respect to externalities. Same as f otherwise.	Same as g but externalities *not* paid for.	Same as h but externalities *not* paid for.	Same as i but externalities *not* paid for.	Same as j but externalities *not* paid for.	Same as l (negative childhood externalities, positive savings but less than rate of population growth), and positive contribution to knowledge and economies of scale effect during adulthood.	Same as n (negative childhood externalities, savings greater than rate of population growth), and positive contribution to knowledge and economies of scale effect during adulthood.
g	h	i	j	k	l	m	n	o	p
				±	±	±	±	±	±
⊕	⊕	⊕	⊕	⊕	⊕	⊕	⊕	±	±
				+	+	+	+	+	+
				+	+	+	+	+	+
				+	+	+	+	+	+
				±	±	±	±	±	±
				−	−	−	−	±	±
				−	−	−	−	±	±
				−	−	−	−	±	±
				−	−	−	−	±	±
				+	+	+	+	+	+
				+	+	+	+	+	+
				±	±	±	±	±	±
				±	±	±	±	±	±
				−	−	−	−	±±	±±
				−	−	−	−	±±	±±

403

(*Continued on next page*)

	Peasant agriculture, no labor force entry, no externalities beyond the family.	Same as column a, but with older siblings.	Labor force entry, but no other externalities, all markets perfect. No end-of-life savings, no creation of knowledge or economies of scale.	Same as column c, except end-of-life *savings positive but less than* rate of population growth contributed by individual and his children.	Same as c, except *savings equal* to contribution to population growth rate.	Same as c, except *savings greater than* contribution to population growth rate.
	a	b	c	d	e	f
31. All workers in same occupation, sum of utilities, assuming concave and positive functions	=	=	+	+	+	+
32. All workers in same occupation, sum of utilities, assuming concave and positive functions, cumulatively	=	=	+	+	+	+
33. All workers in same occupation, sum of utilities, no assumptions about functional form	=	=	±	±	±	±
34. All workers in same occupation, sum of utilities, no assumptions about functional form, cumulatively	=	=	±	±	±	±
35. Others in community (excepting only him and his family), per-capita income	=	=	⊕	+	+	+
36. Others in community (excepting only him and his family), per-capita income, cumulatively	=	=	±	±	±	±
37. Others in community, sum of utilities, functions assumed positive and concave	=	=	⊕	+	+	+
38. Others in community, no assumptions about functions	=	=	+	+	+	+
39. Others in community, no assumptions about functions, cumulatively	=	=	⊕	+	+	+
40. Community as a whole including him, per-capita income	−	−	⊖	−	−	−
41. Community as a whole including him, per-capita income, cumulatively	−	−	−	−	−	−
42. Community as a whole, sum of utilities, functions assumed positive and concave	+	+	⊕	+	+	+
43. Community as a whole, sum of utilities, functions assumed positive and concave, cumulatively	+	+	+	+	+	+
44. Community as a whole, sum of utilities, no assumptions about form of utility function	±	±	±	±	±	±
45. Community as a whole, sum of utilities, no assumptions about form of utility function, cumulatively	±	±	±	±	±	±
46. Community as a whole, expanded Pareto criterion assuming positive and concave functions	+	±	±	±	±	±
47. Community as a whole, expanded Pareto criterion assuming positive and concave functions, cumulatively	+	±	±	±	±	±

the economic situation

	g	h	i	j	k	l	m	n	o	p

Column descriptions:

- **g**: Schooling and child-service externalities, but paid for by parents. Otherwise same as c.
- **h**: Same as g with respect to externalities. Same as d otherwise.
- **i**: Same as g with respect to externalities. Same as e otherwise.
- **j**: Same as g with respect to externalities. Same as f otherwise.
- **k**: Same as g but externalities *not* paid for.
- **l**: Same as h but externalities *not* paid for.
- **m**: Same as i but externalities *not* paid for.
- **n**: Same as j but externalities *not* paid for.
- **o**: Same as l (negative childhood externalities, positive savings but less than rate of population growth), and positive contribution to knowledge and economies of scale effect during adulthood.
- **p**: Same as n (negative childhood externalities, savings greater than rate of population growth), and positive contribution to knowledge and economies of scale effect during adulthood.

g	h	i	j	k	l	m	n	o	p
Same as column 3	Same as column 4	Same as column 5	Same as column 6	+	+	+	+	+	+
				+	+	+	+	+	+
				±	±	±	±	±	±
				±	±	±	±	±	±
				−	−	−	−	±	±
				−	−	−	−	±	±
				−	−	−	−	±	±
				−	−	−	−	±	±
				−	−	−	−	±	±
				−	−	−	−	⊕	±
				+	+	+	+	+	+
				⊕	⊕	⊕	⊕	±	±
				±	±	±	±	±	±
				±	±	±	±	±	±
				±	±	±	±	±	±
				±	±	±	±	±	±

(*Continued on next page*)

	Peasant agriculture, no labor force entry, no externalities beyond the family.	Same as column a, but with older siblings.	Labor force entry, but no other externalities, all markets perfect. No end-of-life savings, no creation of knowledge or economies of scale.	Same as column c, except end-of-life *savings positive but less than* rate of population growth contributed by individual and his children.	Same as c, except *savings equal* to contribution to population growth rate.	Same as c, except *savings greater than* contribution to population growth rate.
	a	b	c	d	e	f

In posterity

	a	b	c	d	e	f
48. Community as a whole, per-capita income	± depends on number of children	–	–	–	=	+
49. Community as a whole, per-capita income, cumulatively through childhood, adulthood, and posterity	±	±	–	–	–	± depends on discount rate
50. Community as a whole, sum of utilities, function assumed positive and concave	+	+	–	±	+	+
51. Community as a whole, sum of utilities, function assumed positive and concave, cumulatively	+	+	±	±	+	+
52. Community as a whole, sum of utilities, no assumptions about utility function	±	±	±	±	±	±
53. Community as a whole, sum of utilities, no assumptions about utility function, cumulatively	±	±	±	±	±	±

NOTE: NA = not applicable; + indicates positive effect; – indicates negative effect; = indicates no effect; ± indicates indeterminate effect. A circle in a cell indicates that the situation is discussed in text.

The table is intended only to show that there are both positive and negative effects for each economic situation. It is *not* intended to be an exhaustive set of analyses (and it could not be); rather each of the analyses is intended to be of special interest. For example, the complication of unemployment, an important argument in people's welfare function, is not taken up at all. Nor does it make any mention of welfare functions which weight the welfare of some persons (e.g., educated persons) higher than that of other persons. Nor does it consider welfare functions which take account of the interest of the state, as distinguished from the welfare of the citizens. Similarly, one would construct many other sorts of welfare functions and factual hypotheses which are not taken up here, but which are accepted by some people. None of these more esoteric possibilities are necessary, however, to establish the central point—indeterminacy until strong assumptions are made.

406

the economic situation

	g	h	i	j	k	l	m	n	o	p
Schooling and child-service externalities, but paid for by parents. Otherwise same as c.										
Same as g with respect to externalities. Same as d otherwise.										
Same as g with respect to externalities. Same as e otherwise.										
Same as g with respect to externalities. Same as f otherwise.										
Same as g but externalities *not* paid for.										
Same as h but externalities *not* paid for.										
Same as i but externalities *not* paid for.										
Same as j but externalities *not* paid for.										
Same as l (negative childhood externalities, positive savings but less than rate of population growth), and positive contribution to knowledge and economies of scale effect during adulthood.										
Same as n (negative childhood externalities, savings greater than rate of population growth), and positive contribution to knowledge and economies of scale effect during adulthood.										

g	h	i	j	k	l	m	n	o	p
↓	↓	↓	↓	−	−	=	+	±	⊕
				±	−	−	± (depends on discount rate)	±	±
				−	±	+	+	±	⊕
				±	±	±	±	±	±
				±	±	±	±	±	±
			↓	+	±	±	±	±	±

407

enjoy positive utility, by assumption; hence his birth would add his own utility, to the community's utility, with no net utility change to his parents, yielding a positive effect on balance. Hence, more children would increase utility.

Even though families do not choose to have enough children to reach the point of zero net marginal social utility, one cannot know *how far* the laissez-faire outcome is from the margin without complete knowledge of people's welfare functions. Hence, it seems that the only sensible course consistent with the foregoing conclusion is to let parents set their own limits on the number of children, subject to consideration of external costs and community values.

The foregoing inference that parents have too few children to maximize community utility applies only to the childhood period and may well hold only on the assumptions that (a) there are no other children in the family, (b) utility is positive; and (c) there are no externalities. It *might*, however, hold even if some of the above assumptions were loosened in some ways.

With the foregoing analysis in hand, one may judge the welfare effect of contraceptive knowledge and of public health measures to reduce infant mortality. Consider contraception first. In a society where no one dies until old age, the ability to practice contraception increases the welfare of *parents* because it allows them to achieve the number of children that will maximize their (parental) utility. That is, ability to contracept increases parents' options, which is a Paretian basic welfare gain. If lack of contraceptive knowledge leads to more children than the couple wants ex ante, this *may* increase the total welfare of the family, and hence of the community. But to argue that people should be hindered from practicing contraception one must argue that (1) one knows the parents' and children's utility functions, and (2) by overcoming the parents' "selfishness" one forces them to a higher level of community utility. (This is implicitly the position of the Catholic Church, as I understand it.) It seems to me that a person outside the couple cannot make such an argument satisfactorily, which implies that an outsider has no welfare grounds to hinder the practice of contraception.

Now consider infant mortality. If the main thrust of this section is correct—that in the simplest agricultural situation with no externalities welfare is maximized by there being at least as many children as parents desire, subject to community values and external costs—and if parents are able to control fertility accurately, then infant mortality is an unmitigated evil. This is because infant mortality must result in the parents often having more or less children than they desire, with consequently lower utility for the parents. Only by luck will the number of children they desire ex ante live to maturity. Even if parents are lucky enough to end up with the number of children they desire, they will have suffered the grief of children's deaths and extra child-raising costs that would not have occurred with a zero infant-mortality regime.

Furthermore, because people are generally averse to risk when it comes to the number of children and to the number of sons they have, the error will likely be on the side of achieving more children than were desired ex ante, as has been shown vividly by Heer and Smith (1968) and May and Heer (1969). Infant mortality might increase total utility by offsetting parental selfishness, but it might also reduce total utility by carrying the process beyond the point of diminishing total utility. Which is true cannot be known a priori.[7]

Now let us consider a case in which the additional child's welfare is said to be *negative*.[8] No judgment about the direction of the community welfare effect can then be made without assigning cardinal values to the individual utility of the additional child and that of his parents, which trade off if the child's utility is said to be negative (Table 18–2 column a, line 13). And if one considers even more complex welfare functions, containing arguments of per-capita income as well as of total utility or total population size (e.g., Meade, 1955; Votey, 1969), they will a fortiori also give indeterminate results in the absence of cardinal specification of the utility function.

---

[7] One might fault the above conclusion because the individual's function does not take account of such important "bads" or "disutilities" as death and suffering. But since we do not have any intimate or metaphysical knowledge of death itself, the only negative effects we can sensibly attach to death are the loss of the welfare that might have occurred if death did not intervene, which is not an operative argument here, and the suffering of survivors, which families surely take into account when they risk having children. Hence the omission of the disutilities of death and suffering is not a defect of the analysis.

[8] If one chooses to reason within the standard logic of consumer-preference theory the available evidence tells us plainly that life does have positive value. That is, people invariably *choose* life in preference to death, no matter what their economic circumstances. Life seems to have more *value* than death for a destitute toothless widowed crone who lives—until the police move her—in a rag-and-newspaper tent by the side of a road in India, just as life seems to have value for you. The rate of suicide is sufficiently low that it is clearly an exception when life ceases to have any value. (And furthermore, suicide is an inverse function of income when such factors as education are not held constant; see Simon, 1968; Barnes, 1975).

To conclude that some people are sufficiently poor that their lives have negative value is quite incompatible with the basic concept of modern economics: that which is chosen is defined to be better. Without this concept all modern economics fall apart. In light of this, it is curious that Meade (1955, Chapter 6) proposes a "welfare-subsistence level" of income below which a person is assumed to have negative utility. But Meade's concept is not only inconsistent with consumer-preference theory. It also is an open door for any income group to eliminate lower-income people or to lower the birth-rate of any lower-income group, by simply choosing a welfare-subsistence level above the income level of the lower-income group. In other words, this concept of negative utility for some low-income people is almost an invitation to snobbish prejudice (about "filthy lives" that "are not worth living") and to justification of self-interested social policies benefiting the rich (though I am sure that this is not Meade's intention).

During His Childhood If There Are Siblings

When a *second* or *subsequent* child is considered to be the additional child, the welfare effect becomes even more complicated (see Table 18–1 or column b, Table 18–2), because consumption by existing children will be reduced by the existence of an additional child. And unlike the parents, there is no reason to assume that the existing children desire the additional child. Hence, the welfare of the previous children is decreased on balance by an additional child (line 4 in Tables 18–1 and 18–2). The over-all welfare judgment must then depend upon the assumption one makes about the utility functions of the people involved.

If the individual utility function of each of the children is assumed positive at all consumption levels, and concave downward[9] and if the utility functions of all the children are assumed to be the same, then the additional child increases total utility of the children in the family (Table 18–1, line 6). This conclusion follows from the mathematical fact that doubling the value on the x (consumption) axis is associated with *less* than doubling the value on the y (utility) axis when the function is concave downward. Hence the *total* utility is greater if one distributes a given amount of consumption among two or more persons with similar utility functions, rather than concentrating the consumption with one person. This is the same reasoning that underlies the conclusion that a more equal distribution of income increases utility, *ceteris paribus*.

If the children's utility functions can be negative at some consumption levels and/or have inflection points, the welfare effect of an additional child upon the children as a group depends on the economic facts and the specific utility functions, and it is indeterminate without cardinal specifications (Table 18–1, line 7). The effect on the family as a whole, and on the community, must also be indeterminate if the effect on the children is indeterminate (Table 18–1, line 15).

Already we can see that even in the very simplest case examined for only a single point in time, the evaluation is thoroughly messy and generally indeterminate. The reader who is convinced of this may quit reading at this point unless he is interested in the additional analyses for their own interest.

During His Adulthood: Subsistence Agriculture

During the additional person's adulthood in this simple world of no externalities, his welfare effect depends upon which reference group is being considered, just as it does during his childhood. An additional

---

[9] Such an assumption is not at all inconsistent with the Friedman-Savage hypothesis, as those authors themselves agree (1952).

peasant in subsistence agriculture affects his brothers and sisters negatively by reducing their inheritance of land (Table 18–1, line 21), and
therefore the expanded-Pareto criterion no longer applies. If, however,
one assumes that the utility of all the siblings is positive and if all their
utility functions are concave, the additional sibling would mean a net
welfare gain to the people constituting the original nuclear family (Table
18–1, line 25), and thence—by the expanded Pareto criterion—to the
society as a whole. But if one assumes that utility can be negative, no such
conclusions can be drawn. Of course, the per-capita-income effect of an
additional person is negative in adulthood in subsistence agriculture
(Table 18–1, line 23).

During His Adulthood If He Enters the Labor Market

Now let us leave idealized subsistence agriculture and move to the
more interesting, but still simple, case in which the additional person
enters the labor force but in which all markets are competitive and the
individual is paid his marginal output (Table 18–2, column c). From the
standpoint of average income, the *rest* of the community as a whole
benefits from the added person's presence (Table 18–2, line 35, column c)
as Berry and Soligo (1969) have shown; the nature of the benefit is exactly
the same as the benefit that occurs when one country opens trade with
another country. But assuming that the incremental person is a *worker*,
the population of *workers* as a whole, and especially the workers in the
trade he enters, will have lower wages because of him (Table 18–2, line
29, column c). Furthermore the average income of the entire community
including the additional person will fall (Table 18–2, line 40, column c).
But if one assumes that all persons' utility functions are positive, concave,
downward, and similar, then the *sum* of the individual utilities in the
community will be *higher* than before, because total output will be greater
(Table 18–2, line 42, column c).

Again even for a single period—adulthood—and in the simplest case
of no externalities and no inheritances, the welfare effect of an incremental
individual can be judged differently from different points of view. Furthermore, if one now wishes to *combine* the judgments about the welfare effects
of the added person during his childhood and during his adulthood the
results are even more mixed and indeterminate.

Thus, ends the story of the man who does not affect society beyond his
family, either during or after his lifetime, with positive or negative savings[10] of any kind, except by working in a perfect market.

---

[10] If he is paid his marginal output, there is some increase in total productivity minus his
consumption. Hence, total saving will rise somewhat, but this can be disregarded for now.

EXTERNALITIES DURING THE ADDED PERSON'S LIFETIME AND BEFORE HIS CHILDREN'S ADULTHOOD

In societies that have advanced economically beyond family subsistence agriculture, an incremental child usually causes effects external to the family. These externalities can be distinguished into two sorts: those whose effects can be appraised and compensated for by way of markets, and those that cannot. The former are treated in the next section, and the latter are treated in the section after that.

Where There Are Compensable Externalities

The main "compensable" externalities are in the labor market, and in social-welfare expenditures, e.g., schooling.[11] The nature of the effect of an additional worker's entrance into the labor force would be difficult to agree upon. But both the labor-force and social-welfare effects of additional children are calculable in principle even if we cannot now agree on how to calculate them. Standard welfare-economics arguments suggest that the total utility of all adults in a society at a given time will be maximized if families pay for all the services used in raising children, and also for neutralizing any labor-market effect. That is, if one considers a median-income family with more than the average number of children, the family would pay taxes to cover the "extra" child-raising services plus the labor-market effect of the "extra" children. The proof of the optimality of this policy is the same as that for other cases of external effects, as shown in a simple way by Coase (1960). As long as the parents pay the full market value of these external effects, a larger number of children produced by a family cannot be said to reduce the utility of the rest of the community. And after the labor-force and social-welfare externalities are taken care of, in which case the utility of existing adults may be assumed to be maximized, the expanded Pareto criterion may be applied again; after compensation no one except older siblings would be made worse off by the added person (Table 18–2, line 16, columns g–j). Hence, if the additional person's own utility is assumed to be positive, and putting siblings aside, parents stop having children before the community's welfare would be maximized, by the same argument as was given earlier. (If the added person's utility is not assumed to be positive, or if other children in the family are considred, no such conclusion can be drawn.)

A technical difficulty which turns into a major political problem arises with respect to compensable externalities, however. It is all very well to talk of parents paying *now* for the *future* effects of their children. But such

[11] I assume here that the society charges the full cost for all consumption products, including the cost of physical pollution prevention and removal. This assumption may be well on the way to becoming fact.

412

payments would have to be discounted for futurity. The community would have to decide on an appropriate discount rate, because economic logic alone reveals none (or a multitude of them). Even if the community were to eventually arrive at agreement on such a discount rate, there would be major conflicts of interest. Old people without children would want a low discount rate and high sums paid immediately. Parents with many children would want the opposite. It might be suggested that the externalities be paid for as they occur; this might work for schooling and medical care, but it would not be feasible for the children's labor-force effect. So, because of this discount-rate problem, together with the difficulty of estimating the future effects of the children, it is quite possible that the community would not arrive at agreement on an externality-neutralizing agreement. If so, it would not be possible for an additional child to effect a Paretian welfare increase, and the total cumulative effect—in his childhood plus his adulthood—is Paretian indeterminate (Table 18–2, line 16, columns k–n). And if externalities are not neutralized, the welfare effect by a total-utility criterion is also indeterminate during his adulthood, and hence indeterminate for his life as a whole (Table 18–2, lines 14, 43, columns k–n).

Now let us consider the *per-capita-income* effect of an additional individual where there are externalities in child services and labor markets. The classical diminishing-returns analysis (same total capital and more labor yield a smaller average product) tells us that the effect is negative during the additional person's adulthood, as it was during his childhood. But in the more-developed world it is not only possible but likely (Kuznets 1960; Chapter 6 above) that after some time in the labor force an additional person will cause enough new knowledge and enough economies of scale that per-capita income will be *higher* than it would otherwise be.[12] If so, by a per-capita-income welfare standard the additional person's effect is positive for at least the latter part of his adulthood (Table 18–2, column o), and the effect may be sufficiently great to make his over-all lifetime effect positive (Table 18–2, line 41, column o). But, given that per-capita income is lower during his childhood because of him, to reckon the lifetime per-capita-income effect one would have to specify the effects for each year and choose a discount rate. A high enough discount rate

---

[12] This *includes* the use of natural resources as raw materials in production, and is supported by the finding by Barnett and Morse (1963) of no increase in natural-resource scarcities. For a quantitative estimate of the interaction of this force with the classical capital-dilution effect, see Chapter 6.

One might argue that the concept of GNP, which underlies the work in Chapter 6, does not measure over-all economic utility sufficiently well, because it leaves out some "quality of life" features. Perhaps so. But in the absence of calculations, or at least cogent reasoning, about the results of using the wider measure, there is no reason to assume the results would be different in any particular way from work based on GNP.

could, of course, be chosen so that the later positive effect would matter little, and hence the lifetime effect would be negative.[13] But with a lower discount rate the lifetime effect *might* well be positive if there are positive externalities from knowledge and economies of scale during the additional person's adulthood—as there is reason to believe there are. So a variety of possible welfare judgments are possible here.

Nonmarket Externalities and Community Values

Let us now consider externalities that realistically would not be compensated through taxes and subsidies, still confining the discussion to the lifetime of the additional person.

As Arrow (1970, p. 153) has made clear, there may be "a difference between the ordering of social states according to the direct consumption of the individual and the ordering when the individual adds his general standards of equity (or perhaps his standards of pecuniary emulation)." The latter states Arrow calls "values," in contrast to the former which he labels "tastes"; the "market mechanisms takes into account only the ordering to tastes" (Arrow, p. 154). Hence it may be appropriate for the community, acting together, to make such laws—which may include taxes on or subsidies for children—as will achieve the sort of society that its members want. For example, someone might suggest that the community hold a referendum as to whether there should be a tax on parents of 100 shekels, say, for each child after the third. People might rationally vote for such a measure if they believe that a lower birth rate would increase the rate of economic development[14] and if they put a positive value on economic development; or if they believe that infant mortality would decrease if each family had fewer children and the death of neighbors' children would cause disutility; or if other people's children,

---

[13] If the lifetime effect were calculated to be negative, on the per-capita-income criterion in such a situation the implication for the society is to get rid of as many people as possible all the way to the point of the "optimum size" population, starting up the income ladder from the poorest person. This increases per-capita income by the magic of arithmetic. Of course, the people being eliminated will not like it, but a simple per-capita-income welfare function is oblivious to their tastes.

From the point of view of any *individual*, now, the implication is to get rid of the *other* people. Particularistic sentiments may not agree with this simple logic, however. An American may find it easy to believe that a small decrease in the number of Indians or Chinese is a good trade-off against a large per-capita income increase in India or China. But would a Jew or a Greek feel the same way about a decrease in the number of Jews or Greeks? The matter becomes more emotional and the social welfare function changes as it gets closer to home; it depends whose ox's fertility is being affected.

[14] Please notice that though the effects people are interested in may occur after the added person's lifetime is over, the values of other people are held and acted upon during (or before) his lifetime. Hence the placement of this discussion in this section.

produce disutility (e.g., because of the noise or for other reasons). If people vote unanimously for the tax, it would imply that each person would be willing to have fewer children if his neighbors also had fewer children.

Similarly, a community might have a positive value for a *larger* number of children in the community than people otherwise choose to bear, given their own tastes. Israel may be an example: Jews there may feel that the continuation of the historical tradition and the values of Judaism can be better served by more people rather than fewer, and they may be prepared to vote subsidies to children, just as a man may try to bribe his married son to have more children to carry on the family name. If people obtain positive utility out of their neighbors' children and vote accordingly, a subsidy on children would be indicated. Or, people may believe that a larger population would contribute to economic growth within a short enough time span so that their subjective discount rate, which might be zero as Ramsey (1928/1969) believed it ought to be, would make the immediate social costs less than the discounted benefits; this is now the state of belief in Australia, as it was in Western United States in the past.

The mechanism for decision—majority vote or monarchy or whatever—will depend upon the group's constitution. *Any* population policy may then be consistent with welfare economics, if voted in accordance with the constitution. The likeliest cause of distortion with respect to a *democratic* constitution is a population policy initiated and executed by bureaucrats who impose *their own* values upon the community while asserting that the rationale for the policy is the "scientific" finding that the policy in question is "provedly" better than noninterference and governmental neutrality with respect to parental decisions about family size. I believe that this danger is great because the officials or legislators may not recognize that their beliefs and values *are* values and beliefs and are not scientifically proven truths. Weckstein (1962, p. 137) put it: "There is a personal bias that colors one's view of the (relatively) poor which comes from appraising others' incomes against the standard of one's own aspirations. This bias is implicit in many conventional economic-welfare judgments, and it seems to me to be both indefensible and in fact without defenders. This is merely shoddy practice, not doctrine." In the past decade so many scientists have made it clear that they favor lower birth rates that one can easily come to think that lower birth rates have indeed been shown to be scientifically better for society in every way, though in fact no such finding has been or could be scientifically arrived at because of the value considerations involved.

In brief, even where externalities are taken into consideration, the welfare effect of an additional child during his own lifetime depends upon

415

so many considerations that, in general, the welfare effect must be said to be indeterminate.

EFFECTS AFTER THE ADDED PERSON'S LIFETIME

Just as a person may affect his society for good or for ill during his lifetime, so may he have effects after he dies. Economists are accustomed to dismissing very long-run effects because of their small weight in calculations made with interest rates of 5%, 10%, or even 15%. But society itself is more ambivalent about the long-run future and sometimes gives it relatively heavy weight, as the current environmental controversy shows.[15] It may well be that the average man's total effects on posterity are more important than his total effects on his contemporaries—who are, after all, smaller in number than his posterity.

There are many sorts of effects one can have on posterity. The simplest and surely most positive is the savings that one leaves to his heirs; usually the savings exceed the debts, as we know from the fact that society's total capital generally grows over time. One may also leave knowledge behind him;[16] the knowledge *might* be satanic, but usually knowledge is positive for the economy, as we know from the higher rate of productivity now than in former millennia. Still another effect is the children that the added person leaves. At first the effect of children seems very complicated. But consider that the effect of each child is expected to be the same as the effect of the added parent *aside from* his children. Therefore, the welfare judgment one makes about the added person is not changed by his having children—aside from their different positions in history, of course, which can be ignored unless there is special information about the course of history.

Another post-life factor is the delayed economies-of-scale effect associated with the creation of additional infrastructure and with changes in the nature of society—perhaps especially in LDC's. As an example, the population-density-induced changes in land-tenure laws and cropping systems shown to occur by Boserup (1965) can have long-run positive effects on productivity.

---

[15] Many of the long-run worries of the contemporary environmentalists may not be real threats, of course, as was the coal shortage foreseen by Jevons (1865). The point here is, rather, the social discount rate.

[16] The argument that some *classes* of people are likely to contribute to knowledge, while others are not, will not be considered here. One reason is that, as a first approximation, this paper assumes the same proportional change in fertility for all classes of the society; this is certainly not unrealistic for the United States, where the poor clearly do *not* account for most of population growth. A second reason is that I have been persuaded by Kuznets' argument (private communication, 1971) that all segments of a society are crucially implicated in the growth of knowledge, and not just the intellectual elite.

416

Let us now get more specific in welfare terms. If the added man leaves a positive net contribution to posterity and if he has no children—that is, if his contribution to subsequent economic growth exceeds his contribution to population growth, then his welfare effect on posterity is positive (Table 18–2, column p, line 50). If he does have children and he and his lineage add proportionately more to saving than to population growth, then the effect on per-capita income of posterity is positive. If he and his heirs each leave something positive, but what they leave contributes less (marginally) to growth than his lineage contributes to population growth, the effect on posterity then is negative in terms of per-capita income unless during his lifetime he contributes greatly in knowledge and otherwise. In such a case, the effect in terms of *total* utility is likely to be positive, however, given a reasonable distribution of income and no negative utilities. If the additional individual leaves a *negative* inheritance, then his effect on posterity is negative.

Each of the sorts of impacts classified above could be combined with impacts of the same *or* opposite sign in earlier periods; if the latter, the over-all evaluation of the added man's welfare impact is indeterminate without numerical specifications of all impacts and an explicit choice of discount rates.

One might ask whether the possibility of a positive inheritance, and especially an inheritance proportionately as large as the population growth he causes, is just a theoretical nicety which may be disregarded. I think the answer is clearly "no;" the possibility of a positive inheritance effect may *not* be disregarded.[17] In LDC's, of which pre-twentieth-century China is the most well-documented example, per-capita income remained at much the same level secularly over 700 years, though it sank seriously during some periods of rapid population growth. This suggests that the added person set in motion events that temporarily increased saving; at some later time, posterity was no worse off (by a per-capita-income test) for the added person's having lived earlier. On the other hand, it is also possible that in some places increased population keeps an economy in stagnation, preventing change and improvement.

In MDC's there is secular growth in per-capita income. If the population had not grown to the present size, contemporary per-person income would be far lower in MDC's than it now is. That is, people leave an amount of productive power to the next generation that is proportionally greater (perhaps 2 or 3 times greater) than the population increase they leave behind. This means that the added man could leave an inheritance

---

[17] In fact, the opposite possibility—that more people *now* mean a negative inheritance for the *future*—is simply assumed without supporting evidence by such writers as Meade (1955) and Votey (1969).

considerably smaller than average and still leave proportionally more productive power than the population growth his lineage contributes.

This raises the question of whether the added man would contribute an inheritance anywhere near as great as the average person would contribute without him, i.e., whether the marginal contribution to posterity is far below the average contribution. First, there is no reason to suppose that the added person is less endowed with intelligence or chance in life than is the average individual. If his endowment is average, then the only factor causing him to lower the average inheritance would be the lesser physical and educational capital endowment per person at labor force entry that population growth probably implies. Given that the average rate of inheritance in MDC's is much greater than the rate of population growth (in proportional terms), this classical capital-dilution effect could be of sizable magnitude without making the marginal inheritance smaller than the population growth contributed by the added person. Furthermore, there are very solid reasons to agree with Kuznets (1960), as noted earlier, that the knowledge and economies-of-scale effects lead to a higher per-capita income before the end of his work life than if the additional person had not been born. If so, the average inheritance left at the time of his death will be *greater* than if he had not been born, which is a positive effect on posterity by any welfare test. Of course, this happy result is much less likely in a LDC than in a MDC, but .his only proves once again the impossibility of making sound a priori welfare judgments about population effects without detailed specification of the conditions, assumptions, and criteria.

SUMMARY AND CONCLUSIONS

There is not one single calculable welfare effect of an additional person. Rather, there are many different reasonable judgments which may be negative or positive. The welfare effect depends upon the particular economic situation into which the child will be born, the point in his life-cycle to which one refers, whether he is expected to have a positive effect upon his particular sort of economy and society during and after his lifetime, and most of all, on the kind of welfare criterion used. Furthermore, no matter which welfare criterion is used, the welfare effect of an added individual *summarized over time* is particularly sensitive to the particular assumptions made. Hence, the welfare effect of an additional child cannot be stated simply and unequivocally.

To put the matter in more popular terms: whether population is now too large, or is growing too fast, *cannot be decided on scientific grounds alone*. One country may take a longer-run view than another country,

418

and be willing to put up with more poverty in the present for the sake of future population than another country. Or, one country may emphasize only the standard of living while another country may feel prepared to accept a somewhat lower level of living in the present for the sake of more population, just as one of us as a parent may decide to have 3 children rather than 2 even though the 3 children will have to get along with less than 2 would. Each country must ultimately decide these value judgments for itself, and neither the calculations of economics nor the opinions of outsiders should or will prevail. This vital point is too often overlooked in discussions of population policy, in my judgment.

Some Additional Issues

*What Kinds of Pro-Natality and Anti-Natality Incentive Plans
Would Best Serve Community Purposes*

EVEN IF there is consensus in a community that an anti-natality or pro-natality tax scheme should be set up, it is not at all obvious which scheme would best accomplish the community's ends. First, consider the possible tax plans themselves. There are many possible ways to apply taxes to reduce the number of children (e.g., a flat-payment tax per child, pro-portional-to-income taxes per child, incentive payments for nonpregnancy funded with any of a variety of taxes). The community might well accept a referendum offering one sort of tax plan, and reject another. And there is no clear relationship between individual and social values in such cases, as Arrow taught us.

We must also consider the possible side-effects of such plans. Other writers have mentioned the possible indirect effects of work incentives, savings rates, and other such "pure" economic variables. The most important and most complex problem, however, is the interrelationship of welfare programs and natality taxes. Take for example a possible pro-natality program in Israel. A country that wants to increase the birthrate is likely to want to concentrate especially on inducing people who would otherwise have 2 or 3 children to have 1 or 2 more than they would otherwise have, rather than wanting to induce high-parity families to have even more children. One reason given by some is that the "biological potential" seems greater for low-parity families. Another reason is that the "additional" child is thought by many to be less likely to be emotionally and materially disadvantaged in a low-parity than in a high-parity family; partly this is because low-parity families have higher family incomes. Related to the last point but somewhat more fashionable ethically, the addition to the society's human capital of another child in a low-parity, high-income, high-education family will be greater than from a child in a poorer high-parity family. Still another possible reason is that payments given only for the third and fourth children would probably be smaller per tax-caused child than if payments were given for the fifth or subsequent children (i.e., the "cost" in transfer sums would be greater per child in the latter case).

But consider the welfare implications of this scheme. A redistribution would take place from families with more children to families with less children, to the disadvantage of the children in big families—who are already in the poorer families.[18] Of course, one might "balance" the matter by increasing the progressivity of the income tax, so that the final distributions among income fractiles would be left untouched. But this adds another order of complexity to the problem.

On the other hand, however, consider the implications of the sort of scheme that is politically likely in most countries: either special amenities for the big family (e.g., rent subsidies), or programs that provide the same benefits for children of all parities (e.g., free higher education). The latter kind of program may have some effect by reducing the parental "cost" of children relative to other "durable goods." But the relative effect is greater for the high-parity families, so one would expect to have more incremental high-parity children than low-parity children as a result of the program. This would not achieve the aims of the pro-natality program.

It is interesting that the opposite sort of confusion is built into the U.S. income-tax child deduction. The original purpose of the $750 deduction per child (as I understand it) was a kind of child-allowance system, for the welfare of children. But the nature of the deduction mechanism is such that it gives little benefit to those who pay little or no income tax (i.e., the poor) who are exactly those families where children might benefit most from higher family income. Rather, the system works as a slight incentive to middle-class families to have more children.

It may help in the design of child-welfare and natality-tax schemes to keep these principles in mind: The most effective welfare payment is one which can be used only by the child, and which does not replace goods the parent would purchase anyway (i.e., not grain or shirts, but rather milk, shoes in cold countries, and social services). Special medical care and education in the broadest sense—including kindergartens, special remedial training, and such—may be the only child-welfare programs that make sense, especially in better-off countries. Such programs are not subsidies to the parents (they do not substitute for what the parents do anyway) and they are of direct benefit to the children. And they do not suffer the many practical difficulties that afflict transfers in kind of food and clothing.

Policies about Persuasion of Others

Until now we have assumed that both tastes and values are fixed. But now we must also consider the possibility that people might undertake to change other people's values about the number of children they want to have. It is consistent with the democratic system that any independent group of citizens should try to persuade others to reduce fertility or to

---

[18] Ansley Coale has emphasized this point in public discussion.

vote for fertility-reducing measures. Of course, it is not legitimate to misrepresent the facts, and most especially not to claim that there are scientific economic reasons why the birth-rate should be lower. Similarly, though it may be in bad taste for outsiders to come into a country and make propaganda to change values, it is not clear that it is unethical to do so. However, outsiders (especially Westerners) are particularly prone to pass themselves off as experts and to argue with gross scientism, in which case there is clearly no justification for their activity.

The trickiest question is whether the government should try to change the prevailing values of the community or desired family size. I suppose it is unfair for the *government* to be the instrument of any one particular small group. But how one would assess the welfare effects I do not know. That is, we have no mechanism for comparing the relative satisfaction of a person before and after his indifference curves shift. Further than this I do not believe an economic analysis can go.

CHAPTER 19

The Per-Capita-Income
Criterion and Natality Policies
in Poor Countries

INTRODUCTION

THE PREVIOUS chapter showed, at a very abstract level of analysis, that evaluations of the economic effect of additional people are very complex. People with different personal values will reach different evaluations about whether additional population is good or bad. Furthermore, the evaluations are likely to be affected by the nature of the particular situation, and also by one's assessment about the likely economic impacts of additional people.

It is nevertheless a fact that there is considerable consensus among economists and planners for LDC's about the criterion to be used in making population policy. Discussions of birth rates in LDC's are almost always couched in terms of income per capita (or income per-consumer-equivalent). The argument generally goes like this: a decrease in population growth will (it is said) lead to a higher per-capita income than would occur with a higher birth rate, and therefore it makes sense to try to get the birth rate down. Per-capita income is accepted as the appropriate criterion for social policy either without discussion or with at most a brief consideration of other criteria. "Let us look these awkward questions squarely in the face and pass rapidly on," said Meade, prefacing his discussion of population policy in Mauritius (1967, p. 236).

It seems to me, however, that to "pass rapidly on" is to run the danger of choosing a course of action that really is not wanted. Therefore this chapter explores the implications of a per-capita-income criterion for population policy. The chapter concludes that per-capita income alone cannot be a satisfactory criterion for a nation's natality policy, because by itself it implies policies that are quite contrary to the wishes of many countries. More specifically, the birth rate that maximizes per-capita income in the short run does not maximize it in the long run, and a per-capita-income criterion is clearly contrary to the revealed preferences of most people, even with respect to the short run.

The earliest appearance of the per-capita-income criterion in the economic theory of population was in the analysis of the "optimum popula-

423

tion size" for a given country.[1] The idea was that by analysis of a country's aggregate production function and of the scale effects, one could find that point at which the decreasing returns to capital balance the increasing returns to scale in such a way that the per-capita income is highest for the country.

THE ARGUMENT

A static analysis of a per-capita-income criterion clearly leads to a short-run optimum which is quite unacceptable to most people. This was made explicit by the Utilitarians and recently by Meade.[2] The argument is simple: One can raise the per-capita income of any given group of people by doing away with all small subgroups that have a lower-than-average per-capita income. The ultimate absurd result is that (economies-of-scale aside) the highest per-capita income would be achieved by leaving just a single person, the richest one at the start. The theoretical mechanism has two elements. First, it is simple arithmetic that getting rid of the lower part of a distribution raises its mean. Second, *ceteris paribus*, the fewer claimants there are to resources, the more for each of them; the fewer the pieces of a pie, the bigger the pieces can be.

Though this static analysis is illuminating, it is not directly relevant to those problems of LDC's to which population policies usually refer. The death rate is not usually considered a major control variable; rather, it is assumed without argument that the government will carry out those public-health measures that will lead rapidly to life-expectancies much higher than heretofore in LDC's—life expectancies at birth of 50 years, 60 years, and higher. This is as it should be, I believe. Nor (unfortunately) is migration a serious possibility at present in LDC's. The only relevant control variable, then, is the birth rate. Hence, there is no practical value

---

[1] The history of this concept may be found at length in Gottlieb (1945, 1956), or more briefly in the United Nations (1953), Hicks (1942, Chapter 5), or Coale and Hoover (1958, pp. 18–19).

Myrdal's overall judgment of the concept was that "since John Stuart Mill the science of economics has, in fact, made only one major contribution to this field [population study]: the theory of optimum population. This theory, which I am inclined to denote one of the most sterile ideas that ever grew out of our science, was, however, already implied in Mill's postulates." (Myrdal, 1940, p. 26). In my judgment, Myrdal is quite right. In recent years the concept has been transformed into that of the optimum *rate of growth* of population, e.g., Meade (1955), Phelps (1966, 1968), Dasgupta (1969), but this concept is also not very useful.

The optimum population has sometimes been discussed with reference to other criteria such as maximum national power (Sauvy, 1969, Chapter 6). Noneconomic optima are beyond the scope of interest of this book, however, and will therefore not be discussed here.

[2] It is interesting that Meade first argued for a per-capita-income criterion (1937), later foreswore it for a total-utility criterion (1955, p. 83), and then proceeded to make his 1967 analysis of Mauritius mostly in terms of per-capita income.

in comparing the present population of a country with a population half as large, say, and the per-capita-income criterion in a static context therefore is useless. Rather, it makes sense to explore the ramifications of different birth rates. This leads into a dynamic analysis.

Evaluation in a dynamic context is much more difficult than in a static context, however. The consequences of births are spread out over a long period of time, and the short-run effect is not at all the same as the long-run effect, as Chapter 13 shows. Therefore, streams of consumption (income) in each future period under various alternatives must somehow be evaluated at the same point in time—the present moment—in order that the total long-run consequences of one natality policy may be compared against the total consequences of another policy.

Let us get to the point quickly. The birth-rate that maximizes income in the short run—say, over the next 15 years—is zero. Not zero growth, but zero births. That is, the optimizing birthrate is *no births at all* if one applies a per-capita-income criterion to a period whose horizon is 15 years from now. The reason is that a child has private and social costs during its growing up, but makes no productive economic contribution during that period.

But to cease having children clearly is unacceptable. Individuals and societies *do* choose to have children despite knowledge that the children will decrease per-capita income while the children are growing up. This behavior by individuals and societies implies that individuals and societies either take into account factors other than per-capita income, (e.g., the pleasure from one's own and other's children) or look further ahead than 15 years or do both, which is surely the case. No matter which of these possibilities is the fact, however, the implication is that per-capita income with a short time horizon (i.e., with a high discount rate) is an inappropriate criterion for population policy.[3] But any low-but-positive birth rate is *less* attractive in the short run than a zero-birth-policy according to a criterion of a per-capita income with a high discount rate. All this implies

---

[3] There is also a more technical reason why a policy of having no (or few) children is optimizing. After the initial period of years t to $t + 15$, during which the additional child Alpha has a net negative effect, and after some transitional period—perhaps long after the child's death—people *then* will be better off, *ceteris paribus*, because of the life of child Alpha. This is because the average child (perhaps especially in MDC's) leaves an increment of savings and knowledge to the community. And growth theory tells us that, aside from the knowledge factor, communities with the same birth rates in later years—$t + 60$, $t + 120$, and after—tend to approach the same level of per-capita income no matter what their earlier birth rates. Hence, a lower birth rate now seems to imply a *lower* per-capita income long in the future, *ceteris paribus*. This is consistent with the idea that we are richer now than if many fewer people had been born 10,000 years ago, or 1000 years ago, or 100 years ago. Hence this is a second reason why a per-capita-income criterion with a high discount rate (a short-time horizon) is inappropriate.

that per-capita income with a high discount rate is an inappropriate criterion.

On the other hand, it is clear that a per-capita-income criterion with a very *long* time horizon (i.e., with a very *low* discount rate) is also an unacceptable criterion. It implies that per-capita income in the short run will not be weighted very heavily in the over-all reckoning. But clearly people *are* very concerned with their incomes in the short run. Though people will make *some* sacrifices for the long run, as we see in social policies that will benefit future generations, they certainly are reluctant to share present wealth with future generations, and obviously do so much less than would be possible. (We do not build all buildings to last 1,000 years). Hence we may conclude that per-capita income with a very *low* discount rate also is not an appropriate criterion.

This brings us to the conclusion—in contrast to the conclusions of Coale-Hoover and similar studies—that *no* birth rate in the present period can be said to "dominate" all other birth rates, (i.e., no birth rate is better at *all* discount rates). This implies that one must choose some discount rate (among those that are between "too low" and "too high") before applying a per-capita-income criterion. The necessity of choosing a discount rate means that a per-capita-income criterion is not the simple straightforward method it seems at first.

How would one choose a discount rate? No procedure has solid claim as the correct way of doing so, as a large literature in economics assures us. The discount rate observed in the market place is probably not appropriate for a variety of reasons. Nor is the discount rate used in other government calculations likely to be appropriate, for these reasons: First there are *many* such government rates. Second, there is no reason to believe that one discount rate is appropriate for different sorts of government policies.[4]

All in all, the choice of an appropriate discount rate must necessarily be difficult and arbitrary. The choice requires a decision about the relative welfares of people at different times in the future. Whatever principle one uses to make this decision, it must be a value judgment. This means that one cannot simply make *one* value judgment to use a per-capita-income criterion, as it seems at first. Rather, *at least two* value judgments must be made, and one of them is very complex and arbitrary. This means that more is involved in the choice of a per-capita-income criterion than most people think when they use it as their criterion.

---

[4] Our apparent concern about not polluting the atmosphere in such a way as to remove the basis for life of future generations suggests that our feelings about the numbers of people who will live in future generations are different—and imply a lower discount rate—than our feelings about providing for their narrowly economic welfare, such as longer-lasting houses.

Still another difficulty is that for any *span* of years in a country there is not just *one* birth rate, but rather an almost-infinite number of permutations of birth rates. Any given birth rate in year t will have different effects in year $t + k$ when combined with different sets of birth rates in the years after t. Thus, one cannot just think of choosing an optimum birth rate for *this* year. Rather, one must choose a whole *structure* of birth rates for future years. This raises a whole host of new questions such as who is to be included in the group whose income is to be maximized—the present population only, or also the people who will be born in the future?

SUMMARY

The per-capita-income criterion leads to nonsensical conclusions in a static immediate context. In a dynamic context, a per-capita-income criterion demands choosing a discount rate to make the criterion applicable. And the choice of discount rate is certainly not obvious; rather, it must be an extraordinarily difficult value judgment. A very high discount rate leads to a population policy of no children at all, which is obviously unacceptable. A very low discount rate makes the present and near future unimportant, which is also unacceptable. No other discount rate has a firm logical foundation. For these reasons, among others, per-capita-income *by itself* seems quite inefficient and unacceptable as a guide to population policies.

CHAPTER 20

The Value of Averted Births
to People in the LDC's

INTRODUCTION

CHAPTER 18 argued that per-capita income is not the only reasonable welfare criterion in the economic analysis of population growth, and Chapter 19 demonstrated that a welfare function based only on per-capita income does not in fact seem to represent the desires of many people in LDC's (or in MDC's, for that matter). Yet per-capita income is *one* of the elements in most people's welfare functions—and the only element in a great many, despite its shortcomings. Therefore, to be practical and helpful to policy-makers, analysts must explore the implications of various alternatives using the per-capita-income criterion.

When policy-makers are considering policies to reduce the birth rate in LDC's, they want to know whether a given policy will increase or decrease the per-capita income of the present population. For example, when considering a family-planning clinic program, they wish to know whether the expenditure will be less or more than the benefit it brings. This implies that one must know how big the cost could be and still not reduce per capita income. This sum is what is meant by "the value of an averted birth." Any expenditure that size or smaller that will achieve an averted birth may therefore be considered to be worth doing.

This chapter considers methods of computing the appropriate value of an averted birth. First there is a critical discussion of the partial-analysis method introduced by Enke (1960a and b), which upon examination seems to be quite inadequate, though it had the great virtue of opening up the subject and leading to better methods. Then the chapter presents a more satisfactory general macroeconomic method of computing the value of an averted birth, in the specific context of the Coale-Hoover model of India.[1] Perhaps unexpectedly, this more general method, free of the flaws of partial-analysis methods, leads to *higher* estimates of the value of an averted birth—estimates of the order of $300, at either 5% and 15% rates of discount, at 1956 prices.

The description of the calculations in the second part of this chapter is quite technical and may be skipped by all those except specialists in this

---

[1] This chapter is an improved version of J. Simon (1969a).

area. But the criticism of the partial-analysis in the next section is not technical and should be of interest to most readers.

In light of the findings in Chapters 13 and 18 that LDC population growth's effects may be judged positive rather than negative—depending on the conditions, the time-horizon, and the value assumptions—the reader may wonder why the book contains chapters such as this one and the next which are intended to help societies reduce their birth rate. The answer is as follows: Extra effort is required in order to raise more children without reducing the material and psychological resources given to the children, even if the children will repay the investment later on. At some point one cannot or will not continue to increase the effort. At the point at which they are not willing to exert more effort and pay the price of having more children, individuals and nations must decide either to stop having children, or to produce more children but to accept a lower standard of living in the near future. If the society as a whole decides that it wishes to limit the number of children that are to be born, then social efforts are necessary in the form of birth-control campaigns. The economics and marketing analysis of such campaigns offered in this chapter and the next is intended to help societies that make a choice in the latter direction; it is not offered as an implicit suggestion that societies ought to limit their rates of population growth.

Several points must be emphasized in connection with the concept of the value of an averted birth: (1) The concept refers only to the per-capita-income criterion of the effect of an additional child. The calculated value of an averted birth therefore is *only one* of the elements that may be taken into account in deciding on population policies; such other aspects as the total size of the population also must be considered. (2) The concept takes into account only the value of the averted births to people who *now* make up the population. This is like the present partners in a firm discussing in terms of their *own* welfare whether to bring in additional partners; the welfare of the possible additional partners is not taken into account in this calculation. (3) The concept is calculated as the *present value* of a stream of future benefits. That is, the stream of future benefits must be adjusted for time preference to find their value in the present; this is the operation of discounting.

The value of an averted birth calculated in terms of the per-capita incomes of the present population may be applied in the evaluation of the various "incentives" schemes which pay people not to have children. The question is: *How much* can a country afford to give as incentive bonuses to those who will have themselves sterilized or who refrain from having children? But such schemes pose a special complication: Bonuses are only transfer payments and do not represent first-order[2] resource costs in the macro-economic accounting. Therefore, why not offer large or even astronomical incentives? What criterion may be used?

Enke (1961a and b) suggested that the ceiling upon bonuses should be fixed on principles of *distributional equity*. More specifically, he suggests that the bonuses should not be so high that a family would lose by the policy *even if that family does not choose to reduce the size of their family and therefor does not earn the bonus*. This ingenious principle really says that *no one* will be allowed to lose, in per-capita income terms. And if the incentive policy really raises per-capita income, then obviously it is possible that at least *some* incentives could be small enough so that the gains from the effect of the policy would outweigh the taxes upon the families that choose not to receive the bonuses. This is the same as asking how much a person could afford to pay out in a resource-cost program and still be better off because of the benefits to be produced by the program. Not only does this system offer a no-loss kind of equity to each person, but it offers him a gain in the choices to him: He can have a choice of doing what he would do otherwise, *or* he can choose the additional option of accepting the bonus and reducing his family size.[3]

The Standard Partial Analysis of the Value of an Averted Birth: An Inadequate Method

The following paragraph is the crux of Enke's argument[4]: "An economy is having too many births for the economic welfare of the *existing* population if the estimated *present value* of infants born this year is negative. This can arise for two reasons. First, the prospective additions to output occasioned by this year's infants may be less than their future subtractions from others' consumption. Second, discounting will reduce the present

---

[2] By "first-order cost" I mean to exclude the effects of redistribution on propensities to save, on foreign trade, etc. An interchange between Demeny (1961) and Enke (1961a) concludes with both men agreeing that such higher-order effects are not likely to affect the appropriate bonus price very much.

Some people have suggested that there might also be a cost if possible tax revenues are limited and if other public investment must therefore be curtailed because of bonuses. This does not seem to me to be an important cost. First, if bonuses are paid in money by the government, it should be easy to extract an equal amount of income in taxes. Second, under some bonus schemes, the actual payment of the bonuses would not occur for many years in the future, e.g., Ridker's bond scheme (1968) under which the bond is given to couples while in the child-bearing age groups but not redeemed until retirement.

[3] One might argue that by changing the nature of the society around him, the person does not have the same original choice, and hence may be disadvantaged. Perhaps. Economic reasoning cannot easily capture such effects.

[4] The general presentation and criticism applies also to writers who have used methods similar to Enke, including Leasure (1967), Repetto (1968), Zaidan (1967). Other criticism may be found in Leibenstein (1969).

value of this year's infants' future production more heavily than that of their future consumption. In many backward countries these two situations combine to give current births a negative present value in economic terms" (1960b).

In other words, Enke figures that the value of a prevented birth is the (negative) present value of an infant's expected stream of consumption and production. Enke then reasons that it makes sense for a society to pay people not to have children down to the point at which the net discounted value of a child is zero rather than negative.

The 15% discount rate used by Enke makes the entire future production of an Indian baby worth only $17 in the present (an undiscounted total of $840 starting 15 years after birth; 1966, p. 47). This makes the "released" *consumption* from the prevented birth the only matter of consequence. But this amount of consumption is primarily (though not completely, as we shall see) a *private* matter, because the child's consumption largely represents a decrease in other consumption by the *parents;* one can therefore think of the child as a durable good that the parents prefer to other consumption outlets. The decision to have the child can then be simply a matter of consumer sovereignty without the public interest being involved.[5]

Enke replies that "the prolific families will not stay on their own subsistence land holdings; some of their young men, desperate to earn, will compete as industrial workers and indirectly for the use of other factors of production. Thus, the improvidence of one set of parents will disadvantage more careful parents" (1962, p. 429). But by Enke's own reasoning, this public cost is no cost at all. If "not many heads of government look beyond 15 years" (1966, p. 47), and if the appropriate discount rate is 15%, then one should not include in the reckoning a public cost that is incurred 15 years after birth.

One might then say that Enke's 15% discount rate is too high, in which case such future public costs are more relevant. And indeed, a much lower discount rate seems more reasonable if one confronts oneself with this thought: income per head in India would probably be maximized in the next 15 years if *no* babies were born in that period,[6] but this would have a cataclysmic effect starting in perhaps 25 or 30 years as the ratio of labor force to dependents began to fall toward zero. Is there any one of us who would accept this as a desirable sequence of events—as would be consistent with a 15% discount rate?

But if the discount rate is taken to be low rather than as high as 15%, then Enke's argument fails on its *internal* logic, because (by his assump-

---

[5] Krueger and Sjaastad (1962) made this same criticism.

[6] This is a crude extrapolation of Coale and Hoover's findings (1958); see Chapter 10 of this book.

tion) marginal babies born now have a positive net value at a low discount rate.[7]

Another major flaw with Enke's method is that it assumes that the public at large pays out and takes in the expenditures and income of the incremental person. But as discussed in Chapter 14, much or all of these sums may not be external to the family, and if the family decides that the overall effect of the child is positive, the rest of society has no interest in the matter (aside from the net external costs, if any).

Leibenstein (1969) has raised other cogent objections to the method of partial analysis in terms of the distributional effects of an incentive scheme. These objections also pertain to the method suggested below, and therefore are given at the end of this chapter.

General Macro-Economic Analysis of the Value of an Averted Birth: Tedious but Necessary

If partial analysis will not work for the aforegoing reasons, we must begin from scratch. The question is: If the discount rate is taken to be 5% or 10% or even 15%, and if most released consumption does not redound to the public benefit, what can one say about the value of preventing births? The answer can only come from a consideration of the entire macro-economic system.[8] This is the complex and arduous task of considering

---

[7] Of course, if the productivity of additional workers is *very* low, then even with a zero discount rate additional babies may have a negative value. Hoover believes that such is indeed the case, stating. "I'd be surprised if in, say, India, additional workers would even pay their own subsistence to say nothing of yielding a *net*" (in correspondence). If this is so, then the simplest possible view suggests that there is economic benefit in lower fertility. But the recent literature seems to run against the idea of the marginal worker's output being so low as to be below subsistence (e.g., Kao *et al.*, 1972).

[8] Demeny (1965) recognized this point, and carried out a macro-economic investigation of the amount of *real resource* costs a society can afford to spend to reduce birth rates. In his study, therefore, the society has less resources to spend on other investments if it spends more on population-control policies. This is not very relevant to incentives programs, however, because the resources available for other investments are not lessened by the transfer payments. And it seems to me rather unlikely that any population-control campaign will spend enough in real resources to significantly affect other investments. Persuasion campaigns do require real resources for salaries, printing, radios, etc. But even expenditures many times any conceivable sum for persuasion would not use up enough resources to make the withdrawal from other investment of any importance. For example, the budget for the Nirodh program for India in 1970–71, was $1.2 million (A. Jain, 1973), which was the biggest promotional campaign of any sort ever carried out in India up until then. But this was only about a fifth of a cent per Indian. And much of the money costs of promotion are not real social costs. Incremental advertising is produced at very low marginal cost in newspapers and radio (which is why so much U.S. television and radio commercial time and street card signs are "contributed free" to Smokey-the-bear-type persuasion.) Other social benefits (e.g. editorial content of periodicals) are paid for through the advertising mechanism. Thus, one can safely disregard the effect of resource expenditures for birth reduction on investment when calculating the value of avoided births.

432

how much more would be saved and invested productively by society if there were fewer children, then calculating the effect of this saving through increases in the capital/labor ratio, and then allowing for the feedback through the circuit by way of the increases in average income. There is no short cut for this exercise in macro-economics; it is because Enke did not take this route, but rather tried to reason at the level of the individual and then simply aggregated individuals, that he ran into trouble.

A macro-economic model with and without the additional children is required. Here the Coale-Hoover model is used for the analysis, despite its drawbacks, for the following reasons: (1) Many readers are familiar with it. (2) When planners consider population policies, and especially bonus schemes, the focus of their interest is the short run and their discount rate is high. The Coale-Hoover model's strength is in the short run, and its shortcomings are in the long run. Hence it is not inappropriate for this context.

The last and most important reason for its use is that the focus of the Coale-Hoover model is upon *per-capita income* and not upon per-worker output, in contrast to the model presented in Chapter 13 which works with the latter concept. And when a welfare rather than an economic-development decision is involved—as seems to be the case in current fertility-reduction programs in LDC's—then per-capita income is the appropriate concept.

For the above reasons there would seem to be no inconsistency in using the Coale-Hoover model for value-of-birth-averted calculations in a welfare context, though (for the reasons cited in Chapters 7, 13 and especially in the Appendix to Chapter 10) the Coale-Hoover model is quite inappropriate for decisions concerning economic development. As is always the case, different models suit different purposes.

And a last point: The main aim of this chapter is to demonstrate a *method* of calculating the value of an averted birth, and the method can be used with *any* macroeconomic model; the Coale-Hoover model is used only for illustration.

Coale and Hoover calculated for India the differences in individual income per-adult-consumer-equivalent, for continued high fertility and for two lower fertility rates. The "high" rate will here be compared with only one "low" rate, the latter a linear decline of 50% in the birth rate over the period 1956–86.[9] These series of crude birth rates are shown in rows 1 and 2, respectively, in Table 20–1.

[9] For convenience and to minimize confusion I have considered the same years as did Coale and Hoover. We pretend we are now in the year 1956 and neglect all subsequent information. Updating would merely require adding, say, 20 years to each date written here.

Table 20–1
Calculations of 1986 Incomes under High and Low Fertility in India, As Seen in 1956

	1961	1966	1971	1976	1981	1986
1. Birth rate (per 1,000 population) "high," i.e. assuming unchanged fertility (Coale and Hoover, p. 38)	41.9	40.9	40.2	40.0	40.0	40.0
2. Birth rate (per 1,000 population) "low," i.e. assuming 50% decline from 1956 to 1981 (Coale and Hoover, p. 38)	38.0	33.8	30.2	26.8	23.0	23.4
3. Total population under high fertility (Coale and Hoover, p. 35)	424,000,000	473,000,000	532,000,000	601,000,000	682,000,000	775,000,000
4. Total population under low fertility (Coale and Hoover, p. 36)	420,000,000	458,000,000	496,000,000	531,000,000	562,000,000	589,000,000
5. Births under high fertility: row 1 × row 3	17,765,600	19,345,700	21,386,400	24,040,000	27,280,000	31,000,000
6. Births under low fertility: row 2 × row 4	15,960,000	15,480,400	14,979,200	14,230,800	12,926,000	13,782,600
7. Difference in number of births between high and low fertility: row 5 − row 6	1,805,600	3,865,300	6,407,200	9,809,200	14,354,000	17,217,400
8. 1956 national income = 108 billion rupees (1952–53 prices) (Coale and Hoover, p. 270)						
9. 1956 number of adult consumer equivalents = 317 million (Coale and Hoover, p. 239)						
10. Per-consumer income index, high fertility (Coale and Hoover, p. 272)	107	114	120	126	132	138
11. Per-consumer income index, low fertility (Coale and Hoover, p. 272)	108	117	126	143	165	195
12. Number of adult consumer equivalents, high fertility, in millions (Coale and Hoover, p. 239)	348	387	434	490	555	629
13. Number of adult consumer equivalents, low fertility, in millions (Coale and Hoover, p. 239)	346	379	415	449	480	507
14. Total income—high fertility (in billions of rupees): $\frac{12}{9} \times 10 \times 8$	127	150	177	210	250	295
15. Total income—low fertility (in billions of rupees): $\frac{13}{9} \times 11 \times 8$	127	151	178	219	270	337
16. Income per-consumer equivalent—high fertility: (14) ÷ (12) = (10 × 8) ÷ (9)	362	388	409	429	450	470
17. Income per-consumer equivalent—low fertility: (15) ÷ (13) = (11 × 8) ÷ (9)	368	399	429	487	562	664
18. Difference in income per-consumer equivalent under the two plans: (16) − (17)	6	11	20	58	112	194

Source: Coale and Hoover, 1958; for page references see above.

The following method will be used:[10] (1) Aggregate income is calculated for each period in the future, separately for the projections of the variants with and without the additional births. (2) The income-per-consumer-equivalent in each future period is computed for the two variants, and the difference between the two is calculated for each period. (3) The differences in each period are discounted to the present using an appropriate discount rate. (4) The present value for each consumer-equivalent *now alive* is multiplied by the present number of consumer-equivalents, to get the total benefit of the fertility reduction. (5) This total benefit is then divided by the difference in (discounted) numbers of births between two variants, to get the value per birth averted. (Using the discounted number of births is a device to get at the discounted value of bonuses to be paid in the future.) In symbolic terms,

$$
\text{Value of an averted birth} = \frac{\left[\left(\dfrac{Y_1}{C_1} - \dfrac{Y_1'}{C_1'}\right)r + \left(\dfrac{Y_2}{C_2} - \dfrac{Y_2'}{C_2'}\right)r^2 \cdots \left(\dfrac{Y_\infty}{C_\infty} - \dfrac{Y_\infty'}{C_\infty'}\right)r^\infty\right]C_0}{(B_1' - B_1)r + (B_2' - B_2)r^2 \ldots (B_\infty' - B_\infty)r^\infty}
$$

$$(20\text{--}1)$$

The terms without a prime stand for the low-fertility alternative, and terms with a prime stand for the high-fertility alternative; the indices indicate years.

Now more specifically for the Coale-Hoover material: Working on one year in each five, we apply the alternative birth rates (rows 1 and 2) to the total populations alive in those years under the alternative assumptions (rows 3 and 4) to get the total number of births in each year (rows 5 and 6).

Next we must have estimates of aggregate income for each year under the alternative assumptions. Coale and Hoover presented only estimates per consumer in index numbers relative to 1956 (rows 10 and 11), as well as estimates of consumer equivalents, and therefore we create aggregate income estimates[11] (rows 14 and 15) by multiplying the index numbers by the ratio of consumer equivalents in years t and 1956, and finally by 1956 national income. Also shown are the incomes per-consumer-equivalents in each year under the two plans (rows 16 and 17). But the key

[10] This method differs from that used in my 1969a paper. The earlier calculation erred by working with *total* income rather than income per-consumer-equivalent.

[11] Notice that *aggregate* income is higher for the low-fertility plan. This stems largely from the fact that entry into the labor force takes place a long time after birth, say, 15 years. During that period the "extra" people born do not produce though they do increase *public* consumption in the form of welfare expenditures (for the "extra" children) that might otherwise go into "productive" investment' (But in fact, parents work harder and produce more when faced with the increased needs of more children. Coale and Hoover make no allowance for this effect.)

amounts for our purposes are the *differences* in per-consumer income between the two fertility plans, which appear in row 18.

Given these numbers of births and these differences in aggregate incomes, the question is how to find the value of any *single* prevented birth. But single births cannot be related to single sets of costs and revenues because their effects ramify and are only felt through the entire growth system; furthermore, the effect of any one prevented birth depends upon how many other births are also prevented. It was by not recognizing these facts that Enke went wrong.

We must relate the differences in births under the two fertility alternatives to differences in aggregate incomes given by the two plans. This cannot be done straightforwardly, because the effects of prevented births are certainly lagged, and our raw data input must end at some point (after 30 years in Coale and Hoover). But at high rates of discount what happens after 30 years is of no import.

Next, the differences in per-consumer-equivalent incomes calculated for each year (i.e., the estimates for the every-fifth years in row 18 each multiplied by 5) are discounted to get the present value of the averted births to each present-day consumer equivalent. Let us try discount rates of 15% and 5%. The results are 95 rupees and 622 rupees at 15% and 5% discount rates, respectively. These sums are then multiplied by the present number of consumer equivalents (317 million as of 1956, as seen in row 9) to get the total present values at 15% and 5%. The results are 30 billion rupees and 197 billion rupees, respectively.

For the relevant number of births we can use the trick of reckoning a discounted number of births, because if a given bonus is paid to all future nonbirths at the time of the nonbirth, the bonus would be discounted; hence a discounted number of births multiplied by the money bonus is the relevant quantity. At 15% the relevant discounted difference in numbers of births between high and low fertility for every fifth year (row 7) is

$$\left(\frac{1}{1+.15}\right)^{4\frac{1}{2}} \times 1{,}805{,}600 + 0.22 \times 3{,}865{,}300 + 0.11 \times 6{,}407{,}200 + 0.05 \times$$

$9{,}809{,}200 + 0.02 \times 14{,}354{,}000 + 0.01 \times 17{,}217{,}400$. Multiplying each of the above by 5 estimates a five-year segment centered on the given year. But we need an adjustment for the years before the first bracket,

and hence we add $\dfrac{1}{1+.15} \times 313{,}600$ and $\left(\dfrac{1}{1+.15}\right)^{2} \times 600{,}000$ births,

giving a grand total at 15% of about 17 million discounted births.[12] At 5% the grand total is 97 million discounted births.

---

[12] Properly, each bracket should be centered at years 4.5, 9.5, etc., instead of 5, 10, etc., years and the first two years should be discounted for 6 months and 18 months instead of one and two years respectively. But the available tables are for full years. And since both of the series are pushed back half a year, the error should be tiny for our purposes here.

Now if we divide the difference in the present value of the income (Rs. 30 billion at 15%, and 197 billion rupees at 5%) by the number of discounted births (17 million and 97 million), we arrive at the finding that the society as a whole would benefit even if it paid up to 1,765 rupees ($294 at the 1956 rate or exchange) and Rs. 2030 ($338) for each birth avoided ($\pm 10\%$ for faulty arithmetic), at 15% and 5% respectively. That is, as of 1956, it was to the advantage of an average Indian to vote at time t for this plan of paying out 1,765 rupees or 2,030 rupees for each birth that would otherwise take place in future years. This assumes that the taxpayer himself does *not* reduce his own birth rate; if his own family size *does* follow the societal mean under the new plan, the taxpayer receives as much bonus money as he pays out in taxes, and has no short-run loss; on balance he is therefore much better off in the long run as the societal benefits begin to accrue and his income rises. And if a much lower payment induces the desired decrease in fertility—as I guess would happen— the benefits to all persons are positive and much higher.

The calculated sums are considerably *higher* than the sum Enke reckoned even though this method figures as a social benefit only a *small portion* of the consumption a child would account for, namely, the part that would be saved and invested and not otherwise consumed by the family, plus the part that the state would spend for education and other social overheads required for children. The reason why this figure grows so large, even though the income difference between the two fertility plans is small in early years, is the power of compounding which is properly built into the Coale-Hoover model but which is absent from Enke's reckoning. The validity of these results depends upon the validity of the macro-economic model, of course, and upon the discount rate.

The value of a prevented birth is a multi-purpose yardstick. First, it indicates how high an incentive bonus the state can afford to pay while still making *everyone* better off; it is therefore relevant to judgments of equity though even higher bonuses might increase average and aggregate income, because the bonus is only a transfer payment. Second, this estimate allows one to compare a given (small) investment in birth control with other welfare investments. Third, the value-of-a-prevented-birth estimate provides a yardstick against which to compare the profitability of various levels of promotion. The fourth and most important use of this estimate is for rhetorical purposes. The large bonus to avoid a birth that is equitable and economically rational (on the criterion of per-capita income) dramatizes the situation.

Qualifications and Limitations

Leibenstein (1969) has discussed some possible sources of error that apply to the method described here as well as to the method of Enke:

1. Various economic classes of people in the society might respond differently to the incentive offer, and perhaps in such a manner as would be detrimental to the economy. More specifically, Leibenstein speculates that the middle-class children yield a larger excess of production over consumption to the economy than do lower-class children, and also are more responsible for improvements in productivity. He speculates further that such middle-class families may be more responsive to an incentive offer than would lower-class families, in which case the incentive scheme might be counter-productive. If such a scheme induces middle-income couples but not lower-income couples to have fewer children, the economy might suffer from the loss of better-educated children who would be net contributors and savers rather than net burdens and dissavers. (It is apparently not true, however, that lower-income and rural people do not save, as was discussed in Chapter 11.) Leibenstein makes the same argument about lower-parity versus higher-parity children. Whether or not these concerns are justified, the value of an averted birth may be misstated if it does not take into account the specific categories of children whose births would be averted, and their specific effects on the economy.

But, *ceteris paribus*, the higher the income of a family, the less responsive it will be to a given sum of money on the assumption of diminishing marginal utility of money—as in fact is seen in the study of R. Simon and J. Simon (1975) described on pages 378–379—which argues against Leibenstein's point.

2. To the extent that higher-income groups already tend to have fewer children—as seems to be the case in LDC's[13]—an incentive plan would redistribute income toward the higher-income families and away from the lower-income families. It would be necessary to employ a progressive income tax to undo this effect if it were considred a social goal not to increase the higher-income group's share of total income.

3. As time goes on, new entrants to the labor force tend to have more education than their elders. If one assumes that (a) this education is not gained at the expense of other social investment, (b) consumption of the new entrants is less-than-proportional to their education, and (c) the entry of the new entrants does not lower the over-all employment average, then the new entrants will benefit the economy. Whether or not these assumptions are reasonable is quite open to question, of course.

These matters, together with the questions raised earlier about the assumptions used in the analysis given here, are strong reason that a policy-maker should use the concept of the value of an averted birth only with extreme caution.

---

[13] Note that this is a *total* relationship. When other variables are held constant for analytic purposes, this relationship may reverse, as discussed in Chapters 14–17. But the total relationship is what matters in this context.

SUMMARY

Chapter 13 found that the short-run negative effect of additional children upon per-worker output is negligible (and the long-run effect often positive). But some countries are more interested in the short-run welfare effect, as measured by per-capita income, than in the long-run effect as measured by per-worker output. In such cases an averted birth may have considerable value, and hence its calculation is a matter of interest. Such a calculation is the subject of this chapter.

An estimate of the value to a developing economy of preventing an incremental birth can be a useful yardstick for decisions about incentive bonuses, information-and-dispensation campaigns, and propaganda campaigns. Enke's method of estimation incorrectly reckons private costs as public costs and attributes all the avoided consumption of the avoided child to the social account, whereas most of it would be otherwise consumed by the child's family. And at the discount rate Enke uses (15%) the effect of an added child on the marginal productivity of other workers is irrelevant. On the other hand, a 15% discount is shown to be inconsistent with other governmental decisions, and a lower discount rate reduces the value of a prevented birth in Enke's scheme. Hence Enke's method is internally inconsistent.

A sounder method is to generate an estimate for the value of an avoided birth on the basis of a complete macro-economic system. Using Coale and Hoover's work on India, at a discount rate of 15%, the value was $294. At a discount rate of 5% the value was $338, *higher* than estimates reached by other inferior methods.

CHAPTER 21

A Cost-Benefit Decision Method
for LDC Fertility Reduction Programs[1]

INTRODUCTION

MANY LDC policy-makers have decided that a lower birth rate is desirable for their countries.[2] And there is reason to think that family-planning campaigns and incentive programs can reduce fertility in some countries at some times.

Decision-makers wish to choose wisely which programs to implement, and how much to spend on them. That is, the decision-makers want cost-benefit analyses of various kinds of family-planning programs. And in response to this need, researchers have begun to develop the data needed for such cost-benefit analyses.

The previous chapter showed how a country can compute the *benefits* of fertility reduction, on particular assumptions. But fertility-reduction campaigns also have *costs*, and both costs and benefits must be taken into account when deciding whether or not to undertake a fertility-reduction campaign. Just how to calculate the cost-benefit comparison is far from a settled question.

This chapter offers an operational framework for the cost-benefit analysis of proposed fertility-reduction programs. It has the disadvantage of depending on assumptions about some parameters whose real values one can only guess at. On the other hand, this framework has the virtue of specificity. It allows decision-makers in any country to insert the values they believe are appropriate for their country, and thereby to arrive at an operational answer with only simple calculations. It must be strongly emphasized, however, that this operational framework, like all others, has many implicit assumptions built into it which may, upon close inspection, turn out to be unacceptable to the reader. The main implicit assumptions of this chapter are: that per-capita income is the welfare criterion; that an additional adjustment must be made if one wishes to add a size-of-population argument to the welfare and decision functions; that the discount factor used in the estimate of the value of an averted birth is appropriate; and that the response and cost functions are reasonable.

---

[1] This chapter is a corrected version of J. Simon (1970c).

[2] One can only hope that the decision-makers really represent the sentiments of their constituencies without imposing their own educated-class values upon them.

The reader who is interested only in the mechanics of making a cost-benefit analysis of fertility may skip to page 448 near the end of the chapter where a list of the operational steps is given.

The alternatives among which any country may choose are as follows:

1. A country can make no special efforts to limit population, but instead it may depend upon natural economic, psychological, and sociological processes to achieve acceptable levels of fertility.

2. A country can emphasize those *programs within the economic development mix* that are thought to reduce fertility (e.g., urbanization and education).

3. A country can carry out programs of *information* about birth-control methods, along with free or inexpensive *dispensation* of birth-control materials and medical treatment.

4. A country can engage in *active propaganda* (i.e., advertising) to persuade people that they ought to have smaller families and ought to use birth-control methods toward that end. Sample persuasive methods include: (i) pointing out that infant mortality has declined, and hence fewer live births are necessary to have surviving sons; and (ii) arguing that the health of children and mother is likely to be better if there are fewer children.

5. A country can give *incentive payments* to families that avoid births.

6. A country may use stronger methods of *coercion*, such as compulsory sterilization.

Alternative 6 will not be considered here because I find such coercion morally unacceptable. Alternatives 4 and 5 will be considered together because they are similar economically (though not ethically). Alternative 2 will not be considered further, for two reasons: First, it is not a substitute for alternatives 3, 4, and 5, but to a considerable extent it provides the structure for them, and hence it is complementary to them. Second, alternative 2 is much more complex because of its interaction with other aspects of economic development; this alternative is simply beyond the scope of this chapter. Alternatives 2–5 are not intended to be mutually exclusive. In fact, alternatives 4 and 5 should never be undertaken without alternative 3, though the converse need not be so. Alternatives 3, 4, and 5 are discussed in much greater detail in Chapter 22.

THE ELEMENTS OF KNOWLEDGE NECESSARY FOR A COST-BENEFIT ANALYSIS OF A FERTILITY-REDUCTION PROGRAM

The elements of knowledge that must enter into a decision about which course of action to urge upon a nation are as follows: (1) the fertility *baseline*, the number of births one estimates would occur in each future

441

year under alternative 1, no family-planning action; (2) the *economic benefits* of the differences between the smaller natality streams and the larger; (3) the *response functions* for each type of campaign, i.e., the number of births that are expected to be averted for expenditures of various sizes on alternatives 3, 4, and 5. We shall proceed by estimating these response functions in two steps: (a) the costs of "standard" campaigns, and (b) the expected effects of standard campaigns in particular places. The first and second of these three elements are relatively easy to estimate compared to the third and will be discussed only briefly. Discussion of the response functions will be in somewhat more detail.

The Baseline: Estimates of Natality Assuming There Will Be No National Family-Planning Programs

Whether or not there is a *reasonable* basis for forecasts of birth rates in the absence of family-planning campaigns, *some* estimates must be made for use as inputs, by one means or another. As part of its 1963 projections, the United Nations estimated the sex-and-age-adjusted birth rates for future periods. And Kirk (1969) calculated the crude birth rates that are implicit in the Medium U.N. forecasts. But hopefully, the country making the cost-benefit analysis has available a set of reasonably accurate projections for itself.

The Economic Benefits of Averted Births

Next, one must estimate the economic *benefit* of fewer births, as discussed in Chapter 20. The benefit levels are assumed to be independent of mortality levels. It is assumed that $150 is paid per averted birth for India. The reason for choosing this figure rather than the estimate calculated in the previous chapter—which is roughly $300, or twice the estimate used here—is that I wish to keep this chapter within the mainstream of discussion of family-planning campaigns. And the $150 figure is of the order of estimates made by many other writers (all of whom used inadequate partial systems similar to that of Enke). Readers for whom my higher estimate is congenial may simply multiply all benefit calculations by a factor of two. Among poor countries there is probably some positive relationship between per-capita income and the value of an avoided birth, so one might transform this estimate for India into the more general estimate that each avoided birth is worth 150% or 300% of per-capita income in a country where fertility is high.

Furthermore, averting a birth is probably worth more to a country when population growth is higher; this assumption reflects the present international concern about population growth rates. When the gross reproduction rate is between 1.7 and 1.3, the value of an averted birth is assumed to be only half of what it is at higher gross reproduction rates and below a gross reproduction rate of 1.3 there is assumed to be no value to an averted birth. (A continuous function would be better, of course, but it would be a nuisance. And, of course, a country should substitute its own estimates for those used here.)

A formal statement of the proposed arbitrary benefit function, V_j, the value of an avoided birth in country j, is as follows:

$$V_j = 1.5Y_j, \text{ if } GRR_j \gtrless 1.7$$

$$= 0.75Y_j, \text{ if } 1.7 \gtrless GRR \gtrless 1.3$$

$$= 0, \text{ if } 1.3 \gtrless GRR \qquad (21\text{--}1)$$

where GRR_j is the gross reproduction rate and Y_j the per-capita income in country j in a given year.

The Response Function

The response function is by far the most difficult to estimate among the elements of knowledge needed for the analysis. It involves both the money costs of carrying out various sorts of programs, and the fertility results to be expected from those programs. It would be best to estimate response functions for many different expenditures on each of the sorts of alternatives, but this would be even more difficult. The discussion will, therefore, be limited to a single "level" of campaign for each alternative, estimating cost and effect for that level.

First, the costs of the "standard" programs. Earlier data on information-and-dispensation campaigns, in Taiwan and South Korea (Berelson, 1969, p. 22) and India and elsewhere (Ross, 1966b), suggested $5 as a fair estimate of the cost per contraceptive acceptor in the late 1960's. In Korea the cost per I.U.D. loop inserted averaged $4.91 in 1967 (Keeny et al., 1968, p. 2), and Potter's "medium" estimate is 0.64 births averted per insertion for women of all ages taken together, per (first segment of) I.U.D. (Potter, 1969, p. 430) which suggest a cost of $7 per birth averted. In 1969, Robinson estimated "between six and nine dollars U. S. to prevent a birth" in Taiwan and South Korea; a "program (that) relies heavily on conventional, [methods[. . . mean(s) . . . 12 to 18 dollars U. S." (W. Robinson, 1969, p. 14); these estimates are the most carefully made among those in the literature. For mobile unit programs in Tunisia, U.A.R., Honduras, South Korea, Turkey, and Pakistan, "cost per acceptor ranged from $16, the median for the Tunisian program, to $1, the median for . . . East Pakistan" (Munroe and Jones, 1971, p. 25) or perhaps from $56 to $2.50 per birth averted. The figure of $15 per averted birth in a country with a per-capita income of $100 is used. To get ahead of our story, this implies a cost of $45 per averted birth under alternatives 4 and 5, propaganda plus incentive. (This is *not* inconsistent with the relatively large incentive payments under bonus schemes; most of an incentive payment represents no real resource cost to the economy, but rather is just a transfer from one person to another, as Enke has taken such pains to point out; see page 430) I have assumed a constant marginal cost for each type of endeavor because the decision unit is the whole campaign, and any campaign would be large enough so that set-up costs would be a relatively small proportion of total costs.

We must also take account of the fact that although most of the countries which are likely to use birth-control programs fall into the lower-income bracket, there may be enough variation in incomes among these countries to affect the costs of the campaigns. There should be a higher cost of averted births in countries with higher per-capita income because of the lower cost of labor (measured in international exchange) in lower per-capita-income countries, despite the greater availability in higher income countries of the communications and transport infrastructure that is used in family-planning campaigns. For example, a girl high-school graduate can be hired for much less in Taiwan than in Europe or the United States. (But even with equal dedication to the job, the girl probably can make fewer calls per day in Taiwan than in Europe or the United States, owing to Taiwan's poorer roads and lack of home telephones with which to make appointments in advance.) Much the same should be true with mass media campaigns. Workers in radio stations are paid less (in exchange-rate terms) in poorer countries. (But fewer homes have radio receivers in the poorer countries.)

The cost of a given unit of sales work (e.g., a home call or a radio message per 1,000 population) are probably fairly proportional (in countries of different incomes) to the costs of a doctor visit, a flower delivery, a postage stamp for domestic mail, and a newspaper. And casual observation suggests to me that the resultant of the forces makes for lower costs of these things in poorer countries, the more so as the charge is for a pure unit of labor input rather than for labor in conjunction with equipment or for an achieved unit of output.

But what about the *slope* of the function? Should the cost function vary as much as per-capita income? Sets of consumer prices for various countries would yield good estimates, but such data are not easy to obtain. In their absence one may note that to a considerable extent the difference in per-capita income in various countries reflects differences in average skill. Hence the cost of a *given* unit of labor input should vary *less* than per-capita income. The individual country should replace these generalized estimates with its own specific estimate, however.

An averted birth must also, *ceteris paribus*, be more expensive to achieve with a persuasion-and-bonus campaign than with information-and-dispensation alone. The reason is that persuasion is really information *plus* persuasion. If the information by itself is sufficient, one need go no further.

444

This is why the first campaign for any new product is invariably just informational, to "skim the cream." And one obviously has less chance of making a sale to a random someone who has already said "no" once than to a random new prospect. This is why the average cost per prevented birth must be higher for persuasion-and-incentive campaigns than for pure information campaigns.

Next we must consider the response functions in different countries, because the cost of a program as measured by the cost per prevented birth clearly depends upon how easy it is to make a "sale." The basis for the estimates that follow is the assumption that people who would be susceptible to natality decline *without* a push will be even *more* susceptible *with* a push. More specifically, the likelihood of making a sale is here assumed to be a function of the likelihood that people will start practicing birth control even without outside influence. The reasoning is as follows: Where everyone has already accepted contraception, the birth rate is not falling, and there is no one left to inform or persuade, so a campaign makes no sales (i.e., it has a high cost). On the other hand, where no one has yet accepted or is now accepting contraception, it would seem likely that no or few people are in the about-to-accept stage. But where many people are presently becoming contraceptors, it would seem likely that there are also many people who are almost-contraceptors, and who constitute a ready market to be induced fairly easily to start controlling fertility. Whether or not this reasoning is sound requires empirical test, however, and the slope of the function is even more in question than its direction, of course. In sum, the following cost-of-an-averted-birth functions may be plausible:[3]

$$C_j^I = \$15 + 0.05(Y_j - \$100)\sqrt{\frac{0.25}{D_j}}$$

$$(21\text{--}2)$$

$$C_j^A = \$45 + 0.15(Y_j - \$100)\sqrt{\frac{0.25}{D_j}}$$

where C_j^I = cost per averted birth in country j with an information-and-dispensation campaign;

C_j^A = cost per averted birth in country j with propaganda-and-bonus campaigns;

Y_j = per-capita income in country j;

D_j = forecast rate of fertility decline per decade if no campaigns are put into effect.

---

[3] Any given country can surely make more precise estimates of the cost of averting births by utilizing the research strategies discussed in Chapter 22, together with field trials using the methods it proposes to use in the campaign itself.

The various cost relationships are summarized in Table 21–1, which shows the cost per averted birth for each combination of per-capita income and rate of independent fertility decline.

TABLE 21–1
ASSUMED COSTS OF AVOIDING A BIRTH UNDER VARIOUS INCOME AND
FERTILITY-DECLINE CONDITIONS

Cost for Information-and-Dispensation Campaigns, Alternative 3

| | % | Per-capita income | | | | |
		$100	$150	$200	$250	$300
		$	$	$	$	$
Expected rate of fertility	25	15.00	17.50	20.00	22.50	25.00
decline per decade if no	20	16.75	19.60	22.40	25.20	28.00
campaigns are undertaken	15	19.30	22.50	25.75	29.00	32.25
	10	23.70	27.60	31.60	35.50	39.50
	5	33.50	39.20	44.75	50.30	55.90

Cost for Propaganda-and-Incentive Campaigns, Alternative 4

| | % | Per-capita income | | | | |
		$100	$150	$200	$250	$300
		$	$	$	$	$
Expected rate of fertility	25	45.00	52.50	60.00	67.50	75.00
decline per decade if no	20	50.30	58.75	67.10	75.50	84.00
campaigns are undertaken	15	58.00	67.60	77.40	87.00	96.00
	10	71.10	83.00	94.80	106.50	118.50
	5	100.70	117.40	134.10	151.00	167.70

Table 21–1 may be read as follows: For a country with a per-capita income of $200, whose expected rate of fertility decline without a family-planning campaign is 20% per decade, each averted birth with an information-and-dispensation campaign may be expected to cost $22.40, and each additional averted birth achieved with a propaganda-and-incentive campaign may be expected to cost $67.10.

One more wrinkle: Planning for individual countries requires an estimate of the effects of the campaigns of the particular sizes that they will undertake. I assume that if an information-and-dispensation campaign *of the sort conducted in Taiwan* is conducted in country *j*, the result in any given year will be again as much as the decline predicted independently (i.e., the total decline will be double that predicted without the information-dispensation campaigns). The basis of this choice of constant is that the Taiwanese cities and villages subject to good information-dispensa-

446

tion campaigns since 1965 have had about double the fertility declines of cities and villages with poor campaigns (Freedman quoted by Berelson, 1969, p. 40). For information-and-dispensation campaigns less or more intensive than Taiwan's, I assume that the response will be proportional to the expenditure per capita on family planning in country j and in Taiwan.[4]

Concerning the effects of alternatives 4 and 5, propaganda plus incentive payments, there is practically no empirical information at all (a situation that desperately needs to be remedied with experiments). I have simply assumed that the effect will be once again as much as for a full information-and-dispensation campaign, which is the same amount as the predicted "independent" fertility decline. That is, full-scale implementation of alternatives 4 and 5, including advertising and incentive payments of perhaps 50% of per-capita income to be paid each year to each fertile woman who does not get pregnant, *plus* a full-scale information campaign, is assumed to *triple* the expected independent fertility decline.

The notion of tripling the "natural" fertility decline may seem doubtful to the reader. But Kirk (1969) has made an interesting reckoning that shows that in more recent decades fertility declines have proceeded faster, once they have begun, than in decades longer ago (see Table 21–2). This indicates that fertility declines can occur much faster than formerly thought.

Now the decision-makers of a particular country should be in a position to compare the cost of a given campaign against the benefits. The

TABLE 21–2

YEARS HISTORICALLY AND PRESENTLY REQUIRED FOR COUNTRIES TO REDUCE ANNUAL CRUDE BIRTH RATES FROM 35 TO 20, 1875 TO PRESENT

Period in which birth rate reached 35 or below	Number of countries	Number of years required to reach birth rate of 20		
		Mean	Median	Range
1875–99	9	48	50	40–55
1900–24	7	39	32	24–64
1925–49	5	31	28	25–37
1950–	6	23	23	11–32

SOURCE: Kirk, 1964, p. 85. Original data from Robert R. Kuczynski, *The Balance of Births and Deaths*; Vol. I, *Western and Northern Europe* (New York: Macmillan, 1928), and Vol. II, *Eastern and Southern Europe* (Washington, D.C.: Brookings Institution, 1931); and United Nations, *Demographic Yearbook, 1965* (New York, 1966).

[4] This probably underestimates the response for low-spending countries and over-estimates it for high-spending countries, because there is apparently no threshold of effectiveness, and in fact, just the opposite (i.e., response to sales promotion is a declining function of marginal expenditure [See J. Simon, 1965]).

former may be found with Equations 21–1 or Table 21–1, and the latter may be found with Equation 21–1. If the benefit of a birth averted with an information-and-dispensation campaign is greater than its cost, the campaign should be undertaken. If the benefit of a propaganda-and-incentive campaign is also higher than the cost, it should also be undertaken.

Three illustrative analyses are shown in Table 21–3 using various estimates and computations for India, Peru, and the Congo, based upon roughly adjusted U.N.–Kirk forecasts (converted into gross reproduction rates) and the above algorithms. These are the steps in the back-of-the-envelope reckoning that goes into a table like Table 21–3, for the alternative of propaganda-and-bonuses for the case of Peru for the year 1980.

(1) Estimate fertility in each future period in the absence of any special campaign. From the U.N. statistics this would be a GRR of 2.17 for Peru. (2) Estimate the value of an averted birth. For Peru's per capita income of about $133, and its GRR well above 1.7, Equation 21–1 gives a value of $200. (3) Estimate the cost-per averted birth from this campaign. This estimate is derived from [a] an estimate of the fertility decline expected per decade *without* special campaigns, the data for which are shown in the GRR forecasts in line 1.1 in Table 21–3, and which is .056 for Peru; [b] an estimate of per-capita income; [c] a combination of these elements as in Equation 21–2, which yields an estimate of $72 for Peru for 1980. (4) Compare the benefit in Step 2 against the cost in Step 3. The former is greater than the latter for propaganda-and-incentives for Peru in 1980, so the compaign should be undertaken.

In all three examples shown in Table 21–3 it apparently makes economic sense to use information-and-dispensation campaigns. But it apparently pays to use propaganda-and-bonus campaigns only in India and Peru, and not in the Congo. We also see that the periods during which such campaigns would be used would be relatively short, perhaps 10 years for propaganda-and-bonus and 20 years for information-and-dispensation, for India and Peru. If the campaigns are as effective as I have assumed, they will work themselves out of a job fairly quickly in those places where there is already some positive climate for fertility decline.

It is important to emphasize again how speculative are the assumptions upon which Table 21–3 is built. Of course, any of the assumptions *may* be quite incorrect. However, if anyone has any better assumptions, let him state them and trace out their consequences.

Though the basic geographic decision unit for this analysis has been the country, this does not imply that policy should be the same for all parts of large countries. In fact, an exactly similar analysis should be applied to the various subdivisions of big countries (e.g., urban versus rural), and

TABLE 21–3

GROSS REPRODUCTION RATES, COSTS, AND BENEFITS FORECAST UNDER
DIFFERENT FAMILY-PLANNING CAMPAIGN POLICIES

India

	Year				
	1963	1970	1980	1990	2000
Alternative					
1. No action					
1.1. G.R.R. forecast	2.8	2.6	2.35	2.0	1.7
3. Information and dispensation					
3.1. G.R.R. forecast	2.8	2.6	2.1	1.4	0.8
3.2. Incremental value per birth avoided	N.A.	N.A.	$150	$100	0
3.3. Cost per birth avoided	N.A.	N.A.	$25	$20	—
4. Propaganda and bonuses					
4.1. G.R.R. forecast	2.8	2.6	1.85	0.8	N.A.
4.2. Incremental value per birth avoided	N.A.	N.A.	$150	$0	—
4.3. Cost per birth avoided	N.A.	N.A.	$72	$72	—

Peru

	1963	1970	1980	1990	2000
Alternative					
1. No action					
1.1. G.R.R. forecast	2.4	2.3	2.17	1.97	1.7
3. Information and dispensation					
3.1. G.R.R. forecast	2.4	2.3	2.04	1.64	1.10
3.2. Incremental value per birth avoided	N.A.	N.A.	$200	$200	$75
3.3. Cost per birth avoided	N.A.	N.A.	$24	$24	$24
4. Propaganda and bonuses					
4.1. G.R.R. forecast	2.4	2.3	1.91	1.31	N.A.
4.2. Incremental value per birth avoided	N.A.	N.A.	$200	$150	—
4.3. Cost per birth avoided	N.A.	N.A.	$72	$72	—

Congo

	1963	1970	1980	1990	2000
Alternative					
1. No action					
1.1. G.R.R. forecast	2.8	2.75	2.7	2.6	2.5
3. Information and dispensation					
3.1. G.R.R. forecast	2.8	2.75	2.65	2.45	3.25
3.2. Incremental value per birth avoided	N.A.	N.A.	$100	$100	$100
3.3. Cost per birth avoided	N.A.	N.A.	$33	$33	$33
4. Propaganda and bonuses					
4.1. G.R.R. forecast	2.8	2.75	2.60	2.30	2.0
4.2. Incremental value per birth avoided	N.A.	N.A.	$100	$100	$100
4.3. Cost per birth avoided	N.A.	N.A.	$99	$99	$99

NOTE: N.A. = Not applicable.

the conclusions that will emerge will be similar: in those areas where the potential for decline is greatest (e.g., usually the cities) it will make sense to use the more powerful and more expensive campaigns. This is in accord with standard marketing thinking that heavier promotion effort should be applied where the response function is higher, because of the phenomenon of diminishing returns in promotion (Simon, 1965).

SUMMARY

This chapter offers an explicit and simple framework for cost-benefit analysis of fertility-control programs, as summarized in four operational steps listed above and illustrated in Table 21–3 for India, Peru and Congo. A cost-benefit analysis for any country requires strong assumptions for which data are lacking, and in lieu of which the chapter offers only some crude speculation. The key assumption is that the extent to which any sort of fertility-reduction campaign will succeed is a function of the speed with which the birth rate is already falling. This assumption has fair weight of evidence behind it as a general proposition. But a better basis for estimation can be developed for an individual country, using methods discussed in Chapter 22. The analysis assumes that averted children represent no loss of noneconomic value to their potential selves or to their potential parents, and I hope that any country will systematically search its collective soul before making a fertility-control decision on the basis of this assumption and cost-benefit analysis.

CHAPTER 22

Birth-Control
Market-Segmentation Strategy, or
How to Increase
Contraceptive Usage

INTRODUCTION[1]

THE SOCIAL planner who wishes to induce more people to use birth-prevention methods of any kind, and the private marketer who wishes to persuade people to buy more of his particular product and brand, both face this general problem: Which variables should one manipulate, in which ways, in the particular situation one is working in, in order to increase contraception? Or to put it differently, the social or private marketer wants to know the proper amounts to use of each of the marketing variables—the quantity and the type of mass-media advertising, the appropriate distribution system, the quantity of personal selling, the price, and so forth. The aim of this chapter, therefore, is to discuss which marketing strategies should be employed to most effectively market birth control in various situations.

A secondary aim is to reconcile the conflict between the advocates of "Only economic development will help" and those of "Campaigns are enough," and between the advocates of the "Mass media can do anything" and those of the "Mass media can do nothing", by showing that neither have all the truth on their side, but that all have partial answers. Too-broad generalizations about what marketing can and cannot do in birth-control campaigns have caused great confusion. The root of the trouble has been people applying their experience with *one* segment to all segments of the market.

The only sure knowledge that marketing offers is that the best marketing strategy must depend upon the place, the time, and especially upon the

This chapter is a revised version of Simon (1974b).

[1] Nothing in this chapter should be construed to mean that the writer believes there are too many births in the United States. And with respect to other countries, I believe that their policies are their business, and it is not my place to urge family-size goals upon others. My hope is that people should be able to exert free choice to the maximum possible and should have the family sizes that they want, in light of the fullest information. As discussed in Chapter 18, planning the diffusion of birth-control knowledge is desirable in itself because it enhances people's ability to achieve their life aims, even if there is no economic reason for a national fertility-control policy. Sound marketing can help people achieve such knowledge and enhanced choice.

sort of people to whom one is trying to market. That is, the optimum strategy is likely to be different for different countries, for different groups within the countries, and at different points in history. This is the concept of market segmentation, which is central in commercial marketing.

It is surprising that there have been no formal attempts to create a segmentation plan for birth-prevention campaigns, or to determine the implications. Schramm (1971) makes some informal references to different "stages of readiness," but no more. And Roberto (1972) has published a segmentation scheme, but it is based only on parity and age of mother.

The scheme presented here offers specific suggestions about the kinds of marketing techniques and advertising themes that will be economically efficient in particular situations. For example, it suggests that in Jamaica, where folk methods of contraception are already widely accepted, the emphasis should be on increasing the availability of modern contraceptive methods and removing the various barriers to their acceptance. In Mexico and urban Brazil, the scheme suggests that the need is for communication of the facts about the decline in infant mortality and the implications for the family of the economic development that is now taking place. In rural Afghanistan and Dahomey only minimal distribution and information are presently warranted, given the high level of infant mortality and the state of economic development.

The ideas in this chapter are summarized in Table 22–6 on p. 471 in the conclusion.

An Idealized Segmentation Scheme

Let us consider an idealized segmentation scheme. This is the way that a marketer, if he were able, would choose to separate his market into segments to which specific marketing campaigns could be addressed. An idealized segmentation cannot be achieved in practice, but such a scheme can be a helpful guide in the development of a workable operating segmentation plan.

One idealized segmentation plan is shown in Figure 22–1. The distinctions, in order of fineness, are:

1. Whether people now regulate fertility. Few couples regulate their fertility perfectly throughout their lives. And few couples conduct their sex lives with no thought at all to the possibility of conception. But certainly couples do differ importantly on this dimension; hence the distinction between those who regulate and those who do not regulate fertility.

2. Among those who regulate fertility, some use artificial, "modern" methods (the *Modern Methods* segment), and some use "folk" methods (the *Folk Method* segment).[2]

[2] *Modern methods* include the oral, the I.U.D., the injectable, the diaphragm, all chemical spermicides, and the condom; folk methods include withdrawal, rhythm, and abstinence.

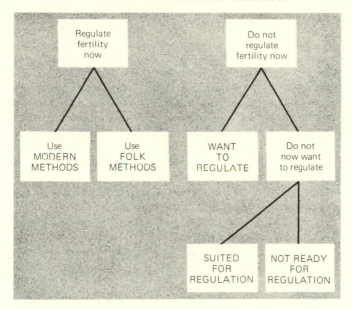

FIGURE 22–1   IDEALIZED OPERATIONAL SCHEME OF
CONTRACEPTIVE MARKET SEGMENTATION

3. Among those who do not regulate fertility, some would like to (the *Want to Regulate* segment), and others do not wish to.

4. Among those who do not wish to regulate fertility, the minds of some may change readily if presented with additional information (the *Suited for Regulation* segment), whereas others are not likely to change their minds no matter what new information is given them (the *Not Ready for Regulation* segment).

Now let us consider which marketing stimuli are most likely to alter the contraceptive practice of people in each one of these market segments.

THE MODERN METHODS SEGMENT

The *Modern Methods* segment is of little interest to social planners because there is not much that the planner can do for them except perhaps help develop better contraceptives. But this segment is of central interest to commercial marketers, because it represents their prime market.

The size of this segment varies greatly from country to country and from time to time, of course. In Sweden in 1972 most adults are part of this segment; in Dahomey, few are.

How should the marketer sell his product to a segment of the market that already uses modern, artificial contraceptive devices? In many places the marketing of contraceptives is (or has been until recently) illegal, for

453

example, in Turkey, in the Arab countries, and in the state of Connecticut. In such circumstances, marketing is a matter of smuggling merchandise across the border. Retail marketing, in turn, is a compound of black-market selling and maintaining discrete behavior. In the United States in the past, condoms generally were marked "Sold only for the prevention of disease," and on the first day at the job, the druggist's assistant learned how to hand the pack of three to the customer in a turned-down palm.

Privacy can apparently still be important in contraceptive marketing in the 1970's in the U.S. Population Planning Associates has sold many millions of condoms by mail in its first years of business largely[3] on the appeal of "privacy—no need to go into a drugstore."

In such an atmosphere of illegality the contraceptive industry is a back-alley trade,[4] the seller being essentially passive.

But people who aready use modern contraceptive devices seem to do rather a good job as consumers, even without aggressive marketing to them. They seek out information from friends, relatives, doctors, and pharmacists about what methods exist and where to get them. An indication of the effectiveness of this market network is the speed with which the oral contraceptive caught on in the United States. In the 5 years from 1960 to 1965, usage went from 0% to 27% of contracepting couples (Whelpton et al., 1966, p. 284; Bogue, 1969, p.722). And the prevalence of illegal abortion in the United States in previous years is an indication that people can get market information even against formidable obstacles.

For the producer, marketing under such conditions seems to be a matter of (1) making a good product; (2) getting wide distribution; (3) in the case of condoms, pricing well, especially giving appropriate discounts to druggists; and (4) in the case of orals and I.U.D.'s, merchandising to doctors, especially "detailing" by drug salesmen.

Once contraception is accepted legally and socially, contraceptive manufacturers can employ the marketing strategies used in other industries, as is now the case in Japan, Sweden, and the United States. They can argue that a new product is more reliable or more convenient than another product, and they can compete with minor product improvements such as color and packaging. The most appropriate strategies for pricing and promotion will differ depending on the type of contraceptive product, the newness of the product, the market share of the brand, and other characteristics of the product and brand.[5]

---

[3] Another important appeal which accounts for an important part of their sales is the offer of condoms that are not sold in drugstores—such as colored condoms and shaped condoms.

[4] It is not surprising that old-line condom firms are taken aback—and in truth, probably feel a sly amusement—as in the 1970's foundations and government agencies turn to them as a "public-service industry," and ask for their aid in social welfare projects.

[5] A general analytic scheme for promoting strategy is given in Simon, 1971, Chapter 14.

THE FOLK METHODS AND WANT TO REGULATE SEGMENTS

The major decline in fertility in Western Europe in the last two centuries was probably accomplished by abstinence (delayed marriage as well as abstinence within marriage) and by coitus interruptus. These effective methods of contraception are still used today by many people all over the world. For example, 18% of married women in Turkey in 1968 were practicing contraception by withdrawal, whereas less than 10% were using any of the modern methods (Özbay and Shorter, 1970).[6]

People in the *Want To Regulate* segment—those who clearly wish to regulate their fertility but do not choose to practice withdrawal or rhythm or occasional abstinence—have much the same consumer characteristics as do those who practice these nonmodern methods (the *Folk Methods* segment); therefore, these 2 segments will be considered together.

Commercial vendors would like to sell contraceptives to these segments of the market. For both economic and historic reasons, however, non-profit organizations do most of the work in getting these 2 segments of people to accept modern methods of contraception. We shall therefore take the point of view of the noncommercial organizations.

As common sense suggests, the key to marketing success with these 2 segments lies in making contraceptives available. This includes physical availability (geographic distribution), economic availability (price), social availability (acceptability and legality), and knowledge of the availability of contraceptives. All 4 aspects of availability must be present at the same time. But it is worthwhile to separate them in the discussion that follows.

Before beginning that discussion, however, the following two examples will show how rapidly contraceptive use can be increased by increasing availability in a situation where there is high interest but low use. In Taiwan, there was a rapid increase in the use of contraceptives from 1965 to 1970, as can be seen in Table 22–1. Apparently as a result, although

TABLE 22–1
PROPORTIONS OF WOMEN PRACTICING BIRTH CONTROL IN TAIWAN

Wife's age	1965	1967	1970	1973
22–24	3	7	13	30
25–29	17	23	30	48
30–34	31	41	55	68
35–39	36	50	63	69

SOURCE: Freedman *et al.*, 1972; 1974, p. 280.

[6] Douching was used by 12% but not with spermicides and probably not for contraceptive purposes.

455

fertility in Taiwan was already falling by 2.3% per year from 1954 to 1963, it fell by more than 5% from 1963 (when the public contraceptive distribution program began) until 1972 (Keeny and Cernada, 1970). In Korea, the proportion of married women practicing contraception (including sterilization) rose from 21% in 1964 to 42% in 1970 (Ross and Smith, 1969; Nortman, 1971; Freedman *et al.*, 1974) during the period of an aggressive government distribution effort. Although some of the contraceptors in these 2 countries were using folk methods, and although much of this increase in contraceptive practice might have occurred without a rapid increase in availability, there is considerable evidence in Korea and in Taiwan that the increased availability of I.U.D.'s and other modern contraceptives through family planning programs helped speed the increase in fertility regulation.[7]

Now let us consider separately the various aspects of availability.

Physical Availability

An increase in contraceptive usage in segments *Folk Methods* and *Want To Regulate* requires that there be enough places where contraceptives can be obtained. Sufficient physical distribution is a necessary element of contraceptive marketing just as with all other marketing. And indeed, physical distribution has been the main thrust of most non-profit birth-control campaigns from the time that Margaret Sanger began to open clinics in New York until the "walking doctors" now reaching every small village in China. Schramm noted: "A program can accomplish very little without adequate clinical services. An unplanned experiment in Seoul, Korea, demonstrated this in 1968. Officials decided to reduce the number of doctors authorized to insert I.U.D.'s from 100 (about 60 of whom were active) to 16, who were working in nine health centers scattered over the city. Within two months the number of new acceptors had fallen to one-fourth of the previous average. When the city brought in six mobile vans to serve as clinics, the performance level rose again" (Schramm, 1971, p. 31). Because there is resistance (as perhaps there should be) in many countries to making oral contraceptives available without a prescription by a doctor, the shortage of doctors limits the physical availability of orals. Likewise the I.U.D. and injectable require a medical network for distribution.

Establishing new outlets requires resources. And keeping outlets open to dispense nothing but contraceptives is very expensive, even for a relatively rich country. An obvious alternative is the vast number of commer-

---

[7] Although it has not yet been shown quantitatively that Koreans and Taiwanese were largely in the *Folk Methods* and *Want to Regulate* segments, there is some reason to presume so, as we shall see later.

cial outlets that already exist in all countries—that is, private shops. In a private-enterprise country in which most of the people are in the *Modern Methods* segment, or even distributed among the segments *Modern Methods, Folk Methods,* and *Want To Regulate,* and where there are no legal barriers, the commercial marketing system is likely to provide a reasonably large number of outlets for condoms. (In such countries the large proportion of the population in urban areas is an important element of infrastructure for the development of an effective private distribution system.)

But in countries with a smaller proportion of people in the segment *Modern Methods,* and also smaller proportions in the segments *Folk Methods* and *Want To Regulate,* the commercial distribution system may not develop quickly enough to service people in the segments *Folk Methods* and *Want To Regulate.* This apparently was the case in Taiwan and Korea, and it would seem to account for the great success of the national programs that increased the physical distribution of contraceptives in those countries.

The pioneer venture in public-sector stimulation of private-sector distribution activity was the Nirodh Marketing Program in India. In the Nirodh scheme, 6 major firms with wide distribution to the smallest villages (Brook Bond Tea, Lipton Tea, Hindustan Lever, India Tobacco, Union Carbide, and Tata Oil Mills) each undertook to stock all their outlets in one area of the country (170,000 in total) with condoms and to charge the retailers a wholesale price so low that they could charge a low retail price ($0.02 for 3) and still make a small profit. The Nirodh scheme has had enough success (see Jain, 1973) to continue, despite the fact that most Indians probably are not yet in the segments *Folk Methods* and *Want To Regulate.* This suggests that such a scheme might be even more successful in a country where more people are in those segments.

Many had hoped that the Nirodh scheme would serve as a model for all other developing countries. Conditions vary, however, between and within countries. In sparsely populated rural Iran, for example, it is much harder to find private companies with distribution networks that reach down to the smallest village.[8] Apparently there are few such networks in Iran—soft drinks, aspirin, cigarettes, matches, kerosene, tea, sugar, and perhaps soap. Cigarettes are a government monopoly, which at first thought would seem to make them particularly accessible if the government wants to distribute condoms—as it does. But the administrators of the monopoly in each area are policital appointees and do not stand to gain personally from an increase in the total volume of business they do. Hence, it would take a considerable amount of bureaucratic ingenuity,

[8] I am grateful to Robert Gillespie for information on Iran.

457

energy, and muscle, which is not yet forthcoming. The sale of kerosene is apparently physically incompatible with the sale of condoms, and the other sorts of firms are reluctant "to associate their company names with condoms" (Little, 1972).

In such a stalemate one's imagination takes flight. Why not simply place one condom in every tenth pack of cigarettes, depending on smokers to get them into the hands of those who want them? At one stroke this would bypass all local distribution problems. But of course such a scheme will not be implemented tomorrow, or even next week.

To repeat, adequate physical distribution is crucial in getting people in segments *Folk Methods* and *Want To Regulate* to implement their desire to regulate fertility with modern methods.

Economic Availability

The price of goods can have a large—or a very small—effect on the quantity bought. We do not know much about the importance of the price of contraceptives to people in the segments *Folk Methods* and *Want To Regulate*. There is reason to think that economic availability is not a barrier to use for people who are "further" from use, that is, in the segment *Not Ready for Regulation,* because offering free contraceptives to people in that segment does not lead to a sudden increase in acceptance by them. On the other hand, there is at least anecdotal evidence that even in MDC's cost can matter. Rainwater (1960, p. 37) quotes this from a lower-class U.S. family: "What does your husband think about contraception?" "He thinks they cost too much and would rather spend it on beer." And in Taiwan, a no-charge I.U.D. offer pulled many more acceptors than a half-price offer, as Table 22–2 shows. (The low-price offer "borrows" some acceptors from future periods, but the over-all effect is almost surely

TABLE 22–2

ACCEPTORS OF INTRAUTERINE DEVICES AND PROGRAM COST
PER ACCEPTOR, BY TYPE OF SOLICITATION AND COST TO
ACCEPTOR, IN TAIWAN, 1964

Type of solicitation	% of acceptors		Program cost per acceptor (in U.S. dollars)	
	No charge	Half price*	No charge	Half price*
Direct mail	2.3	1.2	.75	2.02
Home visits	6.8	4.3	.75	2.00
Meetings	2.4	.8	1.70	4.00

SOURCE: Schramm, 1971, p. 37.
  *U.S. $.75.

an increase in acceptors. And the market is not "spoiled" by the price reductions, because acceptance returns to normal levels after a few months.)

Although we do not have solid knowledge of how much contraceptive practice would increase in the segments *Folk Methods* and *Want To Regulate* if contraceptives were lower-priced, or even completely free, the sketchy evidence suggests that cost can be an import element. Those readers for whom the cost of contraceptives is insignificant should remember that this cost might represent a significant expense relative to per capita income in LDC's.[9]

The issue of economic availability involves more than the customer's response to various retail price structures. If contraceptives are to be given away free, there is no profit margin for a retailer and no incentive for him to carry the product in his store. It will not work to subsidize him just to carry the product, either, because he will accept the merchandise in order to get the subsidy and then not bother to sell the merchandise. The most that can be done is to give the product free to the retailer and perhaps fix the price at which he can sell it. But from the retailer's point of view even the profit-maximizing retail price may not be profitable enough to make the product line desirable to him. And the retailer's profit-maximizing price is almost surely too high from other social points of view.

Cost may be a barrier to contraceptive practice, but we do not know how great a barrier it is, for those in segments *Folk Methods* and *Want To Regulate*.

Social Availability

The sexual behavior of those in the segments *Folk Methods* and *Want To Regulate* can be strongly affected by social beliefs and attitudes about sexual morality. For example, it may be thought immoral not to have children, or to have too many children; contraception may be regarded as a sin; use of the condom may be taboo because of its association with prostitution. Such beliefs and attitudes act as a barrier to contraceptive use, and removing such barriers is an important part of making contraceptives available to these two segments.

But removing social barriers is difficult and complex. For example, anecdotal evidence suggests that condoms are looked down upon in Iranian villages because of their association with prostitution (Little, 1972, p. 14); hence oral contraceptives are accepted more freely than are

---

[9] Monetary incentives given to couples not to have children are increases in the cost of children, not changes in the price of contraception, and therefore are not considered here.

condoms in these villages. Contraceptive users will buy condoms in larger communities if nearby, and otherwise do without.

Another social barrier arises from the lack of privacy in multi-family or overcrowded living quarters. Contraceptives that need no installation or disposal eliminate this deterrent to use if it is important.

Social barriers are not limited to the segments *Folk Methods* and *Want To Regulate*, however. Even in England and the United States, the condom is less publicly acceptable as a product than is, say, soap. Condom manufacturers in England say that, of all the things their government could do to help increase condom sales, a campaign to make condoms "respectable" would do most.

What can be done to increase social availability? Time will probably alter unfavorable attitudes toward contraception as infant mortality declines and urbanization and education spread. But governments do not wish to wait. Products with special characteristics—such as orals, I.U.D.'s, and injectables—can circumvent some social barriers, which is a good reason for further research on prostaglandins and other new contraceptives. It seems likely that adept advertising and propaganda can achieve greater social availability for contraceptive practice in the segments *Folk Methods* and *Want To Regulate*, but there does not seem to be any solid empirical evidence on the matter.

In brief, lowering social barriers to contraceptives can help increase practice in the segments *Folk Methods* and *Want To Regulate*, but not much is known scientifically about how this can be done.

Information Availability

Making information about contraception available goes hand in hand with the other aspects of availability. Increasing distribution and informing people about availability go together, as do reducing cost and telling people about the cost reduction.

A contraceptive marketing campaign to the segments *Folk Methods* and *Want To Regulate* can successfully use relatively short messages in the mass media regarding availability since no arguments for contraception motivation need be communicated. The messages need to communicate primarily the availability and acceptability of contraception.

Information dissemination also can allay some health fears. For one example, the true nature and magnitude of the health dangers from orals and I.U.D.'s can be made clear. For another example, a rumor has arisen, apparently independently, in many countries where I.U.D.'s recently have been introduced, that the vagina of a woman with an I.U.D. can constrict and prevent the exit of her partner's penis. Such fears can be reduced (although not eliminated) by accurate information in the mass media. On the other hand, it may be appropriate to remind people of the dangers of venereal disease and the costs of an unwanted pregnancy in an information campaign to the segments *Folk Methods* and *Want To Regulate*.

At this stage in communication research, it is no longer necessary to prove that people learn from mass media. Many studies of the KAP or cross-media-comparison types testify that they learn about family planning as readily as about other subject matter. To take only one example, when people in Sudong Gu, in Seoul, Korea, were asked where they had learned about family planning, 47% mentioned movies; 8%, magazines; 7%, newspapers; 6%, leaflets; and 3% television. They were permitted to name more than one source if they so wished; 46% of them said that they learned something about it from their neighbors; 22%, from home visits by family planning workers; 18%, from health stations or family planning clinics. These results are typical of other studies of family planning knowledge: where available, the mass media are responsible for an important share of the information that comes to people. (Schramm, 1971, p. 32).

In summary, to increase the use of contraceptives among the segments *Folk Methods* and *Want To Regulate*, there must be increases in the physical, economic, and social availability of contraceptives. These three kinds of availability go hand in hand with each other, as they do with increasing the availability of sound information about contraceptives. New products can help in surmounting social barriers, as may persuasion, but we know little about the latter. Programs that increase availability can have a considerable impact on reducing the gap between the desire to regulate fertility and the realization of that desire. This can be seen in Table 22–3 where the proportion of people wanting no more children but not using contraceptives has gone down sharply over the period of the Taiwan national program.[10]

TABLE 22–3

PROPORTIONS OF TAIWANESE COUPLES WHO SAY THEY WANT NO MORE CHILDREN BUT ARE NOT USING CONTRACEPTION

Age of wife	1965	1967	1970	1973
22–24	8.4	8.0	6.1	14*
25–29	24.2	18.6	17.2	20
30–34	42.0	32.8	25.8	20
35–39	53.7	37.3	30.1	24

SOURCE: Freedman *et al.*, 1972, p. 158; 1974, p. 287.
*Based on ages 20–24.

[10] An example (Chow, 1966) of the combined impact of information, distribution, and economic availability was a reduced-priced ($.50 per cycle) mail-order offer of oral pills in a Taiwan newspaper with a circulation of 140,000: A 2-inch advertisement produced 626 sales. Any mail-order businessman knows that such a response is extraordinary.

461

THE SUITED FOR REGULATION SEGMENT

There is a continuum between the two segments *Suited for Regulation* and *Not Ready for Regulation* that ranges from those who will easily change their minds about desired family size and contraceptive practice if presented with additional information, to those who are unlikely to change their minds no matter what new information is given them. Despite the continuity between these 2 segments, however, for convenience only the 2 extremes of the continuum will be discussed.

Although social attitudes and religious beliefs affect attitudes toward family planning, the available evidence suggests to me that such objective factors as child mortality, income, educational opportunities, and place of residence and associated childrearing costs and benefits are the important, fundamental determinants of desired family size and whether people want to regulate their fertility. According to this view, the only people who do not now wish to regulate fertility, but whose minds might change fairly readily, are people whose objective conditions are appropriate for low fertility but who have not yet realized that these are, in fact, the objective conditions of their lives. Consider infant mortality, for example. Demographers and statisticians find it difficult to know what the "true" infant mortality rates are among various groups in a country, even with considerable scientific apparatus. It seems plausible, therefore, that laymen should require a considerable length of time to recognize changes in infant mortality rates by means of casual observation. Much the same is probably true of educational and occupational opportunities; a subsistence farmer is not likely to learn quickly of changes in the opportunity structure for his children. But advertising may be able to convey these facts effectively and thereby reduce desired family size and increase readiness to contracept.

Mexico may well be a country with a large proportion of its urban—and perhaps rural—population in the segment *Suited for Regulation*. If this is so, the appropriate marketing stretegy for this segment is to point out the relevant objective facts of their situation, telling people about the decline in infant mortality, the growing necessity of a higher education for occupations newly opened up and the costs of such an education, the costs of raising children in the cities, into which many villagers are moving, and so on. It also is relevant to point out the relationship between family size and the health of children in poor communities.

In this kind of promotion, sound advertising is crucial. Some governments and advertising men have thought that songs, slogans, and "image" gimmicks—techniques of the sort used to sell soap or soft drinks—would be appropriate. But such a strategy will surely fail in this kind of situation. And social scientists who have tried to invent the appropriate techniques from scratch have also made some mistakes—for example, dismissing the mass media, assuming that "the total amount of information to be communicated should be reduced to the smallest amount possible," assuming that there is a "communications threshold," and worst of all, paying no attention to the cost of obtaining a response, or testing various advertising copy (see Bogue, 1963; J. Simon, 1968a).

Advertising to the segment *Suited for Regulation* requires messages containing a great deal of factual information about objective circumstances. This implies the use of such techniques as "long copy" or news stories in the media, lengthy discussions and study groups with family planning workers, and educational films. Short, repeated messages on TV or radio of the sort used to sell soap or soft drinks will not be successful with the segment *Suited for Regulation*. The situation is analogous to that of agricultural extension workers trying to persuade farmers in LDC's to try a new variety of seed; farmers will be convinced with facts and logical reasons, not with catchy slogans. As with crop yields, the matter of family size and regulating births is too important to people for anything except serious talk to have much effect. But advertising that educates can have an effect when the circumstances are appropriate for sale and adoption to take place. Again, however, solid empirical support for this assertion is lacking.

The approach suggested here is just the opposite of the approach Indian planners chose: ". . . they decided to find a message that would be a *direct exhortation to have a specific number of children;* to present this message *in the same form in all media;* to keep it *simple and understandable;* and to stay with it until everyone knew, through this message, that family planning is legitimate and what it means" (Wilder and Tyagi, 1968, p. 775).

The Not Ready for Regulation Segment

Many of the world's people live in circumstances that make it sensible to want many children. In agricultural villages where infant mortality is high, additional children can be a sound investment for old age. Rural India is a classic example of the segment *Not Ready for Regulation.* When the typical villager[11] in India is asked, "Why do you have as many as 6 children?" he answers, "Two or 3 may die."

[11] From a close anthropological study—participant observation and surveys—of a village in the Faizabad district of Uttar Pradesh, North India, Gould concluded: "The data provides convincing proof that . . . the fertility behavior of these families is completely rational, and their decision not to adopt family planning, especially in the early stages of the developmental cycle, is based on a realistic appraisal of their social and physical environment" (no date, p. 2).

No marketing effort is likely to convince people to have fewer children in such a situation.[12] It is simply foolishness to believe—as some advertising men, sociologists, and government officials have believed in the past—that achieving lower birth rates under such conditions is simply a matter of "enlightening" the "ignorant" and "primitive" villagers who "breed like animals." Nothing could be further from the truth. Rather, these are sensible people making rational decisions, given the facts of their situation as they see them. This is not to say that they plan perfectly or know how to limit their fertility when they wish to, but most births in such situations are desired by parents.[13]

I have said that this type of campaign "will not be successful" with segment *Not Ready for Regulation*. This requires clarification and more precision: (1) A Madison-Avenue-type campaign will produce fewer acceptors per dollar than will the sort of campaign recommended above for these segments of the market. (2) Any quantity of this sort of campaign will cost more per acceptor, or per birth averted, than the benefits that any government is likely to reckon per acceptor or per averted birth, whereas some quantities of the other sort of campaign *will* appear to be worthwhile (even though the cost per acceptor will be higher than campaigns to segments *Folk Methods* and *Want To Regulate*). To put the proposition more precisely, the cost per acceptor, or per averted birth, of an aggressive marketing campaign to segment *Not Ready for Regulation* will be unacceptably high.[14]

To put in perspective these propositions about the segment *Not Ready for Regulation,* consider this analogy. Assume that you and your spouse plan to have 4 or fewer children. Given your life circumstances, do you think that any kind of marketing campaign, with any sort of persuasive advertising, could convince you to have 6 or 8 children instead of the number you have chosen? Just so is it with those in the segment *Not*

[12] In general, "consumers can't be forced to buy through ads," as an advertising psychologist put it (Dunn, 1973). This is especially true when the action concerns something important; while advertising can shift people with some effectiveness from one brand of beer to another—an unimportant change—it is much harder, to the point of being economically impossible, to get people to change strongly-held views about how to live their lives. The history of "subliminal" advertising is relevant: Despite first beliefs of psychologists, subliminal advertising—advertisements shown in movie-screen flashes so fast one does not perceive them—turns out to be ineffective even in getting people to eat popcorn or drink Coca Cola in the movie theaters. It is a simple fact—of which I feel thoroughly confident as an ex-advertising practitioner and teacher of advertising for 10 years—that it is very difficult to manipulate people with advertising. This is reassuring.

[13] For a summary of the evidence on this matter, see Simon, 1974a, Chapter 1.

[14] It should be noted, however, that in any country at any given time, even if *most* of the population is in segment *Not Ready for Regulation*, at least a few of the people are in segments *Want to Regulate* or *Folk Methods*. Low-key and inexpensive availability programs will enable these people to become acceptors at a relatively low cost per acceptor.

Ready for Regulation, except that their life circumstances are different.[15]

Only a *change in conditions* will alter birth-control practice in such situations as mountain-village Iran or Afghanistan. Where infant and child mortality are high and incomes low, only a change in health and economic conditions will effectively alter desired family size and contraceptive practice. The necessary changes are those generally included in economic development—better health, rising income, more jobs, and better education. As these changes occur, people move into the segment *Suited for Regulation* and become potential responders to marketing efforts. Therefore, there is little point in thinking about marketing contraception aggressively to the segment *Not Ready for Regulation* until the conditions of their lives begin to change.

IDEAL AND PRACTICAL MARKET SEGMENTATION

Thus far we have discussed an idealized situation in which the marketer would be able to separate potential "customers" into homogeneous segments corresponding to the market segments in Figure 22–1. But like most ideals, this one cannot be approached closely. For example, in a country such as Korea, which probably has considerable numbers of people in all six categories in Figure 22–1, there are no printed or electronic media that serve only one segment and no other. This means that the contraceptive campaign planner cannot perfectly match marketing strategies and media to market segments. (To some extent face-to-face family planning workers can flexibly choose the appropriate strategy for each prospect, but the mass media are likely to be an important part of any successful contraceptive marketing campaign.)

The most important contribution of an ideal segmentation scheme is that it forces the planner first to think out the appropriate strategy for each separate segment and then to choose those strategies that best serve the population groups one is dealing with. For example, if most of the people in the West of the country are in the segments *Folk Methods* and *Want To Regulate,* and most of the people in the East of the country are in the segment *Suited for Regulation,* one can apply appropriate and different marketing strategies in West and East.

The really troublesome decision problem arises if the people within one geographic area belong to very different segments. The campaign that is

---

[15] The earliest, longest and perhaps most intensive attempt to "sell" birth control to an Indian village was the Khanna Study. After 15 years it was concluded: "Apparently the chief accomplishment of the programs for family planning had been to induce one quarter to one half of the couples *previously practicing* birth control to switch to modern methods, easier to use and more effective" (Wyon and Gordon, 1971, p. xviii, quoted by Mamdani, 1972, p. 28, italics added).

465

appropriate for some of the people will not be appropriate for others. In such a case, there is no solution except careful and detailed calculations of how much of each kind of campaign to direct to the population group as a whole. If the various groups can be thought of as independent of each other in all ways—and totally unresponsive to campaigns addressed to other groups—then (assuming no budget constraints exist) the appropriate policy is to exert additional marketing effort to each population group until the incremental cost per acceptor becomes higher than the incremental benefit.[16] This will be too cautious a policy, however, because there is at least some benefit to all segments within a group from the marketing effort directed to each segment within any specific group. If this indirect effect is substantial in a given situation, it should be taken into account, of course.

MARKET-RESEARCH IDENTIFICATION OF THE SEGMENTS

Effective segmentation of the market requires that the planner know accurately how many individuals among a given population group are in each segment. To make this determination, it is necessary that there be sound research methods. But this is easier said than done.

It is not difficult to establish accurately how many pople are in the *Modern Methods* and *Folk Methods* segments. Successful methods of questioning people about their contraceptive practice are well established, and most users will tell you what means of contraception they employ. It is harder to determine which segments the rest of the population are in; the research methods are much less well developed. For a while it was thought that questions about the number of children people say they "want" for themselves or think "ideal" for others would be good indicators. But it was soon found that the answers to such questions are not good predictors of actual fertility and contraceptive practice.

Here is some evidence: (1) International cross-sectional data show that, in almost all LDC's, the average completed family size is larger than the average stated ideal family size (Berelson, 1966). And, although there is some association in the international cross-section between actual and ideal family size, the relationship is not strong. This may be seen in Figure 22–2, where the dashed line shows where the dots would be if "actual" equalled "ideal." (2) National cross-sectional data seem to show the same discrepancy between actual and ideal family size. (3) The time-series data for Taiwan from roughly 1965 to 1973 show that "desired" number of children changed much less and much earlier than did the total fertility

---

[16] This assumes that there are always diminishing marginal returns to promotion, which seems plausible (see J. Simon, 1970b, Chapter 1).

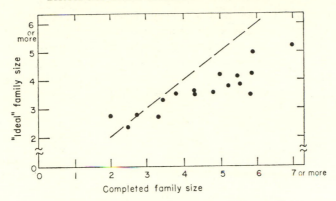

FIGURE 22–2   COMPLETED AND "IDEAL" FAMILY SIZE
(APPROXIMATE) BY COUNTRY, EARLY 1960's
SOURCE: Reproduced from Berelson, 1966, p. 659.

rate and contraceptive practice (though since 1970 there has been a considerable reduction in the former) (see Tables 22–1, 22–4, 22–5).

TABLE 22–4
WIFE'S DESIRED NUMBER OF CHILDREN BY AGE
IN TAIWAN, 1965, 1967, 1970, 1973

Wife's age	1965	1967	1970	1973
22–24	3.73	3.56	3.56	3.0
25–29	3.76	3.59	3.56	3.0
30–34	4.05	3.92	3.80	3.3
35–39	4.3	4.2	4.1	3.6
Total, 22–39	4.01	3.8	3.8	3.2

SOURCE: Freedman *et al.*, 1972, p. 160.

TABLE 22–5
AGE-SPECIFIC BIRTH RATES IN TAIWAN, 1964–69

Type of area	% change in age-specific birth rates 1964–1969						Total fertility rate
	15–19	20–24	25–29	30–34	35–39	40–44	
Cities	−7.7	−11.7	−11.2	−28.1	−43.3	−55.6	−20.4
Towns	+21.9	−2.0	−11.7	−28.5	−47.5	−54.9	−18.4
Rural	+18.4	+2.6	−9.0	−28.8	−47.9	−55.4	−17.4

SOURCE: Freedman *et al.*, 1972, p. 151.

467

Some questions have already been developed, however, that have proven to be reasonably satisfactory predictors (at least in Taiwan) of whether a couple will accept contraception. One such question is whether the couple has ever practiced contraception in the past. The following table shows acceptors in the Taichung program as of mid-1965 classified by past contraceptive experience (Freedman *et al.*, 1969, p. 155):

Past contraceptive experience	% accepting
Never practiced contraception	18
Abortion in past	58
Practiced contraception; no abortion	53
Practiced contraception; had abortion	83

Eighty-three percent of those who had practiced contraception in the past and also had had an abortion accepted a contraceptive method, whereas 18% of those who had never practiced any form of contractption accepted.

Another useful predictor is whether the couple says they "intend" to accept contraception "soon." Classifying acceptors in the Taiwan program according to previous stated intention showed that there was a strong relationship between stated intention to practice contraception some time in the future and subsequent acceptance:

Stated intention	% accepting
Will accept soon	44
Will accept eventually	15
Will never accept	19

Still another effective predictor is whether the couple has more or fewer children than they say they now want. In the Taiwan program as of 1965, the greatest proportion of acceptors was among those who said they already had more children than they wanted:

Desired family size	% accepting
Want at least 2 more children	11
Want at least 1 more child	24
Have number I want	28
Have more than I want	45

If no survey data exist, the planner should have them collected. Even without the proper data, however, he can make some useful guesses from other data. For example, if the birth rate is high and stable and the economy is not developing, most people probably are in the segment *Not Ready for Regulation*. If the birth rate is low, most people probably are in the segment *Modern Methods*. If the birth rate is falling rapidly from a high level, most people are in the segments *Folk Methods*, *Want To Regulate*, or *Suited for Regulation*. But collecting direct data is sufficiently easy that the planner should not rely on such gross indices.

Cost-Benefit Calculations of the Amount That Should Be Spent for Campaigns

The segmentation scheme outlined in this chapter tells which kind of campaign is appropriate in which kinds of conditions. But it does not by itself tell what *size* the campaign should be, i.e., how big the budget should be. That decision can only be made with the apparatus of an explicit cost-benefit analysis such as was outlined in Chapter 21. But by offering primary segment-identification methods that are better than the segment-identification methods described there, this chapter goes one step beyond that analysis. With the primary segment-identification methods, it should be possible to develop much more accurate response functions than are employed there. One may then determine with greater accuracy how much should be spent on a given campaign before the benefit of the incremental response falls below the cost of obtaining it.

A small pilot experiment with the campaign, using several given levels of expenditures in different places, is ideal. Then a straightforward calculation determines which expenditure level is best. One begins with the numbers of acceptors at each expenditure level. Then one must measure the benefit of a single "sale," beginning with one of the general calculations of the *value* of an avoided birth (see Chapter 20). Then the *number* of averted births expected of each acceptor is calculated with various demographic techniques. The total economic valuation of the averted births that may be attributed to the increment of campaign effort may then be found by multiplying the number by the value of each avoided birth. Finally, this calculated *benefit* should be compared against the cost of the campaign to see if the benefits outweigh the costs. For example, Krishnakumar (1972) estimated that each vasectomy performed in the Ernakulam campaigns prevents 2.0–2.2 births. He then multiplied these numbers by 78,423 sterilizations to get 170,798 averted births. Multiplying by 950 rupees estimated benefit per averted birth gives a calculated benefit of 163 million rupees. This was then compared against the estimated cost of 10.9 million rupees, showing that the benefit is much larger than the costs and that projects like this one are worthwhile.

In all cost-benefit calculations, one must be careful to use correct concepts of both benefits *and* costs. For example, the calculation made by Krishnakumar for the Ernakulam vasectomy campaign includes as a cost the value of the money incentives given to acceptors. But from the national point of view, these moneys are *not* a cost because they are simply *transferred* from some people to others (see the dispute between Enke, 1961a, and Demeny, 1961). If these moneys are omitted—as they should be—the campaign is seen to be even more *successful* than it now appears. Of course, if the planner has a fixed budget of funds, he will not think this way because the incentive payments must come out of his budget. But in this—as in all other such budget situations—the planner should not simply work within his fixed budget, spending it all but no more. If he has projects that will yield a handsome return he should request more money, showing how big the payoff is.

Summary and Conclusions

Sound planning for a campaign to market fertility regulation requires that the campaign be fitted to the particular segment of the market at which it aims. Described here is a scheme of categorization into segments that differ on fundamental consumer characteristics with respect to fertility regulation (Table 22–6). Marketing analysis suggests a set of propositions about the best campaign for each of these segments:

Modern Methods

This segment includes those currently using artificial, modern contraceptives. Most people in Sweden fall into this market segment. Relevant marketing techniques are not spelled out here because this segment is of little interest to social planners, and because there are a great many different propositions depending on the product, the brand, and other characteristics of the modern contraceptive market.

Folk Methods and Want To Regulate

These 2 segments include, respectively, those who regulate fertility without artificial devices, and those who want to regulate fertility but do not now do so. Many couples in Taiwan and Korea were in these segments before the massive family planning campaigns of the 1960's. A campaign to these segments must increase the availability of contraception. This includes physical distribution, acceptable prices, lowering of social

Table 22–6
Summary of Contraceptive Market Segmentation Scheme

Segment	Characteristics	Primary identification	Secondary identification	Illustrative areas heavily composed of this segment	Recommended marketing techniques	Recommended marketing themes
Modern methods	Now use modern, artificial contraceptives	Affirmative response to questions on contraceptive practice in survey	Population group has low birth rate	Sweden; urban United States	Varies with type of contraceptive and market position of vendor's brand	Reliability, convenience, safety, pleasure, and others, depending on product and brand characteristics
Folk methods	Now use folk methods of contraception such as withdrawal and abstinence	Individuals say they use folk methods in response to questions in survey	Population group has falling birth rate and rising level of economic development	Jamaica, Taiwan, Korea pre-1965; France in 19th century; perhaps Yugoslavia; parts of Turkey	Increase availability, improve distribution, lower cost, remove social barriers, disseminate information about products available	Availability of products; "legitimacy" of modern contraception
Want to regulate	Do not now contracept but would like to	Individuals say they have contracepted in the past or that they have more children than they wanted	See folk methods segment	See folk methods segment	See folk methods segment	See folk methods segment
Suited for regulation	Do not now wish to contracept, but may change minds readily if presented with additional information	Express little interest in contraception but belong to a population group with declining mortality and rising level of economic development	Same as primary identification method	Mexico; urban Brazil	Communicate that the objective facts of death rate and economic development are appropriate for fertility regulation; ensure physical and economic availability	"Your objective circumstances make it sensible to contracept. Here are the facts of the situation . . . ."
Not ready for regulation	Do not now wish to contracept and will not change minds easily	Belong to population group where mortality remains high and economy is not developing on a per capita basis	Same as primary identification method	Afghanistan; Dahomey	Make contraceptives available for those few whose special life circumstances lead them to want to contracept	"If you want to contracept, effective means are available."

barriers, and dissemination of information about availability. Advertising can successfully use relatively short messages in the mass media because no arguments for contraception motivation need be communicated. The messages need only to communicate the availability and acceptability of contraception.

Suited for Regulation

This segment includes people who currently do not want to regulate fertility but whose minds may change fairly readily if presented with additional information. A large proportion of couples in urban and perhaps rural Mexico may be in this segment. In addition to increasing the availability of contraception, marketing to this segment must communicate to people the relevant, objective facts of their lives (declining infant mortality, rising incomes, rising costs of education) that make it appropriate for them to have fewer children than in the past. The communications campaign to this segment must consist of lengthy, detailed "reason why" copy in the print media or on radio, discussion and study groups with family planning workers, and educational films. Short, repeated messages about availability such as may be sufficient for the segments *Folk Methods* and *Want To Regulate* will be less effective than will lengthy, educational messages.

Not Ready for Regulation

This segment includes people who do not want to regulate fertility and whose minds are not likely to be changed no matter what kind of campaign is directed at them. Rural Afghanistan is composed primarily of people in this segment. No marketing campaign to this segment is likely to produce enough acceptors to be worth the cost of the campaign. It is probable, however, that in any area where people are mostly in the *Not Ready for Regulation* segment there will be some people in other segments. For these people, it will probably be worthwhile in terms of both economics and social welfare to make contraception physically and economically available.

The market segmentation scheme discussed here should help reconcile the differences between those who believe campaigns are sufficient to increase contraceptive practice and those who believe that only economic development will bring lowered fertility. The former view is correct when applied to populations that belong to the *Folk Methods* and *Want To Regulate* categories. When people already recognize the need to regulate their fertility, a promotion campaign can be effective in both numbers of new acceptors and cost per acceptor. Promotion campaigns also may be effective with the segment *Suited for Regulation* where information about

472

prevailing economic and demographic conditions may convince people that family planning is appropriate. But it is also correct that, without economic development, the desire for large families will not be altered, and contraceptive practice will increase very little even with heavy saturation of the best promotion campaign. Concerning any segment, there should be no disagreement between the 2 schools of thought; their disagreement stems from failing to specify or recognize the domains to which their approaches apply.

Similarly, the argument between those who believe that the mass media can do anything and those who believe that the mass media can do nothing derives from not recognizing that what the mass media can accomplish depends on the characteristics of the target population. The mass media will not be effective with the segment *Not Ready for Regulation,* but they can be very useful with the other segments.

The campaign planner must have methods of determining into which of these segments his target market falls. Market-research methods for identification have been suggested, although these methods need considerable improvement.

The segmentation scheme outlined here tells which kind of campaign is appropriate in which kinds of situations. It does not, however, tell what size the campaign should be, that is, how big a budget is necessary. That decision can only be made with the apparatus of an explicit cost-benefit analysis.

CHAPTER 23

Summary and Conclusions

THE MAIN FINDINGS

THE MOST important findings in the book are:

1. In the context of MDC's: when the effects of knowledge, economies-of-scale, and natural resources are taken account of, together with the classical elements such as diminishing returns and the dependency burden, a simulation model shows that faster population growth has at first a negative effect on per-worker income than slower population growth. But after a period of perhaps 30 to 80 years, higher fertility and faster population growth lead to *higher* per-worker income (Chapter 6).

2. In the context of LDC's: moderate population growth leads in the long run to higher per-worker income than does a constant-size population *or* very fast population growth. This is shown in a complex 2-sector simulation model embodying the work-leisure choice and the effect of demand upon investment (Chapter 13).

The optimum LDC population growth rate differs fairly widely within the positive growth range depending upon the parameters chosen, which suggests that no simple analytic model is acceptable and no single answer about the best rate of population goals is reasonable (Chapter 13).

The short-run negative effects of population growth are more severe, and the long-run benefits are slower in appearing, in a country whose population-response parameters are appropriate for India rather than for a more representative LDC. This implies that all things being equal, the argument is stronger for a reduction in population growth in India than in other LDC countries.

3. Within a rather wide range of positive population growth rates in LDC's there is relatively little long-run difference in per-worker-output results—though low or zero population growth rates do much worse, and very high population growth rates do somewhat worse, than do moderate rates (Chapter 13).

4. Population growth has a substantial positive effect upon agricultural investment by farmers in poor countries, and especially upon investment in irrigation (Chapter 11).

5. Population growth in LDC's has a very strong positive effect upon the creation of infrastructure such as roads (Chapter 12). That is, higher population density leads to more roads, which cause an increase in total food production and average income. Roads also facilitate the distribution of food and hence avoid famines of the sort experienced throughout history and recently in the Sahel and Bangladesh.

6. Population growth has a less powerful negative effect upon the level of education than writers on the subject have speculated it would have. The cross-country data suggest that higher population growth has somewhere between some negative effect and no negative effect at all, in MDC's and LDC's, on the proportions of students in school and the schooling expenditures per child.

7. The apparent contradiction between the "population-push" theory of economic development described by Boserup and the "invention-pull" theory attributed to Malthus is only apparent. The former theory fits the labor-using inventions, while the latter fits labor-saving inventions, both of which are important in technology history. The theories complement each other rather than oppose each other (Chapter 8).

8. One cannot deduce from welfare economics alone an answer about whether the welfare effect of an additional child is positive or negative, unless one makes value assumptions that run contrary to the explicit or implicit values of a great many people, no matter which assumptions one makes. Hence, the welfare effect of an additional child, in an MDC or an LDC, cannot be deduced from accepted economic principles alone (Chapter 18).

9. The commonly-accepted criterion of population policy, income per capita (or income per-consumer-equivalent or per-worker), is not satisfactory because it does not coincide with the revealed preferences of people and governments. And implementation of this criterion would require a difficult value judgment about the appropriate discount rate (Chapter 19).

10. The standard partial-equilibrium Enke-type cost-benefit calculations of "the value of an averted birth" are internally inconsistent. A more satisfactory method of reckoning this concept from macro-economic data is shown, though with cautions about its meaningfulness (Chapter 20). Perhaps unexpectedly, this more general macro-economic method, which is free of the flaws of partial-analysis methods, leads to much *higher* estimates of the value of an expected birth—of the order of $300 at 1956 prices, at 5% and 15% rates of discount, using the Coale-Hoover data and model as a basis for analysis.

11. Additional income in MDC's increases the likelihood that a family will have an additional child if it has none or a few, but *decreases* the probability of an additional child if the family already has several (Chapter 14).

12. The long-run total impact of increased income levels in LDC's is to decrease fertility, though the short-run partial effect of rises in income above subsistence is to increase fertility.

13. Findings 1, 2 and 12 jointly refute Malthus' central propositions which are: "(1) Population is necessarily limited by the means of subsistence. (2) Population always increases where the means of subsistence

475

increases" (5th ed., 1817/1963, p. 12). This is not to say that there are no exceptional situations for which these propositions may be relevant, such as small islands not yet reached by modernization. But the Malthusian propositions are not correct for the vast majority of today's world—just as they were not correct for the Western world Malthus had in mind. The models given in this book together with the empirical evidence also refute modern-day computerized Malthusian models such as *The Limits to Growth* (Meadows *et al.*, 1972).

14. With respect to natural resources, the key constraint is energy, because with sufficient energy all other resources can be created. And the key constraint with respect to energy is the human imagination, because the future cost of energy will be determined by new discoveries in the technology of energy production from nuclear fusion and solar energy as well as from conventional sources. More people mean more imagination, other things being equal, so population growth may be expected to have a positive long-run effect on the supply of natural resources. In the short run additional people increase resource scarcity, but the effect is not large (Chapter 5).

15. A key issue in over-all judgments about whether population growth is good or bad is the discount factor one uses, that is, the relative weighting of the shorter-run and the longer-run futures. The effect of population growth upon the standard of living (putting aside the pleasure that children give to their parents) is clearly negative in the short run. In the years while children consume but do not produce, additional children mean less food and less education for each person, and/or additional effort on the part of the parental generation to satisfy the needs of the additional children. During this early period, then, the effect of the additional children upon the standard of living is negative. And if one's horizon is short and one gives importance only to this early period, then it is clear that additional children are a negative economic force.

But if, on the other hand, one gives weight to the more-distant future, then the over-all effect of the additional child may be positive. The positive effects will last much longer than the negative effects (indefinitely, in fact), and hence can outweigh the short-run effects even though it is natural to put less weight on a *given* period of time in the far future than to an equal period of time now.

The device used by economists to summarize a stream of future effects is the "discount rate." A low discount rate indicates that one gives more weight to the future than a high discount rate—though a future period always gets *somewhat* less weight than a present period.

One's judgment about the over-all effect of an additional child, then, depends wholly upon the discount rate one chooses as appropriate (on the assumption that an additional child will have a positive effect after some period of time). If one gives little or no weight to society's welfare in the far future, but rather pays attention only to the present and near future, then additional children have a negative effect. But if one weights the welfare of future generations almost as heavily as the welfare of present generations, then additional children now are a positive economic force. In between, there is some discount rate which, given a given set of circumstances, marks the point at which additional children now are at the borderline of having negative or positive value.

In brief, whether one assesses the effect of additional children now as being negative or positive depends largely upon one's time perspective. And given the economic analysis developed in this book, anyone who takes a long-range view and gives high weight to the welfare of future generations should prefer a growing population to a stationary one now or in the near future.

Furthermore—and this is unarguable—economics alone cannot dictate what policy a country should follow. A country's values and beliefs are fundamental, and they can dictate one decision or another. For example, one country may take a longer-run view than another country, and be more willing to put up with more poverty in the present for the sake of future population. Or, one country may emphasize only the standard of living while another country may feel prepared to accept a somewhat lower level of living in the present for the sake of more population, just as one of us as a parent may decide to have three children rather than two even though the three children will have to get along with less than two would. Each country must ultimately decide these value judgments for itself, and neither the calculations of economics nor the opinions of outsiders should prevail. This vital point is too often overlooked in discussions of population policy, in my judgment.

SUMMARY OF THE BOOK

Now for a summary of the contents of the book as a backwards guide to the reader. The least original research is found in Part II, which is a survey of the extensive and fast-growing literature on the economic determinants of fertility in LDC's and MDC's, in the short run and in the long run. In all countries, economic factors are seen to matter significantly in family decisions about fertility by way of budget effects (Chapter 14). In the short run, higher income leads to more children, and higher expected expenditures per child lead to less children, *ceteris paribus* (Chapters 15 and 16). Money incentives can influence the decision to have more or fewer children, but the incentives probably must be large relative to per-capita income (Chapter 18). Specific estimates of the size of these effects in many different contexts are presented, which may serve as a guide for policy matters.

In the long run, income and economic conditions can lead to structural changes over and beyond the budget effects—changes in child mortality; changes in women's education, and consequent changes in women's opportunity cost; changes in urbanization, and consequent changes in the costs and benefits of children; and so forth. These income-caused structural changes have *negative* effects on fertility on balance in LDC's (Chapter 16). This long-run fertility-reducing effect of income and economic development—the demographic transition—is one fundamental element that invalidates Malthus' "dismal" analysis.

Chapter 14 and its appendix resolve the paradox that the simple cross-sectional relationship of income to fertility is usually negative while the time-series relationship over the business cycle is positive. This is seen to be a statistical artifact due to the embodiment in cross-sectional relationships of the long-run indirect effects of income via education and other fertility-reducing variables, whereas in short-time-series analysis these effects are not operative leaving only the positive direct effect of income to appear.

Part III contains a set of essays on the welfare and marketing economics of economic growth. In contrast to the first two parts of the book which are descriptive and "positive," the third part is normative; it discusses how policy decisions about population size and rates of population growth may be arrived at, and how they may be implemented. Chapter 18 reaches the conclusion that, within the ranges of common values and economic judgments, it is *not possible* to draw any conclusions about whether an increase of population is good or bad from an economic point of view. That is, all studies of welfare economics that purport to draw valid conclusions about population growth are based on a set of implicit value judgments and economic analyses, and other equally plausible judgments or analyses would reverse or render a conclusion indeterminate. The contribution of Chapter 18 is to identify and analyse these frequently hidden assumptions, and to show the indeterminate complexity of the analyses when these assumptions are made explicit and reasonable alternatives are considered. Chapter 18 is intended to limit the scope of classical welfare economics in relation to population growth, and to show that in the matter of population growth value judgments are overwhelmingly important.

In most discussions of welfare economics, per-capita income is used without further ado as the criterion of optimality. Chapter 19 investigates that criterion and shows that it is quite deficient as a general test of population policies. That criterion quickly leads to absurdities when carried

478

beyond a narrow range of fertility, and it does not correspond to people's desires as manifested in their behavior. Therefore, per-capita income by itself can be a badly misleading criterion in discussions of population size and growth.

In some places where there is high fertility, low mortality, and little use of modern methods for the control of conception, there may be a consensus that per-capita income alone can serve as a test for population policies. But birth-control campaigns conducted in such places still need a cost-benefit standard of evaluation to determine if they are worth doing. The concept of the "value of an averted birth," which is based on a per-capita income criteria, is often used. Chapter 20 shows that there are fatal flaws in computing such a value using the standard partial-equilibrium analysis. But it goes on to show how the value may be computed (and actually estimates the value) using a short-run model of an LDC economy—the Coale-Hoover model of India, in this case.

Cost-benefit analysis of a country-wide birth-control campaign in advance of the campaign's start-up is chancy but necessary. Chapter 21 shows how one may combine some assumptions about cost functions for reducing birth rates by different methods, under different conditions, together with the estimated value of an averted birth, to determine which kind of campaign is worth undertaking in various circumstances. Illustrative calculations are shown for a few varied countries.

Chapter 22 gets more specific. It discusses the appropriate marketing and market-segmentation scheme for a birth-control campaign under various conditions. It separately considers each of the market segments—which are defined by contraceptive usage, desire to control birth, and objective health and economic conditions. The over-all scheme recommends the marketing techniques that are likely to be most efficient for each of these segments. The chapter also takes up the difficult problem of how the various market segments may be identified with market research.

Part I of the book is the most ambitious and far-reaching of the three parts. It studies the effects of different rates of population growth upon more-developed and less-developed economies. Chapter 2 provides some intellectual history and a discussion of the general model and the basic variables in the economics of population. The MDC case is the less complex, and hence it is treated first. Chapters 3, 4, and 5 discuss the empirical evidence bearing on the variables necessary for a quantitative model of the effect of population growth on the economy of the MDC world. These variables include the effects of population growth upon saving and education and upon the labor force, as well as the phenomena of classical diminishing returns and economies of scale including the effects on natural resources.

A numerical simulation model is then constructed in Chapter 6. The key issue is how to allow for the additional technological knowledge that additional people create. Two approaches are used. (1) In the Residual approach, it is argued that the knowledge effect is inseparable from economies of scale and natural resource effects. And it is further argued that this complex of effects corresponds to the "residual" in such aggregate production-function studies as those of Solow (1957) and Denison (1967) after increases in physical capital and labor and education have been allowed for. The key assumption is then made that the size of the residual is a function of population size. (2) In the Verdoorn approach, the rate of change of productivity depends upon the (square root of the) total output, an estimate which is derived from empirical evidence of many sorts.

The feedback effect, either from labor-force size in the Residual approach or from total output in the Verdoorn approach, is then combined with a Cobb-Douglas production function. The models are run with various sets of assumptions about the effect of population growth on saving, labor-force participation, and education. Experiments are conducted with several rates of population growth and many different sets of assumed conditions.

The results are unambiguous, and directly opposed to the conventional wisdom as embodied in all classical models in recent simulations. After an initial period of lower per-worker output, the higher-birth-rate variations come to show higher per-worker output after anywhere from less than half a century to somewhat more than a century. That is, when the positive benefits of advances in knowledge together with economies-of-scale and natural resources are combined with the negative capital-diluting effects, the effect of knowledge, economies-of-scale, and natural resources measured by the "residual" or the Verdoorn parameter comes to dominate the diminishing returns from capital fairly quickly. This suggests that in the long run population growth has a positive effect in the standard of living in MDC's.

The general LDC model is outlined in Chapter 7. Unlike the MDC model, the LDC model requires both an agricultural sector and an industrial sector, and in the LDC model the amount of labor supplied per potential worker cannot be assumed to be fixed exogenously. The model is therefore solved by the optimizing tangency of the aggregate production function and the leisure-output indifference curves.

Much work and several chapters had to be devoted to estimation of the key parameters of the LDC model because so little has been done in this area. A key variable in the relationship of population growth and family size to economic development is the amount of labor that farmers are willing to exert to obtain output. This issue is first examined in Chapter 8 in the context of the dispute about the appropriate theory of demographic-

480

economic history. On the one side is the Malthusian "invention-pull" hypothesis, in which the variation in the amount of work done plays no role. The invention-pull view is that exogenous invention is the force that increases output and thereby raises the potential for population growth, and growth then continues until the potential has all been used. In contrast, the "population-push" hypothesis asserts that there is always a stock of available knowledge that can raise output, but at the cost of intensifying labor. These inventions are only adopted when the press of population and the consequent expansion of need makes people willing to exert additional labor, according to the population-push hypothesis. Upon examination, the invention-pull hypothesis is seen to fit inventions which are labor-saving relative to technological practice at the time of invention, while the population-push hypothesis fits inventions which are not immediately labor-saving but become so at higher levels of population. Both sorts of inventions have been important in economic history. Thus the two hypotheses are reconciled and are complementary in the historical explanation. It also makes it clear that the leisure-output choice, and people's tastes about it, is an important element in the productivity of an agricultural economy.

To explain history, however, is quite different than predicting the likelihood that a given group of people will respond with more work to increased population. In order to estimate this parameter, Chapter 9 discusses the various alternatives open to a group when population increases; increasing their work input is only one such alternative. Data were adduced from scattered sources to develop a quantitative estimate of the work-response parameter.

The effect of dependency rates and family size upon monetized nonagricultural saving has been much studied, so that literature is merely reviewed and analyzed in Chapter 10. Investment in agriculture—and especially nonmonetized investment which is done by the cultivator himself—is much less well understood, however. Historical evidence linking population growth and land development is presented in the first part of Chapter 11. Then follows a brief study relating population density to investment in irrigation in various countries. The elasticity estimated in that study jibes with the historical evidence, both lines of evidence suggesting a strong positive response in agricultural saving to an increase in population density. This material on agricultural investment provides the basis for a parametric estimate for the simulation model, and also suggests that in heavily agricultural poor LDC's the positive effect of population growth on agricultural saving may be of the same magnitude as the negative effect on monetized nonagricultural saving, which would imply that population growth's net effect on saving in LDC's should not be said to be negative *or* positive until more is known.

481

Not only private capital but also social capital are important in the economic development of a community. The additional social capital that is needed to shelter and care for additional people may be a drain on social resources; this phenomenon is treated with care by Coale and Hoover and is included in the discussion and estimate of monetized non-agricultural capital in Chapter 12. But some social capital serves *all* people. Such social capital includes roads, harbors, and other "infrastructure," for which the average cost tends to be lower as total use increases. And such infrastructure facilitates all forms of economic activity, a special example being the benefit gained by agriculture from farm-to-market roads. For these reasons it is necessary to estimate the effect of population increase upon the formation of increased infrastructure. The focus of Chapter 12 is upon road construction, and data are adduced to show that increased population density is very strongly related to increases in road mileage. The parameter of this positive effect of population increase is estimated in a form usable in the simulation model.

General investigation of population-related parameters tells much. But the parameters certainly differ from country to country, and to understand the effects of population growth upon a particular economy one must therefore estimate the particular response parameters for that country. This is illustrated in the Appendix to Chapter 9 for the case of India, with concentration upon a key parameter—the response of Indian agriculturalists to population growth. It is concluded that Indian agriculturalists respond to population growth with more work on current crops and farm investment, but that their response is somewhat less rapid than in other LDC's.

Chapter 13 integrates the work on population growth in LDC's. It is a 2-sector simulation model embodying the effects of population growth upon aspirations interacting with the work-leisure choice, and upon investment and technological change in agriculture and industry as well as upon infrastructure and economies of scale—all this together with such classical elements as diminishing returns and the dependency effect. The results are quite different than those arrived at by previous work: zero population growth results in *poorer* long-run results than does moderate population growth in all the experiments with widely different sets of parameters. It is also important that *within* a wide range of moderate population growth rates, there is relatively little difference in output per worker.

In short, Malthus and such neo-Malthusian works such as *The Limits To Growth* (Meadows *et al.*, 1972) are wrong with respect to human society in the assertion that there is a "constant tendency in all animated life to increase beyond the nourishment prepared for it" (Malthus, 5th ed., 1817/1963. p. 1). To put this in Malthus-like terms: If population has a

482

tendency to increase geometrically, output has a tendency to increase geometrically and at least as fast—without apparent limit. Others have reached similar conclusions. But this book is new in giving empirical evidence and quantitative analyses in proof.

WHY DO THE FINDINGS DIFFER FROM PREVIOUS STUDIES?

Why does this book arrive at conclusions that conflict so sharply with the main stream of the research on the economics of population? The findings that conflict most sharply are these: (1) In MDC's, population growth has a long-run *positive* effect on per-worker income, on balance. (2) Population growth in LDC's produces many positive economic effects as well as negative effects. (3) In LDC's, *some* population growth is beneficial in the long run, as compared to *no* population growth. (4) Over a wide range of "moderate" rates of population growth in LDC's, the rate of population growth has a relatively small long-run effect upon per-worker income. (5) Welfare economics by itself can tell nothing useful about the effects of population growth.

Many of the same factors account for several of the differences between these findings and those of other writers. Perhaps most important, the time-horizon in this work is at least 30 and up to more than 100 years, in contrast to almost all quantitative analysis in the economics of population growth whose time-horizon is less than 30 or 50 years. The long time-horizon in my models allows for the influence of those forces that take a long time to begin to work. In LDC's it is the effect on aggregate demand of additional workers and their output that takes effect so slowly. In MDC's it is the knowledge and technological advance that begin to occur only after children enter the labor force, and continue during a person's entire creative lifetime. Then it takes time for such effects to cumulate. Such effects are not captured by a model with a time-horizon of 30 or 50 years. This is why these effects of population growth on demand and on technological advance would not show up in the other models even if these effects had been included in those models.

In the short-run models found in the literature—especially that of Coale and Hoover for the LDC case—it is arithmetically inevitable that the main effect of population growth is lower per-capita income, because much the same output in each population-growth case is divided by more people in the higher-population-growth case. The reduction in per-capita income caused by this arithmetic effect is exacerbated by the dilution of capital during the early years of workers' entry into the labor force. The simulations here are able to arrive at different results because they have a time-horizon long enough for other forces to reveal their full influences.

It is true that the long run—30 to 150 years—is a long way off and therefore of less pressing importance than the short run. But we should remember that our long run will be somone else's short run, just as our short run was someone else's long run. Some measure of unselfishness should impel us to keep this in mind as we make our decisions about population policy.

The models given above also differ from previous models in allowing positive social and individual economic *responses* to the pressure of population growth, whereas such positive responses are absent from other models. In LDC's one response, well-documented in the book, is an increase in the amount of work done toward current output, especially in farming. Another is the increase in agricultural investment and in social investment in infrastructure such as roads, in response to population growth. The only social or individual economic response to more children found in other models is the *negative* response of a reduction in saving. The allowance for these positive feedback responses in my models, together with their longer time-horizons, accounts for the difference between the results of the LDC and MDC models presented here and those of others, and contributes to the difference between the results of my MDC model and that of others. The positive responses, and the positive effects that occur because of them, are not obviated by scarcities of natural resources, because such resources are created by mankind in response to human needs.

The importance of the elements that are responsible for the positive effect of an additional person differ between LDC's and MDC's. And the speed with which they work differs from country to country depending on the country's characteristics. But the historical evidence seems conclusive that sooner or later the effect of an additional person will be positive in every country.

To illustrate, the reader may suggest that India would now be better off if fewer children had been born in the past. But think about this: Over the past four centuries until perhaps half a century ago—a time when India was certainly no better off than it is now—it was the West that experienced fast population growth while population growth in India was nonexistent or slower. But it was the West that forged ahead economically, not India. So in this baldest of cases that is so frequently cited to prove the contrary, it appears that faster population growth was associated with faster economic growth, and slower population growth with slower (or no) economic growth.

Another illustration: Can one doubt that the standard of living in the United States now is higher than it would have been if immigration and fertility in the United States had been lower in the eighteenth and nineteenth centuries than it actually was?

The welfare analysis given in Chapter 18 concludes that no judgment about population growth can be drawn from welfare economics alone, whereas other welfare analyses obtain deterministic results (negative nowadays, positive in the analyses in earlier times by the Utilitarians and others). This conclusion stems both from the longer time-horizon used here, and from the wider set of values which are considered as possible; this welfare analysis makes fewer assumptions than other analyses. Different countries have different needs, of course, even at the same level of economic development. Singapore feels an urgent need to *reduce* fertility, and Rumania feels the need to *increase* fertility. Everything said here should be understood to be subject to the special economic needs of each country, which may suggest a very different course of action than does the general discussion.

Furthermore, economics alone cannot dictate what policy a country should follow. A country's values and beliefs are fundamental, and they can dictate one decision or another.

In brief, the results arrived at here are radically different than those produced by other models because of the inclusion of positive feedback influences left out of other models, because of the long time horizon in which these influences together with others can work out their full effects, and because the importance of value judgments is acknowledged.

CHAPTER 24

Some Speculations

IN THE PROCESS of doing the research for this book, I formed a few conclusions about population growth that I cannot solidly substantiate with a closely argued chain of logical reasoning together with reasonable amounts of empirical evidence. Yet I wish to at least state these conclusions, along with this clear qualification of them. I hope the reader will read them in the spirit in which they are written—as ex-cathedra statements rather than as a part of the scientific material of the book.

1. *Reduced Mortality and Better Health Is the Best Road to a Higher Standard of Living in LDC's.* From time to time, it is suggested (though usually the suggestion is attributed to someone else) that the best way to deal with population growth in LDC's is to allow the death rate to remain high. Ehrlich (1969a) stated: ". . . we should see that the majority of federal support of bio-medical research goes into the broad areas of population regulation, environmental sciences and behavioral sciences, rather than into short-sighted programs of death control." But I am sure that to postpone the drop in mortality will *not* achieve a low population growth rate as effectively as would much-improved death control—besides being morally abhorrent.

Eventually in most of the world parents will be able to expect that all their children will live through maturity. At such time parents will bear just as many children as they want, and no more. And at such time the birth rate will be much lower than it now is in poor countries, instead of being what it is today in the countries where life expectancy is high. The birth rate may still be high enough for population to grow at a substantial rate, but this will respond to what people can afford, just as within industrialized countries a rise in income seems to increase the birth rate, and a drop in income (as in the depression of the 1930's) lowers the birth rate. All this seems sure to be, barring cataclysm; the question is *how soon* it will come about.

(Health also has a very large effect upon the amount of work supplied, Among the poorer respondents to the 1967 survey of Economic Opportunity, a white head of household with good health worked 370 hours (384 for blacks) more than a head of household who was unhealthy—roughly 25% more. Hill, 1971 p. 385).

The quickest and surest route to the rosy situation portrayed above is, I think, through increasing life expectancy, and especially by reducing child mortality. Recent empirical studies have shown that when child mortality falls, the birth rate falls, too (Ben-Porath, 1975; T. P. Schultz,

486

1975; and references cited therein). And better nutrition is the best way to reduce child mortality.

Until mortality falls very low, parents will continue to have *more* children than they want, on the average, because of the conservative but rational desire to err on the high side rather than the low side. That is, parents are more willing to chance having *too many* children rather than *too few*, too many sons rather than none. If people really do behave in this fashion, the effect of a fall to a very low mortality rate could have a terrific effect on the birth rate in poor countries.

It is interesting that many Indians who work in their population program have come around to this general viewpoint of their population situation.

In short, the best way to the demographic situation desired by the human community as a whole is by decreased mortality and increased life expectancy, together with economic development.

2. *The Present Situation Is Not New.* Reading through old books on population gives one a feeling that there is indeed nothing new under the sun. Ideas used in discussing population growth pro and con today are the same ideas found in Godwin and Malthus, as described in Chapter 2. And popular expressions about over-population and under-population use the same concepts and language that appear in all recorded historical discussions. It gives perspective to remember that in the 1930's people worried about under-population. (But Figure 1–4 suggests how unfounded can be fears of population change.) On the other hand, people worried that the earth was over-crowded 3,000 years ago, as the Bible records. And in 1802, when Java had a population of 4 million, a Dutch colonial official wrote that Java was "overcrowded with unemployed" (cited in Myrdal, 1968, p. 974). Now Java has most of Indonesia's 125 million people, and again it is said to be over-crowded. The notion of "standing room only," used so often in recent discussions of population growth, was the title of a book by Ross in 1927, and the idea is found explicitly in Malthus and Godwin.

Some explanations of *why* there have been alternating panics about over-population and under-population are offered in the next sections of this chapter.

3. *Longer-Run Effects Are Misunderstood.* There seems to be a general tendency in all of us to extrapolate present difficulties into the future, and to stay unaware of the forces set in motion by present difficulties that will reverse the situation. Food supplies and food prices are a classic case: For a typical example, in 1973 U.S. housewives organized a boycott against high meat prices, and some people related the "economy of scarcity" to population growth. About a year later there was a photo-

graph in the paper of farmers killing and burying calves because of too-low prices, with this caption: "A farmer at Curtiss, Wisconsin, holds a gun to the head of one calf, while a second farmer prepares to slit the throat of another animal. The calves were among an estimated 600 slaughtered on Tuesday in protest against low prices paid to beef farmers.'" (Associated Press, Oct. 17, 1974.)

The difficulty of foreseeing longer-run effects is especially likely to lead to fear of population growth, because the short-run costs are inevitable and the long-run benefits are hard to foresee. In the very short run—say, next year—it is unquestionable that per-capita income will be lower if there are more children than otherwise. If there are more babies almost the same amount of food will still be produced in the short run, but it will be split among more mouths. Furthermore, more babies mean greater demands on public resources—more health care immediately, and more schooling—which means that resources will be pulled away from other possible uses that might otherwise help raise per-capita income. That is, additional children or a relatively faster rate of population growth create immediate economic problems in the sense of making the available resources more scarce for everyone as compared with a slower rate of population growth. Additional children mean more crowded schoolrooms and less teacher attention per child, or more children getting less or no schooling. More people mean greater pressure on the systems that deliver water, electricity, sanitation, and transportation. Sidewalks and playgrounds are more crowded if an additional child is born. If your neighbor has another child your school taxes will go up, and there will be more noise in your neighborhood.

Later when the child reaches maturity, the additional person causes greater pressure for jobs unless the economy makes costly adjustments to provide more jobs. When the additional child first goes to work, per-worker income will be lower than otherwise, at least for a while.

The short-run effect of an additional child on the society is quite analogous to the short-run effect of an additional child upon a family: less resources available for each person. In the somewhat longer run, more babies today mean that more people will be added to the labor force in a few years, but land and capital will be no larger than otherwise, at least at first. So production output per worker will be lower than otherwise, with negative effects on income per person.

It is more difficult to foresee and understand possible long-run positive benefits. Increased population can stimulate increases in knowledge, pressures for beneficial changes, a youthful spirit, and what are known to economists as "economies-of-scale." The latter means that more people cause bigger markets, which can often be served by more efficient production facilities. And increased population density can make economical the building of transportation, communication, educational systems, and other kinds of "infrastructure" that are uneconomical for a less-dense population. But the connection between population growth and these beneficial changes is indirect and tenuous, and hence these possible benefits do not strike people's minds with the same force as do the short-run disadvantages. The effect of increases in knowledge created by more people is especially immaterial and easy not to notice. Writers about population growth talk about a greater number of mouths coming into the world and more pairs of hands, but never about more brains arriving. This emphasis on physical consumption and production may be responsible for much unsound thinking about population and fear of its growth.

The above paragraphs do *not* imply that *on balance* the effect of increased population is good. Rather, I am arguing that the positive effects tend to be overlooked, causing people to think, without sound basis, that the long-run effects of population growth *surely* are negative, when in fact a good argument can be made that the net effect *may* be positive.

4. *Longer-Run Benefits Are Discounted Too Much.* The previous section argued that the longer-run benefits caused by population growth tend not to be understood, and for that reason the long-run benefits are taken less into consideration than are the immediate costs of population growth. There are, however, additional reasons why the long-run benefits of population growth are given less attention at present than they might receive under other circumstances.

One reason why future benefits are discounted is that many people do not perceive a continuity between past and future, though there is no scientific evidence that this is indeed a time of fundamental discontinuity. Another reason why future benefits are given little weight may be a greater amount of pessimism and despair present in Western society than in the past.

Some discounting of the future is inevitable. Even if there are long-run benefits, the benefits are *less immediate* than are the short-run costs of population growth. Additional public medical care is needed even before the birth of an additional child. But if the baby discovers a theory that will lead to a large body of scientific literature, the economic or social benefits may not be felt for 100 years. All of us tend to put less weight on events in the future compared to those in the present, just as a dollar that you will receive 20 years from now is worth less to you than is a dollar in your hand now.

But the national mood can affect the rate at which the future is discounted, and moods now are not optimistic. For example, a survey in 1972 reported that there is "an increasing belief among students that American society is 'a sick society' . . . [students are] uneasy and worried. . . . Only a handful believe our national policies will lead to peace or economic well-being . . . In 1968, 69 per cent of students believed that 'hard work will always pay off'; in 1971, only 39 per cent" (*New York Times*, April 16, 1972).

Pessimism must be reflected in a relatively high rate of discount of the future, that is, in giving relatively less weight to the far future, compared to the present, than when the mood is more optimistic. "Having children is also evidence of faith in the future . . . Granted, in recent decades this faith has an apocalyptic tinge, colored by visions of atomic holocausts and Armageddons. It is a faith, nevertheless, in the country's future, unless or until terminated by such calamities as transcend the limits of planning of a household, a firm, or even a country. Contrariwise, a constant or slowly growing population is implicit evidence of lack of faith in the future" (Kuznets, 1960, p. 336).

5. *Rhetoric Affects Popular Judgments about Population Growth.* Fear of population growth has been inflamed by the language used by writers and speakers about population growth. Examples are the terms "population explosion," "people pollution," and "population bomb." Nor are these terms just the catchwords of popular wordsmiths, whose rhetoric one is accustomed to discount. Rather, these terms have been coined and circulated by distinguished scientists and professors. An example comes from the justly-famous demographer Kingsley Davis, who began an article in a professional journal: "In subsequent history the Twentieth Century may be called either the century of world wars or the century of the population *plague*" (1970, p. 33, italics added). Such language is loaded, perjorative, and unscientific.[1]

And in a full-page newspaper advertisement of such a prestigious organization as the Campaign to Check the Population Explosion one finds such rhetoric as this: "Our city slums are packed with youngsters—thousands of them idle, victims of discontent and drug addiction. And millions more will pour into our streets in the next few years at the present rate of procreation."

---

[1] Such language also reveals something about the feelings involved in contemporary anti-natalist campaigns. The psychiatrist Wertham (1961) points out that many of these terms have the overtones of violence, e.g., "bomb," and "explosion," and many show contempt for other human beings, e.g., "people pollution." Franz Fanon analyzes such language in another context: "[Colonialism] dehumanizes the native, or to speak plainly, it turns him into an animal. In fact, the terms the settler uses when he mentions the native are zoological terms. He speaks of the yellow man's reptilian motions, of the stink of the native quarter, of breeding swarms, of foulness, of spawn, of gesticulations. When the settler seeks to describe the native fully in exact terms he constantly refers to the bestiary. . . . Those hordes of vital statistics, those hysterical masses, those faces bereft of all humanity, those distended bodies which are like nothing on earth, that mob without beginning or end, those children who seem to belong to nobody, that laziness stretched out in the sun, that vegetative rhythm of life—all this forms part of the colonial vocabulary" (Fanon, 1968, pp. 42–43).

"You go out after dark at your peril. Last year one out of every four hundred Americans was murdered, raped or robbed." ("Birth Control Is an Answer," *New York Times*, May 25, 1969, p. 5E).

There is no campaign of counter-epithets to allay fear of population growth, perhaps because of a Gresham's law of language: Bad terms drive out good. Reasoning by epithet is another likely cause of the current fear of population growth in the United States.[2]

6. My over-all conclusion is: *Economic Demography Is a Cheerful Science*. For more than a century economics was thought of as the "dismal science" because of Malthus' vision that there is a "constant tendency in all animated matter to increase beyond the nourishment prepared for it" (1817/1963, 5th ed., p. 1). That is, population growth would always tend to bring society to the brink of starvation. But the analysis in this book argues that the opposite will happen—that increased population growth eventually helps raise the level of living even higher. If I am correct, then, economic demography is indeed a cheerful rather than a dismal science.

Many writers have argued against Malthus' conclusions. But the central reasons of others are not mine. Some have argued that technology has a built-in mechanism that enables it to win a "race" against population growth. Others (notably Godwin and Marx) have argued that structural changes in society, especially redistribution of wealth, would solve the "problem." Though I do not reject the importance of structural change,[3] or of technological change as an independent force, I (somewhat like Kuznets) give central place to technological and market changes *influenced by* population growth. I see a *deterministic economic causal sequence*, rather than a "race" whose outcome depends upon chance or a structural change that is the outcome of political decisions. And the quantitative analysis contained in this book suggests that the on-balance effect of population growth in the long run is likely to be positive.

Economic demography is also a cheerful science for me personally because I believe it is human life that gives significance to the world. A world with no or few people would, in my view, be a world without meaning or

[2] Such words and ideas can have enormous influence for good or evil in the matter of population. For example, an idealistic young woman chosen as valedictorian of her college class gave a valedictory speech entitled "Saving the Human Race," saying: "Dr. Paul Ehrlich and others say that immediate action must be taken.... The most humane thing for me to do is to have no children at all" (Mills, 1970, p. 11).

[3] Kuznets is certainly right in this respect: "[The] history of economic growth, past and current, suggests strongly the importance of non-economic factors not amenable to economic analysis—the broader social, political, and international decisions that set the conditions for the purely economic decisions and factors. Consequently, in dealing with the relation of population to economic growth, whether in underdeveloped or developed countries, we must note, in addition to the familiar economic factors, some of the broader aspects of social organization, national and international" (1967, p. 184).

491

value. Hence the fact that our economic system can support an ever-increasing number of people seems wonderful to me.

Depending upon one's point of view, contemporary population growth may be thought of either as a failure or as a triumph. One may look at a rapid rate of natural increase as proof that humans have failed to control their numbers in the most sensible fashion. Or, one may view the population of today that is ten, a thousand, a million times bigger than at various times in the past, and say: In earlier times humanity did not have the power to support so much human life, but now humanity has succeeded in the marvelous achievement of creating the means to sustain so many people. Thus, the present spurt in population can be seen as bringing good or evil or both. For me, the present spurt in population is both the sign of success of human civilization and the harbinger of greater success in the future—indeed a cheerful rather than a dismal outlook.

Common Objections to
the Book's Conclusions and
Some Simplified Rebuttals

by Lincoln Pashute and Julian L. Simon

THIS BOOK has reached conclusions which run contrary to prevailing popular opinion as well as to most of the professional literature since before Malthus. Therefore it may be useful to consider some of the objections to these conclusions. Of course the full text of the book, both the analysis and the empirical data, is the basic relevant material in rebuttal to these objections. But this appendix, which is not an integral part of the book, takes up the arguments in a lighter and more casual fashion. It is for the lay reader but not for the professional.

1. "But population growth must stop at *some* point. There is *some* population size at which the world's resources must run out, even standing room."

When someone questions the need to immediately check population growth in the United States or in the world, as does this book, the standard response ever since Malthus has been a series of calculations about how, after a certain number of doublings of population, there will be only standing room, or a solid mass of human bodies, on earth or in the United States. This apparently shows that population growth must stop *sometime*.

Let's agree for now that population growth will stop *sometime*, just as any other growth process will stop sometime. by But what reasoning do people get from "sometime" to "now" and from "will" to "must"? Two aspects of their reasoning can be identified, both containing the premise that individuals and societies cannot be trusted to make rational, timely decisions about fertility rates.

First, the argument assumes that if humans do something now they will inevitably continue to do the same in the future. That is, it is assumed that if society's birth rate is high now, it will continue to be high later. But one need *not* believe that if people decide to have more children now, they will also continue indefinitely to have them at the same rate. By analogy, because a man decides to have another bite of pie today, it does not mean that we should worry that he will eat himself to death. If he is like most people, he will stop after he recognizes a reasonable limit. But many seem to have a "drunkard" model of fertility and society; if he takes one drink, he's down the road to hell.

493

A second common assumption is that people (especially poor people) in the United States and abroad have babies without rational thought, and without wanting them. As discussed in Chapter 14, however, it is plain wrong to think that "primitive" people breed prolifically and without rational control. If one asks men in Indian villages why they have as many or as few children as they do, a typical answer comes from a man with five children: "Two, maybe three, will die, and I want to have at least two that live to become adults." And Krzywicki (1934) and Nag (1962) have found that among many of the *most* "primitive" of peoples observed—Australian tribes, and American Indian tribes just after the coming of the white man—relatively few babies were born and even fewer were raised. This was by deliberate choice of these "primitives," both personal choice (e.g., abstinence, infanticide, and abortion) and social choice (e.g., taboos against intercourse at various periods of time).

It was quite clear even to Malthus—though most Malthusians seem not to have noticed this in his revised *Essay*—that unlike plants and animals, people are capable of foresight and may abstain from having children from "fear of misery." "Impelled to the increase of his species by an equally powerful instinct, reason interrupts his career, and asks him whether he may not bring beings into the world, for whom he cannot provide the means of support" (2nd ed., 1803, p. 3). This implies that when people judge the negative consequences of children to be greater than the positive consequences—personally and collectively—they will then reduce the rate at which they have babies.

Why do so many people who fear population growth, especially in MDC's, not think this way? Perhaps because they liken mankind's behavior to that of animals, who do not seem capable of the foresight needed to refrain from having children because of the consequences. Their models are flies in a bottle or worms in a bucket (Price, 1967, p. 4), meadow mice or cotton rats (Van Vleck, 1970) which will indeed keep multiplying until they die for lack of sustenance. Malthus was quite aware of this "constant tendency in all animated life to increase beyond the nourishment prepared for it. . . ." He discussed this idea as expressed by Benjamin Franklin: "It is observed by Dr. Franklin: that there is no bound to the prolific nature of plants or animals, but what is made by their crowding and interfering with each others' means of substinence. . . . This is incontrovertibly true. . . . In plants and animals the view of the subject is simple. They are all impelled by a powerful instinct to the increase of their species; and this instinct is interrupted by no reasoning or doubts about providing for their offspring . . . the superabundant effects are repressed afterwards by want of room and nourishment . . . and among animals, by their becoming the prey of each other" (Malthus, 2nd ed., 1803, pp. 2–3).

But then Malthus himself destroyed this line of thought: "The effects of this [preventive] check on man are more complicated . . . The preventive check, is peculiar to man, and arises from that distinctive superiority in his reasoning faculties, which enables him to calculate distant consequences . . ." (2nd ed., 1803, pp. 3, 9). The point is that mankind is different from the animals in that we have much more capacity to alter our behavior—including our fertility—to meet the needs of our environment.

Another kind of reasoning that leads people away from thinking that mankind will respond adaptively to population growth is the mathematics of exponential growth functions, the "geometric increase" of Malthus. The usual argument that population will grow to a doomsday point is based on the crudest sort of curve-fitting, a kind of hypnotism by mathematics. Starkly, the argument is that population will grow in the future because it has always grown in the past. Certainly this proposition is not even true historically; population has been stationary or gotten smaller in large parts of the world for long periods of time (e.g., Europe after the Roman Empire, and aborigine tribes in Australia). And many other sorts of trends have been reversed in the past before they have been forced to stop by physical limits (e.g., the length of women's skirts, or the growth of Christianity and Islam).

If one is attracted to the sort of curve-fitting that underlies most arguments about the need for control of population growth, one might do well to consider another long trend: The proportion of people who die each year from famine has probably been decreasing each year since the beginning of mankind, and even the *absolute* number of people who die of famine has been on a decrease despite the large increases in total population (see Chapter 5, page 95, and Chapter 9, p. 198).

An even more reliable and important trend statistic in this connection is the steady increase in life expectancy over recorded history. Why not focus on this trend statistic rather than on the total population trend?

An absurd counterspeculation is instructive. The exponential growth rate of university buildings in the past decade, and perhaps in the past 100 years, has been much faster than the population growth rate. Simple curve-fitting will show that university buildings will over-take and pass the amount of space in which people stand, long before people have "standing room only." This apparently makes university growth the juggernaut to worry about, not population growth!

Some will reply that the analogy is not relevant because universities are built by reasonable men who will stop building when there are enough buildings, whereas people have children acting only out of passion and not subject to the control of reason. This latter assertion is, however, empirically false. Every tribe known to anthropologists, no matter how "primitive," has some effective social scheme for controlling the birth rate, as seen in Chapter 14.

Even the proposition that population growth must stop *sometime* may not be very meaningful. The length of time required to reach any absolute physical limits of space or energy is long in the future, and many unforeseeable things can happen between now and then which could change those apparent limits.

2. "But the earth is finite, and the quantities of resources are finite. This finitude of resources is a compelling reason why growth must cease sometime."

This assertion is dealt with carefully and at length in Chapter 5. This section treats the matter in a more general way. It is a shame to treat this topic in the manner of this section. But the sober argumentation of the point by Resources for the Future and others (outlined in Chapter 5), even though unchallenged by serious economic critics over the past 15 years, has not succeeded in winning people's minds. Therefore, the lighter analogical discussion in this section seems necessary.

It makes excellent common sense that if there are more people, natural resources will inevitably get used up and become scarce. And the idealistic generous side of young people responds to the fear that future people will be disadvantaged by heavy use of resources by more people in this generation. This letter recently appeared in a local newspaper:

> To the Editor:
>
> Sir: To all advertisers: I would like you to know you are wasting paper sending out your door-to-door advertisements. Wasting paper is wasting trees, which leaves animals homeless. Please try to advertise on TV and radio or in the daily newspaper. You will help this world a lot if you do.
>
> Anjali Mittra
> Age 9, 5th grade

(*Champaign-Urbana Courier*, May 3, 1970)

Solzhenitsyn has expressed a similar point of view. "We had to be dragged along the whole of the Western bourgeois-industrial and Marxist path . . . in order to discover, at the end of the twentieth century, and again from progressive Western scholars, what any village gray-beard in the Ukraine or Russia had understood from time immemorial . . . : that a dozen maggots can't go on and on gnawing the same apple *forever;* that if the earth is a *finite* object, then its expanses and resources are finite also, and the *endless, infinite* progress dinned into our heads by the dreamers of the

Enlightenment cannot be accomplished on it. . . ." (*Newsweek*, March 18, 1974, p. 122).

To argue that natural resources will *not* necessarily become more scarce as time goes on is apparently to argue against all logic. But commonsense is just plain wrong in this case. Commonsense gives us "outgo vision," the reasoning of someone who sees only his record of expenditures and assumes that he must be on his way to going broke—failing to see that at the same time there is income, which may well yield a positive balance. Commonsense notices our *use* of resources but fails to see that our needs lead to our *creation* of resources—planting of forests, exploration of new oil fields and invention of ways to obtain oil from rocks, discovery of substitute sources of energy and nutrients, invention of new tools of all kinds. Clearly we now have *available to us* vastly more resources of almost every kind than did people in any preceding age. And there is no reason to doubt that this process of the expansion of resources, caused in part by our growing population, will continue in the foreseeable future—that is, as far into the future as we can sensibly plan for now.

A recent example of outgo vision is the calculation that a baby in the United States exerts 25 to 50 times more "pressure on the environment" than does a baby in India. It goes unnoticed that the United States worker also *creates more resources and thereby puts more resources back* into the environment than does the Indian worker.

Perhaps a doomsday view of natural resources is partly accounted for by the ease of demonstrating incontrovertibly that more people will cause some *particular* negative effects (e.g., if there are more Americans there will be less wilderness to go around). The logic of the rebuttal must be much more global and indirect than the logic of the charge. To show that the loss of wilderness to be enjoyed in solitude is not an argument against more people, one must show that an increase in people may ultimately lead to a general expansion in space and nature available to the person—transportation to the wilderness, high-rise buildings, trips to the moon, plus many other partial responses that would not now be possible if population had been stationary 100 years ago. Obviously, the benefit of the sum effect of these population-caused improvements is harder to show than is the harm of the partial effect of the decrease in wilderness one may enjoy in solitude. Hence the result is a belief in the ill effects of population growth.

Now let us turn to the special subject of *exhaustible* resources such as coal and iron, rather than replenishable resources such as land fertility or water: In the simplest static case, if this generation digs more of the peat from the farm, there will be less left for future generations to dig. But even if this were the complete story, it would not be a warrant for restricting use now. Why should the use of a pound of coal or iron yield more utility if it is used by a person 100 years hence than if it is used now? Of course, one might argue that the resource may be wasted now, but this is a pretty tenuous argument, no matter how "wasted" is defined.

Another objection is, "Yes, but without coal and iron then the people will starve." But why? Future generations will do exactly what this generation does: take resources into account when it reproduces.

To repeat, the idea of a physical limit on a resource does not make sense. When faced with scarcity, people find new sources; such is the history of coal, oil, etc. And people invent new ways to replace one commodity with another (e.g., oil for coal and nuclear power for both). The more people there are to think about the matter, the more likely is discovery and invention of new sources and resources.

3. "But how can we be sure that science and technology will continue to solve our resource problems in the future?"

Especially the young ask: "How do we know that scientific discovery will continue?" Just as they are not convinced by sociological and economic arguments about the continuation of the research-and-development process, they do not believe that the past record of discovery can be extrapolated into the future. It seems to them that the course of human history is not a sound guide to the future, because it seems to them that we are now standing at the point of a sharp discontinuity, a break in history.

If this were so, then there would be no way at all to predict the effects of any population movement, because *any* analysis requires parametric estimates, and the only sensible source of human-behavior parameters is human behavior in the past. But luckily the existing trend data on resource costs, life expectation, knowledge creation and so on give no reason to believe that any such historical break has begun or will take place in the future. Nor do there seem to be indirect effects caused by this trend and working against it. No one has given a sound reason why our time should be one of sudden discontinuity in the historical process of scientific discovery, just as there has been no such discontinuity in the past. But disbelief in historical continuity in the creation of natural resources contributes to fear about population growth.

For perspective it is interesting to read what Macaulay wrote in 1830: "'We cannot absolutely prove that those are in error who tell us that society has reached a turning-point, that we have seen our best days. *But so said all who came before us* [italics added], and with just as much apparent reason. . . . On what principle is it that, when we see nothing but improvement behind us, we are expected to see nothing but deterioration before us? . . .'" (Quoted by Zimmerman, 1965, p. 11.)

498

Judgments about the trend of *pollution* are also affected by the comparison one makes to the past, as Boorstin says:

> We sputter against The Polluted Environment—as if it was invented in the age of the automobile. We compare our smoggy air not with the odor of horsedung and the plague of flies and the smells of garbage and human excrement which filled cities in the past, but with the honeysuckle perfumes of some nonexistent City Beautiful. We forget that even if the water in many cities today is not as spring-pure nor as palatable as we would like, for most of history the water of the cities (and of the countryside) was undrinkable. We reproach ourselves for the ills of disease and malnourishment, and forget that until recently enteritis and measles and whooping cough, diphtheria and typhoid, were killing diseases of childhood, puerperal fever plagued mothers in childbirth, polio was a summer monster (1970, p. 28).

Perhaps the best single quantitative measure of the purity of the environment over time is life expectancy. While pollution may have ugly esthetic effects, its key importance is its effect on health. But history shows a long upward climb of life expectancy in the United States and in the world, up to and through the present. Surely this historical view gives no ground for hysteria. Of course, history may change course as of now, and we may be headed directly into cataclysm. But there is *no evidence* showing that history is indeed changing course.

Perhaps it is normal for the young, especially, to pay little attention to history, and to feel that their own generation and period in history is unique. When their mood is rosy, this leads to unwarranted optimism. When the mood is glum, this leads to unwarranted pessimism. And when one is despairing and pessimistic, one tends to put relatively much weight on the negative aspects of a phenomenon, and relatively little weight on its positive aspects. Perhaps this is the root cause of the present fear of population growth in the United States and in the world.

4. "But more people necessarily mean more pollution."

It has come to seem as if one must be against population growth if one is for pollution control. And pollution control in itself appeals to everyone, for very substantial reasons.

To understand the link-up of population control and pollution control, we must understand the nature of the argumentation on both sides. One can *directly* demonstrate that more people increase a flow of a pollutant (e.g., more people make more trash). But the argument that more people may *reduce* pollution is less direct and not so obvious (e.g., as more people make a bigger pollution problem, there arise forces of reaction to clean up the pollution that may make the situation better than ever before). Furthermore, the ill effects of people and pollution can be understood *deductively* (e.g., more people *must* create more trash). But whether the end-point after a sequence of social steps will be an even cleaner environment can only be shown by an *empirical* survey of experiences in various places (e.g., are city streets in the United States cleaner now than they were a hundred years ago?). Such empirical arguments are usually less compelling to the imagination than are deductive arguments.

An analogy may help. Think how much easier it would be to argue that the automobile is detrimental to life and health than that it is beneficial. To show how terrible cars are for people, all you need are the statistics of the people killed and mained each year, plus a few gory pictures of smash-ups. That's strong stuff. To argue that the auto is beneficial to health you would need to show a lot of relatively small, indirect benefits— the people who can get to a doctor or hospital by car who could not do so otherwise; the therapeutic results of being able to take a trip into the countryside; the gain in efficiency in transporting knowledge that eventually saves lives; and so forth. Our point here is not to say that cars are, in fact, beneficial on balance, but only to illustrate how much easier it is to show their maleficence than their beneficence. So it is with arguments about pollution and population growth.

The discussion is complicated by the fact that pollution makes news, as does all trouble and danger. But depollution is less newsworthy. The consequent imbalance in the press leads to an imbalanced public judgement of the situation. Everyone has read that "Lake Erie is Dead." But how many have read the statement by Philip Handler, President of the National Academy of Sciences, that "the fish catch [from Lake Erie] has been increasing rather than decreasing" (Handler, 1971, p. 33). How many have seen reports that "British rivers . . . have been polluted for a century while in America they began to grow foul only a couple of decades ago . . . The Thames has been without fish for a century. But by 1968 some 40 different varieties had come back to the river" (Friendly, 1970). How many know about London that "Now to be seen are birds and plants long unsighted here. . . . The appearance of long-absent birds is measured by one claim that 138 species are currently identified in London, compared with less than half that number 10 years ago . . . Gone are the killer smogs. . . . Even fog itself—a sometimes romanticized but often ominous aspect of life in London over the centuries—is becoming increasingly a thing of the past. Londoners . . . are breathing air cleaner than it has been for a century . . . effects of air pollution on bronchial patients is diminishing . . . visibility is better, too . . . on an average winter day . . . about 4 miles compared with 1.4 miles in 1958" (*U.S. News and World Report* December 15, 1975).

The mass media, together with the ecologists, produce new pollution threats faster than old ones can be discussed and understood, let alone dealt with. Whoever offers an optimistic assessment of one specific pollution threat is assailed with "But what about X?" where "X" may be thermal radiation, mercury contamination, plastic containers, or human verbosity—all of which a growing population increases, of course. The list of *possible* dangers is infinitely long and contributes to the atmosphere of fear about population increase.

Perhaps the silliest of such pollution threats—but one which was nonetheless taken very seriously for a while about 5 years ago—was the threat of being overcome by our own wastes. But in the course of less than 5 years, engineers found myriad new ways not only to get rid of wastes, but also to get value from them as well. "From their one-time reputation as major pollutants, garbage and sewage now seem to be acquiring the status of national resources" (*Newsweek*, January 28, 1974, p. 83). Within a year after Connecticut set up a Resources Recovery Authority "to manage a garbage collection and re-use program for the entire state" the authorities could judge that "There are no technological problems with garbage any more. All that is needed is initiative" (*Time*, December 2, 1974, p. 59).

Pollution is indeed bad. But as argued with more care in Chapter 5, more people need not imply more pollution, and may imply less pollution; this has been the trend in human history as indicated by the most important general index of pollution—increasing life expectancy.

5. "But do we have a right to live high on the hog, while subsequent generations suffer?"

The facts would seem to be the opposite, however—later generations benefit if population growth is higher in earlier generations. During the Industrial Revolution in England the standard of living might (or might not) have been higher for a while if population growth had been slower. But we today clearly benefit from the high population growth and consequent high *total* economic growth of that period—as the LDC model in Chapter 13 suggests.

The intergenerational issue, specifically with respect to natural resources, is discussed on page 98 in Chapter 5.

6. "But all the experts say the opposite of what this book says. It's not likely that they *all* are wrong and one lone author is right."

It does sometimes seem as if all the experts believe that population growth is an unmitigated evil. Consider, for example, this statement of Ehrlich, as of 1968: "I have yet to meet anyone familiar with the situation who thinks India will be self-sufficient in food by 1971, if ever" (1968, p. 41). And from a *Newsweek* columnist and former high State Department official: "Informed men in every nation now know that, next to population growth and avoidance of nuclear war, the despoiling of nature is the biggest world problem of the next 30 years " (Bundy, 1972).

Nor are the above two quotes isolated examples. Consider this Report from Planned Parenthood supposedly *not* an anti-natalistic organization. Notice the implication that there is only one authoritative point of view:

BIRTH RATES DOWN, BUT POPULATION THREAT CONTIN-UES. Despite indications that birth rates are dropping in the United States and in many other countries, authorities see population growth as a continuing threat to the world. Members of the United Nations Population Commission, meeting in Geneva during November, reviewed predictions that—at the present rate of growth and with steadily increasing life spans—planet earth will reach its alleged population "limit" of 10 billion people in 60 years . . . .

Commenting on the recent sharp drop in the United States birth rate revealed in preliminary results of the 1970 National Fertility Study and other reports, demographic authorities have shied away from expressions of optimism . . . .

[The term "optimism" makes clear that a lower birth rate is a good thing.]

Biologist Paul R. Ehrlich took an equally cautious position, saying "what has come down quickly can go up quickly." The wait-and-see attitude was shared by another noted demographer, Dr. Philip M. Hauser of the University of Chicago. "There is still a bomb there," Dr. Hauser said. "Basic changes in reproductive behavior must be measured in generations, not years."

John C. Robbins, chief executive officer of PP-WP, analyzing the decline in United States fertility rates since 1957 . . . told delegates to the October annual meeting of PP-WP in San Francisco that "the fertility rates of a dozen years, let alone three months, offer no basis whatsoever for bringing down the curtain on the population problem."

This language suggests that all experts agree, and that it is a *fact* that population is growing too fast in the United States.

In fact, however, even when they speak as citizens rather than as scientists, there is *not* consensus among population scientists that there is now over-population in the United States, or that population growth in the United States is too fast for the good of the United States or of the world, despite the absence of these views in the popular press. For example, Coale's presidential address to the Population Association of America was entitled "Should the United States Start a Campaign for Fewer Births?" and his answer was "I do not think that we need to rush into a program of special inducements for lower family-size targets" (1968, p. 474). Coale does not judge that we have a population crisis in the United

States (though he does worry about population in poor countries). And Notestein, the elder statesman of American demographers, finds nothing but "esthetic grounds" for wishing to slow population growth in the United States. "I would like to come to zero population growth, but with no great haste, and without making important sacrifices in the process" (1970, p. 6). But Notestein's and Coale's messages are less exciting than the alarms about impending starvation, misery, death, and oblivion sounded by those who favor population control for MDC's. The drama of such alarms may account for the wider publicity and more popular belief in the latter point of view than in Coale's or Notestein's.

Especially among economists—whose business it is to understand resources and the standard of living—it is not agreed that population growth is bad. And in a number of noteworthy cases, economists have begun by thinking that population growth is bad and then changed their minds after study of the facts. Commenting on one such case in the President's Commission on Population Growth, Easterlin says: "It is instructive, I think, to note Kelley's own statement on the change in his views as a result of this research. Whereas he started out in the expectation that an anti-natal government policy was justifiable on economic and ecological grounds, he ended up in a much more neutral position. In this respect, Kelley's experience is representative, I think, of that of many of us who have tried to look into the arguments and evidence about the "population problem" (1972, p. 45).

So the argument to authority, that population growth must be bad because the experts say so, is wrong on grounds of fact as well as on the logic of legitimate argumentation.

7. "It doesn't make sense to take into account the lives of people who have not yet been born."

This objection is often raised in two contexts: First it is raised with respect to discussion of the long-run effects of population growth upon the economic level 50 or 100 or 200 years in the future; second this objection arises when it is argued that the level of per-capita income is not necessarily a complete criterion, the end-all and be-all of population policy, but that the *number* of people who enjoy life may also enter into the criterion.

In fact, most people and all societies act in ways that show concern about people who have not yet been born, whether or not people justify these actions metaphysically. Governments often build public works to last beyond the life-times of present citizens, explicitly taking future generations into account in such actions. And young families take unborn children into account when they save money or buy a house with space for the children. So taking unborn children into account is a basic fact of life, and it therefore needs no further defense in the context of considering the long-run as well as the short-run impacts of population growth upon economic growth.

But let us go further. Some people say that they cannot feel a concern for unborn people. But this does not imply that it is foolish or impossible if one *does* feel such a concern. It seems to us that there need not be a difference in one's feelings toward a person who is unborn and toward a person whom you do not know. One can clearly feel concern for someone you do not know—and similarly for an unborn person. For example, if one imagines—as prospective parents often do—terrible events in which their future children would be injured or killed, that emotion can be much stronger than an imagined (or real) scene in which a living person on another continent, of another race and nationality, is injured or killed. So again we think that it is a psychological *fact* that some people can feel a sentimental tie to people who are not yet born, and who might not be born.

So far we have only said that one *might* take into account unborn people. But it is very clear that the *importance* of unborn children ranges all the way from low to high, among various individuals. This would seem to be the sort of value or taste about which economics and science generally has nothing to say. As individuals, however, we obviously have a particular value, and since this value is getting so little public expression today that people assume that the value does not even exist, we will take this opportunity of saying a few words about it. Holding the standard of living constant, we think it better to have more rather than less people. And if the price is not too great, we would be in favor of a somewhat lower standard of living if more people were alive to enjoy it (though the analysis of this book suggests that in the long run more people imply a *higher* rather than a lower standard of living).

It is necessary to say what one means by liking the idea of more people. To us it means that we do not mind seeing more people in the cities we live in, seeing more children going to school and playing in the park. We would be even more pleased if there were more cities, more people in unsettled areas—even another planet like this one.

We believe that this particular value is in the spirit of the best of Judeo-Christian-Islamic culture, as well as of the Utilitarian tradition that underlies modern economics (see Chapter 18 for historical documentation), because it is generally consistent with the rest of our values and tastes; that's why we hold this value for more life. It is a value that many other people hold, too. And others, like us, may come to recognize the importance of this value to them as they come to recognize—as we did, in the course of writing this book—that population growth has beneficial rather than ill effects upon civilization's standard of living in the long run.

8. "If population control is undertaken and is successful in preventing births, but it turns out to be unnecessary, then what is lost?" (This argument is found in Ehrlich's *Population Bomb*.)

The answer depends upon one's values. If one believes that additional human lives have value, as discussed in the previous section, and some lives are prevented unnecessarily from occurring, that is an obvious loss.

9. "More children grow up to be more adults who can push the nuclear button and kill civilization."

True. More generally, as Wolfers reduces the matter to an absurdity, "All human problems can be solved by doing away with human beings" (1971, p. 229). But more children also grow up to be more people who can find ways to avert catastrophe.

10. "How can one call upon people in poor countries to reduce their birth rate if we in rich countries go on having many children?"

In fact, though it is not very relevant, the rate of population growth in MDC's is much below that in LDC's, so MDC's cannot be a "bad example." More relevant, there is no reason to assume that MDC's should call on LDC's to lower their growth rate. The LDC growth rate does no economic damage to MDC's. So why should MDC's ask LDC's to reduce fertility, and why should LDC's then not do what is best for them—which *may* be to lower their population growth rates? In short, the MDC population growth rate is not an embarrassment to people in MDC's, no matter what they say to LDC's.

11. "Western science is responsible for decreased LDC mortality and hence for the LDC population growth rate. Therefore, MDC science must take the responsibility for reducing LDC fertility."

How does one idea follow from the other? There is no logical connection.

12. "Zero population growth obviously is the only possible state of affairs in the long-run."

Why? Why should population not get *smaller* if it already is too big? What is sacred about the present population size, or the size that will be attained if it levels off soon? As Wolfers puts it, the concept of ZPG is "a careless example of round number preference" (1971, p. 227). As to whether a larger and/or growing population is plausible or desirable in the long run—the whole of this book is addressed to that topic.

13. "Some people's lives are so poor and miserable that an economic policy does them a service if it discourages their births."

It is a fundamental and irresolvable question whether the poorest man's life is worth living—that is, whether it is better that a very poor man live or not live. The view of many is that some lives are *not* worth living and give "negative utility." This implies that the sum of humanity's happiness would be greater if people with below-threshhold incomes had never been born.

Our aim in this paragraph is not to persuade anyone that all lives do have value, but only that the question is an *open* one, whose answer depends upon one's values and view of the world. The belief that very poor people's lives are not worth living comes out clearly in Ehrlich's language when he talks about India: "I came to understand the population explosion emotionally one stinking hot night in Delhi . . . The streets seemed alive with people. People eating, people washing, people sleeping, people visiting, arguing, and screaming. People thrusting their hands through the taxi window, begging. People defecating and urinating. People clinging to buses. People herding animals. People, people, people, people" (Ehrlich, 1968, p. 15). But Ehrlich writes nothing about those people laughing, loving, being tender to their children, all of which one also sees among these poor Indians.

There *is* misery in India, truly. Intestinal disease and blindness are all around. A 14-year-old girl catches bricks on a construction job for 30 cents per day as her baby lies on a burlap sack, covered with flies and crying on the ground below the scaffold on which the young mother works. A toothless crone of indeterminate age, with no relatives in the world and no home, begins with a cake of wet cow dung to lay a floor for a "dwelling" of sticks and rags, by the side of the road.

And yet these people think their lives are worth living, or else they would choose to stop living. (Note that to choose death does not require suicide. Anthropologists describe people—even young people—who decide they want to die and then do die. People even die on their own schedules, frequently waiting until after weddings and birthdays of relatives to die.) Because people continue to live, we believe that their lives have value to them. And those lives therefore have value in our scheme of things. Hence we do not believe that the existence of poor people—either in poor countries or, a fortiori, in the United States—is a sign of "overpopulation."

14. "But the models in Chapters 6 and 13 take account only of the economic effects of population growth. Higher population density has deleterious psychological and sociological effects."

Scientifically wrong. High population density has been shown to harm animals but not humans; isolation harms humans. See Hawley (1972), Galle (1972) or Choldin and McGinty (1972).

15. "These models emphasize the long-run positive effects of population growth. But as Keynes said, in the long-run we're all dead."

Yes, but others will be alive. And as emphasized earlier, one's over-all judgment about population growth depends upon one's discount factor—how you weight the short-run and the long-run effects.

REFERENCES

Abramovitz, Moses. 1960. Growing up in an affluent society. In *The nation's children*, Vol. 1: *The family and social change*. Eli Ginzberg, ed. New York: Columbia University Press.

Adams, Robert McC. 1965. *Land behind Baghdad*. Chicago: University of Chicago Press.

Adelman, Irma. 1963. An econometric analysis of population growth. *American Economic Review* 53: 314–9.

Adelman, Irma and George Dalton. 1971. A further analysis of modernization in village India. *Economic Journal* 81: 563–79.

Adelman, Irma and Cynthia Taft Morris. 1966. A quantitative study of social and political determinants of fertility. *Economic Development and Cultural Change* 14: 129–57.

Aigner, Dennis J. and Julian L. Simon. 1970. A specification bias interpretation of cross-section vs. time series parameter estimates. *Western Economic Journal* 8: 144–61.

Alonso, William. 1970. The economics of urban size. Mimeo.

Alonso, William and Michael Fajans. 1970. Cost of living and income by urban size. Mimeo.

Andrus, J. Russell. 1948. *Burmese economic life*. Stanford: Stanford University Press.

Anker, Richard. 1973. Socio-economic determinants of reproductive behavior in households of rural Gujurat, India. Ph.D. University of Michigan.

———. 1974. An analysis of International Variations in Birth Rates: Preliminary Analysis. ILO Population and Employment Working Paper 3.

Arensberg, Conrad M. 1968. *The Irish countryman*. 2d ed. New York: Macmillan.

Arney, William Ray. No date. Distributed lag models and the effects of socioeconomic change on fertility. University of Colorado.

Arnold, Fred S. and James T. Fawcett. 1973. The rewards and costs of children: A comparison of Japanese, Filipinos, and Caucasians in Hawaii. Draft paper prepared for the annual meeting of the Population Association of America. New Orleans. April.

Arrow, Kenneth J. 1950. A difficulty in the concept of social welfare. *The Journal of Political Economy* 58: 328–46. Reprinted in K. J. Arrow and T. Scitovsky, eds. *Readings in welfare economics.* Homewood: Irwin, 1969.

———. 1962. The economic implications of learning by doing. *Review of Economic Studies* 29: 155–73.

———. 1963. *Social choice and individual values*. 2d ed. New York: Wiley.

Bahral, Uri. 1965. *The effect of mass immigration on wages in Israel*. Jerusalem: Falk Institute.

Balassa, Bela. 1961. *The theory of economic integration*. Homewood: Irwin.

Balfour, Marshall C. 1962. A scheme for rewarding successful family planners. Mimeo.

507

Balikci, Asen. 1968. The Netsilik Eskimos: adaptive processes. In *Man the hunter*. Richard B. Lee and Irven DeVore, eds. Chicago: Aldine.

Banfield, Edward. 1958. *The moral basis of a backward society*. Chicago: Free Press.

Banks, Joseph A. 1954. *Prosperity and parenthood*. London: Routledge and Kegan Paul.

Barber, William J. 1970. Land reform and economic change among African farmers in Kenya. *Economic Development and Cultural Change* 19: 6–15.

Barclay, William, Joseph Enright, and Reid T. Reynolds. 1970. The social context of U.S. population control programs in the Third World. Mimeo. PAA Meeting.

Barlow, Robin. 1967. *The economic effects of malaria eradication*. Ann Arbor: School of Public Health.

Barnes, Carl B. 1975. The effect of income on suicide: comment. *American Journal of Sociology*, forthcoming.

Barnett, Harold J. and Chandler Morse. 1963. *Scarcity and growth: the economics of natural resource availability*. Baltimore: Johns Hopkins University Press.

Barnett, Larry. 1970. Political affiliation and attitudes toward population limitation. *Social Biology* 17: 124–31.

———. 1971. Zero population growth, Inc. *Bio-Science* 21: 759–65.

Baron, Salo W. 1952. *A social and religious history of the Jews*, Vol. 2. New York: Columbia University Press.

Basavarajappa, K. G. 1971. The influence of fluctuations in economic conditions on fertility and marriage rates, Australia 1920–21 to 1937–38 and 1947–48 to 1966–67. *Population Studies* 25: 39–53.

Bauer, Peter T. and Basil S. Yamey. 1957. *The economics of under-developed countries*. Chicago: University of Chicago Press.

Baumol, William J. 1951. *Economic dynamics*. New York: Macmillan.

Becker, Gary S. 1960. An economic analysis of fertility. In *Demographic and economic change in developed countries*. Princeton: Princeton University Press.

———. 1965. A theory of the allocation of time. *Economic Journal* 75: 493–517.

———. 1966. *Human capital: a theoretical and empirical analysis with special reference to education*. New York: NBER.

———. 1970. Unpublished paper on marriage behavior.

Becker, Gary S. and H. Gregg Lewis. 1973. On the interaction between quantity and quality of children. *Journal of Political Economy* 81 Supplement: S279–88.

Behrman, Jere R. 1968. *Supply response in underdeveloped agriculture: a case study of four major annual crops in Thailand, 1937–1963*. Amsterdam: North Holland.

Belden, G. C. Jr. *et al.* 1964. *The protein paradox*. Boston: Management Report.

Benedict, Burton. 1970. Population regulation in primitive societies. In *Population Control*. Anthony Allison, ed. Harmondsworth: Pelican.

Bennett, John W. 1967. *Hutterian brethren*. Stanford: Stanford University Press.

Bennett, Merrill Kelley. 1954. *The world's food: a study of the interrelationships of world populations, national diets, and food potentials*. New York: Harper.

Ben-Porath, Yoram. 1971. Fertility and economic activity in the short run, Israel 1951–1969. Mimeo. Jerusalem: The Hebrew University.

———. 1972. Fertility in Israel, an economist's interpretation: differentials and trends 1950–1970. In *Economic development and population growth in the*

508

Middle East. Charles A Cooper and Sidney S. Alexander, eds. New York: American Elsevier.

———. 1973. Economic analysis of fertility in Israel: point and counterpoint. *Journal of Political Economy* 81, Supplement: S202–33.

———. 1974. Unpublished paper on mortality and fertility.

———. 1975. Fertility and child mortality over the life cycle evidence from Israel. A paper presented at the Population Research Program Conference sponsored by the Ford and Rockefeller Foundations. Bellagio Study and Conference Center, Lake Como, Italy, May.

Berelson, Bernard. 1964a. National family planning programs: a guide. *Studies in Family Planning*. December.

———. 1964b. Turkey: national survey in population. *Studies in Family Planning*. December.

———. 1966. KAP studies on fertility. In *Family planning and population programs*. Bernard Berelson *et al.*, eds. Chicago: University of Chicago Press.

———. 1969. National family planning programs: where we stand. In *Fertility and family planning: a world view*. S. J. Behrman, Leslie Corsa, and Ronald Freedman, eds. Ann Arbor: University of Michigan Press.

Berelson, Bernard and Ronald Freedman. 1964. A study in fertility control. *Scientific American* 210: 29–38.

Berent, Jerzy. 1970. Fertility decline in eastern Europe and Soviet Union. *Population Studies* 24: 35–58.

Bernhardt, Eva M. 1972. Fertility and economic status—some recent findings on differentials in Sweden. *Population Studies* 26: 175–84.

Berry, R. Albert, and Ronald Soligo. 1969. Some welfare aspects of international migration. *Journal of Political Economy* 77: 778–94.

Berry, Brian J. L. 1972. Population growth in the daily urban systems of the United States, 1980–2000. *Population Distribution and Policy*. The Commission on Population Growth and the American Future, Vol. 5, Research Report. Sara Mills Mazie, ed. Washington: Government Printing Office.

Bethe, Hans A. 1969. Atomic power. *The quality of life*. Cornell University Faculty Members, eds. Ithaca: Cornell University Press.

Bhatia, B. M. 1967. *Famines in India*. 2d ed. New Delhi: Asia.

Bhompore, S. R. *et al.* 1952. A survey of the economic status of villagers in a malarious irrigated tract in Mysore State, India, before and after DDT residual insecticidal spraying. *Indian Journal of Malariology* 6: 355–66.

Birdzell, Ruth A. and Dana C. Hewins. 1971. Unit consolidation to stretch tax dollars. *Illinois Business Review* 28: 6–8.

Blake, Judith. 1966. Ideal family size among white Americans: a quarter of a century's evidence. *Demography* 3: 154–73.

———. 1967. Income and reproductive motivation. *Population Studies* 21: 185–206.

———. 1968. Are babies consumer durables? *Population Studies* 22: 5–27.

Blake, Judith, J. Mayone Stycos and Kingsley Davis. 1961. *Family structure in Jamaica*. Glencoe: Free Press.

Blandy, Richard. 1974. The welfare analysis of fertility reduction. *The Economic Journal* 84: 109–29.

Blyn, George. 1966. *Agricultural trends in India, 1891–1947: output availability and productivity*. Philadelphia: University of Pennsylvania Press.

Bogan, Forrest A. and Thomas E. Swanstrom. 1966. Multiple jobholders in May, 1965. *Monthly Labor Review* 89: 147–54.

Bogue, Donald J. 1953. *Population growth in standard metropolitan areas 1900–1950*. Washington: Housing and Home Finance Agency.

———. 1963. Some tentative recommendations for a 'sociologically correct' family planning communication and motivation program in India. In *Research in family planning*. Clyde V. Kiser, ed. Princeton: Princeton University Press.

———. 1969. *Principles of demography*. New York: Wiley.

Bogue, Donald J. and James A. Palmore. 1964. Some empirical and analytical relations among demographic fertility measures, with regression models for fertility estimation. *Demography* 1: 316–38.

Boorstin, Daniel J. 1970. A case of hypochondria. *Newsweek*, July 6.

Borrie, Wilfrid D, Raymond Firth, and James Spillius. 1957. The population of Tikopia, 1929 and 1952. *Population Studies* 10: 229–52.

Boserup, Ester. 1965. *The conditions of agricultural growth*. London: George Allen and Unwin.

———. 1970. *Woman's role in economic development*. London: George Allen and Unwin.

Bourgeois-Pichat, Jean. 1966. *Population growth and development*. International conciliation 556. January.

Bowden, Witt, Mikhail Karpovitch, and Abbot P. Usher. 1937. *An economic history of Europe since 1750*. New York: American Book Company.

Bowen, Ian. 1954. *Population*. Cambridge: Cambridge University Press.

Bowen, William and T. Aldrich Finegan. 1969. *The economics of labor force participation*. Princeton: Princeton University Press.

Boyd, Robert. 1972. World dynamics: a note. *Science* 177: 516–19.

Bradburn, Norman. 1969. *The structure of psychological well-being*. Chicago: Aldine.

Brady, Dorothy S. 1956. Family saving, 1888 to 1950. In *A study of saving in the United States,* Vol. 3. R. W. Goldsmith, D. S. Brady, and H. Mendershausen, eds. Princeton: Princeton University Press.

Brandis, Royall. 1972. *Principles of economics*. Rev. ed. Homewood: Irwin.

Brandt, R. B. 1972. The morality of abortion. *The Monist* 56: 503–526.

Branson, William H. 1968. Social legislation and the birth rate in nineteenth century Britain. *Western Economic Journal* 6: 134–44.

Brown, Ernest. Henry Phelps, and Sheila V. Hopkins. 1957. Wage rates and prices: evidence for population pressure in the sixteenth century. *Economics* 24: 289–306.

Brown, Lester R. 1968. The agricultural revolution in Asia. *Foreign Affairs* 46: 680–98.

———. 1970. *Seeds of change*. New York: Praeger.

Brown, Randall S. 1972. Population trends in the United States, 1920–1970. Mimeo. University of Illinois.

Buck, John Lossing. 1930. *Chinese farm economy*. Chicago: University of Chicago Press.

———. 1937. *Land utilization in China*. Nanking: The University of Nanking.

REFERENCES

Buer, M. C. 1926. *Health, wealth, and population in the early days of the industrial revolution.* London: George Routledge.

Bundy, William P. 1972. Learning to walk. *Newsweek*, February 28: 35.

Burch, Thomas K. and Murray Gendell. 1971. Extended family structure and fertility: some conceptual and methodological issues. In *Culture and population: a collection of current studies.* S. Polgar, ed. Cambridge: Schenkman.

Cain, Glen G. 1966. *Married women in the labor force.* Chicago: University of Chicago Press.

―――. 1972. *The effect of income maintenance laws on fertility in the United States.* Madison: Institute for Research on Poverty, University of Wisconsin.

Cain, Glen G. and Adriana Weininger. 1972. Economic determinants of fertility. Mimeo. University of Wisconsin.

Calder, Ritchie. 1973. Some views from an expert on experts. *Population Dynamics Quarterly* 1, no. 3 (Summer): 6.

Caldwell, J. C. 1965. Extended family obligations and education: a study of an aspect of demographic transition amongst Ghanaian university students. *Population Studies* 19: 183–204.

―――. 1966. The erosion of the family: a study of the fate of the family in Ghana. *Population Studies* 20: 5–26.

―――. 1967. Fertility attitudes in three economically contrasting rural regions of Ghana. *Economic Development and Cultural Change* 15: 217–38.

―――. 1968a. The control of family size in tropical Africa. *Demography* 5: 598–619.

―――. 1968b. *Population growth and family change in Africa.* Canberra: Australian National University Press.

Campbell, B. O. 1963. Long swings in residential construction: the post-war experience. *American Economic Review* 53: 508–18.

Campbell, Flann. 1960. Birth control and the Christian churches. *Population Studies* 14: 131–47.

Cannan, Edwin. 1928. *Wealth.* London: P. S. King.

Carr-Saunders, A. M. 1922. *The population problem: a study in human evolution.* Oxford: Oxford University Press.

―――. 1925. *Population.* London: Oxford University Press.

―――. 1936. *World population: past growth and present trends.* Oxford: Clarendon Press.

Cassel, Gustav. 1932. *The theory of social economy.* 5th ed., trans. New York: Harcourt Brace.

Centers, Richard, and Hadley Cantril. 1936. Income satisfaction and income aspirations. *Journal of Abnormal and Social Psychology* 41: 64–69.

Chacko, V. I. 1975. Family planners earn retirement bonus on plantations in India. *Population Dynamics Quarterly* 3: 1–8.

Chambers, Jonathan. 1957. The vale of Trent 1760–1800. *Economic History Review* (2d ser.) Supplement No. 3: 1–63.

Chapelle, Anthony, and Georgette Dickey Chapelle. 1956. New life for India's villagers. *The National Geographic Magazine* 109: 572–95.

Chayanov, A. V. 1966. *The theory of peasant economy.* D. Thorner *et al.,* eds. Homewood: Irwin.

511

Chenery, Hollis B. 1960. Patterns of industrial growth. *American Economic Review* 50: 624–54.

Chenery, Hollis B. and Lance Taylor. 1968. Development patterns: among countries and over time. *Review of Economics and Statistics* 50: 391–416.

Chesnais, Jean-Claude and Alfred Sauvy. 1973. Progrès économique et accroissement de la population; une expérience commentée. *Population* 28: 843–57.

Cheung, Steven N. S. 1968. Private property rights and sharecropping. *Journal of Political Economy* 76: 1107–122.

Childe, V. Gordon. 1937. *Man makes himself.* London: Watts.

———. 1950. *What happened in history.* Middlesex, England: Penguin Books.

Cho, Lee-Jay, Wilson H. Grabill, and Donald J. Bogue. 1970. *Differential current fertility in the United States.* Chicago: Community and Family Study Center.

Choldin, Harvey and M. J. McGinty. 1972. Bibliography: population, density, "crowding," and social relations. *Man-Environment Systems* 2: 131–58.

Chow, L. P. 1966. Taiwan: experimental series. *Studies in Family Planning* 13: 3.

Cipolla, Carlo M. 1962. *The economic history of world population.* Baltimore: Pelican.

Clark, Colin. 1951. *Conditions of economic progress.* 2d ed. New York: Macmillan.

———. 1957. *Conditions of economic progress.* 3d ed. New York: Macmillan.

———. 1960. *The economics of irrigation in dry climates.* Oxford: Institute for Research in Agricultural Economics.

———. 1953/1963. Population growth and living standards. *International Labor Review* 68: 99–117. Reprinted in *The economics of underdevelopment.* A. N. Agarwala and S. P. Singh, eds. New York: Oxford.

———. 1967. *Population growth and land use.* New York: St. Martins.

———. 1969a. *Land requirements in peasant agriculture.* International Population Conference, London.

———. 1969b. Misconceptions on hunger, population. *Chicago Sun Times,* October 3: 28.

Clark, Colin and Margaret Haswell. 1967. *The economics of subsistence agriculture.* New York: St. Martins.

Clelland, Wendell. 1936. *The population problem in Egypt.* Lancaster: Science Press.

Coale, Ansley J. 1960. Population change and demand, prices, and the level of employment. In *Demographic and economic change in developed countries.* Ansley Coale, ed. Princeton: Princeton University Press.

———. 1963. Population and economic development. In *The population dilemma.* Philip Hauser, ed. Englewood Cliffs: Prentice-Hall.

———. 1967a. The decline of fertility from the French Revolution to World War II. In *Fertility and Family Planning: A World View.* S. J. Behrman, Leslie Corsa, and Ronald Freedman, eds. Ann Arbor: University of Michigan Press.

———. 1967b. The voluntary control of human fertility. *American Philosophical Society Proceedings* 11: 164–69.

———. 1968. Should the United States start a campaign for fewer births? *Population Index* 34: 467–74.

———. 1970. Man and his environment. *Science* 170: 132–36.

Coale, Ansley J. and Paul Demeny. 1966. *Regional model life tables and stable populations.* Princeton: Princeton University Press.

REFERENCES

Coale, Ansley J. and Edgar M. Hoover. 1958. *Population growth and economic development in low-income countries*. Princeton: Princeton University Press.

Coale, Ansley J. and Melvin Zelnik. 1963. *New estimates of fertility and population in the United States*. Princeton: Princeton University Press.

Coase, Ronald H. 1960. The problem of social cost. *Journal of Law and Economics* 3: 1–44.

Conlisk, John and Donald Huddle. 1969. Allocating foreign aid: an appraisal of a self-help model. *Journal of Development Studies* 5: 245–51.

Connell, K. H. 1950a. The colonization of waste land in Ireland, 1780–1845. *Economic History Review* (2d. ser) 3: 44–71.

———. 1950b. *The population of Ireland, 1750–1845*. Oxford: Clarendon Press.

———. 1965. *Land and population in Ireland, 1780–1845*. In *Population in history*. D. V. Glass and D. E. C. Eversley, eds. Chicago: Aldine.

Cook, Sherburne F. 1947. The inter-relation of population, food supply, and building in pre-conquest central Mexico. *American Antiquity* 13: 45–52.

Cook, Sherburne F. and Woodrow Borah. 1971. *Essays in population history: Mexico and the Carribean*, Vol. 1. Berkeley: University of California Press.

Correa, Hector. 1963. *The economics of human resources*. Amsterdam: North-Holland.

Cummings, Ralph W., Jr. 1970. U.S. expert potentials and prospects with recent trends in world food production and needs: the green revolution in Asia agriculture. Mimeo.

Curwen, E. Cecil and Gudmund Hatt. 1953. *Plough and pasture*. New York: Collier.

Cyert, Richard and James G. March. 1963. *A behavioral theory of the firm*. New York: Wiley.

Dalton, Hugh. 1928. The theory of population. *Economica* 8: 28–50.

Dandekar, V. M. 1969. Overpopulation and the "Asian Drama." *Ceres* 2: 52–55.

Danhof, Clarence. 1941. Farm making costs and the "safety valve" 1850–1860. *Journal of Political Economy* 49: 317–59.

Dasgupta, Partha. 1969. On the concept of optimum population. *The Review of Economic Studies* 36: 295–318.

DaVanzo, Julie. 1971. *The determinants of family formation in Chile, 1960*. Santa Monica: Rand, R-830-AID.

Davis, Joseph S. 1953. The population upsurge and the American economy, 1945–80. *Journal of Political Economy* 61: 369–88.

Davis, Kingsley. 1937. Reproductive instructions and the pressure for population. *Sociological Review* 29: 289–306.

———. 1951. *The population of India and Pakistan*. Princeton: Princeton University Press.

———. 1963. The theory of change and response in modern demographic history. *Population Index* 4: 345–65.

———. 1967. Population policy: will current programs succeed? *Science* 158: 730–39.

———. 1970. The climax of population growth. *California Medicine* 113: 33–39.

Davis, Kingsley and Judith Blake. 1956. Social structure and fertility: an analytical framework. *Economic Development and Cultural Change* 4: 211–35.

Davis, Wayne H. 1970. Overpopulated America. *New Republic* 162: 13–15.

513

Day, Lincoln H. and Alice. 1964. *Too many Americans*. New York: Houghton Mifflin.

Deane, Phyllis. 1967. *The first industrial revolution*. Cambridge: Cambridge University Press.

Deane, Phyllis and W. A. Cole. 1964. *British economic growth, 1688–1959*. Cambridge: Cambridge University Press.

Deevey, Edward S. 1956. The human crop. *Scientific American* 194: 105–12.

———. 1960. The human population. *Scientific American* 203: 195–204.

De Grazia, Sebastian. 1962. *Of time, work and leisure*. New York: Twentieth Century Fund.

De Jong, Gordon. 1965. Religious fundamentalism, socio-economic status, and fertility attitudes in the southern Appalachians. *Demography* 2: 540–48.

Demeny, Paul. 1961. The economics of government payments to limit population: a comment. *Economic Development and Cultural Change* 9: 641–45.

———. 1965. Investment allocation and population growth. *Demography* 2: 203–32.

Denison, Edward F. 1962. *The sources of economic growth in the United States and the alternatives before us*. New York: CED.

———. 1967. *Why growth rates differ*. Washington: The Brookings Institution.

———. 1969. The contribution of education to the quality of labor: comment. *American Economic Review* 59: 935–43.

Denton, Frank T. and Byron G. Spencer. 1974. Household and population effects on aggregate consumption. Mimeo. McMaster University.

De Tray, Dennis N. 1970. *An economic analysis of quantity-quality substitution in household fertility decisions*. Santa Monica, Cal.: Rand, P-4449.

———. 1972. The interaction between parent investment in children and family size: an economic analysis. Mimeo. Rand, R-1003-RF.

———. 1973. Child quality and the demand for children. *Journal of Political Economy* 81, Supplement: S70–95.

Digby, Adrian. 1949. Techniques and the time factor in relation to economic organization. *Man* 49: 16–18.

Dorn, Harold F. 1957. Mortality. In *The study of population*. Philip M. Hauser and Otis Dudley Duncan, eds. Chicago: University of Chicago Press.

———. 1963. World population growth. In *The population dilemma*. Philip M. Hauser, ed. Englewood Cliffs: Prentice-Hall.

Douglas, Mary. 1966. Population control in primitive groups. *British Journal of Sociology* 17: 263–73.

Dovring, Folke. 1965a. *Land and labor in Europe in the twentieth century*. The Hague: M. Nijhoff.

———. 1965b. The transformation of European agriculture. Chapter 6 in *The Cambridge economic history of Europe*, Vol. 6. H. J. Habakkuk and M. Postan, eds. Cambridge: Cambridge University Press.

———. 1966. Review of Boserup. *Journal of Economic History* 26: 380–81.

Dublin, Louis I. 1928. *Health and wealth*. New York: Harper and Bros.

Dublin, Louis I. and A. J. Lotka. 1946. *The money value of a man*. New York: Ronald.

514

Duesenberry, James S. 1960. Comment. In *Demographic and economic change in developed countries*. Ansley J. Coale, ed. Princeton: Princeton University Press.

Dunn, Theodore F. 1973. Quoted in *Advertising Age*, September 3: 6.

Easterlin, Richard A. 1960a. Interregional differences in per capita income, 1840–1950. In *Trends in the American economy in the nineteenth century*. Princeton: Princeton University-NBER, Studies in Income and Wealth 24: 73–141.

————. 1960b. Regional growth of income: long term tendencies. In *Population redistribution and economic growth: United States, 1870–1950*. Vol. II. Simon Kuznets and Dorothy Swaine Thomas, eds. Philadelphia: American Philosophical Society.

————. 1961. The American baby boom in historical perspective. *American Economic Review* 51: 869–911. Reprinted as Chapter 4 in Easterlin 1968.

————. 1967. Effects of population growth in the economic development of developing countries. *The Annals of the American Academy of Political and Social Science* 369: 98–108.

————. 1968. *Population, labor force, and long swings in economic growth*. New York: NBER.

————. 1969. Towards a socio-economic theory of fertility: survey of recent research on economic factors in American fertility. In *Fertility and family planning: a world view*. S. J. Behrman, Leslie Corsa, and Ronald Freedman, eds. Ann Arbor: University of Michigan Press.

————. 1972. Comment on Allen C. Kelley Demographic changes and American economic development: past, present and future. In U.S. Commission on Population Growth and the American Future, *Economic Aspects of Population Change*. Elliot R. Morse and Ritchie H. Reed, eds. Vol. II. Washington: Government Printing Office.

————. In press. Relative economic status and the American fertility swing. In *Social structure, family life styles, and economic behavior*. Eleanor B. Sheldon, ed. Philadelphia: J. B. Lippincott for the Institute of Life Insurance.

Eaton, Joseph W. and Albert J. Mayer. 1953/1968. The social biology of very high fertility among the Hutterites: the demography of a unique population. *Human Biology* 25: 256–62. Reprinted by Charles B. Nam in *Population and society*. New York: Houghton Mifflin.

Edin, K. A. and Edward P. Hutchinson. 1935. *Studies of differential fertility in Sweden*. London: P. G. King.

Ehrlich, Paul R. 1968. *The population bomb*. New York: Ballantine.

————. 1969a. World population: is the battle lost? *Reader's Digest* 94: 137–40.

————. 1969b. Eco-catastrophe. *Ramparts* 7: 24–28.

Eizenga, W. 1961. *Demographic factors and savings*. Amsterdam: North-Holland.

El-Badry, M. A. 1965. Trends in the components of population growth in the Arab countries of the Middle East: a survey of present information. *Demography* 2: 140–86.

Encarnacion, Jose. 1972. Family income, educational level, labor force participation and fertility. Mimeo.

————. 1974. Fertility and labour force participation: Philippines 1968. ILO Population and Employment Working Paper 2.

515

Enke, Stephen. 1960a. The gains to India from population control: some money measures and incentive schemes. *Review of Economics and Statistics* 42: 175–180.

———. 1960b. The economics of government payments to limit population. *Economic Development and Cultural Change* 8: 339–48.

———. 1961a. A rejoiner to comments on the superior effectiveness of vasectomy-bonus schemes. *Economic Development and Cultural Change* 9: 645–47.

———. 1961b. Some reactions to bonuses for family limitation. *Population Review* 5: 33–40.

———. 1962. Some misconceptions of Krueger and Sjaastad regarding the vasectomy-bonus plan to reduce births in overpopulated and poor countries. *Economic Development and Cultural Change* 10: 427–31.

———. 1963. *Economics for development.* New York: Prentice-Hall.

———. 1966. The economic aspects of slowing population growth. *Economic Journal* 76: 44–56.

———. 1969. Birth control for economic development. *Science* 164: 798–802.

Enke, Stephen, et al. 1970. *Economic benefits of slowing population growth.* Santa Barbara: Tempe.

Enke, Stephen, and Richard G. Zind. 1969. Effect of fewer births on average income. *Journal of Biosocial Sciences* 1: 41–55.

Epstein, Trude Scarlett. 1962. *Economic development and social change in South India.* Manchester: Manchester University Press.

———. 1965. Economic change and differentiation in new Britain. *Economic Record* 41: 173–92.

Espenshade, Thomas J. 1972. Estimating the cost of children and some results from urban United States. Mimeo. International Population and Urban Research, University of California, Berkeley.

Eversley, D. E. C. 1965. Population, economy and society. In *Population in history.* D. Glass and D. E. C. Eversley, eds. London: Aldine.

———. 1967. The home market and economic growth in England, 1750–1780. In *Labour and population.* E. L. Jones and G. E. Mingay, eds. London: Arnold.

Fabricant, Solomon. 1963. Study of the size and efficiency of the American economy. In *The economic consequences of the size of nations.* E. Robinson, ed. London: Macmillan.

Fanon, Franz. 1968. *The Wretched of the Earth.* New York: Grove Press.

Farooq, Ghazi M. and Baran Tuncer. 1974. Fertility and economic and social development in Turkey: a cross-sectional and time series study. *Population Studies* 28: 263–76.

Fawcett, James T. 1970. *Psychology and population.* New York: Population Council.

Fei, John C. H. and Gustav Ranis. 1964. *Development of the labor surplus economy.* Homewood: Irwin.

Fellner, William. 1963. Introduction. In *The principles of political economy and taxation.* D. Ricardo. Homewood: Irwin.

———. 1969. Specific interpretations of learning by doing. *Journal of Economic Theory* 1: 119–40.

———. 1970. Trends in the activities generating technological progress. *American Economic Review* 60: 1–29.

516

Felson, Marcus and Mauricio Solaun. 1974. The effect of crowded apartments on fertility in a Colombian public housing project. Mimeo. University of Illinois.

Firth, Raymond W. 1936. *We, the Tikopia*. London: Allen and Unwin.

————. 1939, 1965. *Primitive Polynesian economy*. London: Routledge and Kegan Paul.

Firth, Raymond W. and Basil S. Yamey. 1964. *Capital, saving and credit in peasant societies*. Chicago: Aldine.

Fisher, Joseph L. and Neal Potter. 1969. Natural resource adequacy for the United States and the world. In *The population dilemma*. 2d ed. Philip H. Hauser, ed. Englewood Cliffs: Prentice-Hall.

Fisher, W. Holder. 1971. The anatomy of inflation: 1953–1975. *Scientific American* 225: 15–22.

Fishlow, Albert. 1965. *American railroads and the transformation of the anti-bellum economy*. Cambridge: Harvard University Press.

Fisk, E. K. and R. T. Shand. 1969. The early stages of development in a primitive economy: the evolution from subsistence to trade and specialization. In *Subsistence agriculture and economic development*. C. R. Wharton, Jr., ed. Chicago: Aldine.

Ford, Clellan S. 1952. Control of conception in cross-cultural perspective. *World population problems and birth control. Annals of the New York Academy of Sciences* 54: 763–68.

Forrester, Jay W. 1971. *World dynamics*. Cambridge: Wright Allen.

Frankel, Marvin. 1957. British and American manufacturing productivity, a comparison and interpretation. *University of Illinois Bulletin*. February, 1957.

Frederiksen, Harald. 1966. Determinants and consequences of mortality and fertility trends. *Public Health Reports* 81: 715–27.

————.1960/1968a. Malaria control and population pressure in Ceylon. *Public Health Reports* 75: 865–68. Reprinted in *Readings on population*. David M. Heer, ed. Englewood Cliffs: Prentice-Hall.

————. 1961/1968b. Determinants and consequences of mortality trends in Ceylon. *Public Health Reports* 76: 659–63. Reprinted in *Readings on population*. David M. Heer, ed. Englewood Cliffs: Prentice-Hall.

Freedman, Deborah. 1963. The relation of economic status to fertility. *American Economic Review* 53: 414–26.

————. 1970. The role of the consumption of modern durables in economic development. *Economic Development and Cultural Change* 19: 25–48.

————. 1972a. Consumption of modern goods and services and their relation to fertility: a study in Taiwan. Mimeo. Population Studies Center, University of Michigan.

————. 1972b. Consumption aspirations as economic incentive in a developing economy—Taiwan. Mimeo. Population Studies Center, University of Michigan.

————. 1972c. Family size and economic welfare in a developing economy. Social Statistics Section, American Statistical Association.

Freedman, Ronald. 1961–1962. The sociology of human fertility. *Current Sociology* 10 and 11: 35–121.

———. 1965a. Family planning programs today. *Studies in Family Planning* 8: 1–7.

———. 1965b. The transition from high to low fertility: challenge to demographers. *Population Index* 31: 417–30.

———. 1967. Applications of the behavioral sciences to family planning programs. *Studies in Family Planning* 23: 5–9.

———. 1963/1968. Norms for family size in underdeveloped areas. *Proceedings of the Royal Society*, b. 159: 240–245. Reprinted in *Readings on population*. David M. Heer, ed. Englewood Cliffs: Prentice-Hall.

Freedman, Ronald and Bernard Berelson. 1974. The human population. *Scientific American* 231: 30–39.

Freedman, Ronald and Lolagene Coombs. 1966a. Child spacing and family economic position. *American Sociological Review* 31: 631–48.

———. 1966b. Economic considerations in family growth decisions. *Population Studies* 20: 197–222.

Freedman, Ronald *et al.* 1974. Trends in fertility, family size preferences and practice of family planning: Taiwan, 1965–1973. *Studies in Family Planning* 5: 270–88.

Freedman, Ronald, Albert Hermalin, and J. H. Sun. 1972. Fertility trends in Taiwan: 1961–1970. *Population Index* 38: 141–65.

Freedman, Ronald and Joanna Muller. 1966. The continuing fertility decline in Taiwan: 1965. Mimeo.

Freedman, Ronald and John Y. Takeshita. 1969. *Family planning in Taiwan*. Princeton: Princeton University Press.

Freeman, Orville L. 1969. The green revolution. Statement before the Subcommittee on National Security Policy and Scientific Development, Committee on Foreign Affairs, H.R., 91st Congress, 1st session, December 5.

Friedlander, Dov. 1969. Demographic responses and population change. *Demography* 6: 359–81.

Friedlander, Stanley, and Morris Silver. 1967. A quantitative study of the determinants of fertility behavior. *Demography* 4: 30–70.

Friedman, David. 1972. Laissez-faire in population: the least bad solution. Population Council Occasional Paper.

Friedman, Milton. 1957. *A theory of the consumption function*. Princeton: Princeton University Press.

Friedman, Milton and Leonard J. Savage. 1952. The expected-utility hypothesis and the measurability of utility. *Journal of Political Economy* 60: 463–74.

Friendly, Alfred. 1970. British stand fast in battle against pollution of environment. *Washington Post*, February 5: A10.

Fuchs, Claudio J. and Henry A. Landsberger. 1973. "Revolution of rising expectations" or "traditional life ways"? A study of income aspirations in a developing country. *Economic Development and Cultural Change* 21: 212–26.

Fuchs, Victor R. 1967. *Differentials in hourly earning by region and city size, 1959*. New York: Columbia University Press.

———. 1973. Some notes on the optimum size of population, with special reference to health. In *Is there an optimum level of population?* S. Fred Singer, ed.

New York: McGraw-Hill.

Furnivall, J. S. 1957. *An introduction to the political economy of Burma.* 3d ed. Rangoon: Peoples Literature.

Galbraith, Virginia, and Dorothy S. Thomas. 1941/1956. Birth rates and the inter-war business cycles. *Journal of the American Statistical Association* 36: 465–76. Reprinted in *Demographic analysis.* J. J. Spengler and O. D. Duncan, eds. Glencoe: Free Press.

Gardner, Bruce. 1973. Economics of the size of North Carolina rural families. *Journal of Political Economy* 81, Supplement: S99–122.

Gayer, David. 1974. The effects of wages, unearned income and taxes on the supply of labor. Mimeo. World Institute, Jerusalem.

Gemery, Henry A. No date. Absorption of population pressure in 19th century Sweden. Mimeo. Colby College.

Gendell, Murray. 1967. Fertility and development in Brazil. *Demography* 4: 143–57.

Gilbert, Milton and Irving B. Kravis. 1954. *An international comparison of national products and the purchasing power of currencies.* Paris: OECD.

Gilboy, Elizabeth W. 1932/1967. Demand as a factor in the industrial revolution. In *Facts as factors in economic history.* A. H. Cole, ed. Boston: Harvard University Press. Reprinted in *The causes of the industrial revolution in England.* R. M. Hartwell, ed. London: Methuen.

Gille, Halver. 1949. The demographic history of the northern European countries in the eighteenth century. *Population Studies* 3: 3–70.

Gillespie, Robert. No date. Economic incentives in family planning programs. Mimeo. Population Council.

———. 1969. *Second Five-Year Plan for Economic and Social Development.* United Republic of Tanzania, Dar es Salaam: Government Printing Office. Quoted from Harbison.

———. 1971. Economic dis-incentives for population control. Mimeo. Faculty Working Papers, College of Commerce and Business Administration, University of Illinois.

Gintis, Herbert. 1971. Education, technology and the characteristics of worker productivity. *American Economic Review* 61: 266–79.

Glaser, Daniel and Kent Rice. 1959/1962. Crime, age and employment. *American Sociological Review* 24: 679–86. Reprinted in *The sociology of crime and delinquency.* M. E. Wolfgang, L. Savitz and N. Johnson, eds. New York: Wiley.

Glass, David V. 1940. *Population policies and movements in Europe.* Oxford: Calrendon Press.

———. 1969. Fertility trends in Europe since the Second World War. In *Fertility and family planning: a world view.* S. J. Behrman, Leslie Corsa, and Ronald Freedman, eds. Ann Arbor: University of Michigan Press.

Glass, David V. and D. E. C. Eversley. 1965. *Population in history.* Chicago: Aldine.

Glover, Donald and Julian L. Simon. 1975. The effects of population density upon infra-structure: the case of road building. *Economic Development and Cultural Change* 23: 453–68.

Glueck, Nelson. 1959. *Rivers in the desert.* New York: Farrar Straus.

519

REFERENCES

Godwin, William. 1820. *Of population*. London: J. McGowan.

Goldsmith, Raymond. 1962. *The national wealth of the United States in the postwar period*. Princeton: Princeton University Press.

Gottlieb, Manuel. 1945/1956. The theory of optimum population for a closed economy. *Journal of Political Economy* 53: 289–316. In *Population theory and policy*. J. J. Spengler and O. D. Duncan, eds. Glencoe: Free Press.

Gould, Ketayun H. 1976. The twain never meet: Sherapin and the family planning program. John F. Marshall and Steven Polgas, eds. *Culture, Natality and Family Planning*. Chapel Hill, N.C.: Carolina Population Center, University of N.C.

Gourou, Pierre. 1966. *The tropical world, its social and economic conditions and its future status*. New York: Wiley.

Gregory, Paul R. 1973. Differences in fertility determinants: developed and developing countries. *The Journal of Development Studies* 9: 233–341.

———. In press. A cost-inclusive simultaneous equation model of birth rates. *Econometrica*.

Gregory, Paul R., John M. Campbell, and Benjamin S. Cheng. 1972. A simultaneous equation model of birth rates in the United States. *The Review of Economics and Statistics* 54: 374–80.

Griliches, Zvi. 1960. Congruence versus probability: a false dichotomy. *Rural Sociology* 25: 35–56.

Gronav, Reuben. 1974. The allocation of time of the Israeli married woman. Mimeo, Falk Institute. November.

Grunfeld, Yehuda. 1961. The interpretation of cross-section estimates in a dynamic model. *Econometrica* 29: 397–404.

Gupta, P. B. and C. R. Malaker. 1963. Fertility differentials with levels of living and adjustment of fertility, birth, and death rates. *Sankya*, b, 25: 23–48.

Guthrie, Harold W. 1965. Who moonlights and why? *Illinois Business Review* 21: 6–8.

———. 1966. Some explanations of moonlighting. Business and Economic Statistics Section, *Proceedings of the American Statistical Association*.

Habakkuk, John. 1960. Family structure and economic change in nineteenth century Europe. In *A modern introduction to the family*. N. W. Bell and E. F. Vogel, eds. New York: Free Press.

———. 1963. Population problems and European economic development in the late eighteenth and nineteenth centuries. *American Economic Review* 53: 607–18.

———. 1971. *Population growth and economic development since 1750*. Leicester: Leicester University Press.

Habakkuk, John and Michael Postan, eds. 1941–1967. The industrial revolution and after: income, population and technological change. In *The Cambridge economic history of Europe*, Vol. 6. Cambridge: Cambridge University Press.

Hagen, Everett E. 1953. The incremental capital-output ratio. Mimeo.

———. 1959. Population and economic growth. *American Economic Review* 49: 310–27.

———. 1975. *The economics of development*. Homewood: Irwin.

REFERENCES

Hagen, Everett E. and Oli Hawrylyshyn. 1969. Analysis of world income and growth, 1955–1964. *Economic development and cultural change* 18: Part II.

Hajnal, Jan. 1954. Analysis of changes in the marriage pattern by economic groups. *American Sociological Review* 19: 295–302.

———. 1964. European marriage patterns in perspective. In *Population in history*. David V. Glass and D. E. C. Eversley, eds. Chicago: Aldine.

Handler, Philip. 1971. Interview in *U. S. News and World Report*, January 18: 30–34.

Handlin, Oscar. 1951. *The uprooted*. Boston: Little, Brown.

Hansen, Alvin H. 1939. Economic progress and declining population growth. *American Economic Review* 29: 1–15.

Hansen, W. Lee. 1957. A note on the cost of children's mortality. *Journal of Political Economy* 65: 257–62.

Harbison, Frederick H. and Charles A. Myers. 1964/1969. *Education, manpower and economic growth*. New York: McGraw-Hill. Excerpted in *Economics of education 2*. M. Blaug, ed. Harmondsworth: Penguin.

Hardy, Thomas. *The Mayor of Casterbridge*. New York: Signet, 1962.

Harman, Alvin J. 1970. Fertility and economic behavior of families in the Philippines. Mimeo. Rand, RM-6385-AID.

Harris, John R. and Michael Todare. 1970. Migration, unemployment and development: a two section analysis. *American Economic Review* 60: 126–42.

Hartwell, Robert M. 1965. The causes of the industrial revolution: an essay in methodology. *Economic History Review* 18: 164–82.

Harvey, Philip D. 1969. Development potential in famine relief: the Bihar model. *International Development Review* 11: 7–9.

Hauser, Philip M. 1967. Family planning and population programs: a book review article. *Demography* 4: 397–414.

Hawkins, Edward K. *Roads and road transport in an underdeveloped country*. London: Colonial Office.

Hawley, Amos H. 1950. *Human ecology*. New York: Ronald Press.

———. 1969. Population and society: an essay on growth. In *Fertility and family planning: a world view*. S. J. Behrman, Leslie Corsa, and Ronald Freedman, eds. Ann Arbor: University of Michigan Press.

———. 1972. Population density and the city. *Demography* 9: 521–30.

Hawley, Amos H. and Visid Prachuabmoh. 1966. Family growth and family planning in a rural district of Thailand. In *Family planning and population programs*. B. Berelson *et al.*, eds. Chicago: University of Chicago Press.

Haworth, C. T. and D. W. Rasmussen. 1973. Determinants of metropolitan cost of living variations. *Southern Economic Journal* 40: 183–92.

Hawthorn, Geoffrey. 1970. *The sociology of fertility*. London: Collier-Macmillan.

Heady, Earl O. 1949. Basic economic and welfare aspects of farm technological advance. *Journal of Farm Economics* 31: 293–316.

Heer, David M. 1966. Economic development and fertility. *Demography* 3: 423–44.

———. 1968. *Readings in population*. Englewood Cliffs: Prentice-Hall.

Heer, David M. and Dean O. Smith. 1968. Mortality level, desired family size, and population increase. *Demography* 5: 104–21.

Heisel, Donald R. 1968a. Attitudes and practice of contraception in Kenya. *Demography* 5: 632–41.

———. 1968b. Fertility limitation among women in rual Kenya. Mimeo.

Henderson, A. M. 1949. The cost of a family. *The Review of Economic Studies* 17: 127–48.

———. 1949/1950. The cost of children. Parts I and II. *Population Studies* 3: 130–50 and 4: 267–98.

Herdt, Robert W. 1970. A disaggregate approach to aggregate supply. *American Journal of Agricultural Economics* 52: 512–70.

Herfindahl, Orris C. and Allen V. Kneese. 1965. *Quality of the environment.* Baltimore: Johns Hopkins University Press.

Herlihy, D. 1965. Population, plague, and social change in rural Pistoia, 1201–1430. *Economic History Review* 2: 225–44.

Heuser, Robert L., Stephanie J. Ventura, and Frank H. Godley. 1970. *Natality statistics analysis, 1965–1976.* National Center for Health Statistics, Ser. 21, No. 19.

Hicks, John R. 1942. *The social framework.* Oxford: Oxford University Press.

———. 1969. *A theory of economic history.* Oxford: Oxford University Press.

———. 1974. Capital controversies: ancient and modern. *American Economic Review* 64: 307–16.

Hicks, Whitney W. 1974. Economic development and fertility change in Mexico, 1950–1970. *Demography* 11: 407–21.

Higgs, Robert. 1971. American inventiveness, 1870–1920. *Journal of Political Economy* 79: 661–67.

Hill, Rueben, J. Mayone Stycos, and Kurt B. Back. 1959. *The family and population control.* Chapel Hill: University of North Carolina Press.

Himes, Norman E. 1936. *The medical history of contraception.* Baltimore: Williams and Wilkins.

Hirschman, Albert O. 1958. *The strategy of economic development.* New Haven: Yale University Press.

Ho, Ping-Ti. 1959. *Studies on the population of China.* Cambridge: Harvard University Press.

Ho, Yhi-Min. 1966. *Agricultural development of Taiwan 1903–1960.* Nashville: Vanderbilt University Press.

Hobsbawn, E. J. and R. M. Hartwell. 1963. The standard of living during the industrial revolution: a discussion. *Economic History Review* 16: 120–46.

Hollingsworth, Thomas Henry. 1969. *Historical Demography.* London: Hodder and Stoughton.

Holmberg, Allan R. 1950. *Nomads of the Long Bow: the Sirione of eastern Bolivia.* Washington: The Smithsonian.

Hooley, R. 1967. Measurement of capital formation in underdeveloped countries. *Review of Economics and Statistics* 49: 199–208.

Hoover, Edgar M. 1969. Economic consequences of population growth. *Indian Journal of Economics* 196: 101–11.

Hoover, Edgar M. and M. Perlman. 1966. Measuring the effect of population control in economic development: a case study of Pakistan. *Pakistan Development Review* 6: 545–66.

REFERENCES

Hoselitz, Bert F. 1964. Capital formation and credit in Indian agricultural society. In *Capital, saving and credit in peasant societies*. R. Firth and B. S. Yamey, eds. Chicago: Aldine.

Hubbert, M. King. 1969. Energy resources. In *Resources and man*. San Francisco: Freeman.

Hymer, Stephen and Stephen Resnick. 1969. A model of an agrarian economy with nonagricultural activities. *American Economic Review* 59: 493–506.

Hyrrenius, H. 1946. The relation between birth rates and economic activity in Sweden, 1920–1944. *Bulletin of the Oxford Institute of Statistics* 8: 14–21.

Government of India. Various years. *Studies in Farm Management.*

International Road Federation. Various years. *Highway expenditures, road and motor vehicle statistics*. Washington: International Road Federation.

Shah of Iran. 1974. Quoted in the *Jerusalem Post*, September 27.

Isaac, Julius. 1947. *Economics of migration*. London: Kegan Paul.

Ishii, Ryoichi. 1937. *Population pressure and economic life in Japan*. Chicago: University of Chicago Press.

Iyoha, Milton Ame. 1973. Human fertility, population change, and economic development. Econometric Society paper. December.

Jaffe, A. J. and K. Azumi. 1960. The birth rate and cottage industries in underdeveloped countries. *Economic Development and Cultural Change* 9: 52–64.

Jain, Anrudh. 1973. Marketing research in the Nirodh program. *Studies in Family Planning* 4: 184–90.

Jerome, Harry. 1926. *Migration and business cycles*. New York: NBER.

Jevens, W. Stanley. 1865. *The coal question*. Cambridge: Macmillan and Co.

Johnson, D. Gale. 1974. Population, food, and economic adjustment. *American Statistician* 28: 89–93.

Jones, Eric L. and G. Mingay. 1967. *Land, labour and population in the industrial revolution*. London: Arnold.

Jones, Gavin. 1969. The economic effect of declining fertility in less developed countries. An occasional paper of the Population Council, New York. February.

Jones, K. and A. D. Smith. 1970. *The economic impact of commonwealth immigration*. London: Cambridge University Press.

Jorgenson, Dale W. 1961. The development of a dual economy. *Economic Journal* 71: 309–34.

———. 1967. Surplus agricultural labour and the development of a dual economy. *Oxford Economic Papers* 19: 288–312.

Kanovsky, Eliyahu. 1966. *The economy of the Israeli kibbutz*. Cambridge, Mass.: Harvard University Press.

Kao, Charles, Kurt Anschel, and Carl Eicher. 1972. Disguised unemployment in agriculture: a survey. In *Readings in economic development*. W. L. Johnson and D. R. Kamersohen, eds. Cincinnati: Southwestern.

Kasarda, John D. 1971. Economic structure and fertility: a comparative analysis. *Demography* 8: 307–18.

Katona, George B. and Ernest Zahn. 1971. *Aspirations and affluence*. New York: McGraw-Hill.

Keeny, Samuel M. and George P. Cernada. 1970. Taiwan. *Country Profiles*. February.

Keeny, Samuel M., George P. Cernada, and John Ross. 1968. Korea and Taiwan: the record for 1967. *Studies in Family Planning* 29: 1–9.

Keesing, Donald B. 1968. Population and industrial development: some evidence from trade patterns. *American Economic Review* 57: 448–55.

Keesing, Donald B. and Donald B. Sherk. 1971. Population density in patterns of trade and development. *American Economic Review* 61: 956–61.

Kelley, Allen C. 1965. International migration and economic growth: Australia, 1865–1935. *The Journal of Economic History* 31: 729–76.

———. 1968. Demographic change and economic growth: Australia, 1861–1911. *Explorations in Entrepreneurial History* 5: 207–77.

———. 1969. Demand patterns, demographic change and economic growth. *Quarterly Journal of Economics* 83: 110–26.

———. 1976. Saving, demographic change, and economic development. *Economic Development and Cultural Change* 24: 683–93.

Kelley, Allen C. and Jeffrey G. Williamson. 1971. Writing history backwards: Meiji Japan revisited. *The Journal of Economic History* 31: 729–76.

Kelley, Allen C., *et al*. 1972. *Economic dualism in theory and history*. Chicago: University of Chicago Press.

Keynes, John Maynard. 1937. Some economic consequences of a declining population. *Eugenics Review* 29: 13–17.

———. 1951. *Essays in biography*. New York: Norton.

Kindleberger, Charles P. 1958. *Economic development*. New York: McGraw-Hill.

———. 1965. *Economic development*. 2d ed. New York: McGraw-Hill.

King, Peter S. 1964. *Proposals for family planning promotion: a marketing plan*. Calcutta: Indian Institute of Management. Mimeo.

Kirk, Dudley. 1942/1956. The relation of employment levels to births in Germany. *Milbank Memorial Fund Quarterly* 20: 126–38. Reprinted in *Demographic Analysis*. J. J. Spengler and O. D. Duncan, eds. Glencoe: Free Press.

———. 1960. The influence of business cycles on marriage and birth rates. In *Demographic and economic change in developed countries*. Ansley J. Coale, ed. Princeton: Princeton University Press.

———. 1969. Natality in the developing countries: recent trends and prospects. In *Fertility and family planning: a world view*. S. J. Behrman, Leslie Corsa, and Ronald Freedman, eds. Ann Arbor: University of Michigan Press.

Kiser, Clyde V. 1970. Changing fertility patterns in the United States. *Social Biology* 17: 312–15.

Kiser, Clyde V. *et al*. 1968. *Trends and variations in fertility in the United States*. Cambridge: Harvard University Press.

Kleiman, Ephraim. 1967. A standardized dependency ratio. *Demography* 4: 876–93.

Kleinman, David S. 1961. Fertility variation and resources in rural India. *Economic Development and Cultural Change*. 21: 679–96.

Klein, Lawrence R. 1962. *An introduction to econometrics*. Englewood Cliffs: Prentice-Hall

Klotz, Benjamin P. 1972. Some consequences of declining population growth. Mimeo.

524

Knight, Frank H. 1936. *The ethics of competition and other essays.* New York: Harper.

Knodel, John. 1968. Infant mortality and fertility in three Bavarian villages: an analysis of family histories from the 19th century. *Population Studies* 2: 297–318.

Knodel, John and Etienne Van DeWalle. 1967. Breast feeding, fertility and infant mortality: an analysis of some early German data. *Population Studies* 21: 109–31.

Kocher, James E. 1972. Agricultural development, equity, and fertility declines: a review of the evidence. Mimeo. Population Council.

———. 1973. Rural development, income distribution, and fertility decline. Population Council Occasional Paper.

Koya, Yoshio. 1964. Does the effect of a family planning program continue? *Eugenics Quarterly* 11: 141–47.

Krause, J. T. 1958. Changes in English fertility and mortality, 1781–1850. *Economic History Review* 11: 52–70.

———. 1963. English population movements between 1700 and 1850. *International Population Conference Proceedings,* 1961: 583–90, London.

———. 1967. Some aspects of population change, 1690–1790. In *Land, labour, and population in the industrial revolution.* B. L. Jones and G. E. Mingay, eds. London: Arnold.

Kreps, Juanita M. 1967. *Lifetime allocation of work and leisure.* Research Report No. 22. U. S. HEW, Social Security Administration.

Krishnakumar, S. 1972. Kerala's pioneering experiment in massive vasectomy camps. *Studies in Family Planning* 3: 177–85.

Krishnamurty, K. 1966. Economic development and population growth in low income countries: an empirical study of India. *Economic Development and Cultural Change* 15: 70–75.

Kroeber, Alfred L. *Anthropology.* New rev. ed. New York: Harcourt Brace.

Krueger, Anne O. and Larry A. Sjaastad. 1962. Some limitations of Enke's economics of population. *Economic Development and Cultural Change* 10: 423–26.

Krzywicki, Ludwik. 1934. *Primitive society and its vital statistics.* London: Macmillan.

Kuh, Edwin and John R. Meyer. 1955. Correlation and regression estimates when the data are ratios. *Econometrica* 23: 400–16.

Kumar, Joginder. 1973. *Population and land in world agriculture.* Berkeley: University of California Press.

Kupinsky, Stanley. 1971. Non-familial activity and socio-economic differentials in fertility. *Demography* 8: 353–68.

Kuznets, Simon. 1956. Quantitative aspects of the economic growth of nations. I: Levels and variability of rates of growth. *Economic Development and Cultural Change* 5: 5–94.

———. 1958. Long swings in the growth of population and in related economic variables. *Proceedings of the American Philosophical Society* 102: 25–52.

———. 1960. Population change and aggregate output. In *Demographic and economic change in developed countries.* Princeton: Princeton University Press.

———. 1963. Quantitative aspects of the economic growth of nations. VIII: Distribution of income by size. *Economic Development and Cultural Change* 11: 1–80.

——. 1965. Demographic aspects of modern economic growth. Paper presented at World Population Conference, Belgrade, September.

——. 1966. *Modern economic growth*. New Haven: Yale University Press.

——. 1967. Population and economic growth. *Proceedings of the American Philosophical Society* 111: 170–93.

——. 1968. *Toward a theory of economic growth of nations*. New York: Norton.

——. 1971. *Economic growth of nations*. Cambridge: Harvard University Press.

——. 1973. *Population, capital and growth*. New York: Norton.

——. 1974. Rural-urban differences in fertility: an international comparison. *Proceedings of the American Philosophical Society* 118: 1–29.

Kuznets, Simon *et al*. 1957–1964. *Population redistribution and economic growth, United States 1870–1950*. 3 vols. Philadelphia: University of Pennsylvania Press.

Lambert, Richard D. and Bert F. Hoselitz. 1963. Southern Asia and the West. In *The role of savings and wealth in southern Asia and the West*. Richard D. Lambert and Bert F. Hoselitz, eds. Paris: UNESCO.

Landsberg, Hans H. 1964. *Natural resources for U.S. growth*. Baltimore: Johns Hopkins University Press.

Landsberger, Michael. 1971. An integrated model of consumption and market activity: The children effect. Social Statistics Section. *Proceedings of the American Statistical Association*: 137–42.

Langer, William L. 1963/1968. Europe's initial population explosion. *American Historical Review* 69: 1–17. Reprinted in *Readings on population*. David M. Heer, ed. Englewood Cliffs: Prentice-Hall.

——. 1972. Checks on population growth: 1750–1850. *Scientific American* 226: 93–99.

Lau, Lawrence J. and Pan A. Yotopoulos. 1971. A test for relative efficiency and application to Indian agriculture. *American Economic Review* 61: 94–109.

Leasure, J. William. 1967. Some economic benefits of birth prevention. *The Milbank Memorial Fund Quarterly* 45: 417–26.

Lebergott, Stanley. 1960. Population change and the supply of labor. In *Demographic and economic change in developed countries*. Ansley J. Coale, ed. Princeton: Princeton University Press.

——. 1964. *Manpower in economic growth*. New York: McGraw-Hill.

Lee, Richard B. 1968. What hunters do for a living, or, how to make out on scarce resources. In *Man the hunter*. R. B. Lee and Irvin Devore, eds. Chicago: Aldine.

Lee, Richard B. and Irvin Devore. 1968. *Man the hunter*. Chicago: Aldine.

——. 1968. Problems in the study of hunters and gatherers. In *Man the hunter*. Chicago: Aldine.

Lee, Ronald. 1971. Population in pre-industrial England: an econometric analysis. Mimeo. Ann Arbor: Department of Economics and Population Studies Center, University of Michigan.

——. 1972a. Models of pre-industrial population dynamics, applications to England. Mimeo.

————. 1972b. Spectral implications of a stochastic birth-marriage model with various applications. Mimeo.

Leff, Nathaniel H. 1969. Dependency rates and saving rates. *American Economic Review* 59: 886–96.

Leibenstein, Harvey. 1954. *A theory of economic demographic development*. Princeton: Princeton University Press.

————. 1957. *Economic backwardness and economic growth*. New York: Wiley.

————. 1964. An econometric analysis of population growth: comment. *American Economic Review* 54: 134–35.

————. 1968. The demographic impact of nurture and education on development. Mimeo.

————. 1969. Pitfalls in benefit-cost analysis of birth prevention. *Population Studies* 23: 161–70.

————. 1972. The impact of population growth on the American economy. In *The report of the Commissions on Population Growth and the American Future*. Vol. 2: *Economic aspects of population change*.

Lele, Uma J. and John W. Mellor. 1964. Estimates of change and causes of change in food grains production: India 1949–50 to 1960–61. *Cornell University Agricultural Development Bulletin* 2.

Levine, Gilbert. 1966. Irrigation costs in the Philippines. *Philippine Economic Journal* 5: 28ff.

Lewis, Anthony. 1970. How pointless it all seems now. *The New York Times Magazine*, February 8.

Lewis, Oscar. 1951. *Life in a Mexican village*. Urbana: University of Illinois Press.

Lewis, William Arthur. 1955. *The theory of economic growth*. London: George Allen and Unwin.

Lindert, Peter H. 1973. The relative cost of American children. Mimeo.

————. 1973. Remodeling the household for fertility analysis. Working Paper 73–14. Center for Demography and Ecology. University of Wisconsin. May.

————. 1974. American fertility patterns since the Civil War. Working Paper 74–27. Center for Demography and Ecology. University of Wisconsin, Madison. September.

————. Forthcoming. *Fertility and scarcity in America*. Princeton: Princeton University Press. (forthcoming).

Lipson, Gerald and Dianne Wolman. 1972. Polling Americans on birth control and population. *Family Planning Perspectives* 4: 39–42.

Little, Arthur D., Inc. 1972. Commercial distribution of contraceptives in Columbia, Iran, and the Philippines. *Reports on Population/Family Planning*. March.

Lloyd, Cynthia Brown. 1972. The effect of child subsidies in fertility: an international study. Ph.D. abstract. Columbia University.

Lockridge, Kenneth. 1968. Land, population, and the evolution of N. England society 1630–1790. *Past and Present* 30: 62–80.

Losch, August. 1937/1956. Population cycles as a cause of business cycles. *Quarterly Journal of Economics*: 649–62. In *Population theory and policy*. Spengler and Duncan, eds. Glencoe: Free Press.

Maital, Shlomo. 1971. Economy and population. Mimeo. Tel Aviv University.

527

REFERENCES

Malinvaud, Edmond. 1966. *Statistical methods of econometrics*. New York: Humanities.

Malthus, Thomas R. 1798. *An Essay on the principle of population, as it affects the future improvements of society*. London: J. Johnson.

——. 1798. *Population: The first essay*. Ann Arbor: University of Michigan Press, 1959.

——. 1803. *An essay on the principle of population, or a view of its past and present effects on human happiness*. London: J. Johnson. A new edition, very thick, enlarged.

——. 1817. *Principle of population*. Vol. 2. London: John Murray.

——. 1817/1963. Principles of population. 5th ed. Homewood: Irwin.

Mamdani, Mahmood. 1972. The myth of population control (family, caste, and class in an Indian village). New York and London: Monthly Review Press.

Mandle, Jay R. 1970. The decline in mortality in British Guiana, 1911–1960. *Demography* 7: 301–16.

Masefield, John. 1967. In *The Cambridge economic history of Europe*. B. J. Habakkuk and M. Postan, eds. Vol. 6. Cambridge: Cambridge University Press.

Mason, Karen O. *et al.* 1971. Social and economic correlates of family fertility: a survey of the evidence. Mimeo, Near East-South Asia Bureau/Office of Population Programs, U.S.A.I.D.

Mason, Karen O. and Barbara S. Schultz. No date. Fertility, work experience, potential earnings and occupation of American women age 30–44: evidence in survey data. Research Triangle Park, North Carolina: Research Triangle Institute.

Mathias, Peter. 1969. *The first industrial nation*. London: Methuen.

Matras, Judah. 1973. *Populations and societies*. Englewood Cliffs: Prentice-Hall.

May, David A. and David M. Heer. 1969. Son survivorship, motivation, and family size in India: a computer simulation. *Population Studies* 23: 199–210.

McCarthy, Frederick D. and Margaret McArthur. 1960. The food quest and the time factor in aboriginal economic life. In *Records of the American-Australian scientific expedition to Arnhem Land*, Vol. 2. Melbourne: Melbourne University Press.

McIntyre, Robert J. 1974. Pro-natalist programs in Eastern Europe. PAA.

McIntyre, Robert J. No date. Population policy in Eastern Europe: abortion liberalization and pro-natalist counter measures. Mimeo.

McInnis, R. Marvin. 1972. Birth rates and land availability in 19th century Canada. PAA Paper.

McKeown, Thomas, and R. G. Brown. 1955/1968. Medieval evidence related to English population changes in the eighteenth century. *Population Studies* 9: 119–41. Reprinted in *Readings on population*. David M. Heer, ed. Englewood Cliffs: Prentice-Hall.

McMahon, Walter W. 1970. An economic analysis of major determinants of expenditures on public education. *Review of Economics and Statistics* 52: 242–51.

Mead, Margaret, ed. 1954. *Cultural patterns and technical change*. Paris: UNESCO.

Meade, James E. 1937. An introduction to economic analysis and policy. London: Oxford University Press.

——. 1955. *The theory of international economic policy*. Vol. II: *trade and welfare*. London: Oxford University Press.

528

————. 1961. Mauritius: a case study in Malthusian economics. *The Economic Journal* 71: 521–34.

————. 1967. Population explosion, the standard of living and social conflict. *The Economic Journal* 77: 233–56.

————. 1968. *The growing economy*. Chicago: Aldine.

Meadows, Donella H., Dennis L. Meadows, Jorgen Randers, and William W. Behrens III. 1972. *The limits to growth*. New York: Potomac Assoc.

Mehta, Jamshed K. 1967. *Rhyme, rhythm and truth in economics*. London: Asia.

Meier, Richard L. 1959. *Modern science and the human fertility problem*. New York: Wiley.

Mellor, John W. 1963. The use and productivity of farm family labor in early stages of agricultural growth. *Journal of Farm Economics* 45: 517–34.

————. 1966. *The economics of agricultural development*. Ithaca: Cornell University Press.

Mellor, John W. *et al.* 1968. *Developing rural India*. Ithaca: Cornell University Press.

Mendels, Franklin F. 1970. Industry and marriages in Flanders before the industrial revolution. In *Population and economics*. Paul Deprez, ed. Winnipeg: University of Manitoba Press.

————. 1971. Industrialization and population pressure in eighteenth century Flanders. Ph.D. University of Wisconsin.

Michael, Robert T. 1970a. Education and fertility. Mimeo.

————. 1970b. Education and the derived demand for children. Mimeo.

————. 1971. Dimensions of household fertility: an economic analysis. American Statistics Association Annual Meeting, Social Statistics Section: 126–36.

————. 1973. Education and the derived demand for children. *Journal of Political Economy* 81, Supplement: S128–64.

Michael, Robert T. and Edward P. Lazear. 1971. On the shadow price of children. Mimeo.

Michael, Robert T. and Willis, Robert J. 1973. The "imperfect contraceptive" population: An economic analysis. Preliminary Draft prepared for presentation at the PAA Meeting in New Orleans, La. April 26–28.

Michael, Robert T. and Willis, Robert J. 1973. Contraception and Fertility: household production under uncertainty. Working Paper No. 21. Center for Economic Analysis of Human Behavior and Social Institutions, New York. December.

Mills, Robert. 1826. *Statistics of South Carolina*. Charleston: Hunburt and Lloyd.

Mills, Stephanie. 1970. Saving the human race. In *The Family Planners* (Syntex Laboratory) 3: 11.

Miles, Macura. 1967. The long-range population outlook: a summary of current estimates. Paper presented at the University of Indiana, April.

Mincer, Jacob. 1960. Labor supply, family income, and consumption. *American Economic Review* 50: 574–83.

————. 1962. Labor force participation of married women. In *Aspects of labor economics*. H. Gregory Lewis, ed. Princeton: Princeton University Press.

————. 1963. Market prices, opportunity costs, and income effects. In *Measurement in economics: studies in mathematical economics and econometrics in memory of Yehuda Grunfeld*. C. Christ, ed. Stanford: Stanford University Press.

Miner, Jerry. 1963. *Social and economic factors in spending for public education.* Syracuse: Syracuse University Press.

Mirrlees, James A. 1972. Population policy and the taxation of family size. *Journal of Public Economics* 1: 169–98.

Mishler, E. G. and L. F. Westoff. 1955. A proposal for research in social psychological factors affecting fertility. *Milbank Memorial Fund Quarterly, Current Research in Human fertility* 121–50.

Mitra, Asok. 1969. Possible demographic changes consequent on rising pressure in India of population on land. International Population Conference.

Modigliani, France. 1949. Fluctuations in the saving-income ratio: a problem in economic forecasting. *Studies in Income and Wealth* 11: 371–443.

———. 1966. The life cycle hypothesis of saving, the demand for wealth and the supply of capital. *Social Research* 33: 160–217.

Moore, Barrington, Jr. 1966. *Social origin of dictatorship and democracy.* Boston: Beacon.

Moore, Geoffrey H. and Janice Neipert Hedges. 1971. Trends in labor and leisure. *Monthly Labor Review* 94: 3–11.

Morss, Elliott R. and Susan McIntosh. Family life styles, the childbearing decision, and the influence of federal activities, and quantitative approach. *Economic aspects of population change.* Elliott R. Morss and Ritchie H. Reed, eds. Vol. 2.

Mott, Frank. The dynamics of demographic change in a Nigerian village. Human Resources Research Unit, University of Lagos, Nigeria.

Mott, Paul E. 1965. Hours work and moonlighting. *Hours of work.* Clyde E. Dankert, ed. New York: Harper and Row.

Mountford, Charles P., ed. 1960. *Arnhem Land.* Vol. 2. Melbourne: Melbourne University Press.

Mueller, Eva. 1973. The Impact of Agricultural Change in Demographic Development in the Third World. To be published in a volume on Demographic growth and development in the third world. International Union for the Scientific Study of Population.

———. 1975. The economic value of children in peasant agriculture. Conference on Population Policy, Resources for the Future.

Munroe, Gretel S. and Gavin W. Jones. 1971. Mobile units in family planning. *Reports on Population/Family Planning.* October.

Myint, Hla. 1964. *The economics of the developing countries.* New York: Praeger.

———. 1969. The peasant economies of today's underdeveloped areas. In *Subsistence agriculture and economic development.* Clifford R. Wharton, ed. Chicago: Aldine.

Myrdal, Alva. 1941/1968. *Nation and family.* Cambridge: Massachusetts Institute of Technology Press: re-issued 1968.

Myrdal, Gunnar. 1940. *Population: a problem for democracy.* Cambridge: Harvard University Press.

———. 1968. *Asian drama.* New York: Pantheon.

Nag, Meni. 1962. *Factors affecting fertility in non-industrial societies: a cross-cultural study.* New Haven: Yale University Publishers in Anthropology.

———. 1967. Family type and fertility. *World Population Conference.* Vol. 2: 160–63.

REFERENCES

Nair, Kusum. 1962. *Blossoms in the dust*. New York: Praeger.

Nakajima, Chihiro. 1969. Subsistence and commercial family farms: some theoretical models of subjective equilibrium. In *Subsistence agriculture and economic development*. Clifton R. Wharton, ed. Chicago: Aldine.

Namboodiri, N. Krishnan. 1970. Economic status and family size preference. *Population Studies* 24: 235–37.

———. 1972. Some observations on the economic framework for fertility analysis. *Population Studies* 26: 185–206.

———. 1974. Which couples at given parities expect to have additional births? *Demography* 11: 45–56.

Narveson, Jan. 1967. Utilitarianism and new generations. *Mind* 76: 62–72.

———. 1973. Moral problems of population. *The Monist* 37: 62–86.

Nath, Pran. 1929. *A study in the economic condition of ancient India*. London: Royal Asiatic Society.

Nelson, Richard R. 1956. A theory of the low-level equilibrium trap in underdeveloped economies. *American Economic Review* 46: 894–908.

———. 1970. Microeconomic theory and economic development. Mimeo.

Nerlove, Marc, and T. Paul Schultz. 1970. Love and life between the censuses: model of family decision-making in Puerto Rico, 1950–1960. Mimeo. The Rand Corporation, RM-6322-AID.

Newman, Peter. 1970. Malaria control and population growth. *The Journal of Development Studies* 6: 133–58.

Nordhaus, William D. and James Tobin. 1972. *Is growth obsolete?* New York: NBER.

North, Douglas C. and Robert P. Thomas. 1970. An economic theory of the growth of the western world. *Economic History Review*, 2d ser., 23: 1–17.

Nortman, Dorothy. 1969. Population and family planning programs: a factbook. *Reports on Population/Family Planning*. December.

———. 1971. Population and family planning programs: A factbook. *Reports on Population/Family Planning*, no. 2, June.

Notestein, Frank W. 1966. Closing remarks. *Family planning and population growth*. B. Berelson, *et al.*, eds. Chicago: University of Chicago Press.

———. 1966. Some economic aspects of population change in the developing countries. *Population dilemma in Latin America*. M. Stycos and J. Arias, eds. Washington, D.C.: Potamac Books.

———. 1970. Zero population growth. Mimeo. PAA Meeting.

Oechsli, Frank Wm. and Dudley Kirk. 1975. Modernization and the demographic transition in Latin America and the Caribbean. *Economic Development and Cultural Change* 23: 391–420.

O'Hara, Donald J. 1972a. Mortality and fertility: Three avenues of interaction. University of Rochester.

———. 1972b. Mortality risks, sequential decisions on births, and population growth. *Demography* 9: 485–98.

Ohkawa, K. 1970. Phases of agricultural development and economic growth. In *Agriculture and economic growth, Japan's experience*. K. Ohkawa, B. Johnston and H. Kaneda, eds. Princeton: Princeton University Press.

Ohlin, Goran. 1955. The positive and the preventive checks: a study of the rate of growth of pre-industrial populations. Ph.D. Harvard University.

531

————. 1961. Mortality, marriage and growth in pre-industrial population. *Population Studies* 14: 190–97.

————. 1970. Historical evidence of Malthusianism. In *Population and economics*. Paul Deprez, ed. Winnipeg: University of Manitoba Press.

Okun, Bernard. 1958. *Trends in birth rates in the United States since 1870*. Baltimore: Johns Hopkins University Press.

————. 1960. Comment. In *Demographic and economic change in developed countries*. Ansley J. Coale, ed. Princeton: Princeton University Press.

Olson, E. and G. S. Tolley. 1971. The interdependence between income and education. *Journal of Political Economy*. 79: 461–80.

Olson, Mancur, Jr. 1965. *The logic of collective action*. Cambridge: Harvard University Press.

Olson, Sherry H. 1971. *The Depletion Myth: History of Railroad Use of Timber*. Cambridge, Mass: Harvard University Press.

Olusanya, P. O. 1969. Cultural barriers to family planning among the Yorubas. *Studies in Family Planning* 37: 13–16.

Owen, Wilfred. 1964. *Strategy for mobility*. Washington: The Brookings Institution.

————. 1968. *Distance and development*. Washington: The Brookings Institution.

Ozbay, Ferhunde, and Frederic C. Shorter. 1970. Turkey: changes in birth control practices, 1963–1968. *Studies in Family Planning* 51: 1–7.

Paglin, Morton. 1965. Surplus agricultural labor and development: facts and theories. *American Economic Review* 55: 815–34.

Paige, Deborah, and Cottfried Bombach. 1959. *A comparison of national output and productivity of the United Kingdom and the United States*. Paris: OECD.

Pakrasi, Kanti, and Chitaaranjan Malaker. 1967. The relationship between family type and fertility. *Milbank Memorial Fund Quarterly* 45: 451–60.

Patinkin, Don. 1965. *Money, interest, and prices*. 2d ed. New York: Harper and Row.

Peel, John. 1963. The manufacturing and retailing of contraceptives in England. *Population Studies* 17: 113–25.

Peled, Tsiyona. 1969. Problems and attitudes in family planning. Israel Institute of Applied Social Research, March, in Hebrew, a, and English summary, b.

Peller, Sigismund. 1965. Births and deaths among Europe's ruling families since 1500. In *Population in history*. D. V. Glass and D. E. L. Eversley, eds. Chicago: Aldine.

Perella, Vera C. Moonlighters: their motivations and characteristics. *Monthly Labor Review* 93: 57–64.

Perkins, Dwight. 1969. *Agricultural development in China, 1368–1968*. Chicago: Aldine.

Petersen, William. 1955/1956. Family subsidies in the Netherlands. *Marriage and Family Living*, August. Reprinted in *Population theory and policy*. J. J. Spengler and O. D. Duncan, eds. Glencoe: Free Press.

————. 1961. *Population*. New York: Macmillan.

Pfanner, David E. 1969. A semisubsistence village economy in lower Burma.

Phelps, Edmund S. 1966. The golden rule of procreation. In *Rules of economic growth*. New York: Norton.

———. 1968. Population increase. *Canadian Journal of Economics* 1: 497–518.

Phillips, Llad, Harold L. Votey, Jr., and Darold E. Maxwell. 1969. A synthesis of the economic and demographic models of fertility: An econometric test. *Review of Economics and Statistics* 51: 298–308.

Pilarski, Adam and Julian L. Simon. 1975a. The effect of population growth upon the quantity of education per child. Mimeo.

———. 1975b. A preliminary study of the effect of population growth on unemployment. Mimeo.

Pirie, N. W. 1963. Future sources of food supply: scientific problems. In Royal Statistical Society. Symposium on Food Supplies and Population Growth, London, 1962, *Food supplies and population growth*. Edinburgh: Oliver and Boyd.

Pitchford, J. D. 1974. *Population in Economic Growth*. Amsterdam: North Holland.

Poffenberger, Thomas. 1969. Husband-wife communication and motivational aspects of population control in an Indian village. New Delhi: Central Family Planning Institute.

Pohlman, Edward. 1969. *Psychology of birth planning*. Cambridge: Schenkman.

———. 1971. Incentives and compensations in birth planning. Carolina Population Center Monograph No. 11. Chapel Hill: Carolina Population Center.

Pope Paul VI. 1965. Address to the United Nations, October 5. Reported in *The New York Times*, October 6: 6.

Population Chronicle. July 1972.

Poti, S. J. and S. Datta. 1960/1967. *Pilot study on social mobility and differential fertility*. New Delhi: Government of India. As cited by Nag, 1967.

Potter, Robert G. 1969. Estimating births averted in a family planning program. In *Fertility and family planning: a world view*. S. J. Behrman, Leslie Corsa, and Ronald Freedman, eds. Ann Arbor: University of Michigan Press.

President's Science Committee. 1967. *The world food problem*. Washington, D.C.: Government Printing Office.

Prest, W. 1963. Note on size of states and cost of administration in Australia. In *The economic consequences of the size of nations*. E. A. G. Robinson, ed. London: Macmillan.

Preston, Samuel H. 1972. Marital fertility and female employment opportunity: United States, 1960. Mimeo. Department of Demography, University of California, Berkeley.

Price, Daniel O. ed. *The 99th Hour* Chapel Hill: University of North Carolina Press, 1967.

Price, Derek de Solla. 1972. The relations between science and technology and their implications for policy formation. FOA Reprint. 1972/3:26. Stockholm.

Rainwater, Lee. 1965. *Family design: marital sexuality, family size, and contraception*. Chicago: Aldine.

Rainwater, Lee, and Karen K. Weinstein. 1960. *And the poor get children*. Chicago: Quadrangle.

Ramsey, Frank P. 1928/1969. A mathematical theory of saving. *The Economic Journal* 38: 543–59. Reprinted in *Reading in welfare economics*. K. J. Arrow and T. Scitovsky, eds. Homewood: Irwin.

Rao, V. V. Bhaaeji and B. P. Ley. 1968. Birth rates and economic development: some observations from Japanese data. *Sankhya*, Ser. b, 30: 149–56.

Reddaway, William. 1939. *Economics of a declining population.* New York: Macmillan.

Redfield, Robert. 1930. *Tepoztlan—a Mexican village.* Chicago: University of Chicago Press.

———. 1957. *A village that chose progress.* Chicago: University of Chicago Press.

Redfield, Robert and Villa Rojas. 1934. *Chan Kon: a Maya village.* Washington: Carnegie.

Repetto, Robert. 1968. India: a case study of the Madras vasectomy program. *Studies in Family Planning* 31: 8–16.

———.1972. Micro-economic theories of fertility: prediction and policy aspects. Mimeo.

———. 1974. The interaction of fertility and the size distribution of income. Mimeo.

———. 1975. A survey of policy prospects and research approaches in the relationship between fertility and the direct economic costs and value of children in the less developed countries. Conference on Population Policy, Resources for the Future.

Requena, Mariano B. 1968. The problem of induced abortion in Latin America. *Demography* 5: 785–99.

Research and Marketing Services. 1970/1971. A study in the evaluation of the effectiveness of the Tata incentive program for sterilization. Bombay, unpublished, 1970. Quoted by Rogers, 1971.

Revelle, Roger, ed. 1971. *Rapid population growth: consequences and policy implications.* Baltimore: Johns Hopkins University Press.

———. 1974. Food and population. *Scientific American* 231: 160–71.

Ricardo, David. 1963. *The principles of political economy and taxation.* Homewood: Irwin.

Rich, William. 1973. *Smaller families through social and economic progress.* Washington: Overseas Development Council.

Richthoven, Baron von. 1871/1959. Letter on the Provinces of Chekiang and Nganhwei (Shanghai, 1871). Written for the *North China Daily News:* 12–14. Quoted by Ho, 1959: 244.

Ridker, Ronald. 1968. A scheme for a family planning retirement bond. (not exact title). Mimeo.

———. 1972. Resource and environmental consequences of population growth and the American future. In *Population, resources, and the environment.* The Commission on Population Growth and the American Future. Ronald Ridker, ed. Washington: Government Printing Office.

———. 1974. Incentives and disincentives for fertility reduction. *Population Policies and Economic Development,* IBRD: 481.

Robbins, Lionel. 1927. The optimum theory of population. In *London essays in*

534

economics: in honour of Edwin Lannan. T. Gregory and H. Dalton, eds. London: Routledge.

Roberto, Eduardo L. 1972. Social marketing strategies for diffusing the adoption of family planning. *Social Science Quarterly* 53: 33–51.

Robinson, Edward A. G., ed. 1960. *Economic consequences of the size of nations*. New York: St. Martins.

———. 1963. The size of the nation and the cost of administration. In *The economic consequences of the size of nations*. Robinson, ed. London: Macmillan.

Robinson, S. 1971. Sources of growth in less developed countries: a cross-section study. *Quarterly Journal of Economics* 75: 391–408.

Robinson, Warren C. 1963. Urbanization and fertility: the non-western experience. *Milbank Memorial Fund Quarterly* 41: 291–308.

———. 1969. Some tentative results of a cost effectiveness study of selected national family planning programs. Mimeo.

Rogers, Everett M. 1971. Incentives in the diffusion of family planning observations. *Studies in Family Planning* 2: 241–48.

———. 1972. Field experiments on family planning incentives. Mimeo, Department of Communication, Michigan State University.

Rogers, Everett M. and J. David Stanfield. 1968. Adoption and diffusion of new products: emerging generalizations and hypotheses. In *Applications of the sciences in marketing management*. F. M. Bass *et al.*, eds. New York: Wiley.

Rosenberg, W. 1971. A note on the relationship of family size and income in New Zealand. *Economic Record* 47: 399–409.

Ross, Edward Alsworth. 1927. *Standing room only*. New York: Century.

Ross, John A. 1966a. Cost analysis of the Taichung experiment. *Studies in Family Planning* 10: 6–15.

———. 1966b. Cost of family planning programs. In *Family planning and population programs*. B. Berelson, *et al.*, eds. Chicago: University of Chicago Press.

Ross, John A. and David P. Smith. 1969. Korea: trends in four national KAP surveys, 1964–67. *Studies in Family Planning* 43: 6–10.

Ross, Sue Goetz. 1973. The effect of economic variables on timing and spacing of births. Paper presented to the PAA.

Rostas, Leo. 1948. *Comparative productivity in British and American Industry*. Occasional Paper 13. NBER. Cambridge.

Rozenthal, Alek A. 1970. A note on the sources and uses of funds in Thai agriculture. *Economic Development and Cultural Change* 18: 383–90.

Ruggles, Richard, and Nancy Ruggles. 1960. Differential fertility in United States census data. In *Demographic and economic change in developed countries*. Ansley J. Coale, ed. Princeton: Princeton University Press.

Russett, B. B. *et al.* 1964. *World handbook of social and political indicators*. New Haven: Yale University Press.

Ruttan, Vernon W. 1969. Two sector models and development policy comment. In *Subsistence agriculture and economic development*. Clifford R. Whanton, Jr., ed. Chicago: Aldine.

Ryder, Norman B. 1969. The emergence of a modern fertility pattern: United States 1917–66. In *Fertility and family planning: a world view*. S. J. Behrman, Leslie

535

Corsa, and Ronald Freedman, eds. Ann Arbor: University of Michigan Press.

Ryder, Norman B. and Charles F. Westoff. 1969. Relationships among intended, expected, desired, and ideal family size: United States, 1965. Center for Population Research. Washington, March.

Sahlins, Marshall D. 1968. Notes on original affluent society. In *Man the Hunter*. Richard B. Lee and Iven Devore, eds. Chicago- Aldine.

Salaman, Redcliffe N. 1949. *History and social influence of the potato*. Cambridge: Cambridge University Press.

Salter, Wilfred Edward Graham. 1966. *Productivity and technical change*. Cambridge: Cambridge University Press.

Sanderson, Warren, and Robert J. Willis. 1971. Economic models of fertility: some examples and implications. *NBER Annual Report:* 32–42.

Sato, Ryuzo, and V. Niho. 1971. Population growth and the development of a dual economy. *Oxford Economic Papers* 23: 415–36.

Sauvy, Alfred. 1968. Public opinion and the population problems. In *World views of population problems*. Egon Szabady, ed. Budapest: Akademiai Kiado.

———. 1969. *General theory of population*. New York: Basic Books.

Schmookler, Jacob. 1962. Changes in industry and in the state of knowledge as determinants of industrial invention. In *The Rate and Direction of Inventive Activity: Economic and Social Factors*. Richard R. Nelson, ed. Princeton: Princeton University Press.

Schorr, Alvin. 1965/1970. Income maintenance and the birth rate. *Social Security Bulletin* 27: 22–30. Reprinted in *Social demography*. T. Ford and G. DeJong, eds. Englewood Cliffs: Prentice-Hall.

Schramm, Wilbur. 1971. Communication in family planning. *Reports on Population/Family Planning* April no. 7

Schran, Peter. 1969. *The development of Chinese agriculture 1950–1959*. Urbana: University of Illinois Press.

Schultz, T. Paul. 1969a. An economic perspective on population growth. Mimeo.

———. 1969b. An economic model of family planning and fertility. *Journal of Political Economy* 77: 153–80.

———. 1973. Explanation of birth rate changes over space and time: a study of Taiwan. *Journal of Political Economy* 81, Supplement: S238–74.

———. 1975. Interrelationships between mortality and fertility. Presented to Resources for the Future Conference, February.

Schultz, T. Paul and Julie DaVanzo. 1970. An analysis of demographic change in East Pakistan: a study of retrospective survey data. Mimeo. Rand: R-564-AID.

Schultz, Theodore W. 1964. *Transforming traditional agriculture*. New Haven: Yale University Press.

———. 1965. *Economic crises in world agriculture*. Ann Arbor: University of Michigan Press.

———. 1972. Production opportunities in Asian agriculture: an economist's agenda. In *Readings in Economic Development*. Walter L. Johnson and David R. Kamerschen, eds. Cincinnati: Southwestern.

Schumpeter, Joseph. 1947. The creative response in economic history. *Journal of Economic History* 7: 149–59.

REFERENCES

Scully, John J. 1962. The influence of family size on efficiency within the farm—an Irish study. *The Journal of Agricultural Economics* 5: 116–21.

Second five-year plan for economic and social development of the United Republic of Tanzania. 1969. Dar Es-Salaam: Government Printing Office. Quoted from Rarbison.

Seiver, Daniel A. 1974. An empirical study of declining fertility in the United States: 1960–1970. Ph.D. Yale University.

Selvin, Hanan, and Warren O. Hagstrom. 1963. The empirical classification of formal groups. *American Sociological Review* 28: 399–411.

Sen, Amartya K. 1959. The choice of agricultural techniques in under-developed countries. *Economic Development and Cultural Change* 7: 279–85.

———. 1966. Peasants and dualism with or without surplus labor. *Journal of Political Economy* 74: 425–50.

Seppilli, T. 1960. Social conditions of fertility in a rural community in transition in Central Italy. In *Culture, Science and Health*, Annals of the N.Y. Academy of Sciences. V. Rubin, ed. 84: 959–62.

Sheffer, Daniel. 1970. Comparable living costs and urban size: a statistical analysis. *American Institute of Planners Journal* 36: 417–21.

Sidgwick, Henry. 1901. *The methods of ethics.* London: Macmillan.

Silver, Morris. 1965. Births, marriages, and business cycles in the United States. *Journal of Political Economy* 73: 237–55.

———. 1966. Birth, marriages, and income fluctuations in the United Kingdom and Japan. *Economic Development and Cultural Change* 14: 302–15.

Simmons, George B. 1969. The Indian investment in family planning. Ph.D. University of California, Berkeley.

Simon, Herbert A. 1957. *Administrative behavior.* New York: Macmillan.

Simon, Julian L. 1965. Are there economies of scale in advertising? *Journal of Advertising Research* 5: 15–19.

———. 1966. The demand for liquor in the U.S., and a simple method of determination. *Econometrica* 34: 193–205.

———. 1968. The role of bonuses and persuasive-propaganda in the reduction of birth rates. *Economic Development and Cultural Change*, vol. 16, no. 3.

———. 1968a. Some "marketing correct" recommendations for family planning campaigns. *Demography* 5: 504–07.

———. 1968b. The effect of income on suicide. *American Journal of Sociology* 74: 302–303.

———. 1968c. Income, childlessness, and fertility in America in the census of 1960. Mimeo. PAA Meeting.

———. 1968d. A huge marketing research job—birth control. *Journal of Marketing Research* 5: 21–27.

———. 1969a. The value of avoided births to underdeveloped countries. *Population Studies*, 23: 61–68.

———. 1969b. The effect of income upon fertility. *Population Studies* 23: 327–41.

———. 1970a. *Issues in the economics of advertising.* Urbana: University of Illinois Press.

———. 1970b. The per-capita income criterion and natality policies in poor countries. *Demography* 7: 369–78.

REFERENCES

————. 1970c. Family planning prospects in less developed countries and a cost-benefit analysis of various alternatives. *Economic Journal* 80: 58–71.

————. 1971. *The management of advertising.* Englewood Cliffs: Prentice-Hall.

————. 1972. The effects of income redistribution on fertility in less-developed countries. Feasibility study for the Bureau of Intelligence and Research of the Department of State.

————. 1973. Science does not show that there is over-population in the U.S. In *Population: a clash of prophets.* Edward Pohlman, ed. New York: Mentor.

————. 1974a. *The effects of income upon fertility.* Chapel Hill: Carolina Population Center.

————. 1974b. Segmentation and market strategy in birth-control campaigns. *Studies in Family Planning* 5: 90–97.

————. 1975a. The positive effect of population on agricultural savings in irrigation systems. *Review of Economics and Statistics* 57: 71–79.

————. 1975b. The effect of income on suicide: reply. *American Journal of Sociology* 81: 1460–62.

Simon, Julian L. and Dennis J. Aigner. 1970. Cross sectional budget studies, aggregate time-series studies, and the permanent income hypothesis. *American Economic Review* 60: 341–51.

Simon, Julian L. and Carl E. Barnes. 1971. The middle-class U.S. consumption function: a hypothetical-question study of expected consumption behavior. *Bulletin of the Oxford Institute of Economics and Statistics* 33: 73–80.

Simon, Julian L. and David H. Gardner. 1969. The new proteins and world food needs. *Economic Development and Cultural Change* 17: 520–26.

Simon, Rita James. 1971. Public attitudes toward population and pollution. *Public Opinion Quarterly* 35: 95–101.

Simon, Rita James and Julian L. Simon. 1974/1975. The effect of money incentives on family size: a hypothetical-question study. *Public Opinion Quarterly* (Winter): 585–95.

Simon, Sheldon R. 1968. The village of Senapur. In *Developing rural India.* John W. Mellor, ed. Ithaca: Cornell University Press.

Singer, Hans W. 1959. Differential population growth as a factor in international economic development. *Economic Journal* 69: 820–22.

————. 1964. Population and economic development. In *International development: growth and change.* Singer, ed. New York: McGraw-Hill.

Slicher van Bath, B. H. 1963. *The agrarian history of western Europe, A.D. 500–1850.* London: Arnold.

Smith, Larry J. 1973. *Black-white reproductive behavior: an economic interpretation.* Ph.D. University of Chicago.

Snyder, Donald W. 1974. Economic Determinants of Family Size in West Africa. *Demography* 11: 613–27.

Sollins, Alfred D. and Raymond L. Belsky. 1970. Commercial production and distribution of contraceptives. *Reports on Population/Family Planning* 4:

Solow, Robert. 1957. Technical change and the aggregate production function. *The Review of Economics and Statistics* 39: 312–20.

Spengler, Joseph J. 1952. Population theory. In *A survey of contemporary economics,* Vol. 2. B. Haley, ed. Homewood: Irwin.

REFERENCES

————. 1958. The economic effects of migration. In *Selected studies of migration since World War II*. F. G. Boudreau and C. V. Kiser, eds. New York: Milbank Memorial Fund.

————. 1964. Population and economic growth. In *Population: the vital revolution*. R. Freedman, ed. New York: Doubleday Anchor.

————. 1966. The economist and the population question. *American Economic Review* 56: 1–24.

————. 1967. Population optima. In *The 99th hour*. Daniel O. Price, ed. Chapel Hill: University of North Carolina Press.

————. 1966/1968. Values and fertility analysis. *Demography* 3: 109–30. In *Readings on population*. David M. Heer, ed. Englewood Cliffs: Prentice Hall.

Stafford, Frank P. 1969. Student family size in relation to current and expected income. *Journal of Political Economy* 77: 474–77.

Stearns, J. Brenton. 1972. Ecology and the indefinite unborn. *The Monist* 56: 612–25.

Stevenson, Robert F. 1968. *Population and political systems in tropical Africa*. New York: Columbia University Press.

Stigler, George J. 1961. Economic problems in measuring changes in productivity. *Output, Input, and Productivity Measurement, Studies in Income and Wealth* 25: 42–63. Conference in Research in Science in Wealth. Princeton: Princeton University Press.

Stockwell, M. 1972. Some observations on the relationship between population growth and economic development during the 1960's. *Rural Sociology* 37: 628–32.

Stolnitz, George. 1965. Recent mortality trends in Latin America, Asia, and Africa. *Population Studies* 19: 117–38.

Studies in Family Planning. Roman Catholic fertility and family planning. 34: 1–24.

Stycos, J. Mayone. 1955. *Family and fertility in Puerto Rico*. Ithaca: Cornell University Press.

————. 1968. *Human fertility in Latin America*. Ithaca: Cornell University Press.

Stycos, J. Mayone, and Kurt W. Back. 1964. *The control of human fertility in Jamaica*. Ithaca: Cornell University Press.

Stycos, J. Mayone, Kurt W. Back, and Reuben Hill. 1956. Problems of communication between husband and wife on matters relating to family limitation. *Human Relations* 9: 207–15.

Stys, W. 1957. The influence of economic conditions on the fertility of peasant women. *Population Studies* 11: 136–48.

Subremian Swamy, and Shadid Javer Burki. 1970. Food grain output in the People's Republic of China, 1958–1965. *China Quarterly* 41: 58–63.

Sweet, James A. 1968. *Family composition and the labor force activity of married women in the United States*. Ph.D. University of Michigan.

————. 1970. Family composition and the labor force activity of American wives. *Demography* 7: 195–209.

Sweezy, Alan. 1971. The economic explanation of fertility changes in the United States. *Population Studies* 25: 255–67.

Tabah, Léon, and Raúl Samuel. 1962. Preliminary findings of a survey in fertility and attitudes toward family formation in Santiago, Chile. *Research in family planning.* C. V. Kiser, ed. Princeton: Princeton University Press.

Taeuber, Irene B. 1958. *The population of Japan.* Princeton: Princeton University Press.

———. 1960. Japan's demographic transition re-examined. *Population Studies* 14: 28–39.

Tarver, J. D. 1956. Costs of rearing and educating farm children. *Journal of Farm Economics* 28: 144–53.

Tawney, R. H. 1932. *Land and labour in China.* London: George Allen and Unwin.

Taylor, Carl E. 1965. Health and population. *Foreign Affairs* 43: 475–86.

Thirlwall, Anthony P. 1972. A cross section study of population growth and the growth of output and per capita income in a production function framework. *Manchester School of Economics and Social Studies* 40: 339–56.

Thomas, Brinley. 1954. *Migration and economic growth.* Cambridge: Cambridge University Press.

———. ed. 1959. *Economics of international migration.* New York: St. Martin's.

———. 1961. *International migration and economic development: a trend report and bibliography.* New York: UNESCO.

———. 1973. *Migration and economic growth.* 2d ed. Cambridge University Press.

Thomas, Dorothy S. 1925. *Social and economic effects of business cycles.* London: Dutton.

———. 1941. *Social and economic aspects of Swedish population movements.* New York: Macmillan.

Thomsen, Moritz. 1969. *Living poor.* New York: Ballantine.

Thorner, Daniel and Alice. 1962. *Land and labour in India.* New York: Asia Publishing House.

von Thunen, Johann H. 1966. *The isolated state.* New York: Pergamon.

Tinbergen, Jan. 1967. *Development planning.* New York: McGraw-Hill.

Tolley, G. S. and E. Olson. 1971. The interdependence between income and education. *Journal of Political Economy* 79: 461–80.

Tomasson, Richard. 1946. Why has American fertility been so high? In *Kinship and family organization.* Bernard Farber, ed. New York: Wiley.

Tussing, A. R. 1969/1972. The labor force in Meiji economic growth: a quantitative study of Yamanishi prefecture. In *Agriculture and economic growth: Japan's experience.* K. Ohkawa, B. F. Johnston, and H. Kaneda, eds. Tokyo: University of Tokyo Press.

United Nations. 1953. *The determinants and consequences of population trends.* New York: U.N.

———. 1956. The aging of populations and its economic social implications. *Population studies* 26: 1–168.

———. 1963. *Compendium of social statistics.* Ser. K, No. 2.

———. 1965. *Population bulletin of the United Nations, No. 7, 1963.* New York: U.N.

———. 1973. The determinants and consequences of population trends. *Population Studies.* Vol. 1, No. 50.

———. 1974. *The world food problem—proposals for national and international actions.* Rome.

United Nations Economic Commission for Africa. 1970. *Statistical bulletin for Africa,* Part 1. New York: U.N.

540

REFERENCES

United Nations Statistical Office. 1970. *Yearbook of national accounts, 1969.* Vol. 1: *Individual country data;* and Vol. 2: *International tables.* New York: U.N.

United States Department of Agriculture, Economic Research Service. 1974. The world food situation and prospects to 1985. Washington: Government Printing Office. December.

United States Department of Commerce, Bureau of Public Roads. 1952. *Highway statistics 1950.* Washington: Government Printing Office.

U.S. Department of Commerce, Bureau of the Census. *Statistical abstract of the United States.* Various years. Washington: Government Printing Office.

————. 1960. *Historical statistics of the United States: colonial times to 1957.* Washington: Government Printing Office.

————. 1964. *1960 Census of population: women by number of children ever born.* PC-(2)-3A. Washington: Government Printing Office.

United States, The White House. 1967. *The world food problem.* Washington: Government Printing Office.

————. 1972. Population and the American future. *The report of the Commission on Population Growth and the American Future.* New York: Signet.

Usher, Abbott Payson. 1930/1956. The history of population and settlement in Urasia. In *Demographic analysis.* Spengler and Duncan, eds. Glencoe: Free Press. *Geographical Review,* January, 1930.

Van de Walle, Etienne. 1972. Implications of increases in rural density. In *Population growth and economic development in Africa.* Ominde and Ejiogu, eds. New York: Population Council.

van Vleck, David B. 1970. A biologist urges stabilizing U.S. population growth, *University: A Princeton Quarterly* Spring: 16–18.

Verdoorn, Peter J. 1951. On an empirical law governing the productivity of labor. *Econometrica* 19: 209–10.

Vielrose, Egon. 1968. Family budgets and birth rates. In *World views of population problems.* Egon Szabady, ed. Budapest: Akademiai Kiade.

Votey, Harold L., Jr. 1969. The optimum population and growth: a new look. *Journal of Economic Theory* 1: 273–90.

Vries, Jan de. 1970. The role of the rural section in the development of the Dutch economy: 1500–1700. Ph.D. Yale University.

Wang, L. M. and S. Y. Chen. 1973. Evaluation of the first year of the educational savings program in Taiwan. *Studies in Family Planning* 4: 157–61.

Warriner, Doreen. 1957. *Land reform and development in the Middle East.* New York: Royal Institute of International Affairs.

Weckstein, Richard S. 1962. Welfare criteria and changing tastes. *American Economic Review* 52: 133–53.

Weintraub, Robert. 1962. The birth rate and economic development. *Econometrica* 40: 812–17.

Wertham, Frederick. 1966. *A sign for Cain.* New York: Macmillan.

West, E. G. 1968. Social legislation and the demand for children: comment. *Western Economic Journal* 6: 419–24.

Westoff, Charles and Norman Ryder. 1969. Recent trends in attitudes toward fertility control and in the practice of contraception in the United States. In *Fertility and family planning: a world view.* S. J. Behrman, Leslie Corsa, and Ronald Freedman, eds. Ann Arbor: University of Michigan Press.

541

REFERENCES

Wharton, Clifford R., Jr. 1969a. *Subsistence agriculture and economic development.* Chicago: Aldine.

———. 1969b. The green revolution: cornucopia or Pandora's Box? *Foreign Affairs* 47: 464–76.

Whelpton, P. K., Arthur A. Campbell, and J. E. Patterson. 1966. *Fertility and family planning in the United States.* Princeton: Princeton University Press.

Whelpton, P. K. and C. V. Kiser, eds. 1946/1950/1952/1954/1958. *Social and psychological factors affecting fertility.* Vols. 1–5. New York: Mlbank Memorial Fund.

White, Lynn, Jr. 1962. *Medieval technology and social change.* New York: Oxford.

Wicksell, Knut. 1928. *Forelasninger i nationalekonomi.* Stockholm.

Wilder, Frank, and D. K. Tyagi. 1968. India's new departures in mass motivation for fertility control. *Demography* 5: 773–79.

Wilensky, Harold. 1963. The moonlighter: a product of relative deprivation. *Industrial Relations* 3: 105–24.

Wilkinson, Maurice. 1967. Evidences of long swings in the growth of Swedish population and related economic variables. *Journal of Economic History* 27: 17–38.

———. 1973. An Econometric Analysis of Fertility in Sweden. *Econometrica* 41: 433–641. July.

Willis, Robert J. 1969. A new approach to the economic theory of fertility behavior. Mimeo. Wesleyan University, December.

———. 1973. A new approach to the economic theory of fertility behavior. *Journal of Political Economy* 81, Supplement: S14–65.

Willis, Robert J. and Warren Sanderson. 1970. Is economics relevant to fertility behavior? Mimeo. NBER: New York.

Wilson, George W., Barbara R. Bergmann, Leon V. Hinser, Martin S. Klein. 1966. *The impact of highway investment on development.* Washington: The Brookings Institution.

Winsborough, H. H., and Peter Dickinson. 1970. Age, cohort, and period effects in U.S. fertility. Mimeo.

Winston, Gordon C. 1966. An international comparison of income and hours of work. *Review of Economics and Statistics* 48: 28–39.

Wold, Herman O. 1966. The approach of model building. In *Model building in the human science.* Wold, ed. Monaco.

Wolfers, David. 1971. The case against zero growth. *International Journal of Environmental Studies* 1: 227–32.

Woodburn, James. 1968. An introduction to Hadza ecology. In *Man the hunter.* Richard B. Lee and Irven DeVore, eds. Chicago: Aldine.

Wrigley, Edward A. 1969. *Population and history.* New York: McGraw-Hill.

Wyon, John B. and John E. Gordon. 1971. *The Khanna study: population problems in the rural Punjab.* Cambridge: Harvard University Press.

Yaari, Shmuel. 1974. World over a barrel. *Jerusalem Post Magazine,* October 4: 4.

Yasuba, Yasukichi. 1962. *Birth rates of the white population in the United States, 1800–1860: An economic study.* Baltimore: Johns Hopkins University Press.

542

REFERENCES

Yaukey, David. 1961. *Fertility differences in a modernizing country*. Princeton: Princeton University Press.

Yotopoulos, Pan A. and Lawrence J. Lau. 1974. On modeling the agricultural sector in developing economies: an integrated approach of micro and macro-economics. *Journal of Development Economics* 1: 105–27.

Young, J. H. 1955. Comparative economic development: Canada and the United States. *American Economic Review* 45: 80–93.

Yule, G. U. 1906. On changes in the marriage- and birth-rates in England and Wales during the past half century. *Journal of the Royal Statistical Society* 69: 88–132.

Zaidan, George C. 1967. Benefits and costs of population control with special reference to the United Arab Republic (Egypt). Ph.D. Harvard University.

————. 1968. The foregone benefits and costs of a prevented birth: conceptual problems and an application to the U.A.R. Mimeo. IBRD Economics Department Working Paper.

————. 1969. Population growth and economic development. *Studies in Family Planning* 42. Population Council of New York. May.

Zimmerman, L. J. *Poor Lands, Rich Lands*. New York: Random House, 1965.

Zitter, Meyer. 1970. Population trends in metropolitan areas. *American Statistical Association Proceedings, Social Statistics Section*.

INDEX

Aborigines: Australian, 165
Abortion: and increased income, 351
Accelerator function, 153
Adelman, Irma, 211, 270
Age distribution: effect on per-capita product, 30
Agriculture: population growth, 29; marginal productivity, 29, 138; investment function, 138; goods, 144; population-push/invention-pull hypotheses, 169, 174–75; slash and burn, 172–74; in Middle Ages, 175; traditional Chinese, 179–81; rate of investment, 239; effect of first child in subsistence community, 397–98
    change: and population growth, 204; in India, 208
    subsistence, 34; and capital formation, 238; and additional output over time, 240
Aigner, Dennis J., 326
Allport, Gordon, 214
Alonso, William, 71
Andrus, J. Russell, 252
Anker, Richard, 234, 362
Arensberg, Conrad M., 315
Arnold, Fred S., 321
Arrow, Kenneth J., 117, 414, 420
ART complex, 113–16, 126
Aspirations: function of, 153; increase of and income, 300; increase of and population growth, 300
Attitudes: changes in, toward work, 140; social, concerning birth control market, 462
Averted birth: value of, 428–29, 430–32, 436, 442, 448; value of and per-capita income criterion, 429, 479; macro-economic analysis of value, 432; state incentives for, 437; value of as yardstick for birth control and welfare investments, 437; economic benefits of, 442; cost of, 464; and cost-benefit study, 469–70; and Enke-type calculations, 475

Balikei, Asen, 171
Banfield, Edward, 212, 316–17
Banks, Joseph A., 312
Barlow, Robin, 138, 235
Barnett, Harold, J., 82, 83, 86, 88, 94, 99
Bauer, Peter T., 244
Baumol, William J., 4, 5
Becker, Gary S., 9, 312–13, 331, 333, 387
Behavior: response and scarcity of natural resources, 88, 90; change in agricultural workers, 183; productive, and population growth, 201

Bennett, John W., 54
Ben-Porath, Yoram, xxv, 313, 330, 333, 341–342, 347, 373, 486
Benthamite-Utilitarian-Pigovian meaning of utility, 394
Berelson, Bernard, 443, 447, 466
Berent, Jerzy, 377
Bernhardt, Eva M., 344
Berry, Brian J. L., 73
Berry, R. Albert, 411
Bethe, Hans A., 94
Bhatia, 209
Biblical period and population-push hypothesis, 170
Birnbaum, Bonnie, xxv
Birth control, 195; and social planners, 451; and private marketer, 451; physical availability of methods, 456–458; economic availability of methods, 458–59; religious beliefs concerning, 462
    campaigns, 12–13; and population policy, 429; as fertility-reduction program, 441; in Taiwan, 446; and cost-benefit study, 469–70
    investments: and value of averted births, 437
    market, 452–55; and privacy, 454; and want to regulate segment, 455; folk methods in, 455–56; and availability of products, 457–61; social availability of, 459–60; information availability, 460–61; suited for regulation segment, 462–63; not ready for regulation segment, 463–65; advertising, 465–66; identification of segments, 466–69; market research, 466–69
    See also Averted birth
Birth-incentive programs. *See* Fertility incentive payments
Birth rate, 13, 25–26, 147; change in, 53; in India, 220; relation with accessible land (LDC's), 358; and short-run per-capita income maximization, 425; and long-run per-capita income, 426; and discount rate, 426; relation to mortality rate, 486
    structure: and capital-dilution effect, 297; economic performance, 290
    policy (LDC's): and per-capita income, 428–29
Births: voluntary limitation of, and Malthus, 6; effect of income on additional (MDC's), 342–44
Blake, Judith, 319
Blandy, Richard, 304
Blumberg, Judith, xxv
Bogue, Donald J., 73, 454, 463

545

551

LIBRARY OF CONGRESS CATALOGING IN PUBLICATION DATA

Simon, Julian Lincoln, 1932–
    The economics of population growth.

    Bibliography: p.
    Includes index.
    1. Population.   2.   Fertility, Human—Economic
aspects.   3.   Birth control.   I.   Title.
HB871.S57   301.32   75–15278
ISBN 0–691–04212–8
ISBN(LPE) 0–691–10053–5